EXPOSITORY THOUGHTS ON THE GOSPELS

John 10:31 — John 21:25

J. C. RYLE

BAKER BOOK HOUSE
Grand Rapids, Michigan

Reprinted 2007 by
Baker Books
a division of Baker Publishing Group
P.O. Box 6287
Grand Rapids, MI 49516-6287

ISBN: 978-0-8010-7755-5
ISBN 10: 0-8010-7755-9
4 Volume Set

Printed in the United States of America

TABLE OF CONTENTS

JOHN.			PAGE
X	31—42	Wickedness of human nature,—honour put on Scripture by Christ,—importance attached by Christ to His miracles	5—9
XI	1—6	True Christians may be ill as well as others,—Christ is the best Friend in time of need,—Christ loves all true Christians, however varying in temperament,—Christ knows best the time to help	18—21
	7—16	Christ's ways with His people sometimes mysterious,—Christ's tender language about His people,—natural temperament shows itself in all believers	32—36
	17—29	Mixture of grace and weakness in believers,—need of having clear views of Christ's person, office, and power	44—47
	30—37	Blessing bestowed on sympathy,—depth of sympathy in Christ for His people	57—60
	38—46	Christ's words about the stone over the grave of Lazarus,—Christ's words addressed to Martha when she doubted,—Christ's words to God the Father,—Christ's words addressed to Lazarus in his grave	67—71
	47—57	Wickedness of man's natural heart,—blind ignorance of God's enemies,—importance often attached by bad men to ceremonial	81—85
XII	1--11	Abounding proofs of the truth of Christ's miracles,—discouragement Christ's friends meet with from man,—man's hardness and unbelief	96—100

TABLE OF CONTENTS

JOHN			PAGE
XII	12—19	Christ's sufferings entirely voluntary,-- prophecies about Christ's first advent minutely fulfilled . . .	111—115
	20—26	Death the way to spiritual life,—Christ's servants must follow Him . .	121—125
	27—33	Man's sin imputed to Christ,—Christ's internal conflict,—God's voice heard from heaven,—Christ's prophecy about His being lifted up . . .	131—135
	34—43	Duty of using present opportunities,— hardness of man's heart,—power of the love of this world . .	147—150
	44—50	Dignity of Christ,—certainty of a judgment to come	161—164

31 Then the Jews took up stones again to stone him.

32 Jesus answered them, Many good works have I shewed you from my Father; for which of those works do ye stone me?

33 The Jews answered him, saying, For a good work we stone thee not; but for blasphemy; and because that thou, being a man, makest thyself God.

34 Jesus answered them, Is it not written in your law, I said Ye are gods?

35 If he called them gods, unto whom the word of God came, and the scripture cannot be broken;

36 Say ye of him, whom the Father hath sanctified, and sent into the world, Thou blasphemest; because I said, I am the Son of God?

37 If I do not the works of my Father, believe me not.

38 But if I do, though ye believe not me, believe the works: that ye may know, and believe, that the Father is in me, and I in him.

39 Therefore they sought again to take him: but he escaped out of their hand.

40 And went away again beyond Jordan into the place where John at first baptized; and there he abode.

41 And many resorted unto him, and said, John did no miracle: but all things that John spake of this man were true.

42 And many believed on him there.

WE should observe, in these verses, *the extreme wickedness of human nature*. The unbelieving Jews at Jerusalem was neither moved by our Lord's miracles, nor by His preaching. They were determined not to receive Him as their Messiah. Once more it is written that " they took up stones to stone Him."

Our Lord had done the Jews no injury. He was no robber, murderer, or rebel against the law of the land. He was one whose whole life was love, and who " went about doing good." (Acts x. 38.) There was no fault or inconsistency in His character. There was no crime that could be laid to His charge. So perfect and spotless a man had never walked on the face of this earth. But yet the Jews hated Him, and thirsted for His blood. How true are the words of Scripture : " They hated Him without a cause." (John xv. 25.) How just the remark of an old divine : " Unconverted men would kill God Himself if they could only get at Him."

The true Christian has surely no right to wonder if he meets with the same kind of treatment as our blessed Lord. In fact, the more like he is to his Master, and the more holy and spiritual his life, the more probable is it that he will have to endure hatred and persecution. Let him not suppose that any degree of consistency will deliver him from this cross. It is not his faults, but his graces, which call forth the enmity of men. The world hates to see anything of God's image. The children of the world are vexed and pricked in conscience when they see others better than themselves. Why did Cain hate his brother Abel, and slay him? "Because," says St. John, "his own works were evil, and his brother's righteous." (1 John iii. 12.) Why did the Jews hate Christ? Because He exposed their sins and false doctrines; and they knew in their own hearts that he was right and they were wrong. "The world," said our Lord, "hateth Me, because I testify of it, that the works thereof are evil." (John vii. 7.) Let Christians make up their minds to drink the same cup, and let them drink it patiently and without surprise. There is One in heaven who said, "If the world hate you, ye know that it hated Me before it hated you." (John xv. 18.) Let them remember this and take courage. The time is short. We are travelling on towards a day when all shall be set right, and every man shall receive according to his works. "There is an end: and our expectation shall not be cut off." (Prov. xxiii. 18.)

We should observe, secondly, in these verses, *the high honour that Jesus Christ puts on the Holy Scriptures.* We find Him using a text out of the Psalms as an argument against His enemies, in which the whole point lies in the single word "gods." And then having quoted the text, He lays down the great principle, "the Scripture cannot be broken." It is as though He said, "Wherever the Scripture speaks plainly on any subject, there can be no more question about it. The cause is settled and decided. Every jot and tittle of Scripture is true, and must be received as conclusive."

The principle here laid down by our Lord is one of vast importance. Let us grasp it firmly, and never let it go. Let us maintain boldly the complete inspiration of every word of the original Hebrew and Greek Scriptures. Let us believe that not only every book of the Bible, but every chapter,—and not only every chapter, but every verse,— and not only every verse, but every word, was originally given by inspiration of God. Inspiration, we must never shrink from asserting, extends not only to the thoughts and ideas of Scripture, but to the least words.

The principle before us, no doubt, is rudely assaulted in the present day. Let no Christian's heart fail because of these assaults. Let us stand our ground manfully, and defend the principle of plenary inspiration as we would the apple of our eye. There are difficulties in Scripture, we need not shrink from conceding, things hard to explain, hard to reconcile, and hard to understand. But in almost all these difficulties, the fault, we may justly suspect, is not so much in Scripture as in our own weak minds. In all cases we may well be content to wait for more light, and to believe that all shall be made clear at last. One thing we may rest assured is very certain,—if the difficulties of plenary inspiration are to be numbered by thousands, the difficulties of any other view of inspiration are to be num- bered by tens of thousands. The wisest course is to walk in the old path,—the path of faith and humility ; and say, " I cannot give up a single word of my Bible. All Scrip- ture is given by inspiration of God. The Scripture cannot be broken."

We should observe, lastly, in these verses, *the importance which our Lord Jesus Christ attaches to His miracles.* He appeals to them as the best evidence of His own Divine mission. He bids the Jews look at them, and deny them if they can. " If I do not the works of my Father, believe me not. But if I do, though ye believe not Me, believe the works."

The mighty miracles which our Lord performed during the three years of His earthly ministry are probably not considered as much as they ought to be in the present day. These miracles were not few in number. Forty times and more we read in the Gospels of His doing things entirely out of the ordinary course of nature,—healing sick people in a moment, raising the dead with a word, casting out devils, calming winds and waves in an instant, walking on the water as on solid ground. These miracles were not all done in private among friends. Many of them were wrought in the most public manner, under the eyes of unfriendly witnesses. We are so familiar with these things that we are apt to forget the mighty lesson they teach. They teach that He who worked these miracles must be nothing less than very God. They stamp His doctrines and precepts with the mark of Divine authority. He only who created all things at the beginning could suspend the laws of creation at His will. He who could suspend the laws of creation must be One who ought to be thoroughly believed and implicitly obeyed. To reject One who confirmed His mission by such mighty works is the height of madness and folly.

Hundreds of unbelieving men, no doubt, in every age, have tried to pour contempt on Christ's miracles, and to deny that they were ever worked at all. But they labour in vain. Proofs upon proofs exist that our Lord's ministry was accompanied by miracles; and that this was acknowledged by those who lived in our Lord's time. Objectors of this sort would do well to take up the one single miracle of our Lord's resurrection from the dead, and disprove it if they can. If they cannot disprove that, they ought, as honest men, to confess that miracles are possible. And then, if their hearts are truly humble, they ought to admit that He whose mission was confirmed by such evidence must have been the Son of God.

Let us thank God, as we turn from this passage, that Christianity has such abundant evidence that it is a religion from God. Whether we appeal to the internal evidence of the Bible, or to the lives of the first Christians, or to prophecy, or to miracles, or to history, we get one and the same answer. All say with one voice, "Jesus is the Son of God, and believers have life through His name."

NOTES JOHN X 31—42

31 —[*Then the Jews took up stones, etc.*] The conduct of the Jews is just the same as it was when our Lord said, "Before Abrahas was I am." (John viii. 59.) They regarded His words as blasphemy, and proceeded to take the law in their own hands, as they did in Stephen's case, and to inflict the punishment due to blasphemy. (See Lev. xxiv. 14—16.) "He that blasphemeth the name of the Lord, he shall surely be put to death, and all the congregation shall certainly stone him." (So Num. xv. 36; 1 Kings xxi. 13.) The Jews of course had no power to put any man to death, being under the dominion of the Romans, and if they did stone any one it would have been a sudden tumultuary proceeding, or act of Lynch-law.

Let it be noted that the Greek word for "took up" here, is not the same that is used at viii. 59. Here it rather means "they carried." Parkhurst thinks this implies the great size of the stones they brought. No doubt the stones used in stoning to death, were not pebbles, but large stones. Yet I rather incline to think that it shows that they had to carry stones from some little distance for their murderous purpose. We can hardly suppose there were suitable stones lying about within an old finished building like Solomon's porch, though there might be stones at a little distance on account of the repairs of the temple.

Augustine remarks: "Behold the Jews understood what Arians do not understand."

Maldonatus observes that "these stones cry out against the Arians."

32 —[*Jesus...many good works...shewed...Father, etc.*] Our Lord here appeals to the many miracles He had publicly wrought before the Jews, in discharging His commission as sent by the Father to be the Messiah, all good and excellent works, in which none could find any fault, and He asks whether they proposed to stone Him for any of them. They had often asked

for signs and proofs of His being the Messiah. Well, He had wrought many such signs. Did they really mean to kill Him for His works? He had gone about only doing good. Did they intend to stone him for this?

The expression, " I have shewed," is curious, and we should have expected rather, " I have worked." It probably means, " I have publicly exhibited before your eyes, and not in a corner, but in such a manner as to court the fullest public observation, many wonderful proofs of my Messiahship." (Compare John ii. 18: " What sign shewest Thou? ") So St. Paul says that " God shall in His own time shew the appearing of Jesus Christ." (1 Tim. vi. 15.) The expression is probably a Hebraism. (Compare Psalm iv. 6; lx. 3; lxxi. 20; Exod. vii. 9.)

The expression, " from my Father," points to the great truth continually brought forward by our Lord in this Gospel: viz., that all His works as well as words were given to Him by the Father, to be worked and spoken in the world, and ought therefore to be held in special reverence.

Hengstenberg observes, that the expression, " many good works," evidently supposes that John knew of many other miracles which he does not record, and that many had been done at Jerusalem beside the few that are recorded.

[*For which...works...stone me.*] This could be literally rendered, " On account of which work of all these are you stoning Me? " Some, as Gualter and Tholuck, have thought that there is a slight tinge of sarcasm about the question. " Is it so that you are actually going to stone Me for good actions? Are not men generally stoned for evil doings? " Yet this seems an unlikely idea, and is needless. Is not the meaning made clear by simply inverting the order of words? " For what work or action are you going to stone Me? Justice requires that criminals should be punished for doing evil works; but all the many wonderful works I have done among you have been good, and not evil. You surely will not stone me for any of these; reason and your laws teach that this would be wrong. It is not therefore for my works and life that you are going to stone Me. I challenge you to prove that I have done evil. Which of you convicteth Me of sin? "

Taken in this view, the verse is simply a strong assertion, made by our Lord, of His own entire innocence of any crime for which He could be stoned.

Hutcheson thinks that " some stones were already cast at Christ, and therefore He says, Do you stone Me? " Yet this seems needless. The present tense here implies only, Are ye on the point of stoning Me?

33 —[*The Jews answered, etc.*] Our Lord's confident challenge, as in chap. viii. 46, seems to have been found unanswerable by the Jews. They could not prove any evil work against Him. They

therefore reply that they do not propose to stone Him for His *works*, but for having spoken blasphemous *words*. The precise nature of the blasphemy they say is, that " being nothing but a mere man, He made Himself God, or spoke of Himself in such a way as showed that He claimed to be God."

This is a very remarkable verse. It is like chap. v. 18 : " The Jews sought to kill Him, because He said that God was His Father, making Himself equal with God." It shows clearly that the Jews in our Lord's time attached a much higher and deeper sense to our Lord's frequently used language about God being His Father than modern readers are apt to do. In fact they regarded it as nothing less than a claim to equality with God. Modern Arians and Socinians, who profess to see nothing in our Lord's Sonship but a higher degree of that relationship which exists between all believers and God, would do well to mark this verse. What they say they cannot see, the Jews who hated Christ could see. This "cotemporaneous exposition," to use a legal phrase, of our Lord's words, deserves great respect, and carries with it great weight and authority. As a man, our Lord was a Jew, educated and trained among Jews. Common sense points out that the Jews who lived in His time were more likely to put correct sense on His words than modern Socinians.

Gualter observes, how frequently wicked men and persecutors of Christ's people have affected a zeal for God's glory and pretended a horror of blasphemy. The accusers of Naboth and Stephen are examples : so also the Spanish Inquisition.

A. Clarke observes : " That had the Jews, as many called Christians do, understood our Lord only to mean, by being 'one with the Father,' that He had unity of *sentiment* with the Father, they would not have attempted to treat Him as a blasphemer. In this sense Abraham, Isaac, Moses, David, and all the prophets were one with God. But what irritated them was that they understood him to speak of unity of *nature*. Therefore they say, ' Thou makest Thyself God.' "

34 —[*Jesus answered them, etc.*] Our Lord's defence of his own language against the charge of blasphemy is very remarkable. It is an argument from a lesser to a greater. If princes, who are merely men, are called gods, He who was the eternal Son of the Father could surely not be justly chargeable with blasphemy for calling Himself the " Son of God."

The expression, " your law," means the Scriptures. Sometimes our Lord speaks of two great divisions into which the Jews divided the Old Testament : viz., the law and the prophets. (As Matt. xxii. 40.) The " law " then included not the books of Moses only, but everything down to the end of the Song of Solomon. Sometimes He distributes the Scriptures into three parts : the law, the psalms, and the prophets. (As in Luke xxii. 44.) Here He uses one word for all the Old Tes-

tament, and calls it "the law." By saying "your law," our
Lord reminds His hearers that He appeals to *their own* honoured
sacred writings.

The expression, " I said ye are gods," is drawn from the
82d Psalm, in which Asaph is speaking of princes and rulers,
and their position and duties. Their elevation above other men
was so great, and their consequent responsibility for the state
of nations so great, that compared to other men, it might
be said, "You are as gods." A king is called "the Lord's
anointed." (2 Sam. i. 14.) So "Ye judge not for man, but for
the Lord." (2 Chron. xix. 6.) Princes and magistrates are
ordained of God, derive their power from God, act for God, and
stand between the people and God. Hence, in a sense, they are
called "gods." Those who wish to see this subject fully worked
out, will see it in Hall and Swinnock's Exposition of the 82d
Psalm.

We should observe how our Lord appeals to Scripture as the
judge of controversy : " Is it not written?" A plain text ought
to settle every disputed point. He might have argued : He simply quotes a text. By so doing He puts peculiar honour on
Scripture.

It is worth noticing that the Hebrew word rendered "judges"
in our version of Exodus xxii. 8, 9, might have been rendered
" gods." (Compare Exodus xxii. 28 ; xxi. 6.)

35 —[*If he called them gods.*] Here our Lord proceeds to show
what was the edge and point of His argument. All turned on
the use of the single word "gods" in one single verse of a
Psalm.

It is not very clear what governs the word we render "called,'
in this sentence. Our translators evidently thought it meant
"God." But why should it not refer direct to "your law " in
the last verse : "If your own book of the law in the Psalm has
called certain persons gods."

Chrysostom observes : " What He saith is of this kind : ' If
those who have received this honour by grace are not found
fault with for calling themselves gods, how can He deserve to
be rebuked who hath this by nature.' " Theophylact says the
same.

[*To whom the word of God came.*] This is a rather difficult
expression. Some, as Bullinger and Burgon, think that it refers to the commission from God, which rulers receive : "they
are persons to whom God has spoken, and commanded them to
rule for Him."—Some, as Alford, think it simply means, " if He
called them gods, to whom God spake in these passages." But
it may justly be replied that it does not say " God spake ; " but,
" There was the word of God." Of the two views the former
seems best. The Greek is almost the same as that of Luke iii.
2 : " The word of God came to John,"—meaning a special commission.

Heinsius suggests that the sentence means "*against* whom the word of God was " spoken in the 82d Psalm : that Psalm containing a rebuke of princes. But this seems doubtful.

Pearce thinks that it means "with whom was the word of judgment," and refers to the Septuagint version of 2 Chron. xix. 6.

It deserves notice that it is never said of Christ Himself, that the " Word of God came to Him." He was above all other commissioned judges.

[*And the Scripture cannot be broken.*] In this remarkable parenthesis our Lord reminds His Jewish hearers of their own acknowledged principle, that the " Scripture cannot be annulled or broken : " that is, that everything which it says must be received reverently and unhesitatingly, and that not one jot or tittle of it ought to be disregarded. Every word of Scripture must be allowed its full weight, and must neither be clipped, passed over, nor evaded. If the 82d Psalm calls princes who are mere men "gods," there cannot be any impropriety in applying the expression to persons commissioned by God. The expression may seem strange at first. Never mind, it is in the Scripture and it must be right.

Few passages appear to me to prove so incontrovertibly the plenary inspiration and divine authority of every word in the original text of the Bible. The whole point of our Lord's argument hinges on the divine authority of a single word. Was that word in the Psalms? Then it justified the application of the expression "gods" to men. Scripture cannot be broken. The theories of those who say that the writers of the Bible were inspired, but not all their writings,—or the ideas of the Bible inspired, but not all the language in which these ideas are conveyed,—appear to be totally irreconcilable with our Lord's use of the sentence before us. There is no other standing ground, I believe about inspiration, excepting the principle that it is plenary, and reaches to every syllable. Once leaving that ground, we are plunged in a sea of uncertainties. Like the carefully composed language of wills, settlements, and conveyances, every word of the Bible must be held sacred, and not a single flaw or slip of the pen admitted.

Let it be noted that the literal meaning of the word rendered " broken " is loosed or untied.

Gill observes : " This is a Jewish way of speaking, much used in the Talmud. When one doctor has produced an argument, another says, ' It may be broken,' or objected to, or refuted. But the Scripture cannot be broken."

Hengstenberg says : " It cannot be doubted that the Scripture is broken by those who assert that the Psalms breathe a spirit of revenge—that Solomon's song is a common Oriental love song—that there are in the Prophets predictions never to

be fulfilled—or by those who deny the Mosaic authorship of the
Pentateuch."

36. —[*Say ye of him, etc.*] Our Lord in this verse presses home on
the Jews the force of the expression in the 82d Psalm. "If
princes are called gods, do ye mean to call Me whom the Father
sanctified from eternity to be Messiah, and sent into the world
in due time, a blasphemer, because I have said, I am the Son of
God?"

" Say ye of *him* " would have been better rendered, " Say ye
of *Me*." The Greek leaves it open.

The expression, "whom the Father hath sanctified," must
mean, "whom the Father hath set apart, and appointed from
all eternity in the covenant of grace, as a priest is sanctified and
set apart for the service of the temple." It cannot mean literally " made holy." It implies eternal dedication and appointment to a certain office. This is one of the places which teach
the eternal generation of Christ. Long before He came into
the world, " the Father" (not *God*, observe) had sanctified and
appointed the Son. He did not become the Son when He entered the world: He was the Son from all eternity.

The expression, " sent into the world," means that *mission*
of Christ's to be the Saviour, which took place when he became
incarnate, and came among us in the form of a man. He was
the Father's " sent One," the " Apostle" of our profession. (See
Heb. iii. 1; John iii. 17; and 1 John iv. 14.) He that was so
" sanctified" and " sent," might well speak of Himself as the Son
of God, and equal with God.

Calvin remarks: " There is a sanctification that is common
to all believers. But here Christ claims for Himself something
far more excellent: namely, that He alone was separated from
all others, that the grace of the Spirit and majesty of God might
be displayed in Him; as He said formerly, ' Him hath God the
Father sealed.'" (John vi. 27.)

37. —[*If I do not the works, etc.*] Here our Lord once more appeals
to the evidence of His miracles, and challenges attention to
them. " I do not ask you to believe that I am the Son of God
and the Messiah, if I do not prove it by my works. If I did no
miracles, you might be justified in not believing Me to be the
Messiah, and in calling Me a blasphemer."

Here, again, we should observe how our Lord calls His miracles the " works of His Father." They were works given to Him
by His Father to do. They were such works as none but God
the Father could possibly perform.

Gualter observes, what a proof this verse indirectly supplies
of the nullity of the Pope's claim to be God's vicegerent and
head of the Church! What are his works? What evidence of a
divine mission does he give?

Musculus also remarks that the Pope's high claims and great sounding titles are useless, so long as his works contradict his words.

38 —[*But if I do though, etc.*] Our Lord here concludes His reply to the Jews: "If I do the works of my Father, then, though ye may not be convinced by what I say, be convinced by what I do. Though ye resist the evidence of my words, yield to the evidence of my works. In this way learn to know and believe that I and my Father are indeed one, He in Me, and I in Him, and that in claiming to be His Son I speak no blasphemy."

We should note here, as elsewhere, our Lord's strong and repeated appeals to the evidence of His miracles. He sent to John the Baptist, and desired him to mark His works, if He would know whether He was "the coming One,"—"Go and tell John what ye have seen and heard, the blind receive their sight," etc. Just so He argues here. (Matt. xi. 4.)

Let us note the close and intimate union that exists between the First and Second Persons of the Trinity: "The Father is in Me, and I in Him." Such language can never be reconciled with the views of Socinians.

"By these words," says Bloomfield, "our Lord meant communion of mind and equality of power. It is plain that the Jews clearly understood that He claimed and ascribed to Himself the attributes of Godhead, and made Himself equal with the Father."

Chrysostom remarks, that our Lord seems to say, "I am nothing different from what the Father is, so however as that I remain Son; and the Father is nothing different from what I am, so however as that He remains Father. He that knows Me has known the Father, and learned the Son."

39 —[*Therefore...sought...take him.*] Here we see the utter insensibility of our Lord's hardened enemies to any argument or appeal to their reason. In spite of what He had now said, they showed a determination to go on with their wicked designs, and tried again to lay violent hands on Him. Nothing seems to harden the heart, and take away the reasoning faculty, so completely as obstinate resistance to plain evidence.

[*But he escaped...hand.*] This would be literally rendered, "And He came forth out of their hand," as in Luke iv. 30; and at viii. 59 of this Gospel. The escape seems to have been effected by miracle. A restraint was put on the hands of His enemies, and their eyes were temporarily blinded.

40 —[*And went...again....Jordan....John...baptized.*] I know not to what the expression "again" can refer here, except to the time when our Lord began His ministry by coming to be baptized by John at Bethabara, beyond Jordan. (See John i. 28.) I do not find that He had been there again during the three years of His

ministry. There is something touching and instructive in the choice of this place. Where our Lord began His ministry, there He resolved to enter it. It would remind His Jewish hearers that John the Baptist had repeatedly proclaimed Him as " the Lamb of God," and they could not deny John's Divine mission. It would remind His own disciples of the first lessons which they learned under their Master's teaching, and recall old things to their minds. It is good to revisit old scenes sometimes. The flesh needs many helps to memory.

Henry makes the quaint remark, " The Bishop of our souls came not to be fixed in one See, but to go about from place to place doing good."

[*And there he abode.*] Our Lord must evidently have remained here between three and four months,—from the feast of dedication to the last passover when he was crucified; that is from winter to Easter. Where precisely, and with whom he stayed, we do not know. It must have been a solemn and quiet season to Himself and His disciples.

Musculus observes that this verse teaches us that it is lawful to regard localities in which great spiritual works have been done with more than ordinary reverence and affection.

41 —[*And many resorted, etc.*] Our Lord's choice of an abode seems to have had an excellent effect. It was not so far from Jerusalem but that " many " could come to hear Him, as they did to hear John the Baptist. There on the very spot where John, now no longer living, used to preach to enormous crowds, and baptize, they could not help being reminded of John's repeated testimony to Christ. And the consequence was, that they said, " John, whom we believe to have been a prophet, certainly did no miracles, but everything that he said of this Jesus as the coming One, whose shoes he was not worthy to wear, was true. We believed John to be a prophet sent of God. Much more ought this man to be believed."

Let us observe that John's preaching was not forgotten after his death, though it seemed to produce little effect during his life. Herod could cut short his ministry, put him in prison, and have him beheaded; but he could not prevent his words being remembered. Sermons never die. The Word of God is not bound. (2 Tim. ii. 9.)

We never read of any miracle or mighty work being performed by John. He was only " a voice." Like all other ministers, he had one great work,—to preach, and prepare the way for Christ. To do this is more lasting work than to perform miracles, though it does not make so much outward show.

Besser remarks : " John is a type of every servant of Christ. The gift of working miracles, imparted but to few, we can do without, if only one hearer testify of us, 'All things that they spake of Christ are true.' If only our preaching, though it may last longer than three years, is sealed as the true witness of Christ, through the experience of those who believe and are saved, then we shall have done miracles enough."

42 —[*And many believed...there.*] Whether this was head belief, the faith of intellectual conviction,—or heart belief, the faith of reception of Christ as a Saviour,—we are left in doubt. We have the same expression viii. 30 and xi. 45. Yet we need not doubt that very many Jews, both here and elsewhere, were secretly convinced of our Lord's Messiahship, and after His resurrection came forward and confessed their faith, and were baptized. It seems highly probable that this accounts for the great number converted at once on the day of Pentecost and at other times. (See Acts iv. 4; vi. 7; and xxi. 20.) The way had been prepared in their hearts long before, by our Lord's own preaching, though at the time they had not courage to avow it. The good that is done by preaching is not always seen immediately. Our Lord sowed, and His Apostles reaped all over Palestine.

Chrysostom has a long and curious comment on this verse. He draws from it the great advantage of privacy and quiet to the soul, and the benefit that women especially derive from living a retired life at home, compared to men. His exhortation to wives to use their advantages in this respect, and to help their husbands' souls, is very singular, when we consider the times he wrote in, and the state of society at Constantinople. "Nothing," he says, "is more powerful than a pious and sensible woman, to bring a man into proper order, and to mould his soul as she will."

Henry observes: "Where the preaching of repentance has had success, there the preaching of reconciliation and Gospel grace is most likely to be prosperous. Where John has been acceptable, Jesus will not be unacceptable. The jubilee trumpet sounds sweetest in the ears of those who, in the day of atonement, have afflicted their souls for sin."

JOHN XI 1—6

1 Now a certain *man* was sick, *named* Lazarus, of Bethany, the town of Mary and her sister Martha.

2 (It was *that* Mary which anointed the Lord with ointment, and wiped his feet with her hair, whose brother Lazarus was sick.)

3 Therefore his sisters sent unto him, saying, Lord, behold, he whom thou lovest is sick.

4 When Jesus heard *that*, he said, This sickness is not unto death, but for the glory of God, that the Son of God might be glorified thereby.

5 Now Jesus loved Martha, and her sister, and Lazarus.

6 When he had heard therefore that he was sick, he abode two days still in the same place where he was.

THE chapter we have now begun is one of the most remarkable in the New Testament. For grandeur and simplicity, for pathos and solemnity, nothing was ever written like it. It describes a miracle which is not recorded in the other Gospels,—the raising of Lazarus from the dead. Nowhere shall we find such convincing proofs of our Lord's Divine power. As God, He makes the grave itself yield up its tenants.—Nowhere shall we find such striking illustrations of our Lord's ability to sympathize with His people. As man, He can be touched with the feelings of our infirmities.—Such a miracle well became the end of such a ministry. It was meet and right that the victory of Bethany should closely precede the crucifixion at Calvary.

These verses teach us that *true Christians may be sick and ill as well as others.* We read that Lazarus of Bethany was one " whom Jesus loved," and a brother of two well-known holy women. Yet Lazarus was sick, even unto death! The Lord Jesus, who had power over all diseases, could no doubt have prevented this illness, if He had thought fit. But He did not do so. He allowed Lazarus to be sick, and in pain, and weary, and to languish and suffer like any other man.

The lesson is one which ought to be deeply graven in our memories. Living in a world full of disease and death, we are sure to need it some day. Sickness, in the very nature of things, can never be anything but trying to flesh and blood. Our bodies and souls are strangely linked together, and that which vexes and weakens the body can hardly fail to vex the mind and soul. But sickness, we must always remember, is no sign that God is displeased with us ; nay, more, it is generally sent for the good of our souls. It tends to draw our affections away from this world, and to direct them to things above. It sends us to our Bibles, and teaches us to pray better. It helps to prove our faith and patience, and shows us the real value of our hope in Christ. It reminds us betimes that we are not to live always, and tunes and trains our hearts for our great change. Then let us be patient and cheerful when we are laid aside by illness. Let us believe that the Lord Jesus loves us when we are sick no less than when we are well.

These verses teach us, secondly, that *Jesus Christ is the Christian's best Friend in the time of need.* We read that when Lazarus was sick, his sisters at once sent to Jesus, and laid the matter before Him. Beautiful, touching, and simple was the message they sent. They did not ask Him to come at once, or to work a miracle, and command the disease to depart. They only said, " Lord, he whom Thou lovest is sick," and left the matter there, in the full belief that He would do what was best. Here was the true faith and humility of saints! Here was gracious submission of will!

The servants of Christ, in every age and climate, will do well to follow this excellent example. No doubt when those whom we love are sick, we are to use diligently every reasonable means for their recovery. We must spare no pains to obtain the best medical advice. We must assist nature in every possible manner to fight a good fight against its enemy. But in all our doing, we must never forget that the best and ablest and wisest Helper is in heaven, at God's right hand. Like afflicted Job our first action must be to fall on our knees and worship. Like Hezekiah, we must spread our matters before the Lord. Like the holy sisters at Bethany, we must send up a prayer to Christ. Let us not forget, in the hurry and excitement of our feelings, that none can help like Him, and that He is merciful, loving, and gracious.

These verses teach us, thirdly, that *Christ loves all who are true Christians.* We read that " Jesus loved Martha, and her sister, and Lazarus." The characters of these three good people seem to have been somewhat different. Of Martha, we are told in a certain place, that she was "careful and troubled about many things," while Mary "sat at Jesus' feet, and heard His word." Of Lazarus we are told nothing distinctive at all. Yet all these were loved by the Lord Jesus. They all belonged to His family, and He loved them all.

We must carefully bear this in mind in forming our estimate of Christians. We must never forget that there are varieties in character, and that the grace of God does not cast all believers into one and the same mould. Admitting fully that the foundations of Christian character are always the same, and that all God's children repent, believe, are holy, prayerful, and Scripture-loving, we must make allowances for wide varieties in their temperaments and habits of mind. We must not undervalue others because they are not exactly like ourselves. The flowers in a garden may differ widely, and yet the gardener feels interest in all. The children of a family may be curiously unlike one another, and yet the parents care for all. It is just so with the Church of Christ. There are degrees of grace, and varieties of grace; but the least, the weakest, the feeblest disciples are all loved by the Lord Jesus. Then let no believer's heart fail because of his infirmities; and, above all, let no believer dare to despise and undervalue a brother.

These verses teach us, lastly, that *Christ knows best at what time to do anything for His people*. We read that "when He had heard that Lazarus was sick, He abode two days still in the same place where He was." In fact, He purposely delayed His journey, and did not come to Bethany till Lazarus had been four days in the grave. No doubt He knew well what was going on; but He never moved till the time came which He saw was best. For the sake of the Church and the world, for the good of friends and enemies, He kept away.

The chilrden of God must constantly school their minds to learn the great lesson now before us. Nothing so helps us to bear patiently the trials of life as an abiding conviction of the perfect wisdom by which everything around us is managed. Let us try to believe not only that all that happens to us is well done, but that it is done in the best manner, by the right instrument, and at the right time. We are all naturally impatient in the day of trial. We are apt to say, like Moses, when beloved ones are sick, " Heal her *now*, Lord, we beseech thee." (Num. xii. 13.) We forget that Christ is too wise a Physician to make any mistakes. It is the duty of faith to say, " My times are in Thy hand. Do with me as Thou wilt, how Thou wilt, what Thou wilt, and when Thou wilt. Not my will, but Thine be done." The highest degree of faith is to be able to wait, sit still, and not complain.

Let us turn from the passage with a settled determination to trust Christ entirely with all the concerns of this world, both public and private. Let us believe that He by whom all things were made at first is He who is managing all with perfect wisdom. The affairs of kingdoms, families, and private individuals are all alike overruled by Him. He chooses all the portions of His people. When we are sick, it is because He knows it to be for our good ; when He delays coming to help us, it is for some wise reason. The hand that was nailed to the -cross is too wise and loving to smite without a needs-be, or to keep us waiting for relief without a cause.

NOTES JOHN XI 1—6

The raising of Lazarus, described in this chapter, is one of the most wonderful events recorded in the Gospels, and demands more than ordinary attention. In no part of our Lord's history do we see Him so distinctly both man and God at the

same time, man in sympathy, and God in power. Like each
of the few incidents in our Lord's ministry related by St. John,
it is placed before us with peculiar minuteness and particularity. The story is singularly rich in delicate, tender, and
beautiful expressions. Before entering upon it, I venture to
offer the following preliminary remarks.

(a) The raising of Lazarus was manifestly intended to
supply the Jews with one more incontrovertible proof that
Jesus was the ·Christ of God, the promised Messiah. In the
tenth chapter, at the feast of dedication, Our Lord had been
asked, " If Thou be the Christ, tell us plainly." (John x. 24.)
In reply He had distinctly appealed to His " works," as the best
evidence of His Messiahship. He had deliberately challenged
attention to those works as witnesses to His commission.
And now, after a short interval, we find Him for the last time,
within two miles of Jerusalem before many eye-witnesses,
doing such a stupendous work of Divine power that a man might
have thought any sceptic would have been silenced forever.
After the raising of Lazarus, the Jews of Jerusalem at any rate
could never say that they were left destitute of proofs of
Christ's Messiahship.

(b) The raising of Lazarus was meant to prepare the minds
of the Jews for our Lord's own resurrection. It took place
between· Christmas and Easter, and probably within two
months of His own crucifixion. It proved incontrovertibly that
a person dead four days could be raised again by Divine power,
and that the restoration to life of a corpse was not an impossibility with God. I think it impossible not to see in this a
latent design to prepare the minds of the Jews for our Lord's
own resurrection. At any rate it paved the way for men believing the event to be not incredible. No one could say on Easter
Sunday, when the grave of Jesus was found empty, and the
body of Jesus was gone, that His resurrection was an impossibility. The mere fact that between winter and Easter in that
very year a man dead four days had been restored to life within
two miles of Jerusalem would silence such remarks. Though
improbable, it could not be called impossible.

(c) The raising of Lazarus is of all our Lord's miracles the
one which is most thoroughly credible, and supported by most
incontrovertible evidence. The man who disbelieves it may as
well say plainly that he does not believe anything in the New
Testament, and does not allow that a miracle is possible. Of
course there is no standing-ground between denying the possibility of miracles, and denying the existence of a creating God.
If God made the world, surely He can change the course of
nature at any time, if He thinks fit.

The famous sceptic, Spinosa, declared that if he could be
persuaded of the truth of the miracle before us, he would forsake his own system, and embrace Christianity. Yet it is extremely difficult to see what evidence of a fact a man can desire,

if he is not satisfied with the evidence that Lazarus really was raised from the dead. But, unhappily, none are so blind as those who will not see.

The following passage from Tittman, the German Commentator, is so sensible that I make no apology for giving it at length, though somewhat condensed: "The whole story," he says, "is of a nature calculated to exclude all suspicion of imposture, and to confirm the truth of the miracle. A well-known person of Bethany, named Lazarus, falls sick in the absence of Jesus. His sisters send a message to Jesus, announcing it; but while He is yet absent Lazarus dies, is buried, and kept in the tomb for four days, during which Jesus is still absent. Martha, Mary, and all his friends are convinced of his death. Our Lord, while yet remaining in the place where He had been staying, tells His disciples in plain terms that He means to go to Bethany, to raise Lazarus from the dead, that the glory of God may be illustrated, and their faith confirmed. At our Lord's approach, Martha goes to meet Him, and announces her brother's death, laments the absence of Jesus before the event took place, and yet expresses a faint hope that by some means Jesus might yet render help. Our Lord declares that her brother shall be raised again, and assures her that He has the power of granting life to the dead. Mary approaches, accompanied by weeping friends from Jerusalem. Our Lord Himself is moved, and weeps, and goes to the sepulchre, attended by a crowd. The stone is removed. The stench of the corpse is perceived. Our Lord, after pouring forth audible prayer to His Father, calls forth Lazarus from the grave, in the hearing of all. The dead man obeys the call, comes forth to public view in the same dress that he was buried in, alive and well, and returns home without assistance. All persons present agree that Lazarus is raised to life, and that a great miracle has been worked, though not all believe the person who worked it to be the Messiah. Some go away and tell the rulers at Jerusalem what Jesus has done. Even these do not doubt the truth of the fact; on the contrary, they confess that our Lord by His works is becoming every day more famous, and that He would probably be soon received as Messiah by the whole nation. And *therefore* the rulers at once take counsel how they may put to death both Jesus and Lazarus. The people, in the mean time hearing of this prodigious transaction, flock in multitudes to Bethany, partly to see Jesus, and partly to view Lazarus. And the consequence is that by and by, when our Lord comes to Jerusalem, the population goes forth in crowds to meet Him and show Him honour, and chiefly because of His work at Bethany. Now, if all these circumstances do not establish the truth of the miracle, there is no truth in history."—I only add the remark, that when we consider the place, the time, the circumstances, and the singular publicity, of the raising of Lazarus, it really seems to require more credulity to deny it than to believe it. It is the unbeliever, and not the believer of this miracle, who seems to me the credulous man. The difficulties of disbelieving it are far greater than those of believing it.

(*d*) The raising of Lazarus is not mentioned by Matthew, Mark, and Luke. This has stumbled many persons. Yet the omission of the story is not hard to explain. Some have said that Matthew, Mark, and Luke purposely confine themselves to miracles done in Galilee.—Some have said that when they wrote their Gospels Lazarus was yet alive, and the mention of his name would have endangered his safety.—Some have said that it was thought better for the soul of Lazarus not to draw attention to him and surround him with an unhealthy celebrity till after he left the world.—In each and all of these reasons there is some weight. But the best and simplest explanation probably is, that each Evangelist was inspired to record what God saw to be best and most suitable. No one, I suppose, imagines that the Evangelists record a tenth part of our Lord's miracles, or that there were not other dead persons raised to life, of whom we know nothing at all. "The dead are raised up," was our Lord's own message, at an early period of His ministry, to John the Baptist. (Matt. xi. 5.) "If the works that Jesus did should be written every one," says John, "the world itself could not contain the books that should be written." (John xxi. 25.) Let it suffice us to believe that each Evangelist was inspired to record exactly those events which were most likely to be profitable for the Church in studying his Gospel. Our Lord's ministry and sayings at Jerusalem were specially assigned to John. What wonder, then, that he was appointed to record the mighty miracle which took place within two miles of Jerusalem, and proved incontrovertibly the guilt of the Jerusalem Jews in not receiving Jesus as the Messiah?

Bucer remarks that there is a continually ascending greatness and splendour in those miracles which John was inspired to record in his Gospel, and that the raising of Lazarus was the most illustrious of all. He also observes that our Lord specially chose the great feasts at Jerusalem as occasions of working miracles.

Chemnitius remarks: "There is not in the whole Evangelical narrative a more delightful history, and one more abundant both in doctrine and consolation, than this of the raising of Lazarus. It therefore ought to be studied most closely and minutely by all pious minds."

1 —[*Now a certain man...sick...Lazarus.*] These simple words are the key-note to the whole chapter. All turns on the bodily illness of an obscure disciple of Christ. How much in the history of our lives hinges on little events, and specially on illnesses! Sickness is a sacred thing, and one of God's great ordinances.

This illness took place between winter and Easter, during the time that our Lord was at Bethabara, beyond Jordan. The nature of the disease we are not told; but from its rapid course, it is not unlikely it was a fever, such as is common even now in Palestine.

This is the first time that Lazarus is mentioned in the New Testament, and we know nothing certain of his history. Some have conjectured that he was the young ruler who came to our Lord, asking what he must do to obtain eternal life,—and went away sorrowful at the time, but was afterwards converted. —Some have conjectured that he is the young man who followed our Lord when he was taken prisoner, mentioned by St. Mark, and fled away naked.—But these are mere guesses, and there is really no solid foundation for them. That he was not a poor man, but comparatively rich, seems highly probable from the "feast" in John xii., the number of friends who came to mourn him, the alabaster box of precious ointment used by his sister, and the sepulchre hewn out of rock. But even this is only a conjecture.

The name "Lazarus" no doubt is a Greek form of the Hebrew name "Eleazer." It is worth noticing, that it survives to this day in the modern name of Bethany, "El-Azarizeh." (*See Smith's Biblical Dictionary.*)

[*Of Bethany...town...Mary...Martha.*] The word "town" in this sentence would have been better translated "village," as it is in sixteen other texts in the New Testament. Bethany, in truth, was only a small village, a short two miles from Jerusalem, on the east side; and its situation is perfectly known now. It lies on the eastern slope of the Mount of Olives, on the road to Jericho. It is not once mentioned in the Old Testament, and owes its fame to its being the place where Lazarus was raised, —the place where our Lord rested at night just before the passion,—the place from which He commenced His triumphant entry into Jerusalem,—the place from which He finally ascended into heaven, (Luke xxiv. 10,) and the dwelling-place of Mary and Martha.

Let it be noted that the presence of God's elect children is the one thing which makes towns and countries famous in God's sight. The village of Martha and Mary is noticed, while Memphis and Thebes are not named in the New Testament. A cottage where there is grace, is more pleasant in God's sight than a cathedral town where there is none.

Let it be noted that this verse supplies internal evidence that St. John's Gospel was written long after the other historical parts of the New Testament. He speaks of Martha and Mary as persons whose names and history would be familiar to all Christian readers.

There is a peculiarity in the Greek of this verse, which is hardly conveyed in our English translation. Literally it would be rendered, "Lazarus *from* Bethany, *out of* the town of Mary," etc. That "from" Bethany means exactly what we render it, is

clear from Acts xvii. 13; Heb. xiii. 24. But why "out of the
village, or town of Mary," is said, is not quite so clear. It is
open to the conjecture that it means "Lazarus was now a man
of Bethany, but was originally out of the town of Mary and
Martha;" viz., some other place. But this seems unlikely.—Web-
ster suggests that "out of" is added by way of emphasis, to
show that Lazarus not only lived there, but that it was also the
place of his nativity. Greswell says much the same. It is noteworthy that John i. 44 contains exactly the same form of expression about Philip and Bethsaida.

It is noteworthy that Mary is named before Martha, though
Martha was evidently the older sister, and head of the house.
The reason, I suppose, is that Mary's name and character were
better known of the two.

Chemnitius thinks it possible that all Bethany belonged to
Martha and Mary, and that this accounts for the consideration
in which they were held, and the number of mourners, etc. It
is worth remembering that Bethany was a very small place.
Yet Bethsaida was called the "town of Andrew and Peter,"
(John i. 44,) and clearly did not belong to two poor fishermen.

2 —[*It was that Mary, etc.*] This verse is a parenthetical explanation inserted by St. John after his manner, to make it certain
what Mary he refers to, as the sister of Lazarus. Christians
knew there were in our Lord's time no less than four Maries :
(1) The virgin mother of our Lord, (2) the wife of Cleophas, (3)
Mary Magdalene, (4) Mary the sister of Martha. To prevent,
therefore, any mistake, John says," It was that Mary who anointed our Lord, whose brother Lazarus was dead."

Simple as these words seem, there is a singular diversity of
opinion as to the question who Mary the sister of Martha and
Lazarus was, and how many times our Lord was anointed.

(*a*) Some, as Chrysostom, Origen, and Chemnitius, maintain
that the anointing took place three times : once, in Luke vii., at
the house of Simon the Pharisee; once in Bethany, at the house
of Simon the leper; and once in Bethany, at the house of Martha and Mary. Others, as Ferus, while agreeing with Chrysostom that our Lord was anointed three times, think Mary was the
woman who twice did it.

(*b*) Some maintain that our Lord was anointed twice : once at
the Pharisee's house, (in Luke vii.,) and once at Bethany, at the
house of Simon the leper, where Martha and Mary and Lazarus
lived, for some cause which we do not know.

(*c*) Some, as Augustine, Bede, Toletus, Kightfoot, Maldonatus,
Cornelius à Lapide, and Hengstenberg, maintain that our Lord
was only once anointed,—that the narrative in Luke vii. was inserted out of chronological order,—that Simon the Pharisee and
Simon the leper were the same person, and that the one anointing took place at Bethany. Hengstenberg supports his theory

very ingeniously, and boldly suggests that Simon the Pharisee was also called Simon the leper, was the husband of Martha, and not friendly to Christ:—that this accounts for Martha being more "careful and troubled," in Luke x. 41, than Mary, and for unfriendly Pharisees being present at the raising of Lazarus;—that Mary Magdalene was the same as Mary of Bethany, and that Mary of Bethany was the "sinner," in Luke vii.

Toletus frankly admits that the Romish Church holds that there was only one anointing by one person, as it is plainly declared in one of her formularies: viz., the Breviary.

My own opinion is decidedly against the last of these views. I hold that there were *at least* two anointings,—one at a comparatively early period of our Lord's ministry, and another at the close of it,—one in the house of an unfriendly Pharisee named Simon, and another at the house of Simon the leper, in Bethany, —one by a woman who had been pre-eminently a sinner, another by Mary the sister of Martha, against whose moral character we know nothing.—Why the house of Martha and Mary at Bethany is called the house of Simon the leper, I admit I cannot explain. I can only surmise that there was some relationship of which we know nothing. But this difficulty is nothing in my eyes compared to that of supposing, with Augustine and his followers, that the event described in Luke vii. took place just at the end of our Lord's ministry. There is strong internal evidence that it did not, to my mind. Surely at the end of our Lord's ministry, people would not have said with wonder, "Who is this that forgiveth sins?" Surely Mary would not be spoken of as a notorious "sinner."

On the other hand, if we hold the view that our Lord was only anointed twice, once at the house of Simon the Pharisee, and once at Bethany, it must be frankly admitted that there is a very grave difficulty to be got over. That difficulty is that St. Mark says that a woman anointed our Lord "two days" before the Passover, and poured the ointment on His "head" while John says He was anointed "six days before the passover," and the ointment poured on His "feet."—I do not see how this difficulty can be got over. If, however, we hold that our Lord was anointed twice in the last week before He was crucified, once "six days" before, and once "two days" before, and on each occasion by a woman, the whole thing is clear. That such a thing should be done more than once, in those days, does not strike me as any objection, considering the customs of the age. That our Lord's language in defence of the woman should on each occasion be the same is somewhat remarkable. But it is only a minor difficulty. On the whole, therefore, if I must give an opinion, I incline to agree with Chrysostom, that there were three anointings. I also think there is something in the view, of Ferus, that Mary, sister of Lazarus, anointed our Lord twice, once six days before the passover, and once again two days before.

The use of the past participle in the verse before us seems to me no difficulty at all. It is of course true that at this time Mary had not anointed our Lord. But it is no less true that John evidently mentions it by anticipation, as an historical fact long past and well known in the Church when he wrote his Gospel, which his readers would understand. "It was that Mary which afterwards anointed Christ's feet."

Let us note in this verse, that the good deeds of all Christ's saints are carefully recorded in God's book of remembrance. Men are forgetful and ungrateful. Nothing done for Christ is ever forgotten.

Let us note that sickness comes to Christ's people as well as to the wicked and worldly. Grace does not exempt us from trial. Sickness, on the contrary, is one of God's most useful instruments for sanctifying His saints, and making them bear fruit of patience, and for showing the world that His people do not serve Him merely for what they get of bodily ease and comfort in this life. "Job does not serve God for nought," was the devil's sneer, in the days when Job prospered. "Lazarus and his sisters make a good thing of their religion,"—might have been said if they had had no trials.

Brentius remarks: "God does not go away when bodily health goes away. Christ does not depart when life departs."

3 —[*Therefore his sisters sent...saying.*] This is an example of what all Christians should do in trouble. Like Mary and Martha, we should first send a message to Christ. By prayer we can do it as really as they did. This is what Job did in his trouble: he first of all "worshipped," and said, "Blessed be the name of the Lord." This is what Asa did not do: "He sought not to the Lord, but to the physicians." (Job i. 20; 2 Chron. xv. 12.)

Let it be noted that the Greek would be more literally rendered "the sisters," and not "his." This message, from the expression in next verse, "heard," would seem to have been a verbal and not a written one.

[*Lord...he whom thou lovest is sick.*] This is a very touching and beautiful little message.—Its humble and respectful confidence is noteworthy, "He whom Thou lovest is sick." They do not say, "do something," or "heal him," or "come at once." They simply spread the case before the Lord, and leave Him to do what He thinks wisest and best. It is like Hezekiah spreading Sennacherib's letter before God. (2 Kings xix. 14.)—The name given to Lazarus is noteworthy: they do not say "our brother," or "thy disciple," or even "one who loves Thee," but simply "he whom Thou lovest," one whom Thou hast been pleased to treat graciously and kindly as a beloved friend. Christ's love to us, and not our love to Christ, is the blessed truth which we ought continually to keep before our minds. His love never changes: ours is wavering and uncertain.

The idea of some, that sending a message to Christ was a mark of weak faith in the two sisters, as if it showed doubt of Christ's omniscience, is absurd. At this rate we might never pray, and might say there is no need, because God knows all!

The word " behold " seems either to indicate something " sudden " in the illness of Lazarus, like Mark ii. 21, and to be used adverbially; or else we must take it as an imperative verb. " Behold a case of great affliction: look upon it and see: he whom Thou lovest is sick." This would be like Hezekiah's prayer: " Open Thine eyes and see." (2 Kings xix. 16.) We can hardly suppose that such disciples as Martha and Mary would think it a strange or surprising thing that a disciple of Christ should be ill; yet it is possible they did. However, Theophylact and Ferus suppose that " Behold " implies a degree of wonder and surprise.

Rupertus remarks, on the message containing no request: " To a loving friend it was quite enough to announce the fact that Lazarus was sick." Affectionate friends are not verbose or lengthy in descriptions.

Brentius remarks that the message is like all true prayer: it does not consist in much speaking, and fine long sentences.

Musculus and Chemnitius both remark, that when a man's child falls into a well or pit, it is enough to tell a loving father the simple fact, in the shortest manner possible, without dwelling on it verbosely and rhetorically.

Rollock observes how useful it is to have praying sisters.

Let us note that Christ's friends may be sick and ill, just like other people. It is no proof that they are not beloved, and specially preserved and cared for by God. " Whom the Lord loveth He chasteneth." The purest gold is most in the fire ; the most useful tools are oftenest ground. Epaphroditus and Timothy were both of weak health, and Paul could not prevent it.

4 —[*When Jesus heard that, he said.*] This verse seems to contain the reply which our Lord gave to the messenger. It was to him probably, though in the hearing of all His disciples, that He addressed the words which follow. It is as though He said, " Go, return to thy mistress and say as follows."

[*This sickness is not unto death, etc.*] The meaning of this sentence must evidently be taken with qualification. Our Lord did not mean that Lazarus would not in any sense die. It is as though He said, " The end of this sickness is not Lazarus' death and entire removal from this world, but generally the glory of God, and specially the glorifying of Me, His Son, which will be effected by my raising him again." Death's temporary victory over us is not complete till our bodies perish and return to dust. This was not allowed in the case of Lazarus, and hence death had not full dominion over him, though he ceased to breathe and became unconscious.

It is undeniable that there was something dark and mysterious about our Lord's message. He might of course have said plainly, "Lazarus will die, and then I will raise him again." Yet there is a wonderful likeness between the style of his message and many an unfulfilled prophecy. He said enough to excite hope, and encourage faith and patience and prayer, but not enough to make Mary and Martha leave off praying and seeking God. And is not this exactly what we should feel about many an unfulfilled prediction of things to come? Men complain that prophecies are not so literally fulfilled as to exclude doubt and uncertainty. But they forget that God wisely permits a degree of uncertainty in order to keep us watching and praying. It is just what He did with Martha and Mary here.

Let us remember that the final result of Lazarus' sickness is what we should desire as the result of any sickness that comes on us and our families: viz., that God and Christ may be glorified in us. We cannot say, "It shall not end in death:" but we can say, "By God's help, it shall be for God's glory."

Chrysostom observes: "The expression *that* in this passage denotes not cause, but consequence. The sickness happened from other causes. Christ used it for the glory of God."

Calvin remarks, that God wishes to be honoured by Christ being glorified. "He who does not honour the Son does not honour the Father." (John v. 23.)

5 —[*Now Jesus loved Martha, etc.*] This verse is meant to show that all the members of the family at Bethany were disciples of Jesus and beloved by Him, the brother as well as the sisters, and one sister as well as the other. A happy family, Lampe remarks, in which all the members were objects of Christ's special love.

We know not where Lazarus was at the time when Jesus stopped at Martha's house, in Luke x.: perhaps he was not converted at that time. But this is only conjecture.

We are generally apt to undervalue the grace of Martha and overvalue that of Mary, because of what happened when Jesus was at Martha's house before. Many foolish things are sometimes lightly said against mothers and mistresses as being Marthas, "careful and troubled about many things." Yet people should remember that different positions call out different phases of character. Mary certainly shines more brightly than Martha in the 10th of Luke; but it is a grave question whether Martha did not outshine her in the 11th of John. Active-minded Christians come out better under some circumstances; quiet-minded Christians, in others. Our Lord teaches us here that He loves all who have grace, though their temperaments differ. Let us learn not to judge others rashly, and not to form hasty estimates of Christians, until we have seen them under every sort of circumstances, in winter as well as summer, in dark days as well as bright.

Let it be noted that the Greek word here rendered "loved," is not the same that is rendered "lovest," in the 3d verse. The word describing the love of Jesus to the three in this verse is a word expressing a high, deep, excellent, and noble affection. It is the same as Mark x. 21, and John iii. 16.—The word used in the message of the sisters is a lower word, such as is used to describe the affection between a parent and child, or husband and wife. It is the word used for "kiss" in Matt. xxvi. 48; Mark xiv. 44; and Luke xxii. 47. It is very noticeable that this word is carefully avoided here, when the two sisters are mentioned. The Holy Ghost inspired John to abstain even from the appearance of evil. What a lesson this ought to be to us!

Let it be noted that we see here an example of the broad distinction that ought to be drawn between Christ's general love of compassion which He feels towards all mankind, and His special love of election which He feels towards His own members. He loved all sinners to whom He came to preach the Gospel, and He wept over unbelieving Jerusalem. But He specially loved those who believed on Him.

6 —[*When he had heard therefore, etc.*] It is impossible not to remark an intentional and most instructive connection between this verse and the preceding one. Our Lord loved the family of Bethany, all three of them; and yet when He heard Lazarus was sick, instead of hastening at once to Bethany to heal him, He quietly remained at Bethabara for two days, without moving.

We cannot doubt that this delay was intentional and of purpose, and it throws immense light on many of God's providential dealings with His people. We know that the delay caused immense mental pain and suffering to Martha and Mary, and obliged Lazarus to go through all the agony of death, and the sorrow of parting. We can easily imagine the grief and suspense and perplexity in which the household at Bethany must have been kept for four days, when their loving Master did not appear; and we know that our Lord could have prevented it all, but did not. But we know also that if He had at once hurried to Bethany and healed Lazarus, or spoken a word from a distance at Bethabara and commanded his healing, as in John iv. 50, the mighty miracle of raising him would never have been wrought, and the wonderful sayings of Bethany would never have been spoken. In short the pain of a few was permitted for the benefit of the whole Church of Christ.

We have here the simplest and best account of the permission of evil and suffering. God could prevent it. God does not love to make his creatures suffer. But God sees there are lessons which mankind could not learn unless evil was permitted; therefore God permits it. The suffering of some tends to the good of many. "He that believeth shall not make haste." We shall see at the last day that all was well done. Even the delays and long intervals which puzzle us in God's dealings, are wisely ordered, and are working for good. Like children, we are poor judges of half-finished work.

Chrysostom says: "Christ tarried that none might be able to assert that He restored Lazarus when not yet dead, saying it was a lethargy, a fainting, a fit, but not death. He therefore tarried so long that corruption began."

Calvin observes: "Let believers learn to suspend their desires, if God does not stretch out His hand to help as soon as they think necessity requires. Whatever may be His delays, he never sleeps and never forgets His people."

Quesnel remarks: "God permits evil, that He may make the power of His grace and the might of His love more conspicuous in the conversion of a sinner."

Poole remarks: "We must not judge of Christ's love to us by His mere external dispensations of providence, nor judge that He doth not love us, because He doth not presently come in to our help at our time, and in such ways and methods as we think reasonable."

JOHN XI 7—16

7 Then after that saith he to *his* disciples, Let us go into Judæa again.

8 *His* disciples say unto him, Master, the Jews of late sought to stone thee; and goest thou thither again?

9 Jesus answered, Are there not twelve hours in the day? If any man walk in the day, he stumbleth not, because he seeth the light of this world.

10 But if a man walk in the night, he stumbleth, because there is no light in him.

11 These things said he: and after that he saith unto them, Our friend Lazarus sleepeth; but I go, that I may awake him out of sleep.

12 Then said his disciples, Lord, if he sleep, he shall do well.

13 Howbeit Jesus spake of his death: but they thought that he had spoken of taking of rest in sleep.

14 Then said Jesus unto them plainly, Lazarus is dead.

15 And I am glad for your sakes that I was not there, to the intent ye may believe; nevertheless let us go unto him.

16 Then said Thomas, which is called Didymus, unto his fellow-disciples, Let us also go, that we may die with him.

WE should notice, in this passage, *how mysterious are the ways in which Christ sometimes leads His people.* We are told that when He talked of going back to Judæa, His disciples were perplexed. It was the very place where the Jews had lately tried to stone their Master: to return thither was to plunge into the midst of danger. These timid Galileans could not see the necessity or prudence of such a step. " Goest Thou thither again ? " they cried.

Things such as these are often going on around us. The servants of Christ are often placed in circumstances just as puzzling and perplexing as those of the disciples. They are led in ways of which they cannot see the purpose and object; they are called to fill positions from which they naturally shrink, and which they would never have chosen for themselves. Thousands in every age are continually learning this by their own experience. The path they are obliged to walk in is not the path of their own choice. At present they cannot see its usefulness or wisdom.

At times like these a Christian must call into exercise his faith and patience. He must believe that his Master knows best by what road His servant ought to travel, and that He is leading him, by the right way, to a city of habitation. He may rest assured that the circumstances in which he is placed are precisely those which are most likely to promote his graces and to check his besetting sins. He need not doubt that what he cannot see now he will understand hereafter. He will find one day that there was wisdom in every step of his journey, though flesh and blood could not see it at the time. If the twelve disciples had not been taken back into Judæa, they would not have seen the glorious miracle of Bethany. If Christians were allowed to choose their own course through life, they would never learn hundreds of lessons about Christ and His grace, which they are now taught in God's ways. Let us remember these things. The time may come when we shall be called to take some journey in life which we greatly dislike. When that time comes, let us set out cheerfully, and believe that all is right.

We should notice, secondly, in this passage, *how tenderly Christ speaks of the death of believers*. He announces the fact of Lazarus being dead in language of singular beauty and gentleness: " Our friend Lazarus sleepeth."

Every true Christian has a Friend in heaven, of almighty power and boundless love. He is thought of, cared for, provided for, defended by God's eternal Son. He has an unfailing Protector, who never slumbers or sleeps, and watches continually over his interests. The world may despise him, but he has no cause to be ashamed. Father and mother even may cast him out, but Christ having once taken him up will never let him go. He is the " friend of Christ " even after he is dead! The friendships of this world are often fair-weather friendships, and fail us like summer-dried fountains, when our need is the sorest; but the friendship of the Son of God is stronger than death, and goes beyond the grave. The Friend of sinners is a Friend that sticketh closer than a brother.

The death of true Christians is " sleep," and not annihilation. It is a solemn and miraculous change, no doubt, but not a change to be regarded with alarm. They have nothing to fear for their souls in the change, for their sins are washed away in Christ's blood. The sharpest sting of death is the sense of unpardoned sin. Christians have nothing to fear for their bodies in the change; they will rise again by and by, refreshed and renewed, after the image of the Lord. The grave itself is a conquered enemy. It must render back its tenants safe and sound, the very moment that Christ calls for them at the last day.

Let us remember these things when those whom we love fall asleep in Christ, or when we ourselves receive our notice to quit this world. Let us call to mind, in such an hour, that our great Friend takes thought for our bodies as well as for our souls, and that He will not allow one hair of our heads to perish. Let us never forget that the grave is the place where the Lord Himself lay, and that as He rose again triumphant from that cold bed, so also shall all

His people. To a mere worldly man death must needs be a terrible thing; but he that has Christian faith may boldly say, as he lays down life, "I will lay me down in peace, and take my rest: for it is Thou, Lord, that makest me dwell in safety."

We should notice, lastly, in this passage, *how much of natural temperament clings to a believer even after conversion.* We read that when Thomas saw that Lazarus was dead, and that Jesus was determined, in spite of all danger, to return into Judæa, he said, "Let us also go, that we may die with Him." There can only be one meaning in that expression: it was the language of a despairing and desponding mind, which could see nothing but dark clouds in the picture. The very man who afterwards could not believe that his Master had risen again, and thought the news too good to be true, is just the one of the twelve who thinks that if they go back to Judæa they must all die!

Things such as these are deeply instructive, and are doubtless recorded for our learning. They show us that the grace of God in conversion does not so re-mould a man as to leave no trace of his natural bent of character. The sanguine do not altogether cease to be sanguine, nor the desponding to be desponding, when they pass from death to life, and become true Christians. They show us that we must make large allowances for natural temperament, in forming our estimate of individual Christians. We must not expect all God's children to be exactly one and the same. Each tree in a forest has its own peculiarities of shape and growth, and yet all at a distance look one mass of leaf and verdure. Each member of Christ's body has his own distinctive bias, and yet all in the main are led by one Spirit, and love one Lord. The two sisters Martha and Mary, the apostles Peter and John and Thomas, were certainly very unlike one another in many respects. But they had all one point in common : they loved Christ, and were His friends.

Let us take heed that we really belong to Christ. This is the one thing needful. If this is made sure, we shall be led by the right way, and end well at last. We may not have the cheerfulness of one brother, or the fiery zeal of another, or the gentleness of another. But if grace reigns within us, and we know what repentance and faith are by experience, we shall stand on the right hand in the great day. Happy is the man of whom, with all his defects, Christ says to saints and angels, " This is our friend."

NOTES JOHN XI 7—16

7.—[*Then after that saith...disciples.*] The Greek words which begin this sentence mark an interval of time even more emphatically than our English version does. They would be literally rendered, " Afterwards, after this." The word translated " then " is the same that is translated " after that " in 1 Cor. xv. 6—7.

[*Let us go...Judæa again.*] This is the language of the kind and loving head of a family, and the chief in a party of friends. Our Lord does not say. " I shall go to," or, " Follow Me to Judæa, but, " Let us go." It is the voice of a kind Master and Shepherd proposing a thing to His pupils and followers, as though He would allow them to express their opinions about it. How much depends on the manner and language of a leader !

The familiar, easy manner in which our Lord is said here to tell His disciples what He proposes to do, gives a pleasant idea of the terms on which they lived with Him.

8 —[*His disciples say...Master.*] The answer of the disciples is an interesting illustration of the easy terms on which they were with their Master. They tell him frankly and unreservedly their feelings and fears.

Let it be noted that the word rendered " Master ", here is the well-known word " Rabbi." The use of it shows that there is nothing necessarily insulting, sneering, or discourteous about the term. It was the title of honour and respect given by all Jews to their teachers. Thus John the Baptist's disciples said to him, when jealous for his honour, " Rabbi, he that was with thee," etc. (John iii. 26.)

[*The Jews of late sought to stone thee.*] The " Jews " here mean especially the leaders or principal persons among the Scribes and Pharisees at Jerusalem, as it generally does in St. John's Gospel. The word rendered " of late " is generally trans-

lated "now," or "at this time." There is not another instance
of its being translated "of late" in the New Testament. Hence
the sentence would be more literally rendered, "The Jews even
now were seeking to stone Thee." They allude to the attempt
made at the feast of dedication a few weeks before. The attempt was so recent that it seemed "even now."

[*And goest thou thither again?*] This question indicates surprise and fear,—"Do we hear aright? Dost Thou really talk of
going back again to Judæa? Dost Thou not fear another assault on Thy life?" We can easily detect fear for their own
safety, as well as their Master's, in the question of the disciples:
yet they put it on "thee," and not on "us."

Let us note how strange and unwise our Lord's plans sometimes appear to His short-sighted people. How little the best
can understand His ways!

9, 10 —[*Jesus answered, Are there not twelve hours, etc.*] The answer which our Lord makes to the remonstrance of His timid
disciples is somewhat remarkable. Instead of giving them a direct reply, bidding them not to be afraid, He first quotes a proverbial saying, and then draws from that saying general lessons
about the time which any one who is on a journey will choose for
journeying. He draws no conclusion, and leaves the application to be made by the disciples themselves. To an English ear
the answer seems far more strange than it would to an Eastern
one. To quote a proverb is, even now, a common reply among
Orientals. To fill up the sense of our Lord's elliptical reply, and
draw the conclusions He meant to be drawn, but did not express,
is, however, not very easy. The following may be taken as a
paraphrase of it:—

"Are not the working hours of the day twelve? You know
they are, speaking generally. If a man on a journey walks during these twelve daylight hours, he sees his road, and does not
stumble or fall, because the sun, which is the light of the world,
shines on his path. If, on the contrary, a man on a journey
chooses to walk in the unreasonable hour of night, he is likely
to stumble or fall, for want of light to guide his feet. It is even
so with Me. My twelve hours of ministry, my day of work, is
not yet over. There is no fear of my life being cut off before
the time: I shall not be slain till my work is done. Till mine
hour is come I am safe, and not a hair of my head can be touched.
I am like one walking in the full light of the sun, and cannot fall.
The night will soon be here when I shall walk on earth no longer: but the night has not yet come. There are twelve hours in
my day of earthly ministry, and the twelfth with Me has not
arrived."

This seems to me substantially the correct explanation of our
Lord's meaning. The idea of ancient writers, as Hugo and Ly-
ranus, that our Lord meant, by mentioning the twelve hours of
the day, that men often change their minds as the day goes on,

and that the Jews, perhaps, no longer wished to kill Him, is very improbable and unsatisfactory.

I grant that the conclusion of the tenth verse, "there is no light in him," presents some difficulty. The simplest explanation is, that it only means, "because he has no light."

Pearce conjectures that the clause should be rendered, "Because there is no light in it; viz., the world." The Greek will perhaps bear this interpretation.

Let us note that the great principle underlying the two verses is the old saying in another form, "Every man is immortal till his work is done." A recollection of that saying is an excellent antidote against fears of danger. The missionary in heathen lands, and the minister at home, pressed down by unhealthy climate, or over-abundant work, may take comfort in it, after their Lord's example. Let us only, by way of caution, make sure that our dangers meet us in the path of duty, and that we do not go out of the way to seek them.

Rupertus suggests that our Lord had in His mind His own doctrine, that He was the Light and Sun of the world. Now as the sun continues shining all the twelve hours of the day, and no mortal power can stop it, so He would have the disciples know that until the evening of His own course arrived, no power of the Jews could possibly check, arrest, or do Him harm. As to the disciples, He seems to add, "So long as I am shining on you with my bodily presence, you have nothing to fear, you will not fall into trouble. When I am taken from you, and not till then, you will be in danger of falling into the hands of persecutors, and even of being put to death." Ecolampadius takes the same view.

Melancthon thinks that our Lord uses a proverbial mode of speech, in order to teach us the great broad lesson that we must attend to the duties of our day, station, and calling, and then leave the event to God. In the path of duty all will turn out right. Calvin, Bullinger, Gualter, and Brentius, take much the same view.

Leigh remarks : " Christ comforts from God's providence. God made the day twelve hours. Who can make it shorter? Who can shorten man's life?"

Does it not come to this, that our Lord would have the disciples know that He Himself could not take harm till His day of work was over, and that they could take no harm while He was with them? (Compare Luke xiii. 32, 33.) Bishop Ellicott suggests that this was the very time in our Lord's ministry when He said to the Pharisee, " I do cures to-day and to-morrow, and the third day I shall be perfected. Nevertheless I must walk to-day and to-morrow and the day following." But I doubt this.

It is certain that there came a time when our Lord said, "This

.

is your hour, and the power of darkness," to His enemies. Then
He was taken, and His disciples fled.

11 —[*These things...our friend Lazarus...sleepeth.*] In this verse
our Lord breaks the fact, that Lazarus is dead, to His disciples.
He does it in words of matchless beauty and tenderness. After
saying " these things " about the twelve hours of the day, which
we have considered in the last verse, He seems to make a slight
pause. Then, "after that," comes the announcement, which
would be more literally rendered, " Lazarus, the friend of us,
has been laid asleep."

The word " sleepeth " means, " is dead." It is a gentle and
pathetic way of expressing the most painful of events that can
befall man, and a most suitable one, when we remember that
after death comes resurrection. In dying we are not annihilated.
Like sleepers, we lie down, to rise again. Estius well remarks,
" Sleeping, in the sense of dying, is only applied to men, because
of the hope of the resurrection. We read no such thing of
brutes."

The use of the figure is so common in Scripture, that it is
almost needless to give references. (See Deut. xxxi. 16; Daniel xii. 2; Matt. xxvii. 52; Acts vii. 60; xiii. 36; 1 Cor. vii. 39;
xi. 30; xv. 6—18; 1 Thess. iv. 13, 14.) But it is a striking fact
that the figure is frequently used by great heathen writers, showing clearly that the tradition of a life after death existed even
among the heathen. Homer, Sophocles, Virgil, Catullus, supply
instances. However, the Christian believer is the only one who
can truly regard death as sleep,—that is, as a healthy, refreshing
thing, which can do him no harm. Many among ourselves, perhaps, are not aware that the figure of speech exists among us in
full force in the word " cemetery," applied to burial-ground.
That word is drawn from the very Greek verb which our Lord
uses here. It is literally a " sleeping-place."

The word " friend," applied to Lazarus, gives a beautiful idea
of the relation between the Lord Jesus and all His believing people. Each one is His " friend,"—not servant, or subject only,
but " friend." A poor believer has no cause to be ashamed. He
has a Friend greater than kings and nobles, who will show Himself friendly to all eternity. A dead saint lying in the grave is
not cut off from Christ's love : even in his grave, he is still the
friend of Christ.

The expression " our," attached to friend, teaches the beautiful lesson that every friend of Christ is or should be the friend
of all Christians. Believers are all one family of brothers and
sisters, and members of one body. Lazarus was not " my " friend,
but " our" friend. If any one is a friend of Christ, every other
believer should be ready and willing to hold out his hand to him,
and say, " You are my friend."

When our Lord says, " I go that I may awaken him out of

sleep," He proclaims His deliberate intention and purpose to raise Lazarus from the dead. He boldly challenges the attention of the disciples, and declares that He is going to Bethany, to restore a dead man to life. Never was bolder declaration made. None surely would make it but One who knew that He was very God.

" I go," is equivalent to saying, " I am at once setting forth on a journey to Bethany." The expression, that " I may awake him out of sleep," is one word in Greek, and is equivalent to " that I may unsleep him." What our Lord went to do at Bethany, He is soon coming to do for all our friends who are asleep in Christ. He is coming to awaken them.

Some commentators have thought that Lazarus died in the very moment that our Lord said, " Our friend sleepeth," and that it means, "Lazarus has just fallen asleep and died." But this is only conjecture, though doubtless our Lord knew the moment of his decease.

Let it be noted that our Lord says, " I go," in the singular number, and not " Let us go." Does it not look as if He meant, " Whether you like to go or not, I intend to go?"

Hall remarks : " None can awaken Lazarus out of this sleep, but He that made Lazarus. Every mouse or gnat can raise us up from that other sleep ; none but an omnipotent power from this."

12.—[*Then said...disciples...sleep...well.*] It seems strange that the disciples should misunderstand our Lord's words, considering how commonly death was called sleep. But their unwillingness to go into Judæa probably made them shut their eyes to our Lord's real meaning.

Most writers think that the disciples referred to the general opinion, that sleep in a sickness is a sign of amendment. Some, however, suggest that they had gathered from the messenger sent by Martha and Mary what was the precise nature of Lazarus' illness, and therefore knew that it was one in which sleep was a favourable symptom.

The Greek word for " he shall do well," is curious. It is the same that is often rendered " shall be made whole." Sometimes it is " healed," and generally " saved."

The latent thought is manifest : " If Lazarus sleeps, he is get- ·ting better, and there is no need of our going to Judæa."

13 —[*Howbeit Jesus spake, etc.*] This verse is one of those ex- planatory glosses which St. John frequently puts into his nar- rative parenthetically. The three first words of the verse would be more literally rendered, " But Jesus had spoken."

How the disciples could have " thought " or " supposed " that our Lord meant literal sleep, and not death, seems strange, when we remember that Peter, James, and John, had heard Him use the same expression after the death of the ruler's daughter: "The maid sleepeth." (Matt. ix. 24.) Two probable reasons may be assigned: one is that they had heard from the messenger that Lazarus' recovery turned on his getting sleep, and that if he only got some sleep he might do well; the other is that they were so afraid of returning to Judæa, that they determined to believe Lazarus was getting better, and to construe our Lord's words in the way most agreeable to their fears. It is common to observe that men will not understand what they do not want to understand.

Quesnel remarks here: "The misunderstanding of the Apostles was a great instance of stupidity, and shows plainly how sensual and carnal their minds still were. The knowledge of this is useful in order to convince incredulous persons that the Apostles were not of themselves capable either of converting the world, or of-inventing the wonderful things and sublime discourses which they relate."

The readiness of the disciples to misunderstand figurative language is curiously shown in two other places, where our Lord spoke of "leaven" and "meat." (Matt. xvi. 6; John iv. 32.)

14 —[*Then said...plainly...Lazarus...dead.*] Here at last our Lord breaks the fact of Lazarus' death to His disciples openly, and without any farther reserve. He had approached the subject gently and delicately, and thus prepared their minds for something painful, by steps. First He said simply, " Let us go into Judæa," without assigning a reason. Secondly He said, "Lazarus sleepeth." Lastly He says, "Lazarus is dead." There is a beautiful consideration for feelings in these three steps. It is a comfortable thought that our mighty Saviour is so tender-hearted and gentle. It is an instructive lesson to us on the duty of dealing gently with others, and specially in announcing afflictions.

The word rendered "plainly" is the same as in John x. 24. Here, as there, it does not mean "in plain, intelligible language" so much as "openly, unreservedly, and without mystery."

15 —[*And I am glad...not there...believe.*] This sentence would be more literally rendered, "And I rejoice on account of you, in order that ye may believe, that I was not there." Our Lord evidently means that He was glad that He was not at Bethany when Lazarus became ill, and had not healed him before his death, as in all probability He would have done. The result now would be most advantageous to the disciples. Their faith would receive an immense confirmation, by witnessing the stupendous miracle of Lazarus being raised from the dead. Thus, great good, in one respect, would come out of great evil. The announcement they had just heard might be very painful and distressing, but He as their Master could not but be glad to think how mightily their faith would be strengthened in the end.

Let us note that our Lord does not say, "I am glad Lazarus is dead, but I am glad I was not there." Had He been there, He seems to say, He could not have refused the prayer of Martha and Mary to heal His friend. We are not intended to be so unfeeling as to rejoice in the death of Christian friends; but we may rejoice in the circumstances attending their deaths, and the glory redounding to Christ, and the benefit accruing to saints from them.

Let us note that our Lord does not say, "I am glad for the sake of Martha and Mary and Lazarus that I am not there, but for your sakes." It is no pleasure to Him to see His individual members suffering, weeping, and dying; but He does rejoice to see the good of many spring out of the suffering of a few. Hence He permits some to be afflicted, in order that many may be instructed through their afflictions. This is the key to the permission of evil in the world; it is for the good of the many. When we ourselves are allowed of God to suffer, we must remember this. We must believe there are wise reasons why God does not come to our help at once and take the suffering away.

Let us note our Lord's desire that His disciples "may believe." He did not mean that they might believe now for the first time, but that they might believe more firmly, heartily, and unhesitatingly; that their faith, in short, might receive a great increase by seeing Lazarus raised. We see here the immense importance of faith. To believe on Christ, and trust God's word, is the first step towards heaven. To believe more and trust more, is the real secret of Christian growth, progress, and prosperity. To make us believe more is the end of all Christ's dealings with us. (See John xiv. 1.)

[*Nevertheless let us go unto him.*] The first word here would be more literally rendered "But." It is as though our Lord said, "But let us delay no longer: let us cast aside all fears of danger; let us go to our friend."

It is noteworthy that our Lord says, "let us go to Lazarus," though he was dead, and would be buried by the time they reached Bethany. Can it be that the disciples thought He had David's words about his dead child in His mind, "I shall go to him"? The words of Thomas, in the next verse, seem to make it possible.

We may notice three gradations in our Lord's language about going to Bethany. The first, in the 7th verse: there He says in the plural, "Let us all go into Judæa."—The second, in verse 11: there He says in the singular, "I go to awake him;" as though He was ready to go alone.—The third is here in the plural, "Let us all go."

Toletus thinks that by these words our Lord meant to hint His intention of raising Lazarus.

Burkitt remarks: "O love, stronger than death! The grave cannot separate Christ and his friends. Other friends accompany us to the brink of the grave, and then they leave us. —Neither life nor death can separate from the love of Christ.

Bengel remarks: "It is beautifully consonant with Divine propriety, that no one is ever read of, as having died while the Prince of Life was present."

16 —[*Then said Thomas...go...die with him.*] The disciple here named is also mentioned in John xiv. 5, and John xx. 24, 26, 27. On each occasion he appears in the same state of mind,—ready to look at the black side of everything,—taking the worst view of the position, and raising doubts and fears. In John xiv. 5, he does not know where our Lord is going. In John xx. 25, he cannot believe our Lord has risen. Here he sees nothing but danger and death, if his Master returns to Judæa. Yet he is true and faithful nevertheless. He will not forsake Christ, even if death is in the way. "Let us go," he says to his fellow-disciples, "and die with our Master. He is sure to be killed if He does go; but we cannot do better than be killed with him."

Some, as Brentius, Grotius, Leigh, Poole, and Hammond, think that "with him," refers to Lazarus. But most commentators think that Thomas refers to our Lord; with them I entirely agree.

Let it be noted that a man may have notable weaknesses and infirmities of Christian character, and yet be a disciple of Christ. There is no more common fault among believers, perhaps, than despondency and unbelief. A reckless readiness to die and make an end of our troubles is not grace but impatience.

Let us observe how extremely unlike one another Christ's disciples were. Peter, for instance, overrunning with zeal and confidence, was the very opposite of desponding Thomas. Yet both had grace, and both loved Christ. We must not foolishly assume that all Christians are exactly like one another in details of character. We must make large allowances, when the main features are right.

Let us remember that this same Thomas, so desponding in our Lord's life-time, was afterwards the very Apostle who first preached the Gospel in India, according to ecclesiastical history, and penetrated further East than any whose name is recorded. Chrysostom says, "The very man who dared not go to Bethany in Christ's company, afterwards ran alone through the world, and dwelt in the midst of nations full of murder and ready to kill him."

Some have thought that his Greek name "Didymus," signifying "two" or "double," was given him because of his character being double, viz., part faith and part weakness. But this is very doubtful. In the first three Gospels, in the catalogue of the twelve, he is always named together with Matthew the publican. But why we do not know.

The Greek word for " fellow-disciple " is never used in the New Testament excepting here.

JOHN XI　17—29

17 Then when Jesus came, he found that he had *lain* in the grave four days already.

18 Now Bethany was nigh unto Jerusalem, about fifteen furlongs off:

19 And many of the Jews came to Martha and Mary, to comfort them concerning their brother.

20 Then Martha, as soon as she heard that Jesus was coming, went and met him: but Mary sat *still* in the house.

21 Then said Martha unto Jesus, Lord, if thou hadst been here, my brother had not died.

22 But I know, that even now, whatsoever thou wilt ask of God, God will give *it* thee.

23 Jesus saith unto her, Thy brother shall rise again.

24 Martha saith unto him, I know that he shall rise again in the resurrection at the last day.

25 Jesus said unto her, I am the resurrection and the life: he that believeth in me, though he were dead, yet shall he live:

26 And whosoever liveth, and believeth in me shall never die. Believest thou this?

27 She saith unto him, Yea, Lord: I believe that thou art the Christ, the Son of God, which should come into the world.

28 And when she had so said, she went her way, and called Mary her sister secretly, saying, The Master is come, and calleth for thee,

29 As soon as she heard *that*, she arose quickly, and came unto him.

THERE is a grand simplicity about this passage, which is almost spoilt by any human exposition. To comment on it seems like gilding gold or painting lilies. Yet it throws much light on a subject which we can never understand too well; that is, the true character of Christ's people. The portraits of Christians in the Bible are faithful likenesses. They show us saints just as they are.

We learn, firstly, *what a strange mixture of grace and weakness is to be found even in the hearts of true believers.*

We see this strikingly illustrated in the language used by Martha and Mary. Both these holy women had faith enough to say, " Lord, if Thou hadst been here, my brother had not died." Yet neither of them seems to have re-

membered that the death of Lazarus did not depend on
Christ's absence, and that our Lord, had He thought fit,
could have prevented his death with a word, without coming to Bethany.—Martha had knowledge enough to say,
" I know, that even now, whatsoever Thou wilt ask of God,
God wilt give it Thee,—I know that my brother shall rise
again at the last day,—I believe that Thou art the Christ,
the Son of God."—But even she could get no further. Her
dim eyes and trembling hands could not grasp the grand
truth that He who stood before her had the keys of life and
death, and that in her Master dwelt " all the fulness of the
Godhead bodily." (Colos. ii. 9.) She saw indeed, but
through a glass darkly. She knew, but only in part. She
believed, but her faith was mingled with much unbelief.
Yet both Martha and Mary were genuine children of God,
and true Christians.

These things are graciously written for our learning. It
is good to remember what true Christians really are. Many
and great are the mistakes into which people fall, by forming a false estimate of the Christian's character. Many
are the bitter things which people write against themselves,
by expecting to find in their hearts what cannot be found
on this side of heaven. Let us settle it in our minds that
saints on earth are not perfect angels, but only converted
sinners. They are sinners renewed, changed, sanctified,
no doubt; but they are yet sinners, and will be till they
die. Like Martha and Mary, their faith is often entangled
with much unbelief, and their grace compassed round
with much infirmity. Happy is that child of God who
understands these things, and has learned to judge rightly
both of himself and others. Rarely indeed shall we find
the saint who does not often need that prayer, " Lord, I
believe : help Thou mine unbelief."

We learn, secondly, what need many believers have
of *clear views of Christ's person, office, and power.* This

is a point which is forcibly brought out in the well-known
sentence which our Lord addressed to Martha. In reply
to her vague and faltering expression of belief in the
resurrection at the last day, He proclaims the glorious
truth, " I am the resurrection and the life ; "—" I, even I,
thy Master, am He that has the keys of life and death in
His hands." And then He presses on her once more that
old lesson, which she had doubtless often heard, but never
fully realized : " He that believeth in Me, though he were
dead, yet shall he live ; and whosoever liveth and believeth
in Me shall never die."

There is matter here which deserves the close consideration of all true Christians. Many of them complain of
want of sensible comfort in their religion. They do not
feel the inward peace which they desire. Let them know
that vague and indefinite views of Christ are too often the
cause of all their perplexities. They must try to see more
clearly the great object on which their faith rests. They
must grasp more firmly His love and power toward them
that believe, and the riches He has laid up for them even
now in this world. We are many of us sadly like Martha.
A little general knowledge of Christ as the only Saviour
is often all that we possess. But of the fulness that dwells
in Him, of His resurrection, His priesthood, His intercession, His unfailing compassion, we have tasted little
or nothing at all. They are things of which our Lord
might well say to many, as he did to Martha, " Believest
thou this ? "

Let us take shame to ourselves that we have named
the name of Christ so long, and yet know so little about
Him. What right have we to wonder that we feel so little
sensible comfort in our Christianity? Our slight and
imperfect knowledge of Christ is the true reason of our
discomfort. Let the time past suffice us to have been
lazy students in Christ's school ; let the time to come find

us more diligent in trying to " know Him and the power
of His resurrection." (Philip. iii. 10.) If true Christians
would only strive, as St. Paul says, to " comprehend what
is the breadth, and length, and depth, and height, and to
know the love of Christ, which passeth knowledge," they
would be amazed at the discoveries they would make.
They would soon find, like Hagar, that there are wells of
water near them of which they had no knowledge. They
would soon discover that there is more heaven to be enjoyed
on earth than they had ever thought possible. The root
of a happy religion is clear, distinct, well-defined knowledge of Jesus Christ. More knowledge would have saved
Martha many sighs and tears. Knowledge alone no doubt,
if unsanctified, only " puffeth up." (1 Cor. viii. 1.) Yet
without clear knowledge of Christ in all His offices we
cannot expect to be established in the faith, and steady in
the time of need.

NOTES, JOHN XI 17—29

17 —[*Then when Jesus came.*] We are left entirely to conjecture
as to the time spent by our Lord in His journey from Bethabara
to Bethany. We do not know anything certain of the place where
He was abiding, except that it was beyond Jordan. Probably it
was between twenty and thirty miles from Bethany, and this
distance, to those who travel on foot, would be at least a day's
journey.

[*He found...lain...grave...four days already.*] The Greek form
of language here is peculiar, and a literal translation would be
impossible. It would be, "He found him being already four
days in the grave." It is highly probable that Lazarus was
buried the same day that he died. In a country like Palestine,
with a hot climate, it is quite impossible to keep corpses long
unburied, without danger and discomfort to the living. A man
may talk to his friend one day, and find him buried the next
day.

One thing is abundantly proved by this verse. Lazarus must
certainly have been dead, and not in a trance or swoon. A person lying in a grave for four days, all reasonable people would
admit, must have been a dead man.

The various forms of death which our Lord is recorded to
have triumphed over should not be forgotten. Jairus' daughter

was just dead; the son of the widow of Nain was being carried to the grave; Lazarus, the most extraordinary case of all, had been four days in the tomb.

The expression, "He found," in this verse, must not be thought to imply any surprise. We know that our Lord begun His journey from Bethabara with a full knowledge that Lazarus was dead. What "He found" applies to Lazarus therefore, and to the precise length of time that he had been in the grave. He was not only dead, but buried.

We can well imagine what a sorrowful time those four days must have been to Martha and Mary, and how many thoughts must have crossed their minds as to the reason of our Lord's delay, as to the day He would come, and the like. Nothing so wears us down as suspense and uncertainty. Yet of all graces there is none so glorifying to God and sanctifying to the heart as that of patience or quietly waiting. How long Abraham, Jacob, Joseph, Moses, and David were kept waiting! Jesus loves to show the world that His people can wait. Martha and Mary had to exemplify this. Well if we can do likewise!

Gomarus discusses at length the curious question, where the soul of Lazarus was during those four days. He dismisses as unscriptural the idea that it was yet in the body, and seems to hold that it was in Paradise.

The "four days" are easily accounted for, if we remember the time occupied by the messenger from Bethany, the two days' delay at Bethabara, and the journey to Bethany.

18 —[*Now Bethany...nigh...Jerusalem, about fifteen furlongs off.*] This verse shows that John wrote for readers who were not acquainted with Palestine. According to his manner he gives a parenthetical description of the situation of Bethany, partly to show how very near to Jerusalem the wonderful miracle he relates was worked,—within a walk of the temple, and almost within view; and partly to account for the number of the Jews who came from Jerusalem to comfort Martha and Mary.

The distance, fifteen furlongs, is rather less than two miles. The use of the expression, "about," shows that the Holy Ghost condescends to use man's common form of language in describing things, and that such expressions are not inconsistent with inspiration. (See John ii. 6, and vi. 19.)

19 —[*And many Jews...came...Mary.*] This sentence would be more literally rendered, "Many from among the Jews had come to those around Martha and Mary." Who these Jews were it is impossible to say, except that they evidently came from Jerusalem. One can hardly suppose that they were the leaders and rulers of the Pharisees. Such men would not be likely to care for friends of Jesus, and would hardly have condescended to visit Martha and Mary, who were doubtless known to be His disciples. Of course it is possible that Simon the leper, in

whose house Lazarus died, may have been a man of consideration, and that the Jews may have come out of respect to him.
At any rate it is clear that those who saw the stupendous miracle of this chapter were Jerusalem Jews, and were "many," and
not few.—The expression, "Those around Martha and Mary,"
is a form of language not uncommon ih Greek, and is probably
rightly translated in our version. It can hardly mean, "the
women who had come to mourn with Martha and Mary," though
it is well known that women were the chief mourners at funer-
als. It is, however, only fair to say that Beza decidedly holds
that the women and female friends who had come to mourn with
Mary and Martha are meant in this verse.

[*To comfort them concerning their brother.*] This appears to
have been a common practice among the Jews. When any one
died, friends and neighbours assembled for several days at the
house of the deceased, to mourn with and comfort the relatives.
Lightfoot specially mentions it. The same custom prevails in
many parts of the world at the present day: Hindostan and
Ireland are instances.

We cannot doubt that many of these Jews came to Martha
and Mary from form and custom, and not from any genuine
sympathy or kind feeling, much less from any unity of spiritual
taste. Yet it is striking to observe how God blesses even the
semblance of sympathy. By coming they saw Christ's greatest
miracle. If unbelief can sympathize, how much more should
grace.

One thing at any rate seems very clearly proved by this
verse. Whatever was the rank or position of Martha, Mary,
and Lazarus, they were well-known people, and anything that
happened in their house at Bethany was soon public news in
Jerusalem. Had they been strangers from Galilee, the thing
named in this verse would not have been written.

Chrysostom thinks the Evangelist mentioned the Jews
coming to comfort Martha and Mary, as one of the many circumstances proving that Lazarus was really dead. They evidently thought him dead, or they would not have come.

Lightfoot gives a long and curious account of the customs of
the Jews about comforting mourners. He says that "thirty
days were allotted for the time of mourning. The three first
days were for weeping; seven days for lamentation; and thirty
days for intermission from washing or shaving. The beds in
the house of mourning were all taken down and laid on the
ground, as soon as the coffin left the house. The comforter sat
on the floor; the bereaved sat chief. The comforter might not
say a word till the chief mourner broke silence."

Poole observes that the mourning for Jacob was forty days,
for Aaron and Moses, thirty days. (Gen. l. 3; Num. xx. 29;
Deut. xxxiv. 8.)

20 —[*Then Martha...heard...Jesus...coming...met him.*] The Greek word for "was coming," would 'have been more literally translated, "is coming," or, "comes," in the present tense. It then gives the idea that Martha received from some friend, servant, or watchman, who was on the lookout on the road from Jordan, the message long looked for, "Jesus is in sight:" "He is coming." She then hurried out, and met our Lord outside the village. The Greek is simply, "met Him;" and "went" is needless.

Bullinger thinks that Martha, with characteristic activity, was bustling after domestic duties, and heard from some one that Jesus was coming, and ran to meet Him, without going to tell Mary.

[*But Mary sat still...house.*] While Martha hurried out to meet Jesus, Mary continued sitting in the house. Martha's "met" is a perfect tense; Mary's "sat" is an imperfect. It is impossible not to see the characteristic temperament of each sister coming out here, and doubtless it is written for our learning. Martha—active, stirring, busy, demonstrative—cannot wait, but runs impulsively to meet Jesus. Mary—quiet, gentle, pensive, meditative, contemplative, meek—sits passively at home. Yet I venture to think that of the two sisters, Martha here appears to most advantage. There is such a thing as being so crushed and stunned by our affliction that we do not adorn our profession under it. Is there not something of this in Mary's conduct throughout this chapter? There is a time to stir, as well as to sit still; and here, by not stirring, Mary certainly missed hearing our Lord's glorious declaration about Himself. I would not be mistaken in saying this. Both these holy women were true disciples; yet if Mary showed more grace on a former occasion than Martha, I think Martha here showed more than Mary.

Let us never forget that there are differences of temperament among believers, and let us make due allowance for others if they are not quite like ourselves. There are believers who are quiet, passive, silent, and meditative; and believers who are active, stirring, and demonstrative. The well-ordered Church must find room, place, and work for all. We need Marys as well as Marthas, and Marthas as well as Marys.

Nothing brings out character so much as sickness and affliction. If we would know how much grace believers have, we should see them in trouble.

Let us remember that "sitting" was the attitude of a mourner, among the Jews. Thus Job's friends "sat down with him on the ground." (Job ii. 13.)

Henry remarks: "In the day of affliction Mary's contemplative and reserved temper proved a snare to her, made her less able to grapple with grief, and disposed her to melancholy.

It will be our wisdom to watch against the temptations, and improve the advantages of our natural temper."

21 —[*Then said Martha...if thou...not died.*] This is the first account of Martha's feelings. It was the uppermost thought in her mind, and with honest impulsiveness she brings it out at once. It is easy to detect in it a strange mixture of emotions.

Here is a passion, not unmixed with a tinge of reproach. "I wish you had been here: why did you not come sooner? You might have prevented my brother's death."

Here is love, confidence, and devotion creeping out. "I wish you had been here. We loved you so much. We depended so entirely on your love. We felt if you had been here all would be ordered well."

Here is faith. "I wish you had been here. I believe you could have healed my brother, and kept death from him."

Nevertheless there is something of unbelief at bottom. Martha forgets that the bodily presence of Jesus was not necessary in order to cure her brother, or to prevent his death. She must have known what our Lord did for the centurion's servant, and the ruler of Capernaum. He had but to speak the word anywhere and Lazarus would have recovered. But memories often fail in time of trouble.

Ferus remarks how apt we all are to say, as Martha, "If God had been here, if Christ had been present, this would not have happened; as if Christ was not always present, and everywhere near His people!"

Henry remarks that in cases like Martha's, "we are apt to add to our trouble by fancying what might have been. If such a method had been taken, such a physician employed, my friend had not died! which is more than we know. And what good does it do? When God's will is done, our business is to submit."

22 —[*But I know...even now...ask...give it thee.*] In these words poor Martha's faith and hope shine clearly and unmistakably, though not without serious blemishes. "Even now," she says, "though my brother is dead and lying in the grave, I know, and feel confident, from the many proofs I have seen of Thy power, that whatsoever things Thou mayest ask of God, God will give them to Thee. I must therefore even now cling to the hope that in some way or other Thou wilt help us."

The faith of these words is plain and unmistakable. Martha hopes, desperately against hope, that somehow all will be right, though she knows not how. She has strong confidence in the efficacy of our Lord's prayers.

The presence of dim views and indistinct apprehensions of Christ in Martha's mind is as evident as her faith. She speaks as if our Lord was a human prophet only, and had no independent power of His own, as God, to work a miracle, and as if He could not command a cure, but must ask God for it, as Elisha did. She must have strangely forgotten the manner in which our Lord had often worked His miracles. Chrysostom remarks, that she speaks as if Christ was only " some virtuous and approved mortal."

Let us note here that there may be true faith and love toward Christ in a person, and yet much dimness and ignorance mixed up with it. Love to Christ, in Christian women especially, is often much clearer than faith and knowledge. Hence women are more easily led astray by false doctrine than men. It is of the utmost importance to remember that there are degrees of faith and knowledge. How small a degree of faith may save, and how much of ignorance may be found even in one who is on the way to heaven, are deep points which probably the last day alone will fully disclose.

Let us do Martha the justice to observe that she shows great confidence in the value and efficacy of prayer.

23 —[*Jesus saith...brother...rise again.*] These words, the first spoken by our Lord after arriving at Bethany, are very remarkable. They sound as if He saw the vague nature of Martha's faith, and would gradually lead her on to clearer and more distinct views of Himself, His office, and Person. He therefore begins by the broad, general promise, " Thy brother shall be raised up." He does not say when or how. If his disciples heard him say this, they might have some clue to his meaning, as He had said, " I go that I may awake him out of sleep." But Martha had not heard that.

Let us note that our Lord loves to draw out the faith and knowledge of His people by degrees. If He told us everything at once, plainly, and without any room for misunderstanding, it would not be good for us. Exercise is useful for all our graces.

Rollock sees in this verse a signal example of our Lord's unwillingness to " break the bruised reed, or quench the smoking flax." He nourishes and encourages the little spark of faith which Martha had.

24 —[*Martha...I know...resurrection...last day.*] Martha here reveals the extent of her faith and knowledge. She knows and feels sure that her brother will be raised again from the dead in the last day, when the resurrection takes place. This, as a pious Jewess, she had learned from the old Testament Scriptures, and as a Christian believer, she had gathered even more distinctly from the teaching of Jesus. But she does not say, " I know and feel confident" of anything more. She may perhaps have had some glimmering of hope that Jesus would do something, but she does not say, " I know." General faith is easier than particular.

We see from this verse that the resurrection of the body

formed part of the creed of the Jewish Church, and of the faith of
our Lord's disciples. Martha's "*I know*," sounds as if she remembered the words of Job, " I know that my Redeemer liveth."
What she did not understand, or had failed to remember, was our
Lord's peculiar office as Lord of the resurrection. We cannot
now understand how she can have failed to hear what our Lord
had said before the Sanhedrim. (John v. 25—29.) If she had, she
evidently had not comprehended it. Even our Lord's teaching
was often not taken in by His people! How much less must
His ministers expect all their sermons to be understood!

To my eyes there is an evident tone of disappointment about
Martha's speech. It is as though she said, " I know, of course,
that he will rise again at last; but that is cold comfort. It is a
far-distant event. I want nearer and better consolation."

Hutcheson remarks : " It is no uncommon thing to see men believing great things that are far off, and about which they have
no present exercise, when yet their faith proves weak in the matter of a present trial, though less difficult than that which they
profess to believe."

25 —[*Jesus said...I am...resurrection...life.*] In this and the following verses, our Lord corrects Martha's feeble and inadequate
notions, and sets before her more exalted views of Himself.
As Chrysostom says, " He shows her that He needed none to
help Him." He tells her that He is not merely a human teacher
of the resurrection, but the Divine Author of all resurrection,
whether spiritual or physical, and the Root and Fountain of all
life. " I am that high and holy One who, by taking man's nature
upon Me, have ennobled his body, and made its resurrection
possible. I am the great First Cause and Procurer of man's
resurrection, the Conqueror of death, and the Saviour of the
body. I am the great Spring and Source of all life, and whatever life any one has, eternal, spiritual, physical, is all owing to
Me. All that are raised from the grave will be raised by Me.
All that are spiritually quickened are quickened by Me. Separate from Me there is no life at all. Death came by Adam: life
comes by Me."

All must feel that this is a deep saying, so deep that we see
but a little of it. One thing only is very clear and plain : none
could use this language but one who knew and felt that He was
very God. No prophet or Apostle ever spoke in this way.

I do not feel sure that the two first words of this verse do not
contain a latent reference to the great title of Jehovah, "I am."
The Greek quite permits it.

[*He that believeth...me...dead..:live.*] This sentence receives
two interpretations. Some, as Calvin and Hutcheson, hold that
" dead " here means *spiritually* dead. Others, as Bullinger, Gualter, Brentitus, Musculus, hold that " dead " means *bodily* dead.—
With these last I entirely agree, partly because of the point that
our Lord is pressing on Martha, partly because of the awkward-
ness of speaking of a believer as "dead." Moreover, the ex-

pression is a verb,—"though he has died," and not an adjective,—"is a dead person." The sense I believe to be this : " He that believes in Me, even if he has died, and been laid in the grave, like thy brother, shall yet live, and be raised again through my power. Faith in Me unites such an one to the Fountain of all life, and death can only hold him for a short time. As surely as I, the Head, have life, and cannot be kept a prisoner by the grave, so surely all my members, believing in Me, shall live also."

26 —[*And whosoever liveth...believeth...never die.*] In this verse our Lord seems to me to speak of living believers, as in the last verse He had spoken of dead ones. Here, then, He makes the sweeping declaration, that " every one who believes in Him shall never die : " that is, he " shall not die eternally," as the Burial Service of the Church of England has it. The second death shall have no power over him. The sting of bodily death shall be taken away. He partakes of a life that never ends, from the moment that he believes in Christ. His body may be laid in the grave for a little season, but only to be raised after a while to glory ; and his soul lives on uninterruptedly for evermore, and, like the great risen Head, dieth no more.

That there are great depths in this and the preceding sentence, every reverent believer will always admit. We feel that we do not see the bottom. The difficulty probably arises from the utter inability of our gross, carnal natures to comprehend the mysteries of life, death, and resurrection of any kind. One thing is abundantly clear, and that is the importance of faith in Christ. " He that believeth " is the man who though dead shall live, and shall never die. Let us take care that we believe, and then all shall one day be plain. The simple questions, " What is life, and what is death ? " contain enough to silence the wisest philosopher.

[*Believest thou this?*] This searching question is the application to Martha of the great doctrines just laid down. " Thou believest that the dead will rise. It is well. But dost thou believe that I am the Author of resurrection, and the source of life ? Dost thou realize that I, thy Teacher and Friend, am very God, and have the keys of death and the grave in my hands ? Hast thou yet got hold of this ? If thou hast not, and only knowest me as a prophet sent to teach good and comfortable things, thou hast only received half the truth."

Home questions like these are very useful. How little we most of us know what we really believe, and what we do not ; what we have grasped and made our own, and what we hold loosely ! Above all, how little we know what we really believe about Christ !

Melancthon points out how immensely important it is to know whether we really have faith, and believe what we hold.

27 —[*She saith...Yea, Lord; I believe.*] Poor Martha, pressed

home with the mighty question of the last verse, seems hardly able to give any but a vague answer. In truth, we cannot expect that she would speak distinctly about that which she only understood imperfectly. She therefore falls back on a general answer, in which she states simply, yet decidedly, what was the extent of her creed.

Our English word, "I believe," hardly gives the full sense of the Greek. It would be literally, "I have believed, and do believe." This is my faith, and has been for a long time.

Augustine, Bede, Bullinger, Chemnitius, Gualter, Maldonatus, Quesnel, and Henry, think that the first word of Martha's reply is a full and explicit declaration of faith in everything our Lord had just said. "Yes, Lord, I do believe Thou art the resurrection and the life," etc. I cannot see this myself. The idea seems contradicted by Martha's subsequent conduct at the grave.

Musculus strongly maintains that Martha's confession, good as it was, was vague and imperfect. Lampe takes much the same view.

[*Thou art the Christ...Son of God...came...world.*] Here is Martha's statement of her belief. It contains three great points: (1) that Jesus was the Christ, the anointed One, the Messiah; (2) that He was the Son of God; (3) that He was the promised Redeemer, who was to come into the world. She goes no further, and probably she could not. Yet considering the time she lived in, the universal unbelief of the Jewish nation, and the wonderful difference in the views of believers before the crucifixion and after, I regard it as a noble and glorious confession, and even fuller than Peter's, in Matthew xvi. 16. Melancthon points out the great superiority of Martha's faith to that of the most intellectual heathen, in a long and interesting passage.

It is easy to say that Martha's faith was rather vague, and that she ought to have seen everything more clearly. But we at this period of time, and with all our advantages, are very poor judges of such a matter. Dark and dim as her views were, it was a great thing for a solitary Jewish woman to have got hold of so much truth, when within two miles, in Jerusalem, all who held such a creed as hers were excommunicated and persecuted.

Let us note that people's views of truth may be very defective on some points, and yet they may have the root of the matter in them. Martha evidently did not yet fully realize that Christ was the resurrection and the life: but she had learned the alphabet of Christianity,—Christ's Messiahship and Divinity, and doubtless learned more in time. We must not condemn people hastily or harshly, because they do not see all at once.

Chrysostom says : " Martha seems to me not to understand Christ's saying. She was conscious it was some great thing, but did not perceive the whole meaning, so that when asked one thing she answered another."

Toletus remarks : " Martha thought she believed everything Christ said, while she believed Him to be the true promised Messiah. And she did truly believe, but her faith was implicit and general. It is just as if some rustic, being questioned about some proposition of faith which he does not quite comprehend, replies, 'I believe in the Holy Church.' So here Martha said, 'I believe, Lord, that Thou art the true Christ, and that all things Thou sayest are true;' and yet she did not distinctly perceive them." This is a remarkable testimony from a Romanist.

Ought we not, perhaps, to make some allowance for the distress and affliction in which Martha was when she made her confession? Is it fair to expect a person in her position to speak as distinctly and precisely as one not in trouble?

28. —[*And when she had said this, etc.*] The affection of Martha for her sister appears here. Once assured that her Master was come, and perhaps somewhat cheered by the few words He spoke, she hastens home to tell Mary that Jesus was come, and had called for her. We are not told expressly that Jesus had mentioned Mary, but we may suppose that He did, and had asked where she was.

The word " secretly " may be applied to the word which follows, if we like, and it would then mean that "Martha called Mary, saying secretly." This is probably the correct rendering.

The word rendered " is come " would be more literally translated, " is present : is actually here."

The expression, " the Master," is probably the name by which our Lord was familiarly known by the family at Bethany. It is literally, " the Teacher."

Bullinger remarks that the word " secretly " is purposely inserted, to show that the Jews who followed Mary had no idea that Jesus was come. Had they known it, he thinks, they would not have followed her, and so would not have seen the miracle.

Hall evidently thinks that Martha told Mary " secretly," for fear of the unbelieving Jews who were among the comforters. He remarks : " Christianity doth not bid us abate anything of our wariness and honest policy : yea, it requires us to have no less of the serpent than of the dove."

29 —[*As soon as she heard, etc.*] The two last words in this sentence are both in the present tense. It would be more literally rendered, " She, when she heard, arises quickly and comes to Him." It is evident, I think, that the sudden movement of Mary

was not caused by hearing that Jesus was come, but that Jesus called for her.

It is not unlikely, from the word "arose," that Mary was lying or sitting prostrate on the ground, under the pressure of grief. We may also well suppose that our Lord, who doubtless knew her state, asked for her, in order to rouse her to exertion. When David heard that his child was dead, and nothing left for him to do but to be resigned, he "arose from off the earth." (2 Sam. xii. 20.)

JOHN XI 30—37

30 Now Jesus was not yet come into the town, but was in that place where Martha met him.

31 The Jews then which were with her in the house, and comforted her, when they saw Mary, that she rose up hastily and went out, followed her, saying, She goeth unto the grave to weep there.

32 Then when Mary was come where Jesus was, and saw him, she fell down at his feet, saying unto him, Lord, if thou hadst been here, my brother had not died.

33 When Jesus therefore saw her weeping, and the Jews also weeping, which came with her, he groaned in the spirit, and was troubled.

34 And said, Where have ye laid him? They said unto him, Lord, come and see.

35 Jesus wept.

36 Then said the Jews, Behold how he loved him!

37 And some of them said, Could not this man, which opened the eyes of the blind, have caused that even this man should not have died?

Not many passages in the New Testament are more wonderful than the simple narrative contained in these eight verses. It brings out, in a most beautiful light, the sympathizing character of our Lord Jesus Christ. It shows us Him who is "able to save to the uttermost all who come to God by Him," as able to feel as He is to save. It shows us Him who is One with the Father, and the Maker of all things, entering into human sorrows, and shedding human tears.

We learn, for one thing, in these verses, *how great a blessing God sometimes bestows on actions of kindness and sympathy.*

It seems that the house of Martha and Mary at Bethany was filled with mourners when Jesus arrived. Many of these mourners, no doubt, knew nothing of the inner

life of these holy women. Their faith, their hope, their
love to Christ, their discipleship, were things of which
they were wholly ignorant. But they felt for them in their
heavy bereavement, and kindly came to offer what comfort
they could. By so doing they reaped a rich and unexpected
reward. They beheld the greatest miracle that Jesus ever
wrought. They were eye-witnesses when Lazarus came
forth from the tomb. To many of them, we may well believe, that day was a spiritual birth. The raising of Lazarus led to a resurrection in their souls. How small sometimes are the hinges on which eternal life appears to depend !
If these people had not sympathized they might never
have been saved.

We need not doubt that these things were written for
our learning. To show sympathy and kindness to the
sorrowful is good for our own souls, whether we know it or
not. To visit the fatherless and widows in their affliction,
to weep with them that weep, to try to bear one another's
burdens, and lighten one another's cares,—all this will
make no atonement for sin, and will not take us to heaven.
Yet it is healthy employment for our hearts, and employment
which none ought to despise. Few perhaps are aware that
one secret of being miserable is to live only for ourselves,
and one secret of being happy is to try to make others
happy, and to do a little good in the world. It is not
for nothing that these words were written by Solomon,
" It is better to go to the house of mourning than to the
house of feasting." — " The heart of the wise is in the
house of mourning, but the heart of fools is in the house
of mirth." (Eccl. vii. 2, 4.) The saying of our Lord is
too much overlooked : " Whosoever shall give to drink to
one of these little ones a cup of cold water only in the name
of a disciple, verily I say unto you he shall in no wise lose
his reward." (Matt. x. 42.) The friends of Martha and
Mary found that promise wonderfully verified. In an

age of peculiar selfishness and self-indulgence, it would be well if they had more imitators.

We learn, for another thing, *what a depth of tender sympathy there is in Christ's heart towards His people.* We read that when our Lord saw Mary weeping, and the Jews also weeping with her, " He groaned in the spirit and was troubled." We read even more than this. He gave outward expression to His feelings : He " wept." He knew perfectly well that the sorrow of the family of Bethany would soon be turned into joy, and that Lazarus in a few minutes would be restored to his sisters. But though he knew all this, he " wept."

This weeping of Christ is deeply instructive. It shows us that it is not sinful to sorrow. Weeping and mourning are sadly trying to flesh and blood, and make us feel the weakness of our mortal nature. But they are not in themselves wrong. Even the Son of God wept.—It shows us that deep· feeling is not a thing of which we need be ashamed. To be cold and stoical and unmoved in the sight of sorrow is no sign of grace. There is nothing unworthy of a child of God in tears. Even the Son of God could weep.—It shows us, above all, that the Saviour in whom believers trust is a most tender and feeling Saviour. He is one who can be touched with sympathy for our infirmities. When we turn to Him in the hour of trouble, and pour out our hearts before Him, He knows what we go through and can pity. And He is One who never changes. Though He now sits at God's right hand in heaven, His heart is still the same that it was upon earth. We have an Advocate with the Father, who, when He was upon earth, could weep.

Let us remember these things in daily life, and never be ashamed of walking in our Master's footsteps. Let us strive to be men and women of a tender heart and a sympathizing spirit. Let us never be ashamed to weep with them that weep, and rejoice with them that rejoice. Well would .it be for the Church and the world if there were more Christians of this stamp and character! The Church would be far more beautiful, and the world be far more happy.

30 —[*Now Jesus was not yet come, etc.*] The Greek word for " come " is in the preterperfect tense. The sentence, translated literally, would be, " Jesus had not yet come into the town," when Martha left Him to tell Mary, but was still waiting or remaining in the place outside Bethany, where Martha at first met Him. The word " town " would be more correctly rendered " village," according to our present acceptation of the word. Yet it is fair to remember that words change their meaning with lapse of time. Even at this day a little Suffolk village of 1,400 people, is called a " town " by many of its inhabitants.

Calvin thinks that Jesus remained outside Bethany by Martha's request, that His life might not be endangered.

31 —[*The Jews then...comforted her...saw Mary...followed her.*] It is probable that the persons here mentioned formed a considerable number,—as many as could crowd into the house. " Comforted " in the Greek is the present participle, and implies that they were actually employed. in comforting Mary. Concerning the manner of comforting on such occasions, we know nothing certain. People who only talk common places are miserable comforters, and far worse than Job's friends, who sat for seven days saying nothing at all. It may be that among the Jews the mere presence of courteous and sympathizing people was thought a kind attention, and soothed the feelings of the bereaved. The customs of nations differ widely in such matters.

It is evident these Jews did not hear Martha's message, and knew nothing of Jesus being near. Some of them, perhaps, had they known it, would not have followed Mary; not knowing, they all followed without exception, and unexpectedly became eye-witnesses of a stupendous miracle. All they knew was that Mary went out hastily. They followed in a spirit of kind sympathy, and by so doing reaped a great blessing.

Rupertus shrewdly remarks that the Jews did not follow Martha, when she ran to meet Jesus, but did follow Mary. He conjectures that Mary's affliction was deeper and more overwhelming than Martha's, and her friends devoted themselves more to comfort her, as needing most consolation. Yet the simpler reason seems to be that when *both* sisters had left the house, the friends could hardly do anything else but go out and follow.

[*She goeth...grave...weep there.*] We must suppose from this sentence, that weeping at the grave of dead friends was a custom among the Jews in our Lord's time. In estimating such a custom, which to most thinking persons may seem as useless as rubbing a wound, and very likely to keep up pain without healing, it is only fair to remember that Old Testament views of the state after death were not nearly so well lighted and comfortable as ours. The removal of death's sting, the resurrection and paradise, were things not nearly so well understood even by the best saints before Christ, as they were after Christ rose again. To most of the Jews, in our Lord's time, we can well believe that death was regarded as the end of all happiness and comfort, and the state after death as a dreary blank. When Sadducees, who said there was "no resurrection," were chief rulers and high priests, we may well suppose that the sorrow of many Jews over the death of friends was a "sorrow without hope." Even at this day, "the place of wailing" at Jerusalem, where the Jews assemble to weep over the foundation-stones of the old temple, is a proof that their habit of weeping over crushed hopes is not yet extinct.

32 — [*That when Mary, etc.*] We see in this verse that as soon as Mary met our Lord, the first thing she said was almost exactly what Martha had said in the twenty-first verse, and the remarks made there need not be repeated. The similarity shows, at any rate, that throughout the illness of Lazarus, the thoughts of the two sisters had been running in one and the same direction. Both had built all their hopes on Jesus coming. Both had felt confidence that His coming would have saved their brother's life. Both were bitterly disappointed that He did not come. Both had probably kept saying the same words repeatedly, "If our Master would only come, Lazarus would not die." There are, however, one or two touches of difference between the two sisters, here as elsewhere. Let us note them.

Mary "fell down" at our Lord's feet, and Martha did not. She was made of softer, feebler character than Martha, and was more completely crushed and overcome than her sister.

Mary fell down at our Lord's feet when she "saw" Him. Up to that moment probably she had borne up, and had run to the place where Martha told her Jesus was waiting. But when she actually saw her Master, and remembered how she had longed for a sight of Him for some days, her feelings overcame her, and she broke down. The eyes have a great effect on the feelings of the heart. People often bear up pretty well, till they *see* something that calls up thoughts.

I do not perceive any ground for thinking, as Calvin does, that this "falling at our Lord's feet" was an act of worship, a recognition of our Lord's divinity. It is much more natural and reasonable to regard it as the mere expression of Mary's state of feelings.

Trapp remarks that the words of Mary in this verse and of
Martha in the former one show that we are all naturally disposed to make too much of Christ's bodily presence.

33 —[*When Jesus therefore saw her, etc.*] This is one of those
verses which bring out very strongly the real humanity of our
Lord, and His power to sympathize with His people. As a real
man, He was specially moved when He saw Mary and the Jews
weeping. As God, He had no need to hear their plaintive
language, and to see their tears, in order to learn that they
were afflicted. He knew perfectly all their feelings. Yet as
man He was like ourselves, peculiarly stirred by the *sight* of
sorrow; for human nature is so constituted that grief is
eminently contagious. If one in a company is deeply touched,
and begins to weep, it is extremely likely that others will weep
also. This power of sympathy our Lord evidently had in full
possession. He *saw* weeping and He wept.

Let us carefully remark that our Lord never changes. He did
not leave behind Him His human nature when He ascended up
into heaven. At this moment, at God's right hand, He can be
touched with the feeling of our infirmities, and can understand
tears as well as ever. Our great High Priest is the very Friend
that our souls need, able to save as God, able to feel as man.
To talk of the Virgin Mary feeling for sinners more than Jesus
is to say that which is ignorant and blasphemous. To teach
that we can need any other priest, when Jesus is such a feeling
Saviour, is to teach what is senseless and absurd.

[*He groaned in spirit.*] There is considerable difficulty about
this expression. The word rendered "groaned," is only used
five times in the New Testament. In Matt. ix. 30, and Mark i.
43, it is "straitly charged." In Mark xiv. 5, it is "murmured."
Here, and at the thirty-eighth verse above, it is "groaned."
Now what is precisely meant by the phrase?

(*a*) Some, as Ecolampadius, Brentius, Chemnitius, Flacius,
and Ferus, maintain firmly that the notion of anger, indignation,
and stern rebuke, is inseparable from the word "groaned."
They think that the latent idea is the deep and holy indignation
with which our Lord was moved at the sight of the ravages
which death had made, and the misery sin and the devil had
brought into the world. They say it implies the stern and
righteous wrath with which the deliverer of a country tyran-
nized over and trampled down by a rebel regards the desolation
and destruction which the rebel has caused.

(*b*) Some add to this view the idea that "in spirit" means
that our Lord groaned through the Holy Ghost, or by the
Divine Spirit which dwelt in Him without measure, or by the
power of His Godhead.

(*c*) Some, as Chrysostom, Theophylact, and Euthymius,
think "groaned in spirit" means that Christ rebuked His own

natural feelings by His Divine nature, or restrained His trouble, and in so doing was greatly disturbed.

(*d*) Some, as Gomarus and Lampe, consider that our Lord was moved to holy sorrow and indignation at the sight of the unbelief even of Martha and Mary, (expressed by their immoderate grief, as if the case of Lazarus was hopeless,) as well as at the sight of the unbelief of the Jews.

(*e*) Some, as Bullinger, Gualter, Diodati, Grotius, Maldonatus, Jansenius, Rollock, and Hutcheson, consider that the phrase simply expresses the highest and deepest kind of inward agitation of mind, an agitation in which grief, compassion, and holy detestation of sin's work in the world were all mingled and combined. This agitation, however, was entirely inward at present: it was not bodily, but spiritual; not in the flesh, but in the spirit. As Burgon says, the "spirit" here means Christ's *inward* soul. I prefer this opinion to the former one, though I fully admit it has difficulties. But it is allowed by Schleusner and Parkhurst, and seems the view of Tyndall, Cranmer, and the Geneva version, as well as of our own.

[*And was troubled.*] This expression is to my mind even more difficult than the one which immediately precedes it. It would be literally translated, as our marginal reading has it, " He troubled himself." In fact, Wycliffe translates it so. Now what can this mean?

Some maintain that in our Lord's mysterious Person the human nature was so entirely subordinated to the Divine, that the human passions and affections never moved unless influenced and actuated by the Divine nature, and that here, to show His sympathy, He "troubled Himself." Thus Rupertus remarks that "if He had not troubled Himself, no one else could have troubled Him." I confess that I regard this view with a little suspicion. It seems to me to imply that our Lord's human nature was not like ours, and that His humanity was like an instrument played upon by His divinity, but in itself dead and passive until its music was called out. To my mind there is something dangerous in this.

I prefer to think that our Lord as man had all the feelings, passions, and affections of a man, but all under such perfect control that they never exceeded as ours do, and were never even very demonstrative, excepting on great occasions. As Beza says, there was no "disorder" in His emotions. Here I think He saw an occasion for exhibiting a very deep degree of sorrow and sympathy, partly from the sorrowful sight He beheld, and partly from His love to Mary, Martha, and Lazarus. Therefore He greatly disturbed and "troubled Himself."

It still admits of a question whether the phrase may not be simply a Hebraism for " He was troubled." (Compare 1 Sam. xxx. 6, and 2 Sam. xii. 18.) Hammond says it is a Hebrew idiom.

When all has been said, we must not forget that the phrase touches a very delicate and mysterious subject: that subject is the precise nature of the union of two natures in our Lord's Person.   That He was at the same time perfect God and perfect Man is an article of the Christian faith; but how far the Divine nature acted on the human, and to what extent it checked and influenced the action of human passions and feelings, are very deep points, which we have no line completely to fathom. After all, not the least part of our difficulty is that we can form no clear and adequate conception of a human nature entirely without sin.

One thing, at any rate, is abundantly clear from this passage: there is nothing wrong or wicked in being greatly moved by the sight of sorrow, so long as we keep our feelings under control. To be always cold, unfeeling, and unsympathizing may appear to some very dignified and philosophical.   But though it may suit a Stoic, it is not consistent with the character of a Christian. Sympathy is not sinful, but Christ-like.

Theophylact observes that Christ "teaches us by His own example the due measure of joy and grief.   The absence altogether of sympathy and sorrow is brutal: the excess of them is womanly."

Melancthon observes that none of Christ's miracles seem to have been done without some great mental emotion.   (Luke viii. 46.)   He supposes that here at this verse, there was a great conflict with Satan in our Lord's mind, and that He wrestled in prayer for the raising of Lazarus, and then thanked God afterwards that the prayer was heard.   Calvin takes much the same view.

Ecolampadius observes that we must not think Christ had a human body only, and not a human soul.   He had a soul like our own in all things, sin only excepted, and capable of all our feelings and emotions.

Piscator and Trapp compare the trouble of spirit which our Lord went through, to the disturbance and agitation of perfectly clear water in a perfectly clear glass vessel.   However great the agitation, the water remains clear.

Musculus reverently remarks that after all there is something about this "groaning in spirit and troubling Himself," which cannot be fully explained.

34 —[*And said, Where have ye laid him?*]   We cannot suppose that our Lord, who knew all things, even to the moment of Lazarus' death could really need to be informed where Lazarus was buried.   He asks what He does here partly as a kind friend to show His deep sympathy and interest in the grave of His friend, and partly to give further proof that there was no collusion in the matter of Lazarus' burial, and that He had nothing to do with the choice of his tomb, in order to concert an impos-

ture about raising him. In short, those who heard Him publicly ask this question would see that this was no prearranged and precontrived miracle.

Quesnel remarks : " Christ does not ask out of ignorance, any more than God did when he said, ' Adam, where art thou ? ' "

[*They said...Lord, come and see.*] Who they were that said this, we do not exactly know. It was probably the common saying of all the party of mourners who stood around while Jesus talked with Mary. They did not know why our Lord wished to see the grave. They may possibly have supposed that He wished to accompany Mary and Martha, and to weep at the grave. At any rate the question and answer secured a large attendance of companions, as the disciples and our Lord went to the place where Lazarus was buried.

35 —[*Jesus wept.*] This wonderful little verse has given rise to an enormous amount of comment. The difficulty is to select thoughts, and not to overload the subject.

The Greek word rendered " wept " is not the same as that used for " weeping " in the thirty-third verse, but totally different. There the weeping is a weeping accompanied by demonstrative lamentation. Here the word would be more literally and accurately rendered " shed tears." In fact it is the only place in the New Testament where this word for " weep " is used.

There are three occasions where our Lord is recorded to have wept, in the Gospels : once when he beheld the city, (Luke xix. 41,) once in the garden of Gethsemanè, (Matt. xxvi. 39, and Heb. ✝i. 7,) and here. We never read of His laughing, and only once of His rejoicing. (Luke x. 21.)

The reasons assigned by commentators why our Lord wept here, before He raised Lazarus, are various and curious.

(*a*) Some think that he wept to see the ravages made by death and sin.

(*b*) Some, as Hilary, think that He wept to think of the unbelief of the Jews.

(*c*) Some think that He wept to see how weak and feeble was the faith of Mary and Martha.

(*d*) Some, as Jerome and Ferus, think that He wept at the thought of the sorrow Lazarus would go through by returning to a sinful world.

(*e*) Some think that He wept out of sympathy with the affliction of His friends at Bethany, in order to give an eternal proof to His Church that He can feel with us and for us.

I believe this last opinion is the true one.

We learn the great practical lesson, from this verse, that there is nothing unworthy of a Christian in tears. There is nothing unmanly, dishonourable, unwise, or feeble, in being full of sympathy with the afflicted, and ready to weep with them that weep. Indeed, it is curious to gather up the many instances we have in Scripture of great men weeping.

We may draw great comfort from the thought that the Saviour in whom we are bid to trust is one who can weep, and is as able to feel as He is able to save.

We may learn the reality of our Lord's humanity very strongly from this little verse. He was one who could hunger, thirst, sleep, eat, drink, speak, walk, groan, be wearied, wonder, feel indignant, rejoice, like any of ourselves, and yet without sin; and, above all, He could weep. I read that there is "joy in the presence of the angels of God," (Luke xv.,) but I never read of angels weeping. Tears are peculiar to flesh and blood.

Chrysostom remarks that "John, who enters into higher statements about our Lord's nature than any of the evangelists, also descends lower than any in describing his bodily affections."

36 —[*Then said...Jews...Behold...loved him.*] This sentence is the expression partly of surprise, which comes out in the word "behold;" and partly of admiration,—what a loving and tender-hearted Teacher this is! It gives the idea that those who said this were the few unprejudiced Jews who had come to Bethany to comfort Mary and Martha, and afterward believed when they saw Lazarus raised.

Let us observe that of all graces, love is the one which most arrests the attention and influences the opinion of the world.

37 —[*And some of them said, etc.*] This sentence sounds to me like the language of enemies determined to believe nothing good of our Lord, and prepared to pick a hole or find a fault if possible, in anything that He did. Does not a sarcastic sneer ring throughout it? "Could not this Man, if He really did open the eyes of that blind person at Jerusalem last autumn, have prevented this friend of His from dying? If He really is the Messiah and the Christ, and really does work such wonderful works, why has He not prevented all this sorrow? If He really loved Lazarus and his sisters, why did He not prove His love by keeping him back from the grave? Is it not plain that He is not Almighty? He cannot do everything. He could open the eyes of a blind man, but He could not prevent death carrying off His friend. If He was able to prevent Lazarus dying, why did He not do it? If He was not able, it is clear there are some things He cannot do."

We should note that "the blind" is a word in the singular number. It is evidently the blind man at Jerusalem whose case is referred to.

Let us note that nothing will convince, or satisfy, or silence some wicked men. Even when Christ is before them, they are cavilling, and doubting, and finding fault. What right have Christ's ministers to be surprised if they meet with the same treatment?

Musculus remarks on the Satanic malice which this sentence displays. It is the old sceptical spirit of cavilling and questioning. Unbelief is always saying why? and why? and why? "If this Man was such a friend of Lazarus, and loved him so much, why did He let him die?"

JOHN XI 38—46

38 Jesus therefore again groaning in himself cometh to the grave. It was a cave, and a stone lay upon it.

39 Jesus said, Take ye away the stone. Martha, the sister of him that was dead, saith unto him, Lord, by this time he stinketh: for he hath been *dead* four days.

40 Jesus saith unto her, Said I not unto thee, that, if thou wouldest believe, thou shouldest see the glory of God?

41 Then they took away the stone *from the place* where the dead was laid. And Jesus lifted up *his* eyes, and said, Father, I thank thee that thou hast heard me.

42 And I knew that thou hearest me always: but because of the people which stand by I said *it*, that they may believe that thou hast sent me.

43 And when he thus had spoken, he cried with a loud voice, Lazarus, come forth.

44 And he that was dead came forth, bound hand and foot with graveclothes: and his face was bound about with a napkin. Jesus saith unto them, Loose him, and let him go.

45 Then many of the Jews which came to Mary, and had seen the things which Jesus did, believed on him.

46 But some of them went their ways to the Pharisees, and told them what things Jesus had done.

THESE verses record one of the greatest miracles the Lord Jesus Christ ever worked, and supply an unanswerable proof of His divinity. He whose voice could bring back from the grave one that had been four days dead, must indeed have been very God! The miracle itself is described in such simple language that no human comment can throw light upon it. But the sayings of our Lord on this occasion are peculiarly interesting, and demand special notice.

We should mark, first, *our Lord's words about the stone which lay upon the grave of Lazarus.* We read that He said to those around Him, when he came to the place of burial, " Take ye away the stone."

Now why did our Lord say this? It was ˙ doubtless as easy for Him to command the stone to roll away untouched as to call a dead body from the tomb. But such was not His mode of proceeding. Here, as in other cases, He chose to give man something to do. Here, as elsewhere, He taught the great lesson that His almighty power was not meant to destroy man's responsibility. Even when He was ready and willing to raise the dead, He would not have man stand by altogether idle.

Let us treasure up this in our memories. It involves a point of great importance. In doing spiritual good to others,—in training up our children for heaven,—in following after holiness in our own daily walk,—in all these things it is undoubtedly true that we are weak and helpless. " Without Christ we can do nothing." But still we must remember that Christ expects us to do what we can. " Take ye away the stone " is the daily command which He gives us. Let us beware that we do not stand still in idleness, under the pretence of humility. Let us daily try to do what we can, and in the trying Christ will meet us and grant His blessing.

We should mark, secondly, the *words which our Lord addressed to Martha, when she objected to the stone being removed from the grave.* The faith of this holy woman completely broke down, when the cave where her beloved brother lay was about to be thrown open. She could not believe that it was of any use. " Lord," she cries, " by this time he stinketh." And then comes in the solemn reproof of our Lord : " Said I ˙not unto thee that if thou wouldest believe thou shouldest see the glory of God? "

That sentence is rich in meaning. It is far from unlikely that it contains a reference to the message which had been sent to Martha and Mary, when their brother first fell sick. It may be meant to remind Martha that her Master had sent her word, "This sickness is not unto death, but for the glory of God." But it is perhaps more likely that our Lord desired to recall to Martha's mind the old lesson He had taught her all through His ministry, the duty of always believing. It is as though He said, "Martha, Martha, thou art forgetting the great doctrine of faith, which I have ever taught thee. Believe, and all will be well. Fear not: only believe."

The lesson is one which we can never know too well. How apt our faith is to break down in time of trial! How easy it is to talk of faith in the days of health and prosperity, and how hard to practise it in the days of darkness, when neither sun, moon, nor stars appear! Let us lay to heart what our Lord says in this place. Let us pray for such stores of inward faith, that when our turn comes to suffer, we may suffer patiently and believe all is well. The Christian who has ceased to say, "I must see, and then I will believe," and has learned to say, "I believe, and by and by I shall see," has reached a high degree in the school of Christ.

We should mark, thirdly, *the words which our Lord addressed to God the Father, when the stone was taken from the grave.* We read that He said, "Father, I thank Thee that Thou hast heard Me. And I knew that Thou hearest Me always: but because of the people which stand by I said it, that they may believe that Thou hast sent Me."

This wonderful language is totally unlike anything said by Prophets or Apostles, when they worked miracles. In fact, it is not prayer, but praise. It evidently implies a constant mysterious communion going on between Jesus and His Father in heaven, which it is past the power of man either to explain or conceive. We need not doubt that here, as elsewhere in St. John, our Lord meant to teach the Jews the entire and complete unity there was between Him and His Father, in all that He did, as well as in all that He taught.   Once more He would remind them that he did not come among them as a mere Prophet, but as the Messiah who was sent by the Father, and who was one with the Father.   Once more He would have them know that as the words which He spake were the very words which the Father gave Him to speak, so the works which He wrought were the very works which the Father gave Him to do.   In short, He was the promised Messiah, whom the Father always hears, because He and the Father are One.

Deep and high as this truth is, it is for the peace of our souls to believe it thoroughly, and to grasp it tightly.   Let it be a settled principle of our religion, that the Saviour in whom we trust is nothing less than eternal God, One whom the Father hears always, One who in very deed is God's Fellow.   A clear view of the dignity of our Mediator's Person is one secret of inward comfort.   Happy is he who can say, " I know whom I have believed, and that He is able to keep that which I have committed to Him."   (2 Tim. i. 12.)

We should mark, lastly, *the words which our Lord addressed to Lazarus when he raised him from the grave.* We read that " He cried with a loud voice, Lazarus, come forth ! "   At the sound of that voice, the king of terrors at once yielded up his lawful captive, and the insatiable grave gave up its prey.   At once "He that was dead came forth, bound hand and foot with grave-clothes."

The greatness of this miracle cannot possibly be exaggerated.   The mind of man can scarcely take in the vastness of the work that was done.   Here, in open day, and before many hostile witnesses, a man, four days dead, was restored to life in a moment.   Here was public proof that our Lord had absolute power over the material world !   A corpse, already corrupt, was made alive !—Here was public proof that our Lord had absolute power over the

world of spirits! A soul that had left its earthly tene-
ment was called back from Paradise, and joined once more
to its owner's body.—Well may the Church of Christ maintain that He who could work such works was "God over
all blessed forever." (Rom. ix. 5.)

Let us turn from the whole passage with thoughts of
comfort and consolation.   Comfortable is the thought
that the loving Saviour of sinners, on whose mercy our
souls entirely depend, is one who has all power in heaven,
and earth, and is mighty to save.—Comfortable is the
thought that there is no sinner too far gone in sin for
Christ to raise and convert.   He that stood by the grave
of Lazarus can say to the vilest of men, "Come forth:
loose him, and let him go."—Comfortable, not least, is the
thought that when we ourselves lie down in the grave, we
may lie down in the full assurance that we shall rise again.
The voice that called Lazarus forth will one day pierce our
tombs, and bid soul and body come together.   "The
trumpets shall sound, and the dead shall be raised incorruptible, and we shall be changed." (1 Cor. xv. 52.)

NOTES JOHN XI 38—46

38 —[*Jesus...groaning...cometh...grave.*] The word here rendered
"groaning" is the same that was used at 32d verse, and the
same remarks apply to it. The only difference is that here it is
"groaning in Himself," and there "groaning in the spirit."
This, however, confirms my impression that in the former verse
"in the spirit" simply means "inwardly and spiritually," and
that the general idea is "under the influence of very strong
inward emotion."

The situation of the grave, we need not doubt, was outside
the village of Bethany. There was no such thing as interment
within a town allowed among the Jews, or indeed among ancient
nations generally. The practice of burying the dead among the
living is a barbarous modern innovation, reflecting little credit
on Christians.

Calvin remarks: "Christ approaches the sepulchre as a cham-
pion preparing for a contest; and we need not wonder that He
groans, as the violent tyranny of death, which He had to conquer, is placed before His eyes."

Ecolampadius and Musculus think that the unbelieving, sneering remark of the Jews in the preceding verse is the reason why our Lord "again groaned." Bullinger thinks that the renewed emotion of our Lord was simply occasioned by the sight of the grave.

[*It was a cave, and a stone lay upon it.*] Graves among the Jews seem to have been of three kinds. (1) Sometimes, but rarely, they were holes dug down into the ground, like our own. (See Luke xi. 44.) (2) Most frequently they were caves hewn horizontally into the side of a rock, with a stone placed against the mouth. This was most probably the kind of new tomb in which our Lord was laid. (3) Sometimes they were caves in which there was a sloping, downward descent. This appears to have been the description of grave in which Lazarus was buried. It says distinctly that " a stone lay *upon* it."

No doubt these particulars are specified to supply incidental proof of the reality of Lazarus' death and burial.

39 —[*Jesus said, Take ye away the stone.*] The expression here conveys the idea of " lifting up " to take away. It is the same word that is rendered " lifted up " in 41st verse.

The use of this word greatly strengthens the idea that the grave was a descending cave, and not a horizontal one. When our Lord rose again, the stone was " rolled away from the door," and not lifted up. (Matt. xxviii. 2.)

By calling on the crowd of attendants to take away the stone, our Lord effected two things. Firstly, He impressed on the mind of all engaged the reality and truth of the miracle He was about to perform. Every one who lent a hand to lift the huge stone and remove it would remember it, and become a witness. He would be able to say, " I myself helped to lift up the stone. I myself am sure there was no imposture. There was a dead body inside the grave." In fact, we cannot doubt that the smell rising from the bottom of the cave would tell any one who helped to lift the stone what there was there.—Secondly, our Lord teaches us the simple lesson that He would have man do what he can. Man cannot raise the soul, and give life, but he can often remove the stone.

Flacius points out the likeness between this command and the command at Cana to fill the water-pots with water. (John ii. 7.)

That the stones placed at the mouth of graves in Palestine were very large, and not easily moved, we may see from Mark xvi. 3.

[*Martha, the sister of him, etc., etc.*] This is a remarkable sentence, and teaches several important things.

(*a*) It certifies, for the last time, the reality of Lazarus' death. He was not in a swoon or a trance. His own sister, who had doubtless seen him die, and closed his eyes, declares before the crowd of lookers-on, that Lazarus had been dead four days, and was fast going to corruption. This we may well believe in such a climate as that of Palestine.

(b) It proves, beyond a reasonable doubt, that there was no imposture, no collusion, no concerted deception, arranged between the family of Bethany and our Lord. Here is the sister of Lazarus actually questioning the propriety of our Lord's order, and publicly saying in effect that it is no use to move the stone, that nothing can now be done to deliver her brother from the power of death. Like the eleven Apostles, after Jesus Himself rose, Martha was not a willing and prepared witness, but a resisting and unwilling one.

(c) It teaches, not least, how much unbelief there is in a believer's heart at the bottom. Here is holy Martha, with all her faith in our Lord's Messiahship, shrinking and breaking down at this most critical point. She cannot believe that there is any use in removing the stone. She suggests, impulsively and anxiously, her doubt whether our Lord remembers how long her brother has been dead.

It is not for nothing that we are specially told it was "Martha, the sister of him that was dead," who said this. If even she could say this, and raise objections, the idea of imposture and deception becomes absurd.

Some writers object to putting the full literal meaning on the Greek word rendered "stinketh; " but I can see nothing in the objection. We need not suppose that the body of Lazarus was different to other bodies. Moreover, it was just as easy to our Lord to raise a corpse four days dead, as one only four hours dead. In either case, the grand difficulty to be overcome would be the same : viz., to change death into life. Indeed, it is worth considering, whether this fact about Lazarus is not specially mentioned in order to show our Lord's power to restore man's corrupt and decayed body at the last day, and to make it a glorious body.

Let us note here what a humbling lesson death teaches. So terrible and painful is the corruption of a body, when the breath leaves it, that even those who love us most are glad to bury us out of sight. (Gen. xxiii. 4.)

Musculus suggests that Martha had so little idea what our Lord was going to do, that she supposed He only wanted to see Lazarus' face once more. This is perhaps going too far.

The Greek for "dead four days," is a singular expression, and one that cannot be literally rendered in English. It would be "He is a person of four days," and it may possibly mean, "He has been buried four days." Raphelius gives examples from Herodotus and Xenophon, which make it possible that it means either dead or buried.

Lightfoot mentions a very curious tradition of the Jews :

" They say after death the spirit hovers about the sepulchre, waiting to see if it may return to the body. But when it sees the look of the face of the corpse changed, then it hovers no more, but leaves the body to itself." He also adds, " They do not certify of the dead, except within three days after decease; for after three days the countenance changes."

40 -[*Jesus saith, said I not, etc.*] This gentle but firm reproof is remarkable. It is not clear to what our Lord refers in the words, " Said I not."

(*a*) Some think, as Rupertus, that He refers to the message He sent at the beginning : " This sickness is not unto death, but for the glory of God."

(*b*) Some think that He refers to the conversation He had with Martha when she first met Him outside Bethany.

(*c*) Some think that He refers to words He had often used in discoursing with Martha and Mary, on former occasions.

The point is one which must be left open, as we have no means of settling it. My own impression is that there is probably a reference to the message which our Lord sent back to the sisters at first, when Lazarus was sick. I fancy there must have been something more said at that time which is not recorded, and that our Lord reminded Martha of this. At the same time I cannot doubt that our Lord constantly taught the family of Bethany and all His disciples, that believing is the grand secret of seeing God's glorious works.—" If thou canst believe, all things are possible to him that believeth."—" He did not many mighty works, because of their unbelief." (Mark ix. 23; Matt. xiii. 58.) Unbelief, in a certain sense, seems to tie the hands and limit the power of omnipotence.

Let us note that if we would see much we must first believe. Man's natural idea is just the reverse : he would first see, and then believe.

Let us note that even the best believers need reminding of Christ's sayings, and are apt to forget them. " Said I not unto thee." It is a little sentence we should often call to mind.

41 -[*Then they took away...stone...laid.*] Martha's interruption seems to me to have caused a little pause in the proceedings. She being the nearest relative of Lazarus, and having probably arranged everything concerning his burial, and provided his tomb, we may well believe that her speech made the bystanders hesitate to move the stone. When, however, they heard our Lord's solemn reply, and observed that she was silenced, and made no further objection, " then" they proceeded to do what our Lord desired.

Hall remarks : " They that laid their hands to the stone doubtless held still awhile, when Martha spoke, and looked one while on Christ, another while on Martha, to hear what issue of resolution would follow so important an objection."

[*And Jesus lifted up his eyes, and said.*] We now reach a point of thrilling and breathless interest. The stone had been removed from the mouth of the cave. Our Lord stands before the open grave, and the crowd stands around, awaiting anxiously to see what would happen next. Nothing appears from the tomb. There is no sign of life at present; but while all are eagerly looking and listening, our Lord addressed His Father in heaven in a most solemn manner, lifting up His eyes, and speaking audibly to Him in the hearing of all the crowd. The reason He explains in the next verse. Now, for the last time, about to work His mightiest miracle, He once more makes a public declaration that He did nothing separate from His Father in heaven, and that in this and all His works there is a mysterious and intimate union between Himself and the Father.

We should note how He suits the action to the word. " He lifted up His eyes." (Compare John xvii. 1.) He showed that He was addressing an unseen Father in heaven.

[*Father, I thank thee that thou hast heard me.*] This is a remarkable expression. Our Lord begins with " thanks," when man would have expected Him to offer prayer. How shall we explain it?

(*a*) Some think that our Lord refers to prayer He had put up to the Father concerning the death of Lazarus, from the moment that He heard of his illness, and to His present firm conviction that those prayers had been heard, and were going to receive a public answer.

(*b*) Others think that there is no reason to suppose that our Lord refers to any former and remote prayer,—that there was a constant, hourly, minutely communication between Himself and His heavenly Father,—and that to pray, and return thanks for the answer to prayer, were actions which in His experience were very closely connected.

The subject is a deep and mysterious one, and I shrink from giving a very positive opinion about it. That our Lord constantly prayed, on all occasions, we know from the Gospels. That He prayed sometimes with great agony of mind and with tears, we also know. (Heb. v. 7.) But how far He could know anything of that peculiar struggle which we poor sinners have to carry on with doubt, fear, and anxiety, in our prayers is another question altogether, and very hard to answer. One might suppose that One who was as man, entirely holy, humble, and without sin, might be able to thank for prayer heard, almost as soon as prayer was offered. Upon this theory the sentence before us would be plain: " I pray that Lazarus may be raised; and I thank Thee at the same time for hearing my prayer, as I know Thou dost."

And yet we must not forget two of our Lord's prayers not granted, apparently: " Father, save Me from this hour;"—

"Father, let this cup pass from Me." (John. xii. 47, and Mark xxvi. 29.) It is, however, only fair to say that the first of these prayers is greatly qualified by the context, and the second by the words, "If it be possible."

We may note here, as elsewhere, what an example of thankfulness, as well as prayerfulness, our Lord always supplies. Well if it was followed! His people are always more ready to ask than to thank. The more grace in a heart the more humility, and the more humility the more praise.

Chrysostom remarks : " Who now ever prayed in this manner ? Before uttering any prayer, He saith, ' I thank Thee,' showing that He needed not prayer." He also says that the real cause of our Lord saying this was to show the Jews He was no enemy of God, but did all His works according to His will.

Origen observes : " If to those who pray worthily is given the promise in Isaiah, ' Thou shalt cry, and He shall say, Here I am,' what answer, think we, could our Lord receive ? He was about to pray for the resurrection of Lazarus. He was heard by the Father before He prayed ; His request was granted before it was made ; and, therefore, He begins with thanks."

Musculus, Flacius, and Glassius, think that our Lord refers to prayer He had been putting up secretly when He was "groaning in spirit and troubled," and that He was then wrestling and agonizing in prayer, though those around Him knew it not. We may remember that at the Red Sea we are not told of any audible prayer Moses offered, and yet the Lord says, "Wherefore criest thou unto Me ? " (Exodus xiv. 15.)

Quesnel observes : " Christ being about to conclude His public life and preaching by the last and most illustrious of His miracles, returns solemn thanks to His Father for the power given to His human nature to prove the authority of His mission by miracles."

Hall observes : " Words express our hearts to men, thoughts to God. Well didst Thou know, Lord, out of the self-sameness of Thy will with the Father's, that if Thou didst but think in Thy heart that Lazarus should rise, he was now raised. It was not for Thee to pray vocally and audibly, lest those captious hearers should say, Thou didst all by entreaty, and nothing by power."

42 —[*And I knew that Thou hearest, etc.*] This verse is so elliptical that the meaning can hardly be seen without a paraphrase. " I do not give Thee these thanks as if I had ever doubted Thy willingness to hear Me ; on the contrary, I know well that Thou always hearest Me.—Thou dost not only hear all my prayers as Man, both for myself and my people ; Thou dost also ever hear Me, even as I hear Thee, from the mystical union there is between the Father and the Son. But I have now said this

publicly, for the benefit of this crowd of people standing by the grave, in order that they may see and believe for the last time that I do no miracle without Thee, and that I am the Messiah whom Thou hast sent into the world.   I would have them publicly hear Me declare that I work this last great work as Thy Sent One, and as a last evidence that I am the Christ."

I cannot but think there is a deep meaning about the expression, " Thou hearest Me alway." (Compare John v. 30.)   But I admit the difficulty of the phrase and would speak with diffidence.

It is impossible to imagine a more thorough open challenge to the attention of the Jews, than the language which preceded the raising of Lazarus.   Before doing this stupendous work, our Lord proclaims that He is doing and speaking as He does to supply a proof that the Father sent and commissioned Him as the Christ.   Was He the " Sent One," or not?   This, we must always remember, was the great question, of which He undertook to give proof.   The Jews, moreover, said that He did His miracles by Beelzebub : let them hear that He did all by the power of God.

Bullinger remarks that our Lord seems to say, " The Jews do not all understand that union and communion between Me and Thee, by which we are of the same will, power, and substance.   Some of them even think that I work by the power of the devil.   Therefore that all may believe that I come from Thee, am sent by Thee, am Thy Son, equal to Thee, light of light, very God of very God, I use expressions of this sort."

Poole remarks : " There is a great difference between God's hearing of Christ and hearing us.   Christ and His Father have one essence, one nature, and one will."

The following miracles were wrought by Christ without audible prayer, and with only an authoritative word, Matt. viii. 3 ; ix. 6 ; Mark v. 41 ; ix. 25 ; Luke vii. 14.

Wordsworth observes : " Christ prayed to show that He was not against God, nor God against Him, and that what He did was done with God's approval."

43 —[*And when...cried...come forth.*]   In this verse we have the last and crowning stage of the miracle.   Attention was concentrated on the grave and our Lord.   The crowd looked on with breathless expectation ; and then, while they looked, having secured their attention, our Lord bids Lazarus come forth out of the grave.   The Greek word for " He cried," is only in this place applied to any voice or utterance of our Lord.   In Matt. xii. 19, it is used, where it is said of our Lord, " He shall *not cry*."   Here it is evident that He purposely used a very loud, piercing cry, that all around might hear and take notice.

Theophylact thinks that Jesus " cried aloud to contradict the Gentile fable that the soul remained in the tomb with the body.   Therefore the soul of Lazarus is called to as if it were absent, and a loud voice were necessary to summon it back." Euthymius suggests the same reason. This, however, seems an odd idea.

On the other hand, Brentius, Grotius, and Lampe suggest that Jesus " cried with a loud voice," to prevent the Jews from saying that He muttered or whispered some magical form, or words of enchantment, as witches did.

Ferus observes that our Lord did not say, " In the name of my Father come forth," or " Raise Him, O my Father," but acts by His own authority.

44 —[*And He that was dead came forth.*] The effect of our Lord's words was seen at once. As soon as He " cried," Lazarus was seen coming up out of the cave, before the eyes of the crowd. A more plain, distinct, and unmistakable miracle it would be impossible for man to imagine. That a dead man should hear a voice, obey it, rise up, and move forth from his grave alive is utterly contrary to nature. God alone could cause such a thing. What first began life in him, how lungs and heart began to act again, suddenly and instantaneously, it would be waste of time to speculate. It was a miracle, and there we must leave it.

The idea of some, that Lazarus moved out of the grave without the use of his legs, passing through air like a spirit or ghost, seems to me needless and unreasonable. I agree with Hutcheson, Hall, and Pearce, that though " bound hand and foot," there is no certain proof that his legs were tied together so tightly that he could not move out of the grave, though slowly and with difficulty, like one encumbered, on his own feet. The tardy, shuffling action of such a figure would strike all. Pearce remarks, " He must have come forth crawling on his knees." We are surely not required to multiply miracles.—Yet the idea that Lazarus came out with a supernatural motion seems to be held by Augustine, Zwingle, Ecolampadius, Bucer, Gualter, Toletus, Jansenius, Lampe, Lightfoot, and Alford, who think it part of the miracle. I would not press my opinion positively on others, though I firmly mantain it. My own private feeling is that the slow, gradual, tottering movements of a figure encumbered by grave-clothes would impress a crowd far more than the rapid, ghost-like gliding out in air of a body, of which the feet did not move.

[*His face bound about...napkin.*] This is mentioned to show that he had been really dead, and his corpse treated like all other corpses. If not dead, he would have been unable to breathe through the napkin for four days.

[*Jesus saith...Loose him...let him go.*] This command was given for two reasons : partly that many around might touch Lazarus and see for themselves that it was not a ghost, but a real body that was raised; partly that he might be able to walk to his own house before the eyes of the multitude as a living man. This, until he was freed from grave-clothes and his eyes were unbandaged, would have been impossible.

Very striking is it to remark how in the least minute particulars the objections of infidels and sceptics are quietly forestalled and met in Gospel narrative! Thus Chrysostom remarks that the command to "loose him" would enable the friends who bore Lazarus to the grave, to know from the grave-clothes that it was the very person they had buried four days before. They would recognize the clothes; they could not say, as some had said in the case of the blind man, "This is not he." He also remarks that both hands, eyes, ears, and nostrils would all convince the witnesses of the truth of the miracle.

45 —[*Then many of the Jews...believed on him.*]   This verse describes the good effect which the raising of Lazarus had on many of the Jews who had come from Jerusalem to comfort Mary and Martha.   Their remaining prejudices gave way.   They were unable to resist the extraordinary evidence of the miracle they had just seen.   From that day they no longer denied that Jesus was the Christ.   Whether their belief was faith unto salvation may well be doubted; but at any rate they ceased to oppose and blaspheme.   And it is more than probable that on the day of Pentecost many of those very Jews whose hearts had been prepared by the miracle of Bethany came boldly forward and were baptized.

We should observe in this verse what a signal blessing God was pleased to bestow on sympathy and kindness.   If the Jews had not come to comfort Mary under her affliction, they would not have seen the mighty miracle of raising Lazarus, and perhaps would not have been saved.

Lampe remarks on these Jews: "They had come as the merciful, and they obtained mercy."

Besner observes the beautiful delicacy with which St. John draws a veil over the effect on Martha and Mary of this miracle, while he dwells on the effect it had on strangers.

46 —[*But some of them went...Pharisees, etc.*]   We see in this verse the bad effect which the raising of Lazarus had on some who saw it.   Instead of being softened and convinced, they were hardened and enraged.   They were vexed to see even more unanswerable proofs that Jesus was the Christ, and irritated to feel that their own unbelief was more than ever inexcusable.   They therefore hurried off to the Pharisees to report what they had seen, and to point out the progress that our Lord was making in the immediate neighborhood of Jerusalem.

The amazing wickedness of human nature is strikingly illustrated in this verse.   There is no greater mistake than to suppose that seeing miracles will necessarily convert souls.   Here is a plain proof that it does not.   Never was there a more remarkable confirmation of our Lord's words in the parable of the Rich Man and Lazarus, "If they believe not Moses and the Prophets, neither will they be persuaded, though one rose from the dead."

Musculus observes what a wonderful example we have here of the sovereign grace of God, choosing some, and leading them to repentance and faith, and not choosing others. Here is the same miracle, seen under the same circumstances, and with the same evidence, by a large crowd of persons; yet while some believe, others believe not! It is like the case of the two thieves on the cross, both seeing the same sight, one repenting and the other impenitent. The same fire which melts wax hardens clay.

In leaving this wonderful miracle, there are three things which demand special notice.

(a) We should observe that we are not told of anything that Lazarus said about his state while in the grave, and nothing of his after history. Tradition says that he lived for thirty years after, and was never known to smile; but this is probably a mere apocryphal invention. As to his silence, we can easily see there is a Divine wisdom about it. If St. Paul "could not utter" the things that he saw in the third heaven, and called them "unspeakable things;" it is not strange that Lazarus should say nothing of what he saw in Paradise. (2 Cor. xii. 4.) But there may be always seen in Scripture a striking silence about the feelings about men and women who have been the subjects of remarkable Divine interposition. God's ways are not man's ways. Man loves sensation and excitement, and likes to make God's work on his fellow-creatures a gazing-stock and a show, to their great damage. God almost always seems to withdraw them from the public, both for their own good and His glory.

(b) We should observe that we are told nothing of the feelings of Martha and Mary, after they saw their brother raised to life. The veil is drawn over their joy, though it was not over their sorrow. Affliction is a more profitable study than rejoicing.

(c) We should observe, lastly, that the raising of Lazarus is one of the most signal instances in the Gospels of Christ's Divine power. To Him who could work such a miracle nothing is impossible. He can raise from the death of sin any dead soul, however far gone and corrupt. He will raise us from the grave at His own second appearing. The voice which called Lazarus from the tomb is almighty. "The dead shall hear the voice of the Son of Man, and they that hear shall live." (John v. 25.)

JOHN XI   47—57

47 Then gathered the chief priests and the Pharisees a council, and said, What do we ? for this man doeth many miracles.

48 If we let him thus alone, all *men* will believe on him : and the Romans shall come and take away both our place and nation.

49 And one of them *named* Caiaphas, being the high priest that same year, said unto them, Ye know nothing at all,

50 Nor consider that it is expedient for us, that one man should die for the people, and that the whole nation perish not.

51 And this spake he not of himself : but being high priest that year, he prophesied that Jesus should die for that nation :

52 And not for that nation only, but that also he should gather together in one the children of God that were scattered abroad.

53 Then from that day forth they took counsel together for to put him to death.

54 Jesus therefore walked no more openly among the Jews; but went thence unto a country near to the wilderness, into a city called Ephraim, and there continued with his disciples.

55 And the Jews' passover was nigh at hand : and many went out of the country up to Jerusalem before the passover, to purify themselves.

56 Then sought they for Jesus, and spake among themselves, as they stood in the temple, What think ye, that he will not come to the feast ?

57 Now both the chief priests and the Pharisees had given a commandment, that, if any man knew where he were, he should shew *it*, that they might take him.

THESE concluding verses of the eleventh chapter of St. John contain a melancholy picture of human nature.   As we turn away from Jesus Christ and the grave at Bethany, and look at Jerusalem and the rulers of the Jews, we may well say, " Lord, what is man ? "

We, should observe, for one thing, in these verses, *the desperate wickedness of man's natural heart.* A mighty miracle was wrought within an easy walk of Jerusalem. A man four days dead was raised to life, in the sight of many witnesses.   The fact was unmistakable, and could not be denied ; and yet the chief priests and Pharisees would not believe that He who did this miracle ought to be received as the Messiah.   In the face of overwhelming evidence they shut their eyes, and refused to be convinced. " This man," they admitted, " does many miracles."   But so far from yielding to this testimony, they only plunged into further wickedness, and " took counsel to put Him to death."   Great, indeed, is the power of unbelief !

Let us beware of supposing that miracles alone have any power to convert men's souls, and to make them Christians. The idea is a complete delusion. To fancy, as some do, that if they saw something wonderful done before their eyes in confirmation of the Gospel, they would at once cast off all indecision and serve Christ, is a mere idle dream. It is the grace of the spirit in our hearts, and not miracles, that our souls require. The Jews of our Lord's day are a standing proof to mankind that men may see signs and wonders, and yet remain hard as stone. It is a deep and true saying, " If men believe not Moses and the Prophets, neither would they be persuaded though one rose from the dead." (Luke xvi. 31.)

We must never wonder if we see abounding unbelief in our own times, and around our own homes. It may seem at first inexplicable to us, how men cannot see the truth which seems so clear to ourselves, and do not receive the Gospel which appears so worthy of acceptation. But the plain truth is, that man's unbelief is a far more deeply seated disease than it is generally reckoned. It is proof against the logic of facts, against reasoning, against argument, against moral suasion. Nothing can melt it down but the grace of God. If we ourselves believe, we can never be too thankful. But we must never count it a strange thing, if we see many of our fellow-Christians just as hardened and unbelieving as the Jews.

We should observe, for another thing, *the blind ignorance with which God's enemies often act and reason.* These rulers of the Jews said to one another, " If we let this Christ alone we shall be ruined. If we do not stop His course, and make an end of His miracles, the Romans will interfere, and make an end of our nation." Never, the event afterward proved, was there a more short-sighted and erring judgment than this. They rushed madly on the path they had chosen, and the very thing they feared came to pass. They did not leave our Lord alone, but crucified and slew Him. And what happened then? After a few years, the very calamity they had dreaded took place: the Roman armies did come, destroyed Jerusalem, burned the temple, and carried away the whole nation into captivity.

The well-read Christian need hardly be reminded of many such like things in the history of Christ's Church. The Roman emperors persecuted the Christians in the first three centuries, and thought it a positive duty not to let them alone. But the more they persecuted them, the more they increased. The blood of the martyrs became the seed of the Church.—The English Papists, in the days of Queen Mary, persecuted the Protestants, and thought that truth was in danger if they were let alone. But the more they burned our forefathers, the more they confirmed men's minds in steadfast attachment to the doctrines of the Reformation.—In short, the words of the second Psalm are continually verified in this world: " The kings of the earth set themselves, and the rulers take counsel together against the Lord." But " He that sitteth in the heavens shall laugh; the Lord shall have them in derision." God can make the designs of His enemies work together for the good of His people, and cause the wrath of man to praise Him. In days of trouble, and rebuke, and blasphemy, believers may rest patiently in the Lord. The very things that at one time seem likely to hurt them, shall prove in the end to be for their gain.

We should observe, lastly, *what importance bad men sometimes attach to outward ceremonial, while their hearts are full of sin.* We are told that many Jews " went up out of the country to Jerusalem, before the Passover, to purify themselves." The most of them, it may be feared, neither knew nor cared anything about inward purity of heart. They made much ado about the washings, and fastings, and ascetic observances, which formed the essence of popular Jewish religion in our Lord's time; and yet they were willing in a very few days to shed innocent blood. Strange as it may appear, these very sticklers for outward sanctification were found ready to do the will of the Pharisees, and to put their own Messiah to a violent death.

Extremes like this meeting together in the same person are, unhappily, far from uncommon. Experience shows that a bad conscience will often try to satisfy itself by a show of zeal for the cause of religion, while the "weightier matters" of the faith are entirely neglected. The very same man who is ready to compass sea and land to attain ceremonial purity is often the very man, who, if he had fit opportunity, would not shrink from helping to crucify Christ. Startling as these assertions may seem, they are abundantly borne out by plain facts. The cities where Lent is kept at this day with the most extravagant strictness are the very cities where the carnival after Lent is a season of glaring excess and immorality. The people in some parts of Christendom, who make much ado one week about fasting and priestly absolution, are the very people who another week will think nothing of murder! These things are simple realities. The hideous inconsistency of the Jewish formalists in our Lord's time has never been without a long succession of followers.

Let us settle it firmly in our minds that a religion which expends itself in zeal for outward formalities is utterless worthless in God's sight. The purity that God desires to see is not the purity of bodily washing and fasting, of holy water and self-imposed asceticism, but purity of heart. Will-worship and ceremonialism may "satisfy the flesh," but they do not tend to promote real godliness. The standard of Christ's kingdom must be sought in the sermon on the Mount: "Blessed are the pure in heart, for they shall see God." (Matt. v. 8; Col. ii. 23.)

NOTES JOHN XI 47—57

47 —[*Then gathered...priests...Pharisees...council.*] This council was probably the great sanhedrim, or consultative assembly of the Jewish Church. It was for purely ecclesiastical, and not for civil or political purposes. It is the same assembly before which, it is conjectured with much show of reason, our Lord made His defence, in the fifth chapter of this gospel. On receiving the tidings of the astounding miracle which had been wrought at Bethany, our Lord's bitterest enemies, the chief priests and Pharisees, seem to have been alarmed and enraged, and to have felt the absolute necessity of taking decided measures to check our Lord's progress. Ecclesiastical rulers, unhappily, are often the foremost enemies of the Gospel.

[*And said, What do we?*] This question indicates perplexity and irritation. "What are we about? Are we going to sit still, and let this new Teacher carry all before Him? · What is the use of trifling with this new heresy? We are doing nothing effectual to check it. It grows; and we let it alone."

[*For this man doeth many miracles.*] This is a marvellous admission. Even our Lord's worst enemies confess that our Lord did miracles, and many miracles. Can we doubt that they would have denied the truth of His miracles, if they could? But they do not seem to have attempted it. They were too many, too public, and too thoroughly witnessed, for them to dare to deny them. How, in the face of this fact, modern infidels and sceptics can talk of our Lord's miracles as being impostures and delusions, they would do well to explain! If the Pharisees who lived in our Lord's time, and who moved heaven and earth to oppose His progress, never dared to dispute the fact that He worked miracles, it is absurd to begin denying His miracles now, after eighteen centuries have passed away.

Let us note the desperate hardness and wickedness of man's heart. Even the sight of miracles will not convert any one, without the renewing grace of the Holy Ghost.

Brentius remarks that the simple answer to the question of this verse ought to have been, "Our duty is to believe at once that this worker of many miracles is the Christ of God."

48 —[*If we let him thus alone.*] This means, "If we continue to treat Him as we do now, and take no more active measures to

put Him down,—if we only dispute and reason and argue and cavil and denounce Him, but let Him have His liberty, let Him go where He pleases, let Him do what He pleases, and preach what He pleases."

" Thus " can only mean " as at present, and hitherto."

[*All men will believe on him.*] This means the bulk of the population will believe that He is what He *professes* to be,—the promised Messiah. The number of His adherents will increase, and faith in His Messiahship will become contagious, and spread all over Palestine.

The word " all," in this sentence, must evidently not be taken literally. It only means " the great mass of the people." It is like " all men come unto Him," said by the angry disciples of John the Baptist about Christ. (John iii. 36.) When men lose their tempers, and talk in passion, they are very apt to use exaggerated expressions.

[*The Romans come...take away...place...nation.*] The process of reasoning by which the Pharisees arrived at this conclusion was probably something of this kind. " This man, if let alone, will gather round Him a crowd of adherents, who will proclaim Him a Leader and King. This our governors, the Romans, will hear, and consider it a rebellion against their authority. Then they will send an army, deal with us as rebels, destroy Jerusalem and the temple, and carry away the whole Jewish nation, as the Babylonians did, into captivity."

In this wretched argument it is difficult to say which appears most prominent, ignorance or unbelief.

It was an *ignorant* argument. The Pharisees ought to have known well that nothing was further from our Lord's teaching than the idea of an earthly kingdom, supported by an armed force. He always proclaimed that His kingdom was not of this world, and not temporal, like Solomon's or David's. He had never hinted at any deliverance from Roman authority. He distinctly taught men to render to Cæsar the things that were Cæsar's, and had distinctly refused, when appealed to, to be " a Judge or divider " among the Jews. Such a person, therefore, was not the least likely to excite the jealousy of the Romans.

It was an *unbelieving* argument. The Pharisees ought to have believed that the Romans could never have conquered and put down our Lord and His adherents, if He really was the Messiah, and could work miracles at His will. The Philistines could not overcome David, and the Romans could not have overcome David's greater Son. By their own showing, the Jewish nation would have had protection enough in the miracle-working power of our Lord.

That there was an exception throughout the East, at the time of our Lord's ministry, that some remarkable person was about to arise, and become a great leader, is mentioned by Roman historians. But there is no evidence that the Roman government ever showed jealousy of any one who was merely a religious teacher, like our Lord, and did not interfere with the civil power.

The plain truth is, that this saying of the Pharisees looks like an excuse, caught up as a weapon against our Lord, and a pretext for stirring up enmity against Him. What they really hated was our Lord's doctrine, which exposed their own system, and weakened their authority. They felt that their craft was in danger; but not daring to say this publicly, they pretended a fear that He would excite the jealousy of the Romans, and endanger the whole nation. They did just the same when they finally accused Him to Pilate, as One that stirred up sedition, and made Himself a King. It is no uncommon thing for wicked people to assign very untrue reasons for their conduct, and to keep back and conceal their true motives. Demetrius, and his friends at Ephesus, said that the temple of the great goddess Diana was in danger, when in reality it was their own craft and their own wealth. The Jews at Thessalonica who persecuted Paul, pretended great zeal for "the decrees of Cæsar," when their real motive was hatred of Christ's Gospel. The Pharisees here pretended fear of the Romans, when in reality they found the growing influence of Jesus pulling down their own power over the people.

Calvin observes: "They double their wickedness by a plausible disguise,—their zeal for the public good. The fear that chiefly distressed them was that their own tyranny should be destroyed; but they pretend to be anxious about the temple and worship of God."

Bucer compares the Pharisees' pretended fear of the Romans to the absurd fears of the consequence of printing and literature, which the Papists used to express at the period of the Reformation.

Flacius remarks that "through fear of Cæsar, God is despised and His Son crucified, and this under pretext of preserving religion, the temple, and the nation. Human wisdom preserves itself by appeasing man and offending God!"

Ferus remarks that the council entirely forgot that "rulers, whether the Romans or any others, are not a terror to good works, but to evil. If the Jews had believed and obeyed God, they had nothing to fear."

That the leading Jews at Jerusalem had a strong suspicion that Jesus really was the Messiah, in spite of all their outrageous enmity and unbelief, is evident not only from comparison of other places, but from their nervous anxiety to get rid of Him. They knew that Daniel's seventy weeks were run out. They could not deny the miracles that Jesus did. But they dared not follow out their convictions, and draw the conclusion they ought to have drawn. They willingly shut their eyes against light.

How miserably mistaken the policy of the Pharisees proved to be, it is needless to say. If they had let Jesus alone, and allowed His. Gospel to be received and believed, Jerusalem, humanly speaking, might have stood to this day, and the Jews might have been more mighty and prosperous than in the days of Solomon. By not letting Jesus alone, and by killing Him, they filled up the measure of their nation's sin, and brought destruction on the temple, and scattering on the whole people.

"Take away," applied to place here, must mean "destroy." Thus Matt. xxiv. 39 : " The flood took them all away."

Some, as Heinsius and Bloomfield, think that "our place" means the city, Jerusalem.

Some, as Olshausen and Alford, think that "our place" means "our country."

Others, as Maldonatus, Hutcheson, Poole, and Hammond, with whom I entirely agree, think "our place" means the temple. (Compare Acts vi. 13, 14.) Lampe thinks this view is proved by Micah i. 3.

Calvin observes, how many people in his day were always hanging back from helping the Protestant Reformation, from the very same motives as these Jews,—the fear of consequences. "We must consult public tranquillity. There are dangers in the way."

49 —[*And one of them, named Caiaphas.*] This man, by comparing Acts v. 17, would seem to have been of the sect of the Sadducees. We also know that he was son-in-law to Annas, of whom Josephus specially mentions that he was a Sadducee. If this view be correct (and Guyse, Gill, Scott, and Lampe agree with me in it), it rather accounts for the contemptuous way in which he seems to speak in replying here to the saying of the Pharisees. It is remarkable, however, to observe how Pharisees and Sadducees, who disagreed on so many points, were agreed in hating and opposing Christ. Formalists and sceptics, in all ages, make common cause against the Gospel.

[*Being...high priest...same year.*] This expression shows the disorder and irregularity which prevailed in the Jewish Church in our Lord's time. According to the law of Moses, the office of high priest was tenable for life. In the last days of the Jews the office seems to have been obtainable by election, and to have been held with great variety of term. Caiaphas was high priest when John the Baptist began his ministry, and Annas with him. (Luke iii. 2.) He was also high priest after the Day of Pentecost, and before the persecution of Stephen. No wonder St. Paul says, on a subsequent occasion, of Ananias, "I wist not that he was the high priest." (Acts xxiii. 2.)

Poole remarks: "After Herod's time there was no regard to the family of Aaron, but the Romans made what high priests they pleased. Josephus tells us that the Jews had thirteen high priests from Aaron to Solomon, which was 612 years; eighteen from Solomon to the Babylonian captivity, which was 460 years; fifteen from the captivity to Antiochus, which was 414 years: but they had no less than twenty-eight between the time that Herod began to reign and Jerusalem was destroyed, which was less than a century."

[*Said... Ye know nothing at all.*] The word rendered "ye" is here emphatic in the Greek. It seems not unlikely that it expresses Caiaphas' contempt for the ignorance and helplessness of the Pharisees' question. "You and all your party do not understand what the situation of things requires. You are wasting time in complaints and expressions of vexation, when a sterner, severer policy is imperatively demanded."

Chrysostom remarks, "What others made matter of doubt, and put forth in the way of deliberation, this man cried aloud shamelessly, openly, and audaciously. *One must die.*"

Pearce thinks that some of the Jews in council must have talked of only putting a stop to Christ's preaching, as they afterwards tried to stop the Apostles, (Acts iv. 18,) but that Caiaphas ridiculed such weak counsel, and advised more violent measures. May we not suppose that Nicodemus and others spoke in favour of our Lord?

50 —[*Nor consider.*] The word thus rendered is almost always translated "reason," and is nowhere "consider," except here. It seems to imply that Caiaphas wished the Pharisees to know that they had not reasoned out and properly weighed the right thing to be done. Hence this perplexity. He would not show them the conclusion they ought to have come to.

[*It is expedient...one...die...whole...perish not.*] Caiaphas' conclusion is short and decisive. He gives it elliptically. "This Man must die. It is far better that one should die, whether innocent or not, for the benefit of the whole nation, than that the whole nation should be brought into trouble and perish. You are thinking that if we do not let this Man alone, and interfere, we are injuring an innocent person. Away with such childish scruples. Let Him be put out of the way. It is expedient to kill Him. Better He should die to save the nation from further trouble, than live, and the nation be brought into trouble by Him."

I cannot suppose that Caiaphas meant anything more than this. He simply argues that Christ's death would be a public benefit, and that to spare Him might bring destruction on the nation. Of the full meaning that His words were capable of bearing I do not believe he had the least idea.

Let us carefully note here what crimes and sins may be com-

mitted on the ground of *expediency*. None are so likely to be
tempted to commit such sins as rulers and governors. None
are so likely to do things unjust, dishonest, and oppressive, as a
Government under the pressure of the spurious argument that
it is expedient that the few should suffer, rather than the many
should take harm. For political expediency Christ was crucified.
What a fact that is! Ought we not rather to ask always what is
just, what is right, what is honourable in the sight of God?
That which is morally wrong can never be politically right. To
govern only for the sake of pleasing and benefiting the majority,
without any reference to the eternal principles of justice, right,
and mercy, may be *expedient*, and please man; but it does not
please God.

Calvin observes: " Let us learn never to separate what is useful and expedient from what is lawful, since we ought not to
expect any prosperity and success but from the blessing of God."

Ecolampadius remarks that we must never do evil that good
may come. "If you could, by the slaying of one good man,
work the saving of many, it would be unlawful."

Poole observes: "Never was anything spoken more diaboli-
cally. Like a wretched politician, concerned for nothing but the
people's safety, Caiaphas saith not it is lawful, but it is expedient for us that one Man, be He never so good, never so innocent
and just, should die."

Doddridge remarks: " When will the politicians of this world
learn to trust God in His own ways, rather than to trust themselves and their own wisdom, in violation of all rules of truth,
honour, and conscience ? "

51, 52 —[*And this spake he not of himself, etc.*] These two verses
contain a parenthetical comment by St. John, on the address of
Caiaphas to the Pharisees. It is a peculiar passage, and not
without difficulty. That a man like Caiaphas should be said to
prophesy, and that his prophecy should be of so wide and exten-
sive a character, is undoubtedly strange. I offer a few remarks
that may help to throw light on the passage.

That God can employ a wicked man to declare prophetical
truth is clearly proved by the case of Balaam. But the positions of Balaam and Caiaphas were very different.

That the Jewish high priest at any time possessed, by virtue
of his office, the power of predicting things to come, I can nowhere find. David certainly speaks of Zadok as "a seer."
(2 Sam. xv. 27.) The high priest's ephod conveyed a certain
mysterious power to the wearer, of foreseeing things immediately near. (1 Sam. xxiii. 9.) The "urim and thummin," whatever
they were, which dwelt in the breast-plate of the high priest,
appear to have given the wearer peculiar powers of discernment. But even they were withdrawn at the destruction of the
first temple. In short, there is an utter absence of proof that a

Jewish high priest, in the time of our Lord, had any power of prophesying.

I believe that the verses before us are very elliptical, and require much to be supplied in order to convey the meaning of St. John. The only satisfactory sense I can put upon the passage will be found in the following free paraphrase.

[*This spake he not of himself.*] He spoke these words, though he was not aware of it, under the influence of an overruling power, making him say things of far deeper meaning than he was conscious of himself. As Ecolampadius says, "God used him as an instrument." (See Isa. x. 15.)

[*But being high priest that year, he prophesied.*] He spoke words which, as the event showed afterwards, were eminently prophetical; and the fact that they fell from his lips when he was high priest made them more remarkable, when afterwards remembered and noted.

[*That Jesus should die for that nation.*] He actually foretold, though the fulfilment was in a manner very different from his intentions, that Jesus would die for the benefit of the Jewish nation.

[*And not for that nation only, etc.*] And He also foretold what was practically fulfilled afterwards, though in a way marvellously unlike what he thought,—that Jesus would not only die for the Jewish nation, but for the benefit of all God's children at present scattered all over the world.

The utmost, in fact, that I can make of John's explanatory comment, is that he remarks on the extraordinary manner in which Caiaphas' words proved true, though in a way that he never intended, wished, or expected. He lets fall a saying on a great public occasion, which comes from his lips with great authority, on account of his office as high priest. That saying was afterwards fulfilled in the most marvellous manner by the overruling providence of God, but in a way that the speaker never dreamed of. The thing was afterwards remembered and remarked on; and it seemed, says St. John, as if being high priest that year, he was miraculously compelled by the Holy Ghost to prophesy the redemption of mankind, at the very time that he thought he was only speaking of putting Christ to death. Caiaphas, in short, meant nothing but to advise the murder of Christ. But the Holy Ghost obliged him unconsciously to use words which were a most remarkable prediction of Christ's death bringing life to a lost world.

The Greek word rendered "should die," would be more literally, "was about to die." It simply expresses a future coming event.

The "children of God scattered abroad," I believe, mean the elect of God among the Gentiles. They are put in contrast with "that nation," or "the nation," as it would be more literally rendered.

The "gathering together in one," I believe to be that final gathering of all Christ's members which is yet to come at His second advent. (See Eph. i. 10; John xii. 32; Gen. xlix. 10.)

Lightfoot says, the Jews thought the greatest work of Messiah was to be the "reduction, or gathering together of the captivities."

I leave the passage with a very deep sense of its difficulty, and desire not to press my views on others dogmatically, if they are not satisfied with them.

Chrysostom remarks, "Caiaphas prophesied, not knowing what he said; and the grace of God merely made use of his mouth, but touched not his accursed heart."

Musculus and Ferus remark how striking the resemblance is between Caiaphas unintentionally using language fulfilled in a sense totally unlike what he meant, and the Jews saying of Christ to Pilate, "His blood be on us and on our children." They little knew the awful and tremendous extent of the saying.

The absurdity of the Roman Catholic claim, that the Pope's words and decrees are to be received as partially inspired because of his office, on the ground of this passage, is noted and exposed by all the Protestant commentators of the seventeenth century.

Lightfoot thinks we should lay great emphasis on the expression, "that same year," and justly so.—He observes that it was the very year when the high priest's office ended, and the veil was rent, and the Jewish dispensation wound up, and the Mosaic priesthood abrogated by Christ's becoming manifestly our Priest.—He thinks St. Paul, in Acts xxiii. 5, "I wist not that he was the high priest," may have meant "that he did not know there was any high priest at all." He also observes that this very year at Pentecost, the Holy Ghost was poured out as the spirit of prophecy and revelation in an extraordinary measure. What wonder if "that year" the last high priest, like Balaam, should prophesy.

53 —[*Then from that day...counsel...death.*] We see here the result of Caiaphas' counsel. His stern, bold, outspoken proposal carried all the council with him, and even if Gamaliel, Nicodemus, and Joseph were there, their voices were silenced. From that very day it became a settled thing with the Jewish leaders at Jerusalem, that Jesus was to be put to death. The only difficulty was to find the way, the time, and the means of doing it without creating a tumult. The great miracle just wrought at Bethany would doubtless increase the number of our Lord's adherents, and make it necessary to use caution in carrying out the murderous plan.

The conclusions of great ecclesiastical councils are seldom wise and good, and sometimes are wicked and cruel. Bold, forward, unscrupulous men, like Caiaphas, generally silence the quieter members, and carry all before them.

54 —[*Jesus therefore walked...Jews.*] From this time our Lord found it necessary to give up appearing openly at Jerusalem, and came there no more till the week of his crucifixion. He knew the result of the council just held, either from His own Divine knowledge, or from the information of friends like Nicodemus; and as His time was not fully come, he retired from Judæa for a season.

The expression, "no more," is literally "not yet." It must mean "no more at present."

May we not learn from our Lord's conduct, that it may be a duty sometimes not to court danger or death? There are seasons when it is a duty to retire, as well as seasons for going forward. There are times to be silent, as well as times to speak.

Hutcheson remarks: "It is lawful for Christ's servants to flee when their death is decreed by enemies, and the persecution is personal."

[*Went thence...wilderness...Ephraim...disciples.*] Nothing whatever is known for certain of the distinct locality to which our Lord retired, or of the city here named. It seems, purposely, to have been a quiet, isolated, and little frequented place. The probability is that it was beyond Jordan, in Perea, because when our Lord came to Jerusalem the last time He passed through Jericho.

Ellicott suggests that Ephraim was a town called also Ophrah, about twenty miles north of Jerusalem, on the borders of Samaria. He also thinks that on leaving Ephraim those words of St. Luke (chapter xvii. 11) come in, which say, that our Lord "passed through the midst of Samaria and Galilee." After that he thinks He went through Perea, to Jericho. But I am not satisfied that he proves these points.

It is worth noticing that our Lord chose a scene of entire quiet and seclusion as His last abode, before going up to His last great season of suffering at the crucifixion. It is well to get alone and be still, before we take in hand any great work for God. Our Saviour was not above this. How much more should His disciples remember it! In saying this, I would not be thought to commend the ostentatious "retreats" of the Romish Church and its followers. It is of the very essence of Christian retirement, if it is to be profitable, that it should be without parade, and should not attract the notice of men. The life of the Eremite has no warrant in Scripture.

When it says that our Lord continued or tarried at Ephraim "with His disciples," it is worth noticing that we do not hear a word of any public works that he did there. It looks as if He

devoted the last few quiet days that remained before His crucifixion, to uninterrupted communion with the Father, and private instruction of His disciples.

55 —[*And...Jews' passover...nigh at hand.*] This expression, like
many others in John's Gospel, shows that he wrote for the
Church generally, and for many readers who were not familiar
with Jewish feasts and customs.

[*And many went...country...before...passover.*] This seems
mentioned as a simple matter of custom among the Jews, and
not as a thing done this year more than any other. They always
did so; and thus drew together, for seven days before the passover, a larger collection of people at Jerusalem than at any
other time of the year. Hence the crowds and expectation
when our Lord appeared. He had been talked of by people
from all parts of Palestine.

[*To purify themselves.*] This refers to the ceremonial washings, purifications, and atonements for ceremonial uncleanness,
which all strict Jews were careful to go through before eating
the passover. (See 2 Chron. xxx. 18, 19.) It is impossible to
read the book of Leviticus carefully, and not to be struck with the
almost endless number of ways in which an Israelite could become ceremonially unclean, and need going to the priest to
have an atonement made. (See Numbers ix. 6—11.) That the
Pharisees, in such matters, added to legal strictness by their
absurd scrupulosity, such as "straining at a gnat," we cannot
doubt; but the simple law as it stood was a yoke that was very
hard to bear. No wonder that thousands of devout Jews came
anxiously before the passover, to Jerusalem, to be made ceremonially clean and fit for the feast.

It is worth noting how singular particular men are sometimes about forms and ceremonies, and outward correctness,
while they coolly plan and execute enormous crimes. The Jews,
zealous about "purifying" themselves while they were planning
the murder of Christ, have had imitators and followers in
every age of the Church. Strictness about forms and ceremonies, and utter recklessness about gross sin, are found quite
compatible in many hearts.

56 —[*Then sought they...Jesus, and spake, etc., etc.*] The persons
here mentioned seem to me to have been the Jews from all
parts of Palestine, mentioned in the last verse, who had come
up to prepare for the passover. The fame and history of our
Lord were probably so great throughout Palestine, that one of
the first inquiries the comers would make of one another would
be about Him. And as they stood in the temple court, waiting
for their turn to go through ceremonial purification, or talking
with old friends and acquaintances who had come up, like themselves, from the country, Jesus would probably be a principal
topic of conversation.

[*What think ye...that...not come...feast.*] This is mentioned as one of the principal inquiries made by the Jews of one another. Our Lord, on a former occasion, had not come up to the passover. (See John vi.) They might, therefore, naturally feel doubtful whether He would come now.

It is noteworthy that the question admits of being taken as one, or divided into two distinct ones.

Some think that it means, " What think ye of the question, whether He will come to the feast or not?"

Others hold that it means, " What think ye of Christ, and especially of His position at this time? Do you think that He will not come to the feast?" I myself prefer this view.

It is noteworthy that the very question with which our Lord confounded the Pharisees a few days after, as recorded in St. Matthew xxii. 42, begins with precisely the same Greek words as those here used, " What think ye of Christ?"

57 —[*Now both...priests...Pharisees, etc., etc.*] This verse shows the first steps which had been taken after the session of the council which adopted the advice of Caiaphas to kill Jesus. A general order had been given that if any man knew where Jesus lodged in Jerusalem, he was to give information, in order that He might be apprehended.

I cannot help thinking myself that this order must only have referred to Jerusalem, and the house where our Lord might lodge when He came to the passover, if He did come. I cannot suppose that our Lord's enemies could be ignorant where He was between the miracle of Bethany and the passover. But I fancy they dared not run the risk of a tumult or rebellion, which might be caused if they sent into the rural districts to apprehend Him. Indeed, it is doubtful whether the jurisdiction of the priests and Pharisees extended beyond the walls of Jerusalem, and whether they could lay hands upon our Lord anywhere outside the city. This might have been the reason why He often lodged at Bethany.

Musculus here discusses the question, whether obedience to the powers that be obliges us to give up a man to those who are seeking to apprehend him. He answers, " Decidedly not; if we believe him to be an innocent man."

JOHN XII 1—11

1 Then Jesus six days before the passover came to Bethany, where Lazarus was which had been dead, whom he raised from the dead.

2 There they made him a supper; and Martha served: but Lazarus was one of them that sat at the table with him.

3 Then took Mary a pound of ointment of spikenard, very costly, and

anointed the feet of Jesus, and wiped his feet with her hair: and the house was filled with the odour of the ointment.

4 Then saith one of his disciples, Judas Iscariot, Simon's *son*, which should betray him,

5 Why was not this ointment sold for three hundred pence, and given to the poor?

6 This he said, not that he cared for the poor; but because he was a thief, and had the bag, and bare what was put therein.

7 Then said Jesus, Let her alone: against the day of my burying hath she kept this.

8 For the poor always ye have with you: but me ye have not always.

9 Much people of the Jews therefore knew that he was there: and they came not for Jesus' sake only, but that they might see Lazarus also, whom he had raised from the dead.

10 But the chief priests consulted that they might put Lazarus also to death;

11 Because that by reason of him, many of the Jews went away, and believed on Jesus.

THE chapter we have now begun finishes a most important division of St. John's Gospel. Our Lord's public addresses to the unbelieving Jews of Jerusalem are here brought to an end. After this chapter, St. John records nothing but what was said in private to the disciples.

We see, for one thing, in this passage, *what abounding proofs exist of the truth of our Lord's greatest miracles.*

We read of a supper at Bethany, where Lazarus " sat at the table " among the guests,—Lazarus, who had been publicly raised from the dead, after lying four days in the grave. No one could pretend to say that his resurrection was a mere optical delusion, and that the eyes of the bystanders must have been deceived by a ghost or vision. Here was the very same Lazarus, after several weeks, sitting among his fellow-men with a real material body, and eating and drinking real material food. It is hard to understand what stronger evidence of a fact could be supplied. He that is not convinced by such evidence as this may as well say that he is determined to believe nothing at all.

It is a comfortable thought, that the very same proofs which exist about the resurrection of Lazarus are the proofs which surround that still mightier fact, the resurrection of Christ from the dead. Was Lazarus seen for several weeks by the people of Bethany, going in and coming out among them? So was the Lord Jesus seen by His disciples.—Did Lazarus take material food before the eyes of his friends? So did the Lord Jesus eat and drink before His ascension.—No one, in his sober senses, who saw Jesus take "broiled fish and a honeycomb," and eat it before several witnesses, would doubt that He had a real body. (Luke xxiv. 42.)

We shall do well to remember this. In an age of abounding unbelief and scepticism, we shall find that the resurrection of Christ will bear any weight that we can lay upon it. Just as He placed beyond reasonable doubt the rising again of a beloved disciple within two miles of Jerusalem, so in a very few weeks He placed beyond doubt His own victory over the grave. If we believe that Lazarus rose again, we need not doubt that Jesus rose again also. If we believe that Jesus rose again, we need not doubt the truth of His Messiahship, the reality of His acceptance as our Mediator, and the certainty of our own resurrection. Christ has risen indeed, and wicked men may well tremble. Christ has risen from the dead, and believers may well rejoice.

We see, for another thing, in this passage, *what unkindness and discouragement Christ's friends sometimes meet with from man.*

We read that, at the supper in Bethany, Mary, the sister of Lazarus, anointed the feet of Jesus with precious ointment, and wiped them with the hair of her head. Nor was this ointment poured on with a niggardly hand. She did it so liberally and profusely that "the house was filled with the odour of the ointment." She did it under the influence of a heart full of love and gratitude. She thought nothing too great and good to bestow on such a Saviour. Sitting at His feet in days gone by, and hearing His words, she had found peace for her conscience, and pardon for her sins. At this

very moment she saw Lazarus, alive and well, sitting by
her Master's side,—her own brother Lazarus, whom He
had brought back to her from the grave. Greatly loved,
she thought she could not show too much love in return.
Having freely received, she freely gave.

But there were some present who found fault with
Mary's conduct, and blamed her as guilty of wasteful
extravagance. One especially, an apostle, a man of
whom better things might have been expected, declared
openly that the ointment would have been better employed if it had been sold, and the price " given to the
poor." The heart which could conceive such thoughts
must have had low views of the dignity of Christ's
person, and still lower views of our obligations to Him. A
cold heart and a stingy hand will generally go together.

There are only too many professing Christians of a
like spirit in the present day. Myriads of baptized
people cannot understand zeal of any sort for the
honour of Christ. Tell them of any vast outlay of
money to push trade or to advance the cause of science,
and they approve of it as right and wise. Tell them of
any expense incurred for the preaching of the Gospel
at home or abroad, for spreading God's Word, for extending the knowledge of Christ on earth, and they tell
you plainly that they think it waste. They never give
a farthing to such objects as these, and count those
people fools who do. Worst of all, they often cover
over their own backwardness to help purely Christian
objects, by a pretended concern for the poor at home.
Yet they find it convenient to forget the notorious fact
that those who do most for the cause of Christ are precisely those who do most for the poor.

We must never allow ourselves to be moved from
" patient continuance in well-doing," by the unkind remarks of such persons. It is vain to expect a man to do

much for Christ, when he has no sense of debt to Christ. We must pity the blindness of our unkind critics, and work on. He who pleaded the cause of loving Mary, and said, "Let her alone," is sitting at the right hand of God, and keeps a book of remembrance. A day is soon coming when a wondering world will see that every cup of cold water given for Christ's sake, as well as every box of precious ointment, was recorded in heaven, and has its rewards. In that great day those who thought that any one could give too much to Christ will find they had better never have been born.

We see, lastly, in this passage, *what desperate hardness and unbelief there is in the heart of man.*

Unbelief appears in the chief priests, who " consulted that they might put Lazarus to death." They could not deny the fact of his having been raised again. Living, and moving, and eating, and drinking within two miles of Jerusalem, after lying four days in the grave, Lazarus was a witness to the truth of Christ's Messiahship, whom they could not possibly answer or put to silence. Yet these proud men would not give way. They would rather commit a murder than throw down the arms of rebellion, and confess themselves in the wrong. No wonder that the Lord Jesus in a certain place " marvelled " at unbelief. Well might He say, in a well-known parable, "If they believe not Moses and the Prophets, neither will they be persuaded though one rose from the dead." (Mark vi. 6 ; Luke xvi. 31.)

Hardness appears in Judas Iscariot, who, after being a chosen Apostle, and a preacher of the kingdom of heaven, turns out at last a thief and a traitor. So long as the world stands this unhappy man will be a lasting proof of the depth of human corruption. That any one could follow Christ as a disciple for three years, see all His miracles, hear all His teaching, receive at His

hand repeated kindnesses, be counted an Apostle, and
yet prove rotten at heart in the end, all this at first
sight appears incredible and impossible! Yet the case of
Judas shows plainly that the thing can be. Few things,
perhaps, are so little realized as the extent of the fall
of man.

Let us thank God if we know anything of faith, and
can say, with all our sense of weakness and infirmity,
"I believe." Let us pray that our faith may be real,
true, genuine, and sincere, and not a mere temporary
impression, like the morning cloud and the early dew.
Not least, let us watch and pray against the love of the
world. It ruined one who basked in the full sunshine
of privileges, and heard Christ Himself teaching every
day. Then " let him that thinketh he standeth take heed
lest he fall." (1 Cor. x. 12.)

NOTES JOHN XII 1—11

1.—[*Then Jesus six days...passover...Bethany.*] Every intelligent
reader of the Gospel will see that John purposely omits at this
point certain events which are recorded by Matthew, Mark, and
Luke. He passes at once from our Lord's retirement to the city
called Ephraim to His return to Bethany for the last time. In
this interval will be found the things related in Matthew x. 17
—34; Mark x. 32—52; Luke xviii. 31, to xix. 1—28. In whatever
part of Palestine this city Ephraim was, it is almost certain that
between it and Bethany Jesus passed through Jericho, healed
two blind men there, converted the publican Zaccheus, and
spoke the parable of the nobleman who went into a far country,
after giving to his ten servants ten pounds.

Why St. John did not record these facts we do not know, and
it is mere waste of time to inquire. A reverent mind will be content to remember that John wrote by inspiration of God, and
was guided by infallible direction, both as to what he recorded
and what he did not record. Reason and common sense, moreover, tell us that if the four Evangelists had all narrated exactly
the same things, their value as independent witnesses would
have been greatly damaged. Their variations and diversities are
a strong indirect proof of their credibility. Too close an agreement would raise a suspicion of collusion, and look like an attempt to deceive.

The expression, " six days before the passover," is remarkable, because at first sight it seems to contradict Mark's narrative of the anointing, which Mark expressly says was "two days before the passover." (Mark xiv. 1.) Hence some maintain that the Greek words should be translated, "Before the six days of the passover feast," leaving the precise day indefinite and uncertain. To this, however, it is reasonably objected that the passover feast was more than six days, and that the proposed translation is not a probable rendering of the Greek words.—To this I must add, that in my opinion there seems no necessity for departing from the English version. It is not only possible, but probable, as Lightfoot maintains, that there were two distinct anointings of our Lord, one six days before the passover, and the other two days before. [The reader is requested to refer back to the notes on John ii. 2, where he will find this point fully discussed.]

The passover was slain on the Thursday evening. At this rate our Lord must have arrived at Bethany on Friday, the afternoon or evening before the Sabbath. Thus he must have spent His last earthly Sabbath with Mary, Martha, and Lazarus, at Bethany.

That the disciples must have journeyed to Bethany with a full impression that a great crisis was at hand, and the end of their Master's ministry approaching, one can hardly doubt, after reading the plain warnings recorded in Matthew, Mark, and Luke. But whether they really thought their Master would be put to death, or whether they did not secretly expect He would soon manifest His Divine power, take His kingdom and reign, is more than questionable.

A more deliberate, voluntary, calm walking up to death than our Lord's last journey into Judæa, it is impossible to conceive.

[*Where Lazarus...been dead...raised from the dead.*] These words seem to show that Lazarus lived at Bethany, and was not merely a visitor or lodger there. They also show the immense importance of the miracle wrought on him. Within two miles of Jerusalem and the temple, there lived for weeks, if not for months, a man well known to many Jews, who had been actually raised from his grave after being four days buried. He had not been raised only, and then disappeared from public notice, but he lived where He was raised.

Lightfoot draws out the following interesting scheme of our Lord's disposal of time during the last six days before His crucifixion: (1) On Saturday He supped with Lazarus. (2) On Sunday He rode into Jerusalem publicly on an ass. This was the day when the Jews used to take out a lamb from the flock, for each family, and to keep it separate for the passover. On this day the Lamb of God publicly presented Himself in Zion. (3) On Monday He went to Jerusalem again, and cursed the barren fig-tree on the way. (4) On Tuesday He went again to Jerusalem, and spoke for the last time to the people. Returning, He sat on the Mount of Olives and delivered the famous prophecy

of Matthew xxiv. and xxv., and supped that night with Simon
the leper. (5) On Wednesday He tarried in Bethany. (6) On
Thursday He went to Jerusalem, ate the passover, appointed the
Lord's Supper, and the same night was taken before the priests
as a prisoner. (7) On Friday He was crucified.

2 —[*There they made him a supper.*] These words show the joyful
hospitality with which the Master was received by the disciples.
The expression, " they," may perhaps be used indefinitely, according to a common Hebraism. (Compare Matthew v. 15; x.
10; xiii. 48, and John xv. 6.) It then simply means, " a supper
was made." If not so used, it evidently can apply to none but
Mary, Martha, and Lazarus.—Whether the supper was on Friday
evening, when our Lord arrived, after the Sabbath began, or on
the Saturday, or the Sabbath Day, is immaterial. It is evident
that hospitality was thought no breach of the Sabbath among
the Jews.

Lightfoot says the feast of the Jews, on this particular day,
six days before the passover, was always peculiarly liberal and
sumptuous.

Hutcheson observes : " It is not unlawful at some times to enjoy
the liberal use of the creatures in a sober manner. Christ doth
not decline this supper; sometimes He went to the feasts of
Pharisees, and sometimes of Publicans." (Luke vii. 36; Matt.
ix. 11.)

[*And Martha served.*] The natural temperament of this good
woman comes out here as elsewhere. She could not sit still and
do nothing while her Lord was in her house. She must be
actively stirring and trying to do something. Grace does not
take away our peculiar characteristics.

[*But Lazarus...sat at the table with him.*] This appears to most
commentators, from Chrysostom downwards, to be purposely
mentioned, in order to show the reality of Lazarus' resurrection.
He was not a ghost or a spirit. He had really been raised to life
with a real body, and flesh and bones, and all the wants and
conditions of a body. Thus we are practically taught that though
a man's body dies, it may yet live again.

°   Is not this feast a faint type of the Marriage Supper of the
Lamb? Jesus Christ will be there; those believers who died
and are raised again at His second advent will be there; and
those ʼwho never died, but are found alive and believing when
He comes, will be there. Then the number of guests will be
complete.

3 —[*Then took Mary...ointment...anointed...feet...Jesus, etc., etc.*]
This remarkable action of Mary, which, according to our Lord's
saying in Matthew and Mark, is related all over the world, deserves our special consideration.

The action itself was not an uncommon one in Eastern countries, where the heat is very great, and the feet exposed to it by

wearing sandals are liable to suffer much from dryness and scorching. There was nothing, moreover, out of the common way in a woman doing this service. To " wash the saints' feet," St. Paul names among the good works of a Christian widow. (1 Tim. v. 10.)

The motive of Mary, in doing what she did, was evidently strong and grateful love to her Lord and Saviour. Not only from what she had learned from Him for her own spiritual benefit, but also for what He had done for her brother Lazarus, she felt there was nothing too great or too good to do for Him. Her feelings made her anxious to do her Master the highest honour, regardless of expense, and indifferent to any remark that witnesses might make.

The extent of her gratitude is shown by the lavish profuseness with which she used the ointment on this occasion, although it was very costly. This seems indicated by her " wiping our Lord's feet with her hair," having poured on them so much ointment that they needed wiping; and also by the " house being filled with the odour of the ointment." She poured out so much ointment that the scent of it filled the whole apartment and the whole house where the guests were. Any one who knows the powerful odour of otto of roses, in the present day, will easily understand this.

What this " ointment of spikenard " was has puzzled the commentators in every age, as the Greek word throws no certain light on the question. Some think that it means " potable " ointment, that might be drunk; some that it means perfectly " pure " ointment, that might be trusted as genuine and unadulterated. Augustine thinks that the expression denotes the place from which the ointment came. The question is of no importance, and must be left unexplained for want of materials to explain it. Enough for us to know that it was something very valuable and costly. How costly an ointment might be, any one can guess who knows the value of pure otto of roses.

I can only repeat the opinion already expressed, that this anointing was certainly not the anointing which is described in Luke vii.; and most probably was not the anointing of Mark xiv. The anointing in Mark was two days before the passover, while this was six. In Mark the ointment was poured on the head, and here it was poured on the feet. In Matthew and Mark several " disciples " murmured, but here only Judas is named. These discrepancies, in my judgment, are insuperable, and make it necessary to believe that there were two distinct anointings at Bethany during the last six days preceding the crucifixion. I grant that it is a choice between difficulties, and that there are difficulties in the view I maintain. But I do not think them so weighty as those of the other view. At any rate, I am supported by the great authority of Chrysostom, Chemnitius, and Lightfoot, as well as of Whitby and Henry.

What the significance of Mary's wiping our Lord's feet with the hairs of her head may be, is a difficult question. Perhaps, from our ignorance of Eastern customs in the days of our Lord's earthly ministry, we are hardly qualified to give an opinion about it now. On points like these, where we are ignorant, it is wisest not to conjecture.

Calvin says: "The usual practice was to anoint the head, and on this account Pliny reckons it an instance of excessive luxury that some anointed the ankles. What John says about the feet amounts to this, that the whole body of Christ, down to the feet, was anointed."

Rollock observes that at this time Mary seems to have had a deeper and more intimate perception of what there was in Christ, and of the real dignity of His person, than any of His disciples.

4 —[*Then saith...Judas Iscariot, Simon's son.*] We know nothing of this Simon, who he was, or why he is specially mentioned here. It is worth notice, that hardly any name occurs so frequently in the New Testament as this. We have the following:—

1. The Apostle Simon, called also Peter.

2. The Apostle Simon, called also Zelotes, and the Canaanite.

3. Simon the brother of our Lord, mentioned with James and Joses. (Matt. xiii. 55.)

4. Simon the leper, in whose house the anointing took place. (Matt. xxvi. 6.)

5. Simon the Cyrenian, who carried the cross. (Matt. xxvii. 32.)

6. Simon the Pharisee. (Luke vii. 40.)

7. Simon the sorcerer at Samaria. (Acts viii. 9.)

8. Simon the tanner. (Acts ix. 43.)

It would, of course, be interesting to know if Judas Iscariot was son of any of these. But we have no clue to guide us.

Wordsworth sees in the mention of Judas by name a strong internal evidence of the late date of St. John's Gospel. Compare with this the fact that John alone mentions Peter and Malchus by name. (John xviii. 10.)

[*Which should betray him.*] These words would be more literally rendered, "the one who was about to betray Him."

On the occasion of the anointing related in Matt. xxvi. and Mark xiv., it is worth noticing that "some of the disciples," and not Judas only, found fault with the action. It rather adds probability to the theory that there were two anointings at Bethany.

Chrysostom remarks, that Jesus knew from the beginning that Judas was a traitor, and often rebuked him with such words as, "One of you is a devil." (John vi. 64.) Augustine also remarks that we must not suppose Judas never fell till he received money from the Jews. He was false from the beginning. He also says that he was present at the institution of the Lord's Supper, and was a communicant.

5 —[*Why was not this ointment sold for three hundred pence...poor?*] This carping question is a specimen of the way in which wicked men often try to depreciate a good action, and specially in the matter of giving money. When the deed is done they do not say downright that it ought not to have been done, but suggest that something better might have been done! Those who do good must be prepared to find their actions carped at and their motives depreciated, and themselves charged with neglecting one class of duties in over-zeal for doing others. If we do nothing until everybody commends and praises us, we shall never do any good in the world.

We may learn from this verse the costly nature of Mary's ointment. If workmen's wages were "a penny a day," (Matt. xx. 2,) about 7½d. of our money, this holy woman must have poured on our Lord's feet what was worth between £9 and £10 of our money, according to the estimate of Judas. But allowances must perhaps be made for an exaggerated statement being made by an envious and wicked man.

We may note here that giving to the poor was evidently assumed to be a part of every Christian's duty. Compare this with Gal. ii. 10. In a country like England, where there is a poor law, Christians are sadly apt to forget this. The duty of "giving to the poor," and not merely paying rates in obedience to law, is just as obligatory now as it was 1800 years ago.

Ecolampadius remarks that the more wicked and graceless people are, the more ready they are to find fault with and blame others, and to see no beauty in what they do.

Quesnel remarks, that Judas made a great ado about 300 pence,—viz., £10, and a little ointment, when he was about to sell the Son of God for 30 pieces of silver,—viz., £3 15s.

Henry observe, "Coldness of love to Christ, and a secret contempt of serious piety, when they appear in professors of religion, are sad presages of final apostasy."

Stier remarks : "We have in the words of Judas an example of those judgments which have their foundation in the favourite principles of utilitarianism, and which may too often be applied falsely, to the wounding of pious hearts."—"This lays bare the root of that suspicion with which missionary offerings for the extension of Christ's kingdom are looked at, because of the poor whom we have at home."—"We have here, furthermore, an example of all cold judgments passed on the virtuous emotions of warm hearts, of all more or less conscious or unconscious censures of the artless outgoings and acts of honest feelings, and of all narrow-hearted criticism of others according to our own mind and temper."

6 —[*This he said not...cared for the poor.*] This is one of those parenthetical explanations or glosses, which are so frequent in St. John's Gospel. The Evangelist tells us the true character of Judas, and the reason he said what he did. He did not really care about the poor, but put their interest forward as a special and plausible argument for depreciating Mary's action, and discouraging such actions in others.

There is something very instructive in this. The argument of Judas is frequently reproduced in the present day. Hundreds of people excuse themselves from one class of duties by pretended zeal for others, and compensate for neglecting Christ's cause by affecting great concern for the poor. Yet in reality they care nothing for the poor, and only want to save their own money, and to be spared contributing to religious objects.

Some, for instance, will never give money to benefit the souls of their fellow-countrymen, and tell us we must first relieve their property and feed their bodies.—Some again will give nothing to help missions abroad, and tell us we must first mind the poor at home.—Even the shareholders of some great joint stock companies have been known to express great concern for the poor and working-classes, as an excuse for carrying on their business on Sundays.—The language of St. John about Judas Iscariot shows us that this apparent zeal for the poor should always be regarded with suspicion, and submitted to close analysis and cross-examination. He talked brave words about the poor, as if he cared more for them than any one! Yet there is not the slightest proof in the Gospels that he cared more for them than others. Above all, the conclusion of the verse lets out the truth, and the unerring pen of inspiration reveals the man's true motives. These things are written for our learning. There are few greater impostors in the world than some of those who are pretending perpetually to care about the poor. The truest and best friends of the working-classes and the poor, the people who give most and do most for them, will always be found among those who do most for Christ. It is the successors of Mary of Bethany, and not of Judas Iscariot, who really " care for the poor." But they do not talk about it. While others talk and profess, they act.

[*But because he was a thief.*] This is strong language, and a very heavy accusation. It seems to indicate that this was the habitual character of Judas. He always had been, and always was, a dishonest man. So says an inspired Apostle. In the face of this expression, it appears to me impossible to prove that Judas ever had the grace of God at any time, and that he only fell away at last. He was inwardly wrong at heart all the way through. Again, I find it impossible to believe that Judas was a high-souled and noble-minded, though greatly erring man, and that his motive in betraying his Lord was to hasten His kingdom, and to cut short the period of his humiliation. I cannot reconcile this with the word "thief."

Let us note here how far a man may go in Christian profession without any inward grace. There is no evidence that Judas up to this time was unlike other Apostles. Like them he had seen all Christ's miracles, heard Christ's teaching, lived in Christ's company, and had himself preached the kingdom of God. Yet he was at bottom a graceless man. Privileges alone convert nobody.

Ferus remarks: "Let us never put confidence in man, or in any sanctity of position, office, or dress. If apostleship did not make Judas a saint, neither will position, office, or dress make thee a saint. In fact, unless you first have inward holiness, and have sought it from God, it may be that your office may render you more wicked."

Let us note the amazing power of the love of money. No besetting sin seems so thoroughly to wither up and blight and harden the heart. No wonder it is called "the root of all evil." (1 Tim. vi. 10.) However many the faults and infirmities recorded of saints in the Bible, we have not a single example of one that was covetous.

Chrysostom observes: "A dreadful thing is the love of money! It disables both eyes and ears, and makes man worse to deal with than a wild beast, allowing a man to consider neither conscience, nor friendship, nor fellowship, nor salvation."

Quesnel observes that "Christ allows His money to be taken from Him, but never His sheep."

[*And had the bag.*] The Greek word rendered "bag" is a curious one. The original idea is that of a bag in which musicians kept the mouthpieces or reeds of their instruments. From that, the idea evidently was attached to it, of a bag carried about by any member of a company, such as that of the disciples, on behalf of his companions. Whether the common stock of provisions as well as of money was not kept in this bag perhaps admits of a question.

Theophylact says, that some think that Judas was trusted with the care of the money as one of the meanest and most inferior of Christian duties. Thus in Acts, the Apostles would not "serve tables." (Acts vi. 2.)

[*And bare what was put therein.*] The last words would be more literally rendered, "the things put therein." Some, as Origen, Theophylact, Pearce, Lampe, Tittman, Bloomfield, and Clarke, have thought that the word "bare" means "took away, carried off, stole, secreted, or set apart for himself."—I doubt this. I prefer the simple idea of " carrying about." It was the office of Judas to be the purse-keeper of the little company of disciples. The contributions in money and provisions of those friends who ministered to our Lord, such as " Joanna, Susanna, and many others," (Luke viii. 3,) were probably meant by the things here mentioned. It is clear that our Lord had no earthly wealth, nor His disciples. It is equally clear that His friends, scattered all over Palestine, must have thought it a privilege, whenever He came among them, to contribute to His maintenance and support. Of these contributions in all probability Judas was treasurer.

Let professing Christians note that to have money passing through their hands is a snare and a temptation. It is a snare by which many in every age have been cast down.

7 —[*Then said Jesus, Let her alone.*] This is unquestionably a rebuke to Judas, and a somewhat sharp one. It shows how jealously our Lord regards any attempt to hinder, check, or discourage the zeal of His own people. Even now, when some of His weak disciples undertake work which calls forth enmity and opposition, He can make all difficulties vanish, and say, " Let them alone."

[*Against the day...burying...kept this.*] The first word here would be more literally rendered, " for " the day. I believe we must not interpret this sentence as if our Lord meant that Mary really knew that our Lord's burial was at hand. I think it rather signifies, " The ointment which Mary has poured on my feet, though she meant it only as a mark of honour, happens to be a most suitable thing, as my death and burial are approaching. She little knew, in doing what she did, the nearness of my death ; but, as it happens, her action is most seasonable."

Some, as Chrysostom, think that our Lord intended to prick the conscience and soften the feelings of Judas by talking of His " burial," and by the language of the next verse, " Me ye have not always." It may possibly be so. But I rather think that in both instances He intended to direct the minds of all around Him, as He had evidently been doing for some weeks, to His approaching death and the conclusion of His ministry. He brings that conclusion in at every turn now.

Some think that the word " kept " refers to the ointment having been originally got by Mary for her brother Lazarus, and that there had been a long hoarding up of it from the day when Lazarus died, and that Judas blamed Mary for having " kept " it so long, and not having sold it. But this is purely conjectural.

May we not learn, from our Lord's words here, that Christians do not always know the full meaning of what they do? God uses them as His instruments, without their being aware of it at the time. (Compare John xii. 16.)

Calvin says: "Those are absurd interpreters who infer from Christ's reply, that costly and magnificent worship is pleasing to God. He rather excuses Mary, on the ground of her having rendered an extraordinary service, which ought not to be regarded as a perpetual rule for the worship of God."

8 —[*For the poor always...with you.*] It is clear from these words that poverty will always exist; and we need not wonder. So long as human nature is what it is, some will always be rich and some poor, because some are diligent and some idle, some are strong and some weak, some are wise and some foolish. We need never dream that by any arrangement, either civil or ecclesiastical, poverty can ever be entirely prevented. The existence of pauperism is no proof whatever that States are ill governed, or that churches are not doing their duty.

Ecolampadius thinks that our Lord here refers to the poor as being His members, and that there is a latent reference to the language of the twenty-fifth chapter of Matthew, about works of mercy being regarded as works done to Christ's brethren and to Christ Himself. (Matt. xxv. 40.)

It is noteworthy that Jesus in this sentence passes from a singular verb to a plural one, and seems to address not Judas only, but all present.

[*But me ye have not always.*] These words show, for one thing, that our Lord's bodily presence on earth was a great and miraculous event, and as such deserved to be marked with peculiar honour; and for another thing, that His departure was at hand, so that the opportunities for doing Him honour were becoming very few. Moreover, if words mean anything, the sentence completely overthrows the whole theory of Christ's body being present under the forms of bread and wine, in the Lord's Supper. That favourite Romish doctrine can never be reconciled with "Me ye have not always."

We may surely learn, from this verse, that relieving the poor, however good a work, is not so important a work as doing honour to Christ. In times like these it is well to remember this. Not a few seem to think all religion consists in giving temporal help to the poor. Yet there are evidently occasions when the relief of the poor must not be allowed to supersede the direct work of honouring Christ. Doubtless it is well to feed, and clothe, and nurse the poor; but it is never to be forgotten, that to glorify Christ among them is far better. Moreover, it is much easier to give temporal than spiritual help, for we have our reward in thanks, and gratitude, and the praise of man. To honour Christ is far harder, and gets us no praise at all.

Augustine remarks: "In respect of the presence of His Majesty, we have Christ always; in respect to the presence of the flesh, it was rightly said, 'Me ye will not have always.' The Church had Him in respect of the flesh for a few days; now by faith it holds, not with eyes beholds Him."

Zwingle observes that this sentence "excludes Christ's corporal presence from the Lord's Supper. According to His Divine nature, Christ is always present with His people. According to His human nature, He is in one place in heaven, at the right hand of God." Most of the other reformers make the same comment.

Rollock remarks, that our Lord's defence of Mary in this passage must not be alleged as a warrant for extravagant and profuse expenditure in the public worship of Christians. Jesus Himself points out that the occasion was extraordinary and singular; viz., on the eve almost of His burial, an occasion which could only happen once. This seems to imply that on ordinary occasions such an expenditure as that of Mary would not have been justifiable.

9 —[*Much people...knew...there.*]   We need not doubt that the news of our Lord's arrival at Bethany would soon spread, like lightning, partly because Bethany was so near Jerusalem, partly because of the recent miracle wrought there, partly because of the order of the rulers to give information where Christ was, partly because of the approach of the Passover, and the crowds assembling all around Jerusalem.

[*They come...not...Jesus' sake...see Lazarus...dead.*]   This sentence is a genuine exhibition of human nature. Curiosity is one of the most common and powerful motives in man. The love of seeing something sensational and out of the common way is almost universal.   When people could see at once both the subject of the miracle and Him that worked the miracle, we need not wonder that they resorted in crowds to Bethany. Yet within ten days a far greater miracle was to take place, viz., our Lord's own resurection.

10 —[*But the chief priests consulted.*]   It admits of doubt whether the word rendered " consulted " would not be better rendered " purposed " or "determined," as in Acts xv. 37; xxvii. 39; 2 Cor. i. 17.   This is the view of Schleusner and Parkhurst.

[*That they might put Lazarus... death.*]   It is difficult to conceive a greater proof of hardened and incorrigible wickedness of heart than this sentence exhibits. The chief priests could not possibly deny the fact of Lazarus having been raised, or explain it away. He was a witness whose testimony against their unbelief was overwhelming. They must therefore stop his mouth by killing him. And these were the chief ecclesiastical leaders of Israel!—Moreover Lazarus had done them no harm.   Though a disciple, there is no proof that he was a leading follower of Christ, much less a preacher of the Gospel. But he was an inconvenient standing evidence, and so he must be removed!

11 —[*Because...many...Jews went away.*]   This sentence shows the immense effect that the raising of Lazarus had on the public mind, in spite of all the priests could do to prevent it. In every

age people will think for themselves, when God's truth comes into a land. Prisons and threats and penalties cannot prevent men thinking. Mind and thought cannot be chained. When ecclesiastical tyrants burn martyrs, and destroy Bibles, and silence preachers, they forget there is one thing they cannot do. They cannot stop the inward machinery of people's thoughts.

The expression, " went away," will hardly bear the sense put on it by Pearce, of " withdrawing themselves from the service of the synagogue." It probably only means " went to Bethany." Bloomfield says, " it denotes their ceasing to pay that regard to the teaching of the Scribes, which they formerly had done."

[*And believed in Jesus.*] I dare not think that this " believing " means more than intellectual conviction that Jesus must be the Messiah. I see no evidence that it means the faith of the heart. Yet it is probable this was exactly the state of mind in which many hundreds or thousands of Jews were before the crucifixion, the resurrection, and the day of Pentecost, convinced but not converted, persuaded that Jesus was the Christ of God, but afraid to confess Him. Hence on the day of Pentecost we cannot doubt that many hundreds of Peter's hearers were prepared to believe. The stony ground of prejudice and ignorant adhesion t. Judaism had been broken to pieces, and the seed fell into so.: prepared for it.

Poole thinks that Lazarus after his marvellous resurrection, "possibly spake of it, to the honour and glory of God," and that this excited the special anger of the priests.

JOHN XII 12—19

12 On the next day much people that were come to the feast, when they heard that Jesus was coming to Jerusalem,

13 Took branches of palm trees, and went forth to meet him, and cried, Hosanna: Blessed *is* the King of Israel that cometh in the name of the Lord.

14 And Jesus, when he had found a young ass, sat thereon; as it is written,

15 Fear not, daughter of Sion: behold, thy King cometh, sitting on an ass's colt.

16 These things understood not his disciples at the first: but when Jesus was glorified, then remembered they that these things were written of him, and *that* they had done these things unto him.

17 The people therefore that was with him when he called Lazarus out of his grave, and raised him from the dead, bare record.

18 For this cause the people also met him, for that they heard that he had done this miracle.

19 The Pharisees therefore said among themselves, Perceive ye how ye prevail nothing? behold, the world is gone after him.

A CAREFUL reader of the Gospels can hardly fail to observe that our Lord Jesus Christ's conduct, at this stage of His earthly ministry, is very peculiar. It is unlike anything else recorded of Him in the New Testament. Hitherto we have seen Him withdrawing as much as possible from public notice, retiring into the wilderness, and checking those who would have brought Him forward and made Him a king. As a rule He did not court popular attention. He did not " cry or strive, or cause His voice to be heard in the streets." (Matt. xii. 19.) Here, on the contrary, we see Him making a public entry into Jerusalem, attended by an immense crowd of people, and causing even the Pharisees to say, " Behold, the world has gone after Him."

The explanation of this apparent inconsistency is not hard to find out. The time had come at last when Christ was to die for the sins of the world. The time had come when the true passover Lamb was to be slain, when the true blood of atonement was to be shed, when Messiah was to be " cut off" according to prophecy, (Dan. ix. 26,) when the way into the holiest was to be opened by the true High Priest to all mankind. Knowing all this, our Lord purposely drew attention to Himself. Knowing this, He placed Himself prominently under the notice of the whole Jewish nation. It was only meet and right that this thing should not be " done in a corner." (Acts xxvi. 26.) If ever there was a transaction in our Lord's earthly ministry which was public, it was the Sacrifice which He offered up on the cross of Calvary. He died at the time of year when all the tribes were assembled at Jerusalem for the passover feast. Nor was this all. He died in a week when, by His remarkable public entry into Jerusalem, He had caused the eyes of all Israel to be specially fixed upon Himself.

We learn, for one thing, in these verses, *how entirely voluntary the sufferings of Christ were.*

It is impossible not to see in the history before us that our Lord had a mysterious influence over the minds and wills of all around Him, whenever He thought fit to use it. Nothing else can account for the effect which His approach to Jerusalem had on the multitudes which accompanied Him. They seem to have been carried forward by a secret constraining power, which they were obliged to obey, in spite of the disapproval of the leaders of the nation. In short, just as our Lord was able to make winds, and waves, and diseases, and devils obey Him, so was He able, when it pleased Him, to turn the minds of men according to His will.

For the case before us does not stand alone. The men of Nazareth could not hold Him when He chose to " pass through the midst of them and go His way." (Luke iv. 30.) The angry Jews of Jerusalem could not detain him when they would have laid violent hands on Him in the Temple ; but, " going through the midst of them, He passed by." (John viii. 59.) Above all, the very soldiers who apprehended Him in the garden, at first " went backward and fell to the ground." (John xviii. 6.) In each of these instances there is but one explanation. A Divine influence was put forth. There was about our Lord during His whole earthly ministry a mysterious " hiding of His power." (Hab. iii. 4.) But He had almighty power when He was pleased to use it.

Why, then, did He not resist His enemies at last? Why did He not scatter the band of soldiers who came to seize Him, like chaff before the wind? There is but one answer. He was a willing Sufferer in order to procure redemption for a lost and ruined soul. He had undertaken to give His own life as a ransom, that we might live forever, and He laid it down on the cross with all the desire of His heart. He did not bleed and suffer and die because He was vanquished by superior force, and could not help Himself, but because He loved us, and rejoiced to give Himself for us as our Substitute. He did not die because He could not avoid death, but because He was willing with all His heart to make His soul an offering for sin.

Forever let us rest our hearts on this most comfortable thought. We have a most willing and loving Saviour. It was His delight to do His Father's will, and to make a way for lost and guilty man to draw near to God in peace. He loved the work He had taken in hand, and the poor sinful world which He came to save. Never, then, let us give way to the unworthy thought that our Saviour does not love to see sinners coming to Him, and does not rejoice to save them. He who was a most willing Sacrifice on the cross is also a most willing Saviour at the right hand of God. He is just as willing to receive sinners who come to Him now for peace, as He was to die for sinners, when He held back His power and willingly suffered on Calvary.

We learn, for another thing, in these verses, *how minutely the prophecies concerning Christ's first coming were fulfilled.*

The riding into Jerusalem on an ass, which is here recorded, might seem at first sight a simple action, and in no way remarkable. But when we turn to the Old Testament, we find that this very thing had been predicted by the Prophet Zechariah five hundred years before. (Zech. ix. 9.) We find that the coming of a Redeemer some day was not the only thing which the Holy Ghost had revealed to the Fathers, but that even the least particulars of His earthly career were predicted and written down with precise accuracy.

Such fulfilments of prophecy as this deserve the special attention of all who love the Bible and read it with reverence. They show us that every word of Holy Scripture was given by inspiration of God. They teach us to beware of the mischievous practice of spiritualizing and explaining away the language of Scripture. We must settle it in our minds that the plain, literal meaning of the Bible is generally the true and correct meaning. Here is a prediction of Zechariah literally and exactly fulfilled. Our Lord was not merely a very humble person, as some spiritualizing interpreters would have explained Zechariah's words to mean, but He literally rode into Jerusalem on an ass. Above all, such fulfilments teach us what we may expect in looking forward to the second advent of Jesus Christ. They show us that we must look for a literal accomplishment of the prophecies concerning that second coming, and not for a figurative and a spiritual one. Forever let us hold fast this great principle. Happy is that Bible-reader who believes the words of the Bible to mean- exactly what they seem to mean. Such a man has got the true key of knowledge in looking forward to things to come. To know that predictions about the second advent of Christ will be fulfilled literally, just as predictions about the first advent of Christ were fulfilled literally, is the first step towards a right understanding of unfulfilled prophecy.

NOTES JOHN XII 12—19

12.—[*On the next day.*] This day must have been the Sunday before Easter, which is commonly known in England as " Palm Sunday," from the circumstance here related.

[*Much people...come to the feast.*] This must include many of the Jews who had come up to the passover from Galilee, and were doubtless well acquainted with our Lord's ministry and the numerous miracles He had wrought in Galilee. Some of them in all human probability had formed part of the multitude whom He fed with a few loaves in the wilderness.

[*When they heard that Jesus was coming to Jerusalem.*] We must suppose that by some means our Lord's intention of coming to Jerusalem must have become known, either by Himself communicating it, or by His disciples learning it and telling others. This information would be carried back to the city by those who came from thence to Bethany on Saturday. Bethany, however, was on the direct road from Jericho to Jerusalem, and the tidings of our Lord's approach may have travelled before Him for some days.

Rollock thinks this multitude must have been chiefly composed of Jews not residing in Jerusalem. The Jerusalem Jews, he thinks, are an instance of the old proverb, which he quotes, "The nearer the Church the further from God."

13 —[*Took branches of palm-trees, and went...meet him.*] The precise motive of this action we are left to conjecture. Palm branches were carried by processions attending kings or victorious generals on public occasions. The triumphant host in heaven, which John saw in vision, was composed of persons having "palms in their hands." (Rev. vii. 9.) It may be that some of the crowd on this occasion believed that Jesus was the Messiah. Others, we may be sure, did what the rest did, without any special motive at all. At most we can only suppose that the multitude had a vague idea that Jesus was somebody very remarkable, a prophet, or some one raised up by God, and as such did Him honour.

Rollock thinks the custom of carrying branches at the feast of tabernacles, as the expression of joy, was the motive of the crowd here.

[*And cried, Hosanna.*] This Hebrew word is taken from Psalm cxviii. 25, and signifies "Save now, we beseech thee."

Calvin thinks this phrase testified that they acknowledged Christ to be the Messiah, and considers that the cxviii. Psalm had special reference to Messiah's coming.

[*Blessed...King of Israel that cometh...name...Lord.*] This sentence would be more literally rendered "Blessed is He that cometh in the name of the Lord, the king of Israel." It is partly taken from Psalm cxviii. 26; but there the words are simply "Blessed be He that cometh in the name of the Lord," and no mention is made of "the king."—We can only conjecture that some of the multitude had a vague idea that Jesus had come to be a temporal King, and a conquering Messiah, who would set Israel free from all foreign dominion. These few caught up the words of the Psalm, and their cry was taken up by the many around them, perhaps without knowing distinctly what they did or said. Nothing is so soon caught up as a popular cry. From "Hosanna" to "Crucify Him" there was only an interval of a very few days! Nothing is so worthless as popular applause.

Theophylact holds decidedly that the multitude honoured our Lord as God. But I cannot think it.

14.—[*And Jesus...found...ass, sat thereon.*] That there was no chance or accident in the ass being found, we know from St. Matthew's Gospel, where we read that the disciples were sent to get the ass ready. (Matt. xxi. 7.) Every step of this triumphal progress into Jerusalem was prearranged.

To ride upon an ass, we must always remember, was not so low and ignominious a mode of travelling as it may seem to us. The Eastern ass is a very different creature to the English ass, larger, stronger, and far more valuable. Asses are specially named as part of the wealth of Abraham, Jacob, and Job. (Gen. xii. 16; xxx. 43; Job xlii. 12.) Solomon had an officer specially over the asses. (1 Chron. xxvii. 30.) Abraham, Balaam, Achsah, Abigail, and the Shunamite rich woman, all rode on asses. To ride on white asses was a mark of great men in the days of the Judges. (Judges v. 10.) The idea therefore of anything degrading in riding on an ass must be entirely dismissed from our minds.

On the other hand, it is undeniable that the ass is not the animal that a king or ruler, in any age, has ever chosen to use, on public occasions, in heading a procession. The horse has always been preferred. The use of an ass, we cannot doubt, was meant to show that our Lord's kingdom was utterly unlike the kingdoms of this world. No Roman soldier in the garrison of Jerusalem, who, standing at his post or sitting in his barrack-window, saw our Lord riding on an ass, could report to his centurion that He looked like one who came to wrest the kingdom of Judæa out of the hand of the Romans, drive out Pontius Pilate and his legions from the tower of Antonia, and achieve independence for the Jews with the sword!

The Greek word rendered "young ass" here, is a diminutive, and seems used intentionally to show that it was a very young or small ass.

[*As it is written.*] By riding on an ass our Lord had fulfilled the prophecy of Zechariah, in which, 500 years before, the prophet had foretold that the King of Zion would one day appear "riding upon an ass." At the time when he prophesied this, there were no kings in Jerusalem. The kingdom had ceased at the captivity. We cannot doubt that this prophecy was well known among the Scribes and Pharisees, and taken together with the fact that Daniel's 70 weeks were expiring, our Lord's entry into Jerusalem in this fashion must have raised many thoughts in their hearts.

Let it be noted that many like events in our Lord's earthly ministry were foreknown and foretold long before they happened, and with increasing minuteness and particularity as the roll of prophecy drew near to an end.

15.—[*Fear not, daughter of Sion, etc.*] It will be observed, of course, that John does not quote literally and exactly all that Zechariah said. He omits several words. The explanation is simple.

He did not quote from memory only, and so forget part; but he purposely only quoted that part of the prediction which was now specially fulfilled; viz., "the riding on the ass." The object of the prophecy, when it was first delivered, was to comfort the Jews in their low and decayed state, after their return from Babylon, by a promise of Messiah. Therefore Zechariah was taught by the Holy Ghost to say things which may be paraphrased as follows: "Fear not; be not cast down or depressed, O daughter of Sion, or inhabitants of Jerusalem. Low and depressed as your condition may be now, there will be a day when you shall have a King again. There shall come One who will ride on a certain public occasion into thy gates,—a King on an ass's colt, not as a warrior, with a sword in hand, but as a peaceful Prince, a just and holy King, better even than David, Solomon, Hezekiah, or Josiah, and bringing with Him salvation for souls. Therefore think not thyself forsaken, because thou art poor now, and hast no king. Look forward to thy coming King."

Let it be noted that Christ's coming, first or second, is always the great topic of comfort in prophetical writings.

16 —[*These things understood not...disciples...first.*] It is clear from this and other kindred passages, that our Lord's own immediate followers had a very imperfect knowledge of our Lord's Person and work, and of the fulfilment of Scripture which was going on around them. Brought up amidst Jewish notions of a glorious temporal Messiah, they failed to see the full meaning of many of our Lord's doings.

Let us never forget that men may be true Christians, and right hearted, and yet be very ignorant on some points. "Faith," says Zwingle, on this verse, "admits of degrees and increase." In estimating others, we must make great allowance for early training and associations.

[*But when Jesus was glorified.*] This must mean, as Theophylact says, our Lord's ascension. After that time, and the day of Pentecost, the minds of the disciples were greatly enlightened. Compare John vii. 39 : "The Holy Ghost was not yet given, because Jesus was not yet glorified."

[*Then remembered...these things...written of him.*] The power of memory to see things, long after they happen, in a new light, and then to recollect them vividly, is very remarkable. In no case does it appear more curiously than in the rising again in our minds of texts and sermons heard long ago, which at the time apparently left no impression on us. Preachers and teachers may take comfort in this. All is not lost that they say, although their hearers and scholars may seem at the time to pay no attention. Their words in many cases shall have a resurrection. One great cause of this is, that it is part of the Holy Ghost's office "to bring things to remembrance." (John xiv. 26.)

[*And...they...done these things...him.*]   The disciples found, long after the triumphant entry into Jerusalem, that they had been unconscious actors in a mighty accomplishment of Scripture.   This is a thought for us all.   We have not the least idea, during the greater part of our lives, how much of God's great purposes on earth are being carried on through us and by us, without our being conscious of it.   The full extent to which they are carried on we shall never know till we wake up in another world.   We shall then discern with wonder and amazement the full meaning of many a thing in which we were unconscious agents during our lives.

Calvin remarks : " Then, after the ascension, did it occur to the disciples that Christ did not do these things rashly, and that these men were not employed in idle amusement, but that the whole transaction had been regulated by the providence of God."

Poole observes, that here St. John " confesseth his own ignorance."   He was present, and saw all that was done, but did not understand it at the time.

17 —[*The people therefore...Lazarus...bare record.*]   I feel no doubt that this verse describes one part of the multitude which met our Lord, and the following verse describes another part.   One part, and of course a small one, consisted of those who had seen the raising of Lazarus.   The other, and a much larger one, consisted of those who had only heard the report.

That there must have been a very large number of persons present at the miracle of Bethany is, I think, indirectly proved by the expression here used, " people that were with Him."

The words, " bare record," must mean that they testified that a great miracle really had been wrought, and that this same Jesus, now riding on an ass before the eyes of the people, was that very Person who had wrought it.   I do not see that we can possibly get more out of the expression, and I cannot suppose that these people testified their belief in Christ's Messiahship.

The double expression, " called out of his grave," and " raised from the dead," deserves notice.   It is doubtless meant to keep before our minds the mighty simplicity of the means used by our Lord.   He spoke, and it was done.   He " called " to Lazarus to come forth, and he was " raised " at once.

18 —[*For this cause...people met him, etc.*]   This verse describes the state of mind of the larger part of the multitude which surrounded our Lord at His entry into Jerusalem.   It consisted of those who had heard the report of His raising Lazarus,—a story magnified, no doubt, in the telling.   Strong curiosity to see the Person who had done such a miracle would call forth an immense crowd in any city.   But among Jews, familiar with Old Testament miracles, assembled in enormous numbers for the Passover, excited by the rumour of Messiah coming,—

among such we may well believe that the report of Jesus coming in from Bethany would draw together many myriads of spectators to meet Him.

The Greek words, " for this cause," here seem to refer forward to the latter part of the verse, and not backward to the preceding verse. Compare x. 17, where the same form of language is used.

19 —[*The Pharisees...said...prevail nothing.*] This is the language of men baffled, angry, and at their wits' end from vexation, to see their plans defeated. Instead of finding people willing to lay hands on Jesus as a malefactor, and to deliver Him up into their power, they beheld a large multitude surrounding Him with joyful acclamations, and saluting Him as a King! Of course they could do nothing but sit still and see it. The least attempt to use violence against our Lord would have raised a tumult, and endangered their own lives. So that they were obliged to see their most hated enemy entering Jerusalem in triumph, like Mordecai led by Haman. (Esther vi. 11.)

" Perceive ye," I believe, should be taken as an imperative, and not as an interrogative indicative. It sounds like the language of men looking on from the city walls or the temple courts, as the huge procession wound slowly through the gates of the city. " Behold this sight! Behold how you do nothing effectual to stop this fellow's course! Your order to denounce Him, and have Him apprehended, is utterly useless and unprofitable."

Chrysostom and Theophylact think that those who said this had some faith and felt rightly, but had not courage enough to confess Christ. But I cannot agree with them. Calvin and other reformers think, on the contrary, that it was the language of Christ's enemies.

Bullinger observes that wicked men show their wickedness especially by their dislike of true religion, and their annoyance when, as in the case before us, it seems to enjoy a temporary popularity. For neglect and contempt of religion they show no concern at all.

[*Behold...world...gone after him.*] Some allowance of course must be made for the exaggerated language which angry and disappointed men use under the influence of passion. Nevertheless the word " world " may not be really so extravagant as it appears at first, when we consider the immense number of Jews who attended the passover feast. According to a computation made by Josephus there were nearly three millions of people assembled on such occasions at Jerusalem. At this rate we can understand that the crowd drawn together by our Lord's public entry might well be so large as to warrant the saying, " The world is gone after him." Most of the crowd, it may be remembered, were not dwellers in Jerusalem, but strangers, who were only visitors or sojourners, absent from home, and would materially swell a crowd.

In leaving this passage it is impossible not to feel that there must have been an overruling, constraining influence on the minds of the Jewish people on the occasion of our Lord's triumphant entry into Jerusalem. This, no doubt, was an influence miraculously exercised by our Lord in order to draw all men's attention to Himself, and to make His approaching Sacrifice on the cross as public an event as possible.

Rollock observes: "A secret power of royal authority stirred up the minds of the multitude to receive Christ as a king." He also observes that it is the same power which Christ will put forth when He comes at the last day to judge the world.

JOHN XII   20—26

20 And there were certain Greeks among them that came up to worship at the feast:

21 The same came therefore to Philip, which was of Bethsaida of Galilee, and desired him, saying, Sir, we would see Jesus.

22 Philip cometh and telleth Andrew: and again Andrew and Philip tell Jesus.

23 And Jesus answered them, saying The hour is come, that the Son of man should be glorified.

24 Verily, verily, I say unto you, Except a corn of wheat fall into the ground and die, it abideth alone: but if it die, it bringeth forth much fruit.

25 He that loveth his life shall lose it; and he that hateth his life in this world shall keep it unto life eternal.

26 If any man serve me, let him follow me; and where I am, there shall also my servant be: if any man serve me, him will *my* Father honour.

THERE is more going on in some people's minds than we are aware of. The case of the Greeks before us is a remarkable proof of this. Who would have thought when Christ was on earth, that foreigners from a distant land would have come forward in Jerusalem, and said, "Sir, we would see Jesus"? Who these Greeks were, what they meant, why they desired to see Jesus, what their inward motives were,—all these are questions we cannot answer. Like Zaccheus, they may have been influenced by curiosity. Like the wise men from the East, they may have surmised that Jesus was the promised King of the Jews, whom all the eastern world was

expecting. Enough for us to know that they showed
more interest in Christ than Caiaphas and all his companions. Enough to know that they drew from our
Lord's lips sayings which are still read in one hundred
and fifty languages, from one end of the world to the
other.

We learn, for one thing, from our Lord's words in this
passage, that *death is the way to spiritual life and glory.*
" Except a corn of wheat fall into the ground, it abideth
alone ; but if it die, it bringeth forth much fruit."

This sentence was primarily meant to teach the wondering Greeks the true nature of Messiah's kingdom. If
they thought to see a King like the kings of this world, they
were greatly mistaken. Our Lord would have them know
that He came to carry a cross, and not to wear a crown.
He came not to live a life of honour, ease, and magnifi-
cence, but to die a shameful and dishonoured death. The
kingdom He came to set up was to begin with a crucifixion, and not with a coronation. Its glory was to take
its rise not from victories won by the sword, and from
accumulated treasures of gold and silver, but from the
death of its King.

But this sentence was also meant to teach a wider
and broader lesson still. It revealed, under a striking
figure, the mighty foundation truth, that Christ's death
was to be the source of spiritual life to the world. From
His cross and passions was to spring up a mighty harvest
of benefit to all mankind. His death, like a grain of
seed-corn, was to be the root of blessings and mercies
to countless millions of immortal souls. In short, the
great principle of the Gospel was once more exhibited,—
that Christ's vicarious death (not His life, or miracles, or
teaching, but His *death*) was to bring forth fruit to the
praise of God, and to provide redemption for a lost
world,

This deep and mighty sentence was followed by a practical application, which closely concerns ourselves. " He that hateth his life shall keep it." He that would be saved must be ready to give up life itself, if necessary, in order to obtain salvation. He must bury his love of the world, with its riches, honours, pleasures, and rewards, with a full belief that in so doing he will reap a better harvest, both here and hereafter. He who loves the life that now is so much that he cannot deny himself anything for the sake of his soul, will find at length that he has lost everything. He, on the contrary, who is ready to cast away everything most dear to him in this life, if it stands in the way of his soul, and to crucify the flesh with its affections and lusts, will find at length that he is no loser. In a word, his losses will prove nothing in comparison to his gains.

Truths such as these should sink deeply into our hearts, and stir up self-inquiry. It is as true of Christians as it is of Christ,—there can be no life without death, there can be no sweet without bitter, there can be no crown without a cross. Without Christ's death there would have been no life for the world. Unless we are willing to die to sin, and crucify all that is most dear to flesh and blood, we cannot expect any benefit from Christ's death. Let us remember these things, and take up our cross daily, like men. Let us for the joy set before us endure the cross and despise the shame, and in the end we shall sit down with our Master at God's right hand. The way of self-crucifixion and sanctification may seem foolishness and waste to the world, just as burying good seed-corn seems waste to the child and the fool. But there never lived the man who did not find that, by sowing to the Spirit, he reaped life everlasting.

We learn, for another thing, from our Lord's words, that *if we profess to serve Christ, we must follow Him.*

"If any man serve Me," is the saying, "let him follow Me."

That expression, "following," is one of wide signification, and brings before our minds many familiar ideas. As the soldier follows his general, as the servant follows his master, as the scholar follows his teacher, as the sheep follows its shepherd, just so ought the professing Christian to follow Christ. Faith and obedience are the leading marks of real followers, and will always be seen in true believing Christians. Their knowledge may be very small, and their infirmities very great; their grace very weak, and their hope very dim. But they believe what Christ says, and strive to do what Christ commands. And of such Christ declares, "They serve Me, they are mine."

Christianity like this receives little from man. It is too thorough, too decided, too strong, too real. To serve Christ in name and form is easy work, and satisfies most people, but to follow Him in faith and life demands more trouble than the generality of men will take about their souls. Laughter, ridicule, opposition, persecution, are often the only reward which Christ's followers get from the world. Their religion is one, "whose praise is not of men, but of God." (Rom. ii. 29.)

Yet to him that followeth, let us never forget, the Lord Jesus holds out abundant encouragement: "Where I am," He declares, "there also shall my servant be; if any man serve Me, him will my Father honour." Let us lay to heart these comfortable promises, and go forward in the narrow way without fear. The world may cast out our name as evil, and turn us out of its society; but when we dwell with Christ in glory, we shall have a home from which we can never be ejected.—The world may pour contempt on our religion, and laugh us and our Christianity to scorn; but when the Father honours us at the last day, before the assembly of angels and men, we shall find that His praise makes amends for all.

20 —[*And there were certain Greeks, etc., etc.*] Who these Greeks were has exercised the conjectural ingenuity of commentators. They were not downright heathens, it is clear, from the expression that they were of those "that came to worship" at the feast. No heathen would be admitted to the passover.—They were not in my judgment Jews who had lived among Greeks until they were more Grecian than Jewish in their language. The word we have rendered "Greeks" seems to me to make that impossible.—I believe they were men who were by birth heathens, but had become proselytes to Judaism, and as such were regular attendants on the Jewish feasts. That there were many such proselytes wherever Jews lived, is a simple matter of fact. So in Acts xvii. 4, we read of "devout" or "worshipping" Greeks. The leavening influence of Judaism, in every part of the heathen world where the scattered Jews dwelt, before the coming of Christ, was probably very considerable. It is worth notice that as Gentiles, the wise men from the East, were among the first to honour our Lord when He was born, so Gentiles were among the first to show interest in Him just before His crucifixion.

Whether the circumstance recorded in the passage before us took place the same day that our Lord rode in triumph into Jerusalem, or whether there was not a break or interval of a day or two, admits of question. Judging from the inquiry of the Greeks, "We would see Jesus," it seems unlikely that it happened the same day. It stands to reason that our Lord, at a time when He was riding into Jerusalem on an ass, and was the object of popular enthusiasm, would easily have been distinguished and recognized by the Greeks. Moreover, one cannot suppose that the words spoken in the following verse, and the miracle of the voice from heaven, belong to a time of noise, shouting, and popular acclamation, such as there must have been during the procession. For these reasons I incline to the opinion that we must suppose an interval of a day or two between this verse and the preceding one.

21 —[*The same came...Philip...Bethsaida...Galilee.*] Why the Greeks came to Philip more than any other disciple we do not know. It is conjectured that Philip, being an inhabitant of a town in North Galilee, was more likely than the other disciples to be acquainted with Greeks, from being near Tyre and Sidon. But this reason applies quite as much to Andrew, Peter, James, and John, who were all Galileans, as it does to Philip.—Is it not worth noticing that Philip's name is a more purely Greek name than that of any of the apostles? Does not this indicate that he probably had Greek relatives and connections?

The mention of Bethsaida accounts for Philip speaking to Andrew, in the next verse. Bethsaida was the native place of Andrew and Peter, and Philip therefore was their fellow-townsman.

[*And desired him, saying, Sir.*] The Greek word rendered "desired" is more frequently translated, "asked," "besought," "prayed." It implies the desire of an inquirer who expresses a wish for a thing, and asks whether it is possible for him to have it.

The word we render " sir " is almost always rendered "lord." When rendered " sir " it is addressed by an inferior to a superior. Thus the servant of the householder says, " Sir, didst thou not sow good seed? " (Matt. xiii. 27.) The Pharisees said to Pilate, " Sir, we remember that deceiver said." (Matt. xxvii. 63.) The Samaritan woman says to Jesus three times, " Sir." (John iv. 11, 13, 19.) Here the use of the word marks the respect of the Greeks for our Lord and His apostles.

[*We would see Jesus.*] The English here fails to express the Greek fully. It is literally, " we wish, we desire to see."

Concerning the motive of the Greeks, in asking to see our Lord, we know nothing certain. It may have been nothing but curiosity, like that of Zaccheus, aroused by hearing rumours about Jesus, and sharpened by seeing the procession of the palm-bearing multitude at His entry into the city. This alone was enough to excite the attention of Greeks accustomed to the demonstrations of their own countrymen on public occasions.— It may possibly be that, like the Canaanitish woman, the centurion of Capernaum, and Cornelius, they had, as proselytes, got hold of the great truths which underlaid Judaism, and were actually looking for a Redeemer. But we do not know.

Bengel thinks that at this moment " Jesus was engaged in the inner part of the temple, to which an entrance was not open to the Greeks," and for this reason the Greeks could not get at Him, and have a personal interview.

These Greeks, we should note, sought to see Jesus at the very time when the Jews sought to kill Him.

22 —[*Philip cometh and telleth Andrew.*] This expression seems to favour the idea that this whole transaction was not on the same day that Jesus entered Jerusalem. On such a day there would hardly be an opportunity for one disciple coming quietly and telling a thing to another. Why Philip chose to tell Andrew we have seen. He was His fellow-townsman.

[*And again Andrew and Philip tell Jesus.*] This expression seems to imply that the two Apostles consulted together before they told our Lord. Perhaps, as thorough Jews, they did not feel sure that our Lord would care to give an interview to Gentiles, and at first hesitated about telling Him. They remembered that at one time Jesus had said, "Go not into the way of the Gentiles." (Matt. x. 5.) On reflection they probably remembered our Lord's kindness to the Canaanitish mother, and the Roman centurion, and resolved to tell Him.

Of course it is possible that the Greeks only wanted to look at our Lord and see what He was like, and not to converse with Him. If this was all, the disciples may have doubted whethei it was worth mentioning to Jesus.

23 —[*And Jesus answered them, saying.*] It is doubtful whether this was spoken to the two disciples only,—or to them and the Greeks before mentioned,—or to the twelve alone. I incline to think it must mean to the twelve, and specially to Andrew and Philip.

[*The hour is come...Son of man...glorified.*] The true key-note to this verse, and the two which follow, is probably this. Our Lord saw the state of mind in which His followers were. He saw them excited by His triumphant entry into Jerusalem, and the desire of strangers like the Greeks to see their Master. He saw they were secretly expecting a glorious kingdom to be immediately set up, in which they would have chief places, power, and authority. He proceeds to rectify their conceptions, and to remind them of what He had repeatedly told them, His own death.

The hour has certainly arrived for my being glorified. I am about to leave the world, ascend up to my Father, finish the work I came to do, and be highly exalted. My earthly ministry of humiliation is ending, and my time of glory is drawing nigh. But all this is to be brought about in a way very different from that which you are thinking about. I am going to a cross first, and not a throne. I am going first to be condemned, crucified, and slain.

That "glorified" means "to be crucified," I cannot admit, with such texts as John vii. 39 and xii. 16 before me. That the cross led to glory, and that through the crucifixion came the glorification, I believe firmly. But the glory came after the suffering. (Luke xxiv. 26.)

Let us note that " the hour " or season for Christ to finish His ministry was fixed and appointed. Till it came the Jews could do nothing to stop His preaching or harm His person. Just so it is with His people in one sense. Each is immortal till his work is done.

Does it not seem that the inquiry of the Greeks has much to do with our Lord's opening words?—" The Gentiles are beginning to inquire after Me. Thus the hour is manifestly come that my work should be finished, and my kingdom fully set up in the world, by my crucifixion, resurrection, and ascension."

24 —[*Verily, verily I say unto you.*] This is one of those solemn

prefaces which are so frequent in John's Gospel, and indicate some very weighty truth coming. I think "to you" must surely include not only Andrew and Philip, but all the company around our Lord.

[*Except a corn of wheat, etc., etc.*] Our Lord here illustrates a great Scriptural truth by a very familiar fact in nature. That fact is, that in plants and seeds life comes by death. The seed must be put into the ground, must rot, decay, and die, if we want it to bear fruit and produce a crop. If we refuse to bury the seed, and will keep it without sowing it, we shall never reap any harvest. We must be content to let it die if we want corn.

The wealth of spiritual truth which this beautiful figure unfolds is very great. The death of Christ was the life of the world. From it, as a most prolific seed, was to spring an enormous harvest of blessing to souls, and of glory to God. His substitution on the cross, His atoning death, were to be the beginning of untold blessings to a lost world. To wish Him not to die, to dislike the idea of His death, (as the disciples evidently did,) was as foolish as to keep seed-corn locked up in the granary, and to refuse to sow it. "I am the corn of wheat," Jesus seems to say. "Unless I die, whatever you in your private opinion may think, my purpose in coming into the world will not be accomplished. But if I die, multitudes of souls will be saved."

Let us carefully mark here the immense importance which our Lord attaches to His death. Nothing can explain this but the old foundation doctrine of the Bible, that Christ's sacrificial death on the cross is the only satisfaction and atonement for the sin of the world. A passage like this can never be thoroughly explained by those who regard Christ's death as nothing more than a martyrdom or an example of self-denial. It was something far greater and more important than this. It was the dying of a corn of wheat, in order that out of its death should spring up an enormous spiritual harvest. Christ's vicarious death is the world's life.

Let us notice here, as elsewhere, the Divine wisdom with which our Master illustrated spiritual truth by earthly figures. Illustrations, fitly chosen, strike men much more than abstract arguments. Ministers and teachers of religion should study to "use similitudes."

Theophylact thinks our Lord meant, by this beautiful figure, to encourage His disciples not to be offended and shaken in mind by His coming death. In His case, as in the natural world, they must remember life comes through death.

Zwingle thinks that as with the corn, when sown, so it is with the body of Christ. It does us good by dying for us, and not by our eating it.

Gill remarks, that by "abiding alone," in this simile, Christ meant that if He did not die, He would be "alone" in heaven with the Father and the elect angels, but without any of the sons of men. Scott says the same.

25 —[*He that loveth his life, etc.*] There are few of our Lord's sayings more frequently recorded by the Holy Ghost than this pair of paradoxes. The repetition shows its great importance. It will be found in Matt. x. 39; xvi. 25: Mark viii. 35; Luke ix. 24; xvii. 33; as well as here.

The meaning is plain : " He that loves his life, or thinks more of the life that now is than that which is to come, shall lose that which is the best part of his life, his soul. He that hateth his life, or cares little for it compared to the life to come, shall preserve to eternal glory that which is the best part of his life, to wit, his soul."

One object of our Lord in saying these words was evidently to prevent His disciples looking for good things in this life, if they followed Him. They must give up their Jewish ideas about temporal rewards and honours in Messiah's service. They must understand that His kingdom was entirely spiritual, and that if they were His disciples they must be content to lose much in this life, in order to gain the glory of the life to come. So far from promising them temporal rewards, He would have them distinctly know that they must give up much and sacrifice much, if they wanted to be saved.

The other object our Lord had in view in saying these words was to teach all Christians in every age, that like Him they must make up their minds to sacrifice much, and to die to the world, in the hope of a harvest of glory in a world to come. Through death we must seek life. Eternal life must be the great end a Christian looks to. To attain it he must be willing to give up everything.

The practical condemnation which this verse passes on the life lived by many should never be overlooked. How few hate their lives here ! How many love them, and care for nothing but how to make them comfortable and happy ! The eternal loss or the eternal gain are often entirely forgotten.

Augustine gives a wise caution : " Take heed lest there steal upon thee a will to make away with thyself, while thou takest in the sense that it is a duty to hate thine own life in this world. Hence certain malignant and perverse men give themselves to the flames, choke themselves in the water, dash themselves in pieces, and so perish. Christ taught not this. Not by himself, but by another, must that man be put to death who would follow in Christ's footsteps."

The word " hate " here must be taken comparatively. It is a Hebraism, like " Jacob have I loved, and Esau have I hated." " Your appointed feasts my soul hateth." (Rom. ix. 13; Isai. i. 14.)

Scott thinks this verse was meant to teach the Greeks and all the disciples to arm themselves with a mind like their Master's if they wanted to follow Him.

26 —[*If any man serve me...follow me.*] This verse seems spoken for the benefit and information of the Greeks who sought to see Jesus, and of all who desired to become His disciples. If any man desires to serve Christ, and be a Christian, he must be content to follow His Master, walk in His footsteps, share His lot, do as He did, and partake of His Master's inheritance in this world. He must not look for good things here,—for crowns, kingdoms, riches, honours, wealth, and dignity. Like His Master, he must be content with a cross. He must, in a word, "take up his cross and follow Me." (Matt. xvi. 24.) As St. Paul says, "we are heirs of God, and joint-heirs with Christ; if so be that we suffer with Him, that we may be also glorified together." (Rom. viii. 17.)

[*And where I am, there...my servant be.*] This is the first thing that Christ promises to those who follow Him. They shall be with Christ wherever He is, in paradise, and in His glorious kingdom. He and His servant shall not be parted. Whatever the Master has, the servant shall have also.

It is a comfortable thought, that however little we know of the life to come and the state after death, we do know that we shall be " with Christ, which is far better." (Phil. i. 23.)

[*If any man serve me...my Father honour.*] This is the second thing which Jesus promises to His disciples. The Father shall give, to those who love Christ, such honour as eye hath not seen nor ear heard. Honour from the men of this world they may not have. Honour from the Father shall make amends for all.

It is impossible not to see throughout this verse that our Lord's intention is to discourage the carnal and earthly expectation of His Jewish followers, and yet to encourage them by showing what they might confidently look for. They must follow in His steps if they were his true servants, and in so following they would find a cross, and not a crown, whatever they might be thinking, at that moment, while the hosannas of an excited crowd were sounding in their ears. But though they had a cross, they should not miss a reward finally, which would make amends for all. They would be with Christ in glory. They would be honoured by God the Father.

The words, "Him will my Father honour," of course admit of being applied to this life in a certain sense: "Them that honour Me I will honour." (1 Sam. ii. 30.) But it is much more agreeable to the context, I think, to apply them to the honour which shall be given in another world.

The clearest conception we can form of heaven is that which is here stated. It is being with Christ, and receiving honour from God. Heaven is generally described by negatives. This

is, however, an exceptional positive. It is being "with Christ."
(Compare John xiv. 3; xvii. 24; 1 Thess. iv. 17.)

Let us note how wisely and mercifully our Lord always damped
and checked the unscriptural expectations of His disciples.
Never on any occasion do we find Him keeping back the cross,
or bribing men to follow Him, as Mahomet did, by promising
temporal comfort and happiness.

JOHN XII   27—33

27 Now is my soul troubled: and
what shall I say? Father, save me
from this hour: but for this cause came
I unto this hour.

28 Father, glorify thy name. Then
came there a voice from heaven *saying*,
I have both glorified *it*, and will glorify *it* again.

29 The people therefore, that stood
by, and heard *it*, said that it thundered:
others said, An angel spake to him.

30 Jesus answered and said, This
voice came not because of me, but for
your sakes.

31 Now is the judgment of this
world: now shall the prince of this
world be cast out.

32 And I, if I be lifted up from the
earth, will draw all *men* unto me.

33 This he said, signifying what
death he should die.

THESE verses show us what St. Peter meant, when he said,
"There are some things hard to be understood" in Scripture. (2 Pet. iii. 16.)   There are depths here which we
have no line to fathom thoroughly. This need not surprise
us, or shake our faith. The Bible would not be a book
"given by inspiration of God," if it did not contain many
things which pass man's finite understanding. With all
its difficulties it contains thousands of passages which the
most unlearned may easily comprehend. Even here, if we
look steadily at these verses, we may gather from them
lessons of no mean importance.

We have, first, in these verses, *a great doctrine indirectly
proved.* That doctrine is the imputation of man's sin to
Christ.

We see the Saviour of the world, the eternal Son of
God troubled and disturbed in mind: " Now is my soul
troubled." We see Him who could heal diseases with a

touch, cast out devils with a word, and command the waves and winds to obey Him, in great agony and conflict of spirit. Now how can this be explained?

To say, as some do, that the only cause of our Lord's trouble was the prospect of His own painful death on the cross, is a very unsatisfactory explanation. At this rate it might justly be said that many a martyr has shown more calmness and courage than the Son of God. Such a conclusion is, to say the least, most revolting. Yet this is the conclusion to which men are driven if they adopt the modern notion, that Christ's death was only a great example of self-sacrifice.

Nothing can ever explain our Lord's trouble of soul, both here and in Gethsemane, except the old doctrine, that He felt the burden of man's sin pressing Him down. It was the mighty weight of a world's guilt imputed to Him and meeting on his head, which made Him groan and agonize, and cry, " Now is my soul troubled." Forever let us cling to that doctrine, not only as untying the knot of the passage before us, but as the only ground of solid comfort for the heart of a Christian. That our sins have been really laid on our Divine Substitute, and borne by Him, and that His righteousness is really imputed to us and accounted ours,— this is the real warrant for Christian peace. And if any man asks how we know that our sins were laid on Christ, we bid him read such passages as that which is before us, and explain them on any other principle if he can. Christ has borne our sins, carried our sins, groaned under the burden of our sins, been " troubled " in soul by the weight of our sins, and really taken away our sins. This, we may rest assured, is sound doctrine: this is Scriptural theology.

We have, secondly, in these verses, *a great mystery unfolded*. That mystery is the possibility of much inward conflict of soul without sin,

We cannot fail to see in the passage before us a mighty mental struggle in our blessed Saviour. Of its depth and intensity we can probably form very little conception. But the agonizing cry, " My soul is troubled,"—the solemn question, " What shall I say?"—the prayer of suffering flesh and blood, " Father, save Me from this hour,"—the meek confession, " For this cause came I unto this hour," —the petition of a perfectly submissive will, " Father, glorify Thy name,"—what does all this mean? Surely there can be only one answer. These sentences tell of a struggle within our Saviour's breast, a struggle arising from the natural feelings of one who was perfect man, and as man could suffer all that man is capable of suffering. Yet He in whom this struggle took place was the Holy Son of God. " In Him is no sin." (1 John iii. 5.) There is a fountain of comfort here for all true servants of Christ, which ought never to be overlooked. Let them learn from their Lord's example that inward conflict of soul is not necessarily in itself a sinful thing. Too many, we believe, from not understanding this point, go heavily all their days on their way to heaven. They fancy they have no grace, because they find a fight in their own hearts. They refuse to take comfort in the Gospel, because they feel a battle between the flesh and the Spirit. Let them mark the experience of their Lord and Master, and lay aside their desponding fears. Let them study the experience of His saints in every age, from St. Paul downwards, and understand that as Christ had inward conflicts, so must Christians expect to have them also. To give way to doubts and unbelief, no doubt is wrong, and robs us of our peace. There is a faithless despondency, unquestionably, which is blameworthy, and must be resisted, repented of, and brought to the fountain for all sin, that it may be pardoned. But the mere presence of fight and strife and conflict in our hearts is in itself no sin. The believer may be known by his inward warfare as well as by his inward peace.

We have, thirdly, in these verses, *a great miracle exhibited*. That miracle is the heavenly Voice described in this passage,—a voice which was heard so plainly that people said it thundered,—proclaiming, "I have glorified my name, and will glorify it again."

This wondrous Voice was heard three times during our Lord's earthly ministry. Once it was heard at His baptism, when the heavens were opened and the Holy Ghost descended on Him. Once it was heard at His transfiguration, when Moses and Elias appeared for a season with Him, before Peter, James, and John. Once it was heard here at Jerusalem, in the midst of a mixed crowd of disciples and unbelieving Jews. On each occasion we know that it was the Voice of God the Father. But why and wherefore this Voice was only heard on these occasions we are left to conjecture. The thing was a deep mystery, and we cannot now speak particularly of it.

Let it suffice us to believe that this miracle was meant to show the intimate relations and unbroken union of God the Father and God the Son, throughout the period of the Son's earthly ministry. At no period during His incarnation was there a time when the eternal Father was not close to Him, though unseen by man.—Let us also believe that this miracle was meant to signify to bystanders the entire approval of the Son by the Father, as the Messiah, the Redeemer, and the Saviour of man. That approval the Father was pleased to signify by voice three times, as well as to declare by signs and mighty deeds, performed by the Son in His name. These things we may well believe. But when we have said all, we must confess that the Voice was a mystery. We may read of it with wonder and awe, but we cannot explain it.

We have, lastly, in these verses, *a great prophecy*

delivered. The Lord Jesus declared, "I, if I be lifted up from the earth, will draw all men unto me."

Concerning the true meaning of these words there can be but one opinion in any candid mind. They do not mean, as is often supposed, that if the doctrine of Christ crucified is lifted up and exalted by ministers and teachers, it will have a drawing effect on hearers. This is undeniably a truth, but it is not the truth of the text. They simply mean that the death of Christ on the cross would have a drawing effect on all mankind. His death as our Substitute, and the Sacrifice for our sins, would draw multitudes out of every nation to believe on Him and receive Him as their Saviour. By being crucified for us, and not by ascending a temporal throne, He would set up a kingdom in the world, and gather subjects to Himself.

How thoroughly this prophecy has been fulfilled for eighteen centuries, the history of the Church is an abundant proof. Whenever Christ crucified has been preached, and the story of the cross fully told, souls have been converted and drawn to Christ, just as iron-filings are drawn to a magnet, in every part of the world. No truth so exactly suits the wants of all children of Adam, of every colour, climate, and language, as the truth about Christ crucified.

And the prophecy is not yet exhausted. It shall yet receive a more complete accomplishment. A day shall come when every knee shall bow before the Lamb that was slain, and every tongue confess that He is Lord to the glory of God the Father. He that was "lifted up" on the cross shall yet sit on the throne of glory, and before Him shall be gathered all nations. Friends and foes, each in their own order, shall be "drawn" from their graves, and appear before the judgment-seat of Christ. Let us take heed in that day that we are found on His right hand!

NOTES   JOHN XII 27—33

27 —[*Now is my soul troubled, etc., etc.*] This remarkable verse
comes in somewhat abruptly. Yet the connection is not hard
to trace. Our Lord had just been speaking of His own atoning
death. The thought and prospect of that death appears to
draw from Him the expressions of this verse, which I will now
examine in order.

[*Now is my soul troubled.*] This sentence implies a sudden,
strong mental agony, which came over our Lord, troubling,
distressing, and harassing Him.—What was it from? Not from
the mere foresight of a painful death on the cross, and the
bodily suffering attending it. No doubt human nature, even
when sinless, naturally revolts from pain and suffering. Yet
mere bodily pain has been endured for weeks by many a
martyr, and even by heathen fanatics in India, without a groan
or a murmur.—No! it was the weight of the world's imputed
sin laid upon our Lord's head, which pressed Him downward,
and made Him cry, "Now is my soul troubled." It was the
sense of the whole burden of man's transgression imputed to
Him, which, as He drew near to the cross, weighed Him down
so tremendously. It was not His bodily sufferings, either an-
ticipated or felt, but our sins, which here, at Gethsemane, and
at Calvary, agonized and racked His soul.

Let us notice here the reality of Christ's substitution for us.
He was made "a curse" for us, and sin for us, and He felt it
for a time most deeply. (Gal. iii. 13; 2 Cor. v. 21.) Those
who deny the doctrine of substitution, imputation, and atonement can never explain the expressions before us satisfactorily.

Poole remarks: "There is a vast difference between this
trouble of spirit in Christ, and that which is in us. Our
troubles are upon reflection for our own sins, and the wrath of
God due to us therefor; His troubles were for the wrath of
God due to us for our sins.—Our troubles are because we have
personally grieved God; His were because those given to Him
had offended God. We are afraid of our eternal condemnation;
He was only afraid by a natural fear of death, which naturally
riseth higher according to the kind of death we die.—Our
troubles have mixture of despair, distrust, sinful horror; there
was no such thing in His trouble.—Our troubles, in their natural tendency, are killing and destroying; only by accident and
the wise ordering of Divine providence do they prove advantageous, and lead us to Him; His trouble, in the very nature of
it, was pure, and clean, and sanative, and healing.—But that He
was truly troubled, and that such a trouble did truly agree to
His office as Mediator, and is a great foundation of peace, quiet,
and satisfaction to us, is out of question. By some of these
stripes we are healed."

We should remember and admire the prayer in the Litany of

the Greek Church,—" By Thine unknown sufferings, good Lord, deliver us."

Rollock observes here, " If you ask me what the Divine nature in Christ was doing when He said, 'My soul is troubled,' and whether it was divided asunder from His human nature, I reply that it was not divided, but contained itself, or held itself passive, while the human nature was suffering. If it had exercised itself in its full power and glory, our Lord could not possibly have suffered."

(The whole of Rollock's remarks on this difficult verse are singularly good, and deserve close study.)

Hutcheson observes : " The rise and cause of this trouble was thus : the Godhead hiding itself from the humanity's sense, and the Father letting out not only an apprehension of sufferings to come, but a present taste of the horror of His wrath due to man for sin. Christ was amazed, perplexed, and overwhelmed with it in His humanity. And no wonder, since He had the sins of all the elect laid upon Him, by imputation, to suffer for."

Hengstenberg remarks : " The only solution of this extreme trouble is the vicarious significance of the sufferings and death of Christ. If our chastisement was upon Him, in order that we might have peace, then in Him must have been concentrated all the horror of death. He bore the sin of the world, and the wages of that sin was death. Death therefore must to Him assume its most frightful form. The physical suffering was nothing compared to the immeasurable suffering of soul which impended over the Redeemer, and the full greatness and depth of which He clearly perceives. Therefore, in Heb. v. 7, ' a fear ' is described as that which pressed with such awful weight upon our Lord. When God freed Him from that, He saved Him from death. Thus, when the suffering of Christ is apprehended as vicarious and voluntary, all the accompanying circumstances can be easily understood."

Let us note the exceeding guilt and sinfulness of sin. The thing which made even God's own Son, who had power to work works that none else did beside Him, groan and cry, " My soul is troubled," can be no light thing. He that would know the full measure of sin and guilt should mark attentively this verse, and the expressions used by our Lord at Gethsemane and Calvary.

It is worth noticing that this verse, Matt. xxvi. 38, and Mark xiv. 34, are the only three places in the Gospels where our Lord speaks of " My soul."

The word " now," I suspect, is emphatic: " Now, at this special time, my soul has begun to be specially troubled."

[*And what shall I say ?*] These words are thought by some,

as Theophylact, Grotius, Bloomfield, and Barnes, to be wrongly
translated in our English version. They would render them,
" And what? What is my duty? What does the hour require
of Me? Shall I say, Save Me," etc., etc.—I much prefer our
English version as it is. I believe the question is strongly significant of the agony and conflict through which our Lord's soul
was passing.—" What shall I say under this sense of pressing,
overwhelming trouble? My human nature bids me say one
thing, acting alone and urging me alone. My knowledge of the
purpose for which I came into the world bids me say another
thing. What, then, shall I say?" Such a question as this is a
strong proof of our Lord's real, true humanity.

Rollock observes: "'What shall I say?' is the language of
the highest perplexity and anxiety of mind. In the height of
anguish is the height of perplexity, so that a man knows not
what to say or do. The Lord found deliverance in prayer. But
the perpetual cry of the lost will be, 'What shall I say? What
shall I do?' From that perplexity and anguish they will never
be delivered."

Bengel remarks: " Jesus says, 'What shall I say?' not, What
shall I choose? Compare with this the different expression of
St. Paul, 'What I shall choose I wist not, for I am in a strait
betwixt two, having a desire to depart.'" (Phil. i. 22.)

Ecolampadius thinks the question means, "In what words
shall I unfold my pain, or the bitterness and ingratitude of the
Jews?" I prefer taking it as the language of perplexity and
distress.

The presence of two natures, in our Lord Jesus Christ's
person, seems clearly taught, when we compare the language
used by our Lord in this verse, with the language of the fifth
and seventeenth chapters of this Gospel. *Here* we see unmistakably our Lord's true humanity. *There*, on the other hand, we
see no less plainly His divinity. Here He speaks as man; there
as God.

[*Father, save me from this hour.*] This is undoubtedly a
prayer to be saved from, or delivered from, the agony and
suffering of this hour. It is the language of a human nature,
which, though sinless, could suffer, and instinctively shrank
from suffering. It would not have been real human nature if it
had not so shrunk and recoiled.

The idea of the prayer is just the same as that of the prayer
in Gethsemane,—" Let this cup pass from me." (Matt. xxvi. 39.)

Let us learn from our Lord's example that there is nothing
sinful in praying to be delivered from suffering, so long as we
do it in submission to the will of God. There is nothing wrong
in a sick person's saying, " Father, make me well," so long as
the prayer is offered with proper qualification.

Rollock observes: " In agony there is a certain forgetfulness of all things except present pain. This seems the case of our Lord here. Yet even here He turns to His Father, showing that He never loses the sense of the Father's love. The lost in hell will never turn to the Father."

It is worth noticing that our Lord speaks of " the Father " and "My Father" at least one hundred and ten times in John's Gospel.

[*But for this cause came I unto this hour.*] This sentence is an elliptical way of declaring our Lord's entire submission to His Father's will, in the matter of the prayer He had just prayed. " But I know that for this cause I came into the world and have reached this hour, to suffer as I am now suffering, and to agonize as I am now agonizing. I do not refuse the cup. If it be Thy will, I am willing to drink it. Only I tell Thee my feelings, with entire submission to Thy will."

We may surely learn from the whole verse that Christians have no cause to despair because they feel trouble of soul,—because they feel perplexed, and know not what to say in the agony of inward conflict,—because their nature shrinks from pain, and cries to God to take it away. In all this there is nothing wicked or sinful. It was the expression of the human nature of our Lord Jesus Christ Himself, and in Him was no sin.

Rollock says : " This is the language of one recollecting himself, and collecting his thoughts to remember something besides his agony and pain."

[*Father, glorify thy name.*] This passage seems the conclusion of the strife and agony of soul which came over our Lord at this particular period. It is as though He said, "I leave the matter in Thy hand, O My Father. Do what Thou seest best. Glorify Thy name and Thy attributes in Me. Do what is meet for setting forth Thy glory in the world. If it be for Thy glory that I should suffer, I am willing to suffer even unto the bearing of the world's sins."

I see in the whole event here described, a short summary of what took place afterwards more fully at Gethsemane. There is a remarkable parallelism at every step.

(*a*) Does our Lord say here, " My soul is troubled"? Just so He said in Gethsemane, " My soul is exceeding sorrowful, even unto death." (Matt. xxvi. 38.)

(*b*) Does our Lord say here, " Father, save Me from this hour"? Just so he says in Gethsemane, " O my Father, if it be possible, let this cup pass from Me." (Matt. xxvi. 39.)

(*c*) Does our Lord say here, " For this cause came I unto this hour"? Just so he says in Gethsemane, " If this cup may not pass away from Me except I drink it, Thy will be done." (Matt. xxvi. 42.)

(*d*) Does our Lord say, finally, " Father, glorify Thy name " ?

Just so our Lord says, lastly, " The cup which my Father hath given Me, shall I not drink it ? "   (John xviii. 11.)

The brief prayer which our Lord here offers, we should remember, is the highest, greatest thing that we can ask God to do.   The utmost reach of the renewed will of a believer is to be able to say always, "Father, glorify Thy name in Me. Do with Me what Thou wilt, only glorify Thy name."   The glory of God after all is the end for which all things were created. Paul's joyful hope, he told the Philippians, when a prisoner at Rome, was " that in all things, by life or by death, Christ might be magnified in his body."   (Philip i. 20.)

Rollock says : " This is the language of one who now forgets the agony and pain, remembers only His Father's glory, and desires it even together with His own passion and death."—He also remarks that the experience of God's saints in great trouble, is in a sense much the same.   For a time they forget everything but present pain.   By and by they rise above their sufferings, and remember only God's glory.

[*Then came there a voice from heaven.*]   This voice was undoubtedly a great miracle.   God the Father was heard speaking audibly with man's voice to the Son.   Three t'mes in our Lord's ministry this miracle took place : first, at His baptism ; secondly, at His transfiguration ; thirdly, just before His crucifixion. Rarely has the voice of God been heard by large crowds of unconverted men.   Here, at Mount Sinai, and perhaps at our Lord's baptism, are the only three occasions on record.

Of course we can no more explain this wonderful miracle than any other miracle in God's Word.   We can only reverently believe and admire it.   The intimate nearness of the Father to the Son, all through His ministry, is one of the many thoughts which may occur to our minds as we consider the miracle. Our Lord was never left alone.   His Father was alway with Him, though men knew it not.   How could it be otherwise? So far as concerned His Divine nature, He and the Father were " one."

How any one, in the face of this passage, can deny that the Father and the Son are two distinct Persons, it is very hard to understand.   When one person is heard speaking to another, common sense seems to point out that there are two persons, and not one.

Hammond maintains that there really was a loud clap of thunder, as well as a voice from heaven.   Burkitt also seems to think the same, and compares it to the thunder which accompanied the giving of the law at Sinai.

[*I have both glorified it and will glorify it again.*]   This solemn sentence—far more solemn in the pithy and expressive Greek language than it can possibly be made in our translation— admits, as Augustine says, of being interpreted two ways.

(a) It may be applied solely and entirely to the Lord Jesus Christ Himself. It would then be a special declaration of the Father to the Son: "I have glorified my name in Thy incarnation, Thy miracles, Thy words, Thy works. I will yet glorify it again in Thy voluntary suffering for mankind, Thy death, Thy resurrection, and Thy ascension."

Lightfoot thinks there is a special reference to our Lord's conflict with the devil. "I have glorified my name in the victory Thou formerly didst obtain over Satan's temptation in the wilderness. I will glorify my name again, in the victory Thou shalt have in this conflict also."

(b) It may be applied to the whole course of God's dealings with creation from the beginning. It would then be a declaration of the Father: "I have continually glorified my name in all the dispensations which have been,—before the flood, in the days of the patriarchs, in the time of Moses, under the law, under the judges, under the kings. I will yet glorify it once more at the end of this dispensation, by finishing up the types and figures, and accomplishing the work of man's redemption."

Which of these views is the true one, I cannot pretend to decide. Either makes excellent divinity, and is reasonable and consistent. But we have no means of ascertaining which is correct. If I have any opinion on the point, I lean to the second view.

29 —[*The people therefore, etc.*] This verse apparently is meant to describe the various opinions of the crowd which stood around our Lord, about the voice which spoke to Him. Some, who were standing at some little distance, and were not listening very attentively, said it thundered. Others, who were standing close by, and paying great attention, declared that an invisible being, an angel, must have spoken. Both parties entirely agreed on one point. Something uncommon had happened. An extraordinary noise had been heard, which to some sounded like thunder, and to others like words. But nobody said they heard nothing at all.

That the voice must have been very loud, seems proved by the supposition that it was "thunder." That the reality and existence of angels formed part of the popular creed of the Jews, seems proved by the readiness of some to take up the idea that an angel had spoken.

Some think that the Greeks before mentioned, not knowing the Hebrew language in which probably the voice spoke, fancied the voice was thunder, and the Jews of the crowd thought it an angel's voice.

30 —[*Jesus answered... This voice...not...me...your sakes.*] In this verse our Lord tells the Jews the purpose of this miraculous voice. It was not for His sake,—to comfort Him and help Him;

but for their sakes,—to be a sign and a witness to them. The
voice could tell Him nothing that He did not know. It was
meant to show them what they did not know, or doubted.
The sentence would be more literally rendered, "Not on account of Me was this voice, but on account of you." It was
just one more public miraculous evidence of His Divine mission,
and apparently the last that was given. The first evidence was
a voice at His baptism, and the last a voice just before His
crucifixion.

Augustine remarks: "Here Christ shows that his voice was
not to make known to Him what He already knew, but to them
to whom it was meet to be made known."

1 —[*Now is the judgment of this world.*] This is undeniably a
difficult saying. The difficulty lies principally in the meaning of
the word "judgment."

(*a*) Some, as Barnes, think that it means, "This is the crisis,
or most important time in the world's history." I cannot receive
this. I doubt whether the Greek word used here, will ever bear
the signification of our word "crisis." That our Lord's atoning
death was a crisis in the world's history, is undoubtedly true.
But that is not the question. The question is, what do the Greek
words mean?

(*b*) Some, as Theophylact and Euthymius, think it means,
"Now is the vengeance of this world."—"I will cast out him
by whom the world has been enslaved."—I doubt this also.

(*c*) Some, as Zwingle, think that "judgment" means the dis-
crimination or separation between the believing and the unbelieving in the world. (Compare John ix. 39.)

(*d*) Some, as Calvin, Brentius, Beza, Bucer, Hutcheson,
Flacius, and Gualter, think that "judgment" means the reformation, or setting in right order of the world.

(*e*) Some, as Grotius, Gerhard, Poole, Toletus, and à Lapide,
think "judgment" means the deliverance, and setting free from
bondage, of this world.

(*f*) Some, as Pearce, think it means, "Now is the Jewish
world or nation about to be judged or condemned for rejecting
Me."

(*g*) Some, as Bengel, think it means, "Now is the judgment
concerning this world, as to who is hereafter to be the rightful
possessor of it."

I take it that the word we render "judgment" can only mean
condemnation, and that the meaning of the sentence is this:
"Now has arrived the season when a sentence of condemnation
shall be passed by my death on the whole order of things which
has prevailed in the world since the creation. The world shall
no longer be let alone, and left to the devil and the powers of

darkness. I am about to spoil them of their dominion by my redeeming work, and to condemn and set aside the dark, godless order of things which has so long prevailed upon earth. It has been long winked at and tolerated by my Father. The time has come when it will be tolerated no longer. This very week, by my crucifixion, the religious systems of the world shall receive a sentence of condemnation." This seems Bullinger and Rollock's view, and I agree with it.

In order to realize the full meaning of this sentence, we must call to mind the extraordinary condition of all the world, with the exception of Palestine, before Christ's death. To an extent of which now we can form no conception, it was a world without God, plunged in idolatry, worshipping devils,—in open rebellion against God. (Compare 1 Cor. x. 20.) When Christ died, this order of things received its sentence of condemnation.

Rollock says: "I understand, by this judgment, the condemnation of that sin of which the world was so full when Christ came, and which had reigned from Adam to Moses." Of this undisturbed reign of idolatry Christ's advent made an end.

Augustine, on this verse, says: "The devil kept possession of mankind, holding men as criminals bound over to punishment by the handwriting of their sins, having dominion in the hearts of the unbelieving, dragging them, deceived and captive, to the worship of the creature, for which they had deserted the Creator. But by the faith of Christ, confirmed by His death and resurrection, through His blood shed for the remission of sins, thousands of believing persons obtain deliverance from the dominion of the devil, are joined to the body of Christ, and quickened by His Spirit as faithful members, under so great a Head. This it was that He called *judgment*."

[*Now shall...prince of this world...cast out.*] In this remarkable sentence there can be no doubt that Satan is meant by the "prince of this world." Up to the time of our Lord's redeeming work, the entire world was in a certain sense completely under his dominion. When Christ came and died for sinners, Satan's usurped power was broken, and received a deadly blow. Heathenism, and idolatry, and devil-worship no longer governed all the earth except Palestine, as they had done for four thousand years, because undisturbed. In a wonderful and mysterious manner Christ on the cross "spoiled principalities and powers, and made a show of them openly, triumphing over them." (Coloss. ii. 15.) To this victory our Lord clearly refers. "Now in this week, by my vicarious death as man's Redeemer on the cross, Satan, the Prince of this world, shall receive a deadly blow, and be dethroned from his supremacy over man, and cast out. The head of the serpent shall be bruised."

Of course our Lord did not mean that Satan would be "cast out" of this world entirely, and tempt it no more. That will be done at the second advent, we know from Rev. xx. ; but it was not done at the first. It only means that he should be cast out of a large portion of the dominion, and power, and undisturbed authority he had hitherto exercised over men's souls.—The result of the change which took place in this respect, when Christ died, is perhaps not enough considered by Christians. We probably have a very inadequate idea of the awful extent to which Satan carried his dominion over men's souls before the "kingdom of heaven" was set up. Bodily possession, familiar spirits, wizards, heathen oracles, heathen mysteries,—all these are things which before the crucifixion of Christ were much more real and powerful than we suppose.—And why ? Because the "prince of this world" had not yet been cast out. He had a power over men's bodies and minds far greater than he has now. When Christ came to the cross He did battle with Satan, won a victory over him, stripped him of a large portion of his authority, and cast him out of a large portion of his dominion. Does not the whole of the vision in Rev. xii. 7—17, point to this ? This view is supported by Lightfoot.

This sentence shows clearly the reality and power of the devil. How any one can say there is no devil, in the face of such expressions as "the prince of this world," is strange. How any one can scoff and think lightly of a being of such mighty power, is stranger still. The true Christian, however, may always take comfort in the thought that Satan is a vanquished enemy. He was stripped of a large part of his dominion at Christ's first advent. He is still "going to and fro," seeking whom he may devour; but he shall be completely bound at the second advent. (1 Pet. v. 8; Rom. xxvi. 20; Rev. xx. 2.)

The whole verse appears to me inexplicable, unless we receive and hold the doctrine of Christ's death being an atonement and satisfaction for man's sin, and a payment of man's debt to God. That thought underlies the deep statement here made of the mighty work about to be done by our Lord, in the week of His crucifixion, against the prince of this world. Once adopt the modern notion that Christ's death was only a beautiful example of self-sacrifice and martyrdom for truth, like that of Socrates, and you can make nothing of this verse. Hold, on the other hand, the old doctrine that Christ's death was the payment of man's debt, and the redemption of man's soul from the power of sin and the devil, and the whole verse is lighted up and made comparatively clear.

Augustine observes: "The Lord in this verse was foretelling that which He knew,—that after His passion and glorifying, throughout the whole world many a people would believe, within whose hearts the devil once was, whom when by faith they renounce, then is he cast out." He also says that what formerly took place in a few hearts, like those of the patriarchs and prophets, or very few individuals, is now foretold as about to take place in many a great people.

Euthymius remarks, that as the first Adam by eating of the

tree was cast out of Paradise, so the second Adam by dying on the tree cast the devil out of his usurped dominion in the world.

Bucer thinks there is a latent reference to our Lord's former words about the "strong man armed keeping his house," till a stronger comes upon him and spoils him. (Luke xi. 21, 22.)

32.—[*And I...lifted up...draw all men unto me.*]. In this remarkable verse our Lord plainly points to His own crucifixion, or being lifted up on the cross. It is the same expression that He used to Nicodemus: "As Moses lifted up the serpent in the wilderness, even so must the Son of man be lifted up." (John iii. 15.)

The promise, "I will draw all men unto Me," must, I think, mean that our Lord after His crucifixion would draw men of all nations and kindreds and tongues to Himself, to believe on Him and be His disciples. Once crucified, He would become a great centre of attraction, and draw to Himself, and release from the devil's usurped power, vast multitudes of all peoples and countries, to be His servants and followers. Up to this time all the world had blindly hastened after Satan and followed him. After Christ's crucifixion great numbers would turn away from the power of Satan and become Christians.

The promise doubtless looks even further than this. It points to a time when every knee shall bow to the crucified Son of God, and every tongue confess that Jesus is the Lord. The whole world shall finally become the kingdom of our God and of His Christ.

Of course the words must not be pressed too far. We must not think that they support the deadly heresy of universal salvation. We must not suppose them to mean that all men shall be actually saved by Christ's crucifixion, any more than we must suppose that Christ actually "lights" every one in the world. (See John i. 9.) The analogy of other texts shows plainly that the only reasonable sense is, that Christ's crucifixion would have a "drawing" influence on men of all nations, Gentiles as well as Jews. Scripture and facts under our eyes both show us that all persons are not actually drawn to Christ. Many live and die and are lost in unbelief.

The word "draw" is precisely the same that is used in John vi. 44: "No man can come to Me except the Father draw him." Yet I doubt whether the meaning is precisely the same. In the one case it is the drawing of election, when the Father chooses and draws souls. In the other case, it is the drawing influence which Christ exercises on labouring and heavy-laden sinners, when He draws them by His spirit to come to Him and believe. The subjects of either "drawing" are the same men and women, and the drawing in either case is irresistible. All who are drawn to believe are drawn both by the Father and the Son. Without this drawing no one would ever come to Christ.

The idea of some, that the verse may be applied to the lifting up or exalting of Christ by ministers in their *preaching*, is utterly baseless, and a mere play upon words. That the preaching of Christ will always do good, more or less, and draw souls to Christ by God's blessing, is no doubt true. But it is not the doctrine of this text, and ought to be dismissed as an unfair accommodation of Scriptural language.

Euthymius observes that the mission of Christ began to draw souls at once, as in the case of the penitent thief and the centurion.

33 —[*This he said...what death...die.*] This explanatory comment of St. John on our Lord's words is evidently intended to make His meaning plain. He spoke of " being lifted up " with a special reference to His being lifted up on the cross.—Of course it is just possible that the reference is to the drawing all men, and that it means, " He spoke of drawing all men, with a reference to His death being a sacrificial and atoning death, which would affect the position of all men." But I doubt this being so correct a view as the other.

" He should die," is literally, He was " about to die."

It is curious that, in the face of this verse, some, as Bucer and Diodati, maintain that our Lord by " being lifted up," refers to His exaltation into heaven after His resurrection. They think that then, and not till then, could He be said to " draw " men. I cannot see anything in this. Our Lord appears to me to teach plainly, that after His crucifixion, and through the virtue of His crucifixion, He would draw men. That " lifting up " means crucifixion is, in my judgment, plainly taught by John iii. 15.

JOHN XII. 34—43

34 The people answered him, We have heard out of the law that Christ abideth forever: and how sayest thou, The Son of man must be lifted up? who is this Son of man?

35 Then Jesus said unto them, Yet a little while is the light with you. Walk while ye have the light, lest darkness come upon you; for he that walketh in darkness knoweth not whither he goeth.

36 While ye have light, believe in the light, that ye may be the children of light. These things spake Jesus, and departed, and did hide himself from them,

37 But though he had done so many miracles before them, yet they believed not on him:

38 That the saying of Esaias the prophet might be fulfilled, which he spake, Lord, who hath believed our report? and to whom hath the arm of the Lord been revealed?

39 Therefore they could not believe, because that Esaias said again,

40 He hath blinded their eyes, and hardened their heart; that they should not see with *their* eyes, nor understand with *their* heart, and be converted, and I should heal them.

41 These things said Esaias, when he saw his glory, and spake of him.

42 Nevertheless among the chief rulers also many believed on him: but because of the Pharisees they did not confess *him*, lest they should be put out of the synagogue:

43 For they loved the praise of men more than the praise of God.

WE may learn, from these verses, the *duty of using present opportunities.* The Lord Jesus says to us all, " Yet a little while is the light with you. Walk while ye have the light, lest darkness come upon you.—While ye have light believe in the light." Let us not think that these things were only spoken for the sake of the Jews. They were written for us also, upon whom the ends of the world are come.

The lesson of the words is generally applicable to the whole professing Church of Christ. Its time for doing good in the world is short and limited. The throne of grace will not always be standing : it will be removed one day, and the throne of judgment will be set up in its place. The door of salvation by faith in Christ will not always be open : it will be shut one day forever, and the number of God's elect will be completed. The fountain for all sin and uncleanness will not always be accessible ; the way to it will one day be barred, and there will remain nothing but the lake that burns with fire and brimstone.

These are solemn thoughts ; but they are true. They cry aloud to sleeping Churchmen and drowsy congregations, and ought to arouse great searchings of heart. " Can nothing more be done to spread the Gospel at home and abroad? Has every means been tried for extending the knowledge of Christ crucified? Can we lay our hands on our hearts, and say that the Churches have left nothing undone in the matter of missions? Can we look forward to the Second Advent with no feelings of humiliation, and say that the talents of wealth, and influence, and opportunities have not been buried in the ground?"—Such questions may well humble us, when we look, on one side, at the state of professing Christendom, and, on the other, at the state of the heathen world. We must confess with shame that the Church is not walking worthy of its light.

But the lesson of the words is specially applicable to ourselves as individuals. Our own time for getting good is short and limited; let us take heed that we make good use of it. Let us " walk while we have the light." Have we Bibles? Let us not neglect to read them. —Have we the preached Gospel? Let us not linger halting between two opinions, but believe to the saving of our souls.—Have we Sabbaths? Let us not waste them in idleness, carelessness, and indifference, but throw our whole hearts into their sacred employments, and turn them to good account.—Light is about us and around us and near us on every side. Let us each resolve to walk in the light while we have it, lest we find ourselves at length cast out into outer darkness forever. It is a true saying of an old divine, that the recollection of lost and misspent opportunities will be the very essence of hell.

We may learn, secondly, from these verses, *the desperate hardness of the human heart.* It is written of our Lord's hearers at Jerusalem, that, " though he had done so many miracles before them, yet they believed not on Him."

We err greatly if we suppose that seeing wonderful things will ever convert souls. Thousands live and die in this delusion. They fancy if they saw some miraculous sight, or witnessed some supernatural exercise of Divine grace, they would lay aside their doubts, and at once become decided Christians. It is a total mistake. Nothing short of a new heart and a new nature implanted in us by the Holy Ghost, will ever make us real disciples of Christ. Without this, a miracle might raise within us a little temporary excitement; but, the novelty once gone, we should find ourselves just as cold and unbelieving as the Jews.

The prevalence of unbelief and indifference in the present day ought not to surprise us. It is just one of the evidences of that mighty foundation-doctrine, the total corruption and fall of man. How feebly we grasp and realize that doctrine is proved by our surprise at human incredulity. We only half believe the heart's deceitfulness. Let us read our Bibles more attentively, and search their contents more carefully. Even when Christ wrought miracles and preached sermons, there were numbers of His hearers who remained utterly unmoved. What right have we to wonder if the hearers of modern sermons in countless instances remain unbelieving? "The disciple is not greater than his Master." If even the hearers of Christ did not believe, how much more should we expect to find unbelief among the hearers of His ministers! Let the truth be spoken and confessed. Man's obstinate unbelief is one among many indirect proofs that the Bible is true. The clearest prophecy in Isaiah begins with the solemn question, " Who hath believed? " (Isai. liii. 1.)

We may learn, thirdly, from these verses, *the amazing power which the love of the world has over men*. We read that " among the chief rulers many believed on Christ; but because of the Pharisees they did not confess Him, lest they should be put out of the synagogue. For they loved the praise of men more than the praise of God."

These unhappy men were evidently convinced that Jesus was the true Messiah. Reason, and intellect, and mind, and conscience, obliged them secretly to admit that no one could do the miracles which He did, unless God was with Him, and that the preacher of Nazareth really was the Christ of God. But they had not courage to confess it.   They dared not face the storm of ridicule, if not of persecution, which confession would have entailed. And so, like cowards, they held their peace, and kept their convictions to themselves.

Their case, it may be feared, is a sadly common one. There are thousands of people who know far more in religion then they act up to. They know they ought to come forward as decided Christians. They know that they are not living up to their light. But the fear of man keeps them back.   They are afraid of being laughed at, jeered at, and despised by the world. They dread losing the good opinion of society, and the favourable judgment of men and women like themselves.   And so they go on from to year to year, secretly ill at ease and dissatisfied with themselves,—knowing too much of religion to be happy in the world, and clinging too much to the world to enjoy any religion.

Faith is the only cure for soul ailments like this. A believing view of an unseen God, and unseen Christ an unseen heaven, and an unseen judgment-day,—this is the grand secret of overcoming the fear of man. The expulsive power of a new principle is required to heal the disease. "This is the victory that overcometh the world, even our faith." (1 John v. 4.) Let us pray for faith, if we would conquer that deadly enemy of souls, the fear of man and the love of man's praise. And if we have any faith, let us pray for more. Let our daily cry be, "Lord, increase our faith."   We may easily have too much money, or too much worldly prosperity; but we can never have too much faith.

NOTES JOHN XII 34—43

34 —[*The people answered, etc.*]   This verse supplies a remarkable instance of the perverse and hardened blindness of the Jews in our Lord's time. They pretended to be unable to reconcile the Lord's language about being "lifted up," with the Old Testa-

ment prophecies about the eternity and never dying of Christ.—
That " lifted up " meant being put to death on the cross, they
seem to have understood. That our Lord, or the Son of man, as
He called Himself, claimed to be the Christ, they quite understood. What they stumbled at was the idea of the eternal Christ
being put to death. They had got hold of the idea of a glorious,
eternal Messiah. They had not got hold of the idea of a suffering, dying Messiah.

Of course they were right in holding that " Christ abideth forever." It is the universal doctrine of the Old Testament. (Compare Isai. ix. 7; Psalm cx. 4; Ezek. xxxvii. 25; Daniel vii. 14;
Micah iv. 7.) Our Lord had never for a moment denied this.
He was the promised Saviour, who, as Gabriel said to Mary, was
to "reign over the house of Jacob forever." (Luke i. 33.)

On the other hand, they were entirely wrong in not understanding that Christ had to suffer before He reigned, and to go to
the cross before He wore the crown. They were wrong in not
seeing that His sacrifice as our Substitute and our Passover was
the very corner-stone of revealed religion, and that the very
" law" of which they made so much, pointed to His sacrifice as
clearly as to His eternal glory. They forgot that Isaiah says that
Messiah is to be " brought as a lamb to the slaughter," and that
Daniel speaks of His being " cut off." (Isai. liii. 7; Dan. ix. 26.)

The words " we " and " thou," in this verse, in the Greek are
emphatic. " WE Jews have always been taught to believe the
eternity of Messiah. THOU, on the other hand, sayest that Messiah must be put to death, and lifted up on the cross. How is
this? How are we to understand it? "

" The law," in this verse, must evidently be taken for the
whole of the Old Testament Scriptures.

It is worthy of remark that the Jews charge our Lord with
saying " the Son of Man must be lifted up." Yet our Lord in
the last verse but one had not mentioned the Son of man, but
had only said, " I, if I be lifted up."—It is also singular that
our Lord nowhere uses the expression " lifted up " except in His
conversation with Nicodemus, in John iii. 14. We must therefore either suppose that the Jews referred to the saying of
Christ when He spoke to Nicodemus, (which is very unlikely;) —
or else that the expression, "The Son of man must be lifted
up," was so frequently on our Lord's lips, that the Jews caught it
up and pressed it on Him here;—or else that our Lord so frequently spoke of Himself as the Son of man, that when He
said, " If I be lifted up," the Jews thought it equivalent to saying, " If the Son of man be lifted up."

The question " Who is this Son of man?" can hardly imply
that the Jews did not know that Christ was speaking of Himself. Does it not rather mean, " Who, and what kind of a person dost Thou claim to be, calling Thyself the Son of man, and
yet talking of being lifted up on the cross? Dost Thou really

mean that one and the same person can be a dying person, and yet also the eternal Christ? Dost Thou claim to be the eternal Christ, and yet talk of being lifted up on a cross? Explain this apparent contradiction, for we cannot understand it."—It is just the old story over again. The Jews could not and would not understand that Messiah was to suffer as well as to reign, to die as a Sacrifice as well as to appear in glory. They could not and would not see that the two things could be reconciled, and could meet in one person. Hence their perplexity exhibited in the question of the text.

The title, "Son of man," is first found applied to Messiah in Daniel vii. 13. We cannot doubt that the Jews understood and remembered that passage.

Let us note that a half knowledge of Scripture, a suppression of some texts, and a misapplication of other texts, will account for a large portion of mistakes in religion. In this way people get a heresy or a crotchet into their heads on some doctrinal point, and seem blind to the truth. No heresies are so obstinately defended, and so difficult to meet, as those which are based on a perverted view of some portion of Scripture. In reading our Bibles, we must be careful to give every part and portion its due weight.

Let us remember, before we judge the blindness of the Jews too severely in this place, that many Christians are just as slow to see the whole truth about the second advent of Christ and His coming glory, as the Jews were to see the whole truth about the first advent and the cross. Multitudes apply texts to the first advent which only belong to the second advent, and are just as much prejudiced against the second personal coming of Christ to reign, as the Jews were against the first personal advent to suffer. Not a few Christians, I fear, are ready to say, "We have heard out of the Scriptures that Christ was to come in humiliation to be crucified; and how say ye, then, that Christ must come in power to reign?"

The expression, "this," is rather emphatic, and has something contemptuous about it. "We have heard of a Son of man who is eternal. Who is THIS Son of man about to be lifted up on the cross, of whom you speak?"

35 [*Then Jesus said unto them..light with you.*] It is noteworthy that our Lord makes no direct answer to the question of the Jews. He only warns them, in a very solemn manner, of the danger they were in of letting their day of grace slip away unimproved. He draws a figure from the light of day, and the acknowledged importance of walking and journeying while we have the light. By "the light" He evidently means Himself. "I, the Light of the world, am only going to be with you a very little longer. My day is drawing to a close. The sun will soon set." (Compare Jer. xiii. 15.)

Here, as elsewhere, we see how clearly and distinctly our

Lord saw His own approaching death and withdrawal from the world.

Ecolampadius thinks that there is a latent connection between this verse and the question of the Jews. " You ask who is this Son of man? I reply that He is the Light of the world, as I have often told you. Like the sun, He is about to be eclipsed, or withdrawn from your eyes very shortly. Make haste, and delay not to believe on Him."

Gerhard justly remarks on this sentence, how far from infallibility the best of the Fathers were. Even Augustine, from his slight acquaintance with Greek, renders the sense, " There is yet a *little light* in your *hearts !* "

A German commentator remarks, that Christ seems here to rebuke this quibbling and questioning about phrases. " There was no time now for sophistry and circumlocution. It was a solemn matter. How differently ought they to demean themselves in their little residue of time, and not to fritter it away with affected contradictions ! How earnestly they ought to seek at once for refuge to the light, and shield themselves against coming darkness ! "

[*Walk while ye have the light.*] This solemn exhortation was meant to urge the Jews to do for their souls' safety, what a wise traveller would do to get safely to his journey's end. "Enter in at the strait gate: walk in the narrow way: flee from the city of destruction: set out on your journey towards eternal life: rise, and be moving, while I and my Gospel are close to you, shining on you, and within your reach."

Hengstenberg remarks, that " walking here denotes activity, and stands opposed to an idle and indifferent rest."

[*Lest darkness come upon you.*] Our Lord here warns the Jews of the things to be feared, if they neglected His advice. Darkness would overtake, catch, and come upon them. He would leave the world, and return to His Father. They would be left in a state of judicial darkness and blindness as a nation, and, with the exception of an election, would be given over to untold calamities, scattering, and misery. How true these words were, we know from the history of the Jews, written by Josephus, after our Lord left the world. His account of the extraordinary state of the inhabitants of Jerusalem, during the siege of the city by Titus, is the best commentary on the text before us. The state of the Jews, as a nation, during the last days of Jerusalem, can only be described as "darkness that might be felt."

[*For he...darkness...knoweth not...goeth.*] This is an argument drawn from the acknowledged helplessness of one who attempts a difficult journey in a dark night. He cannot see his way. He only gets into trouble, and perhaps loses his life. This was exactly the case of the Jewish nation, after our Lord left the world. Up to the time of the destruction of the temple, they seemed like a nation of madmen, and a people judicially blinded,—conscious that they were in a wrong position, struggling furiously to get out of it, and yet only plunging deeper into the mire of hopeless misery, till Titus took the city, and carried the whole race into captivity. They had put out their own eyes by rejecting Christ, and were like a strong man blinded, maddened by a sense of his own misery, and yet impotent to get out of it.

36 —[*While light...believe...children of light.*] This sentence would have been more accurately rendered, "While ye have THE Light;" that is, "while ye have ME, the Light of the world, with you." It is a final, affectionate entreaty to the Jews repeating in more plain words the exhortation of the last verse, "To walk in the light." It is as though our Lord said, "Once more I beseech you to believe in Me as the Light of the world, while I am with you." The end and object for which they are to believe is also added, "That ye may become my children, have light in your hearts, light in your consciences, light in your lives, light on your present path, light in your future prospects." There can be no doubt that the expression "children of light" is a Hebraism, signifying "to be brought in close connection with or under the full influence of light."

Let us note that here, as elsewhere, believing is the first step, the one thing needful. The exhortation is still to be offered to every sinner directly and personally,—"Believe, that thou mayest be a child of light."

[*These things...spake...departed...hide...them.*] We know not exactly on what day in the last week of our Lord's life the words just recorded had been spoken. The sentence before us certainly seems to mark a break and interval, and we can hardly suppose that the short address from the forty-fourth verse to the end of the chapter was spoken the same day, or was continuously connected with the discourse ending in this verse.

To me it seems probable that our Lord "departed" to Bethany after the miracle of the Voice from the heavens, and the commotion that followed it.—The words of our English version "Did hide Himself," seem to me rather stronger than the Greek warrants. It would be more literally, "Was concealed from them." Whether this was by miracle, as on other occasions, is not clear.

Calvin seems to think that our Lord only departed from the hearers immediately round Him, and went to the temple, where He met with another audience, of a more believing kind. Flacius, too, thinks it was only a short and temporary withdrawal. Poole, on the contrary, takes the view that I adopt, and says that our Lord withdrew to Bethany.

37 —[*But though...so many miracles...them.*] This verse begins a long parenthetical comment, which John was inspired to make

at this point, on the peculiar unbelief of the Jerusalem Jews. He remarks on the singular hardness of this section of the nation, in the face of the singularly strong evidence which they enjoyed of Christ's Messiahship.

The expression, "So many miracles," seems to point out that the miracles recorded by St. John are by no means all the miracles that our Lord performed in and near Jerusalem. Beside the purifying of the temple, John only records three : the healing of the impotent man, the healing of the blind, and the raising of Lazarus. (John v., ix., xi.) Yet John expressly speaks of *miracles*, (both here, and in John ii. 23,) and the Pharisees say, " This Man doeth many miracles." (John xi. 47.)

The Greek word rendered " before," is very strong. It is the same that is " In the sight of," in 1 Thess. i. 3 ; and " In the presence of," in 1 Thess. ii. 19.

[*Yet they believed not on him.*] In estimating the peculiar hardness and unbelief of the Jews at Jerusalem, it is worth remembering that all experience proves that where there is the greatest quantity of the form of religion, there is often the greatest proportion of formality and unbelief. The places where men become most familiar with the outside and ceremonial of Christianity are precisely the places where the heart seems to become most hard. Witness the state of Rome at this day. Witness too often the state of cathedral cities in our own land. We need not wonder that the city in which was the temple, the daily sacrifice, and the priesthood, was the most unbelieving place in Palestine.

38 —[*That...saying...Esaias...fulfilled...spake.*] We must not suppose this means that the Jews did not believe, *in order that* the prophecy of Isaiah might be fulfilled. This would be teaching sheer fatalism, and would destroy man's responsibility. The true meaning is, " So that by this unbelief the saying of Isaiah was fulfilled." (See John v. 20 ; Rom. v. 20 ; 2 Cor. i. 17.)

Chrysostom observes : " It was not because Isaiah spake that they believed not, but because they were not about to believe, that he spake."

Augustine says : " The Lord, by the prophet, did predict the unbelief of the Jews,—predict, however, not cause. It does not follow that the Lord compels any man to sin, because He knows men's future sins."

Theophylact and Euthymius say much the same.

[*Lord, who...believed our report.*] This question begins the well-known fifty-third chapter of Isaiah, which describes with such extraordinary accuracy our Lord's sufferings. It is certainly a most singular fact, that the very chapter which the Jews in every age have been most obstinately unwilling to believe, should begin with this question. It is a Hebraism, tantamount to saying, " Nobody believes our report." The unbelief of the

Jews was a thing as clearly foretold in Scripture as the sufferings of Christ. If they had not been unbelieving, the Scriptures would have been untrue.

[*To whom...arm of...Lord revealed.*] The expression, "Arm of the Lord," is thought by Augustine to mean Christ Himself. It may be so. If not, it must mean, "To whom is the Lord's power in raising up a Redeemer and an atoning sacrifice revealed?" That is, the Lord's power is revealed to and received by none. The question here again is a Hebraism, equivalent to an assertion.

Bullinger observes, that "some might perhaps wonder that the Jews did not believe Jesus to be the Messiah. To this John replies, that Isaiah long ago foretold that they would prove an unreasonable and unbelieving nation."

The quotation of Isaiah in this place is strong evidence that the fifty-third chapter of this prophecy applies to Christ, and none else.

39 —[*Therefore they could not believe, because, etc.*] This is undeniably a difficult verse. It cannot of course mean that the Jews were unable to believe, although really desirous to do so, and were prevented by the prophecy of Isaiah. What, then, can it mean? The following paraphrase is offered: "This was the cause why they could not believe,—they were in that state of judicial blindness and hardness which Isaiah had described. They were justly given over to this state, because of their many sins, and for this cause they had no power to believe."

"Therefore," is literally, "on account of this." It cannot, I think, look backward, but forward. (Compare x. 17, and xii. 18.)

"They could not," is literally, "they were not able." It precisely describes the moral inability of a thoroughly hardened and wicked man to believe. He is thoroughly under the mastery of a hardened and seared conscience, and has, as it were, lost the power of believing.—They had no will to believe, and so they had no power. They could have believed if they would, but they would not, and so they could not. The expression is parallel to the well-known words, "No man can come to Me, except the Father which hath sent Me draw him." There the meaning is, "No man has any will to come unless he is drawn, and so no man can come."

Even in our own English language the expression, "could not," is sometimes used in the sense of "would not." Thus the brethren of Joseph "hated him, and could not speak peaceably of him." (Gen. xxxvii. 4.)

The word "because" is a needlessly strong rendering of the Greek. It would be just as correctly translated "for."

Chrysostom observes; "In many places Christ is wont to term

choice power. So, " The world *cannot* hate you, but Me it hateth." So in common conversation a man says, " I cannot love this or that person, calling the force of his will power."

Augustine says : " If I be asked why they could not believe, I answer in a word, Because they would not."—He also says, " It is said of the Omnipotent, He *cannot* deny Himself : and this is the power of the Divine will. So ' they could not believe ' is the fault of the human will."

Zwingle also says that " could not " means " would not."

Ecolampadius observes : " They would not, and therefore they could not believe. God is wont to punish those who commit some sin by giving them up to other sins." This, he remarks, is the heaviest judgment to which we can be given up,—to have sins punished by sins, that is, by being let alone to commit them.

Bishop Hall says : " They could not believe, because, as Isaiah says, in a just punishment for their maliciousness and contempt, God had stricken them with a reprobate sense, so that their eyes were blinded."

Quesnel says here : " Let us bewail this inability of will with which, by means of Adam's sin, we are all born, and which, by our own sins, we daily increase. Let us continually have recourse to Him who said, ' without Me ye can do nothing,' and, ' No man can come to Me, unless the Father draw him.' "

40 —[*He hath blinded their eyes, etc.*] This quotation is a free paraphrase of the general view of a verse in Isaiah vi. 9, 10. I think it can only have one meaning. That meaning is, that " God had given over the Jews to judicial blindness, as a punishment for their long-continued and obstinate rejection of His warnings." That God does in some cases give people over. as a punishment for obstinate unbelief, and that He may ' be justly termed the cause of such unbelief, is I think, quite plain in Scripture. Pharaoh is a case in point. He obstinately refused God's warnings, and so at last He was given over, and God is said to have " hardened his heart. " Compare Joshua xi. 20 : " It was of the Lord to harden their hearts, that they should come against Israel in battle, that He might destroy them." (So Deut. ii. 30; 1 Sam. ii. 25; Rom. ix. 18.)

This is no doubt a very solemn and awful subject. It seems at first sight to make God the author of man's destruction, But surely a moment's reflection will show us that God is a Sovereign in punishing, and may punish in any way he pleases. Some He cuts off suddenly the moment they sin. Others He gives over to judicial blindness, and ceases to strive with their consciences. " The Judge of all the earth will certainly do right." Those whom He is said to " harden and blind " will always be found to be persons whom He had previously warned, exhorted, and constantly summoned to repent. And never is He said to harden and blind, and give men up to judicial hardness and

blindness, till after a long course of warnings.   This was
certainly the case with Pharaoh and with the Jews.

The consequence of God blinding and hardening a person is
that he does not "see" his danger with his eyes, or "understand" his position with his heart.   The result is that he holds
on his way unconverted, and dies without his soul's disease
being healed.—"Seeing" and "understanding" are essential
parts of conversion.   No simpler reason can be given why
myriads of church-goers continue careless, unaffected, unmoved, and unconverted: they neither "see" nor "understand." God alone can give them seeing eyes and understanding
hearts, and ministers cannot.   And one solemn reason why
many live and die in this state is, that they have resisted God's
warnings, and are justly punished already with a judicial blindness and hardness, by Him whom they have resisted.

The key to the whole difficulty, after all, lies in the answer
we are prepared to give to the question, "Is God just in
punishing the sinner?"—The true Christian and honest Bible
reader will find no difficulty in answering that question in the
affirmative.   Once grant that God is just in punishing the ungodly, and there is an end of the problem.   God may punish by
giving over the obstinate sinner to a reprobate mind, as really
as by sentencing him to everlasting fire at the last day.

One thing only must never be forgotten. God "willeth not the
death of any sinner." He is willing to soften the hardest heart,
and to open the blind eyes of the greatest sinner. In dealing
with men about their souls we must never forget this. We may
well remind them that by hardened impenitence they may pro-
voke God to give them up. But we must also press on them
that God's mercies in Christ are infinite, and that, if they are
finally lost, they will have none but themselves to blame.

Burgon thinks that the nominative to "blinded" at the beginning of the verse is not God, but "the Jewish people;" and
that the meaning is, "This people hath blinded their own
eyes." But I cannot see that this idea can be supported by reference to Isaiah, and though it smooths over difficulties, I dare
not receive it.

Calvin thinks that the passage applies to the hardness by
which God punishes the wickedness of an ungrateful people.
They are given over justly to an unbelieving and judicially
blinded state of mind.

Poole observes: "We have this text, than which there is
none more terrible, no less than six times quoted in the New
Testament. In all places it is quoted and given as a reason for
the Jews' unbelief in Christ. (Matt. xiii. 14, 15; Mark iv. 12;
Luke viii. 10; Acts xxviii. 26, 27; Rom. xi. 8.) It is not quoted
alike in all places, but for substance it is the same. In the
original, Isaiah is made the instrumental cause. Matthew and
Luke, in Acts, mention the people themselves as the cause.

All the other texts speak of it as God's act. The thing is easily reconciled."—He then says: "The Jews first shut their own eyes, and hardened their own hearts. Thus behaving themselves, God judicially gave them up to their own lusts, permitted their hearts to harden, and suffered them to close their own eyes, so that they could not repent, believe, or return. God did not infuse any malice into their hearts, but withdrew His grace from them."

Rollock makes the wise and deep remark, that "Darkness does not blind men so much as light, unless God renews their minds by His Spirit."

It is of course noteworthy that this quotation is not given literally and exactly as it stands in the Old Testament. But it is particularly mentioned by Surenhusine, in his book upon the quotations in the New Testament, that it was a common thing with the Hebrew doctors to abbreviate texts in quoting them, and to be content with giving the general sense. The abbreviation, therefore, in the text quoted before us, would not strike John's cotemporaries as at all extraordinary.

Let us not fail to remark how "seeing, understanding, being converted, and being healed," are linked together.

41 —[*These things...Esaias...his glory...him.*] To see the full force of this verse we should read the sixth chapter of Isaiah in its entirety. We should there see a magnificent description of the Lord's glory, before which even the seraphim veiled their faces. We should observe their cry, "Holy, holy, is the Lord of Hosts!" We should mark how Isaiah says, "My eyes have seen the King, the Lord of Hosts." And then let us remember that John says, "Esaias saw Christ's glory, and spake of Christ!"—How any one, in the face of this evidence, can say that Jesus Christ is not very God, it seems hard to understand.

Lightfoot thinks that Isaiah in this chapter had a view of the glory which our Lord would have when He came to punish the Jewish nation. He thinks this is pointed out by "the posts of the door being shaken;" by "the temple being filled with smoke;" and by "the cities being wasted." (See Isaiah vi.)

42 —[*Nevertheless...rulers...many believed him.*] Here St. John mentions a fact which he would have us take together with his account of the hardened unbelief of most of the Jews. There were some who were not so utterly hardened as the rest. They were in a different state of mind: not blind, but convinced; not hardened against our Lord, but secretly persuaded that He was the Christ. Many even of the chief people at Jerusalem believed, in their own secret minds, that Jesus was the Christ. This faith no doubt was only the faith of the head, and not of the heart. But they did believe.

Let us note that there is often far more going on in people's minds than preachers are aware of. There is much secret conviction.

[*But because...Pharisees...not confess him.*] They dared not openly confess their faith in our Lord, for fear of the persecution of the Pharisees. They were cowards, and influenced by the fear of man. No wonder that our Lord spoke so strongly in other places about the duty of confessing Him.

[*Lest...put out of...synagogue.*] The thing that they feared was excommunication. We can have little idea perhaps of the extreme dread with which a Jew regarded exclusion from the visible Jewish Church. Unlike ourselves, he knew no other Church in the whole world. To be shut out of this Church was equivalent to being shut out of heaven. The dread of excommunication in the Irish Catholic Church is perhaps the nearest thing to it in our days.

43.—[*For...loved..praise...man more...God.*] St. John here tells us plainly the prevailing motive in the minds of the cowardly Jews. They loved above everything to be well thought of by their fellow-men. They thought more of having the good opinion of man than the praise of God. They could not bear the idea of being laughed at, ridiculed, reviled, or persecuted by their fellow-men. To keep in with them and have their praise, they sacrificed their own convictions, and acted contrary to their conscience. How much this feeling injures the soul is shown by our Lord's words in a former place: "How can ye believe which receive honour one from another?" (John v. 44.)

Let us remember that all over the world the same miserable motive is still ruining myriads of souls. "The fear of man bringeth a snare." (Prov. xxix. 25.) Nothing seems so difficult to overcome as the desire of pleasing man, keeping in with man, and retaining man's praise. Nothing will overcome it but thorough faith. "This is the victory that overcometh the world, even our faith." (1 John v. 4.) The expulsive power of a new principle, making us see God, Christ, heaven, hell, judgment, eternity, as realities, is the grand secret of getting the victory over the fear of man.

Poole says: "They were not willing to part with their great places in the magistracy, which brought them respect, honour, and applause from men. They valued this more than God's praise."

JOHN XII. 44—50

44 Jesus cried and said, He that believeth on me, believeth not on me, but on him that sent me.

45 And he that seeth me seeth him that sent me.

46 I am come a light into the world that whosoever believeth on me should not abide in darkness.

47 And if any man hear my words, and believe not, I judge him not: for I came not to judge the world, but to save the world.

48 He that rejecteth me, and receiveth not my words, hath one that judgeth him: the word that I have spoken, the same shall judge him in the last day.

49 For I have not spoken of myself, but the Father which sent me, he gave me a commandment, what I should say, and what I should speak.

50 And I know that his commandment is life everlasting: whatsoever I speak therefore, even as the Father said unto me, so I speak.

THESE verses throw light on two subjects which we can never understand too well. Our daily peace and our practice of daily watchfulness over ourselves are closely connected with a clear knowledge of these two subjects.

One thing shown in these verses is, *the dignity of our Lord Jesus Christ*. We find Him saying, " He that seeth Me, seeth Him that sent Me. I am come a Light into the world, that whosoever believeth on Me should not abide in darkness." Christ's oneness with the Father, and Christ's office, are clearly exhibited in these words.

Concerning the unity of the Father and the Son, we must be content to believe reverently what we cannot grasp mentally or explain distinctly. Let it suffice us to know that our Saviour was not like the prophets and patriarchs, a man sent by God the Father, a friend of God, and a witness for God. He was something far higher and greater than this. He was in His Divine nature essentially one with the Father: and in seeing Him, men saw the Father that sent Him. This is a great mystery ; but a truth of vast importance to our souls. He that casts His sins on Jesus Christ by faith is building on a rock. Believing on Christ, he believes not merely on Him, but on Him that sent Him.

Concerning the office of Christ, there can be little doubt

that in this place He compares Himself to the sun. Like the sun, He has risen on this sin-darkened world with healing on His wings, and shines for the common benefit of all mankind. Like the sun, He is the great source and centre of all spiritual life, comfort, and fertility. Like the sun, He illuminates the whole earth, and no one need miss the way to heaven, if he will only use the light offered for his acceptance.

Forever let us make much of Christ in all our religion. We can never trust Him too much, follow Him too closely, or commune with Him too unreservedly. He has all power in heaven and earth. He is able to save to the uttermost all who come to God by Him. None can pluck us out of the hand of Him who is one with the Father. He can make all our way to heaven bright and plain and cheerful, like the morning sun cheering the traveller. Looking unto Him, we shall find light in our understandings, see light on the path of life we have to travel, feel light in our hearts, and find the days of darkness, which will come sometimes, stripped of half their gloom. Only let us abide in Him, and look to Him with a single eye. There is a mine of meaning in His words, " If thine eye be single, thy whole body shall be full of light." (Matt. vi. 22.)

Another thing shown in these verses is, *the certainty of a judgment to come*. We find our Lord saying, " He that rejecteth Me, and receiveth not my words, hath One that judgeth him : the word that I have spoken, the same shall judge him in the last day."

There is a last day ! The world shall not always go on as it does now. Buying and selling, sowing and reaping, planting and building, marrying and giving in marriage,— all this shall come to an end at last. There is a time appointed by the Father when the whole machinery of creation shall stop, and the present dispensation shall be changed for another. It had a beginning, and it shall also

have an end. Banks shall at length close their doors forever. Stock exchanges shall be shut. Parliaments shall
be dissolved. The very sun, which since Noah's flood has
done his daily work so faithfully, shall rise and set no
more. Well would it be if we thought more of this day!
Rent-days, birth-days, wedding-days, are often regarded
as days of absorbing interest; but they are nothing compared to the last day.

There is a judgment coming! Men have their reckoning days, and God will at last have His. The trumpet
shall sound. The dead shall be raised incorruptible. The
living shall be changed. All, of every name and nation,
and people and tongue, shall stand before the judgment-
seat of Christ. The books shall be opened, and the evidence brought forth. Our true character will come out
before the world. There will be no concealment, no evasion, no false colouring. Every one shall give account of
himself to God, and all shall be judged according to their
works. The wicked shall go away into everlasting fire,
and the righteous into life eternal.

These are awful truths! But they are truths, and ought
to be told. No wonder that the Roman governor Felix
trembled when Paul the prisoner discoursed about "righteousness, temperance, and judgment to come." (Acts
xxiv. 25.) Yet the believer in the Lord Jesus Christ has
no cause to be afraid. For him, at any rate, there is no
condemnation, and the last assize need have no terrors.
The bias of his life shall witness for him; while the short-
comings of his life shall not condemn him. It is the man
who rejects Christ, and will not hear His call to repentance,
— he is the man who in the judgment-day will have reason to be cast down and afraid.

Let the thought of judgment to come have a practical
effect on our religion. Let us daily judge ourselves with
righteous judgment, that we may not be judged and con-

demned of the Lord. Let us so speak and so act as men
who will be judged by the law of liberty. Let us make
conscience of all our hourly conduct, and never forget that
for every idle word we must give account at the last day.
In a word, let us live like those who believe in the truth of
judgment, heaven, and hell. So living, we shall be Christians indeed and in truth, and have boldness in the day of
Christ's appearing.

Let the judgment-day be the Christian's answer and
apology when men ridicule him as too strict, too precise, and too particular in his religion. Irreligion may do
tolerably well for a season, so long as a man is in health
and prosperous, and looks at nothing but this world. But
he who believes that he must give account to the Judge of
quick and dead, at His appearing and kingdom, will never
be content with an ungodly life. He will say, "There is
a judgment. I can never serve God too much. Christ
died for me. I can never do too much for Him."

NOTES. JOHN XII 44—50

44 —[*Jesus cried and said.*] The connection between the address
which begins here and the preceding verse is not very plain or
easy to understand.

Some think that it is a continuation of the address which
ended at the thirty-sixth verse, and that John's comment and
explanation in the last seven verses must be regarded entirely
as a parenthesis. This is rather an awkward supposition, when
we look at the thirty-sixth verse, and see at the end, "These
words spake Jesus and departed, and did hide Himself." Unless
we suppose that as He was walking away, "He cried and said,
He that believeth on Me," etc., the connection seems incapable
of proof. Yet it appears most unlikely that our Lord would
have said such things as he was departing.

Others, as Theophylact, think that the address before us is an
entirely new and distinct one, and delivered on a different day
from that ending at the thirty-sixth verse: viz., on the Tuesday,
Wednesday, or Thursday, in Passion Week. This certainly appears to me the least difficult view of the subject. It would
then mean that the day after the miracle of the voice from heav-
en, Jesus appeared again publicly in Jerusalem, and "cried
and said."

However, it is useless to deny that the abrupt manner in which the verse before us and the following verses come in is a difficulty, and one which we know not exactly how to explain. One thing only is very clear: this was probably one of the last public discourses which our Lord delivered in Jerusalem, and forms a kind of conclusion to His ministry in that city. It is a short but solemn winding up of all His public testimony to the Jews.

It deserves notice, that some, as Tittman, Stier, Olshausen, Tholuck, Bloomfield, and Alford, consider the whole of the passage, from verse forty-four to the end of the chapter, to be not the words of Jesus Christ, but a statement of John the Baptist himself, concerning the doctrine Jesus taught throughout His ministry, and specially at Jerusalem. From this view, however, I strongly dissent. The beginning, "Jesus cried," etc., seems utterly inconsistent with the theory. There seems no special necessity for adopting it. A plain reader of the chapter would never dream of it.

It is worth remarking, that the Greek expression, "He cried," is very seldom applied to our Lord in the New Testament. It is found in Matt. xxvii. 50; Mark xv. 39; John vii. 28—37, and here. In every instance it means a loud cry, such as any one uses to call attention to what he has to say.

Flacius thinks that the address beginning here is a kind of peroration and summing up of all our Lord's public teaching to the Jews. In it He repeats the proclamation of His own Divine office and dignity,—the purpose for which He came, to be a "light,"—the danger of neglecting His testimony,—the certainty of a final judgment,—and the direct procession of His doctrine from the Father.

[*He that believeth...me...Him that sent me.*] This remarkable expression seems meant to proclaim, for the last time, the great truth so often insisted on by our Lord,—the entire unity between Himself and the Father. Once more Jesus declares that there is such a complete and mysterious oneness between Himself and the Father, that he who believes on Him believes not only on Him, but on Him that sent Him.—Of course the sentence cannot literally mean that the man who believes on Christ does *not* believe on Christ. But according to a mode of speech not uncommon in the New Testament, our Lord taught that all who in obedience to His call put their trust in Him, would find that they were not trusting in the Son only, but in the Father *also*. In short, to trust in the Son, the sent Saviour of sinners, is to trust also in the Father, who sent Him to save. The Son and the Father cannot be divided, though they are distinct Persons in the Trinity; and faith in the Son gives an interest in the Father. (Compare John v. 24: "He that heareth my word, and believeth on Him that sent Me." And 1 Peter i. 21: "Who by Him do believe in God.")

To draw a wide line of separation between the Father and the Son, as some do, and to represent the Father as an angry Being whom the Son appeases, is very poor theology, and the high road to Tritheism. The true doctrine is that the Godhead of Father, Son, and Holy Ghost is one, and that in the unity of the Godhead there are three Persons, and yet that there is such entire unity between the Persons, that He who believes in the Son believes also in the Father.

Zwingle thinks the latent idea is, "Do not think it is a small and insignificant thing to believe on Me. To believe on Me is the same thing as believing on God the Father, and to know Me is to know the Father."

Bucer seems to think that the address in this verse was meant to encourage those who believed Christ to be the Messiah, but were afraid of confessing Him, to come forward boldly, and acknowledge their belief.

Poole says, that in like manner God says to Samuel, "They have not rejected thee, but have rejected Me," meaning not thee *alone.* (1 Sam. viii. 7.)

45.—[*And he...seeth me seeth him that sent me.*] This deep and mysterious verse proclaims even more distinctly than the last verse the unity of the Father and the Son. It cannot mean that any one who saw Christ with his bodily eyes, did, in so seeing, behold the First Person in the Trinity. Such beholding we are distinctly told is impossible. He is one "whom no man hath seen or can see." (1 Tim. vi. 16.) What our Lord seems to mean is this: "He that seeth Me seeth not Me only, as an ordinary man or a Prophet, like John the Baptist. In seeing Me he beholds one who is one with the Father, the brightness of His glory, and the express image of His Person." (Heb. i. 3.) Of course our Lord did not literally mean, "He that sees Me does not see Me." But He meant, "He that sees Me sees not only Me, but through Me and by Me he sees Him that sent Me, for we cannot be divided."

The divinity of Jesus Christ seems incontrovertibly proved by this verse and the preceding one. If to believe in Christ is to believe in the Father, and to see Christ is to see the Father, then Jesus Christ must be equal with the Father,—very and eternal God.

The supposition of some, that the first "seeth" in this verse means nothing more than "seeth by faith," appears rather incredible. At this rate the verse would be only a repetition of the one preceding it. I prefer the idea that "seeth" means literally, "Seeth with his bodily eyes." Yet Bengel says that "seeth" refers to that vision which faith accompanies, and compares it to John vi. 40.

The object our Lord had in view in this and the preceding verse appears to have been twofold. It was partly to proclaim once more the unity of Himself and the Father. It was partly to encourage all believers in Himself, for the last time, before He was crucified. Let them know that in resting their souls on Him, they were resting not on Him alone who died on Calvary, but on one who was one with the Father, and therefore were resting on the Father.

Chrysostom observes on the expression " seeth Him that sent me,"—" What then? Is God a body? By no means. The seeing of which Jesus here speaks is that of the mind, thence showing the consubstantiality."

Barnes observes, that this language could not have been used about any mere man. To say it of Paul or Isaiah would have been blasphemy.

46 —[*I am come a light into the world, etc.*] In this sentence our Lord proclaims once more the great end and object of His coming into the world. He does it by using His favourite figure of light, and comparing Himself to the sun.—" I have come into a world full of darkness and sin, to be the source and centre of life, peace, holiness, happiness to mankind, so that every one who receives and believes in Me may be delivered from darkness and walk in full light."

Let us note that the form of language used here seems to teach that our Lord existed before He entered the world. The saints " are the light of the world," but they do not " come a light into the world." This could only be said of Christ, who was light before His incarnation, just as the sun exists and shines before it rises above the eastern horizon.

Let us note that our Lord's language seems to teach that He came to be a common Saviour and Messiah for all mankind, just as the sun shines for the good of all. It is as though He said, " I have arisen on the world like the sun in the firmament of heaven, in order that every one who is willing to believe in Me should be delivered from spiritual darkness, and be enabled to walk in the light of spiritual life."

Once more we may remember that none could give such a majestic description of His mission, but one who knew and felt that He was very God. We never find Moses, or John the Baptist, or Paul, or Peter, using such language as this.

The quantity of precious truth taught and implied in this verse is very noteworthy.—The world is in darkness.—Christ is the only light.—Faith is the only way to have interest in Christ.—He that believeth no longer abides in darkness, but has spiritual light.—He that does not believe remains and continues in a state of darkness, the prelude to hell.

The expression, " not abide in darkness," seems to have a latent reference to those Jews who were convinced of Christ's Messiahship, but were afraid to confess Him openly. Such persons are here exhorted not to remain, stick fast, and continue in darkness.

Burgon remarks on this verse: "This verse shows that (1) Christ existed before His incarnation, even as the sun exists before it appears above the eastern hills; (2) that Christ is the one Saviour of the world, even as there is only one sun; (3) that He came not for one nation, but for all, as the sun shines for all the world."

47 —[*And if any...hear...believe not.*] Having shown the privilege of those who believe in Him, our Lord now shows the danger and ruin of those who hear His teaching and yet believe not.

[*I judge him not.*] These words can only mean, "I judge him not now." To put more on them would contradict the teaching of other places, where Christ is spoken of as the Judge of all at the last day. Our Lord's meaning evidently is to teach that His First Advent was not for judgment, but for salvation, not to punish and smite as a conqueror, but to heal and save as a physician.

[*For I am not...judge...save the world.*] These words are an expansion and explanation of the preceding sentence, "I judge him not." They are evidently meant to correct the Jewish impression that Messiah was to come only to judge, to execute vengeance, to smite down His enemies, and to punish His adversaries. This impression arose from misapplied views of the Second Advent and the judgment yet to come. Our Lord, for the last time, declares that He came for no such purpose. Wicked as unbelief was, He did not come to punish it now. He came not as a judge at His First Advent, but as a Saviour.

We must take care, however, that we do not misinterpret this sentence. It affords no countenance to the dangerous doctrine of universal salvation. It does not mean that Christ came in order to actually save from hell all the inhabitants of the whole world. Such a meaning would flatly contradict many other plain passages of Scripture. What, then, does it mean?

It means that our Lord came at His First Advent not to be a judge, but a Saviour not to inflict punishment, but to provide mercy. He came to provide salvation for all the world, so that any one in the world may be saved. But no one gets any benefit from this salvation excepting those that believe.—The true key to the meaning of the sentence is the contrast between Christ's first coming and His second one. The first was to set up a throne of grace: the second will be to set up a throne of judgment. The expression in John iii. 17 is precisely parallel, —"God sent not His Son into the world to condemn the world, but that the world through Him might be saved." If it were lawful to coin a word, the true exposition of the sentence would be, "I came that the world might be *salvable.*"

But while I say all this, I am unable to see how such expressions as this, and John iii. 16, 17, can possibly be reconciled with an extreme view of particular redemption. To say, on the one hand, that Christ's death is efficacious to none but the elect and believers, is strictly true. Not all men are finally saved by Christ. There is a hell, and unbelievers and impenitent people will be found there.—But to say, on the other hand, that in no sense did Christ do anything at all for the whole world, but that He did everything for the elect alone, seems to me utterly irreconcilable with this text. Surely Christ came to provide a salvation *sufficient* for the whole " world."

I am aware that the advocates of an extreme view of particular redemption say that " the world " here does not mean " the world," but the elect of all nations, as compared to the Jews. But this view is not satisfactory, and looks very like an evasion of the plain meaning of words.

Why the same Greek word is rendered by our English translators, "judge" in this verse, and "condemn" in the parallel place in John iii. 17, it is not easy to see.

48 —[*He that rejecteth me...receiveth not my words...judgeth him.*] In this verse our Lord declares positively the future judgment and condemnation of those who reject Him, and refuse to believe His teaching.

The word we render " rejecteth " is only used here in St. John's Gospel. The idea is that of " despising, setting at naught." (See Luke x. 16.) The person described is one who despises and sets at naught Christ Himself, after seeing Him, and deliberately refuses to acknowledge Him as the Messiah, in spite of all the evidence of His miracles. He is also one who will not receive and take into his heart the doctrines preached by Christ. In short, he despises His person, and refuses to believe His teaching.—" Such a man will find at last, though I punish him not now, that there is a judgment and condemnation of him. He will not find that rejection of Me, and his unbelief, will go unpunished. He has a Judge prepared already. There is one already, though he knows it not, who will witness against him and condemn him."

[*The word...I have spoken...judge him...last day.*] Our Lord here declares that the things He publicly preached to the Jews while He was upon earth would witness finally against those who did not believe, at the last day, and be their condemnation. They will not then be able to deny that they were words of wisdom, words of mercy, words subversive of their false views, words fully explaining Christ's kingdom, words entirely in accordance with the Scriptures. And the result will be that they will be speechless. The witness of Christ's words will be unanswerable, and in consequence of that witness they will be condemned.

We see here that the words of those who speak for God are not thrown away, because they seem not believed at the time.

Christ's words, though despised and rejected by the Jews, did not fall to the ground. Those whom they did not save they will condemn. There will be a resurrection of all faithful sermons at the last day.—Great is the responsibility of preachers! Their words are always doing good, or adding to the condemnation of the lost. They are a savour of life to some, and of death to others. Great is the responsibility of hearers! They may ridicule and despise sermons; but they will find to their cost at last that they must give account of all they hear. The very sermons they now despise may be witnesses against them to their eternal ruin.

Let us note that our Lord speaks of judgment and the last day as great realities. Let us take care that we always account them such, and live accordingly. The Christian's best answer to those who ridicule his religion is to say, "I believe in a judgment and a last day."

Let us note that condemnation is taken for granted, if not directly expressed, as the portion of some at the last day. Then let us not listen to those who say that there is no future punishment, and that all persons of all characters, both good and bad, are at last going to heaven.

Zwingle remarks that the expression, " My word shall judge," is parallel to such expressions as, " The law puts a man to death," though it is not actually the law, but the executioner that does it. The law only shows him to be worthy of death. So the works and words of Christ will show the unbelieving to be worthy of judgment and condemnation.

49 —[*For I have not spoken of myself.*] In these words our Lord once more, as if for the last time, declares that mighty truth which we find so often in St. John,—the intimate union between Himself and His Father. " I have not spoken of myself, of my own independent mind, and without concert with my Father in heaven."

The object of saying this is evident. Our Lord would have the Jews know what a serious sin it was to refuse His words, and not believe them. In so doing men did not refuse the words of a mere man, or a prophet, like Moses or John the Baptist. They were refusing the words of Him who never spake alone, but always in closest union with the Father. To refuse to receive the words of Christ was to reject not merely His words, but the words of God the Father.

Here, as in many other places in St. John's Gospel, the Greek does not mean, " I have not spoken *concerning* myself, but out of or from myself."

[*But the Father...gave...commandment...speak*.] Here our Lord explains and enforces more fully what He said of " not speaking from Himself." He declares that when He came into the world, the Father gave Him a " commandment " or a commission, as to what He should say and speak to men. The things that He had spoken were the result of the eternal counsels of the ever-blessed Trinity. The works that He had done were works which the Father gave Him to do. The words which He spoke were words which the Father gave Him to speak. Both in His doing and speaking nothing was left to chance, unforeseen, unprovided, or unpremeditated. All was arranged by perfect wisdom, both His words and His works.

When we read of the Father "sending" Christ, and giving Christ a "commandment," we must carefully dismiss from our minds all idea of any inferiority to God the Father on the part of God the Son. The expressions are used in condescension to our weak faculties, to convey the idea of perfect oneness. We are not speaking of the relation that exists between two human beings like ourselves, but between the Persons in the Divine Trinity.—The "*sending*" of the Son was the result of the eternal counsel of that blessed Trinity, in which Father, Son, and Holy Ghost are co-equal and co-eternal. The eternal Son was as willing to be "sent" as the eternal Father was to "send" Him.—The "*commandment*" given by the Father to the Son as to what He should teach and do, was not a commandment in which the Son had no part but to obey. It was simply the charge or commission arranged in the covenant of redemption, by all three Persons in the Trinity, which the Son was as willing to execute as the Father was willing to give.

The distinction between "say" and "speak" in the Greek is not very clear. Burgon thinks the phrase is meant to include "every class of discourse; as well the words of familiar intercourse, as the grave and solemn addresses." But I am not satisfied that this can be proved,—"À Lapide" says that "to say is to teach, and publish a thing gravely, and to speak is to utter a thing familiarly."—Bengel, however, distinguishes them in precisely the contrary way!

There certainly seems to be an intention in the verse to refer the Jews to the well-known words of Deuteronomy, concerning the Prophet like unto Moses. "I will raise up a Prophet from among their brethren, like unto thee, and will put my words into His mouth, and he shall speak unto them all that I shall command Him." Our Lord's hearers, familiar from their infancy with Scripture, would see at once that Jesus claimed to be the promised Prophet. The Father's words were in His mouth. He spoke what was commanded Him. (See Deut. xviii. 18.)

50 —[*And I know...his commandment...life everlasting.*] The meaning of this sentence seems to be,—"I know, whether you like to believe it or not, that this message, commandment, or commission, which I have from my Father, is life everlasting to all who receive it, and believe. You, in your blindness, see no beauty or excellence in the message I bring, and the doctrine I preach. But I know that in rejecting it you are rejecting life

everlasting."—Thus Peter says to our Lord, "Thou hast the words of eternal life," (John vi. 68;) that is, we know Thou hast a commission to proclaim and publish eternal life.—Thus our Lord says, "The words that I speak are spirit and life." (John vi. 63.)

Poole and others say this sentence means, "I know that the way to life everlasting is to keep His commandments." But I cannot think this is the meaning.

Hall paraphrases the sentence, "The doctrine which by His commandment I preach unto you, is that which will surely bring you to everlasting life."

[*Whatsoever I speak...as Father...so I speak.*] This sentence seems intended to wind up our Lord's public discourses to the unbelieving Jews at Jerusalem. "Whatsoever things I am teaching now, or have spoken to you all through my ministry, are things which the Father gave to Me to speak to you. I am only speaking to you what the Father said to Me. If therefore you reject or refuse my message, know once more, for the last time, that you are rejecting a message from God the Father Himself. I speak nothing but what the Father said to Me. If you despise it, you are despising the God of your fathers, the God of Abraham, and Isaac, and Jacob."

Let us remember that the holy boldness of this last verse should be a pattern to every minister and preacher of the Gospel. Such a man ought to be able to say confidently, "I know and am persuaded that the message I bring is life everlasting to all who believe it; and that, in saying what I do, I say nothing but what God has showed me in His Word."

EXPOSITORY THOUGHTS ON THE GOSPELS

John 13:1—21:25

J. C. RYLE

PREFACE

THE volume now in the reader's hands completes a work which I began sixteen years ago, entitled "Expository Thoughts on the Gospels." By the good hand of God that work is now finished. For this I desire to be deeply thankful. "Better is the end of a thing than the beginning of it." (Eccles. vii. 8.)

In concluding that portion of the work which is devoted to St. John's Gospel, I think it right to make a few prefatory remarks about the "Notes." They occupy so large a part of my three volumes on St. John, that my readers may not unreasonably expect me to give some account of them. Filling up, as they do, at least two-thirds of the work, and necessarily increasing its cost, they require some defence and explanation. Questions such as these will naturally arise in some minds,—"What are these notes? What is their object? What is their doctrinal tone? What helps have been used in preparing them?"—These questions I propose to answer.

(1) My *object* in writing these notes on St. John's Gospel is soon stated. I have tried to explain, in simple language, everything in the text which needs explanation, and to bring all available light to bear on every verse in the book. In trying to attain this object, I have given not only my own thoughts and opinions, but also the results of a patient study of about seventy Commentators, both ancient and modern, of almost every Church and school in Christendom. I have en-

deavored to handle every subject raised by the text,
however high and deep, and to meet the requirements
of every class of readers, whether educated or uneducat-
ed. I have evaded no hard passage, and turned away
from no difficulty. I am very sensible that I have often
failed to hit the mark, and I have not been ashamed in
many places to confess my ignorance. Competent critics will probably detect in the work not a few errors
and mistakes. I lay no claim to infallibility. But I
can honestly say that I have never handled the Word
partially or deceitfully, and have done my best to show
"the thing as it is." (Job xxvi. 3.) Some controverted points I have ventured to discuss in annotations of
more than ordinary length, and of these a list will be
found appended to this concluding volume. On the
whole I cannot help hoping, that, in spite of many defi-
ciencies, the notes will be found a help to thoughtful
readers of St. John's Gospel.

(2) The *doctrinal tone* of the notes, I must frankly
avow, is thoroughly and unmistakably evangelical. After patiently studying St. John's Gospel for twelve
years, with much thought, much labor, much examination of the writings of others, and, I hope I may add,
with some earnest prayers, my theological opinions are
what they were when I began to write. In these twelve
years I trust I have learned many things : but I can
truly say that I have seen no reason to alter my views
of doctrine. My conviction is firm and decided, that
the theology of that religious school in the Church of
England, which, rightly or wrongly, is called Evangelical, is thoroughly Scriptural, and a theology of which
no Christian man need be ashamed.

I freely confess that, with increasing years and experience, I have learned to think more kindly and charitably than I once did, of theologians who belong to

other schools than my own. I am more and more convinced every year I live, that there are many Christians
whose hearts are right in the sight of God, while their
heads are very wrong. I am more and more convinced,
that the differences between schools of religious thought
are frequently more nominal than real, more verbal than
actual, and that many of them would melt away and
disappear, if men would only define the terms and words
they use with logical accuracy. But, for all this, I cannot shrink from saying, as in the sight of God, that at
present I know no theology which appears to me so
thoroughly in accordance with Scripture as Evangelical
theology. In the belief of this I have written my notes
on St. John, and in the faith of this I hope to die.
With the Bible only in my hands, I find difficulties in
the systems of non-Evangelical schools, which to my
mind appear insuperable.

(3) Concerning *the Commentators* I have consulted,
in preparing my notes on St. John, I wish to make a
few remarks for the benefit of my younger readers, and
of those who have not access to large libraries. I see
no reason to alter the opinions which I expressed seven
years ago, in the Preface to my first volume. After patiently studying Cyril, Chrysostom, Augustine, and
Theophylact, for twelve years, it is my deliberate conviction that their Commentaries on the Gospels are
often overrated and overpraised, and that those who
lead young students of theology to expect to find "all
wisdom" in the Fathers, are neither wise nor kind.
After an equally patient examination of the modern
German Commentators, Tittman, Tholuck, Olshausen,
Stier, and Hengstenberg, I am obliged to say that I
leave them with a feeling of disappointment. About
them also I raise a warning cry for the benefit of young
students. I advise them not to expect too much.

Writers like Hengstenberg and Stier are well worth reading; but I cannot say that any modern German Commentators seem to me to deserve the extravagant commendation which is often bestowed on them. In fact I have a strong suspicion that many praise German theology without having read it !

For throwing light on the meaning of the text of St. John, and for raising just and beautiful thoughts out of it, my opinion is distinct and decided, that there are no Commentaries equal to those of the Continental divines who lived immediately after the Protestant Reformation. Unfortunately they wrote in Latin, which few persons care to read ; and their books are, generally, huge, lumbering folios, which few care to handle. Moreover, they are sometimes defective in verbal criticism, and were, most of them, more familiar with Latin than Greek. But taking them for all in all, as Expositors and Elucidators of God's Word, in my judgment, there is nothing like them. The man who has carefully read the expositions of Brentius, Bullinger, Gualter, Musculus, and Gerhard, will find that later Commentaries rarely contain any good thoughts which are not to be found in these five writers, and that they say many excellent things which have not occurred to later writers at all. Why these great Expositors are so totally ignored and neglected in the nineteenth century, I do not pretend to explain. Some modern theologians seem not even to be aware that such Commentators as Brentius, Musculus, and Gerhard, ever existed ! But the fact is one which reflects little credit on our times.

I shall say little or nothing about the works of British Commentators. This is a department of theological literature in which, I must plainly say, I do not think my fellow-countrymen shine. With rare exceptions, they appear to me to fall below the level of their reputation. I shall therefore content myself with naming a few Commentaries, which appear to me more than ordinarily useful and suggestive, and which I have seldom consulted in vain.—Rollock on John is excellent ; and it is a great pity that the whole work is not translated, instead of lying buried in Latin.—Hutcheson is always good ; but his value is sadly marred by his interminable divisions, uses, applications, and inferences.—Matthew Henry is generally rich in pious thoughts and pleasing illustrations, and sometimes exhibits more learning and acquaintance with books, than he is commonly credited with.—Poole's " Annotations " are sound, clear, and sensible ; and, taking him for all in all, I place him at the head of English Commentators on the whole Bible. —Alford and Wordsworth have done good service to the Church by their works on the Greek Testament, and I know none at present that I can sooner recommend to a student of the original. But they both say, occasionally, things with which I cannot agree, and they often seem to me to leave important texts very scantily expounded, or entirely unnoticed.* A fuller and more satisfactory commentary on the Greek Testament appears to me to be still wanted.—Burgon's " Plain Commentary on the Gospels " is an excellent, suggestive, and devout work. But I cannot agree with him, when he touches such subjects as the Church, the Sacraments, and the Ministry.—In fact, the conclusion I arrive at, after a diligent examination of many Commentators, is always one and the same. I trust none of them unreservedly, and I expect nowhere to find perfection. All must be read with caution. They are good helps, but they are not infallible. They are useful assistants, but

* As examples of what I mean, I refer the reader to Words worth on John xvii. 4–20, very scantily expounded, in my judgment ; and to Alford on John x. 27, 28, not expounded at all !

they are not the pillar of cloud and fire. I advise my younger readers to remember that. Use your own judgment prayerfully and diligently. Use commentaries; but be a slave to none. Call no man master.*

It only remains for me now to express my regret, that the completion of my "Expository Thoughts on the Gospels" has been so long delayed. The delay has arisen from causes entirely beyond my control. The work was first begun in a little quiet parish of three hundred people, and then brought to a standstill by heavy domestic affliction. It has been resumed, and carried on, amidst many interruptions, in an isolated rural parish of 1,300 souls, in which, after coming into residence, I found a parsonage had to be repaired, large schools had to be built, and a huge old dilapidated church had to be restored. In the face of these difficulties and distractions, I can only wonder that I have been enabled to finish my work on St. John at all.

The book is now sent forth, with a deep conviction in the author's mind, that it contains many defects, inaccuracies, and blemishes, but with an earnest desire and prayer that it may help some readers to a better understanding of one of the most interesting portions of Holy Scripture. I never felt more persuaded than I do in the present day of the truth of the old saying, "Ignorance of Scripture is the root of all error." If I can lessen that ignorance a little I shall be very thankful.

The concluding paragraph of Dean Alford's "Prolegomena" to his "Commentary on the Book of Revela-

---

* A full list of Commentators, whom I have consulted, more or less, in preparing my notes on St. John, will be found in the preface to my first volume. From that list the following authors were omitted,—Hengstenberg on "John," Manton, Newton, Burgess, and Traill, on the "17th chapter of John," and Bishop Andrews' Sermons.

tion," so thoroughly expresses my own feelings, on completing my work on St. John's Gospel, that I make no excuse for inserting it here, with the omission of a few words:—

"I have now only to commend to my gracious God and Father this feeble attempt to explain a most glorious portion of His revealed Scripture. I do it with hnmble thankfulness, but with a sense of utter weakness before the power of His word, and of inability to sound the depth even of its simplest sentence. May he spare the hand which has been put forward to touch the ark ! May He, for Christ's sake, forgive all rashness, all perverseness, all uncharitableness, which may be found in this book ! And may He sanctify it to the use of His Church: its truth, if any, for teaching ; its manifold defects for warning."

J. C. RYLE

Stradbroke Vicarage, Suffolk,
  February, 1873

TABLE OF CONTENTS

	JOHN		PAGE
XIII	1—5.	Christ's patient and continuing love,—the deep corruption of some professors	1—4
	6—15.	Peter's ignorance,—plain practical lessons,—deep spiritual lessons .	12—16
	16—20.	Christians should not be ashamed to imitate Christ,—uselessness of knowledge without practice, — Christ's perfect knowledge of all His people,—the dignity of discipleship . . .	22—26
	21—30.	The troubles which Christ endured,—the power and malignity of the devil,—the hardness of a backslider , .	29—33
	31—38.	The crucifixion glorifying to the Father and the Son,—the importance of brotherly love,—the self-ignorance that may be in a true believer . . .	39—43
XIV	1—3.	Remedy for heart-trouble,—an account of heaven,—ground for expecting good things	49—53
	4—11.	Believers better thought of by Christ than by themselves,—glorious names given to Christ,—only one way to God, —close union of Father and Son .	57—61

JOHN   PAGE

12—17. Works that Christians may do,—things that prayer may obtain,—promise of the Comforter .   .   .   .   66—70

_18—20. Christ's second coming,—Christ's life the life of His people,—perfect knowledge not attained till second advent of Christ .   .   .   .   .   .   74—77

21—26. Keeping Christ's commandments the best test of love,—special comforts of those who love Christ,—Holy Ghost's teaching and reminding work .   .   79—82

27—31. Christ's last legacy to His people, — Christ's perfect sinlessness .   .   86—89

XV   1—6. Close union of Christ and believers,— false Christians,—fruit only safe evidence of life,—God increases holiness by providential chastisement   .   93—97

7—11. Promises to prayer, — fruitfulness the best evidence,—obedience the secret of sensible comfort .   .   .   .   103—107

12—16. Brotherly love,—relation between Christ and believers,—election   .   .   109—113

17—21. What Christians must expect from the world,—reasons for patience   .   117—118

22—27. Misuse of privileges,—the Holy Ghost,— office of the Apostles -   .   .   121—125

XVI   1—7. A remarkable prophecy, --warning against taking offence at trouble,—reasons why Christ went away .   .   .   .   129—134

8—15. Holy Ghost's work for the the Jews,— Holy Ghost's work for the world .   139—142

JOHN   **PAGE**

16—24. Christ's absence a sorrow to believers,—
Christ's second coming a joy to believers, — duty of prayer in Christ's absence   .   .   .   .   .   .   149—153

25—33. Importance of knowing the Father,—
Christ's kindness to those who have
weak grace, — believers ignorant of
their own hearts, — Christ the true
source of peace   .   .   .   .   158—163

XVII   1—8.   Christ's office and dignity,—Christ's gracious account of His people .   .   167—170

9—16. Christ's special work for believers,—believers not taken out of the world, but
kept   .   .   .   .   .   .   181—185

17—26. Christ's prayer for His people's sanctification,—Christ's prayer for His people's
unity,—Christ's prayer for His people's
glorification   .   .   .   .   .   194—198

XVIII   1—11.   Hardness of a backslider's heart,—voluntariness of Christ's sufferings,—Christ's
care for His people's safety,—Christ's
submission to His Father's will   .   208--212

12—27. Desperate wickedness of unconverted
men,—Christ's condescension,— weakness of some real Christians   .   224—228

28—40. False scrupulosity of hypocrites,—nature
of Christ's kingdom,—Christ's mission,
—Pilate's question   .   .   241—247

XIX   1—16.   Portrait of Christ,—portrait of the Jews,
—portrait of Pilate   .   .   .   265—268

17—27. Christ bearing His cross,—Christ crucified as a King,—Christ's care for His
mother   .   .   .   .   .   .   290—294

JOHN   **PAGE**

28—37. Scripture fulfilled in every part of the crucifixion,—It is finished,—reality of Christ's death   .   .   .   .   314—318

38—42. Some Christians little known,—some end better than they begin .   .   .   333—338

XX   1—10. Those love Christ most who have got most from Him,—different temperaments of believers,—much ignorance remaining in believers .   .   .   346—350

11—18. Love receives most privileges, — fear and sorrow often needless,—earthly thoughts even in true believers .   365—370

19—23. Christ's kind greeting,—evidence of resurrection,—commission of the Apostles .   .   .   .   .   .   386—390

24—31. Danger of not attending assemblies of Christians,—Christ's kindness to dull believers,—Thomas's glorious confession   .   .   .   .   .   403—408

XXI   1—14. Poverty of first Disciples,—difference in characters of Disciples,—abundant evidence of Christ's resurrection   . . 422—426

15—17. Christ's question to Peter,—Peter's answer to Christ,—Christ's command to Peter   .   .   .   .   .   442—445

18—25. The future of Christians foreknown to Christ,—believer's death glorifies God, —our own duty should be our first thought, — number and greatness of Christ's works   .   .   .   .   454—460

EXPOSITORY THOUGHTS

ON THE GOSPELS

JOHN XIII 1—5

1 Now before the feast of the passover, when Jesus knew that his hour was come that he should depart out of this world unto the Father, having loved his own which were in the world, he loved them unto the end.

2 And supper being ended, the devil having now put into the heart of Judas Iscariot, Simon's *son*, to betray him;

3 Jesus knowing that the Father had given all things into his hands, and that he was come from God and went to God;

4 He riseth from supper, and laid aside his garments; and took a towel, and girded himself.

5 After that he poureth water into a bason, and began to wash the disciples' feet, and to wipe *them* with the towel wherewith he was girded.

THE passage we have now read begins one of the most interesting portions of St. John's Gospel. For five consecutive chapters we find the Evangelist recording matters which are not mentioned by Matthew, Mark, and Luke. We can never be thankful enough that the Holy Ghost has caused them to be written for our learning! In every age the contents of these chapters have been justly regarded as one of the most precious parts of the Bible. They have been the meat and drink, the strength and comfort of all true-hearted Christians. Let us ever approach them with peculiar reverence. The place whereon we stand is holy ground.

We learn, for one thing, from these verses, *what patient and continuing love there is in Christ's heart to-*

wards His people. It is written that " having loved
His own which were in the world, He loved them unto
the end." Knowing perfectly well that they were about
to forsake Him shamefully in a very few hours, in full
view of their approaching display of weakness and infirmity, our blessed Master did not cease to have loving
thoughts of His disciples. He was not weary of them:
He loved them to the last.

The love of Christ to sinners is the very essence and
marrow of the Gospel. That He should love us at all,
and care for our souls,—that He should love us before
we love Him, or even know anything about Him,—that
He should love us so much as to come into the world
to save us, take our nature on Him, bear our sins, and
die for us on the cross,—all this is wonderful indeed !
It is a kind of love to which there is nothing like among
men. The narrow selfishness of human nature cannot
fully comprehend it. It is one of those things which
even the angels of God "desire to look into." It is a
truth which Christian preachers and teachers should
proclaim incessantly, and never be weary of proclaiming.

But the love of Christ to saints is no less wonderful,
in its way, than His love to sinners, though far less considered. That He should bear with all their countless
infirmities from grace to glory,—that He should never
be tired of their endless inconsistencies and petty prov-
ocations,—that He should go on forgiving and forgetting incessantly, and never be provoked to cast them off
and give them up,—all this is marvellous indeed ! No
mother watching over the waywardness of her feeble
babe, in the days of its infancy, has her patience so
thoroughly tried, as the patience of Christ is tried by
Christians. Yet His longsuffering is infinite. His com-

passions are a well that is never exhausted. His love is " a love that passeth knowledge."

Let no man be afraid of beginning with Christ, if he desires to be saved. The chief of sinners may come to Him with boldness, and trust Him for pardon with confidence. This loving Saviour is One who delights to "receive sinners." (Luke xv. 2.) Let no man be afraid of going on with Christ after he has once come to Him and believed. Let him not fancy that Christ will cast him off because of failures, and dismiss him into his former hopelessness on account of infirmities. Such thoughts are entirely unwarranted by anything in the Scriptures. Jesus will never reject any servant because of feeble service and weak performance. Those whom He receives He always keeps. Those whom He loves at first He loves at last. His promise shall never be broken, and it is for saints as well as sinners : " Him that cometh unto Me I will in no wise cast out." (John vi. 37.)

We learn, for another thing, from these verses, *what deep corruption may sometimes be found in the heart of a great professor of religion.* It is written that "the devil put into the heart of Judas Iscariot, Simon's son, to betray Christ."

This Judas, we must always remember, was one of the twelve Apostles. He had been chosen by Christ Himself, at the same time with Peter, James, John, and their companions. For three years he had walked in Christ's society, had seen His miracles, had heard His preaching, had experienced many proofs of His loving-kindness. He had even preached himself and wrought miracles in Christ's name; and when our Lord sent out His disciples two and two, Judas Iscariot no doubt must have been one of some couple that was sent. Yet here we see this very man possessed by the devil, and rushing headlong to destruction.

On all the coasts of England there is not such a beacon to warn sailors of danger as Judas Iscariot is to warn Christians. He shows us what length a man may go in religious profession, and yet turn out a rotten hypocrite at last, and prove never to have been converted. He shows us the uselessness of the highest privileges, unless we have a heart to value them and turn them to good account. Privileges alone without grace save nobody, and will only make hell deeper. He shows us the uselessness of mere head-knowledge. To know things with our brains, and be able to talk and preach and speak to others, is no proof that our own feet are in the way of peace. These are terrible lessons: but they are true.

Let us never be surprised if we see hypocrisy and false profession among Christians in modern days. There is nothing new in it, nothing peculiar, nothing that did not happen even among Christ's own immediate followers, and under Christ's own eyes. Bad money is a strong proof that there is good coin somewhere. Hypocrisy is a strong indirect evidence that there is such a thing as true religion.

Above all, let us pray daily that our own Christianity may at any rate be genuine, sincere, real and true. Our faith may be feeble, our hope dim, our knowledge small, our failures frequent, our faults many. But at all events let us be real and true. Let us be able to say with poor, weak, erring Peter, "Thou, Lord, who knowest all things, knowest that I love Thee." (John xxi. 17.)

Notes John xiii 1—5

There are peculiarities in St. John's narrative of the end of our Lord's life on earth, which seem to require a few introductory remarks before entering into the substance of the thir-teenth chapter.

A careful reader of the four Gospels can hardly fail to re-mark that in St. John's account of the last six days of our Lord's ministry, many things mentioned by Matthew, Mark, and Luke, are entirely omitted.

The parables of the two sons,—of the householder who let out a vineyard,—of the wedding garment,—of the ten virgins, —of the talents,—of the sheep and goats, are left out. The second cleansing of the temple,—the cursing of the barren fig-tree,—the public discussion with the chief priests and elders about John's baptism,—the silencing of the Pharisees, the Sad-ducees, and the lawyers,—the public denunciation to the mul-titude of the Scribes and Pharisees,—all these interesting mat-ters are found in the first three Gospels, but passed over in silence in the fourth. We cannot doubt that there were wise reasons.

But the most striking thing in St. John's narrative at this point, is the entire absence of our Lord's famous prophecy upon the Mount of Olives, and of the institution of the Lord's Sup-per. Both these deeply interesting portions of our Lord's last doings before His crucifixion, which are most fully given in the three Gospels, are completely omitted in the fourth.

The reason of these two remarkable omissions we are left to conjecture. "God giveth no account of His matters." If we once admit that all Scripture is given by inspiration of God, we need not doubt that the Gospel writers were equally guided and directed by the Holy Ghost, both in the things they omitted and the things they recorded. Nevertheless a few remarks on the subject may be interesting to some readers.

(a) Concerning the omission of the prophecy on the Mount of Olives, I venture the following conjecture. I think it is partly accounted for by the time when St. John's Gospel was given to the Church. That must have been very near the tak-ing of Jerusalem, the destruction of the temple, and the com-plete overthrow of the Jewish ceremonial. Now if St. John had just at this crisis inserted anew this prophecy in his Gospel, it would have confirmed the erroneous notion which many have always held, that it refers only to the destruction of Jerusalem, and does not extend to the second advent of Christ, and the end of the world. His marked silence about it would be a testi-mony against the misapplication of the prophecy. The second reason of the omission, I think, is the striking fact that the writer of the fourth Gospel was inspired to write the Book of Revelation. No wonder, therefore, that he was directed to pass over our Lord's prophecy, when he was about to write at a later date the most striking prophetical book in the Bible.

(b) Concerning the omission of the Lord's Supper, I venture the following conjecture. I think it was specially intended to be a witness forever against the growing tendency of Christians to make an idol of the sacraments. Even from the beginning there seems to have been a disposition in the Church to make Christianity a religion of forms and ceremonies rather than of heart, and to exalt outward ordinances to a place which God never meant them to fill. Against this teaching St. John was raised up to testify. The mere fact that in his Gospel he leaves out the Lord's Supper altogether, and does not even name it, is strong proof that the Lord's Supper cannot be, as many tell us, the first, foremost, chief, and principal thing in Christianity. Its perfect silence about it can never be reconciled with this favorite theory. It is a most conspicuous silence, which the modern advocates of the so-called sacramental system, can never get over or explain away. If the Sacrament of the Lord's Supper really is the first and chief thing in Christianity, why does St. John tell us nothing about it? To that question I can only see one answer: it is because it is not a primary, but a secondary thing in Christ's religion.

The reason assigned for the omission by many commentators, viz., that St. John thought it needless to repeat the account of the institution, after it had been recorded by three evangelists and St. Paul, appears to me entirely insufficient.

1 —[*Now before...passover.*] We should observe that the feast of the passover is always carefully mentioned by each Gospel writer, as the precise time of the year when Jesus was crucified. It was ordered of God that it should be at this particular time, for two good reasons. For one thing, the passover lamb was the most striking and remarkable type in the whole Jewish ceremonial of Christ Himself, and the history of the passover of Christ's work of redemption. For another thing, it secured the greatest assembly of Israelites to be eye-witnesses of our Lord's crucifixion. At no time of the Jewish year were so many Jews gathered at Jerusalem. Anything that happened at the passover would be reported by Jewish worshippers, on returning home, all over the civilized world. For these two reasons " the Lamb of God " was slain at this feast, in spite of the priests, who said, " Not on the feast day."

Let us remember that one of the few dates we know for certainty of the events in our Lord's life, is the time of His crucifixion. Of the time of His birth and baptism we know nothing. But that he died at Easter, we may be quite sure.

[*When Jesus knew...hour...come.*] Let us note that our Lord knew perfectly beforehand when and how He should suffer. This, whatever we may think, is a great addition to suffering. Our ignorance of things before us is a great blessing. Our Lord saw the cross clearly before Him, and walked straight up to it. His death was not a surprise to Him, but a voluntary, foreknown thing.

[*That...depart...world...Father.*] Let us observe how death is spoken of here. It is taking a journey—a going from one place to another. In the case of our Lord, it was a return to His Father's house, and a going home, after finishing the work He came to do. So a believer's death, in a lower sense, is going home.

Calvin observes, "This definition of death belongs to the whole body of the Church. It is to the saints a passage to the Father, an inlet to eternal life."

[*Having loved his own...world...loved...end.*] The meaning of this seems to be, "Having always loved His own disciples, and having given many proofs of his singular affection, He now, before leaving them alone like orphans in the world, gave one more striking proof of His love by washing their feet, and thus on the last evening before His death, showed that He loved them to the very end of His ministry, and was not weary of them."

He knew perfectly that they were going to forsake Him and act like cowards, but that did not prevent Him loving them, with all their weakness, to the very end.

He knew perfectly that He was about to suffer within twenty-four hours, but the knowledge and foresight of it did not absorb His thoughts so as to make Him forget His little flock of followers. Saints, when they are dying, often ask to be left alone and let alone; Christ, on the trial of His crucifixion, thought of others, and loved His disciples to the end.

The love of Christ to Christians who really believe on Him, is a great depth. "It passeth knowledge." It is something that our poor corrupt nature cannot fully comprehend or measure.

The expression, "His own," applied to believers, is very noteworthy. They are Christ's peculiar property, given to Him by the Father, and His own special care as members of His body. Tittman's idea that "His own" means all mankind, is preposterous and weak, and ignores the privileges of believers.

The expression, "which were in the world," is another great depth. Believers are not in heaven yet, and find it out to their cost. They are in a cold, unkind, persecuting world. Let them take comfort in the thought, that Jesus knows and remembers it. "I know thy works and where thou dwellest." (Rev. ii. 13.)

Theophylact thinks that our Lord purposely deferred this act of washing the disciples' feet to the last evening of His ministry, in order to leave in their minds a pleasant impression of His love and condescension.

Melancthon shows that the three greatest marks of pity and compassion are (1) to tolerate the wicked for a season; (2) to abstain from exposing their sins as long as possible; (3) to warn them plainly and gently before leaving them for ever. All this appears in our Lord's dealing with Judas in this chapter.

2 —[*And supper being ended.*] These words would have been more literally rendered, " while supper was going on," or, " supper being in progress." That this is the true meaning seems clear from the twenty-sixth verse. If supper had really been ended, we should not have heard of a sop being given out of the dish, etc.

It is only fair to say that Scaliger and other learned men insist that the Jews had more than one supper at the passover,—one a legal one, strictly according to ritual ; the other a social one. They think these two suppers are both in this chapter. Gerhard gives this opinion at length. Whitby seems to lean to this view, and maintains that our Lord *twice* pointed out Judas as the traitor,—once privately and once publicly.

Let it be noted that our Lord's ministry ended with a supper, —that the last ordinance He appointed was a supper,—that one promise He has left to a believer is, " I will come and sup with him " (Rev. iii. 20),—and that the first thing that will take place at His second advent will be the marriage supper of the Lamb. All point to the same great truth,—the close union, familiarity, and comfortable intimacy between Christ and His people. It is a thing far too little known.

What supper this was we are not told, and are left to conjecture. It is a point on which opinions widely differ.

Some, as Lightfoot, think that the supper was the same that took place at Bethany, in the house of Simon the leper, two days before the passover. Rollock also thinks it was not the passover.

Others think it was the ordinary passover supper, which our Lord was eating with His disciples the night before His crucifixion. This certainly, in my judgment, seems the more probable view.

One thing at any rate is pretty clear. It was not the institution of the Lord's Supper. It seems highly improbable that the washing of the disciples' feet would take place after the Lord's Supper. That blessed ordinance appears to come in after the twentieth verse. Brentius stands alone in maintaining that it was the Lord's Supper.

[*The devil ... put .. heart.*] This does not mean that Judas now for the first time left the faith, and became an apostate. Our Lord long before had spoken of him as one that " was a devil." (John vi. 70.) But it means that now at length the devil suggested into the heart of this unhappy man the atrocious idea of betraying his Master. It was the last and final heading up of his apostasy.

The personality of Satan, and his old character as the father of all wickedness, are forcibly brought out here.

The word rendered "put" is literally "cast." This graphically describes the way in which Satan works. He casts into the heart of those he tempts the seeds of evil. The heart is the seed plot which he sows. Suggestion is one of his chief weapons. The sin of man consists in opening his heart to the suggestion; giving it a place, and letting it sink down. This is obvious in the first temptation of Eve in the garden of Eden.

Tittman's idea that the expression is only a "popular form of speaking," is utterly untenable, and cannot be reconciled with the general teaching of the Bible about the devil.

[*Judas Iscariot, Simon's son.*] Here, as in three other places, the false apostle is called emphatically "Simon's son." Doubtless this was to mark him out as not the Judas who was brother of James and son of Alphæus. Who this Simon was we do not know. (See note on John vi. 71.)

[*To betray him.*] There seems no need for regarding Judas's betrayal of his Master as anything but the wicked act of a wicked man, who loved money more than his soul. The theory that he was a high-minded, impatient disciple, who wished his Master no harm, but desired to hasten His kingdom, and expected Him to work a miracle, and save Himself at the last, is ingenious, but lacks foundation. Our Lord's word applied to him, "a devil," and the word of St. John, "a thief," appear to me to overturn the theory altogether. Judas betrayed Jesus because he loved money better than His Master. He probably did not realize the full consequence of his act. But this is often the case with wicked men.

3 —[*Jesus, knowing that the Father, etc.*] The reason why this verse comes in here is not very plain. Why are we told that Jesus "washed His disciples' feet," knowing all these wonderful things? What is the special point and object of the sentence?

Some think that the words mean that our Lord knew the end of His ministry was at hand, that all His work was accomplished, that the Father had now committed to Him all power in heaven and earth, and that having come from God, He was about to return to God very shortly. Knowing this, He seized the last opportunity that remained to give His disciples a practical example of love and humility. He knew that His time was short, and that He must give the lesson this night, if it was to be given at all.

Others, as Chrysostom, Augustine, and Zwingle, think that the object of the words is to show the extent and depth of our Lord's infinite condescension and love to His disciples. With a full knowledge that the Father had committed all power into His hands, that He had been from eternity with God, and was going back to God,—knowing all the dignity and majesty of His person and office, He yet condescended to perform the most menial office, and to minister like a servant to His disciples.

Either view is good sense and good divinity, and admissible as a fair interpretation of the words. For myself I prefer the latter view.

Theophylact points out that to argue our Lord's inferiority to the Father from the expression, " Delivered· all things into His hand," is' unfair. He justly remarks that you might as well infer the Father's inferiority to the Son from the expression in Corinthians, " When He shall have delivered up the kingdom to the Father."

Bernard remarks that " Jesus came from God, not leaving Him, and went to God, not leaving us."

4 —[*He riseth from supper, etc.*] The minuteness with which every action of our Lord is related here is very striking. No less than seven distinct things are named,—rising, laying aside garments, taking a towel, girding Himself, pouring water into a bason, washing and wiping. This very particularity stamps the whole transaction with reality, and is the natural language of an astonished and admiring eye-witness.

The " laying aside garments " of course only means the laying aside the long, loose, outer garment which people in the East always wear, and which must be laid aside if any bodily exertion is used.

The " girding Himself " refers to the well-known practice of tying tightly round the person any loose garment before taking any action requiring bodily exertion. A good servant is said to have " his loins girded and his lamp burning," ready for any errand or duty.

The likeness between our Lord's action here and the words in Luke xii. 37, are very striking : " He shall gird Himself—serve them," etc.

Jansenius remarks, that the " rising " here mentioned seems like a. clear proof that this supper could not be the paschal supper. That was to be eaten standing.

The use of the present tense all through this description is noteworthy. It brings the whole transaction before us like a picture.

Hengstenberg says here, " Jesus had seated himself at the table, and Peter probably enjoyed the honor of washing His feet. After this he, with the other disciples, sat down also at table, expecting that the younger would spontaneously assume the function of feet-washer for all the rest. But pride evoked pride. The younger Apostles, following a quick impulse, seated themselves also at table. Thus a situation of deep embarrassment resulted in murmuring and contest. Who would be the first to rise up again ? Jesus put an end to the embarrassment, by rising from supper and washing the feet of His disciples." This is possible; but it is only conjecture.

5 —[*After that he poureth water, etc., etc.*] Wonderful as all this transaction seems, and no doubt is, when we remember who our Lord was, one thing must never be forgotten. The actions here described would not seem nearly so strange to the disciples as they do to us. They were simply the courteous actions of a host who desired to show the utmost degree of hospitable attention to the guests. Thus Abraham washed the feet of the three angelic messengers. (Gen. xviii. 4. So also 1 Sam. xxv. 41.) In a hot country like Palestine, where people wore no stockings, and the heat was very scorching to the skin, frequent washing of the feet was an absolute necessity, and to wash the feet of guests was a common piece of hospitality. It is one mark of a deserving widow, that she has " washed the saints' feet." (1 Tim. v. 10.) The real wonder was that such a Master, on such a solemn occasion, should do such a condescending act to such weak disciples. It was not so much the action as the doer of it, that was remarkable.

After all there was a touching fitness in our Lord's choice of an instructive action on this solemn occasion. He knew that He was leaving His disciples, like poor feeble travellers, in a weary, wicked world. He would therefore wash their feet before parting, and strengthen and refresh them for their journey.

It will be observed that the work was not left unfinished and half-done. Like a perfect servant, our Lord " wiped " the feet as well as " washed " them.

JOHN XIII 6—15

6 Then cometh he to Simon Peter: and Peter saith unto him, Lord, dost thou wash my feet ?

7 Jesus answered and said unto him, What I do thou knowest not now; but thou shalt - know hereafter.

8 Peter saith unto him, thou shalt never wash my feet. Jesus answered him, If I wash thee not, thou hast no part with me.

9 Simon Peter saith to him, Lord, not my feet only, but also *my* hands and *my* head.

10 Jesus saith unto him, He that is washed needeth not save to wash *his* feet, but is clean every whit: and ye are clean, but not all.

11 For he knew who should betray him; therefore said he, Ye are not all clean.

12 So after he had washed their feet, and had taken his garments, and was set down again, he said unto them, Know ye what I have done to you ?

13 Ye call me Master and Lord : and ye say well ; for *so* I am.

14 If I then, *your* Lord and Master, have washed your feet; ye also ought to wash one another's feet.

15 For I have given you an example, that ye should do as I have done to you.

THE verses we have now read conclude the story of our Lord's washing the feet of His disciples, the night before He was crucified. It is a story full of touching interest, which for some wise reason no Evangelist records except St. John. The wonderful condescension of Christ, in doing such a menial action, can hardly fail to strike any reader. The mere fact that the Master should wash the feet of the servants might well fill us with surprise. But the circumstances and sayings which arose out of the action are just as interesting as the action itself. Let us see what they were.

We should notice, firstly, *the hasty ignorance of the Apostle Peter.* One moment we find him refusing to allow his Master to do such a servile work as He is about to do :—" Dost thou wash my feet ? " " Thou shalt never wash my feet."—Another moment we find him rushing with characteristic impetuosity into the other extreme :—" Lord, wash not my feet only, but my hands and my head." But throughout the transaction we find him unable to take in the real meaning of what his eyes behold. He sees, but he does not understand.

Let us gather from Peter's conduct that a man may have plenty of faith and love, and yet be sadly destitute of clear knowledge. We must not set down men as graceless and godless because they are dull, and stupid, and blundering in their religion. The heart may often be quite right when the head is quite wrong. We must make allowances for the corruption of the understanding as well as of the will. We must not be surprised to find that the brains as well as the affections of Adam's children have been hurt by the fall. It is a humbling lesson, and one seldom fully learned except by long experience. But the longer we live the more true shall we find it, that a believer, like Peter, may make many mistakes and lack understanding, and yet, like Peter, have a heart right before God, and get to heaven at last.

Even at our best estate we shall find that many of Christ's dealings with us are hard to understand in this life. The "why" and "wherefore" of many a providence will often puzzle and perplex us quite as much as the washing puzzled Peter. The wisdom, and fitness, and necessity of many a thing will often be hidden from our eyes. But at times like these we must remember the Master's words, and fall back upon them :—"What I do thou knowest not now, but thou shalt know hereafter." There came days, long after Christ had left the world, when Peter saw the full meaning of all that happened on the memorable night before the crucifixion. Even so there will be a day when every dark page in our life's history will be explained, and when, as we stand with Christ in glory, we shall know all.

We should notice, secondly, in this passage, *the plain practical lesson which lies upon its surface.* That lesson is read out to us by our Lord. He says, "I have given you an example, that ye should do as I have done to you."

Humility is evidently one part of the lesson. If the only-begotten Son of God, the King of kings, did not think it beneath Him to do the humblest work of a servant, there is nothing which His disciples should think themselves too great or too good to do. No sin is so offensive to God, and so injurious to the soul as pride. No grace is so commended, both by precept and example, as humility. "Be clothed with humility." "He that humbleth himself shall be exalted."—"Let this mind be in you, which was also in Christ Jesus; who, being in the form of God, thought it not robbery to be equal with God : but made Himself of no reputation, and took upon Him the form of a servant, and was made in the likeness of men: and being found in fashion as a man, He humbled Himself." (1 Pet. v. 5 ; Luke xviii. 14 ; Phil. ii. 5—8.) Well would it be for the Church if this very simple truth was more remembered, and real humility was not so sadly rare. Perhaps there is no sight so displeasing in God's eyes as a self-conceited, self-satisfied, self-contented, stuck-up professor of religion. Alas, it is a sight only too common ! Yet the words which St. John here records have never been repealed. They will be a swift witness against many at the last day, except they repent.

Love is manifestly the other part of the great practical lesson. Our Lord would have us love others so much that we should delight to do anything which can promote their happiness. We ought to rejoice in doing kindnesses, even in little things. We ought to count it a pleasure to lessen sorrow and multiply joy, even when it costs us some self-sacrifice and self-denial. We ought to love every child of Adam so well, that if in the least trifle we can do anything to make him more happy and comfortable, we should be glad to do it. This was the mind of the Master, and this the ruling principle of His conduct upon earth. There are but few who walk in His steps, it may be feared ; but these few are men and women after His own heart.

The lesson before us may seem a very simple one ; but its importance can never be overrated. Humility and love are precisely the graces which the men of the world can understand, if they do not comprehend doctrines. They are graces about which there is no mystery, and they are within reach of all classes. The poorest and most ignorant Christian can every day find occasion for practicing love and humility. Then if we would do good to the world, and make our calling and election sure, let no man forget our Lord's example in this passage. Like Him, let us be humble and loving towards all.

We should notice, lastly, in this passage, *the deep spiritual lessons which lie beneath its surface.* They are three in number, and lie at the very root of religion, though we can only touch them briefly.

For one thing, we learn that all need to be washed by Christ. " If I wash thee not, thou hast no part in Me." No man or woman can be saved unless his sins are washed away in Christ's precious blood. Nothing else can make us clean or acceptable before God. We must be " washed, sanctified, and justified, in the name of the Lord Jesus, and by the Spirit of our God." (1 Cor. vi. 11.) Christ must wash us, if we are ever to sit down with saints in glory. Then let us take heed that we apply to Him by faith, wash and become clean. They only are washed who believe.

For another thing, we learn that even those who are cleansed and forgiven need a daily application to the blood of Christ for daily pardon. We cannot pass through this evil world without defilement. There is not a day in our lives but we fail and come short in many things, and need fresh supplies of mercy. Even "he that is washed needs to wash his feet," and to wash them in the same fountain where he found peace of conscience when he first believed. Then let us daily use that fountain without fear. With the blood of Christ we must begin, and with the blood of Christ we must go on.

Finally, we learn that even those who kept company with Christ, and were baptized with water as His disciples, were " not all " washed from their sin. These words are very solemn,—" Ye are clean: but not all." Then let us take heed to ourselves, and beware of false profession. If even Christ's own disciples are not all

cleansed and justified, we have reason to be on our
guard. Baptism and Churchmanship are no proof that
we are right in the sight of God.

NOTES JOHN XIII 6—15

6 —[*Then cometh he to Simon Peter.*] Whether our Lord began
with Simon Peter, is not quite clear from the words before us.
The word " then," however, certainly does not mean " then," in
the sense of " in order."

Chrysostom and Theophylact hold that Jesus washed Judas
Iscariot's feet, and then came to Peter. From the subsequent
action of dipping and giving a morsel to Judas, it certainly
seems probable that he sat very near our Lord.

Augustine holds that Jesus began with Peter. Bellarmine
eagerly grasps at this, and gives it as one of twenty-eight alleged
proofs that Peter always had a primacy among the Apostles !

[*And Peter saith unto him.*] The word " Peter " is not in the
Greek text here, but simply " he," or " that man." Our translators seem to have inserted it to make the meaning plain.

[*Lord, dost thou wash my feet ?*] The English language here
fails to give the full emphasis of the Greek. It would be literally rendered, " Dost Thou, of me, wash the feet ?" Such an
one as Thou art, wash the feet of such an one as I am ! It is
like John the Baptist's exclamation when our Lord came to his
baptism : " Comest thou to me ? " (Matt. iii. 14.)

7 —[*Jesus answered and said, etc.*] The famous saying of this
verse stretches far beyond the literal application of the words.
Primarily, of course, it means, " This action of mine has a
meaning which in a few minutes I will explain and you will
understand, though at present it may seem to you strange and
unsuitable."—But in every age true Christians have seen a
higher, deeper, broader meaning in the words, and a pious
mind cannot doubt that they were intended to bear that meaning. It supplies the key to many things which we cannot understand in the providential government of the world, in the
history of the Church, in the events of our own lives. We
must make up our minds to see many things happening which
we do not know and understand now, and of which we cannot
at present see the wisdom. But we must believe that "we shall
know hereafter" the full purposes, the why and wherefore and
needs-be, of each and all. It is a golden sentence to store up in
our memories. God's eternal counsels, the wisdom of the great
Head of the Church, must never be forgotten. All is going on
well, even when we think all is going on ill. When we cannot
see it we must believe. In sickness, sorrow, bereavement, disappointment, we must summon up faith and patience, and hear

Christ saying to us, " What I do thou knowest not now, but thou shalt know hereafter."

Musculus has some happy remarks here on the applicability of this expression to infant baptism, which are most just and true.

8 —[*Peter saith...thou...never wash my feet.*] Here, again, the English version fails to give the full strength of the Greek words. This sentence would be rendered literally, " Thou shalt never wash my feet for ever," or unto eternity.

We may note here, in Peter's language, that there is such a thing as " a voluntary humility," which runs into extremes.

Hutcheson remarks, " Men may have much seeming humility in the matters of God, which is yet but preposterous and sinful, and learned from carnal reason." Rollock compares with Peter's conduct here the Romish worship of saints and angels, under the pretence of deep humility and unworthiness to approach God.

[*Jesus answered . . . If I wash . . . not . . . no part . . . me.*] We need not doubt that this sentence was meant to bear a deep and full meaning, and to reach far beyond the primary application. It would be a very cold and tame exposition to say that our Lord only meant, " Unless thy feet are washed by Me to-night, thou art not one of my disciples."—It means a great deal more. Our Lord seems in effect to say, " Thou wilt not be wise to object to the symbolical action which I am performing. Remember no one can be saved, or have any part in Me and my work of redemption, unless I wash away his sins. Except I wash away thy many sins, even thou, Simon Peter, hast no part in Me. I must wash every saved soul, and every saved soul must be washed. Surely, therefore, it does not become thee to object to my doing an instructive and figurative act to thy feet, when I must needs do a far greater work to thy soul."

The sentence is one of wide, deep, and sweeping application. It is true of every Christian of every rank and position. To each one Christ says, " If I wash thee not, thou hast no part in Me." It is not enough that we are Churchmen, professed communicants, and the like. The great question for every one is this : " Am I washed and justified ? "

The common assertion that this " washing " here spoken of is baptism, seems to me unwarrantable. Our Lord never baptized any one, so far as we can learn from Scripture. Where is it said that He baptized Peter ? Moreover, if baptism were meant, the past tense would have been used : " If I had not washed thee, thou wouldst have no part in Me." The washing here spoken of is something far above baptism.

9 —[*Simon Peter saith, etc.*] The exclamation of Peter in this verse is highly characteristic of the man. Impulsive, excita-

ble, zealous, ardent, with more love than knowledge, and more feeling than spiritual discernment, he is horrified at the very idea of "having no part in Christ." Anything rather than that! Not seeing clearly the deep meaning of His Master's words, and still sticking to a carnal, literal interpretation of the word "washing," he cries out that his Master may wash him all over, hands and head as well as feet, if an interest in Christ depends on that.

Great zeal and love are perfectly consistent with great spiritual ignorance and dulness, and great slowness to comprehend spiritual truth.

Rollock remarks that Peter erred as much in one extreme now, as he had erred before in another.

Stier remarks that the passionate, strong expression of Peter in this verse, is just the language of a warm-hearted but dull-minded disciple, just beginning to understand, as if light had suddenly flashed on him.

10 —[*Jesus saith to him, He that is washed, etc.*] This sentence of our Lord's conveys a latent rebuke of Peter's spiritual dulness. It is as though Jesus said, "The washing of head and hands whereof thou speakest is not needed. Even assuming that a literal washing is all I meant in saying, 'If I wash thee not,' it is well known that he who is washed needs only to wash his feet after a journey, and is accounted clean entirely after such a partial washing. But this is far more true of the washing of pardon and justification. He that is pardoned and justified by Me is entirely washed from all his sins, and only needs the daily forgiveness of the daily defilement he contracts in travelling through a sinful world. Once washed, justified, and accepted by Me, ye are clean before God: although not all of you. There is one painful exception."

The great practical truth contained in this sentence ought to be carefully noted and treasured up by all believers. Once joined to Christ and cleansed in His blood, they are completely absolved and free from all spot of guilt, and are counted without blame before God. But for all this they need every day, as they walk through this world, to confess their daily failures, and to sue for daily pardon. They require, in short, a daily washing of their feet, over and above the great washing of justification, which is theirs the moment they first believe. He that neglects this daily washing is a very questionable and doubtful kind of Christian. Luther remarks pithily, "The devil allows no Christian to reach heaven with clean feet all the way."

"Every whit," in this verse, means literally "the whole man."

The deep mine of meaning which often lies under the surface of our Lord's language is strikingly exemplified in this verse, as well as in the seventh and eighth. There is far more in many of His sayings, we may believe, than has ever yet been discovered.

It is striking to observe that even of His poor, weak, erring disciples Jesus says, " Ye are clean."

Bullinger observes that the words of the Lord's Prayer, " Forgive us our trespasses," are a daily confession of the very thing here mentioned,—*viz.*, the need of daily washing of our feet.

Casaubon remarks that those who come out of a bath, as a matter of constant experience, only need to wash their feet, which, stepping on the ground as they come out, must needs contract some defilement. In Eastern countries, where bathing was very common, all could see the force of this.

Hengstenberg remarks, that " the expression, ' but not all,' was intended to pierce the conscience of Judas, whom the Redeemer did not give up until the last good impulse died within him."

The common idea that the " washing " here spoken of refers to the baptism, seems to me quite untenable. He that is washed must mean only " washed in a spiritual sense from his sins ; " as Psalm li. 4. Hengstenberg's discussion of the point is worth reading.

Burgon observes, " The traitor, Judas, though washed by the hands of Christ Himself, was filthy still."

11 —[*For he knew...betray him, etc.*] Our Lord's perfect fore-knowledge of His sufferings and the manner of them, and His thorough discernment of the real characters of all His disciples, are alike shown in this verse. He did not suffer because he did not foresee it, and was taken by surprise. He walked up to death knowing every step he was about to tread.

The sentence is an example of the explanatory glosses which are so characteristic of St. John's Gospel.

The Greek words rendered " who should betray Him," are literally, " the person betraying Him," in the past participle.

12 —[*So after...washed...feet.*] After the conversation between our Lord and Peter, the washing seems to have gone on without interruption. The disciples were accustomed to see their Master do things they did not understand, and they submitted in silence.

[*And had taken...garments...set down again.*] This refers to His putting on again the long loose outer robe, which was laid aside on performing any action requiring exertion in the East. Then our Lord took His place once more at the table, and commenced a discourse which seems to have ushered in the Lord's Supper. Whether the washing of the feet was meant, among

other things, to teach the need of special preparation for that
blessed ordinance, is an interesting thought, and worth consideration. It certainly seems our Lord's last *action* before He
gave the bread and wine.

[*He said...know ye what...done...you.*] This question was meant
to stir up in the disciples' minds inquiry as to the meaning of
what they had just seen. Understanding and intelligent perception of all we do in religion, should be sought after and
valued by all true Christians. There is no real religion in blind
devotion. "What mean I by this service?" should be the
question often impressed on our minds.

13 —[*Ye call me Master and Lord.*] These words would be more
literally rendered, " Ye call Me, or speak of Me, as the Master
and the Lord." The expression seems to show that this was the
habitual language of the disciples while our Lord was on earth.
So Martha says to Mary, " The Master is come." (John xi. 28.)

[*Ye say well : for so I am.*] The word " so " is not in the
Greek. It is simply "for I am." The expression is a beautiful warrant for applying to Jesus especially the appellation
" the Lord." He has Himself endorsed it, by the words, " Ye
say well."

14 —[*If 1 then, your Lord, etc.*] The argument of this verse is
one which our Lord very frequently uses : " If I do a thing,
much more ought ye to do it." Literally rendered the meaning
is, " If I, the Person whom ye speak of as ' the Lord ' and ' the
Master,' have washed your feet, and condescended to perform
the most menial act of attention to you, ye also ought to feel it
a duty to do acts of the same kind for one another,—acts as
condescending as washing one another's feet."

The words " Your Lord and Master " in the Greek are literally, " The Lord and the Master."

" Ye ought " is a very strong expression. It is tantamount to
saying, " It is your duty and debt,—ye are under an obligation
to do it."

Paley on Evidences, p. 2, ch. iv., has a remarkable passage,
showing the close affinity between our Lord's conduct here, and
His conduct when taking a little child and putting him in the
midst of the disciples. In both he taught humility, that rare
grace, by action.

15 —[*For 1 have given you an example, etc.*] " I have, in my own
person, given you a pattern of what your own conduct should
be. The duty I want you to learn is of such vast importance
that I have not left it to a general precept, but have given you
an example of my meaning."

Of course the question at once rises,—What did our Lord
really mean ? Did he mean that we all ought literally to do the

very same thing that He did ? Or did he only mean that we are to imitate the spirit of his action ?

The Church of Rome, it is well-known, puts a literal sense on our Lord's language. Once every year, about Easter, the head of the Romish Church publicly washes the feet of certain poor persons got ready for the occasion. The absurdity, to say the least, of this view is evident on a moment's reflection.

It seems absurd to take our Lord's words literally, and to suppose that the Pope's literal washing of a few feet at Easter can supersede the duty of all Christians to do the same. Yet it is only fair to remember that the Moravians to this day take a literal view of those words, and have a custom called " pedilavium."

It is in any case absurd to suppose that our Lord would require His disciples to perform a duty which the young and the feeble would be physically unable to do.

It is inconsistent with the general tenor of our Lord's teaching to suppose that He would ever attach so much importance to a mere bodily action. " Bodily exercise profiteth little." (1 Tim. iv. 8.) A formal performance of bodily acts of religion is just the easiest thing that can be imposed on people. The thing that is really hard, and yet always required, is the service of the heart.

The true interpretation of the two verses is that which places a spiritual sense on our Lord's words. It is a practical illustration of Matt. xx. 26—28. He wished to teach His disciples that they ought to be willing to wait on one another, serve one another, minister to one another, even in the least and lowest things. They should think nothing too low, or humble, or menial to undertake, if they can show love, kindness, and condescension to another. If He, the King of kings, condescended to leave heaven to save souls, and dwell thirty-three years in this sin-defiled world, there is nothing that we should think too lowly to undertake.

Pride, because we possess wealth, rank, position, place, education, or high-breeding, is condemned heavily in this passage. He who would shrink from doing the least kindness to the poorest Christian, has read these verses to little purpose, and does not copy his Master's example.

One caution only we must remember. Let us not suppose that an ostentatious attention to the poor constitutes the whole of obedience to the law of this passage. It is easy work comparatively to care for the poor. We are to be ready to do the least acts of kindness to our equals quite as much as to the poor. There is nothing about temporal poverty in the passage. The disciples were told their duty to " one another." This is a very important point. It is much easier and more self-satisfying to play the part and do the work of a Christian to the poor than to our equals.

How entirely the passage overthrows the claim of mere talking, head-learned professors of sound doctrine, to be accounted true Christians, it is needless to show. Doctrinal orthodoxy, without practical love and humility, is utterly worthless before God.

Bullinger remarks, how singularly full of Christian truth the passage is which ends at this verse. That we are washed clean from all sins, by Christ our Saviour,—that although washed, the remainder of infirmity sticks to us, and obliges us to wash our feet daily,—that the duty of a disciple is to make Christ his example in all things,—these three great lessons stand forth most prominently.

Gurnall observes, " The master here doth not only rule the scholar's book for him ; but writes him a copy with his own hand."

JOHN XIII 16—20

16 Verily, verily, I say unto you, The servant is not greater than his lord ; neither he that is sent greater than he that sent him.

17 If ye know these things, happy are ye if ye do them.

18 I speak not of you all: I know whom I have chosen ; but that the scripture may be fulfilled, He that eateth bread with me hath lifted up his heel against me.

19 Now I tell you before it come, that, when it is come to pass, ye may believe that I am *he*.

20 Verily, verily, I say unto you, He that receiveth whomsoever I send receiveth me ; and he that receiveth me receiveth him that sent me.

IF we would understand the full meaning of these verses, we must mark carefully where they stand in the chapter. They follow hard after the remarkable passage in which we read of Christ washing His disciples' feet. They stand in close connection with His solemn command, that the disciples should do as they had seen Him do. Then come the five verses which we have now to consider.

We are taught, for one thing, in these verses, that *Christians must never be ashamed of doing anything that Christ has done.* We read, " Verily, I say unto you, The servant is not greater than his Lord ; neither he that is sent greater than he that sent him."

There seems little doubt that our Lord's all-seeing eye saw a rising unwillingness in the minds of the Apostles to do such menial things as they had just seen Him do. Puffed up with their old Jewish expectation of thrones and kingdoms in this world, secretly self-satisfied with their own position as our Lord's friends, these poor Galileans were startled at the idea of washing people's feet! They could not bring themselves to believe that Messiah's service entailed work like this. They could not yet take in the grand truth, that true Christian greatness consisted in doing good to others. And hence they needed our Lord's word of warning. If He had humbled Himself to do humbling work, His disciples must not hesitate to do the same.

The lesson is one of which we all need to be reminded. We are all too apt to dislike any work which seems to entail trouble, self-denial, and going down to our inferiors. We are only too ready to depute such work to others, and to excuse ourselves by saying, " It is not in our way." When feelings of this kind arise within us we shall find it good to remember our Lord's words in this passage, no less than our Lord's example. We ought never to think it beneath us to show kindness to the lowest of men. We ought never to hold our hand because the objects of our kindness are ungrateful or unworthy. Such was not the mind of Him who washed the feet of Judas Iscariot as well as Peter. He who in these matters cannot stoop to follow Christ's example, gives little evidence of possessing true love or true humility.

We are taught, for another thing, in these verses, *the uselessness of religious knowledge if not accompanied by practice.* We read, " If ye know these things, happy are ye if ye do them." It sounds as if our Lord would warn His disciples that they would never be really happy in His service if they were content with a barren head-knowledge of duty, and did n^t live according to their knowledge.

The lesson is one which deserves the continual remembrance of all professing Christians. Nothing is more common than to hear people saying of doctrine or duty,—" We know it, we know it;" while they sit still in unbelief or disobedience. They actually seem to flatter themselves that there is something creditable and redeeming in knowledge, even when it bears no fruit in heart, character, or life. Yet the truth is precisely the other way. To know what we ought to be, believe, and do, and yet to be unaffected by our knowledge, only adds to our guilt in·the sight of God. To know that Christians should be humble and loving, while we continue proud and selfish, will only sink us deeper in the pit, unless we awake and repent. Practice, in short, is the very life of religion. " To him that knoweth to do good, and doeth it not, to him it is sin." (James iv. 17.)

Of course we must never *despise* knowledge. It is in one sense the beginning of Christianity in the soul. So long as we know nothing of sin, or God, or Christ, or grace, or repentance, or faith, or conscience, we are of course nothing better than heathens. But we must not *overrate* knowledge. It is perfectly valueless unless it produces results in our conduct, and influences our lives, and moves our wills. In fact knowledge without practice does not raise us above the level of the devil. He could say to Jesus, "I know Thee who Thou art, the Holy One of God." The devils, says St. James, "believe and tremble." (James ii. 20.) Satan knows truth, but has no will to obey it, and is miserable. He that would be happy in Christ's service must not only know, but do.

We are taught, for another thing, in these verses, *the perfect knowledge which Christ has of all His people.* He can distinguish between false profession and true grace. The Church may be deceived, and rank men as Apostles who are nothing better than brethren of Judas Iscariot. But Jesus is never deceived, for He can read hearts. And here He declares with peculiar emphasis, " I know whom I have chosen."

This perfect knowledge of our Lord Jesus Christ is a very solemn thought, and one which cuts two ways. It ought to fill the hypocrite with alarm, and drive him to repentance. Let him remember that the eyes of the all-seeing Judge already see him through and through, and detect the want of a wedding garment. If he would not be put to shame before assembled worlds, let him cast aside his false profession, and confess his sin before it is too late. Believers, on the other hand, may think of an all-knowing Saviour with comfort. They may remember, when misunderstood and slandered by an evil world, that their Master knows all. He knows that they are true and sincere, however weak and failing. A time is coming when He will confess them before His Father, and bring forth their characters clear and bright as the summer sun at noon-day.

We are taught, finally, in these verses, *the true dignity of Christ's disciples.* The world may despise and ridicule the Apostles because they care more for works of love and humility than the pursuits of the world. But the Master bids them remember their commission, and not be ashamed. They are God's ambassadors, and have no cause to be cast down. " Verily, verily," He declares, " He that receiveth whomsoever I send receiveth Me ; and he that receiveth Me receiveth Him that sent Me."

The doctrine here laid down is full of encourage-

ment. It ought to cheer and hearten all who lay themselves out to do good, and specially to do good to the
fallen and the poor.   Work of this kind gets little
praise from men, and they who give themselves up to
it are often regarded as miserable enthusiasts, and meet
with much opposition.   Let them however work on,
and take comfort in the words of Christ which we are
now considering.   To spend and be spent in trying to
do good makes a man far more honorable in the eyes of
Jesus than to command armies or amass a fortune.   The
few who work for God in Christ's way have no cause to
be ashamed.   Let them not be cast down if the children
of the world laugh and sneer and despise them.   A day
comes when they will hear the words, "Come ye blessed children of my Father, inherit the kingdom prepared
for you." (Matt. xxv. 34.)

Notes. JOHN XIII 16—20

16 —[*Verily, verily, I say unto you, etc.*]   This well-known mode
of expression is doubtless used here to show the importance of
the lessons which our Lord is imposing on the disciples at this
point.   It is as though He said, "Do not think lightly of what
I am teaching you now.   It is no trifling matter.   Love and
humility are weighty things in my service.   I solemnly charge
you to remember that, as I have often told you, the servant is
not greater than his master, but must strictly follow his example.
The messenger sent on an errand is not greater than him that
sends him, and must carefully do as he is bid.   If I, your Master and Head, have done these actions of love and humility,
never be ashamed of doing the same, or similar ones.   If you
are really my disciples and messengers, you must prove it by
shrinking from nothing which you have seen Me do."

The Greek word which we render here, "He that is sent," is
the same that is elsewhere rendered "the Apostle."   Our
translators seem to have translated the word as they have to
show more forcibly the connection between "the sender" and
"the sent," which, to a reader ignorant of Greek, would not
have appeared if the word "apostle" had been used.

17 —*If ye know...happy...do them.*]   The object of this verse seems
to be the confirmation of the preceding one.   "Be not content
with knowing these things with your heads.   See that you
actually practice them.   If you really know and understand

my meaning, you will find it your happiness to put it in practice." The latent idea seems to be, " Wretched and miserable Christians are ye, if you know these things, and then stop short, and do not practice them."

Let us note the solemn principle which lies beneath the verse. Knowledge without practice is the character of the devil. None knows more truth, and none does more evil than he. Let us not forget that !

18 —[*I speak not of you all.*] It is not quite clear what our Lord meant by these words. Some think, as Bishop Hall, that the connection is with the verse before, and that our Lord meant, " When I speak of happiness, knowledge, and practice, I do not speak as if there was no false Apostle among you."

Others think that the sense should be carried forward. " I am not speaking as if you were all equally faithful, and equally sent by Me."

[*I know whom I have chosen.*] This sentence again admits of being taken in two senses. Some think, as Calvin, Poole, Rollock, and Hutcheson, that it refers to the eternal election and choice of those disciples who were true believers. " I know whom I have really called and chosen to be mine by my Spirit."

Others think, as Zwingle, Musculus, Hall, Whitby, Hengstenberg, and Burgon, that it only refers to the official choice and calling of the twelve when our Lord selected them to be His disciples, and has no reference to the inward call of grace. It would then mean, " I know the real inward character of all those whom I have called to be my professing disciples." It certainly favors this view, that our Lord uses precisely the same expression in John vi. 70 : " Have not I chosen you twelve, and one of you is a devil ? "

Any one who cares to see the question well discussed, will find it ably examined by Gomarus.

[*But that the Scripture...fulfilled.*] Our Lord's meaning seems to be filled up in the following way : " I speak not of you all, as if I thought you all faithful. I know that ye are not all clean and trustworthy, and I know that in this way you will see the words of Scripture fulfilled."

Here, as in many places where the expression occurs, " This was done that the Scripture might be fulfilled,'' we must not for a moment suppose that " things were done in order that Scripture might be fulfilled," but that " when things were done the Scripture was fulfilled." " I know the characters of all my disciples,'' our Lord seems to say, " and I know that very soon something will happen by which the Scripture will be fulfilled."

[*He that eateth bread, etc.*] The forty-first Psalm is here shown to apply to one greater than David, and one worse than

Ahitophel. The ninth verse here quoted says, "Mine own familiar friend, which did eat of my bread, hath lifted up his heel against me." The expression implies the act of one who like a stubborn and vicious horse, suddenly turns round against his master and kicks at him. "This," our Lord says, "is about to be fulfilled in the conduct of Judas Iscariot to Me."

It cannot of course be said that this quotation is positive proof that Judas ate the Lord's Supper. But it certainly rather increases the probability of it. The words, "eateth bread with Me," used in such close juxtaposition to the institution of the Lord's Supper, are very remarkable.

The grand lesson, that we must be prepared for much disappointment in friends and companions in this life, is very plain in this passage. The less we expect from man the better.

19 —[*Now I tell you before, etc.*] There can be little doubt that this verse applies to the warning of Judas' approaching apostasy which our Lord had just given. "I tell you of the coming fall of one of your number before it takes place, in order that when it takes place you may not be confounded, but may see fresh reason for believing that I am the promised Messiah."

The expression, "I am He," in the Greek is literally, "I am." Is there any reference to the famous "I AM" hath sent me in Exodus? It comes in close connection with "sending" in the next verse.

20 —[*Verily, verily I say, etc.*] Our Lord's purpose in this verse seems to be to encourage and cheer His faithful disciples. "Be not dismayed" he seems to say, "though one of your number is unfaithful and falls away. Persevere and fear not. Remember the high dignity of your office. I solemnly declare to you that he who receives you or any one else whom I send forth to preach the Gospel, receives Me, because ye are my representatives. Nor is this all. He that receives Me, receives not Me only, but God the Father who sent Me. Ye have no cause therefore to be ashamed of your calling however unworthily some may behave."

Let us note that it is no light matter to reject and despise a faithful minister of Christ. A weak and ignorant servant may carry a message for a royal master, and for his master's sake, ought not to be lightly esteemed. Contempt for Christ's ministers, when they are really faithful, is a bad symptom in a church or nation.

The connection of this verse with the preceding passage is certainly not easy to see, and has puzzled all commentators. Some, as Alford, have thought that our Lord intended to show the wickedness of Judas in giving up such an honorable office as that of the Apostleship. This seems far-fetched.—Some refer it back to the command to imitate our Lord's humility by washing one another's feet, and think it is meant to remind them that even they are Christ's ambassadors. I prefer the view already given, that the words are meant to cheer and comfort the disciples. Though not all were faithful, the true-hearted ones were Christ's commissioned ambassadors.

Stier says. "The whole circle of the Apostles seemed to be disgraced and broken up by the treachery of Judas, and therefore our Iord confirms the faithful in their election, and that very fitly by repeating an earlier promise."

JOHN XIII 21—30

21 When Jesus had thus said, he was troubled in spirit, and testified, and said, Verily, verily, I say unto you, that one of you shall betray me.

22 Then the disciples looked one on another, doubting of whom he spake.

23 Now there was leaning on Jesus' bosom one of his disciples, whom Jesus loved.

24 Simon Peter therefore beckoned to him, that he should ask who it should be of whom he spake.

25 He then lying on Jesus' breast saith unto him, Lord who is it?

26 Jesus answered, he it is, to whom I shall give a sop, when I have dipped *it*. And when he had dipped the sop, he gave *it* to Judas Iscariot, *the son* of Simon.

27 And after the sop Satan entered into him. Then said Jesus unto him, That thou doest, do quickly.

28 Now no man at the table knew for what intent he spake this unto him.

29 For some *of them* thought, because Judas had the bag, that Jesus had said unto him, Buy *those things* that we have need of against the feast; or, that he should give somethin to the poor.

30 He then having received the sop went immediately out: and it was night.

THE subject of the verses before us is a very painful one. They describe the last scene between our Lord Jesus Christ and the false Apostle Judas Iscariot. They contain the last words which passed between them before they parted forever in this world. They never seem to have met again on earth, excepting in the garden when our Lord was taken prisoner. Within a short time both the holy Master and the treacherous servant were dead. They will never meet again in the body till the trumpet sounds, and the dead are raised, and the judgment is set, and the books are opened. What an awful meeting will that be!

Let us mark, firstly, in this passage, *what trouble our*

Lord Jesus went through for the sake of our souls. We
are told that shortly after washing the disciples' feet,
He " was troubled in spirit, and said, One of you shall
betray Me."

The whole length and breadth and depth of our
Master's troubles during His earthly ministry are far
beyond the conception of most people. His death and
suffering on the cross were only the heading up and
completion of His sorrows. But all throughout His
life,—partly from the general unbelief of the Jews,—
partly from the special hatred of the Pharisees and Sadducees,—partly from the weakness and infirmity of
His few followers,—He must have been in a peculiar
degree "a Man of sorrows and acquainted with grief."
(Isa. liii. 3.)

But the trouble before us was a singular and exceptional one. It was the bitter sorrow of seeing a chosen
Apostle deliberately becoming an apostate, a backslider,
and an ungrateful traitor. That it was a foreseen
sorrow from the beginning we need not doubt ; but
sorrow is not less acute because long foreseen. That
it was a peculiarly cutting sorrow is very evident.
Nothing is found so hard for flesh and blood to bear
as ingratitude. Even a poet of our own has said that
it is " sharper than a serpent's tooth to have a thankless
child." Absalom's rebellion seems to have been David's
heaviest trouble, and Judas Iscariot's treachery seems to
have been one of the heaviest trials of the Son of David.
When He saw it drawing near He was " troubled in
spirit."

Passages like these should make us see the amazing
love of Christ to sinners. How many cups of sorrow
He drained to the dregs in working out our salvation,
beside the mighty cup of bearing our sins. They
show us how little reason we have for complaining

when friends fail us, and men disappoint us. If we share our Master's lot we have no cause to be surprised. Above all, they show us the perfect suitableness of Christ to be our Saviour. He can sympathize with us. He has suffered Himself, and can feel for those who are ill-used and forsaken.

Let us mark, secondly, in these verses, *the power and malignity of our great enemy the devil.* We are told in the beginning of the chapter that he "put it into the heart" of Judas to betray our Lord. We are told here that he "entered into" him. First he suggests : then he commands. First he knocks at the door and asks permission to come in : then, once admitted, he takes complete possession, and rules the whole inward man like a tyrant.

Let us take heed that we are not "ignorant of Satan's devices." He is still going to and fro in the earth, seeking whom he may devour. He is about our path, and about our bed, and spies out all our ways. Our only safety lies in resisting him at the first, and not listening to his first advances. For this we are all responsible. Strong as he is, he has no power to do us harm, if we cry to the stronger One in heaven, and use the means which He has appointed. It is a standing principle of Christianity, and will ever be found true. "Resist the devil, and he will flee from you." (James iv. 7.)

Once let a man begin tampering with the devil, and he never knows how far he may fall. Trifling with the first thoughts of sin,—making light of evil ideas when first offered to our hearts,—allowing Satan to talk to us, and flatter us, and put bad notions into our hearts,—all this may seem a small matter to many. It is precisely at this point that the road to ruin often begins. He that allows Satan to sow wicked thoughts will soon find

within his heart a crop of wicked habits. Happy is
he who really believes that there is a devil, and believing,
watches and prays daily that he may be kept from his
temptations.

Let us mark, lastly, in these verses, *the extreme
hardness which comes over the heart of a backsliding
professor of religion.* This is a thing which is most
painfully brought out in the case of Judas Iscariot.
One might have thought that the sight of our Lord's
trouble, and the solemn warning, "One of you shall
betray Me," would have stirred the conscience of this
unhappy man. But it did not do so. One might
have thought that the solemn words, "That thou
doest, do quickly," would have arrested him, and made
him ashamed of his intended sin. But nothing seems
to have moved him. Like one whose conscience was
dead, buried, and gone, he rises and goes out to do his
wicked work, and parts with his Lord for ever.

The extent to which we may harden ourselves by resisting light and knowledge is one of the most fearful
facts in our nature. We may become past feeling, like
those whose limbs are mortified before they die. We
may lose entirely all sense of fear, or shame, or remorse,
and have a heart as hard as the nether millstone, blind
to every warning, and deaf to every appeal. It is a
sore disease, but one which unhappily is not uncommon
among professing Christians. None seem so liable to it
as those who, having great light and privilege, deliberately turn their backs on Christ, and return to the world.
Nothing seems likely to touch such people, but the voice
of the archangel and the trump of God.

Let us watch jealously over our hearts, and beware
of giving way to the beginnings of sin. Happy is he
who feareth always, and walks humbly with his God.
The strongest Christian is the one who feels his weakness

most, and cries most frequently, " Hold Thou me up, and I shall be safe." (Psalm cxix. 117 ; Prov. xxviii. 14.)

Notes John xiii 21—30

21 —[*When Jesus had thus said.*] This would be more literally rendered, " had said these things," referring to all He had just been saying.

There seems to be a kind of break or pause in the narrative here. This is the point in St. John's narrative where the institution of the Lord's Supper seems to come in. At any rate there seems no point, comparing his account of this evening with that of Matthew, Mark, and Luke, where it can be so well fitted in. This is the view of Jansenius, Lampe, and Burgon.

[*He was troubled in spirit.*] This expression applied to our Lord is peculiar to St. John. We find it only in his Gospel, here and at xi. 33 and xii. 27. Here it seems to mean principally the pain and sorrow which our Lord experienced, on seeing one of his own chosen Apostles about to betray him. In addition to this, it probably includes that peculiar agony and distress of soul which our Lord was subject to under the presence of a world's sin laid upon Him, and which we see intensified in the garden of Gethsemane.

Let it be noted, that of all the Gospel writers John is the one who dwells most fully on the Divine nature of our Lord, and also is the one who describes most fully the reality of His human affections.

Observe that to be troubled and disturbed in mind is not in itself sinful. Brentius remarks, after Augustine, how foolish were the Stoic philosophers, who taught that a wise man is never disturbed in mind.

Musculus thinks that our Lord's distress and sorrow at the sight of the wickedness of Judas had much to do with this " trouble of spirit." Nothing so sad as the sight of a hardened, incorrigible backslider.

[*And testified, and said.*] The frequency with which John used the word " testified " is very remarkable. It occurs thirty-three times in his Gospel, and only three times in all the other three Gospels. Why our Lord is said to " testify " in this place is hard to see. We must suppose that it means He made an open, solemn declaration in a very impressive manner, like a witness bearing testimony to some great and unexpected fact.

[*Verily...I say...one of you...betray me.*] The solemn " Amen, amen," here, as elsewhere, was calculated to arrest the attention of the disciples to the declaration our Lord was going to make. " One out of you (*i. e.*, out of your number) shall betray Me. My last and crowning trial draws near. I am about to bear a world's sins, in my own body on the tree; and painful as it is to say, the first step in the history of my passion shall be my betrayal by one of yourselves."

Let us note our Lord's thorough foreknowledge of all the details of His sufferings, as well as of the great fact that He was about to be killed.

22 —[*Then the disciples looked...another.*] The first effect of our Lord's declaration seems to have been silence. Like men stunned and amazed, the disciples looked at one another in astonishment. The thing announced was the last thing they expected to hear.

[*Doubting of whom he spake.*] The word " doubting " hardly conveys the full force of the Greek here. It is rather, as 2 Cor. iv. 8, " perplexed," " puzzled."

Let us note that neither here nor afterwards does any suspicion appear to have fallen on Judas. For anything we can see he looked as good as Peter, James, and John, and as unlikely to betray his Master. The length to which hypocrisy can go is very awful.

23 —[*Now...leaning...Jesus' bosom.*] To understand this we must remember the customs of the East, in the time of our Lord, about the position and attitude of the guests at a meal. They did not sit, but reclined. The famous picture of the Last Supper, by Leonardo Da Vinci, gives a totally inaccurate idea of the scene.

[*One...disciples...Jesus loved.*] There can be no doubt this was John, the writer of this Gospel. It is the first time he speaks of himself in this way, and the expression occurs afterwards four times, xix. 26, xx. 7, xx. 20.

The Greek word rendered " loved " deserves notice. It signifies the higher, nobler, and more refined kind of love. There are two words in the Greek language translated " love " in the New Testament.

Let it be noted that the general special love with which our Lord loved all His disciples did not prevent His having a particular love for one individual. Why He specially loved John we are not told. Gifts certainly do not appear so much in John as grace. But it is worth noticing that love seems more the characteristic of John than of any disciple, and that in this he showed more of the mind of Christ. It is quite clear that special friendship for one individual is quite consistent with love for all.

It is noteworthy that of all the writers of the New Testament, none goes so deep and reveals so much of the hidden things of God as he who lay in the bosom of Christ.

24 —[*Simon Peter therefore beckoned, etc.*] The characteristic for

wardness and zeal of Peter come out strikingly in this verse. None seem so excited by our Lord's announcement as he is. None is so anxious to know of whom our Lord can be speaking. He cannot wait silently like the others. He makes a sign to John to ask privately who it can be. A fisherman by early training, like John, he was probably intimate with him, and could make himself understood by signs.

Let us note that the whole transaction seems to show that Peter did not sit next our Lord in the post of honor and favor. That place was given to John.

Rollock here observes, that so far from Peter having any primacy among the Apostles, he here uses the intercession of John !

25 —[*He then lying on Jesus' breast, etc.*] The Greek words here would be more literally rendered, "He having fallen upon." It is so translated in eleven out of twelve other places where it occurs in the New Testament. The idea is evidently of one moving and leaning towards another, so as to get closer to him and whisper a question, so as not to be heard or observed. That this is what John did is evident. It is plain that he did not say out aloud, " Lord, who is it ? "

26 —[*Jesus answered... He... sop... dipped it.*] The action by which our Lord told John He would indicate the traitor to him, was probably so common at an Eastern banquet, that no one at the table would remark anything about it. That it was a common way of eating is shown by Ruth ii. 14, " Dip thy morsel in the vinegar." The word " sop," the marginal reading tells us, might be translated "morsel." To give a morsel, as our Lord did, was probably a mark of favor or compliment.

That our Lord's answer was whispered, is evident. No one seems to have noticed it, except John.

Hengstenberg observes, that by this act of kindness and attention Jesus " would touch the heart of Judas once more, if haply he might be susceptible of better emotions."

[*And when...dipped...gave....Judas...Simon.*] The word " gave " is literally " gives," in the present tense, showing the immediate action which followed our Lord's reply to John's question.

Here, as elsewhere, it is noteworthy that John specially calls Judas " the son of Simon," in order to make it quite clear what Judas it was who did this foul deed.

Bengel remarks, " How very near to Jesus was Judas on this occasion ! But in a short time after, by what a wide gulf did glory separate Jesus from Judas, and destruction separate Judas from Jesus."

27 —[*And after the sop...Satan entered...him.*] Of course this does not mean that now for the first time Satan entered, but

that from this moment Satan got full and entire possession of the heart of Judas. Up to this time he was in it, but now he possessed it.

The word " then " is emphatically given in the Greek, but omitted by our translators. It should be, " After the Supper, then Satan entered into him."

Let us note the reality, personality, and awful power of our great spiritual enemy the devil. There are degrees in his power and dominion over us. If his first temptations are not resisted, he may in the end gain full and entire possession of every part of our soul, and lead us captive to be his slaves. This seems the history of Judas.

Musculus observes that even at the first communion Satan was present, and busy in a heart.

[*Then said Jesus...that...doest...do quickly.*] The full meaning and purport of this solemn saying it is not easy to define positively. It is evidently a very elliptical saying, and we can only conjecture about it.

Of course we cannot suppose that our Lord desired to hasten on an act of wickedness, nor yet can we suppose for a moment that there was any impatience in our Lord, or unwillingness to await the hour of His sufferings.—But we must remember that our Lord foreknew perfectly all that was before Him in the next twenty-four hours. Does He not then speak to Judas as to one of the instruments in the great work which was about to be accomplished? Does He not seem to say, " If thou must indeed do this wicked act—and I know now that the prince of this world has got full possession of thy heart,—go on and do it. There need be no delay. I am ready to suffer and to die. Do thy part, and I will do mine. The Sacrifice is ready to be slain. Do thy part in the transaction, and let there be no unnecessary waste of time."

Chrysostom says, " This is not the expression of one commanding, nor advising, but of one reproaching, and showing him that He desired to correct him; but that since he was incorrigible, He let him go.

Augustine says, " This was a word rather of glad readiness than of anger."

Calvin says, " Hitherto Jesus tried by various methods to bring Judas back, but to no purpose. Now He addresses him as a desperate man : ' Go to destruction, since you have resolved to go to destruction.' In doing so He performs the office of a Judge who condemns to death not those whom He drives of His own accord to ruin, but those who have already ruined themselves by their own fault."

Cyril starts the odd idea that our Lord addresses these words to Satan rather than Judas, and as it were challenges him to do his worst!

Gerhard sees a likeness in the expression, to God's words to Balaam, when He says, "Rise up and go." (Num. xxii. 20.) They did not signify approbation, but only a permission. Yet God's anger was kindled when Balaam went with Balak's ambassadors.

Musculus observes the use of the present tense here. It is not "What thou art going to do," but "What thou art doing now." Even at the Lord's table wickedness was going on in Judas' heart.

Lightfoot says, "I take this expression for a tacit, severe threat, pronounced not without scorn and indignation : 'I know well what thou art contriving against Me. What thou doest, do quickly, else thy own death may prevent thee; for thou hast but a very short time to live. Thy own end draws on apace."

Whitby compares it to Ezek. xx. 39: "Go ye, serve every one his idols."

Some, as Hengstenberg, would render the Greek word for quickly "more quickly," as if our Lord wished him to hasten his work. But there seems no necessity for this.

After all it is noteworthy that the disciples did not know what the saying meant ; and even John, though writing forty or fifty years afterwards, by inspiration of God, was not directed to explain it, though he does explain our Lord's sayings in other places. We may therefore safely leave the meaning somewhat uncertain.

That our Lord spoke these mysterious words aloud and openly, so that all the company heard, is quite evident from the context. John's question was a whisper ; his reply was another whisper, and neither was remarked or heard by others. But the address to Judas was heard by all.

28 —[*Now no man at the table, etc.*] This verse would be more literally rendered, "Now this thing no one knew, of them that were sitting at table, for what purpose He said it to him." The sentence confirms the statement above made, that both John's question and our Lord's answer were spoken in a whisper or undertone, and not noticed by any one. This sudden address of our Lord to Judas would therefore take the disciples by surprise.

29 —[*For some of them thought, etc.*] This whole verse is interesting, and throws light on some curious points.

The statement that "Judas had the bag," shows the position he occupied among the Apostles. He was so far from being suspected, that he had the charge of the common store of mon-

ey. Bullinger even thinks that he must have been a man remarkable for wisdom, prudence, economy, and faithfulness.

The supposition of some, that Jesus told Judas to " buy the
things needed against the feast," shows clearly that our Lord
did not work miracles in order to procure the necessaries required by Himself and His disciples. Christians must buy and
sell like other people, and must manage their money affairs
with prudence and economy. It shows how little the disciples
realized that their Master's death was close at hand.

The supposition of others, that Jesus told Judas to "give
something to the poor," shows plainly what was our Lord's custom in the matter of almsgiving. He sanctified and adorned
the practice of caring for the poor by His own example. This
passage, and Gal. ii. 10, deserve careful consideration. It may
be doubted whether the English Poor Law has not tended to
shut up English almsgiving far more than is right before God.

Let us mark the snares which attend the possession, finger-
ing, and handling of money. The man who has care of the
money in our Lord's little company of followers, is the very
man who makes shipwreck of his soul forever, through the
love of money. " Give me neither poverty nor riches," should
be a Christian's frequent prayer. (Prov. xxx. 8.)

Bullinger points out that the possession of money is evidently
not in itself sinful and wicked, and argues from the verse that
the Romish mendicant friars, and others who made a merit of
self-imposed poverty, are under a complete delusion. It is not
the having, but the misusing money which is sinful.

30 —[*He then...received...sop...immediately out.*] The hasty departure of Judas as soon as our Lord had given him the morsel, and spoken the remarkable words already commented on,
may easily be explained. He saw at once that our Lord knew
all his plot, and dreaded exposure. His conscience condemned
him, and he dared no longer sit in our Lord's company. He at
any rate understood what our Lord meant, if nobody else did.
He felt himself detected and discovered, and for very shame
got up and went away.

It is curious and noteworthy that John, at all events, must
have known Judas to be the traitor, and yet he seems to have
said nothing.

It seems very difficult to me to explain this part of the history of this memorable evening, unless we admit that Judas
Iscariot received the Lord's Supper with the other Apostles.—
From this point to the seizure of our Lord in the garden, the
narrative flows on without break or interruption, and I cannot
see any place at which the Lord's Supper can come in. I therefore hold strongly that Judas was actually a communicant.—
The subject is very fully discussed by Gerhard, who takes this
view, and confirms it by quotations from Cyprian, Jerome Au-

gustine, Chrysostom, Cyril of Jerusalem, Theodoret, Euthymius, Aquinas, Ferus, Toletus, Bellarmine, Jansenius, Baronius, Maldonatus, Calvin, Beza, Martyr, Bucer, and Whittaker. After all the expression of Luke xxii. 21 appears to me unanswerable.

[*And it was night.*] This emphatic little sentence of course is not inserted without a meaning ; but why, we are left to conjecture.

Perhaps it was meant to show us that Judas purposely waited till darkness, to accomplish his deed of darkness. " This is your hour, and the power of darkness." (Luke xxii. 53.)

Perhaps it was meant to show that Judas slunk off at a time when nobody could see where he went, follow him, or observe his movements.

Perhaps it was meant to show that the time was hastening on, and that our Lord had reason to say, " That thou doest, do quickly."

Perhaps it was only meant to mark the precise time when our Lord delivered the exquisite address of the next three chapters. St. John loves to mark time and places in his narrative.

One thing, at any rate, is very clear. The expression shows that the first Lord's Supper was not celebrated by day, but by night. The objections to an evening sacrament commonly made by certain persons, are really so untenable in the face of this passage, that one marvels how men of common sense can make them.

JOHN XIII 31—38.

31 Therefore, when he was gone out, Jesus said, Now is the Son of Man glorified, and God is glorified in him.

32 If God be glorified in him, God shall also glorify him in himself, and shall straightway glorify him.

33 Little children, yet a little while I am with you. Ye shall seek me: and as I said unto the Jews, Whither I go, ye cannot come ; so now I say to you.

34 A new commandment I give unto you, that ye love one another ; as I have loved you, that ye also love one another.

35 By this shall all *men* know that ye are my disciples, if ye have love one to another.

36 Simon Peter said unto him, Lord, whither goest thou? Jesus answered him, Whither I go, thou canst not follow me now ; but thou shalt follow me afterwards.

37 Peter said unto him, Lord, why cannot I follow thee now ? I will lay down my life for thy sake.

38 Jesus answered him, Wilt thou lay down thy life for my sake ? Verily, verily, I say unto thee, The cock shall not crow, till thou hast denied me thrice.

In this passage we find the Lord Jesus at last alone

with His eleven faithful disciples. The traitor, Judas Iscariot, had left the room, and gone out to do his wicked deed of darkness. Freed from his painful company, our Lord opens His heart to His little flock more fully than He had ever done before. Speaking to them for the last time before His passion, He begins a discourse which for touching interest surpasses any portion of Scripture.

These verses show us *what glory the crucifixion brought both to God the Father and to God the Son.* It seems impossible to avoid the conclusion that this was what our Lord had in His mind when He said, "Now is the Son of man glorified, and God is glorified in Him."—It is as though He said, "The time of my crucifixion is at hand. My work on earth is finished. An event is about to take place to-morrow, which, however painful to you who love Me, is in reality most glorifying both to Me and My Father."

This was a dark and mysterious saying, and we may well believe that the eleven did not understand it. And no wonder ! In all the agony of the death on the cross, in all the ignominy and humiliation which they saw afar off, or heard of next day, in hanging naked for six hours between two thieves,—in all this there was no appearance of glory ! On the contrary, it was an event calculated to fill the minds of the Apostles with shame, disappointment, and dismay. And yet our Lord's saying was true.

The crucifixion brought glory to the Father. It glorified His wisdom, faithfulness, holiness, and love. It showed Him wise, in providing a plan whereby He could be just, and yet the Justifier of the ungodly.—It showed Him faithful, in keeping His promise, that the seed of the woman should bruise the serpent's head.—It showed Him holy, in requiring His law's demands to be satisfied

by our great Substitute.—It showed Him loving, in providing such a Mediator, such a Redeemer, and such a
Friend for sinful man as His co-eternal Son.

The crucifixion brought glory to the Son. It glorified His compassion, His patience, and His power. It
showed Him most compassionate, in dying for us, suffering in our stead, allowing Himself to be counted sin and
a curse for us, and buying our redemption with the price
of His own blood.—It showed Him most patient, in not
dying the common death of most men, but in willingly
submitting to such horrors and unknown agonies as no
mind can conceive, when with a word he could have
summoned His Father's angels, and been set free.—It
showed Him most powerful, in bearing the weight of all
a world's transgressions, and vanquishing Satan and
despoiling him of his prey.

For ever let us cling to these thoughts about the
crucifixion. Let us remember that painting and sculp-
ture can never tell a tenth part of what took place on
the cross. Crucifixes and pictures at best can only
show us a human being agonizing in a painful death.
But of the length and breadth and depth and height of
the work transacted on the cross,—of God's law honored, man's sins borne, sin punished in a Substitute, free
salvation bought for man,—of all this they can tell
nothing. Yet all this lies hid under the crucifixion. No
wonder St. Paul cries, "God forbid that I should glory,
save in the cross of our Lord Jesus Christ." (Gal. vi. 14.)

These verses show us, secondly, *what great importance our Lord Jesus attaches to the grace of brotherly
love.* Almost as soon as the false Apostle had left the
faithful eleven, comes the injunction, "Love one another." Immediately after the sad announcement that
He would leave them soon, the commandment is given,
"Love one another." It is called a "new" command-

ment, not because it had never been given before, but because it was to be more honored, to occupy a higher position, to be backed by a higher example than it ever had been before. Above all, it was to be the test of Christianity before the world. " By this shall all men know that ye are my disciples, if ye have love one to another."

Let us take heed that this well-known Christian grace is not merely a notion in our heads, but a practice in our lives. Of all the commands of our Master there is none which is so much talked about and so little obeyed as this. Yet, if we mean anything when we profess to have charity and love toward all men, it ought to be seen in our tempers and our words, our bearing and our doing, our behavior at home and abroad, our conduct in every relation of life. Specially it ought to show itself forth in all our dealing with other Christians. We should regard them as brethren and sisters, and delight to do anything to promote their happiness. We should abhor the idea of envy, malice, and jealousy towards a member of Christ, and regard it as a downright sin. This is what our Lord meant when He told us to love one another.

Christ's cause in the earth would prosper far more than it does if this simple law was more honored. There is nothing that the world understands and values more than true charity. The very men who cannot comprehend doctrine, and know nothing of theology, can appreciate charity. It arrests their attention, and makes them think. For the world's sake, if for no other cause, let us follow after charity more and more.

These verses show us, lastly, *how much self-ignorance there may be in the heart of a true believer.* We see Simon Peter declaring that he was ready to lay down his life for his Master. We see his Master telling him that in that very night he would "deny Him thrice." And we all know how the matter ended. The Master was right, and Peter was wrong.

Let it be a settled principle in our religion, that there is an amount of weakness in all our hearts, of which we have no adequate conception, and that we never know how far we might fall if we were tempted. We fancy sometimes, like Peter, that there are some things we could not possibly do. We look pitifully upon others who fall, and please ourselves in the thought that at any rate we should not have done so. We know nothing at all. The seeds of every sin are latent in our hearts, even when renewed, and they only need occasion, or carelessness and the withdrawal of God's grace for a season, to put forth an abundant crop. Like Peter, we may think we can do wonders for Christ, and like Peter, we may learn by bitter experience that we have no power and might at all.

The servant of Christ will do wisely to remember these things. "Let him that thinketh he standeth, take heed lest he fall." (1 Cor. x. 12.) A humble sense of our own innate weakness, a constant dependence on the Strong for strength, a daily prayer to be held up, because we cannot hold up ourselves,—these are the true secrets of safety. The great Apostle of the Gentiles said, "When I am weak, then I am strong." (2 Cor. xii. 10.)

Notes John xiii 31—38

31 —[*Therefore, when...gone out, Jesus said.*] The withdrawal of Judas from the company of the disciples, at that point, forms a distinct break in the narrative. At once, from this time, our Lord seems to speak as one relieved by the absence of an uncongenial mind. There is a manifest alteration in the tone of all He says. It seems pitched in a higher key.

Bengel, at this point, interposes an entire interval of a night, and thinks that a new discourse begins here. It seems a needless view, and is very unnatural.

[*Now is the Son of Man glorified, etc., etc.*] This is a deep
saying, and not least so because both the verbs are in the past
tense. Literally rendered in each case, the verb should be
" has been glorified." This is not an uncommon mode of
speech. The glorification is so near, so certain, so complete,
that it is spoken of as a thing accomplished, and even past. It
was accomplished in purpose, and in a few hours would be accomplished in reality. (So John xvii. 4.) The meaning of our
Lord may probably be paraphrased thus : " Now has the time
come that I, the Son of Man, should be glorified, by actually
dying as man's substitute, and shedding my blood for the sins
of the world. Now has the time come that God the Father
should receive the highest glory by my sacrifice on the cross."

Let it be noted that the Lord regards His own atoning death
on the cross as the most glorious part of His work on earth ;
and that nothing so tends to glorify the Father's attributes of
justice, holiness, mercy, and faithfulness to His promises, as
the death of the Son.

Let it be noted that the Lord does not speak of His death as
a punishment, or disgrace, or humiliation, but as an event most
glorious,—glorifying both to Himself and to the Father. So
Christians should learn to " glory in the cross."

If we do not take this view, and adhere to a strictly literal
rendering of the verb glorified, as past, as Hengstenberg does,
we must suppose it to mean, " Now at last, by my perfect
righteousness in life and willingness to suffer in death, I, the
Son of man, have received glory, and my Father at the same
time has received glory through Me." But the other interpretation, taking the past tense for the present or future, is
better. "The sacrifice has begun. The last act of my redeeming work,—specially glorifying myself and my Father,—has
actually commenced or is commencing."

Augustine and Ecolampadius hold that the expression, " Now
is the Son of Man glorified," has a special reference to the glory which surrounds our Lord when the wicked are all put
away from Him, and He is attended only by saints. This peculiar glory was on Him when Judas Iscariot went out, and
left Him and His faithful disciples alone.

32.—[*If God be glorified in him, etc.*] This verse may be paraphrased as follows : " If God the Father be specially glorified
in all His attributes by my death, He shall proceed at once to
place special glory on Me, for my personal work, and shall do
it without delay, by raising Me from the dead, and placing Me
at His right hand." It is like the famous passage in Philippians : " Wherefore God also hath highly exalted Him." It is
the same idea that we have in the seventeenth chapter more
fully : " I have glorified Thee on the earth ;—now, O Father,
glorify Thou Me with Thine own self." (Phil. ii. 9 ; John
xvii, 5.)

If the Son, on the one hand, specially glorifies the Father's attributes of holiness, justice, and mercy, by satisfying all His demands with His own precious blood on the cross, so, on the other hand, the Father specially glorifies the Son, by exalting Him above all Kings, raising Him from the dead, and giving Him a name above every name.

" In Himself" must refer to that special and peculiar glory which, in the counsels of the blessed Trinity, is conferred on the Second Person, on account of His incarnation, cross, and passion.

It is hardly needful to remind Christians that " if " does not imply any doubtfulness, but is rather equivalent to " since " as in Coloss. iii. 1 : " If ye then be risen with Christ."

If any one wishes to adhere rigidly to the past tense in the first " glorified " of this verse, it undoubtedly makes excellent meaning. " If God the Father has been glorified on the earth by my life and perfect obedience to His law, He will also glorify Me in my own person, by raising Me from the dead, and placing Me at His own right hand, and that very soon." But I doubt this being the full meaning, for the reasons given in the preceding verse.

The perfect harmony and co-operation of the Persons in the blessed Trinity shine out here. The Son glorifies the Father, and the Father glorifies the Son. The Son shows the world by His death how holy and just is the Father, and how He hates sin. The Father shows the world, by raising and exalting the Son to glory, how He delights in the redemption for sinners which the Son has accomplished.

Chrysostom thinks, that " straightway glorify Him " must refer to the special signs and wonders which appeared from the very time that our Lord was on the cross. " So the sun was darkened, the rocks rent, the veil of the temple parted, many bodies of the saints arose, the tomb had its seal, the guards sat by, and while a stone lay on the grave, the body rose."

Musculus remarks, that here you have the great principle asserted which is always true : " Those who glorify God shall be glorified by God."

33 —[*Little children*.] This is the only time our Lord ever calls His disciples by this name. It was evidently a term of affection and compassion, like the language of a father speaking to children whom he is about to leave alone as orphans in the world. " My believing followers, whom I love and regard as my children."

Observe that the expression is not used till Judas has gone away. Unbelievers are not to be addressed as Christ's children.

[*Yet a little while I am with you.*] This seems to mean, " I am only staying a very little longer with you. The time is short. The hour approaches when we must part. Give me your best attention while I talk to you for the last time before I go."

[*Ye shall seek Me.*] It is not quite clear what this means. Of course it cannot refer to the time after the resurrection, when the disciples were fully convinced that " the Lord had risen." Much less can it refer to the time after the ascension. I can only suppose it means, " After my death ye shall be perplexed, amazed, and confounded for a little season, wanting Me, seeking Me, wishing for Me, and wondering where I am gone. The very moment the little child is left alone by mother or nurse, it begins to cry after her and want her. So will it be with you."

[*And as I said unto the Jews, etc.*] This sentence can only mean, " The words that I said to the Jews will soon apply to you also, though in a very different sense. Whither I am going you cannot follow Me. You will follow Me hereafter; but at present there is a gulf between us, and you will not see Me."

Of course the words applied to the Jews meant that Jesus was going to a place where spiritually and morally the Jews were unfit to go, and in their impenitent state could not go. The words applied to the disciples only meant that Jesus was going into a world where they could not follow Him till they died. They were remaining on earth, and He was going to heaven.

Hengstenberg observes, that this is the only place in which Jesus ever spoke to His disciples concerning " the Jews." Elsewhere He uses the expression in speaking to the Samaritan woman (John iv. 22) and before Caiaphas and Pilate.

34 —[*A new commandment, etc.*] The immense importance of Christian love or charity cannot possibly be shown more strikingly than by the way that it is urged on the disciples in this place. Here is our Lord leaving the world, speaking for the last time, and giving His last charge to His disciples. The very first subject He takes up and presses on them, is the great duty of loving one another, and that with no common love ; but after the same patient, tender, unwearied manner that He has loved them. Love must needs be a very rare and important grace to be so spoken of ! The want of it must needs be a plain proof that a man is no true disciple of Christ. How vast the extent of Christian love ought to be ! The measure and standard of it is the love wherewith Christ loved us. His was a love even to death.

Melancthon points out our Lord's great desire to promote unity and concord among professing Christians, by His dwelling so much on love before He left the world.

Why did our Lord call love a "new" commandment? This is a rather difficult question, and has called forth great variety of opinions. One thing only is very clear. Jesus did not mean to say that "love" was a grace peculiar to the Gospel, and was nowhere taught in the law of Moses. To say this, is a mark of great ignorance. The point is set at rest by the words in Lev. xix. 18: "Thou shalt love thy neighbor as thyself." What then does this word "new" mean?

Some think, as Chrysostom, that our Lord refers to the degree with which Christians should love,—even as He had loved them. This was a new and higher standard than had been yet known. Hitherto, as Cyril says, men were to love others as themselves. Now they were to love them more than themselves.—Some think that our Lord refers to the great duty of Christians to love one another, and cling to one another with a special and peculiar love, over and above the love they had generally to all mankind. This was in a sense a novelty.— Some think that our Lord only meant that He renewed and re-created the great law of love, and raised it to so much higher a position than it had ever held among the Jews, that it might be truly called a "new commandment." The parable of the good Samaritan shows how little the Jews realized the duty of loving their neighbors. He had in view the utter neglect into which the law of love had fallen among Jewish teachers like the Pharisees, and like Isaac digging the earth out of the old well, would give the law a second beginning, as if it were new.

Some, as Maldonatus and Suicer, think that the expression is only a Hebraism, and that "new," "rare," and "excellent" are synonymous. Thus a new name, a new song, a new wine. (Rev. ii. 17 ; Psalm xcv. 1 ; Matt. xxvi. 29.)

Perhaps there is something in each and all of these views. One thing is very certain : nothing could exalt the value of love so highly as to call it a "new commandment."

Scott observes that the law of. love to others " was now to be explained with new clearness, enforced by new motives and obligations, illustrated by a new example, and obeyed in a new manner.

35 —[*By this shall all men know, etc.*] There can be no mistake about these words. Love was to be the grand characteristic, the distinguishing mark of Christ's disciples.

Let us note that our Lord does not name gifts, or miracles, or intellectual attainments, but love, the simple grace of love, a grace within reach of the poorest, lowliest believer, as the evidence of discipleship. No love, no grace, no regeneration, no true Christianity !

Musculus observes, with withering scorn, how little likeness there is between our Lord's mark of discipleship, and the dresses, beads, fastings, and self-imposed austerities of the Church of Rome.

Let us note what a heavy condemnation this verse pronounces on sectarianism, bigotry, narrow-mindedness, party-spirit, strife, bitterness, needless controversy between Christian and Christian.

Let us note how far from satisfactory is the state of those who are content with sound doctrinal opinions, and orthodox correct views of the Gospel, while in their daily life they give way to ill-temper, ill-nature, malice, envy, quarrelling, squabbling, bickering, surliness, passion, snappish language, and crossness of word and manner. Such persons, whether they know it or not, are daily proclaiming that they are not Christ's disciples. It is nonsense to talk about justification, and regeneration, and election, and conversion, and the uselessness of works, unless people can see in us practical Christian love.

Whitby remarks that in the primitive ages the mutual love of Christians was notorious among heathens. "See how these Christians love one another," was a common saying, according to Tertullian. Even Julian the apostate proposed them to the heathen as a pattern in this respect.

36 —[*Simon Peter...Lord, whither goest Thou?*] Here as elsewhere, the forward, impulsive spirit of Peter prompts him to ask anxiously what our Lord meant by talking of going: " Whither goest Thou?" Can we doubt however that in this question he was the spokesman of all?

How very little the disciples had ever comprehended our Lord's repeated saying that He must be taken prisoner, crucified, and die, we see in this place. Often as He had told them He must die, they had never realized it, and are startled when He talks of going away. It is marvellous how much religious teaching men may have, and yet not take it in, receive, or believe it, especially when it contradicts preconceived notions.

[*Jesus answered him, etc.*] Our Lord graciously explains here a part of His meaning. He does not explicitly tell Peter where He is going; but He tells him He is going to a place where Peter cannot follow Him now during his lifetime, but will follow Him after his death, at a future date. It is not unlikely, as Cyril observes, that these words, "Thou shalt follow Me," pointed to the manner of Peter's death by crucifixion. He was to walk in his Master's steps, and enter heaven by the same road.

37 —[*Peter said...Lord, why...follow Thee now, etc.*] This question shows how little Peter realized what our Lord fully meant, and the nearness of His death on the cross. "Why cannot I follow Thee now? Where is the place Thou art going to on earth, where I am not willing and ready to follow Thee? I love Thee so much, and am so determined to cling to Thee, that I am ready to lay down my life rather than be separate from Thee."

These words were well meant, and Peter never doubted, perhaps, that he could stand to them. But he did not know his own heart. There was more feeling than principle in his declaration. He did not see all that was in himself.

Let us note the mischief of self-ignorance. Let us pray for humility. Let us beware of over-confidence in our own courage and steadfastness. Pride goeth before a fall.

38 —[*Jesus answered him, Wilt thou, etc.*] Our Lord's meaning appears to be, " Wilt thou really and truly lay down thy life for Me ? Thou little knowest thy own weakness and feebleness. I tell thee in the most solemn answer, that this very night, before the cock crow, before sunrise, thou, even thou, wilt deny three times that thou knowest Me. So far from laying down thy life, thou wilt try to save thy life by cowardly denying that thou hast anything to do with Me."

Let us note the wonderful foreknowledge of our Lord. What an unlikely thing it seemed that such a professor should fall so far and so soon. Yet our Lord foresaw it all !

Let us note the wonderful kindness and condescension of Jesus. He knew perfectly well the weakness and feebleness of His chief disciple, and yet never rejected him, and even raised him again after his fall. Christians should be men of very pitiful and tender feelings toward weak brethren. Their inconsistencies may be very great and provoking, but we must never forget our Lord's dealing with Simon Peter.

JOHN XIV 1—3

1 Let not your heart be troubled : ye believe in God, believe also in me.

2 In my father's house are many mansions : if *it were* not *so*, I would have told you. I go to prepare a place for you.

3 And if I go and prepare a place for you, I will come again, and receive you unto myself : that where I am, *there* ye may be also.

THE three verses we have now read are rich in precious truth. For eighteen centuries they have been peculiarly dear to Christ's believing servants in every part of the world. Many are the sick rooms which they have lightened ! Many are the dying hearts which they have cheered ! Let us see what they contain.

We have, first, in this passage *a precious remedy against an old disease.* That disease is trouble of heart. That remedy is faith.

Heart-trouble is the commonest thing in the world. No rank, or class, or condition is exempt from it. No bars, or bolts, or locks can keep it out. Partly from inward causes and partly from outward,—partly from the body and partly from the mind,—partly from what we love and partly from what we fear, the journey of life is full of trouble. Even the best of Christians have many bitter cups to drink between grace and glory. Even the holiest saints find the world a vale of tears.

Faith in the Lord Jesus is the only sure medicine for troubled hearts. To believe more thoroughly, trust more entirely, rest more unreservedly, lay hold more firmly, lean back more completely,—this is the prescription which our Master urges on the attention of all His disciples. No doubt the members of that little band which sat round the table at the last supper, had believed already. They had proved the reality of their faith by giving up everything for Christ's sake. Yet what does their Lord say to them here? Once more He presses on them the old lesson, the lesson with which they first began: "Believe! Believe more! Believe on Me!" (Isai. xxvi. 3.)

Never let us forget that there are degrees in faith, and that there is a wide difference between weak and strong believers. The weakest faith is enough to give a man a saving interest in Christ, and ought not to be despised, but it will not give a man such inward comfort as a strong faith. Vagueness and dimness of perception are the defect of weak believers. They do not see clearly what they believe and why they believe. In such cases more faith is the one thing needed. Like Peter on the water, they need to look more steadily at Jesus, and less at the waves and wind. Is it not written,

" Thou wilt keep him in perfect peace whose mind is stayed on Thee "? (Isai. xxvi. 3.)

We have, secondly, in this passage *a very comfortable account of heaven, or the future abode of saints.* It is but little that we understand about heaven while we are here in the body, and that little is generally taught us in the Bible by negatives much more than positives. But here, at any rate, there are some plain things.

Heaven is " a Father's house,"—the house of that God of whom Jesus says, " I go to my Father, and your Father." It is, in a word, home : the home of Christ and Christians. This is a sweet and touching expression. Home, as we all know, is the place where we are generally loved for our own sakes, and not for our gifts or possessions; the place where we are loved to the end, never forgotten, and always welcome. This is one idea of heaven. Believers are in a strange land and at school in this life. In the life to come they will be at home.

Heaven is a place of " mansions,"—of lasting, permanent, and eternal dwellings. Here in the body we are in lodgings, tents, and tabernacles, and must submit to many changes. In heaven we shall be settled at last, and go out no more. " Here we have no continuing city." (Heb. xiii. 14.) Our house not made with hands shall never be taken down.

Heaven is a place of "many mansions." There will be room for all believers and room for all sorts, for little saints as well as great ones, for the weakest believer as well as for the strongest. The feeblest child of God need not fear there will be no place for him. None will be shut out but impenitent sinners and obstinate unbelievers.

Heaven is a place where Christ Himself shall be present. He will not be content to dwell without His people :—" Where I am, there ye shall be also." We need not think that we shall be alone and neglected. Our Saviour,—our elder Brother,—our Redeemer, who loved us and gave Himself for us, shall be in the midst of us forever. What we shall see, and whom we shall see in heaven, we cannot fully conceive yet, while we are in the body. But one thing is certain : we shall see Christ.

Let these things sink down into our minds. To the worldly and careless they may seem nothing at all. To all who feel in themselves the working of the Spirit of God they are full of unspeakable comfort. If we hope to be in heaven it is pleasant to know what heaven is like.

We have, lastly, in this passage *a solid ground for expecting good things to come.* The evil heart of unbelief within us is apt to rob us of our comfort about heaven. " We wish we could think it was all true."—" We fear we shall never be admitted into heaven."—Let us hear what Jesus says to encourage us.

One cheering word is this,—" I go to prepare a place for you." Heaven is a prepared place for a prepared people : a place which we shall find Christ Himself has made ready for true Christians. He has prepared it by procuring a right for every sinner who believes to enter in. None can stop us, and say we have no business there.—He has prepared it by going before us as our Head and Representative, and taking possession of it for all the members of His mystical body. As our Forerunner He has marched in, leading captivity captive, and has planted His banner in the land of glory.—He has prepared it by carrying our names with Him as our High Priest into the holy of holies, and making angels ready to receive us. They that enter heaven will find they are neither unknown nor unexpected.

Another cheering word is this,—" I will come again and receive you unto myself." Christ will not wait for believers to come up to Him, but will come down to them, to raise them from their graves and escort them to their heavenly home. As Joseph came to meet Jacob, so will Jesus come to call His people togethei and guide them to their inheritance. The second advent ought never to be forgotten. Great is the blessedness of looking back to Christ coming the first time to suffer for us, but no less great is the comfort of looking forward to Christ coming the second time, to raise and reward His saints.

Let us leave the whole passage with solemnized feelings and serious self-examination. How much they miss who live in a dying world and yet know nothing of God as their Father and Christ as their Saviour ! How much they possess who live the life of faith in the Son of God, and believe in Jesus ! With all their weaknesses and crosses they have that which the world can neither give nor take away. They have a true Friend while they live, and a true home when they die.

NOTES. JOHN XIV 1—3

1 —[*Let not...heart...be troubled.*] We must carefully remember that there is no break between the end of the thirteenth and beginning of the fourteenth chapters. Our Lord is continuing the discourse He began after the Lord's Supper and the departure of Judas, in the presence of the eleven faithful disciples. A slight pause there certainly seems to be, since He turns from Peter, to whom He had been speaking individually, to the whole body of the Apostles, and addresses them collectively. But the place, the time, and the audience are all one.

Our Lord's great object throughout this and the two following chapters seems clear and plain. He desired to comfort, stablish, and build up His downcast disciples. He saw their " hearts were troubled" from a variety of causes,—partly by seeing their Master "troubled in Spirit " (xiii. 21),—partly by hearing that one of them should betray Him,—partly by the mysterious departure of Judas,—partly by their Master's announcement that He should only be a little time longer with them, and that at last they could not come with Him,—and partly by the warning addressed to Peter, that he would deny his Master thrice. For all these reasons this little company of weak believers was disquieted and cast down and anxious. Their gracious Master saw it, and proceeded to give them encouragement : " Let not your heart be troubled." It will be noted that He uses the singular number " your heart," not " your hearts." He means " the heart of any one of you."

Hengstenberg gives the following list of the grounds of comfort which the chapter contains, in systematic order, which well deserves attention. (a) The first encouragement is, that to the disciples of Christ heaven is sure (v. 2, 3). (b) The second encouragement is, that disciples have in Christ a certain way to heaven (v. 4—11). (c) The third encouragement is, that disciples need not fear that with the departure of Christ His work will cease (v. 12—14). (d) The fourth encouragement is, that in the absence of Christ disciples will have the help of the Spirit (v. 15—17). (e) The fifth encouragement is, that Christ will not leave His people for ever, but will come back again (v. 18—24). (f) The sixth encouragement is, that the Spirit will teach the disciples and supply their want of understanding when left alone (v. 25, 26). (g) Finally, the seventh encouragement is, that the legacy of peace will be left to cheer them in their Master's absence (v. 27.) These seven points are well worthy the attention of all believers in every age, and are as useful now as when first pressed on the eleven.

Lightfoot thinks one principal cause of the disciples' trouble, was their disappointment at seeing their Jewish expectations of a temporal kingdom under a temporal Messiah failing and coming to an end.

[*Ye believe...God...believe...Me.*] The Gospel words rendered " Ye believe," and " believe," in this place, admit of being differently translated ; and it is impossible to say certainly whether our English version is right. Some, as Luther, think both words should be indicative : " ye believe and ye believe." Some think both should be imperative : " believe and believe." My own opinion is decided, that the English version is right. It seems to me to express exactly the state of mind in which the disciples were. They did, as pious Jews, believe in God already. They needed, as young Christians, to be taught to believe more thoroughly in Christ.

Among those who think that both verbs are imperative are Cyril, Augustine, Lampe, Stier, Hengstenberg, and Alford. Among those who adhere to our English version, and make the first " believe " indicative, and the second imperative, are Erasmus, Beza, Grotius, and Olshausen.

Let us note that faith, and specially more strong and distinct faith in Christ, is the truest remedy for trouble of heart. But we must never forget that true faith admits of growth and degrees. There is a wide gulf between little and great faith.

Ferus remarks that our Lord does not say "Believe my divinity," but, Believe personally in Me.

Toletus observes that our Lord here teaches that Jewish faith was somewhat distinct from Christian faith. The Jew, not seeing clearly the Trinity, dwelt chiefly on the unity of God. The Christian was intended to see three Persons in the Godhead.

Wordsworth remarks that the verb " to believe," followed by a preposition and an accusative, is never applied to any but God in the New Testament.

2 –[*In my Father's house.*] This phrase can bear only one meaning. It is my Father's house in Heaven: an expression accommodated to our weakness. God needs no literal house, with walls and roof, as we do. But where He dwells is called His house. (See Deut. xxvi. 15; Psalm xxxiii. 14; 2 Chron. xxxviii. 27; 2 Cor. v. 1.) There is something very touching and comforting in the thought that the heaven we go to is " our Father's house." It is home.

[*There are many mansions.*] The word rendered " mansions" means literally " abiding-places." It is only used here, and in the twenty-third verse of this chapter, " abode." We need not doubt that there is an intentional contrast between the un changing, unvarying house in heaven, and the changing, uncer tain, dwellings of this world. Here we are ever moving : there we shall no more go out. (See also Heb. xiii. 14.)

Our Lord's intention seems to be to comfort His disciples by the thought that nothing could cast them out of the heavenly house. They might be left alone by Him on earth ; they might be even cast out of the Jewish Church, and find no resting-place or refuge on earth ; but there would be always room enough for them in heaven, and a house from which they would never be expelled. " Fear not. There is room enough in heaven."

Chrysostom, Augustine, and several other ancient writers think the " many mansions " mean the degrees of glory. But the argument in favor of the idea does not appear to me satisfactory. Bishop Bull, Wordsworth, and some few modern writers take the same view. That there are degrees of glory in heaven is undoubtedly true, but I do not think it is the truth of this text.

The modern idea, that our Lord meant that heaven was a place for all sorts of creeds and religions, seems utterly unwarranted by the text. From the whole context He is evidently speaking for the special comfort of Christians.

Lightfoot's idea, that our Lord meant to teach the passing away of the Jewish economy, and the admission of all nations into heaven by faith in Christ, seems fanciful.

[*If it were not so...told you.*] This is a gracious way of assuring the disciples that they might have confidence that what their Lord said was true. It is the tender manner of a parent speaking to a child. "Do nòt be afraid because I am leaving you. There is plenty of room for you in heaven. You will get there safe at last. If there was the least uncertainty about it, I would tell you." We may remember that our Lord called the Apostles "little children" only a few minutes before. (John xiii. 33.)

[*I go...prepare...place...you.*] This sentence is meant to be another ground of comfort. One of the reasons why our Lord went away, He says, was to get ready a dwelling-place for His disciples. It is like the expression in the Hebrews, "the fore-runner." (Heb. vi. 20; see also Num. x. 33.)

The manner in which Christ prepares a place for His people is mysterious and yet not inexplicable. He enters heaven as their High Priest, presenting the merit of his sacrifice for their sins. He removes all barriers that sin made between them and God. He appears as their proxy and representative, and claims a right of entry for all His believing members. He intercedes continually for them at God's right hand; and makes them always acceptable in Himself, though unworthy in themselves. He bears their names mystically, as the High Priest, on His breast; and introduces them to the court of heaven before they get there.

That heaven is a prepared place for a prepared people is a very cheering and animating thought. When we arrive there we shall not be in a strange land. We shall find we have been known and thought of before we got there.

3 —[*And if I go...come again...receive...myself.*] These words contain another strong consolation. Our Lord tells the disciples that if He does go away, they must not think it is forever. He means to come again and take them all home, and gather them round Him in one united family to part no more.

Poole remarks "the particle 'if' in this place denotes no uncertainty of the thing, but hath the force of although, or after that." (See also Col. iii. 1.)

Many think, as Stier, that the "coming again" here spoken of means Christ's coming to His disciples after His resurrection, or Christ's coming spiritually to His people in comfort and help even now, or Christ's coming to remove them at last by death. I cannot think so. I believe that, as a rule, when Christ speaks of *coming again*, both here and elsewhere, He means His own personal second advent at the end of this dispensation. The Greek word rendered "I will come," is in the present tense, and the same that is used in Rev. xxii. 20: "I come quickly." The first and second advents are the two great events to which the minds of all Christians should be directed. This is Cyril's view of the passage, and Bishop Hall's.

[*That where I am...ye...also.*] Here is one more comfort. The final end of Christ's going away and coming again is, that at last His disciples may be once more with Him, and enjoy His company forever. "We part; but we shall meet again, and part no more."

Let us note that one of the simplest, plainest ideas of heaven is here. It is being "ever with the Lord." Whatever else we see or do not see in heaven, we shall see Christ. Whatever kind of a place, it is a place where Christ is. (Phil. i. 23. 1 Thess. iv. 17.)

JOHN XIV 4—11

4 And whither I go ye know, and the way ye know.

5 Thomas saith unto him, Lord, we know not whither thou goest; and how can we know the way?

6 Jesus saith unto him, I am the way, the truth, and the life: no man cometh unto the Father, but by me.

7 If ye had known me, ye should have known my Father also: and from henceforth ye know him, and have seen him.

8 Philip saith unto him, Lord, show us the Father, and it sufficeth us.

9 Jesus saith unto him, Have I been so long time with you, and yet hast thou not known me, Philip? He that hath seen me hath seen the Father; and how sayest thou *then*, Show us the Father?

10 Believest thou not that I am in the Father, and the Father in me? The words that I speak unto you I speak not of myself: but the Father that dwelleth in me, he doeth the works.

11 Believe me that I *am* in the Father and the Father in me: or else believe me for the very works' sake.

WE should mark in these verses *how much better Jesus speaks of believers than they speak of themselves.* He says to His disciples, "Ye know whither I go, and ye know the way." And yet Thomas at once breaks in with the remark, "We know neither the whither nor the way." The apparent contradiction demands explanation. It is more seeming than real.

Certainly, in one point of view, the knowledge of the disciples was very small. They knew little before the crucifixion and resurrection compared to what they might have known, and little compared to what they afterwards knew after the day of Pentecost. About our Lord's purpose in coming into the world, about His sacrificial death and substitution for us on the cross, their ignorance was glaring and great. It might well be said, that they "knew in part" only, and were children in understanding.

And yet, in another point of view, the knowledge of the disciples was very great. They knew far more than the great majority of the Jewish nation, and received truths which the Scribes and Pharisees entirely rejected. Compared to the world around them, they were in the highest sense enlightened. They knew and believed that their Master was the promised Messiah, the Son of the living God; and to know Him was the first step towards heaven. All things go by comparison. Before we lightly esteem the disciples because of their ignorance, let us take care that we do not underrate their knowledge. They knew more precious truth than they were aware of themselves. Their hearts were better than their heads.

The plain truth is, that all believers are apt to undervalue the work of the Spirit in their own souls, and to fancy they know nothing because they do not know everything. Many true Christians are thought more of in heaven while they live than they think of themselves, and will find it out to their surprise at the last day. There is One above who takes far more account of heart-knowledge than head-knowledge. Many go mourning all the way to heaven because they know so little, and fancy they will miss the way altogether, and yet have hearts with which God is well pleased.

We should mark, secondly, in these verses, *what glorious names the Lord Jesus gives Himself.* He says,

"I am the way, the truth, and the life." The fulness of these precious words can probably never be taken in by man. He that attempts to unfold them does little more than scratch the surface of a rich soil.

Christ is " the way,"—the way to heaven and peace with God. He is not only the guide, and teacher, and lawgiver, like Moses; He is Himself the door, the ladder, and the road, through whom we must draw near to God. He has opened the way to the tree of life, which was closed when Adam and Eve fell, by the satisfaction He made for us on the cross. Through His blood we may draw near with boldness, and have access with confidence into God's presence.

Christ is " the truth,"—the whole substance of true religion which the mind of man requires. Without Him the wisest heathen groped in gross darkness and knew nothing about God. Before He came even the Jews saw " through a glass darkly," and discerned nothing distinctly under the types, figures, and ceremonies of the Mosaic law. Christ is the whole truth, and meets and satisfies every desire of the human mind.

Christ is " the life,"—the sinner's title to eternal life and pardon, the believer's root of spiritual life and holiness, the surety of the Christian's resurrection life. He that believeth on Christ hath everlasting life. He that abideth in Him, as the branch abides in the vine, shall bring forth much fruit. He that believeth on Him, though he were dead, yet shall he live. The root of all life, for soul and for body, is Christ.

Forever let us grasp and hold fast these truths. To use Christ daily as the way,—to believe Christ daily as the truth,—to live on Christ daily as the life,—this is to be a well-informed, a thoroughly furnished and an established Christian.

We should mark, thirdly, in these verses, *how ex-*

pressly the Lord Jesus shuts out all ways of salvation but Himself. "No man," He declares, "No man cometh unto the Father but by Me."

It avails nothing that a man is clever, learned, highly gifted, amiable, charitable, kind-hearted, and zealous about some sort of religion. All this will not save his soul if he does not draw near to God by Christ's atonement, and make use of God's own Son as his Mediator and Saviour. God is so holy that all men are guilty and debtors in His sight. Sin is so sinful that no mortal man can make satisfaction for it. There must be a mediator, a ransom-payer, a redeemer, between ourselves and God, or else we can never be saved. There is only one door, one bridge, one ladder, between earth and heaven,—the crucified Son of God. Whosoever will enter in by that door may be saved; but to him who refuses to use that door the Bible holds out no hope at all. Without shedding of blood there is no remission.

Let us beware, if we love life, of supposing that mere earnestness will take a man to heaven, though he know nothing of Christ. The idea is a deadly and ruinous error. Sincerity will never wipe away our sins. It is not true that every man will be saved by his own religion, no matter what he believes, so long as he is diligent and sincere. We must not pretend to be wiser than God. Christ has said, and Christ will stand to it, "No man cometh unto the Father but by Me."

We should mark, lastly, in these verses, *how close and mysterious is the union of God the Father and God the Son.* Four times over this mighty truth is put before us in words that cannot be mistaken. "If ye had known Me, ye would have known my Father."—"He that hath seen Me hath seen the Father."—"I am in the Father, and the Father in Me."—"The Father that dwelleth in Me, He doeth the works."

Sayings like these are full of deep mystery. We have no eyes to see their meaning fully,—no line to fathom it,—no language to express it,—no mind to take it in. We must be content to believe when we cannot explain, and to admire and revere when we cannot interpret. Let it suffice us to know and hold that the Father is God and the Son is God, and yet that they are one in essence though two distinct Persons,—ineffably one, and yet ineffably distinct. These are high things, and we cannot attain to a full comprehension of them.

Let us however take comfort in the simple truth, that Christ is very God of very God ; equal with the Father in all things, and One with Him. He who loved us, and shed His blood for us on the cross, and bids us trust Him for pardon, is no mere man like ourselves. He is " God over all, blessed for ever," and able to save to the uttermost the chief of sinners. Though our sins be as scarlet, He can make them white as snow. He that casts his soul on Christ has an Almighty Friend,—a Friend who is One with the Father, and very God.

NOTES. JOHN XIV 4—11

4 —[*And whither I go ye know...way ye know.*] This remarkable sentence was evidently meant to stir and cheer the disciples, by reminding them of what their Master had repeatedly told them. It is as though our Lord said, " Do not be cast down by my going away, as if you had never heard Me say anything about heaven and the way to heaven. Awake from your despondency, stir up your memories. Surely you know, if you reflect a little, that I have often told you all about it." Is it not, again, like a tender parent saying to a frightened child, who says he knows not what to do, and is ready to sit down in despair, " Come, you know well enough, if you will only consider " ?

Poole observes on this verse, " It is pleasant to notice how Christ continueth His discourse to the disciples, like a mother speaking to a little child crying after her when she prepares to go abroad. The child cries ; the mother bids it be still, for she is only going to a friend's house. It still cries ; she tells it she is only going to prepare a place for it there, where it will be much happier than at home. It is not yet satisfied ; she tells it again, that though she goes, she will come again, and then it shall go with her, and she will part from it no more. The child is yet impatient ; she endeavoreth to still it, telling it that it knoweth whither she goeth, and it knows the way by which, if need be, it may come to her."

Let us note that disciples often know more than they suppose or admit, but do not use their knowledge, or keep it ready for use. Ferus compares them to infants lying in their cradles, who have fathers and fortunes, but do not know it.

Let us note that Christ looks graciously on the little knowledge His people possess, and make the most of it. He can make allowance for their minds being clouded by grief or trouble, and their consequent forgetfulness of truth for a season.

5 —[*Thomas saith unto Him, etc.*] This verse shows how foolishly a disciple may talk under the influence of despondency. Here is one of the eleven faithful Apostles declaring flatly that they neither knew where their Master was going, nor the way ! The saying is characteristic of the man. Thomas always appears a doubting, slow-minded believer. But we must not judge disciples too sharply for words spoken under deep distress. When the passions and affections are much stirred, the tongue often runs away with a man, and he speaks unadvisedly. Nor must we forget that disciples have very different gifts. All have not equally strong faith, clear understanding, and good memory.

Trapp quaintly remarks that believers in the frame of Thomas are like people who hunt for their keys and purses, when they have got them in their pockets.

6 —[*Jesus saith...I...way...truth...life.*] This wonderful saying is a brilliant example of a foolish remark calling out a great truth from our Lord's lips. To the ill natured remark of the Pharisees we owe the parable of the Prodigal Son (See Luke chapter xv.) ; to the fretful complaint of Thomas we owe one of the grandest texts in Scripture. It is one of those deep utterances which no exposition can thoroughly unfold and exhaust.

When our Lord says, "I am the way," He means, "the Father's house is to be reached through my mediation and atonement. Faith in Me is the key to heaven. He that believeth in Me is in the right road."

When our Lord says, "I am the truth," He means, "The root of all knowledge is to know Me. I am the true Messiah to whom all revelation points, the truth of which the Old Testament ceremonies and sacrifices were a figure and shadow. He that really knows Me, knows enough to take him safe to heaven, though he may not know many things, and may be troubled at his own ignorance."

When our Lord says "I am the life," He means, "I am the

Root and Fountain of all life in religion, the Redeemer from death and the Giver of everlasting life. He that knows and believes in Me, however weak and ignorant he may feel, has spiritual life now, and will have a glorious life in my Father's house hereafter."

Some think that the three great words in this sentence should be taken together, and that our Lord meant, " I am the true and living way." Yet the general opinion of the best commentators is decidedly unfavorable to this view of the sentence. To my own mind it cuts down and impoverishes a great and deep saying.

Musculus remarks that no prophet, teacher, or apostle ever used such words as these. They are the language of one who knew that He was God.

[*No man...cometh...Father...by me.*] Here our Lord teaches that He is not merely the way to our Father's home in heaven, but that there is no other way, and that men must either go to heaven by His atonement or not go there at all. It is a clear distinct limitation of heaven to those who believe on Christ. None else will enter in there. Rejecting Christ they lose all.

We should mark carefully what an unanswerable argument this sentence supplies against the modern notion that it does not matter what a man believes,—that all religions will lead men to heaven if they are sincere,—that creeds and doctrines are of no importance,—that heaven is a place for all mankind—whether heathen, Mahometan, or Christian,—and that the Fatherhood of God is enough to save all at last, of all sects, kinds, and characters ! Our Lord's words should never be forgotten. " There is no way to the Father but by Me." God is a Father to none but to those who believe in Christ. In short, there are not many ways to heaven. There is only one way.

" Coming to the Father," in this place, we must remark, includes not only coming to Him in glory at the last, but coming to Him in a friendly relation for peace and comfort now in this life.

" By Me," is literally, " through " Me,—as a door, a gate, a road, a path, an entrance. It is an expression which would be peculiarly expressive to the Jews, taught from their childhood to draw near to God only through the priests.

7 —[*If...known me...Father also.*] This is a deep saying, like every saying which handles the mysterious union of the Father and the Son in St. John's Gospel. The meaning seems to be, " If you had rightly, properly, and perfectly known Me, as the Divine Messiah, in all the fulness of my nature, you would then have known more of that Father to whom I am inseparably united. No one can rightly know Me without knowing the Father, because I and the Father are One."

[*And from henceforth...known....seen Him.*]   The meaning of these words seems to be, " Understand from this time forward, that in knowing Me you know the Father, and in seeing Me see the Father, so far as the Father can be seen and known by man." Although the Son and the Father are two distinct persons in the Trinity, yet there is so close and mysterious a union between them that he who sees and knows the Son, in a certain sense, sees and knows the Father. Is it not written of the Son that " He is the express image of the Father." (Heb. i. 2.)

The whole difficulty of the verse arises from the extreme mysteriousness of its subject. The relation between the eternal Father and the eternal Son and the eternal Spirit, who, while three Persons, are one God, is precisely one of those things which we have no minds to take in, and no language to express. We must often be content to believe and reverence it, without attempting to explain it. This only we may lay down with certainty, as a great canon and maxim,—the more we know of Christ, " the more we know of the Father."

8 —[*Philip...shew us the Father...sufficeth us.*]   We are not told Philip's motive in making this request. Perhaps, like Moses, he and the other disciples had a pious desire to see a more full vision and revelation of God's glory, as an authentication of their Master's Divine mission. " Show me Thy glory." (Ex. xxxiii. 18.) Perhaps Philip's petition is recorded to show how little clear knowledge the Apostles yet had of their Master's nature, and how little they realized that He and the Father were One :—" If we could only see once for all the Divine Being whom Thou dost call the Father, it would be sufficient. We should be satisfied and our doubts would be removed." At any rate we have no right to think that Philip spoke like the unbelieving Jews, who always pretended to want signs and wonders. Whatever sense we put on the words, we must carefully remember not to judge Philip too harshly. Living as we do in the nineteenth century, amidst light and creeds and knowledge, we can have faint ideas of the extreme difficulty that must have been felt by the disciples in fully realizing their Master's nature, in the days when He was " in the form of a Servant," and under a veil of poverty, weakness, and humiliation.

Melancthon remarks that Philip's petition represents the natural wish of man in every age. Men feel an inward craving everywhere to see God.

9 —[*Jesus saith...so long time...Philip.*]   This verse is undoubtedly a gentle rebuke. The expression, " so long time," is noteworthy, when we remember that Philip was one of the very first disciples whom Jesus called. (See John i. 43.) The meaning seems to be, " After three long years, Philip, dost thou not yet thoroughly know and understand who I am ?"

[*He...seen me...seen the Father.*] This deep sentence can only mean, " He that hath thoroughly seen me with the eye of faith, and realized that I am the eternal Son, the Divine Messiah, hath seen as much of my Father, whose express image I am, as mortal man can comprehend." There is so close and intimate a union between persons in the Trinity, that he who sees the Son sees the Father. And yet we must carefully beware that we do not, like some heretics, " confound the Persons." The Father is not the Son, and the Son is not the Father.

Musculus observes that to see with bodily eyes is one thing, and to see with the eyes of faith quite another.

[*And how sayest thou...show...Father.*] This question is a further gentle rebuke of Philip's ignorance. " What dost thou mean by saying, Show us the Father? What clear knowledge of Me canst thou have if thou canst ask such a question ? "

Let us note how Jesus calls " Philip " by his name. It was doubtless meant to prick his conscience. " Thou, Philip, an old disciple, so ignorant! Ought not thou, after following and hearing Me for three years to have known better than this ? "

10 —[*Believest thou not...I...in Father...in Me.*] This question continues the rebuke to Philip. It means, " Dost thou not yet believe and realize what I have taught,—that there is a mystical union between Me and the Father, and that He is in Me and I in Him ? "

This question surely seems to indicate that our Lord had often taught His disciples about the union between Himself and the Father. But, like many of the things He taught, the mighty truth passed over their heads at first, and was not remembered till afterwards. How little reason have ministers to complain if their teaching is little regarded, when this was Christ's experience !

[*The words that I speak...Father...works.*] There can be little doubt that this is a very elliptical sentence. The full meaning must be supplied in this way. " The words that I speak to you I speak not independently of the Father ; and the works that I do I do not do them independently of the Father. The Father who dwells in Me, speaks in Me and works in Me. My words are words given Me to speak, and my works are works given Me to do, in the eternal counsel between the Father and the Son. Both in speaking and working I and my Father are one. What I speak He speaks, and what I work He works."

The whole difficulty of the verse arises from forgetting the close and mysterious and insoluble union between the Persons of the Trinity. How little we realize the fulness of the expression, " The Father dwelleth in Me."

11 —[*Believe Me...in the Father...in Me.*]   Direct instruction follows the rebuke of the preceding verse.   Our Lord repeats for
the benefit not of Philip only, but of all the eleven, the great
doctrine He had so often taught them.   " Once more, I say,
Believe, all of you, my words, when I say that I and the Father are so closely united that I am in Him and He in Me."

The word rendered " believe " in this verse is in the plural
number.   Our Lord does not address Philip only, but the
whole company of the Apostles.

What an example we have here of the necessity of repeating
instruction over and over again.   Our Lord had evidently
taught these things before to the eleven, and yet they had
either not understood or not remembered.

[*Or else believe...works' sake.*]   Here our Lord condescends to
the weakness of the disciples.   ".If you will not believe the
close union of Myself and the Father because of my word, believe it because of the works I work.   They are such works as
no one could work of himself, and without the Father."

Let us carefully observe how our Lord here, as elsewhere,
specially names His works, or miracles, as testimonies of His
nature and Divine mission.   To leave out miracles in the list
of the evidences of Christianity is a great mistake.

JOHN XIV 12—17

12 Verily, verily, I say unto you, He that believeth on me, the works that I do shall he do also; and greater *works* than these shall he do; because I go unto my Father.

13 And whatsoever ye shall ask in my name, that will I do, that the Father may be glorified in the Son.

14 If ye shall ask anything in my name, I will do *it*.

15 If ye love me keep my commandments.

16 And I will pray the Father, and he shall give you another Comforter, that he may abide with you forever;

17 *Even* the Spirit of truth; whom the world cannot receive, because it seeth him not, neither knoweth him; but ye know him : for he dwelleth with you, and shall be in you.

THESE verses are an example of our Lord's tender
consideration for the weakness of His disciples.   He
saw them troubled and faint-hearted at the prospect of
being left alone in the world.   He cheers them by three
promises, peculiarly suited to their circumstances.   " A
word spoken in season, how good is it ! "

We have first in this passage, a striking promise
about *the works that Christians may do.*   Our Lord

says, "He that believeth on Me, the works that I do shall he do also ; and greater works than these shall he do ; because I go unto my Father."

The full meaning of this promise is not to be sought in the miracles which the Apostles wrought after Christ left the world. Such a notion seems hardly borne out by facts. We read of no Apostle walking on the water, or raising a person four days dead, like Lazarus. What our Lord has in view seems to be the far greater number of conversions, the far wider spread of the Gospel, which would take place under the ministry of the Apostles, than under his own teaching. This was the case, we know from the Acts of the Apostles. We read of no sermon preached by Christ, under which three thousand were converted in one day, as they were on the day of Pentecost. In short, " greater works " mean more conversions. There is no greater work possible than the conversion of a soul.

Let us admire the condescension of our Master in allowing to the ministry of His weak servants more success than to His own. Let us learn that His visible presence is not absolutely necessary to the progress of His kingdom. He can help forward His cause on earth quite as much by sitting at the right hand of the Father, and sending forth the Holy Ghost, as by walking to and fro in the world. Let us believe that there is nothing too hard or too great for believers to do, so long as their Lord intercedes for them in heaven. Let us work on in faith, and expect great things, though we feel weak and lonely, like the disciples. Our Lord is working with us and for us, though we cannot see Him. It was not so much the sword of Joshua that defeated Amalek, as the intercession of Moses on the hill. (Ex. xvii. 11.)

We have, secondly, in this passage, a striking promise *about things that Christians may get by prayer.* Our

Lord says, "Whatsoever ye shall ask in my name, that will I do. . . . If ye shall ask anything in my name, I will do it."

These words are a direct encouragement to the simple, yet great duty of praying. Every one who kneels daily before God, and from his heart "says his prayers," has a right to take comfort in these words. Weak and imperfect as his supplications may be, so long as they are put in Christ's hands, and offered in Christ's name, they shall not be in vain. We have a Friend at Court, an Advocate with the Father; and if we honor Him by sending all our petitions through Him, He pledges His word that they shall succeed. Of course it is taken for granted that the things we ask are for our souls' good, and not mere temporal benefits. "Anything" and "whatsoever" do not include wealth, and money, and worldly prosperity. These things are not always good for us, and our Lord loves us too well to let us have them. But whatever is really good for our souls, we need not doubt we shall have, if we ask in Christ's name.

How is it that many true Christians have so little? How is it that they go halting and mourning on the way to heaven, and enjoy so little peace, and show so little strength in Christ's service? The answer is simple and plain. "They have not, because they ask not." They have little because they ask little. They are no better than they are, because they do not ask their Lord to make them better. Our languid desires are the reason of our languid performances. We are not straitened in our Lord, but in ourselves. Happy are they who never forget the words, "Open thy mouth wide, and I will fill it." (Ps. lxxxi. 10.) He that does much for Christ, and leaves his mark in the world, will always prove to be one who prays much.

We have, lastly, in this passage, a striking promise *about the Holy Ghost.* Our Lord says, " I will pray the Father, and He shall give you another Comforter, ... even the Spirit of truth."

This is the first time that the Holy Ghost is mentioned as Christ's special gift to his people. Of course we are not to suppose that He did not dwell in the hearts of all the Old Testament saints. But He was given with peculiar influence and power to believers when the New Testament dispensation came in, and this is the special promise of the passage before us. We shall find it useful, therefore, to observe closely the things that are here said about Him.

The Holy Ghost is spoken of as " a Person." To apply the language before us to a mere influence or inward feeling, is an unreasonable strain of words.

The Holy Ghost is called " the Spirit of truth." It is His special office to apply truth to the hearts of Christians, to guide them into all truth, and to sanctify them by the truth.

The Holy Ghost is said to be one whom " the world cannot receive and does not know." His operations are in the strongest sense foolishness to the natural man. The inward feelings of conviction, repentance, faith, hope, fear, and love, which He always produces, are precisely that part of religion which the world cannot understand.

The Holy Ghost is said to " dwell in " believers, and to be known of them. They know the feelings that He creates, and the fruits that He produces, though they may not be able to explain them, or see at first whence they come. But they all are what they are,—new men, new creatures, light and salt in the earth, compared to the worldly, by the indwelling of the Holy Ghost.

The Holy Ghost is given to the Church of the elect,

"to abide with them" until Christ comes the second time. He is meant to supply all the needs of believers, and to fill up all that is wanting while Christ's visible presence is removed. He is sent to abide with and help them until Christ returns.

These are truths of vast importance. Let us take care that we grasp them firmly, and never let them go. Next to the whole truth about Christ, it concerns our safety and peace to see the whole truth about the Holy Ghost. Any doctrine about the Church, the ministry, or the Sacraments, which obscures the Spirit's inward work, or turns it into mere form, is to be avoided as deadly error. Let us never rest till we *feel* and *know* that He dwells in us. "If any man have not the Spirit of Christ, he is none of His." (Rom. viii. 9.)

NOTES. JOHN XIV 12—17

12 —[*Verily...works...shall he do also.*] Here we have another comforting word addressed to the disciples. They must not suppose there would be an end of miraculous works when their Master went away, and that they would be left weak and help-less, and unable to do any thing to arrest the attention of an unbelieving world. On the contrary, our Lord assures them, with two emphatic "verilys," that miracles would not cease with His departure. He would take care that believers should have power to do works like His own, and to confirm their word by signs following.

I cannot doubt that this promise refers to the miraculous gifts which the first generation of Christians had power to exercise, as we read everywhere in the Acts of the Apostles. That the sick were healed, the dead raised, and devils cast out by disciples after the Lord ascended, is quite plain, and this fulfilled the words now before us.

I can see no reason to suppose that our Lord meant the prom-ise to be fulfilled after the generation He left on earth was dead. If miracles were continually in the Church, they would cease to be miracles. We never see them in the Bible except at some great crisis in the Church's history. The Irvingite theory, that the Church would always have miraculous gifts if men only had faith seems to me a violent straining of this text.

[*And greater works...do.*] The meaning of these words must

be sought in the moral and spiritual miracles which followed the preaching of the Apostles after the day of Pentecost. It could not be truly said that the physical miracles worked by the Apostles in the Acts were greater than those worked by Christ. But it is equally certain that after the day of Pentecost they did far more wonderful works in converting souls than our Lord did. On no occasion did Jesus convert 3,000 at one time, and a " great company of priests."

[*Because I go...Father.*] These words must point to the great outpouring of the Holy Ghost which took place after our Lord's ascension into heaven, whereby the miracles of conversion were wrought. There was an immediate and mysterious connection, we must remember, between our Lord ascending up on high and " receiving gifts for men." If He had not gone to the Father the Spirit would not have been sent forth. (Ephes. iv. 8.)

Melancthon thinks the promise of this text is clearly bound up with the following verse, " He shall do greater works because I go to the Father, and because then whatsoever ye shall ask I will do."

13 —[*And whatsoever...ask...will I do.*] Here comes another great piece of comfort for the troubled disciples : viz., a promise that Christ will do everything for them which they pray for in His name and for His sake. Whatever help, or strength, or support, or guiding they need, if they ask God for it in Christ's name, Christ will give it.

This is one of those texts which authorizes all prayers being made through Christ's mediation, as in Prayer-book collects.

The " whatsoever " must of course be taken with the qualifying condition, " whatsoever really good thing ye ask."

The connection with the end of the preceding verse should not be overlooked, " When I go to the Father I will do whatsoever ye ask."

[*That...Father... glorified...Son.*] This is a difficult sentence. The meaning probably is, " I will do whatsoever ye ask, that my Father may be glorified by my mediation, by sending into the world a Son through whom sinners can obtain such blessings." Christ's power to do anything that He is asked, brings glory to Him who sent Him.

14 —[*If...ask anything...will do it.*] This verse is a repetition of the preceding, to give emphasis and assurance to the promise. It is as if our Lord saw how slow the disciples would be to believe the efficacy of prayer in His name. " Once more I tell you most emphatically, that if you ask anything in my name, I will do it."

We should notice both in this verse and the preceding one,

that it is not said "If ye ask in my name, the Father will do it:" but "I will do it."

15 —[*If ye love...keep...commandments.*] Here we have a direct practical exhortation. "If ye really love Me, prove your love not by weeping and lamenting at my departure, but by striving to do my will when I am gone. Doing, and not crying, is the best proof of love." The commandments here mentioned must include all the Lord's moral teaching while on earth, and specially such rules and laws as He had laid down in the "Sermon on the Mount."

I cannot but think that in this verse our Lord had in view the disposition of His disciples to give way to grief and distress at His leaving them ; and to forget that the true test of love was not useless and barren lamentation, but practical obedience to their Master's commands.

Let us notice how our Lord speaks of "my commandments." We never read of Moses or any other servant of God using such an expression. It is the language of one who was one with God the Father, and had power to lay down laws and make statutes for His Church.

16 —[*And I...pray the Father, etc.*] This verse holds up to the eleven another grand consolation, viz, the gift of another abiding Comforter in place of Christ, even the Holy Ghost. "When I go to heaven I will ask the Father to give you another friend and helper, to be with you and support you in my stead, and never leave you as I do." In this remarkable verse several points demand special notice.

One principal point is the mention of all the three persons in the blessed Trinity, the Son praying, the Father giving, the Spirit comforting.

When our Lord says, "I will pray the Father and He shall give," we must needs suppose that He accommodates language to our minds. The gift of the Holy Ghost was appointed in the eternal counsels of the Trinity ; and we cannot literally say that the gift depended on Christ asking. Moreover, in another place our Lord says, "I will send Him."

Burkitt remarks that the future tense here points to Christ's continual intercession. As long as Christ is in heaven, Christians shall not want a supply of comfort.

When we read of the Holy Ghost being "given," we must not think that He was in no sense in the Church before the day of Pentecost. He was ever in the hearts of Old Testament believers. No one ever served God acceptably, from Abel downwards, without the grace of the Holy Ghost. John the Baptist was "filled" with Him. It can only mean that He shall come with more fulness, influence, grace, and manifestation, than He did before.

When we read of the "Spirit abiding forever" with disciples, it means that He will not, like Christ after His resurrection, return to the Father, but will always be with God's people until Christ comes again.

The word "Comforter" is the same that is translated "Advocate," and applied to Christ Himself in 1 John ii. 2. This has caused much difference of opinion. The word is only used five times in the New Testament, and is four times applied to the Holy Spirit.

Some, as Lightfoot, Bishop Hall, and Doddridge, maintain that our translation here is right, and that it is the office of the Spirit to comfort and strengthen Christ's people.

Others, as Beza, Lampe, De Dieus, Gomarus, Poole, Pearce, Stier, and Alford, maintain that the word here should have been rendered "Advocate," as in John's Epistle; and that this word aptly expresses the office of the Spirit as pleading our cause, and making intercession for the saints, and helping them in prayer and preaching. (See Rom. viii. 26; Matt. x, 19, 20.) I decidedly prefer this latter view. Those who wish to see an able argument in its favor, should study Canon Lightfoot's volume on New Testament Revision (p. 55).

Lampe sensibly remarks that the word "another" points to the phrase meaning "Advocate" rather than "Comforter." That Jesus is our "Advocate" all allow. "Well," our Lord seems to say, "you shall have another 'Advocate' beside myself." Why use the word "another" at all, if "Comforter" is the meaning?

It is only fair to say that "the consolation of Israel" was a Jewish name of Messiah (Luke ii. 25,) and that some think that Christ was one Comforter and the Holy Ghost another. But I do not see much in this.

17 —[*Even the Spirit of truth.*] The Holy Ghost is most probably so called because He brings truth specially home to men's hearts,—because truth is His great instrument in all His operations,—and because He bears witness to Christ the truth. Elsewhere we read, "It is the Spirit that beareth witness, because the Spirit is truth." (1 John v. 6.)

[*Whom...world cannot receive...knoweth Him.*] Here our Lord teaches that it is one great mark of the unbelieving and worldly that they neither receive, nor know, nor see anything of the Holy Ghost. This is strikingly true. Many false professors and unconverted people receive Christ's name and talk of Him, while they know nothing experimentally of the operations of the Holy Spirit. It is written, "The natural man receiveth not the things of the spirit of God, for they are foolishness to him; neither can he know them." (1 Cor. ii. 14.)

[*But ye know...dwelleth...shall be in you.*] Our Lord's mean-

ing here must be that the eleven knew something experimentally of the Spirit's work. They might not be fully acquainted
with Him; but He was actually in them, making them what
they were, and He would remain in them, and carry on the
work He had begun to a glorious end. " Whether you know it
thoroughly and rightly or not, He is actually in you now, and
shall always be in you and never leave you."

Let us mark in this and in the preceding verse how our Lord
speaks of the Holy Spirit as " a Person." We should never
speak of Him as a mere " influence," or dishonor Him by calling Him " it."

Let us never forget that " having the Spirit, or not having
the Spirit," makes the great distinction between the children of
God and the children of the world. Believers have Him.
Worldly and wicked people have Him not. (Jude 19.)

JOHN XIV 18—20

18 I will not leave you comfort-less : I will come to you.
19 Yet a little while, and the world seeth me no more ; but ye see me ; because I live, ye shall live also.
20 At that day ye shall know that I *am* in my Father, and ye in me, and I in you.

THE short passage before us is singularly rich in
" precious promises." Twice our Lord Jesus Christ
says, " I will." Twice He says to believers, " Ye shall."

We learn from this passage, that *Christ's second
coming is meant to be the special comfort of believers.*
He says to His disciples, " I will not leave you comfortless : I will come to you."

Now what is the " coming " here spoken of? It is
only fair to say that this is a disputed point among
Christians. Many refer it to our Lord's coming to
His disciples after His resurrection. Many refer it to
His invisible coming into the hearts of His people by
the grace of the Holy Spirit. Many refer it to His coming by the outpouring of the Holy Ghost on the day of
Pentecost. It may well be doubted, however, whether
any one of these three views conveys the full meaning
of our Lord's words, " I will come."

The true sense of the expression appears to be the second personal coming of Christ at the end of the world. It is a wide, broad, sweeping promise, intended for all believers, in every age, and not for the Apostles alone :—" I will not stay always in heaven : I will one day come back to you." It is like the message which the angels brought to the disciples after the ascension : —" This same Jesus shall come in like manner as ye have seen Him go." (Acts. i. 11.) It is like the last promise which winds up the Book of Revelation :— " Surely I come quickly." (Rev. xxii, 20.) Just in the same way the parting consolation held out to believers, the night before the crucifixion, is a personal return :— " I will come."

Let us settle it in our minds that all believers are comparatively "orphans," and children in their minority, until the second advent. Our best things are yet to come. Faith has yet to be exchanged for sight, and hope for certainty. Our peace and joy are at present very imperfect. They are as nothing to what we shall have when Christ returns. For the return let us look and long and pray. Let us place it in the forefront of all our doctrinal system, next to the atoning death and the interceding life of our Lord. The highest style of Christians are the men who look for and love the Lord's appearing. (2 Tim. iv. 8.)

We learn for another thing, that *Christ's life secures the life of His believing people.* He says, " Because I live ye shall live also."

There is a mysterious and indissoluble union between Christ and every true Christian. The man that is once joined to Him by faith, is as closely united as a member of the body is united to the head. So long as Christ, his Head, lives, so long he will live. He cannot die unless Christ can be plucked from heaven, and Christ's life destroyed. But this, since Christ is very God, is totally impossible ! " Christ being raised from the dead, dieth no more : death hath no more dominion over Him." (Rom. vi. 9.) That which is divine, in the very nature of things, cannot die.

Christ's life secures the continuance of *spiritual life* to His people. They shall not fall away. They shall persevere unto the end. The divine nature of which they are partakers, shall not perish. The incorruptible seed within them shall not be destroyed by the devil and the world. Weak as they are in themselves, they are closely knit to an immortal Head, and not one member of His mystical body shall ever perish.

Christ's life secures the *resurrection life* of His people. Just as He rose again from the grave, because death could not hold Him one moment beyond the appointed time, so shall all His believing members rise again in the day when He calls them from the tomb. The victory that Jesus won when He rolled the stone away, and came forth from the tomb, was a victory not only for Himself, but for His people. If the Head rose, much more shall the members.

Truths like these ought to be often pondered by true Christians. The careless world knows little of a believer's privileges. It sees little but the outside of him. It does not understand the secret of his present strength, and of his strong hope of good things to come. And what is that secret ? Invisible union with an invisible Saviour in heaven ! Each child of God is invisibly linked to the throne of the Rock of Ages. When that throne can be shaken, and not till then, we may despair. But Christ lives, and we shall live also.

We learn, finally, from this passage, that *full and perfect knowledge of divine things will never be attained by believers until the second advent.* Our Lord says, "At that day," the day of my coming, "ye shall know that I am in my Father, and ye in Me, and I in you."

The best of saints knows but little so long as he is in the body. The fall of our father Adam has corrupted our understandings, as well as our consciences, hearts, and wills. Even after conversion we see through a glass darkly, and on no point do we see so dimly as on the nature of our own union with Christ, and of the union of Christ and the Father. These are matters in which we must be content to believe humbly, and, like little children, to receive on trust the things which we cannot explain.

But it is a blessed and cheering thought that when Christ comes again, the remains of ignorance shall be rolled away. Raised from the dead, freed from the darkness of this world, no longer tempted by the devil and tried by the flesh, believers shall see as they have been seen, and know as they have been known. We shall have light enough one day. What we know not now, we shall know hereafter.

Let us rest our souls on this comfortable thought, when we see the mournful divisions which rend the Church of Christ. Let us remember that a large portion of them arise from ignorance. We know in part, and therefore misunderstand one another. A day comes when Lutherans shall no longer wrangle with Zwinglians, nor Calvinist with Arminian, nor Churchman with Dissenter. That day is the day of Christ's second coming. Then and then only will the promise receive its complete fulfilment,—" At that day ye shall know."

NOTES   JOHN XIV 18—20

18 —[*I will not leave you comfortless.*]   The word we render " comfortless," means literally " orphans," and is so translated in the

marginal reading of the English version. It beautifully describes the helpless, solitary, friendless state, by comparison, in which the disciples of Christ were left, when He died and was withdrawn from their bodily eyes. " In that condition," says Jesus, " I will not leave you. You shall not always be orphans." It adds to the beauty of the expression to remember that He had already called them " little children : " hence there was a special fitness in the word " orphans."

[*I will come to you.*] The verb here is in the present tense : " I do come." About the meaning of the sentence there is much difference of opinion. Even the Fathers, as Burgon says, " explain the words diversely." There is no more unanimity, we must remember, among the Fathers than among modern divines. The " consent of Catholic antiquity," about which many make so much ado, is more imaginary than real.

Some think, as Chrysostom, that the " coming " means only the reappearing of Christ after His resurrection from the grave on the third day.

Others think, as Hutcheson, that our Lord only means His coming by His Spirit, as a pledge of his presence.

Others think, as Augustine and Bede, that our Lord looks far forward to His second coming at the end of the world, and speaks the words to the whole company of believers in every age : " I am coming again. I come quickly."

I decidedly prefer this last view. The first and second seem to me to cramp, narrow, and confine our Lord's promise. The last is in harmony with all His teaching. The second advent is the great hope of the Church. In the last chapter of the Bible, the Greek for " I come quickly," is precisely the same verb that is used here. (Rev. xxii. 20.)

In saying this I would not be mistaken. I admit fully that Jesus came to His Church after His ascension, invisibly, does come to His Church continually, is with His Church even to the end of the world. But I do not think this is the meaning of the text.

19.—[*Yet a little while...ye see Me.*] Again the meaning of our Lord is somewhat obscure. I think He must mean, " Very shortly the wicked unbelieving world will no longer behold and gaze on Me, as I shall be withdrawn from it, and ascend into heaven. But even then ye see Me, and will continue seeing Me with the eyes of faith." I cannot think that the present tense here, " Ye behold Me," can apply to the second advent. It must surely refer to the spiritual vision of Christ which believers would enjoy. The world could not prevent them seeing Him. The Greek word for " ye see " implies a fixed, steady, habitual gaze.

Bishop Hall says, " Ye by the eye of faith shall see and acknowledge Me."

[*Because I live, ye shall live also.*] This great deep saying of Christ seems to admit of a very wide and full signification " Your spiritual life now, and your eternal life hereafter, are both secured by my life. The life of the Head guarantees the life of the members. I live, have life in myself, can never die, can never have my life destroyed by my enemies, and live on to all eternity. Therefore ye shall live also. Your life is secured for you, and can never be destroyed. You have everlasting life now, and shall have everlasting glory hereafter."

That word " I live," is a great full saying, and we cannot fathom it all. It does not merely mean " I shall rise from the dead." It is certainly far more than the future tense. It implies that Christ is " the Living One," the source and fountain of life. It is like " In Him was life,"—and " as the Father hath life in Himself, even so hath He given to the Son to have life in Himself." (John i. 4 ; v. 26.)

20 —[*On that day ye shall know, etc.*] Here, again, I believe, with Cyril and Augustine, that our Lord specially refers to the day of His own second advent. Then, and not till then, His disciples will have perfect knowledge. Now they see and know in part, and through a glass darkly. Then they shall fully understand the mystical union between the Father and Son, and between the Son and all His believing members.

To confine the " day," as Chrysostom does, to the resurrection of Christ from the dead, seems to me to fall short of its full meaning.

JOHN XIV 21—26

21 He that hath my commandments, and keepeth them, he it is that loveth me: and he that loveth me shall be loved of my father, and I will love him, and will manifest myself to him.

22 Judas saith unto him, not Iscariot, Lord, how is it that thou wilt manifest thyself unto us, and not unto the world?

23 Jesus answered and said unto him, If a man love me he will keep my words, and my father will love him, and we will come unto him, and make our abode with him.

24 He that loveth me not keepeth not my sayings; and the word which ye hear is not mine, but the Father's which sent me.

25 These things have I spoken unto you, being *yet* present with you.

26 But the Comforter, *which is* the Holy Ghost, whom the Father will send in my name, he will teach you all things, and bring all things to your remembrance whatsoever I have said unto you.

WE learn from these verses that *keeping Christ's commandments is the best test of love to Christ.*

This is a lesson of vast importance and one that

needs continually pressing on the attention of Christians. It is not talking about religion, and talking fluently and well too, but steadily doing Christ's will and walking in Christ's ways, that is the proof of our being true believers. Good feelings and desires are useless if they are not accompanied by action. They may even become mischievous to the soul, induce hardness of conscience, and do positive harm. Passive impressions which do not lead to action, gradually deaden and paralyze the heart. Living and doing are the only real evidence of grace. Where the Holy Spirit is, there will always be a holy life. A jealous watchfulness over tempers, words, and deeds, a constant endeavor to live by the rule of the Sermon on the Mount, this is the best proof that we love Christ.

Of course such maxims as these must not be wrested and misunderstood. We are not to suppose for a moment that "keeping Christ's commandments" can save us. Our best works are full of imperfection. When we have done all we can, we are feeble and unprofitable servants. "By grace are ye saved through faith,—not of works." (Ep. ii. 8.) But while we hold one class of truths, we must not forget another. Faith in the blood of Christ must always be attended by loving obedience to the will of Christ. What the Master has joined together, the disciple must not put asunder. Do we profess to love Christ? Then let us show it by our lives. The Apostle who said, "Thou knowest that I love Thee!" received the charge, "Feed my lambs." That meant, "Do something. Be useful: follow my example." (John xxi. 17.)

We learn, secondly, from these verses, that *there are special comforts laid up for those who love Christ, and prove it by keeping His words.* This, at any rate, seems the general sense of our Lord's language: "My

Father will love him, and we will come unto him, and make our abode with him."

The full meaning of this promise, no doubt, is a deep thing. We have no line to fathom it. It is a thing which no man can understand except he that receives and experiences it. But we need not shrink from believing that eminent holiness brings eminent comfort with it, and that no man has such sensible enjoyment of his religion as the man who, like Enoch and Abraham, walks closely with God. There is more of heaven on earth to be obtained than most Christians are aware of. "The secret of the Lord is with them that fear Him, and He will show them His covenant."—"If any man hear my voice and open the door, I will come in to him, and sup with him, and he with Me." (Ps. xxv. 14; Rev. iii. 20.] Promises like these, we may be sure, mean something, and were not written in vain.

How is it, people often ask, that so many professing believers have so little happiness in their religion? How is it that so many know little of "joy and peace in believing," and go mourning and heavy-hearted towards heaven? The answer to these questions is a sorrowful one, but it must be given. Few believers attend as strictly as they should to Christ's practical sayings and words. There is far too much loose and careless obedience to Christ's commandments. There is far too much forgetfulness, that while good works cannot justify us they are not to be despised. Let these things sink down into our hearts. If we want to be eminently happy, we must strive to be eminently holy.

We learn, lastly, from these verses, that *one part of the Holy Ghost's work is to teach, and to bring things to remembrance.* It is written, "The Comforter shall teach you all things, and bring all things to your remembrance."

To confine this promise to the eleven Apostles, as some do, seems a narrow and unsatisfactory mode of interpreting Scripture. It appears to reach far beyond the day of Pentecost, and the gift of writing inspired books of God's Holy Word. It is safer, wiser, and more consistent with the whole tone of our Lord's last discourse, to regard the promise as the common property of all believers, in every age of the world. Our Lord knows the ignorance and forgetfulness of our nature in spiritual things. He graciously declares that when He leaves the world, His people shall have a teacher and remembrancer.

Are we sensible of spiritual ignorance? Do we feel that at best we know in part and see in part? Do we desire to understand more clearly the doctrines of the Gospel? Let us pray daily for the help of the "teaching" Spirit. It is His office to illuminate the soul, to open the eyes of the understanding, and to guide us into all truth. He can make dark places light, and rough places smooth.

Do we find our memory of spiritual things defective? Do we complain that though we read and hear, we seem to lose as fast as we gain? Let us pray daily for the help of the Holy Ghost. He can bring things to our remembrance. He can make us remember "old things and new." He can keep in our minds the whole system of truth and duty, and make us ready for every good word and work.

NOTES. JOHN XIV 21—26

21.—[*He that hath...commandments...loveth Me.*] Our Lord seems to return to the lesson of the fifteenth verse, and to repeat it because of its importance. There, however, He spoke specially to His disciples; here He lays it down as a general principle applicable to all Christians in all time :—" He that not only possesses and knows my commandments, but also does and practices them, he is the man that really loves Me." Obedi-

ence is the true test of real love to Christ, and not knowledge
and talk only. Many HAVE, but do not KEEP Christ's will.

Burgon observes, " This amounts to a declaration that the
sad hearts and weeping eyes of the Apostles would not be accepted by their Lord as any proof of their love. Obedience
was the test He chose."

[*He...loveth Me...loved...Father.*] Here follows an encouragement to practical obedience : " He that really loves Me, and
proves his love by his life, shall be specially loved by my Father. My Father loves those who love Me."

Let us carefully note that there is a special love of God the
Father which is peculiarly set on believers, over and above the
general love of pity and compassion with which He regards all
mankind. In the highest sense God is a " Father " to none but
those who love Christ. The modern doctrine of a " Fatherhood " of God which is soul-saving to those who neglect Christ,
is a mere delusion of man.

[*And I...love...manifest...him.*] Here follows another encouragement to the man who strives to keep Christ's commandments. Christ will specially love that man, and will give him
special manifestations of His grace and favor, invisibly and
spiritually. He shall feel and know in his own heart comforts
and joys that wicked men and inconsistent professors know
nothing of. That the " manifesting " of Himself here spoken
of is a purely unseen and spiritual thing, is self-evident. It is
one of those things which can only be known by experience,
and is only known by holy and consistent Christians.

We should carefully observe here, that Christ does more for
the comfort of some of His people than He does for others.
Those who follow Christ most closely and obediently will always follow Him most comfortably, and feel most of His inward presence. It is one thing, as St. John says, to know
Christ, another to know that we know Him. (1 John ii. 3.)

22 —[*Judas saith...not Iscariot.*] Jude, the writer of the Epistle,
and brother of James, was the Apostle who speaks here. He
is called elsewhere Lebbeus and Thaddeus. Remembering
that James is called in Galatians " the Lord's brother," there
must have been some relationship between him and our Lord.
Probably he was a cousin. Whether a recollection of this may
have been in His mind when asking the question, admits of
conjecture. This is the only word recorded to have been spoken by Jude in the Gospels.

We should mark the careful manner in which St. John reminds us that it was not the false Apostle who asked.

Let us note that out of each saying of the three Apostles
who spoke to our Lord, interrupting Him in His last discourse,
a great truth was elicited for the benefit of the Church.

Thomas, Philip, and Jude, ignorant and slow as they were, drew out of our Lord's mouth rich and precious sayings.

[*How is it...manifest...us...not...world.*] This question is the simple inquiry of one guessing after the truth, and not able to see clearly what our Lord's words meant,—whether a visible or an invisible manifestation of Himself :—" What is the precise distinction of privilege between ourselves and the world to which you point ?"

The Greek for "how is it?" would be literally, "What has happened ?" The Greek for "Thou wilt," is literally, "Thou art about."

Whitby thinks that Jude, like most Jews of his time, expected Messiah's kingdom to be a visible temporal kingdom over all the earth. He could not therefore understand a manifestation of Christ confined to the disciples.

23 —[*Jesus answered...will love him.*] This sentence is simply a repetition of the truth contained in the fifteenth and twenty-first verses : " I tell you again emphatically that the man who really loves Me will keep my words, and obey my commandments. And I repeat that such a man will be specially loved and cared for by my heavenly Father."

Let us note that in this verse our Lord does not say, " Keep my commandments," but my " word " generally, in the singular number, including all His whole teaching.

[*And we will come...abide with him.*] These words can only admit of one sense,—a spiritual and invisible coming and abiding. The Father and the Son will come spiritually into the heart and soul of a true saint, and will make their continual dwelling with him. This, again, is a purely experimental truth, and one that none can know but he that has felt it.

Let us note the condescension of the Father and the Son, and the high privileges of a believer. No matter how poor and lowly a man may be, if he has faith and grace, he has the best of company and friends. Christ and the Father dwell in his heart, and he is never alone, and cannot be poor. He is the temple of Father, Son, and Holy Ghost. The use of the plural number " we," is very noteworthy in this place.

24 —[*He...loveth Me not...my sayings.*] Once more the same great principle already taught, is laid down again from the negative side. Where there is no obedience to Christ, there is no love. Nothing can be more plain than our Lord's repeated warnings that practical obedience, keeping His commandments and sayings, doing His will, is the only sure test of love to Him. Without this obedience, profession, talk, knowledge, Churchmanship, yea, even feeling, conviction, weeping and crying, are all worthless things.

[*And word...not mine...Father...sent Me.*] The purpose of this sentence is to remind the disciples of the authority and dignity of our Lord's sayings and commandments. They are not His words only, but His Father's. He that despises them despises the Father, and He that honors them by obedience honors the Father.

25 —[*These things...spoken...present with you.*] Our Lord seems here to begin to wind up the first part of His discourse to a conclusion. Whether "these things" mean only the things He spoke this evening, or all the things He had taught them during His ministry, admits of doubt. I rather incline to the view that the expression must be taken in the widest sense : " These and many other things I have spoken to you, while abiding and dwelling among you. Your hearts are troubled, perhaps, by the thought that you cannot remember them, and do not understand them. Here there are some grounds of comfort."

26 —[*But...Comforter...Holy Ghost...my name.*] Here comes one more grand consolation : " When I am gone, the Holy Ghost, the promised Advocate, whom the Father will send on my account, through my intercession, and to glorify Me, shall supply all your need, and provide for all your wants."

Let us note how distinctly the Holy Spirit is spoken of here as a Person, and not an influence.

Let us note how the Father sends the Spirit, but also sends Him in Christ's name, and with a special reference to Christ's work.

[*He shall teach you all things.*] The first word here rendered " He " is unmistakably applicative to none but a person, being a masculine pronoun. The " teaching " here promised must mean, firstly, that fuller and more complete instruction which the Holy Ghost evidently gave to believers after our Lord's ascension. No one can read the "Acts " without seeing that the eleven were different men after the day of Pentecost ; and saw and knew and understood things of which they were very ignorant before. But, secondly, the " teaching " most probably includes all that teaching and enlightening which the Spirit imparts to all true believers in every age. Light is the first thing we need, and He gives it. It is His special office to " open the eyes of our understandings."

The expression " all things " must plainly be limited to all things needful to be known by the soul, and does not include all knowledge of every kind.

[*And bring all things...remembrance...told you.*] This is a special consolation for the weak memories of the troubled disciples. Our Lord promises that the Spirit would bring back to their memories the many lessons, both doctrinal and practical, which they had heard from Him but forgotten. This was a very needful promise. How often we find it recorded that the disciples did not understand our Lord's sayings and doings at the time they heard and saw them, it is almost needless to point out. (John ii. 22 ; xii. 16.)

Some apply these words especially to the gift of inspiration by which the New Testament Scriptures were written. I cannot see this. The promise was to the whole eleven, of whom only five were allowed to write ! This is strongly dwelt on by Alford.

Some apply these words exclusively to the eleven. I cannot see this either. To my eyes they seem a general promise, primarily no doubt applying specially to the eleven, but after them belonging also to all believers in every age. As a matter of experience I believe that the awakening of the memories of true Christians is one of the peculiar works of the Holy Ghost on their souls. Once converted, they understand things and remember things in a way they did not before.

Does any one complain of his own ignorance and bad memory ? Let him not forget that there is One whose office it is to "teach and to bring to remembrance." Let him pray for the Holy Spirit's help.

JOHN XIV 27–31

27 Peace I leave with you, my peace I give unto you; not as the world giveth, give I unto you. Let not your heart be troubled, neither let it be afraid.

28 Ye have heard how I said unto you, I go away, and come *again* unto you. If ye loved me, ye would rejoice, because I said, I go unto the Father; for my Father is greater than I.

29 And now I have told you before it come to pass, that, when it is come to pass, ye might believe.

30 Hereafter I will not talk much with you: for the prince of this world cometh, and hath nothing in me.

31 But that the world may know that I love the Father; and as the Father gave me commandment, even so I do. Arise, let us go hence.

WE ought not to leave the closing portion of this wonderful chapter without noticing one striking feature in it. That feature is the singular frequency with which our Lord uses the expression, " My Father," and " the Father." In the last five verses we find it four times. In the whole chapter it occurs no less than twenty-two times. In this respect the chapter stands alone in the Bible.

The reason of this frequent use of the expression, is a

deep subject. Perhaps the less we speculate and dog-matize about it the better. Our Lord was one who never spoke a word without a meaning, and we need not doubt there was a meaning here. Yet may we not reverently suppose that He desired to leave on the minds of His disciples a strong impression of his entire unity with the Father ? Seldom does our Lord lay claim to such high dignity, and such power of giving and sup-plying comfort to His Church, as in this discourse. Was there not, then, a fitness in His continually reminding His disciples that in all His giving He was one with the Father, and did nothing without the Father ? This, at any rate, seems a fair conjecture. Let it be taken for what it is worth.

We should observe, for one thing, in this passage, *Christ's last legacy to His people.* We find Him saying, "Peace I leave with you, my peace I give unto you ; not as the world giveth give I unto you."

Peace is Christ's peculiar gift : not money, not worldly ease, not temporal prosperity. These are at best very questionable possessions. They often do more harm than good to the soul. They act as clogs and weights to our spiritual life. Inward peace of con-science, arising from a sense of pardoned sin and recon-ciliation with God, is a far greater blessing. This peace is the property of all believers, whether high or low, rich or poor.

The peace which Christ gives He calls "my peace." It is specially His own to give, because He bought it by His own blood, purchased it by His own substitution, and is appointed by the Father to dispense it to a per-ishing world. Just as Joseph was sealed and commis-sioned to give corn to the starving Egyptians, so is Christ specially commissioned, in the counsels of the Eternal Trinity, to give peace to mankind.

The peace that Christ gives is not given as the world gives. What He gives the world cannot give at all, and what He gives is given neither unwillingly, nor sparingly, nor for a little time. Christ is far more will-ing to give than the world is to receive. What He gives He gives to all eternity, and never takes away. He is ready to give abundantly above all that we can ask or think. " Open thy mouth wide," He says, " and I will fill it." (Psalm lxxxi. 10.)

Who can wonder that a legacy like this should be backed by the renewed emphatic charge, " Let not your heart be troubled, neither let it be afraid ? " There is nothing lacking on Christ's part for our comfort, if we will only come to Him, believe, and receive. The chief of sinners has no cause to be afraid. If we will only look to the one true Saviour, there is medicine for every trouble of heart. Half our doubts and fears arise from dim perceptions of the real nature of Christ's Gospel.

We should observe, for another thing, in this passage, *Christ's perfect holiness.* We find Him saying, " The prince of this world cometh, and hath nothing in Me."

The meaning of these remarkable words admits of only one interpretation. Our Lord would have his dis-ciples know that Satan, " the prince of this world," was about to make his last and most violent attack on Him. He was mustering all his strength for one more tre-mendous onset. He was coming up with his utmost malice to try the second Adam in the garden of Geth-semane, and on the cross of Calvary. But our blessed Master declares, " He hath nothing in Me."—" There is nothing he can lay hold on. There is no weak and de-fective point in Me. I have kept my Father's command-ment, and finished the work He gave me to do. Satan, therefore, cannot overthrow Me. He can lay nothing to my charge. He cannot condemn Me. I shall come forth from the trial more than conqueror."

Let us mark the difference between Christ and all others who have been born of woman. He is the only one in whom Satan has found "nothing." He came to Adam and Eve, and found weakness. He came to Noah, Abraham, Moses, David, and all the saints, and found imperfection. He came to Christ, and found "nothing" at all. He was a Lamb "without blemish and without spot," a suitable Sacrifice for a world of sinners, a suitable Head for a redeemed race.

Let us thank God that we have such a perfect, sinless Saviour ; that His righteousness is a perfect righteousness, and His life a blameless life. In ourselves and our doings we shall find everything imperfect ; and if we had no other hope than our own goodness, we might well despair. But in Christ we have a perfect, sinless, Representative and Substitute. Well may we say, with the triumphant Apostle, "Who shall lay anything to our charge?" (Rom. viii. 33.) Christ hath died for us, and suffered in our stead. In Him Satan can find nothing. We are·hidden in Him. The Father sees us in Him, unworthy as we are, and for His sake is well pleased.

NOTES. JOHN XIV 27—31

27 —[*Peace 1 leave with you.*] In this verse our Lord gives His disciples one more consolation. He bequeaths them as a legacy, "peace ;" not riches or worldly honor, but peace,—peace of heart, conscience, and inward man,—peace from a sense of pardoned sin, a living Saviour, and a home in heaven.

Matthew Henry remarks here, "When Christ left the world, He made His will. His soul He bequeathed to His Father, and His body to Joseph. His clothes fell to the soldiers. His mother He left to the care of John. But what should He leave to His poor disciples, who had left all for Him? Silver and gold He had none ; but He left them what was far better, His peace."

[*My peace give I unto you.*] The expression "my peace," seems to indicate something peculiar in the gift here promised. Does it not mean " a sense of that peace with God which I am purchasing with my blood,—that inward calm and rest of soul which faith in Me procures for believers,—that peace which it is my special prerogative to give to my people "?

[*Not as...world giveth...I...you.*] The first and fullest meaning of this sentence seems to lie in the kind of things which Christ gives : " I give you possessions which the world cannot give, because it has not got them to give." The world can give temporary carnal satisfaction and excitement, and can gratify the passions and affections and pride of the natural man. But the world cannot give inward peace and rest of conscience.

Some, however, think that the point of the sentence lies in the manner of the world's giving,—temporarily, defectively, imperfectly, grudgingly, and the like. But, however true this may be, I prefer the view that the chief point is in the nature of the world's gifts compared to Christ's.

[*Let not your heart be troubled.*] This is a repetition of the words which began the long list of consolations in this chapter : "Once more I say to you, in view of the many grounds of comfort which I have just named, do not give way to trouble of heart."

[*Neither let it be afraid.*] These words are added to the opening charge, not to be "troubled." They point to a frame of mind which our Lord saw creeping over the disciples : " Let not your heart give way to cowardice. Let it not be fearful." It is the only place in the New Testament where this word is used.

We need not doubt that the whole of this consoling verse is meant to be the property of all believers in every age.

28 —[*Ye have heard...said...go away.*] This sentence must refer to ch. xiii. 33—36, and xiv. 2, 3, 12. The disciples seem to have understood clearly that our Lord was leaving them, and that seems to have been one chief reason of their trouble and distress.

[*And come...to you.*] I must retain the opinion that this coming refers to the second advent, and not to the resurrection of Christ. " My leaving the world until my second advent, you have heard me plainly teach and declare."

[*If ye loved...rejoice...go...Father.*] These words mean,—" if you really loved Me with an intelligent love, and thoroughly understood my person, nature, and work, you would rejoice to hear of my leaving the world and going to the Father, because you would see in it the finishing and completion of the work which the Father sent Me to do." Our Lord cannot of course mean that the disciples did not " love " Him at all, but that they did not rightly and intelligently love Him ; otherwise they would have rejoiced at His completion of His work.

[*For my Father is greater than I.*] This famous sentence has always been an occasion of controversy and dispute. It presents two difficulties.

(*a*) What did our Lord mean by saying, " My Father is greater than I " ? I answer that the words of the Athanasian Creed contain the best reply. Christ is no doubt "equal to the Father as touching His Godhead, and inferior to the Father as touching His manhood." This we may freely and fully admit, and yet not give up a hair's breadth to Arians and Socinians, who always throw this text in our teeth. The enemies of the doctrine of Christ's divinity forget that Trinitarians maintain the humanity of Christ as strongly as His divinity ; and never shrink from admitting that while Christ as God is equal to the Father, as man He is inferior to the Father. And it is in this sense that He here says truly, " My Father is greater than I." It was specially spoken of the time of His incarnation and humiliation. When the Word was " made flesh " He took on Him " the form of a servant." This was temporary inferiority. (Phil. ii. 7.)

(*b*) But what did our Lord mean by saying that the disciples ought to rejoice at His going to the Father, BECAUSE " the Father is greater than I " ? This is a hard knot to untie, and has received different solutions. My own impression is that the meaning must be something of this kind :—"Ye ought to rejoice at my going to the Father, because in so going I shall resume that glory which I had with Him before the world was, and which I laid aside on becoming incarnate. Here on earth, during the thirty-three years of my incarnation, I have been in the form of a servant, and dwelling in a body as one inferior to my Father. In leaving this world I go to take up again the equal glory and honor which I had with the Father before my incarnation ; and to lay aside the position of inferiority in which I have tabernacled here below. I go to be once more Almighty with the Almighty, and to share once more my Father's throne, as a Person in that Trinity in which ' none is afore or after other, none is greater or less than another.' I go to receive the kingdom and honor which in eternal counsels the Father has prepared for the Son ; and on this account, if you really knew and understood all, you would rejoice at my going. If I had not voluntarily placed myself in a position of inferiority to the Father by becoming man for man's sake, you would have no hope for your souls. But now the work is finished. I return to the Father, and leave my position of inferiority and humiliation, and you ought to rejoice and be glad."

29 —[*And now...told...before...to pass, etc.*] This seems to refer to our Lord's going away. " I have told you plainly that I am leaving you and about to die on the cross, in order that when I·

do die and go, you may continue believing, and not have your faith shaken."

30 —[*Hereafter...not talk much with you.*] This must mean that our Lord would not talk much more before His crucifixion. The time was short, and the betrayal and suffering drew nigh. It does not refer to the time after our Lord's resurrection, and the forty days before His ascension.

[*For...prince...cometh...nothing in me.*] This means that Satan was drawing nigh for his last final assault on our Lord; and that he would find nothing to lay hold on, and no weak point.

It is very striking to observe that our Lord does not say "Judas, the Romans, the Pharisees are coming." It is only the devil. He, as at the fall, is at the bottom of all. Others are only his tools.

We should note how the devil is called "the prince of this world." He rules and reigns in the hearts of the vast majority of mankind. The whole world "lieth in the wicked one." Of the extent and intensity of Satan's influence on earth, even now we have probably very little idea.

When it says that he "cometh," we must not suppose that it means "cometh for the first time." All through our Lord's earthly ministry He was tempted and assailed and opposed by Satan. It must mean, "He is coming with special violence and bitter wrath to make his last attack on Me both in Gethsemane and on Calvary." There are evidently degrees at different seasons in the intensity and virulence of Satan's attacks.

When it says "hath nothing in Me," it must mean that our Lord's heart and life were equally without spot of sin. He knew and felt that He the second Adam, had nothing about Him that Satan could lay hold on. No one but Christ our Head could say that. The holiest saint could never say it !

Sanderson observes, " a cunning searcher had pried narrowly into every corner of His life ; and if there had been anything amiss, would have been sure to have spied it, and proclaimed it. But he could find nothing."

31 —[*But that the world...so I do.*] This is a somewhat dark and obscure passage. The meaning is probably something of this kind: "I do all I am doing now, and go to the cross voluntarily, though innocent, that the world may have full proof that I love the Father who sent Me to die, and am willing to go through everything which He has commanded Me to go through. Innocent as I am, and without one spot of sin that Satan can lay to my charge, I willingly go forward to the cross, to show how I love the Father's will, and am determined to do it by dying for sinners."

[*Arise, let us go hence.*] These words seem to indicate a change of position, and probably mean that our Lord at this point rose from the table where He had been speaking, and walked out towards the garden of Gethsemane. The rest of His discourse He seems to have delivered in the act of walking, without a single interruption from any of the disciples, until the end of the sixteenth chapter; and then, at some point unknown to us, He probably paused and offered up the prayer of the seventeenth chapter.

This is the view of Cyril and Augustine, and most commentators. Yet Jansenius, Maldonatus, Alford, and some others, think that our Lord never left the house, and only rose from table at this point, and went on with His discourse standing!

Lightfoot, almost alone, maintains the strange and improbable notion that the place where this discourse was delivered was Bethany, that the interval of a week comes into the narrative here, that at the end of this week the paschal supper and the institution of the Lord's Supper took place, and then came the discourse of the fifteenth chapter.

No commentator perhaps can leave this chapter without deeply feeling how little he knows and understands of the full meaning of much of its contents. May we not however fairly reflect that one great cause of the chapter's difficulty is man's entire inability to grasp the great mystery of the union of the Father, the Son and the Spirit in the Trinity? We are continually handling matters which we cannot fully comprehend, and cannot therefore fully explain, and must be content humbly to believe.

JOHN XV. 1—6.

1 I am the true vine, and my Father is the husbandman.

2 Every branch in me that beareth not fruit he taketh away: and every *branch* that beareth fruit, he purgeth it, that it may bring forth more fruit.

3 Now ye are clean through the word which I have spoken unto you.

4 Abide in me, and I in you. As the branch cannot bear fruit of itself, except it abide in the vine; no more can ye, except ye abide in me.

5 I am the vine, ye *are* the branches: He that abideth in me, and I in him, the same bringeth forth much fruit: for without me ye can do nothing.

6 If a man abide not in me, he is cast forth as a branch, and is withered; and men gather them, and cast *them* into the fire, and they are burned.

THESE verses, we must carefully remember, contain a parable. In interpreting it we must not forget the great rule which applies to all Christ's parables. The general lesson of each parable is the main thing to be noticed. The minor details must not be tortured and pressed to an excess, in order to extract a meaning from them. The mistakes into which Christians have fallen by neglecting this rule, are neither few nor small.

We are meant to learn first, from these verses, that *the union between Christ and believers is very close.* He is "the Vine," and they are "the branches."

The union between the branch of a vine and the main stem, is the closest that can be conceived. It is the whole secret of the branch's life, strength, vigor, beauty, and fertility. Separate from the parent stem, it has no life of its own. The sap and juice that flow from the stem are the origin and maintaining power of all its leaves, buds, blossoms, and fruit. Cut off from the stem, it must soon wither and die.

The union between Christ and believers is just as close, and just as real. In themselves believers have no life, or strength, or spiritual power. All that they have of vital religion comes from Christ. They are what they are, and feel what they feel, and do what they do, because they draw out of Jesus a continual supply of grace, help, and ability. Joined to the Lord by faith, and united in mysterious union with Him by the Spirit, they stand, and walk, and continue, and run the Christian race. But every jot of good about them is drawn from their spiritual Head, Jesus Christ.

The thought before us is both comfortable and instructive. Believers have no cause to despair of their own salvation, and to think they will never reach heaven. Let them consider that they are not left to themselves and their own strength. Their root is Christ, and all that there is in the root is for the benefit of the branches. Because He lives, they shall live also. Worldly people have no cause to wonder at the contin-nance and perseverance of believers. Weak as they are in themselves, their Root is in heaven, and never dies. "When I am weak," said Paul, "then am I strong." (2 Cor. xii. 10.)

We are meant to learn, secondly, from these verses, that *there are false Christians as well as true ones.* There are " branches in the vine " which appear to be joined to the parent stem, and yet bear no fruit. There are men and women who appear to be members of Christ, and yet will prove finally to have had no vital union with Him.

There are myriads of professing Christians in every Church whose union with Christ is only outward and formal. Some of them are joined to Christ by baptism and Church-membership. Some of them go even further than this, and are regular communicants and loud talkers about religion. But they all lack the one thing needful. Notwithstanding services, and sermons, and sacrament, they have no grace in their hearts, no faith, no inward work of the Holy Spirit. They are not one with Christ, and Christ in them. Their union with Him is only nominal, and not real. They have " a name to live," but in the sight of God they are dead.

Christians of this stamp are aptly represented by branches in a vine which bear no fruit. Useless and unsightly, such branches are only fit to be cut off and burned. They draw nothing out of the parent stem, and make no return for the place they occupy. Just so will it be at the last day with false professors and nominal Christians. Their end, except they repent, will be destruction. They will be separated from the company of true believers, and cast out, as withered, useless branches, into everlasting fire. They will find at last, whatever they thought in this world, that there is a worm that never dies, and a fire that is not quenched.

We are meant to learn, thirdly, from these verses, that the *fruits of the Spirit are the only satisfactory evidence of a man being a true Christian.* The disciple that " abides in Christ," like a branch abiding in the vine, will always bear fruit.

He that would know what the word "fruit" means, need not wait long for an answer. Repentance toward God, faith toward our Lord Jesus Christ, holiness of life and conduct, these are what the New Testament calls " fruit." These are the distinguishing marks of the man who is a•living branch of the true Vine. Where these things are wanting, it is vain to talk of possessing dormant grace and spiritual life. Where there is no fruit there is no life. He that lacketh these things is " dead while he liveth."

True grace, we must not forget, is never idle. It never slumbers and never sleeps. It is a vain notion to suppose that we are living members of Christ, if the example of Christ is the only satisfactory evidence of saving union between Christ and our souls. Where there is no fruit of the Spirit to be seen, there is no vital religion in the heart. The Spirit of Life in Christ Jesus will always make Himself known in the daily conduct of those in whom He dwells. The Master Himself declares, "Every tree is known by his own fruit." (Luke vi. 44.)

We are meant, lastly, to learn from these verses, that *God will often increase the holiness of true Christians by His providential dealings with them.* "Every branch," it is written, "that beareth fruit, He purgeth it, that it may bear more fruit."

The meaning of this language is clear and plain. Just as the vine-dresser prunes and cuts back the branches of a fruitful vine, in order to make them more fruitful, so does God purify and sanctify believers by the circumstances of life in which He places them.

Trial, to speak plainly, is the instrument by which our Father in heaven makes Christians more holy. By trial He calls out their passive graces, and proves whether they can suffer His will as well as do it. By trial He weans them from the world, draws them to Christ, drives them to the Bible and prayer, shows them their own hearts, and makes them humble. This is the process by which He "purges" them, and makes them more fruitful. The lives of the saints in every age, are the best and truest comment on the text. Never, hardly, do we find an eminent saint, either in the Old Testament or the New, who was not purified by suffering, and, like His Master, a "man of sorrows."

Let us learn to be patient in the days of darkness, if we know anything of vital union with Christ. Let us remember the doctrine of the passage before us, and not murmur and complain because of trials. Our trials are not meant to do us harm, but good. God chastens us "for our profit, that we may be partakers of His holiness." (Heb. xii. 10.) Fruit is the thing that our Master desires to see in us, and He will not spare the pruning-knife if He sees we need it. In the last day we shall see that all was well done.

NOTES JOHN xv 1—6

1 —[*I am... Vine...Father...husbandman.*] In this and the following chapter, our Lord proceeds to give instruction rather than consolation. Having cheered and comforted the timid disciples in the fourteenth chapter, He now presses on their attention certain great truths which He would have them specially remember when He was gone. And He begins by urging the absolute necessity of close union and communion with Himself, by means of the illustration of a vine and its branches.

We must always remember that the passage before us is a parable, and as a parable must be interpreted. We must be careful not to press each sentence in it too far; and, in all parables, we must look at the great lesson which it contains, rather than at each clause.—The old saying is most true, that no parable stands on four legs;" and in all parables there are parts which are only the drapery of the figure, and not the figure itself. Neglect of this caution does much harm to the souls of Christians, and is the cause of much crude and unsound doctrine.—In the passage before us we must remember that our Lord Jesus Christ is not literally a vine, nor are believers literal branches, nor is the Father literally a husbandman. We are dealing with figures and pictures, mercifully used in order to meet our weak capacities; and we must take care we do not draw doctrinal conclusions from them, which contradict other plain passages of Scripture.

Even Maldonatus, the Romish commentator, here remarks: "All the several parts of a parable are not always meant to be fitted to the thing signified by the parable. Many things in parables are said to fill up or adorn the narrative." Toletus says just the same.

Burgon remarks, " Let us, instead of perplexing ourselves with minor details, bear in mind that in interpreting each of our Lord's parables, the great *purpose* for which it was delivered is ever to be borne in mind, if we would understand it rightly."

Our Lord's reason for choosing the illustration of " a vine " has caused much speculation. Some think that He drew the figure from a vine trained over the walls and windows of the upper chamber which He and His disciples were leaving.—Some think that He drew it from the famous golden vine, which ornamented the principal gate of the temple.—Some think that He drew it from the vines which He saw by the wayside as He walked to the garden of Gethsemane.—Some refer it to the " fruit of the vine " at the Lord's Supper.—After all, these are only guesses and conjectures. It was night when our Lord spoke, and of course nothing could be seen very distinctly. Nor is it necessary to suppose that our Lord drew His illustration from anything but His own mind.

The expression " the true " applied to the vine is an argument much used by those who think our Lord founded His parable on a vine under His eyes. But is it not more likely that our Lord had in view those places in the Old Testament where the Jewish Church is compared to a vine? (See Psalm lxxx. 8; Jer. ii. 21; Ezek. xv. 2; Hosea x. 1.) It would then mean: " I, and not the decaying Jewish Church, am the true source of spiritual life." This to Jewish minds would be a very useful lesson.

For the use of the word " true " in a precisely similar way, see John vi. 32; " the true bread." It means the true, original, type vine, of which all other vines are only types and shadows.

Lightfoot says, "Hitherto Israel had been the vine, into which every one that would worship the true God must be grafted. But from henceforward they were to be planted into the profession of Christ."

The meaning of the verse seems to be this:—" The relation between you and Me is that of a vine and its branches. I am the true source of all your life and spiritual vigor; and you are as entirely dependent on Me, as the branches of the vine are on the parent stem: and there is as close union between you and Me, as between a vine and its branches. My Father takes the same tender interest in you that the vine-dresser does in the branch of the vine; and is continually watching over your health, fruitfulness, and fertility. Think not for a moment that my Father is not as deeply interested in your spiritual prosperity as I am myself."

The interpretation adopted by Alford and many others, that the vine means "the visible Church," of which Christ is the *inclusive Head*, appears to me thoroughly unsatisfactory. Our Lord is speaking specially to eleven believers, and treating of their relation to himself. To apply all the language of this parable to so mixed and defective a body as the "visible Church," seems to me to lower and degrade the whole passage.

2 —[*Every branch...not fruit...taketh away.*] Perhaps no sentence in the parable is more perverted, and wrested, and misapplied than this. Many assert that it teaches that a man may be a real true branch of the vine, a member of Christ, and yet lose all His grace, and be finally cast away. In short, the sentence is the favorite weapon of all Arminians, of all who maintain an inseparable connection between grace and baptism, and of all who deny the perseverance in faith of believers.

I will not urge in reply that this view of the sentence cannot be reconciled with other plainer texts of Scripture, which are not parts of a parable like this; and that we should always shrink from interpreting Scripture so as to make one part contradict another. I prefer saying that the sentence before us will not bear the sense commonly put on it.

The plain truth is that this text is precisely that part of the parable which will not admit of a literal interpretation. As a matter of fact it is not true that the Father "taketh away" all unfruitful branches. When does He do it? When does He remove from the Church all graceless Christians? On the contrary, for 1800 years He has allowed them to exist in the Church, and has not taken them away. Nor will He take them away till the day of judgment. If the expression "taketh away" cannot be interpreted literally we must beware of interpreting literally the expression, "branch in Me." As the one phrase is figurative, so also is the other. In short it cannot be shown that a "branch in Me" must mean a believer in Me. It means nothing more than "a professing member of my Church, a man joined to the company of my people, but not joined to me."

The true meaning of the verse I believe to be this: " My Father deals with my mystical body just as the vine-dresser deals with the vine and its branches. He will no more allow any of my members to be fruitless and graceless, than a vine-dresser will allow barren branches to grow on the vine. My Father will take care that all who are in Me give proof of their union by their fruitful lives and conversation. He will not tolerate for a moment such an inconsistent being as an unfruitful believer, if such a being could be found. In a word, fruitfulness is the great test of being one of my disciples ; and he that is not fruitful is not a branch of the true vine."

Calvin remarks, " Many are supposed to be in the vine, according to man's opinion, who actually have no root in the vine."

Hengstenberg thinks that the Jewish Church is primarily meant here, as a fruitless branch compared to the Christian Church.

[*And every branch...purgeth...fruit.*] The meaning of this part of the verse is happily more easy than the other. " Just as a vine-dresser prunes and cuts all healthy branches of a vine, in order to prevent it running to wood and have it bear more fruit, so does my Father deal with all my believing members. He prunes and purifies them by affliction and trouble, in order to make them more fruitful in holiness."

Let us remember that this sentence throws light on many of the afflictions and trials of God's people. They are all part of that mysterious process by which God the Father purifies and sanctifies Christ's people. They are the " pruning " of the vine-branches, for good and not for harm, to increase their fruitfulness. All the most eminent saints in every age have been men of sorrows, and often pruned.

Clement of Alexandria, and many writers in all ages, remark, on this verse, that the vine-branch, which is not sharply pruned, is peculiarly liable to run to wood and bear no fruit.

After all, in leaving this difficult verse, we must not forget that a man may *appear* to us to be a " branch in Christ," and a true believer, and yet not be one in the sight of God. The end of that man will be death. He will be " taken away " at last to punishment. " Every one that seems and appears to be a branch of the true vine, and yet is not really one, will be lost."—Two principles in any case we must never let go. One principle is that no one can be a branch in Christ, and a living member of His body, who does not bear fruit. Vital union with Christ not evidenced by life is an impossibility, and a blasphemous idea.—The other principle is that no living branch of the true vine, no believer in Christ, will ever finally perish. They that perish may have looked like believers, but they were not believers in reality.

3 —[*Now ye are clean...word...unto you.*] Having described the relation between Himself and His people generally, our Lord now turns to His disciples, and shows them their present position and immediate duty. "Now you are comparatively cleansed and purified by the doctrine which I have taught, and you have received and believed. But do not be content with past attainments. Attend to the counsel which I am about to give you."

When our Lord calls His disciples "clean" or "pure" in this place, we cannot doubt that He uses the phrase in a comparative sense. Compared to the unbelieving Scribes and Pharisees, compared indeed with themselves before their Lord called and taught them, the disciples were a cleansed and purified people,—imperfectly and very partially cleansed no doubt, but cleansed.

We should carefully note how our Lord speaks of His "Word" as the great instrument of cleansing His disciples. It is the same mighty principle that is found in Eph. v. 26 and 1 Peter i. 22. God's Word is God's grand means of converting and sanctifying souls.

Henry remarks here, "Those who are justified by the blood, and sanctified by the Spirit of Christ, are in Christ's account clean already, notwithstanding many spots and manifold imperfections."

4 —[*Abide in Me....I in you.*] Now comes the direct instruction which our Lord desired the disciples to receive:—"Abide in Me. Cling to Me. Stick fast to Me. Live the life of close and intimate communion with Me. Get nearer and nearer to Me. Roll every burden on Me. Cast your whole weight on Me. Never let go your hold on Me for a moment. Be as it were rooted and planted in Me. Do this, and I will never fail you. I will ever abide in you."

This word "abide," or "remain," is used no less than ten times in the first eleven verses of this chapter. It implies a constant remaining or continuing in one spot or place. A true Christian must be always "in Christ," as a man dwelling always inside the walls of a fortified city.

[*As the branch...abide in Me.*] Here our Lord returns once more to the figure of the parable:—"Just as the branch of the vine cannot bear fruit separately and of itself, and must keep up living union with the parent stem, and out of it draw life and strength, just so you cannot bear Christian fruit and walk in Christian ways, and live a Christian life, except you keep up constant union and communion with Me."

5 —[*I am... Vine...ye...branches.*] Once more our Lord repeats the

leading idea of the parable, in order to impress the lesson He is teaching on the disciples' minds :—" I repeat the assertion I made. The relation between you and Me must be as close and intimate as that between a vine and its branches."

[*He that abideth...much fruit.*] Here our Lord gives encouragement to the disciples to keep up the habit of closest union with Him. This is the secret of bearing " much fruit," and being an eminently holy and useful Christian. The experience of every age of the Church proves the truth of this saying. The greatest saints have always lived nearest to Christ.

Do we not see here that there is a difference in the degrees of fruitfulness to which Christians attain? Is there not a tacit distinction here between " fruit " and " much fruit " ?

[*For without Me...do nothing.*] The marginal reading gives our Lord's meaning more completely : " Severed from Me, separate from Me, you have no strength, and can do nothing. You are as lifeless as a branch cut off from the parent stem."

We must always take care that we do not misapply and misinterpret this text. Nothing is more common than to hear some ignorant Christians quoting it partially, as an excuse for indolence, and neglect of means of grace. " You know we can do nothing," is the cry of such people.—This is dragging out of the text a lesson it was never meant to teach. He that spoke these words to His eleven chosen Apostles, is the same Lord who said to all men who would be saved,—" Strive to enter in ; "—" Labor for the meat which endureth to everlasting life ; "—" Repent and believe."

6 —[*If a man abide not...burned.*] The consequence of not abiding in Christ, of refusing to live the life of faith in Christ, are here described under a terrible figure. The end of such false professors will be like the end of fruitless and dead branches of a vine. Sooner or later they are cast out of the vineyard as withered, useless things, and gathered as firewood to be burned. Such will be the last end of professing Christians who turn their backs on Jesus, and bear no fruit to God's glory. They will finally come to the fire that is never quenched in hell.

These are awful words. They seem, however, to apply specially to backsliders and apostates, like Judas Iscariot. There must be about a man some *appearance* of professed faith in Christ, before he can come to the state described here. Doubtless there are those who seem to depart from grace, and to go back from union with Christ ; but we need not doubt in such cases that the grace was not real, but seeming, and the union was not true, but fictitious. Once more we must remember that we are reading a parable.

That there is a hell, and that God can punish, seems plainly taught in this verse.

It is noteworthy that the Greek would be more literally rendered, " He has been cast out," and " Has been withered," in the past tense. Alford thinks that this is because the whole is spoken as if the great day of judgment were come.—Also the word "men" is supplied in our translation. Literally it would be, " They gather," " They cast," without referring to any person in particular. This is a Hebraism which will be found in Matt. v. 15; Luke xvi. 9; Acts vii. 6.

After all, the final, miserable ruin and punishment of false professors, is the great lesson which the verse teaches. Abiding in Christ leads to fruitfulness in this life and everlasting happiness in the life to come. Departure from Christ leads to the everlasting fire of hell.

JOHN XV 7—11

7 If ye abide in me, and my words abide in you, ye shall ask what ye will, and it shall be done unto you.

8 Herein is my Father glorified, that ye bear much fruit; so shall ye be my disciples.

9 As the Father hath loved me, so have I loved you : continue ye in my love.

10 If ye keep my commandments, ye shall abide in my love; even as I have kept my Father's commandments, and abide in his love.

11 These things have I spoken unto you, that my joy might remain in you, and *that* your joy might be full.

THERE is a wide difference between believers and believers. In some things they are all alike. All feel their sins; all trust in Christ; all repent and strive to be holy. All have grace, and faith, and new hearts. But they differ widely in the degree of their attainments. Some are far happier and holier Christians than others, and have far more influence on the world.

Now what are the inducements which the Lord Jesus holds out to His people, to make them aim at eminent holiness? This is a question which ought to be deeply interesting to every pious mind. Who would not like to be a singularly useful and happy servant of Christ? The passage before us throws light on the subject in three ways.

In the first place, our Lord declares, "If ye abide in Me, and my words abide in you, ye shall ask what ye will, and it shall be done unto you." This is *a distinct promise of power and success in prayer.* And what does it turn upon? We must "abide in Christ," and Christ's "words must abide in us."

To abide in Christ means to keep up a habit of constant close communion with Him,—to be always leaning on Him, resting on Him, pouring out our hearts to Him, and using Him as our Fountain of life and strength, as our chief Companion and best Friend.—To have His words abiding in us, is to keep His sayings and precepts continually before our memories and minds, and to make them the guide of our actions and the rule of our daily conduct and behavior.

Christians of this stamp, we are told, shall not pray in vain. Whatever they ask they shall obtain, so long as they ask things according to God's mind. No work shall be found too hard, and no difficulty insurmountable. Asking they shall receive, and seeking they shall find. Such men were Martin Luther, the German Reformer, and our own martyr, Bishop Latimer. Such a man was John Knox, of whom Queen Mary said, that she feared his prayers more than an army of twenty thousand men. It is written in a certain place, "The effectual fervent prayer of a righteous man availeth much." (James v. 16.)

Now, why is there so little power of prayer like this in our own time? Simply because there is so little close communion with Christ, and so little strict conformity to His will. Men do not "abide in Christ," and therefore pray in vain. Christ's words do not abide in them, as their standard of practice, and therefore their prayers seem not to be heard. They ask and receive not, because they ask amiss. Let this lesson sink down into our hearts. He that would have answers to his prayers, must carefully remember Christ's directions. We must keep up intimate friendship with the great Advocate in heaven, if our petitions are to prosper.

In the second place, our Lord declares, "Herein is my Father glorified, that ye bear much fruit ; so shall ye be my disciples." The meaning of this promise seems to be, that *fruitfulness in Christian practice will not only bring glory to God, but will supply the best evidence to our own hearts that we are real disciples of Christ.*

Assurance of our own interest in Christ, and our consequent eternal safety, is one of the highest privileges in religion. To be always doubting and fearing is miserable work. Nothing is worse than suspense in any matter of importance, and above all in the matter of our souls. He that would know one of the best receipts for obtaining assurance, should diligently study Christ's words now before us. Let him strive to bear much fruit in his life, his habits, his temper, his words, and his works. So doing he shall feel the "witness of the Spirit" in his heart, and give abundant proof that he is a living branch of the true Vine. He shall find inward evidence in his own soul that he is a child of God, and shall supply the world with outward evidence that cannot be disputed. He shall leave no room for doubt that he is a disciple.

Would we know why so many professing Christians have little comfort in their religion, and go fearing and doubting along the road to heaven ? The question receives a solution in the saying of our Lord we are now considering. Men are content with a little Christianity, and a little fruit of the Spirit, and do not labor to be holy in all manner of conversation. They must not wonder if they enjoy little peace, feel little hope, and leave behind them little evidence. The fault lies with themselves. God has linked together holiness and happiness; and what God has joined together we must not think to put asunder.

In the third place, our Lord declares, "If ye keep my commandments, ye shall abide in my love." The meaning of this promise is near akin to that of the preceding one. The man who *makes conscience of diligently observing Christ's precepts, is the man who shall continually enjoy a sense of Christ's love in his soul.*

Of course we must not misunderstand our Lord's words when He speaks of "keeping His commandments." There is a sense in which no one can keep them. Our best works are imperfect and defective, and when we have done our best we may well cry, "God be merciful to me a sinner." Yet we must not run into the other extreme, and give way to the lazy idea that we can do nothing at all. By the grace of God we may make Christ's laws our rule of life, and show daily that we desire to please Him. So doing, our gracious Master will give us a constant sense of His favor, and make us feel His face smiling on us, like the sun shining on a fine day. "The secret of the Lord is with them that fear Him, and He will show them His covenant." (Ps. xxv. 14.)

Lessons like these may be *legal* to some, and bring down much blame on those who advocate them. Such is the narrow-mindedness of human nature, that few can look on more than one side of truth! Let the servant of Christ call no man his master. Let him hold on his way, and never be ashamed of diligence, fruitfulness, and jealous watchfulness, in his obedience to Christ's commands. These things are perfectly consistent with salvation by grace and justification by faith, whatever any one may say to the contrary.

Let us hear the conclusion of the whole matter. The Christian who is careful over his words and tempers and works, will generally be the most happy Christian. "Joy and peace in believing" will never accoi pany an inconsistent life. It is not for nothing that oui Lord concludes the passage : "These things have 1 spoken unto you, that your joy might be full."

NOTES JOHN V 7-11

7 —[*If ye abide in Me...done unto you.*] In this verse our Lord continues to encourage the disciples to "abide in Him," by holding up to them a gracious promise. Abiding in Christ, their prayers will obtain signal and special replies. They shalt ask what they will, and it shall be done for them.

The doctrine here laid down and implied is a very remarkable one. There are some Christians whose prayers are more powerful and effectual than those of others. The nearer a man lives to Christ, and the closer his communion with Him, the more effectual will his prayers be. The truth of the doctrine is so self-evident and reasonable, that no one on reflection can deny it. He that lives nearest to Christ will always be the man that feels most, and prays most earnestly, and fervently, and heartily. Common sense shows that such prayers are most likely to get answers. Many believers get little from God, because they ask little, or ask amiss. The holiest saints are the most earnest in prayer, and they consequently get the most.

We should note that our Lord says not only "if ye abide in Me," but adds, "and my words abide in you." This means, "If my doctrine and teaching abide fresh in your memories, and is continually influencing your lives." Our Lord guards us against supposing that a mere indolent abiding in Him, with a dreamy, mystical kind of religion, is what He means. His words must be burning like fire within us, and constantly actuating our characters and lives.

When He says "ye shall ask what ye will," we must of course understand that His promise only includes things according to God's mind and for God's glory. Paul asked for the "thorn in the flesh" to depart; but his prayer was not granted. We need not, however, hesitate to believe that there is a special and peculiar power in the prayers of eminent saints. "The effectual fervent prayer of a righteous man availeth much." (James v. 16.) The prayers of Luther, Latimer, Knox, Welsh, Baxter, Herbert, Romaine, and other great saints, are specially noted by their contemporaries as possessing power.

The Greek word rendered " it shall be done," means literally " it shall come to pass."

8 —[*Herein...Father glorified...disciples.*] In this verse our Lord
supplies two more reasons why His disciples should abide in
Him, and strive to bring forth much fruit of holiness. One
reason is, that it will glorify His Father in heaven. Their good
works will recommend their religion, and make the world honor
the God who has such servants. The other reason is, that it
will give evidence of their being real, true, genuine disciples.
Their lives will prove plainly that they are followers of Christ.

The expression " so shall ye be," is literally " all ye shall be."
It must mean, " Ye shall be known and recognized by all men
as my disciples, and shall feel in your own hearts the witness
of the Spirit that ye are such."

Poole remarks, " In Scripture, being often signifieth appearing," as in John viii. 31, and Romans iii. 4.

9 —[*As...Father...loved...I...you.*] This remarkable statement
seems intended to show the depth and magnitude of our Lord's
love to His people. We can form no adequate idea of the love
of the Father towards the Son. The feeling of one eternal
Person in the Trinity to another Person is a high thing into
which we cannot enter. Yet even such is the love of Christ towards those who believe in Him,—a vast, wide, deep, unmeas-
urable love that passeth knowledge, and can never be fully
comprehended by man.

[*Continue ye in my love.*] This must mean,—" Continue resting your souls on this love of mine towards you, and live under a constant sense of it. Remain clinging to it, as within a
fortress and place of refuge." Christ's free, and continued,
and mighty love should be the home and abiding place of a believer's soul.

The word rendered " continue " is the same that is rendered
" abide " in verse 4, and ought to have been the same here.

10 —[*If...keep commandments...love.*] Once more our Lord returns
to the subject of practical obedience to His laws, as the grand
secret of a happy and comfortable religion. " If you keep my
commandments, you will live in the enjoyment of a continued
sense of my love to your souls, and feel inwardly that you are
my saved people." The doctrine here laid down is one of the
great principles of experimental Christianity. Holy living and
assurance of an interest in Christ are closely connected. Our
own happiness and enjoyment of religion are inseparably bound
up with our daily practical living. He that expects assurance,
while he neglects Christ's commandments, and gives way to
daily inconsistencies of temper and conduct, is expecting what
he will never get. " Hereby we know that we know Him, if we
keep His commandments." (1 John ii. 3.) Let those who will
call such doctrine " legal." As a matter of fact, it will always
be found true.

[*Even as I...his love.*] The statement of this sentence is one of those which man can never fully grasp. That Christ kept the Father's commandments perfectly, while we can only keep His imperfectly, and that He abides in the Father's love continually and without defect, while our abiding in His love is at least fitful and uncertain, are truths which no intelligent Christian can dispute. In this, as in everything else, our Lord's example and pattern are propounded to us as things which we must strive to follow, though at a long distance, and not always with sensible comfort. But we may remember that, even when Jesus said on the cross,—" My God, why hast thou forsaken Me ? "—He was still abiding in the Father's love.

11 —[*These things...might be full.*] In this verse our Lord gives two reasons why all the things in His discourses were addressed to the disciples. One was that " his joy might abide " or remain " in them,"—that they might have a comfortable share of their Master's joy in their salvation and redemption. The other was that their own individual joy might be filled up and perfected. Two joys are named, we must observe. One is that special joy mentioned in Hebrews xii. 2, which our Lord feels in the redemption of His people. The other is that joy which His people feel from a sense of Christ's love to their souls.

Here, as elsewhere, we should note, that the joy of believers is a thing that admits of degrees and increase.

Cyril, on this verse, remarks that it is the mark of prosperous Christians to rejoice in those things in which Christ rejoices ; and that this is the special object of the phrase, " my joy,"— " that ye may continually rejoice in those things in which I rejoice, and so your own inward happiness may be increased."

JOHN XV 12—16

12 This is my commandment, That ye love one another, as I have loved you.

13 Greater love hath no man than this, that a man lay down his life for his friends.

14 Ye are my friends, if ye do whatsoever I command you.

15 Henceforth I call you not servants ; for the servant knoweth not what his Lord doeth : but I have called you friends ; for all things that I have heard of my Father I have made known unto you.

16 Ye have not chosen me, but I have chosen you, and ordained you, that ye should go and bring forth fruit, and *that* your fruit should remain : that whatsoever ye shall ask of the Father in my name, he may give it you.

THREE weighty points demand our attention in this passage. On each of these the language of our Lord Jesus Christ is full of striking instruction.

We should observe first, *how our Lord speaks of the grace of brotherly love.*

He returns to it a second time, though He has already spoken of it in the former part of His discourse. He would have us know that we can never think too highly of love, attach too much weight to it, labor too much to practice it. Truths which our Master thinks it needful to enforce on us by repetition, must needs be of first-class importance.

He commands us to love one another. " This is my commandment." It is a positive duty laid on our consciences to practice this grace. We have no more right to neglect it than any of the ten precepts given on Mount Sinai.

He supplies the highest standard of love : " Love one another as I have loved you." No lower measure must content us. The weakest, the lowest, the most ignorant, the most defective disciple, is not to be despised. All are to be loved with an active, self-denying, self-sacrificing love. He that cannot do this, or will not try to do it, is disobeying the command of his Master.

A precept like this should stir up in us great searchings of heart. It condemns the selfish, ill-natured, jealous, ill-tempered spirit of many professing Christians, with a sweeping condemnation. Sound views of doctrine, and knowledge of controversy, will avail us nothing at last, if we have known nothing of love. Without charity we may pass muster very well as Churchmen. But without charity we are no better, says St. Paul, than "sounding brass and tinkling cymbal." (1 Cor. xiii. 1.) Where there is no Christ-like love, there is no grace, no work of the Spirit, and no reality in our religion. Blessed are they that do not forget Christ's commandment! They are those who shall have right to the tree of life, and enter the celestial city. The unloving Christian is unmeet for heaven.

We should observe, secondly, *how our Lord speaks of the relation between Himself and true believers.* He says, " Henceforth I call you not servants . . . . but I have called you friends."

This is indeed a glorious privilege. To know Christ, serve Christ, follow Christ, obey Christ, work in Christ's vineyard, fight Christ's battles, all this is no small matter. But for sinful men and women like ourselves to be called " friends of Christ," is something that our weak minds can hardly grasp and take in. The King of kings and Lord of lords not only pities and saves all them that believe in Him, but actually calls them His " friends." We need not wonder, in the face of such language as this, that St. Paul should say, the " love of Christ passeth knowledge." (Ephes. iii. 19.)

Let the expression before us encourage Christians to deal familiarly with Christ in prayer. Why should we be afraid to pour out all our hearts, and unbosom all our secrets, in speaking to one who calls us His "friends"? Let it cheer us in all the troubles and sorrows of life, and increase our confidence in our Lord. " He that hath friends," says Solomon, " will show himself friendly." (Prov. xviii. 24.) Certainly our great Master in heaven will never forsake His " friends." Poor and unworthy as we are, He will not cast us off, but will stand by us and keep us to the end. David never forgot Jonathan, and the Son of David will never forget His people. None so rich, so strong, so independent, so well off, so thoroughly provided for, as the man of whom Christ says, " This is my friend ! "

We should observe, lastly, *how our Lord speaks of the doctrine of election.* He says, " Ye have not chosen Me, but I have chosen you, ... that ye should go and bring forth fruit." The choosing here mentioned is evidently twofold. It includes not only the election to the Apostolic office, which was peculiar to the eleven, but the election to eternal life, which is the privilege of all believers. To this last "choosing," as it specially concerns ourselves, we may profitably direct our attention.

Election to eternal life, is a truth of Scripture which we must receive humbly, and believe implicitly. Why the Lord Jesus calls some and does not call others, quickens whom He will, and leaves others alone in their sins, these are deep things which we cannot explain. Let it suffice us to know that it is a fact. God must begin the work of grace in a man's heart, or else a man will never be saved. Christ must first choose us and call us by His Spirit, or else we shall never choose Christ. Beyond doubt, if not saved, we shall have none to blame but ourselves. But if saved, we shall certainly trace up the beginning of our salvation, to the choosing grace of Christ. Our song to all eternity will be that which fell from the lips of Jonah : "Salvation is of the Lord." (Jonah ii. 9.)

Election is always to sanctification. Those whom Christ chooses out of mankind, He chooses not only that they may be saved, but that they may bear fruit, and fruit that can be seen. All other election beside this is a mere vain delusion, and a miserable invention of man. It was the faith and hope and love of the Thessalonians, which made St. Paul say, " I know your election of God." (1 Thess. i. 4.) Where there is no visible fruit of sanctification, we may be sure there is no election.

Armed with such principles as these, we have no cause to be afraid of the doctrine of election. Like any other truth of the Gospel, it is liable to be abused and perverted. But to a pious mind, as the seventeenth Article of the Church of England truly says, it is a doctrine "full of sweet, pleasant, and unspeakable comfort."

NOTES JOHN XV 12—16

12 —[*This...commandment...love...loved you.*] In this verse our Lord returns to the old lesson which He has taught before : the great duty of love towards other Christians. He backs the command by His own example. Nothing less than His matchless love towards sinners should be the measure and standard of love to one another.

The frequent repetition of this command teaches the vast importance of Christian charity, and the great rarity of it. How any one can pretend to Christian hope who is ignorant of Christian love, it is hard to understand. He that supposes he is right in the sight of God, because his doctrinal views are correct, while he is unloving in his temper, and sharp, cross, snappish, and ill-natured in the use of his tongue, exhibits wretched ignorance of the first principles of Christ's Gospel. The crossness, spitefulness, jealousy, maliciousness, and general disagreeableness of many high professors of " sound doctrine," are a positive scandal to Christianity. Where there is little love there can be little grace.

13 —[*Greater love...for his friends.*] In this verse our Lord teaches what should be the measure and degree of the love which Christians should have to one another. It should be a self-sacrificing love, even to death, as His was. He proved the greatness of His love by dying for His friends, and even for His enemies. (Rom. v. 6—8.) It would be impossible for love to go further. There is no greater love than willingness to lay down life for those we love. Christ did this, and Christians should be willing to do the same.

Let us note here that our Lord clearly speaks of His own death as a sacrificial and propitiatory death. Even His friends need a substitute to die for them.

14 —[*Ye are my friends...command you.*] This verse seems closely connected with the preceding one. " You are the friends for whom I lay down my life, if you do whatever things I command you." We are not to dream that we are Christ's friends, if we do not habitually practice His commands. Very striking is it to observe how frequently our Lord returns to this great principle, that obedience is the great test of vital Christianity, and doing the real mark of saving faith. Men who talk of being " the Lord's people," while they live in sin and neglect Christ's plain commands, are in the broad way that leads to destruction.

15 —[*Henceforth I call you not servants, &c.*] Having used the word "friends," our Lord tells His disciples that He has used that word purposely to cheer and encourage them. "Observe that I call you friends. I do so intentionally. I no longer call you servants ; because the servant from his position knows not all his master's mind, and is not in his confidence. But to you I have revealed all the truths which my Father sent me to teach the world, and have kept nothing back. I may therefore justly call you friends."

When our Lord speaks of "having made known all things" to the disciples, we must reasonably suppose that He means all things needful to their spiritual good, and all things that they were able to bear.

The high privilege of a believer is strikingly taught here. He is a friend of Christ, as well as a child of God. No one need ever say I have no "friend" to turn to, so long as Christ is in heaven. Once only before this place does Christ call the disciples "friends." (Luke xii. 4.)

It is noteworthy that Abraham is the only person in the Old Testament who is called "the friend of God" (Isa. xli. 8,) and of him the Lord says, "Shall I hide from Abraham that thing which I do?" (Gen. xviii. 17.)

16 —[*Ye have not chosen Me, etc., etc.*] The connecting link between this verse and the passage preceding it is not very clear.

Hengstenberg thinks that it refers to the commandment just laid down, to love one another. "I may fairly lay down laws and rules for your conduct, because I first chose and called you to be members of my church."

I much prefer thinking that our Lord's object is to exalt the privilege of discipleship in the eyes of the eleven. "Remember, when I call you friends, that I called you into the number of my people, and chose you before you chose Me. See then how great and free and deep is my love to you."

When our Lord speaks of "choosing" in this verse, I think that He means two things : viz., His choice of the eleven to be His apostles, and their eternal election to salvation. There seems to be a peculiar fulness in the phrase. The choice of the believer to eternal life is not the whole idea that our Lord means to convey. True as that glorious doctrine is, it is not the whole doctrine of this verse. The "choosing" includes a choosing for an office, like John vi. 70, and seems to have a special reference to the choice of the eleven faithful apostles to be the first children of Christ's Church.

Calvin certainly says, "the subject now in hand is not the ordinary election of believers, by which they are adopted to be God's children ; but that special election by which Christ sets apart His disciples to the office of preaching the gospel." (See

John vi. 70.) This also is the view of Chrysostom and Cyril.—But most of the Latin fathers apply the " choice " to eternal election. So also does Lampe. My own impression is, that, for once, the expression includes both official and eternal election.

The Greek word rendered " ordained " means simply, " I have placed you " in a certain position as my apostles.

When our Lord says, " I have chosen and ordained you that ye should go and bring forth fruit," I think He refers to the work of conversion and building a Church in the world. " I chose and set you apart for this great purpose, that ye should go into all the world preaching the Gospel, and gathering in the harvest and fruit of saved souls ; and that this work begun by you might remain and continue long after your deaths." And then to encourage the eleven, He adds, " It was part of my plan that so bringing forth fruit, ye should obtain by prayer everything that ye need for your work."

It is vain to deny that the verse is a very difficult one both as to its connection and contents. As a general rule I hold strongly that the things spoken by our Lord in this last discourse decidedly belong to all believers in every age, and not to the eleven only. Yet there are perhaps exceptions, and this verse may be one.—The expression " Go and bring forth fruit " certainly seems to apply peculiarly to the eleven, who were to " GO " into all the world and preach the Gospel. It is as though our Lord said " Take comfort in the thought that I chose you as my friends for this great purpose, to go and preach, to reap an abundant harvest of souls, to do lasting work, and to obtain a constant supply of grace and help, by prayer."—I cannot see how the word " go " can apply to any but the eleven to whom the Lord was speaking ; and this weighs heavily with me in interpreting it.—" That your fruit should remain," again, is a phrase that I cannot apply to anything but the lasting and abiding work which the Apostles did when they went through the world preaching the Gospel. But I freely admit that I find in the verse " things hard to be understood."

JOHN XV 17-21

17 These things I command you, that ye love one another.

18 If the world hate you, ye know that it hated me before *it hated* you.

19 If ye were of the world, the world would love his own: but because ye are not of the world, but I have chosen you out of the world, therefore the world hateth you.

20 Remember the word that I said unto you, The servant is not greater than his lord. If they have persecuted me, they will also persecute you; if they have kept my saying, they will keep yours also.

21 But all these things will they do unto you for my name's sake, because they know not him that sent me.

THE passage before us opens with a renewed exhortation to brotherly love. For the third time in this discourse our Lord thinks it needful to press this precious grace on the attention of His disciples. Rare, indeed, must genuine charity be, when such repeated mention of it is made! In the present instance the connection in which it stands should be carefully observed. Christian love is placed in contrast to the hatred of the world.

We are shown first, in this passage, *what true Christians must expect to meet in this world,—hatred and persecution.* If the disciples looked for kindness and gratitude from man they would be painfully disappointed. They must lay their account to be ill-treated like their Master.—"The world hateth you. Be not moved or surprised. If they have persecuted Me, they will also persecute you; if they have kept my saying, they will keep yours also."

Facts, painful facts in every age, supply abundant proof that our Lord's warning was not without cause. Persecution was the lot of the Apostles and their companions wherever they went. Not more than one or two of them died quietly in his bed.—Persecution has been the lot of true believers throughout the eighteen Christian centuries of history. The doings of Roman Emperors and Roman Popes, the Spanish inquisition, the martyrdoms of Queen Mary's reign, all tell the same story.—Persecution is the lot of all really godly people at this very day. Ridicule, mockery, slander, misrepresentation, still show the feeling of unconverted people against the true Christian. As it was in St. Paul's day, so it is now. In public and in private, at school and at college, at home and abroad, " all that will live godly in Christ Jesus shall suffer persecution." (2 Tim. iii 12.) Mere churchmanship and outward profession are a cheap religion, of course, and cost a man nothing. But real vital Christianity will always bring with it a cross.

To know and understand these things is of the utmost importance to our comfort. Nothing is so mischievous as the habit of indulging false expectations. Let us realize that human nature never changes, that "the carnal mind is enmity against God," and against God's image in His people. Let us settle it in our minds that no holiness of life or consistency of conduct will ever prevent wicked people hating the servants of Christ, just as they hated their blameless Master. Let us remember these things, and then we shall not be disappointed.

We are shown secondly, in this passage, *two reasons for patience under the persecution of this world.* Each is weighty, and supplies matter for much thought.

For one thing, persecution is the cup of which Christ Himself drank. Faultless as He was in everything, in temper, word, and deed,—unwearied as He was in works of kindness, always going about doing good,—never was any one so hated as Jesus was to the last day of His earthly ministry. Scribes and High Priests, Pharisees and Sadducees, Jews and Gentiles, united in pouring contempt on Him, and opposing Him, and never rested till He was put to death.

Surely this simple fact alone should sustain our spirits and prevent our being cast down by the hatred of man. Let us consider that we are only walking in our Master's footsteps, and sharing our Master's portion. Do we deserve to be better treated ? Are we better than He ? Let us fight against these murmuring thoughts. Let us drink quietly the cup which our Father gives us. Above all, let us often call to mind the saying, " Remember the word that I spake unto you, The servant is not greater than his Master."

For another thing, persecution helps to prove that we are children of God, and have treasure in heaven. It supplies evidence that we are really born again, that we have grace in our hearts, and are heirs of glory : "If ye were of the world, the world would love his own: but because ye are not of the world, but I have chosen you out of the world, therefore the world hateth you." Persecution, in short, is like the Goldsmith's Hall mark on real silver and gold: it is one of the marks of a converted man.

Let us nerve our minds with this cheering thought, when we feel ready to faint and give way under the world's hatred. No doubt it is hard to bear, and the more hard when our conscience tells us we are innocent. But after all let us never forget that it is a token for good. It is a symptom of a work begun within us by the Holy Ghost, which can never be overthrown. We may fall back on that wonderful promise, "Blessed are ye when men shall revile you, and persecute you, and shall say all manner of evil against you falsely, for my sake. Rejoice, and be exceeding glad: for great is your reward in heaven." (Matt. v. 11, 12.) When the world has said and done its worst, it cannot rob believers of that promise.

Let us leave the whole subject with a feeling of deep pity for those who persecute others on account of their religion. Often, very often, as our Lord says, they do it because they know no better. "They know not Him that sent Me." Like our Divine Master and His servant Stephen, let us pray for those who despitefully use us and persecute us. Their persecution rarely does us harm, and often drives us nearer to Christ, the Bible, and the throne of grace. Our intercession, if heard on high, may bring down blessings on their souls.

NOTES JOHN XV 17—21

17 —[*These things I command...love one another.*] The expression
"these things," must either refer backwards to what has just
been said, or forwards to what is going to be said. I prefer the
latter view. " I press on you these repeated charges to love one
another, because you must expect the hatred of the world.
The more the world hates you, the more you ought to love one
another and stick together."

18 —[*If...world hate...hated Me...you.*] The object of this verse is
to encourage and comfort the disciples under the hatred and
enmity of the unbelieving Jews. " Do not be surprised and
discouraged if you find yourselves hated and persecuted by an
unbelieving world. Do not think the fault is yours. You know,
and have seen, and must remember that this same world has
always hated and persecuted Me before you, although it could
lay no fault to my charge."

The principle of the verse will be found true in every age.
It is not the weaknesses and inconsistencies of Christians that
the world hates, but their grace. Christians should carefully
remember that their spotless and blameless Master was bitterly
hated by the world when He was on earth, and they must count
it no strange thing if they are treated in the same way.

Hengstenberg thinks that the words " ye know " should be
taken as an imperative, and not an indicative, like " remember," in verse 20. I doubt this; but the construction of the
Greek language makes it an open question.

The Greek word rendered " before " is literally " first." It is
the same that is translated " before " in John i. 15 and 30.

19 —[*If ye were of the world, etc.*] In this verse our Lord shows
the disciples that the hatred of the world, however painful to
bear, is a satisfactory evidence of their state before God. It is
like " Blessed are ye when men shall revile you and persecute
you," and " Woe unto you when all men shall speak well of
you." This comes out more clearly if we invert the order of
the verse. " The world hates you because you are not like
itself, but have a different faith and live a different life, and
because I have drawn you out of it to be my disciples and apostles. The world always loves what is like itself, and would
love you if your standard of faith and life was like its own.
The very hatred of the world, therefore, is a satisfactory evidence that you are my disciples."

Luther remarks, " Towards each other, apart from Christ, the
men of the world are as little friends as dogs and cats. In all
that concerns Christ they are unanimous in hatred."

The expression " his own," means literally " its own thing," its own spirit, tone, character, faith, and life.

The whole verse contains rich experimental comfort for true Christians. There are few things that we are so slow to realize as the enmity of natural man against God, and all that have anything of God's image ; and forgetfulness of it often brings believers into much trouble and perplexity of mind. They do not expect the world's hatred, and are surprised when they meet with it. This verse teaches plainly that they ought not to be surprised.

Burgon quotes a saying of Bishop Sanderson : " The godly are in the world as strangers, and in a foreign, yea in an enemy's country ; and they look upon the world, and are looked upon by it, as strangers ; and are used by it accordingly."

20 —[*Remember the word, etc.*] Our Lord continues in this verse the same subject: viz., what the disciples must expect from the world. He reminds the eleven of the things He had said before, when He first sent them out to preach. (Matt. x. 24 ; Luke vi. 40.) He had always told them that they must not expect to be better treated than He had been Himself. He quotes the proverbial saying that " a servant must not expect to fare better than his master." " Did they persecute Me ? Then they will persecute you. Did they keep, mind, and attend to my teaching ? As a rule the greater part did not, and you must expect the same."

We ought to observe carefully how strongly this lesson about the world is laid down by our Lord. It was doubtless spoken for all time, and with a special reference to believers' slowness to realize it. If there is anything that true Christians seem incessantly forgetting, and seem to need incessantly reminding of, it is the real feeling of unconverted people towards them, and the treatment they must expect to meet with. Wrong expectations are one great cause of Christians feeling troubled and perplexed. That word " remember,"—" do you remember," —has a mine of meaning in it.

Gataker, Bengel, and some others, think that the Greek word rendered " keep," here means " to observe with a malicious intention" to carp at it : but this seems improbable. Whether, however, there is not a latent irony in the sentence is doubtful.

21 —[*But all these things...name's sake.*] Our Lord here tells His disciples that He Himself was the cause of all the enmity and hatred they would meet with. They would be hated on account of their Master, more than on account of themselves.

" These things " must refer apparently to the expression, "hate, persecute, and keep your saying."

It may be some comfort to a persecuted Christian to think that it is for his Master's sake that he is ill used. He is

"filling up that which is behind of the afflictions of Christ."
(Coloss. i. 24.) He is "bearing the reproach of Christ." (Heb.
xi. 26.)

[*Because they know not...sent Me.*] This sentence is elliptical. It means that dark ignorance was the great cause of the
conduct of the unbelieving Jews. They did not rightly know
God the Father who had sent Christ into the world. They did
not know that Christ was the Messiah whom the Father had
promised to send. In this state of ignorance they blindly persecuted Christ and His disciples.

This judicial blindness and hardness of the Jewish nation in
the time of our Lord and His Apostles is a thing that ought to
be carefully observed by all Bible-readers. (See Acts iii. 17 ;
xiii. 27 ; xxviii. 25–27 ; 1 Cor. ii. 8 ; 2 Cor. iii. 14.) It was a
peculiar judicial blindness, we must remember, to which the
whole nation was given over, like Pharaoh, as a final punishment for many centuries of idolatry, wickedness and unbelief.
Nothing but this seems thoroughly to account for the extraordinary unbelief of many of our Lord's hearers.

In leaving this passage we should not fail to notice the singular frequency with which our Lord speaks of "the world."
Six times he mentions it. We should also notice the singular
resemblance between the line of argument adopted in the passage, and the line of St. John in the third chapter of his first
Epistle. The Apostle writes his Epistle in that part, as if he
had this chapter before him.

JOHN XV 22—27

22 If I had not come and spoken
unto them, they had not had sin :
but now they have no cloke for
their sin.
23 He that hateth me hateth my
Father also.
24 If I had not done among them
the works which none other man
did, they had not had sin : but now
have they both seen and hated both
me and my Father.
25 But *this cometh to pass,* that the
word might be fulfilled that is written in their law, They hated me
without a cause.
26 But when the Comforter is
come, whom I will send unto you
from the Father, *even* the Spirit of
truth, which proceedeth from the
Father, he shall testify of me :
27 And ye also shall bear witness,
because ye have been with me from
the beginning.

IN these verses our Lord Jesus Christ handles three
subjects of great importance. They are difficult subjects, no doubt, subjects on which we may easily fall
into error. But the words before us throw much light
upon them.

We should observe, for one thing, how our Lord speaks of *the misuse of religious privileges.* It intensifies man's guilt, and will increase his condemnation. He tells His disciples that if He had not "spoken" and "done" among the Jews things which none ever spoke or did before, "they had not had sin." By this, we must remember, He means, "they had not been so sinful and so guilty as they are now." But now they were utterly without excuse. They had seen Christ's works, and heard Christ's teaching, and yet remained unbelieving. What more could be done for them? Nothing ––absolutely nothing! They wilfully sinned against the clearest possible light, and were of all men most guilty.

Let us settle it down as a first principle in our religion, that religious privileges are in a certain sense very dangerous things. If they do not help us toward heaven, they will only sink us deeper into hell. They add to our responsibility. "To whomsoever much is given, of him shall much be required." (Luke xii. 48.) He that dwells in a land of open Bibles and preached Gospel, and yet dreams that he will stand in the judgment day on the same level with an untaught Chinese, is fearfully deceived. He will find to his own cost, except he repents, that his judgment will be according to his light. The mere fact that he had knowledge and did not improve it, will of itself prove one of his greatest sins. "He that knew His Master's will and did it not, shall be beaten with many stripes." (Luke xii. 47.)

Well would it be for all professing Christians in England, if this point was more thoroughly considered! Nothing is more common than to hear men taking comfort in the thought that they "know what" is right, while at the same time they are evidently unconverted, and unfit to die. They rest in that unhappy phrase, "We know it, we know it," as if knowledge could wash away all their sins,—forgetting that the devil has more knowledge than any of us, and yet is no better for it. Let the burning words of our Lord in the passage now before us, sink down into our hearts, and never be forgotten: "If I had not come and spoken unto them, they had not had sin: but now they have no cloke for their sin." To see light and not use it, to possess knowledge and yet not turn it to account, to be able to say "I know," and yet not to say "I believe," will place us at the lowest place on Christ's left hand, in the great day of judgment.

We should observe, for another thing, in these verses, how our Lord *speaks of the Holy Ghost.*

He speaks of Him as a Person. He is "the Comforter" who is to come; He is One sent and "proceeding;" He is One whose office it is to "testify." These are not words that can be used of a mere influence or inward feeling. So to interpret them is to contradict common sense, and to strain the meaning of plain language. Reason and fairness require us to understand that it is a personal Being who is here mentioned, even He whom we are justly taught to adore as the third Person in the blessed Trinity.

Again, our Lord speaks of the Holy Ghost as One whom He "will send from the Father," and One "who proceedeth from the Father." These are deep sayings, no doubt, so deep that we have no line to fathom them. The mere fact that for centuries the Eastern and Western Churches of Christendom have been divided about their meaning, should teach us to handle them with modesty and reverence. One thing, at all events, is very clear and plain. There is a close and intimate connection between the Spirit, the Father, and the

Son. Why the Holy Ghost should be said to be *sent* by the Son, and to *proceed* from the Father, in this verse, we cannot tell. But we may quietly repose our minds in the thought expressed in an ancient creed, that "In this Trinity none is afore or after other : none is greater or less than another."—"Such as the Father is such is the Son, and such is the Holy Ghost."—Above all, we may rest in the comfortable truth that in the salvation of our souls all three Persons in the Trinity equally co-operate. It was God in Trinity who said, "Let us create," and it is God in Trinity who says, "Let us save."

For ever let us take heed to our doctrine about the Holy Spirit. Let us make sure that we hold sound and Scriptural views of His nature, His Person, and His operations. A religion which entirely leaves Him out, and gives Him no place, is far from uncommon. Let us beware that such a religion is not ours. "Where is the Lamb, the Lord Jesus Christ ?" should be the first testing question about our Christianity. Where is the Holy Ghost?" should be the second question. Let us take good heed that the work of the Spirit is not so buried under extravagant views of the Church, the ministry, and the Sacraments, that the real Holy Ghost of Scripture is completely put out of sight. "If any man have not the Spirit of Christ, he is none of His." (Rom. viii. 9.) No religion deserves to be called Scriptural and apostolic, in which the work of the Spirit does not stand forth prominently, and occupy a principal place.

We should observe lastly, in these verses, how our Lord speaks of *the special office of the Apostles.* They were to be His witnesses in the world. "Ye also shall bear witness."

The expression is singularly instructive and full of meaning. It taught the eleven what they must expect their portion to be, so long as they lived. They would have to bear testimony to facts which many would not believe, and to truths which the natural heart would dislike. They would often have to stand alone, a few against many, a little flock against a great multitude. None of these things must move them. They must count it no strange thing to be persecuted, hated, opposed, and discredited. They must not mind it. To witness was their grand duty, whether men believed them or not. So witnessing, their record would be on high, in God's book of remembrance; and so witnessing, sooner or later, the Judge of all would give them a crown of glory that fadeth not away.

Let us never forget, as we leave this passage, that the position of the Apostles is that which, in a certain sense, every true Christian must fill, as long as the world stands. We must all be witnesses for Christ. We must not be ashamed to stand up for Christ's cause, to speak out for Christ, and to persist in maintaining the truth of Christ's Gospel. Wherever we live, in town or in country, in public or in private, abroad or at home. we must boldly confess our Master on every opportunity, So doing, we shall walk in the steps of the Apostles, though at a long interval. So doing, we shall please our Master, and may hope at last that we shall receive the Apostles' reward.

NOTES JOHN XV 22—27

22.—[*If I had not come, etc.*] In this and the three following verses our Lord shows the peculiar guilt and wickedness of the Jews in not believing Him.—" If I had not come among them and spoken such words as no one ever spake before, and taught such truths as no one ever taught before, they would not have been so guilty as they are. But now they have no excuse for their unbelief. They cannot say that they were not taught in the plainest way who I am and who sent Me."

Does not our Lord in this verse point to the famous prophecy

(Deut. xviii. 18, 19) of a Prophet to be raised up like Moses, to whom the Jews were to hearken? Does He not seem to say, "I have come as that Prophet, and have spoken my Father's words, and they ought to have received and hearkened to them? The refusal of the promised Prophet is of itself their condemnation, and leaves them without excuse."

The word rendered "cloke," would have been better as in the margin, "excuse." The clause literally is, "They have now no excuse concerning their sin."

When our Lord says "they had not had sin," He does not of course mean they would not have been sinners at all. It is only another way of putting the degree of their guilt. "They would have been less guilty than they are now. To have heard Me and not believed will increase their condemnation." (Compare John ix. 41.)

Let us note that there are degrees of sin, and that nothing seems to increase man's guiltiness so much as to have privileges, and not use them aright.

23 —[*He...hateth Me...Father also.*] The object of this verse is to supply a reason why the guilt of hearing Christ without believing was so great. It was because Christ's words were not only His words but the Father's also.—"He that hears Me, and hates and refuses my teachings, is hating not Me only but my Father, because I and my Father are one."—Once more we are reminded of the close union between the first and second Persons of the Trinity. The idea that we can worship and serve God while we neglect Christ, is a baseless dream. Neglecting Christ, we neglect the Father. (See Psalm lxix. 9.)

Poole remarks, "It is a common error of the world, that many pretend to love God, while yet they are manifest haters of Christ and His Gospel. Our Saviour saith, this is impossible; whosoever hateth him who is sent, hateth also him who sent him."

Hengstenberg observes, "The Jews professed that they loved God, and that on the ground of that love they hated Christ; the God, however, whom they loved was not the true God, but a phantom which they named God. The fact that they rejected Christ, in spite of all His words of spirit and truth, showed them to be enemies of the Father."

24 —[*If I had not done, etc.*]—In this verse our Lord gives another proof of the exceeding wickedness of the Jews. They had seen works and miracles done under their eyes, in confirmation of Christ's Divine mission, more numerous and mighty than any one had ever worked before, and yet they continued unbelieving. The more they saw of Him the more they hated Him; and in so hating Him, they hated not Him only, but the Father which sent Him.—"The Jews would not be so guilty as

they now are, if they had not seen my miracles as well as heard my words. But now they have both seen and heard over-whelming proofs of my Divine mission, and yet remain unbe-lieving. They have had the clearest evidence that could be given—the evidence of works and words; and yet they have persisted in hating both Me and the Father which sent Me."

Burgon here remarks, " It is not meant that every single miracle which our Lord performed, surpassed in wonder any single miracle recorded of Moses, Elijah, or Elisha; for that would not be true. But Christ's works were made so great by the way He wrought them. Without effort, by a mere word, He showed that all creation was obedient to His will."

Let us carefully observe how our Lord appeals to His mira-cles as a proof of His Messiahship, which ought to have con-vinced the Jews. They are a part of the evidences of Chris-tianity which ought never to be kept back or omitted.

25 —[*But this cometh to pass, etc.*] The manner in which our Lord quotes Scripture here is so common in the Gospels that it needs little remark. The things He mentions did not happen in order that Scripture might be fulfilled, but by their happen-ing Scripture was fulfilled.

" Their law " here is a general expression denoting the Old Testament Scripture.

" Without a cause " means literally " gratuitously, as a free gift." The word occurs only nine times in the New Testa-ment. Six times it is rendered " freely," once " in vain," once " for nought," and once " without a cause."

What precise text our Lord had in view is not quite clear, and some have thought that He only referred generally to Scripture testimony, like Matt. ii. 23. Others however point to Psalm xxxi. 19, and Psalm lxix. 4.

Let us note that gratuitous, ceaseless hatred was our Lord's portion on earth; and His true disciples in every age must never wonder if they share His lot.

26 —[*But when the Comforter, etc.*] The object of this verse ap-pears to be the encouragement of the disciples. They were not to despond or feel hopeless because of the unbelief and hard-ness of the Jews. A witness would be raised up by and by, whose evidence the Jews would not be able to resist. There would come One who would give such testimony to the Divine mission of Christ, that even the wicked Jews would be silenced and crushed, although unconverted. Who was this promised witness ? It was the Holy Ghost, who was to come forth with peculiar power in the day of Pentecost, and to abide in the early Church. The second chapter of Acts was the first fulfil-ment of the verse. The irresistible influence which the Gos-pel obtained in Jerusalem, in spite of all the efforts of scribe

and priest, and Pharisee and Sadducee, was another fulfilment.

The " proceeding " here spoken of, we must remember, does not merely mean that the Spirit is sent by the Father, and comes from the Father. All the best interpreters agree in thinking, that it means the eternal procession of the Holy Spirit.

We should carefully note in this verse the language which our Lord uses concerning the Holy Ghost. He is the " Comforter," or rather the Advocate, as we have seen before. He is the " Spirit of truth," also, as we have seen before. But we should specially mark that Christ says, " I will send Him ; " and also says, He " proceedeth from the Father." The singular number is used : " He proceedeth," not " will proceed."— This then is one of those texts which appears to supply evidence of the Holy Ghost proceeding both from the Father and from the Son, though not direct evidence. The whole Greek Church, however, denies the procession from the Son ; and it must be honestly conceded that the Scripture does not so distinctly and directly assert it as the procession from the Father. Yet, on the other hand, it is hard to understand how the Son can *send* the Spirit, and the Spirit in no sense *proceed* from the Son. The subject is a deep and mysterious one, and we have not eyes to see everything about it. The difference between the Eastern and Western Churches may after all be more apparent than real ; and we must beware of denouncing men as heretics, whom perhaps God has received. But in any case the text before us is one which ought to be carefully noted, as one on which much of the controversy hinges. Let us take that care we ourselves have the Holy Spirit in our hearts; and when we die we shall know all about the point in dispute.

One thing at any rate comes out very plainly here, and that is the personality of the Holy Ghost. In the Greek it stands out very prominently in the gender of the pronouns, which our English language cannot reach. The word we render " whom," in the Greek text is masculine ;—" which " is neuter ;—and " he " is masculine again.

27 —[*And ye also shall bear witness.*] In this verse our Lord continues the line of encouragement which He began in the preceding verse. Notwithstanding all the hardness and unbelief of the Jews, even the disciples would be enabled to bear a testimony to their Lord's Divine mission, which none of their enemies would be able to gainsay or resist. How remarkably this was fulfilled we know from the first seven chapters of the Acts of the Apostles. For instance, the verse, " with great power gave the Apostles witness of the resurrection of the Lord Jesus " (Acts iv. 32), is an exact accomplishment of the promise of the text.

It is noteworthy that both the verbs in this verse are in the present tense. They would be naturally rendered, " Ye do bear witness," and, " Ye are with Me." Does this point to the certainty of the testimony being borne ?   " Ye do bear witness : " you are sure to be enabled to do it.

In leaving this chapter, let us not fail to note how systematically our blessed Master gave His disciples instruction on three most important points. The *first* was their relation to Himself. They were to abide in close union with Him, like branches in a vine. The *second* was their relation to one another. They were to love one another with a deep, self-sacrificing love, like their Master's. The *third* was their relation to the world. They were to expect its hatred, not be surprised at it ; to bear it patiently, and not be afraid of it.

JOHN XVI 1—7

1 These things have I spoken unto you, that ye should not be offended.

2 They shall put you out of the synagogues : yea, the time cometh, that whosoever killeth you will think that he doeth God service.

3 And these things will they do unto you, because they have not known the Father, nor me.

4 But these things have I told you, that when the time shall come, ye may remember that I told you of them. And these things I said not unto you at the beginning, because I was with you.

5 But now I go my way to him that sent me ; and none of you asketh me, Whither goest thou ?

6 But because I have said these things unto you, sorrow hath filled your heart.

7 Nevertheless I tell you the truth ; It is expedient for you that I go away : for if I go not away, the Comforter will not come unto you ; but if I depart, I will send him unto you.

THE opening verses of this chapter contain three important utterances of Christ, which deserve our special attention.

For one thing, we find our Lord *delivering a remarkable prophecy.* He tells His disciples that they will be cast out of the Jewish Church, and persecuted even to the death:—" They shall put you out of the synagogues : yea, the time cometh, that whosoever killeth you will think that he doeth God service."

How strange that seems at first sight !   Excommunication, suffering, and death, are the portion that the Prince of Peace predicts to His disciples. So far from receiving them and their message with gratitude, the world would hate them, despitefully use them, and put them to death. And, worst of all, their persecutors would actually persuade themselves that it was right to persecute, and would inflict the cruelest injuries in the sacred name of religion.

How true the prediction has turned out ! Like every other prophecy of Scripture, it has been fulfilled to the very letter. The Acts of the Apostles show us how the unbelieving Jews persecuted the early Christians. The pages of history tell us what horrible crimes have been committed by the Popish Inquisition. The annals of our own country inform us how our holy Reformers were burned at the stake for their religion, by men who professed to do all they did from zeal for pure Christianity. Unlikely and incredible as it might seem at the time, the great Prophet of the Church has been found in this, as in everything else, to have predicted nothing but literal truth.·

Let it never surprise us to hear of true Christians being persecuted, in one way or another, even in our own day. Human nature never changes. Grace is never really popular. The quantity of persecution which God's children have to suffer in every rank of life, even now, if they confess their Master, is far greater than the thoughtless world supposes. They only know it who go through it, at school, at college, in the counting-house, in the barrack-room, on board the ship. Those words shall always be found true: " All that will live godly in Christ Jesus, shall suffer persecution." (2 Tim. iii. 12.)

Let us never forget that religious earnestness alone is no proof that a man is a sound Christian. Not all zeal is right: it may be a zeal without knowledge. No one is so mischievous as a blundering, ignorant zealot. Not all earnestness is trustworthy: without the leading of God's Spirit, it may lead a man so far astray, that, like Saul, he will persecute Christ himself. Some bigots fancy they are doing God service, when they are actually fighting against His truth, and trampling on His people. Let us **pray** that we may have light as well as zeal.

For another thing, we find our Lord *explaining His special reason for delivering the prophecy just referred to,* as well as all His discourse. "These things," He says, "I have spoken unto you, that ye should not be offended."

Well did our Lord know that nothing is so dangerous to our comfort as to indulge false expectations. He therefore prepared His disciples for what they must expect to meet with in His service. Forewarned, forearmed! They must not look for a smooth course and a peaceful journey. They must make up their minds to battles, conflicts, wounds, opposition, persecution, and perhaps even death. Like a wise general, He did not conceal from His soldiers the nature of the campaign they were beginning. He told them all that was before them, in faithfulness and love, that when the time of trial came, they might remember His words, and not be disappointed and offended. He wisely forewarned them that the cross was the way to the crown.

To count the cost is one of the first duties that ought to be pressed on Christians in every age. It is no kindness to young beginners to paint the service of Christ in false colors, and to keep back from them the old truth, "Through much tribulation we must enter the kingdom of God." By prophesying smooth things, and crying "Peace," we may easily fill the ranks of Christ's army with professing soldiers. But they are just the soldiers, who, like the stony-ground hearers, in time of tribulation will fall away, and turn back in the day of battle.

No Christian is in a healthy state of mind who is not prepared for trouble and persecution. He that expects to cross the troubled waters of this world, and to reach heaven with wind and tide always in his favor, knows nothing yet as he ought to know. We never can tell what is before us in life. But of one thing we may be very sure: we must carry the cross if we would wear the crown. Let us grasp this principle firmly, and never forget it. Then, when the hour of trial comes, we shall "not be offended."

In the last place, we find our Lord *giving a special reason why it was expedient for Him to go away from His disciples.* "If I go not away," He says, "the Comforter will not come unto you."

We can well suppose that our gracious Lord saw the minds of His disciples crushed at the idea of His leaving them. Little as they realized His full meaning, on this, as well as on other occasions, they evidently had a vague notion that they were about to be left, like orphans, in a cold and unkind world, by their Almighty Friend. Their hearts quailed and shrunk back at the thought. Most graciously does our Lord cheer them by words of deep and mysterious meaning. He tells them that His departure, however painful it might seem, was not an evil, but a good. They would actually find it was not a loss, but a gain. His bodily absence would be more useful than His presence.

It is vain to deny that this is a somewhat dark saying. It seems at first sight hard to understand how in any sense it could be good that Christ should go away from His disciples. Yet a little reflection may show us that, like our Lord's sayings, this remarkable utterance was wise, and right, and true. The following points, at any rate, deserve attentive consideration.

If Christ had not died, risen again, and ascended up

into heaven, it is plain that the Holy Ghost could not have come down with special power on the day of Pentecost, and bestowed His manifold gifts on the Church. Mysterious as it may be, there was a connection in the eternal counsels of God, between the ascension of Christ and the outpouring of the Spirit.

If Christ had remained bodily with the disciples, He could not have been in more places than one at the same time. The presence of the Spirit whom He sent down, would fill every place where believers were assembled in His name, in every part of the world.

If Christ had remained upon earth, and not gone up into heaven, He could not have become a High Priest for His people in the same full and perfect manner that He became after His ascension. He went away to sit down at the right hand of God, and to appear for us, in our human nature glorified, as our Advocate with the Father.

Finally, if Christ had always remained bodily with His disciples, there would have been far less room for the exercise of their faith and hope and trust, than there was when He went away. Their graces would not have been called into such active exercise, and they would have had less opportunity of glorifying God, and exhibiting His power in the world.

After all there remains the broad fact that after the Lord Jesus went away, and the Comforter came down on the day of Pentecost, the religion of the disciples became a new thing altogether. The growth of their knowledge, and faith, and hope, and zeal, and courage, was so remarkable, that they were twice the men they were before. They did far more for Christ when He was absent, than they had ever done when He was present. What stronger proof can we require that it was expedient for them that their Master should go away !

Let us leave the whole subject with a deep conviction that it is not the carnal presence of Christ in the
midst of us, so much as the presence of the Holy Spirit
in our hearts, that is essential to a high standard of
Christianity. What we should all desire and long for
is not Christ's body literally touched with our hands
and received into our mouths, but Christ dwelling spiritually in our hearts by the grace of the Holy Ghost.

NOTES   JOHN XVI 1—7

1 —[*These things...spoken...not...offended.*] The chapter we now
begin is a direct continuation of the last chapter, without break
or pause. Our Lord's object in this first verse is to cheer and
revive the minds of the Apostles, and to prevent them being
discouraged by the persecution of the unbelieving Jews. " I
have spoken the things which I have just been speaking, in
order to obviate the depressing effect of the treatment you will
receive. Lest you should be stumbled and offended by the
conduct of your enemies, I have told you the things you have
just heard."

Stier remarks that " these things " include both the warning
of the world's hatred and the promise of the witnessing Spirit.
Foreknowledge of the world's hatred would prevent the disciples being surprised and disappointed. The promise of the
Spirit would cheer and encourage.

The word " offended " is literally " scandalized." It is a remarkable instance of a word which has greatly changed its
meaning since the last translation of the Bible, to the great
perplexity and injury of many Bible readers.

How great a stumbling-block it often is to young and unes-
tablished Christians to find themselves persecuted and ill-used
for their religion, it is needless to point out. Our Lord knew
this, and took care to arm the eleven apostles with warnings.
He never kept back the cross, or concealed the difficulties in
the way to heaven.

2 —[*They shall put...out...synagogue.*] In this verse our Lord
tells the disciples most plainly what they must expect. " They
will excommunicate you, and cast you out of the Jewish
Church, and expel you from their assemblies." The Greek
words are curious : " They will make you out-of-synagogue
men." How great a grief and loss this was to a Jew we have
little idea, unless we have studied the work of Christianity
among the Jews in modern times. Nothing affects a Jew so
much as expulsion from the synagogue, or excommunication.

There is no nominative here to which we can refer " they."
It is an Hebraism equivalent to " You will be put out."

Hengstenberg observes, " The disciples were not to depart
voluntarily out of the synagogue, but to await what would
happen to them on a full proclamation of the Gospel. This
gives a very intelligible hint to the faithful in times of the
Church's decline : viz., that they should keep far from their
thoughts the idea of arbitrary secession. The new formation
is right only when the casting out has gone before."

Calvin remarks, " We have no reason to be alarmed at the
Pope's excommunications, with which he thunders against us
on account of the Gospel. They will do us no more injury
than those ancient excommunications which were made against
the apostles." The curse causeless shall not come.

[*Yea...time cometh...killeth...service.*] In this clause our Lord
warns the eleven that they must not be surprised if even death
was the final result of discipleship. There would be no length
of persecution to which their enemies would not go. " The
hour comes when he who has killed you will think that in so
doing he offers God an acceptable service."

How true this has proved, the history of all religious persecution has abundantly showed. Who can doubt that Saul before his conversion was sincere ? " I verily thought that I
ought to do many things contrary to the name of Jesus of Nazareth." (Acts xxvi. 9.) The persecutions carried on in Spain,
and Portugal, and France, and England, by Romanists against
Protestants, are painful examples of the same thing. Men
have actually thought that killing people was doing a holy and
a good action.

The extent to which conscience may be blinded, until a man
actually thinks that he is doing a godly deed, when in reality
he is committing a huge sin, is one of the most painful phe-
nomena in human nature. Many of those who burned our Reformers in the days of Queen Mary were sincere and in earnest.
" Earnestness " is not the slightest proof that a man is right in
his religion. It is one of the most monstrous idols of modern
times. The folly of those who are content with " earnestness,"
and say that all " earnest " men go to heaven, is abundantly
shown by this text.

Ferus remarks that " good intentions and meanings are no
better than impiety, if they do not spring from God's Word."

3 —[*And these things will they do, etc.*] Here, as in a former
verse, our Lord points to blind ignorance as the true cause of
the enmity of the Jews against Himself and His disciples.
" They do not rightly know my Father, in spite of their profes-
sions of religious knowledge ; nor Me, whom the Father hath
sent. Hence they hate and persecute." (See Ch. xv. 21.)

4 —[*But these things have I told, etc.*] Here once more our Lord repeats His reasons for telling the disciples what they must expect. " I have told you what treatment you will receive, in order that you may not be surprised when the time of trial comes, but may remember that I foretold you all, and not be cast down. Nothing unforeseen, nothing unpredicted, you will feel, happens to us. Our Master told us it would be so."

The word " I," in the sentence, " that ye may remember that I told you," is emphatic in the Greek. It seems to mean, " Remember that I myself, your Master, told you."

Our Lord adds the reason why He had not dwelt on these trials before. " I did not tell you much of these things at the beginning of your discipleship, because I was with you, and would not disturb your minds with painful tidings while you were learning the first principles of the Gospel. But now that I am about to leave you, it is needful to forewarn you of things you are likely to meet with."

Of course it cannot be said that our Lord had never and in no sense before this time foretold persecution and the cross to His disciples. But it must mean that He did not think it needful to dwell much on the subject, so long as He was with them and taking care of them.

5 —[*But now I go...whither goest thou ?* "] These words seem to convey a reproof to the disciples for not inquiring more earnestly about the heavenly home to which their Master was going. Peter, no doubt, had said with vague curiosity, " Whither goest Thou ? " (John xiii. 36); but his question had not originated in a desire to know the place, so much as in surprise that His Lord was going at all. Our Lord seems here to say, " If your hearts were in a right frame, you would seek to understand the nature of my going and the place to which I go."

Let us observe that the disciples, with all their grace, were slow to use their opportunities, and to seek the knowledge which they might have obtained. They had not because they asked not.

Let us observe that our Lord spoke of His departure as a " going back to Him that sent Him," His mission being finished and His work done.

6 —[*But because...sorrow...your heart.*] Here our Lord continues the reproof of the last verse. The minds of the eleven were absorbed and overwhelmed with sorrow at the thought of their Master going, and they could think of nothing else. Instead of seizing the little time that was left, in order to learn more from His lips about His place and work in heaven, they were completely taken up with sorrow, and could think of nothing else but their Master's departure.

We should do well to mark how mischievous overmuch sorrow is, and to seek grace to keep it in proper control. No affection, if uncontrolled, so disarranges the order of men's minds, and unfits them for the duties of their calling.

7 —[*Nevertheless, I tell you the truth, etc.*] In this verse we see our Lord mercifully condescending to show His disciples the necessity for His leaving them. It was expedient. It was for their good. It was for the real ultimate benefit of themselves and the whole Church that He should go away. If He did not go away the great outpouring of the Holy Ghost, so often promised, could not come down on them and the world. If He went away He would send the Comforter. If he did not go away the Comforter would not come.

There is undeniably much that is deep and mysterious about the contents of this verse. We can only speak with reverence of the matter it unfolds. It seems clearly laid down that the Holy Ghost's coming down into the world with influence and grace, was a thing dependent on our Lord's dying, rising again, and ascending into heaven. It seems to be part of the eternal covenant of man's salvation that the Son should be incarnate, die, and rise again ; and that then, as a consequence, the Holy Spirit should be poured out with mighty influence on mankind, and the Gentile Churches be brought into the fold, and christianity spread over a vast portion of the world. This seems plainly taught, and this we must simply believe. If any one asks " why the Holy Ghost could not be poured down without Christ's going away ?" it is safest to reply, that we do not know.

One thing is very clear. The universal invisible presence of the Holy Ghost in the Church, is better than the visible bodily presence of Christ with the Church. Christ's body could only be in one place. The Holy Ghost can be everywhere at one and the same time.—Whatever the disciples might think, it was far better for Christ to go up to heaven, and sit at God's right hand as their Priest, and send down the Holy Ghost to be with the Church till He came again, than for Christ to tarry with them as He had done.—Flesh and blood might have liked better to keep Christ on earth, eating and drinking, and walking and talking in Palestine. But it was far better for the souls of men that Christ should finish His work, go up to heaven, take up His office there in the holy of holies, and send down the Holy Spirit on the Church and the world.

Calvin remarks, " Far more advantageous and far more desirable is that presence of Christ, by which He communicates Himself to us through the grace and power of His Spirit, than if He were present before our eyes."

Alford remarks, " The dispensation of the Spirit is a more blessed manifestation of God than was ever the bodily presence of the risen Saviour.

Bishop Andrews remarks, " We shall never see the absolute necessity of the Holy Ghost's coming, until we see the inconvenience of His not coming."

The expression, " I tell you the truth," is a very solemn, emphatic one. It is like, " Verily, verily I say, whether you believe me or not, it is true."

The expression, " I will send," seems again to point to the equal procession of the Holy Ghost from the Son and the Father. In another place it is, " The Father will send." Here, " I will send."

After all no text throws more light on this deep verse than Psalm lxviii. 18: " Thou hast ascended up on high, and received gifts for men; that the Lord God might dwell among them." These words surely point out that the Holy Ghost's dwelling among men was a gift purchased by the Son.

Does not the verse teach us that those who make much of the " corporal presence " of Christ, so called in the Lord's Supper, as a thing we should hold and believe, are in great error? There is something of far more importance to the Church, between the first and second advents, than any corporal presence of Christ, and that is the presence of the Holy Ghost. This is the *real presence* we should make much of, and desire to feel more. Our question should be not, " Is Christ's body here ? "—but, " is the Spirit, the Comforter here? "—Excessive craving after Christ's bodily presence before the second advent, is in reality a dishonoring of the Holy Ghost. We should make much of the Spirit.

Ecolampadius remarks, " Those who try to defend an eating of Christ, or a presence of Christ, in the Sacramental bread, as if His body was at the same time with us and in heaven, are manifestly at variance with this text."

Henry remarks here : " The presence of the Holy Spirit is a greater comfort and advantage to us than the presence of Christ in the flesh. Christ's bodily presence was comfortable, but the Spirit is more intimately a Comforter than Christ in His fleshly presence ; because the Spirit can comfort all believers at once in all places, while Christ's bodily presence can comfort but few, and that only in one place at once. The benefit of Christ's presence was great, but the advantage of the Spirit's renovation and holy inspiration is much greater."

JOHN XVᵀ 8—15

8 And when he is come, he will reprove the world of sin, and of righteousness, and of judgment.

9 Of sin, because they believe not on me ;

10 Of righteousness, because I go to my Father and ye see me no more ;

11 Of judgment, because the prince of this world is judged.

12 I have yet many things to say unto you, but ye cannot bear them now.

13 Howbeit when he, the Spirit of truth, is come, he will guide you into all truth : for he shall not speak of himself; but whatsoever he shall hear, *that* shall he speak ; and he will shew you things to come.

14 He shall glorify me : for he shall receive of mine, and shall shew *it* unto you.

15 All things that the Father hath are mine : therefore said I, that he shall take of mine, and shall shew *it* unto you.

WHEN our Lord in this passage speaks of the Holy Spirit " coming," we must take care that we do not misunderstand His meaning. On the one hand, we must remember that the Holy Ghost was in all believers in the Old Testament days, from the very beginning. No man was ever saved from the power of sin, and made a saint, except by the renewing of the Holy Ghost. Abraham, and Isaac, and Samuel, and David, and the Prophets, were made what they were by the operation of the Holy Ghost. On the other hand, we must never forget that after Christ's ascension the Holy Ghost was poured down on men with far greater energy as individuals, and with far wider influence on the nations of the world at large, than He has ever poured out before. It is this increased energy and influence that our Lord has in view in the verses before us. He meant that after His own ascension the Holy Ghost would "come" down into the world with such a vastly increased power, that it would seem as if He had " come " for the first time, and had never been in the world before.

The difficulty of rightly explaining the wondrous sayings of our Lord in this place is undeniably very great. It may well be doubted whether the full meaning of His words has ever been entirely grasped by man, and whether there is not something at the bottom which has not been completely unfolded. The common, superficial explanation, that our Lord only meant that the work of the Spirit in saving individual believers is to convince them of their own sins, of Christ's righteousness, and of the certainty of judgment at last, will hardly satisfy thinking minds. It is a short-cut and superficial way of getting over Scripture difficulties. It contains excellent and sound doctrine, no doubt, but it does not meet the full meaning of our Lord's words. It is truth, but not the truth of the text. It is not individuals here and there whom He says the Spirit is to convince, but *the world*. Let us see whether we cannot find a fuller and more satisfactory interpretation.

For one thing, our Lord probably meant to show us *what the Holy Ghost would do to the world of unbelieving Jews*. He would convince them "of sin, and righteousness, and judgment."

He would convince the Jews "of sin." He would compel them to feel and acknowledge in their own minds, that in rejecting Jesus of Nazareth they had committed a great sin, and were guilty of gross unbelief.

He would convince the Jews of "righteousness." He would press home on their consciences that Jesus of Nazareth was not an impostor and a deceiver, as they had said, but a holy, just, and blameless Person, whom God had owned by receiving up into heaven.

He would convince the Jews of "judgment." He would oblige them to see that Jesus of Nazareth had conquered, overcome, and judged the devil and all his host, and was exalted to be a Prince and a Saviour at the right hand of God.

That the Holy Ghost did actually so convince the Jewish nation after the day of Pentecost, is clearly shown by the Acts of the Apostles. · It was He who gave the humble fishermen of Galilee such grace and might in testifying of Christ, that their adversaries were put to silence. It was His reproving and convincing power which enabled them to "fill Jerusalem with their

doctrine." Not a few of the nation, we know, were savingly convinced, like St. Paul, and "a great company
of priests" became obedient to the faith.   Myriads more,
we have every reason to believe, were mentally convinced, if they had not courage to come out and take
up the cross.   The whole tone of the Jewish people
towards the end of the Acts of the Apostles is unlike
what it is at the beginning.   A vast reproving and convincing influence even where not saving, seems to have
gone over their minds.   Surely this was partly what our
Lord had in view in these verses when He said, "The
Holy Ghost shall reprove and convince."

For another thing, our Lord probably meant to foretell *what the Holy Ghost would do for the whole of mankind, both Gentiles as well as Jews.*

He would reprove in every part of the earth the current ideas of men about sin, righteousness, judgment,
and convince people of some far higher ideas on these
points than they had before acknowledged.   He would
make men see more clearly the nature of sin, the need
of righteousness, the certainty of judgment.   In a word,
He would insensibly be an Advocate and convincing
Pleader for God throughout the whole world, and raise
up a standard of morality, purity and knowledge, of
which formerly men had no conception.

That the Holy Ghost actually did so in every part
of the earth, after the day of Pentecost, is a simple matter of fact.   The unlearned and lowly Jews, whom He
sent forth and strengthened to preach the Gospel after
our Lord's ascension, " turned the world upside down,"
and in two or three centuries altered the habits, tastes,
and practices of the whole civilized world.   The power
of the devil received a decided check.   Even infidels
dare not deny that the doctrines of Christianity had an
enormous effect on men's ways, lives, and opinions, when

they were first preached, and that there were no special graces or eloquence in the preachers that can account for it. In truth, the world was "reproved and convinced," in spite of itself; and even those who did not become believers became better men. Surely this also was partly what our Lord had in view when He said to His disciples, "When the Holy Ghost comes, He shall convince the world of sin, and righteousness, and judgment."

Let us leave the whole passage, deep and difficult as it is, with a thankful remembrance of one comfortable promise which it contains. "The Spirit of truth," says our Lord to His weak and half-informed followers, "shall guide you into all truth." That promise was for our sakes, no doubt, as well as for theirs. Whatever we need to know for our present peace and sanctification, the Holy Ghost is ready to teach us. All truth in science, nature, and philosophy of course is not included in this promise. But into all spiritual truth that is really profitable, and that our minds can comprehend and bear, the Holy Spirit is ready and willing to guide us. Then let us never forget, in reading the Bible, to pray for the teaching of the Holy Ghost. We must not wonder if we find the Bible a dark and difficult book, if we do not regularly seek light from Him by whom it was first inspired. In this, as in many other things, "we have not because we ask not."

NOTES. JOHN XVI 8–15

8 —[*And when he is come.*] These words would be rendered more literally, "And He having come." Here, as in other places, we must remember that the "coming" of the Holy Ghost does not mean His coming for the first time into the world. He was in all the old Testament saints, and no one ever believed or served God without His grace. Wherever there has been a true servant of God, there has been the Holy Ghost. The "coming" here mentioned means His coming down with larger power and influence on all mankind after the ascension of Christ, and spe-

cially on the day of Pentecost. From that day began an enormous extension of His influence and operation on human nature : an influence so much wider than it ever was before, that He is said to have " come."

Lightfoot remarks that "the Holy Spirit had absented Himself from the Jewish nation for four hundred years!" Hence the phrase " come " had a special significance..

[*He will reprove..judgment.*] This sentence is perhaps one of the most difficult in the whole of St. John's Gospel. Men will probably never agree about it entirely till the Lord comes. There is something in it which seems to baffle all interpreters.

The commonest explanation is that which regards the passage as describing the ordinary operations of the Holy Ghost in saving God's people. It is He who convinces people that they are sinners ; convinces them that they must be saved by Christ's righteousness, and not their own ; and convinces them that there is a judgment to come. This interpretation is the one adopted by Alford and many others.—No doubt it contains truth, but it is not at all clear to me that it is the truth of the passage. It is open, in short, to grave objections, and, in common with some commentators, I cannot feel satisfied with it. For popular addresses this view may do pretty well. But, I venture to think, no man who sits down and calmly weighs the meaning of words, can fail to see that it is open to very serious objections.

Inward conviction is certainly not the meaning of the word rendered " reprove." It is rather refutation by proofs, convicting by unanswerable argument as an advocate, that is meant.

Believers and God's people are not said to be the subjects of the Spirit's reproving work. It is the " world " that is to be reproved ; and this very world, in this last sermon, is continually put in contrast with Christ's people.

Add to all this, that the latter part of the ninth, tenth, and eleventh verses can hardly be said to suit and square in with the verse we are considering. If our Lord had simply said, " The Spirit shall convince your hearers of their own sins, of my imputed righteousness, and of a day of judgment," it would have been plain enough. But unfortunately there are several things added which really do not chime in with this mode of interpretation. I repeat, that no intelligent Christian, of course, will think of denying that conviction of sin is a special and saving work of the Holy Ghost on the hearts of believers. But it does not therefore follow that it is the thing taught in this passage. It is truth, but not the truth of the text.

I believe the meaning to be something of this kind.—" After

the day of Pentecost the Holy Ghost, the great Advocate of Me and my people, shall come into this world with such mighty power that He shall silence, convince, and stop the mouths of your enemies, and oblige them, however unwillingly, to think of Me and my cause very differently from what they think now. In particular, He shall convince them of their own sin, of my righteousness, and of the victory which I have won over Satan. He shall, in short, be a crushing Advocate whom the world shall not be able to resist or gainsay."

That this was one effect of the Holy Ghost coming down on the day of Pentecost, appears so frequently in the Acts of the Apostles that it is needless to quote texts. It is clear from the whole narrative of the earlier portion of Acts, that after the day of Pentecost there was a peculiar, restraining, irresistible power accompanying the work of the Apostles, which the unbelieving Jews, in spite of all their numbers and influence, were unable to withstand. Nor was this work of the Holy Ghost confined to the Jews. Wherever the Apostles and their fellow-laborers went, the same convincing power accompanied them, and obliged even the heathen to acknowledge Christianity as a great fact, even when they did not believe. Pliny's famous letter to Trajan about the Christians, is a remarkable illustration of this.

I prefer this interpretation to the one above mentioned, as held by Alford and most commentators, for two simple reasons. One is that it suits the language of the passage, and the other view does not. The other reason is that it harmonizes with the context. Our Lord is encouraging the disciples against the world by the presence of the Comforter. And one special part of the encouragement is, that the Comforter shall do for them the work of an advocate, by silencing, crushing, refuting, and convincing their enemies.

After all, the enormous change which took place in the state of " the world " within a few centuries after Pentecost, is a strong proof to my own mind of the correctness of the view I advocate. About sin, Christ, and judgment, the opinions of men were completely transformed, even though men were unconverted. And who did this ? The Holy Ghost. Nothing can account for the change but the miraculous interposition of the Holy Ghost.—I frankly confess that this view of the passage before us is not that of the vast majority of commentators. But in these matters I dare not call any man master, and must say what I think. Those who wish to see the view I maintain more fully argued out and supported, are advised to consult " Poole's Annotations," and Suicer's " Thesaurus " on the Greek word which we translate " reprove." Schleusner also seems to support the view.

Scott remarks here, " It is worthy of notice that an immense proportion of the human race, since the pouring out of the

Holy Spirit after our Lord's ascension, have been led to form such sentiments about sin, righteousness, and a future judgment, as the world up to that time had not the most remote conception of ; so that a far higher standard of morals has been fixed throughout numerous nations than was at all thought of before."

9 —[*Of sin...believe not...Me.*] I think this verse means, " The Holy Ghost shall first and foremost convince the world concerning sin, by obliging my enemies to see, though too late, that in not believing Me they made an enormous mistake, and committed a great sin. He shall make them feel at last that in rejecting Me, they rejected One whom they ought to have believed."

10 —[*Of righteousness...no more.*] I think this verse means, " The Holy Ghost, secondly, shall convince the world concerning my righteousness, that I was a righteous Man, and not a deceiver. And this He will do after I have left the world, when the Jews can no longer see Me, and form any opinion of Me. I go to the Father, you know, and you will soon see me no more. But after I am gone the Holy Ghost will oblige my enemies to feel that I was a just and righteous Person, and was unjustly slain." Even the centurion who saw our Lord crucified, declared, " Certainly this was a righteous man." (Luke xxiii. 46.)

11 —[*Of judgment...judged*] I think this verse means, " The Holy Ghost, in the last place, shall convince the world concerning the judgment and overthrow of Satan's usurped power, by setting up a new kingdom everywhere, even my Church, by emptying the heathen temples of their worshippers, and by drying up the power of idolatry, and delivering vast portions of the world from its dominion."

The " Prince of this world," of course means the devil. How great His power was over mankind before Christ came into the world, and how great a change Christ's death and resurrection produced in the general condition of mankind, are things which at this period of time we can hardly realize. The coming of the " kingdom of God," or " kingdom of heaven," was a reality 1800 years ago, of which we can now form little idea. The Holy Ghost produced a general conviction that a new order of things had begun, and that the old king and tyrant of the world was dethroned and stripped of much of his power.

Such is the view that I take of this passage. I do not pretend to deny that there are difficulties about it. I only maintain that these difficulties are fewer than those which surround the common idea attached to the passage.

Poole's " Annotations " perhaps throw more light on the passage than any commentary I have met with. But even he says things which appear to me not warranted by the words of the evangelist.

12 –[*I have yet many things...you.*] This clause seems to refer to the higher, fuller, deeper views of Christian truth which our Lord doubtless revealed to His disciples during the forty days between His resurrection and ascension, when He was continually " speaking of the things pertaining to the kingdom of God."

The absurdity and unreasonableness of concluding from this text that there are many other truths which Christ after His resurrection revealed to the Apostles, but which are not recorded in Scripture, is well exposed by Ecolampadius and other Protestant commentators.

[*Ye cannot bear them now.*] This word " bear " means literally " carry." It does not therefore signify things that the disciples could not " apprehend," but things that their minds were not yet strong enough to endure and digest.

Do we not see here that there are steps and degrees in Christian attainment ? A man may be a good man, and yet not able to endure the whole truth. We must teach people as they are able to bear, and be patient.

13 –[*Howbeit...He...guide...all truth.*] Here our Lord gives another promise concerning the Holy Ghost. He shall guide disciples into all truth. He will lead and direct them into the full knowledge of all the doctrines of the Gospel, and all the truth they need to know.

It is needless to say that " all truth " here does not mean all scientific truth. It applies specially to spiritual truth.

This great promise does not appear to me to signify " inspiration," or the imparting of that power to write and teach infallibly which the Apostles possessed. I much prefer the view, that it is a wide promise belonging to the whole Church in every age. It means that special office of " teaching " by which the Spirit illuminates, guides, and informs the understandings of all believers. That the minds of true Christians are taught and enlightened in a manner wonderful to themselves as well as others, is a simple matter of Christian experience. That enlightenment is the gift of the Holy Spirit, and the first step in saving religion. At the same time we must never forget that the disciples received an immense increase of spiritual knowledge after the day of Pentecost, and saw everything in religion far more clearly than they did before.

Alford observes, " No promise of universal knowledge, nor of infallibility, is hereby conveyed ; but it is a promise to them and us, that the Holy Spirit shall teach and lead us, not as children under the tutors and governors of legal and imperfect knowledge, but as sons, making known to us all the truth of God. (Gal. iv. 6.)

It is worth notice that in the Greek it is literally, " guide into all THE truth ; " as if it specially meant " the truth concerning Me."

Poole remarks that the Greek word rendered " guide," is one of great emphasis, signifying not only a guide who will discover truth as the object of the understanding, but one who will bow the will to the doctrines of truth.

[*For...not speak...Himself...hear...speak.*] Here begins a list of things said about the Holy Ghost, which our weak capacities can hardly take in.

The clause before us seems meant to show the close and intimate union existing between the Spirit and the two other Persons in the blessed Trinity. " He shall not speak from Himself, independently of Me and my Father. He shall only speak such things as He shall hear from us."

The phrases " speak " and " hear " are both accommodations to man's weakness. The Spirit does not literally " speak " or literally " hear." It must mean, " His teachings and guidings shall be those of One who is in the closest union with the Father and the Son."

" Of Himself " does not mean " about Himself," but " from Himself."

[*He will show...things to come.*] The second thing said about the Spirit, is that He will show " things to come." I can only suppose that this points to the prophetical revelation of the future of the Church which the Spirit was to impart to the disciples. He did so when He inspired St. Paul, St. Peter, St. Jude, and St. John to prophecy. The expression probably includes the destruction of Jerusalem, the removal of the Mosaic dispensation, the scattering of the Jews, the calling in of the Gentile Churches, and the whole history of their rise, progress, and final decay.

14 —[*He...glorify Me.*] The third thing said of the Spirit, is that He shall " glorify " Christ." He shall continually teach, and lead, and guide disciples to make much of Christ. Any religious teaching which does not tend to exalt Christ, has a fatal defect about it. It cannot be from the Spirit.

[*He shall receive...mine...show you.*] This is the fourth thing said of the Spirit in this place. He will take of the truth about Christ, and show it or reveal it to disciples. I can attach no other meaning to the phrase " mine." It is in the singular number,—" that thing which is mine,"—and I cannot see what it can mean but " truth concerning Me."

Alford remarks, " This verse is decisive against all additions and pretended revelations, subsequent to and beside Christ ; it being the work of the Spirit to testify to the things of Christ, and not to anything new or beyond Him."

15 —[*All things...Father...mine, etc.*] The object of this deep verse seems to be to show the entire unity between Father, Son, and Holy Spirit in the revelation of truth made to man. " The Holy Spirit shall show you things concerning Me, and yet things at the same time concerning the Father, because all things that the Father hath are mine."

Both this verse and the preceding one are strikingly calculated to humble a Bible reader, and make him feel how little he knows, at his very best, of the full meaning of some Scriptures. There are things in them which we must feel we do not comprehend. Beyond the great principle, that it is the special office of the Holy Spirit to glorify Christ, and to show disciples the whole truth concerning Christ, it is very hard to get.

May not the clause, " All things that the Father hath are mine," be specially put in to prevent our supposing that there can be any real separation between the things of Christ and the things of the Father ? It is like " I and my Father are One." " All mine are Thine, and Thine are mine."—" Think not," our Lord seems to say, " when I speak of the Spirit showing you ' my things,' that He will not show you the things of my Father. That would be impossible. There is so close an union between the Father and the Son, that the Spirit cannot show or teach the things of the one without the things of the other. In a word, He proceeds from the Father as well as from the Son."

JOHN XVI 16—24

16 A little while, and ye shall not see me : and again, a little while, and ye shall see me, because I go to the Father.

17 Then said *some* of his disciples among themselves, What is this that he saith unto us, A little while, and ye shall not see me : and again, a little while, and ye shall see me : and, Because I go to the Father ?

18 They said therefore, What is this that he saith, A little while ? we cannot tell what he saith.

19 Now Jesus knew that they were desirous to ask him, and said unto them, Do ye enquire among yourselves of that I said, A little while, and ye shall not see me : and again, a little while, and ye shall see me ?

20 Verily, verily, I say unto you, That ye shall weep and lament, but the world shall rejoice : and ye shall be sorrowful, but your sorrow shall be turned into joy.

21 A woman when she is in travail hath sorrow, because her hour is come : but as soon as she is delivered of the child she remembereth no more the anguish, for joy that a man is born into the world.

22 And ye now therefore have sorrow : but I will see you again, and your heart shall rejoice, and your joy no man taketh from you.

23 And in that day ye shall ask me nothing. Verily, verily I say unto you, Whatsoever ye shall ask the Father in my name, he will give *it* you.

24 Hitherto have ye asked nothing in my name : ask, and ye shall receive, that your joy may be full.

Not all Christ's sayings were understood by His disciples. We are told this distinctly in the passage we have now read.—" What is this that he saith ? We cannot tell what he saith."—None ever spake so plainly as Jesus. None were so thoroughly accustomed to His style of teaching as the Apostles. Yet even the Apostles did not always take in their Master's meaning. Surely we have no right to be surprised if we cannot interpret ·Christ's words. There are many depths in them which we have no line to fathom. But let us thank God that there are many sayings of our Lord recorded which no honest mind can fail to understand. Let us use diligently the light that we have, and not doubt that " to him that hath more shall be given."

We learn, for one thing, in these verses, that *Christ's absence from the earth will be a time of sorrow to believers, but of joy to the world.* It is written, " Ye shall weep and lament, but the world shall rejoice." To confine these words to the single point of Christ's approaching death and burial, appears a narrow view of their meaning. Like many of our Lord's sayings on the last evening of His earthly ministry, they seem to extend over the whole period of time between His first and second advents.

Christ's personal absence must needs be a sorrow to all true-hearted believers. " The children of the bride-chamber cannot but fast when the bridegroom is taken from them." Faith is not sight. Hope is not certainty. Reading and hearing are not the same as beholding. Praying is not the same as speaking face to face. There is something, even in the hearts of the most eminent saints, that will never be fully satisfied as long as they are on earth and Christ is in heaven. So long as they dwell in a body of corruption, and see through a glass darkly,—so long as they behold creation groaning under

the power of sin, and all things not put under Christ ;—
so long their happiness and peace must needs be incomplete. This is what St. Paul meant when he said, " We
ourselves, which have the first fruits of the Spirit, groan
within ourselves, waiting for the adoption, to wit, the
redemption of our body." (Rom. vii. 23.)

Yet this same personal absence of Christ is no cause
of sorrow to the children of this world. It was not to the
unbelieving Jews, we may be sure. When Christ was
condemned and crucified, they rejoiced and were glad.
They thought that the hated reprover of their sins
and false teaching was silenced for ever. It is not to
the careless and the wicked of our day, we may be sure.
The longer Christ keeps away from this earth, and lets
them alone, the better will they be pleased. " We do
not want this Christ to reign over us," is the feeling of
the world. His absence causes them no pain. Their
so-called happiness is complete without Him. All this
may sound very painful and startling. But where is
the thinking reader of the Bible who can deny that it is
true ? The world does not want Christ back again, and
thinks that it does very well without Him. What a
fearful waking up there will be by-and-by !

We learn, for another thing in this verse, that *Christ's
personal return shall be a source of boundless joy to
His believing people.* It is written, " I will see you
again, and your heart shall rejoice, and your joy no man
taketh from you." Once more we must take care that
we do not narrow the meaning of these words by tying
them down to our Lord's resurrection. They surely
reach much further than this. The joy of the disciples
when they saw Christ risen from the dead, was a joy
soon obscured by His ascension and withdrawal into
heaven. The true joy, the perfect joy, the joy that can
never be taken away, will be the joy which Christ's

people will feel when Christ returns the second time, at the end of this world.

The second personal advent of Christ, to speak plainly, is the one grand object on which our Lord, both here and elsewhere, teaches all believers to fix their eyes. We ought to be always looking for and " loving His appearing," as the perfection of our happiness, and the consummation of all our hopes. (2 Peter iii. 12; 2 Tim. iv. 8.) That same Jesus who was taken up visibly into heaven, shall also come again visibly, even as He went. Let the eyes of our faith be always fixed on this coming. It is not enough that we look *back-ward* to the cross, and rejoice in Christ dying for our sins; and *upwards* to the right hand of God, and rejoice in Christ's interceding for every believer. We must do more than this. We must look *forward* to Christ's return from heaven to bless His people, and to wind up the work of redemption. Then, and then only, will the prayer of eighteen centuries receive its complete answer,—" Thy kingdom come, Thy will be done on earth as it is in heaven." Well may our Lord say that in that day of resurrection and reunion our "hearts shall rejoice."—" When we awake up after His likeness we shall be satisfied." (Psalm xvii. 15.)

We learn, lastly, in these verses, that *while Christ is absent believers must ask much in prayer*. It is written, " Hitherto have ye asked nothing in My name : ask and ye shall receive, that your joy may be full."

We may well believe that up to this time the disciples had never realized their Master's full dignity. They had certainly never understood that He was the one Mediator between God and man, in whose name and for whose sake they were to put up their prayers. Here they are distinctly told that henceforward they are to " ask in His name." Nor can we doubt that our Lord

would have all His people, in every age, understand
that the secret of comfort during His absence is to be
instant in prayer. He would have us know that if we
cannot see Him with our bodily eyes any longer, we can
talk with Him, and through Him have special access to
God. "Ask and ye shall receive," He proclaims to
all His people in every age; "and your joy shall be
full."

Let the lesson sink down deeply into our hearts. Of
all the list of Christian duties there is none to which
there is such abounding encouragement as prayer. It
is a duty which concerns all. High and low, rich and
poor, learned and unlearned,—all must pray. It is a
duty for which all are accountable. All cannot read, or
hear, or sing; but all who have the spirit of adoption
can pray. Above all, it is a duty in which everything
depends on the heart and motive within. Our words
may be feeble and ill-chosen, and our language broken
and ungrammatical, and unworthy to be written down.
But if the heart be right, it matters not. He that
sits in heaven can spell out the meaning of every
petition sent up in the name of Jesus, and can make
the asker know and feel that he receives.

"If we know these things, happy are we if we do
them." Let prayer in the name of Jesus be a daily
habit with us every morning and evening of our lives.
Keeping up that habit, we shall find strength for duty,
comfort in trouble, guidance in perplexity, hope in
sickness, and support in death. Faithful is He that
promised, "Your joy shall be full;" and He will keep
His word, if we ask in prayer.

NOTES. JOHN XVI 16—24

16.—[*A little while, and ye shall, etc.*] There is a difficulty in this
verse which requires consideration. To what time does our Lord

refer when He says, " a little while and ye shall not see Me,"
and " ye shall see Me " ? There are two answers.

(a) Some think, as Chrysostom, Cyril, and Hengstenberg, that
our Lord only meant, " in a few hours I shall be removed by
death, and buried, and then you will not see Me ; and again after
three days I shall rise again, and then you will see Me."

(b) Others think, as Augustine, Maldonatus, and Wordsworth,
that our Lord meant, " In a short time I shall leave the world,
ascend up to heaven, and go to my Father, and you will see Me
no more ; and again, in comparatively short time, I shall return
to the world at my second advent, and you will see Me again."

I decidedly prefer the second of these interpretations. To
explain the words, " Ye shall not see Me," and " Ye shall see
Me," by our Lord's death and resurrection, seems to me a forced
and unnatural interpretation. Moreover it completely fails to
explain the words, " I go to the Father." Both here and all
through the passage, I believe our Lord is speaking for the
benefit of the whole Church until His coming again, and not
merely for the benefit of the eleven apostles. The true sense
is best seen by inverting the order of the words. " The time
has arrived when I must leave the world, and go back again to
my Father. The consequence is that in a little time you will
no longer see Me with your bodily eyes, for I shall be in heaven
and you on earth. But take comfort ! In a little time I shall
return again with power and great glory, and then you and all
my believing people will see Me again."

It is worth notice, in support of the view I maintain, that the
expression in Greek, " a little while," is almost the same as in
Heb. x. 37, when the second advent is clearly spoken of. Moreover the expression " I go," is distinctly applied in several places
to our Lord's final departure from the world, and seldom, if ever,
to our Lord's death on the cross.

Alford thinks His meaning is manifold, and says, " ' Ye shall
see Me ' began to be fulfilled at the resurrection, then received
its main fulfilment at Pentecost, and shall have its final fulfilment at the return of our Lord." This strikes me as a very
untenable view.

It is curious that the first " Ye shall see " is in the present
tense, and is an entirely different word to the second, which is
a future. The first would be rendered literally, " Ye behold, or
gaze upon Me ! "

17.—[*Then said some, etc.*] This whole verse shows how little the
disciples realized or understood our Lord's meaning at present,
when He spoke of His second advent. Yet when we consider
how widely different are the meanings put on our Lord's words
by Christians in *this* day, we can hardly feel surprised that
eleven weak believers, like the apostles, could not take in the

full sense of the words when they first heard them, the night before the crucifixion.

18 —[*They said therefore...little while.*] This sentence shows that it was the "time" mentioned—"a little while"—which perplexed the disciples. We may conjecture that they could not make out whether it meant " literally " a few days or hours, or figuratively a comparatively short time. And is not this precisely the point on which all students of unfulfilled prophecy disagree? The verse before us is curiously applicable to many a prophetical controversy.

[*We cannot tell...saith.*] The words would be more literally rendered, " We do not know what he is speaking of."

19.—[*Now Jesus knew...ask Him.*] Here, as in other places, our Lord's perfect knowledge of the hearts and thoughts of all around Him is pointed out. The word "ask," we should carefully note, is literally " to ask questions about a thing." It is the same word that is used in verse 23: " at that day ye shall ask Me nothing."

[*And said, etc.*] The word rendered, " Do ye inquire among yourselves of that ? " would be more literally, "Concerning this, do ye seek with each other ? "

20 —[*Verily...say unto you.*] It should be observed in this verse that our Lord gives no reply to the inquiry of the disciples. He does not tell them what He meant by saying " a little while." Questions about times and dates are rarely answered in Scripture. Our attention is rather turned to practical things.

[*Ye shall weep and lament, etc.*] I believe, with Augustine and Bede, that the whole verse is meant to be a general description of the state of things between the first and second advents of Christ. " During my absence from the world after my ascension, you, my beloved disciples, and believers after you, shall have many reasons to lament and mourn, like a bride separate from her husband, while the wicked world around you shall rejoice in my absence, and not wish to see Me return. During this long weary interval, you and all believers after you often have sorrow and tribulation; but at last, when I come again, your sorrow shall be turned into joy." In support of this view I advise the reader to study Matt. ix. 15. The idea in each place seems the same. (Compare also Is. lxv. 14.)

Poole remarks, " The time of this life is the worldling's hour, while it is for the most part the power of darkness fo all who love and fear God. But as the worldling's joy shall at last be turned into sorrow, so the godly man's sorrow shall be turned into joy." (Isai. l. 11 ; Matt. xxv. 23.)

The interpretation of Chrysostom, Cyril, and others, which makes the whole verse fulfilled by the crucifixion and resurrection of our Lord, appears to me very unsatisfactory. It hardly affords time for the weeping and rejoicing which is here described. Nor is it quite clear that the day during which our Lord lay in the grave was a day of rejoicing to His enemies, if we may judge their anxiety to prevent, if possible, His resurrection from the dead.

21 —[*A woman, etc.*] This verse is an illustration of the whole state of the Church between the first and second advents of Christ. It was to be a time of pain, anxiety, and desire for deliverance, from which the only cessation would be at the personal return of Christ.

We are distinctly told in Rom. viii. 22, that "the whole creation groaneth and travaileth in pain until now." It is the normal state of things while Christ is absent. The second coming of the second Adam can alone restore joy to the world. The Church in Rev. vii. 2, is compared to a woman "travailing in birth, and pained to be delivered." The wars and disturbances of the world are called in Matt. xxiv. 8, the beginning of " sorrows ;" and the word " sorrows " there means literally " the pains of a travailing woman."

The whole idea of the verse seems to be that the interval between Christ's first and second advent will be, to the Church, a period of pain, sorrow, and anxiety, like the state of a woman expecting her delivery,—that the end of this period will be the appearance of our Lord Jesus Christ the second time,—and that when our Lord does come the second time, the joy of the true Church will be so great, that the former sorrow and tribulation will be comparatively forgotten. The joy of seeing Christ will swallow up the afflictions of His absence. (Compare Rom. viii. 18—22 ; 2 Cor. iv. 17.)

22 —[*And ye now therefore, etc.*] I apply to this verse the same principle of interpretation that I have applied to the preceding ones. I think our Lord is speaking of the sorrow and pain which believers would feel during the interval between His first and second advent. " You are now entering on a period of pain, sorrow, and tribulation. But fear not. It shall not be for ever. I will return and see you again. In that day your heart shall be filled and satisfied with joy, a joy which no one can ever take from you, a joy which shall be for ever."

I cannot bring myself to believe that this " see you again " can possibly refer to the short period of forty days between the resurrection and the ascension ! Above all, I feel strongly that the words, " Your joy no man taketh from you," could certainly not be applied to the times of trouble, and tribulation, and persecution even unto death, which the primitive Church passed through in the beginning of its existence. The sensible joy of the primitive Church, beyond doubt, was often taken away, as when Stephen was martyred, James slain with the sword, and Peter put in prison. The second coming of Christ is the only time of universal and unbroken joy to which believers can look forward. Now we are in the wilderness, and our sorrowless home is yet to be reached. Then, and then only, will tears be wiped from all eyes.

23 —[*And in that day...ask...nothing.*] In the first part of this verse I believe, with Augustine, that the " day " spoken of is the day of our Lord's second advent. The " asking " is asking questions, or making inquiries, such as the disciples had wanted to make in verse 19. " They were desirous to ask Him." The Greek word is the same, and quite different from the word rendered " ask " in the latter part of this verse. The meaning of the sentence is, " In the day of my second advent you will not need to ask Me any questions. You will then fully understand the meaning of many things which you do not understand now." The far superior light which believers will enjoy in the day of Christ's second coming, is the chief point of the promise, as in 1 Cor. xiii. 12.

Cyril and Chrysostom, however, apply " that day " to our Lord's resurrection and the forty days following it.

[*Verily, verily...whatsoever...ask...give it you.*] In this portion of the verse our Lord renews and repeats His former promise about prayer. " Until that day when I come again, I solemnly declare that whatsoever things you shall ask in prayer from the Father in my name, He will give them to you."

The word " ask " in the Greek, in the latter part of this verse, is entirely different from the word rendered " ask " in the former part. Here it signifies seeking or petitioning in prayer. There it meant asking questions.

It is worth noticing here how very frequent and full are the encouragements to prayer which our Lord holds out in the Gospels.

The " whatsoever " of the text must of course be limited to whatsoever things are really for God's glory, the disciples' good and the interests of Christ's cause in the world.

24 —[*Hitherto...nothing in my name.*] This sentence means that up to this time the disciples had not prayed for anything through the name and mediation of Christ. They had followed Him as a teacher, looked up to Him as a Master, loved Him as a friend, believed Him as the Messiah predicted by the prophets. But they had not fully realized that He was the one Mediator between God and man, through whom alone God's mercy could come down to sinners, and sinful creatures could draw near to God. They were now to learn that their Master was one far higher than any prophet, yea, even than Moses himself.

Daniel's prayer, " Shine on Thy sanctuary for the Lord's sake," is almost the only instance of a prayer in Messiah's name in the Old Testament. (Dan. ix. 17.)

[*Ask...receive..joy...full.*] This sentence means, " From henceforth begin the practice of asking everything in my name and through my mediation. Ask fully and confidently, and you shall receive fully and abundantly. So asking, you shall find the joy and comfort of your own souls enlarged and filled up."

John Gerhard here remarks: " The benefit of prayer is so great that it cannot be expressed!—Prayer is the dove which, when sent out, returns again, bringing with it the olive-leaf, namely peace of heart. Prayer is the golden chain which God holds fast, and lets not go until He blesses. Prayer is the Moses' rod, which brings forth the water of consolation out of the rock of salvation. Prayer is Samson's jaw-bone, which smites down our enemies. Prayer is David's harp, before which the evil spirit flies. Prayer is the key to Heaven's treasures."

The Greek word rendered " full " means literally " filled up," being the perfect participle of the verb " to fill or fulfil."

The sentence teaches us that the joy and happiness of believers admit of degrees, and may be fuller at one time than at another. It also teaches that the joy of a believer depends much on his fervency and earnestness in prayer. He that prays little and coldly must not expect to know much of " joy and peace in believing."

We should not fail to observe how prayer is set before believers here as a plain duty, in the imperative mood, and also how desirous our Lord is that His people should be rejoicing Christians even now in the midst of a bad world. That religion which makes people melancholy and miserable and wretched-looking, is a very low type of Christianity, and far below the standard of Him who wished " joy to be full." (Compare 1 John i. 4.)

JOHN XVI 25—33

25 These things have I spoken unto you in proverbs : but the time cometh, when I shall no more speak unto you in proverbs, but I shall shew you plainly of the Father.

26 At that day ye shall ask in my name : and I say not unto you, that I will pray the Father for you :

27 For the Father himself loveth you, because ye have loved me, and have believed that I came out from God.

28 I came forth from the Father, and am come into the world : again, I leave the world, and go to the Father.

29 His disciples said unto him, Lo, now speakest thou plainly, and speakest no proverb.

30 Now are we sure that thou knowest all things, and needest not that any man should ask thee : by this we believe that thou camest forth from God.

31 Jesus answered them, Do ye now believe ?

32 Behold, the hour cometh, yea, is now come, that ye shall be scattered, every man to his own, and shall leave me alone ; and yet I am not alone, because the father is with me.

33 These things I have spoken unto you, that in me ye might have peace. In the world ye shall have tribulation ; but be of good cheer ; I have overcome the world.

THE passage we have now read is a very remarkable portion of Scripture, for two reasons. On the one hand, it forms a suitable conclusion to our Lord's long parting address to His disciples. It was meet and right that such a solemn sermon should have a solemn ending. On the other hand it contains the most general and unanimous profession of belief that we ever find the Apostles making :—"Now are we sure that Thou knowest all things :....by this we believe that thou camest forth from God."

That there are things hard to be understood in the passage it would be useless to deny. But there lie on its surface three plain and profitable lessons, to which we may usefully confine our attention.

We learn, for one thing, that *clear knowledge of God the Father is one of the foundations of the Christian religion.* Our Lord says to His disciples, "The time cometh when I shall show you plainly of the Father." He does not say, we should mark, "I will show you plainly about myself." It is the Father whom He promises to show.

The wisdom of this remarkable saying is very deep. There are few subjects of which men know so little in reality as the character and attributes of God the Father. It is not for nothing that it is written, "No man knoweth the Father save the Son, and he to whomsoever the Son shall reveal Him." (Matt. xi. 27.) "The only begotten Son, which is in the bosom of the Father, He hath declared Him." (John i. 18.) Thousands fancy they know the Father because they think of Him as great, and almighty, and all-hearing, and wise, and eternal, but they think no further. To think of Him as just and yet the justifier of the sinner who believes in Jesus,—as the God who sent His Son to suffer and die,—as God in Christ reconciling the world unto Himself,—as God specially well-pleased with the atoning sacrifice of His Son, whereby His law is honored; to think of God the Father in this way is not given to most men. No wonder that our Master says, "I will show you plainly of the Father."

Let it be part of our daily prayers, that we may know more of " the only true God," as well as of Jesus Christ whom He has sent. Let us beware alike of the mistakes which some make, who speak of God as if there was no Christ ; and of the mistakes which others make, who speak of Christ as if there was no God. Let us seek to know all three Persons in the blessed Trinity, and give to each One the honor due to him. Let us lay hold firmly of the great truth, that the Gospel of our salvation is the result of the eternal counsels of Father, Son, and Holy Ghost ; and that we are as thoroughly debtors to the love of the Father, as to the love of the Spirit, or the love of the Son. No one has learned of Christ so deeply as the man who is ever drawing nearer to the Father through the Son,—ever feeling more childlike confidence in Him,—and ever understanding more thoroughly that in Christ God is not an angry judge, but a loving Father and Friend.

We learn, for another thing, in this passage, that *our Lord Jesus Christ makes much of a little grace, and speaks kindly of those who have it.* We see Him saying to the disciples : "The Father Himself loveth you, because ye have loved Me, and have believed that I came out from God."

How weak was the faith and love of the Apostles ! How soon, in a very few hours, they were buried under a cloud of unbelief and cowardice ! These very men whom Jesus commends for loving and believing, before the morning sun arose forsook Him and fled. Yet, weak as their graces were, they were real and true and genuine. They were graces which hundreds of learned priests and scribes and Pharisees never attained, and, not attaining, died miserably in their sins.

Let us take great comfort in this blessed truth. The Saviour of sinners will not cast off them that believe in Him, because they are babes in faith and knowledge. He will not break the bruised reed or quench the smoking flax. He can see reality under much infirmity, and where He sees it He is graciously pleased. The followers of such a Saviour may well be bold and confident. They have a Friend who despises not the least member of His flock, and casts out none who come to Him, however weak and feeble, if they are only true.

We learn, for another thing, in this passage, that the *best Christians know but little of their own hearts.* We see the disciples professing loudly, "Now Thou speakest plainly,—now we are sure,—now we believe." Brave words these! And yet the very men that spoke them, in a very short time were scattered like timid sheep, and left their Master alone.

We need not doubt that the profession of the eleven was real and sincere. They honestly meant what they said. But they did not know themselves. They did not know what they were capable of doing under the pressure of the fear of men and of strong temptation. They had not rightly estimated the weakness of the flesh, the power of the devil, the feebleness of their own resolutions, the shallowness of their own faith. All this they had yet to learn by painful experience. Like young recruits, they had yet to learn that it is one thing to know the soldier's drill and wear the uniform, and quite another thing to be steadfast in the day of battle.

Let us mark these things, and learn wisdom. The true secret of spiritual strength is self-distrust and deep humility. "When I am weak," said a great Christian,

"then am I strong." (2 Cor. xii. 10.) None of us, perhaps, have the least idea how much we might fall if
placed suddenly under the influence of strong temptation. Happy is he who never forgets the words, " Let
him that thinketh he standeth take heed lest he fall ; "
and, remembering our Lord's disciples, prays daily :
" Hold Thou me up and then I shall be safe."

We learn, lastly, from this passage, that *Christ is
the true source of peace.* We read that our Lord winds
up all His discourse with these soothing words: " These
things have I spoken unto you, that ye might have
peace." The end and scope of His parting address, He
would have us know, is to draw us nearer to Himself as
the only fountain of comfort. He does not tell us that
we shall have no trouble in the world. He holds out
no promise of freedom from tribulation while we are in
the body. But He bids us rest in the thought that He
has fought our battle and won a victory for us. Though
tried, and troubled, and vexed with things here below,
we shall not be destroyed. " Be of good cheer," is His
parting charge: " Be of good cheer; I have overcome
the world."

Let us lean back our souls on these comfortable
words, and take courage. The storms of trial and persecution may sometimes beat heavily on us ; but let them
only drive us closer to Christ. The sorrows, and losses,
and crosses, and disappointments of our life may often
make us feel sorely cast down; but let them only make
us tighten our hold on Christ. Armed with this very
promise let us, under every cross, come boldly to the
throne of grace, that we may obtain mercy, and find
grace to help in time of need. Let us often say to our
souls, " Why art thou cast down, and why art thou disquieted ? " And let us often say to our gracious Mas-

ter,—" Lord, didst not Thou say, Be of good cheer?
Lord, do as Thou hast said, and cheer us to the end."

NOTES   JOHN XVI   25—33

25 —[*These things...proverbs.*]   Our Lord seems here to begin
winding up and concluding His discourse.   The expression
" these things," seems to me to apply to all that He had been
saying since Judas went out, and He was alone with the elev-
en.   " All these things I have been saying to you in language
which you have not been able fully to understand, insomuch
that I seem to have been speaking to you in parables or proverbs."   The Greek word rendered " proverb " is only used five
times in the New Testament, and in John x. 6 is translated parable.

Besser observes here, " From the very first words of our
Lord's farewell discourse,— ' In my Father's house are many
mansions,'—up to the words concerning the travailing woman,
the heavenly purport of the discourse is enwrapped in various
similes and parables."

Do we not learn here that ministers must not refrain from
telling their hearers many truths, which at the time they do
not fully comprehend, in the hope that they will seek more
knowledge, and comprehend afterwards the meaning of the
things taught ?

[*But the time cometh...Father.*]   I believe the " time " here
mentioned must be the time between our Lord's resurrection
and ascension, the great forty days when He taught the eleven
disciples more fully than He had taught them before, and
spoke more openly of the things of His Father.—I say this
with diffidence.   But I can see no other time to which our
Lord could refer excepting this.   It is evidently some personal
instruction that He means, and not instruction by the invisible
agency of the Holy Ghost.   " The time is very close at hand,
when my sacrifice on the cross having been accomplished, and
my resurrection having taken place, I will show you openly
and plainly the things concerning my Father, who I am, and
what my relation to Him, and will no longer use parables and
figures to convey my meaning."

The promise MAY possibly include the continual teaching of
the Holy Spirit, which our Lord would give His disciples after
His ascension ; but the language seems rather to point to direct teaching from our Lord's own mouth.   Moreover, it is an
" hour " that cometh, in the Greek, and not a continuous period
of time.   So in ver. 32, " the hour " means a time close at hand.

26 —[*At that day...ask in my name.*]   I believe this sentence
must mean, " In the day following my resurrection, when the
full nature of my mission and office is at last understood, you

will begin to pray and ask in my name. Hitherto you have not done it. When I have risen from the dead, and opened your understandings, you will begin to do it."

I see insuperable objection to any other view. The "day" spoken of cannot be the day of Christ's second advent, because prayer will not be needed then. Nor yet can it be the whole period of time between Christ's first and second advent, because the passage which it is here bound up with belongs specially to the Apostles. (See ver. 27.) There remains, in my judgment, no reasonable explanation except the one already given.

[*And I say not...pray...Father...you.*] The meaning of this sentence seems to be, " It is not necessary to say that I will pray the Father to hear you and grant your requests. Not only shall I of course do this, but my Father also will willingly hear your prayer." This is the most natural meaning of the passage, in my judgment.

It is singular that the Greek word rendered " pray " at the end of the verse, is the same that is used to signify " ask questions," or " make inquiry," in ver. 23. But it is worth notice that the word seems specially used when our Lord is described as " praying " to the Father. (See John xvii. 9 ; xv. 20.)

27 —[*For the Father Himself, etc.*] This verse is a continuation of the encouragement contained in the verse before. " You need not doubt the Father doing for you all that you ask in my name, because he loveth you for having loved Me, and believed my divine mission. He loves all who love Me, and believe on Me." (See John xiv. 23.)

Anton paraphrases the verse, " ye need not so think of my intercession as if the Father were not Himself well disposed, but must first be coerced into kindness. No! He Himself loveth you, and Himself ordained my intercession."

We should notice here how graciously our Lord acknowledges the grace there was in the disciples, with all their weakness. When myriads of Jews regarded Jesus as an impostor, the eleven loved Him and believed in Him. Jesus never forgets to honor true grace, however much it may be mingled with infirmity.

28 —[*I came forth, etc.*] This verse seems a farewell summary of the true nature of our Lord's office and mission. It grows out of the last clause of the preceding verse. " You have believed that I came out from God. In so believing you have done well, for so it is. For the last time I repeat that my mission is divine. I came forth from the Father, and came into the world to be man's Redeemer ; and now, my work being finished, I am about to leave the world, and to go back again to my Father." This deep sentence contains more than at first sight appears. It points backward to our Lord's persecution ; it points forward to His resurrection and ascension into glory.

Augustine, quoted by Burgon, remarks, " When Christ came forth from the Father, He so came into the world as never to leave the Father ; and He so left the world and went unto the Father as never to leave the world."

29 —[*His disciples said, etc.*] The words of the disciples seem to be a reference to our Lord's statement in the twenty-fifth verse, that " the time was coming when He would no more speak in proverbs, but show them plainly concerning the Father." The eleven appear to catch at that promise. " Even now Thou art speaking to us more plainly that we have ever heard Thee speaking before, and not in figurative language."

30 —[*Now are we sure, etc.*] This is a peculiar verse. It is hard to see what there was in our Lord's statement in ver. 28, to carry such conviction to the minds of the eleven, and to make them see things about their Master so much more clearly than they had seen them before. But the precise reason why words affect men's minds, and lay hold on their attention at one time and not at another, is a deep mystery, and hard to explain. The very same truths which a man hears from one mouth and is utterly unimpressed, come home to him with such power from another mouth, that he will declare he never heard them before ! Nay, more : the very same speaker who is heard without attention one day, is heard another day teaching the very same things with the deepest interest, by the same hearers, and they will tell you they never heard them before !

The words, " We are sure," are literally, " We know." They mean, " We know now that Thou knowest all things concerning Thyself, Thy mission, and the Father."

The words, " Thou needest not that any man should ask Thee," mean, " Thou hast told us so plainly who and what Thou art, that there is no need for any one to ask Thee questions, or seek further explanation."

The words, " By this we believe," must mean, " We are convinced and persuaded by the statement Thou hast just made," in ver. 28.

31 —[*Jesus answered...now believe.*] In this verse our Lord warns the eleven of their self-ignorance. They thought they believed. They did not doubt their own faith. Let them not be too confident. They would soon find they had an evil root of unbelief within. Never do we find our Lord flattering His disciples. Warnings against self-confidence need to be continually pressed on believers. Nothing is so deceptive as feeling and excitement in religion. We know not the weakness of our hearts.

Alford thinks that " do ye now believe," should not be rendered as a question, but as an affirmation. " You now believe, I know." The Greek admits of either view. I prefer the question.

32 —[*Behold the hour...leave Me alone.*] In this sentence our Lord reveals to his confident hearers, the amazing fact that they, even they, would in a very short time forsake Him, desert Him, run away and fail in faith altogether. " Behold ! " He begins, to denote how wonderful it was, " the hour cometh, yea, is now come. This very night, before the sun rises, the thing is immediately going to take place. Ye shall be scattered, like sheep fleeing from a wolf, one running one way and another another, every man going off to his own things, his own friends, or his own house, or his own place of refuge. Ye shall leave Me alone. You will actually allow Me to be taken off by myself as a prisoner to the high priests and to Pontius Pilate, and not so much as one of you will stand by Me."

How little the best of believers know of their own hearts, or understand how they may behave in times of trial ! If any men were ever fully and fairly warned of their coming failure, the disciples were. We can only suppose that they did not understand our Lord, or did not realize the magnitude of the trial coming on them, or fancied that He would work some miracle at the last moment, for His deliverance.

The Greek phrase rendered " His own," means literally, " His own things." It may either be " His own business," or as the margin renders it, " His own home."

[*And yet...not alone...with Me.*] In this teaching and touching sentence, our Lord reminds His disciples that their desertion would not deprive Him of all comfort. " And yet, when you are scattered, and have left Me, I am not entirely alone, because the Father is always with Me."

We need not doubt that one great need of the sentence was to teach the disciples where they must look themselves in their own future trials. They must never forget that God the Father would always be near them and with them, even in the darkest times. A sense of God's presence is one great source of the comfort of believers. The last promise in Matthew, before the ascension, was, " I am with you alway, even unto the end of the world." (Matt. xxviii. 20.)

John Huss, the famous martyr, who was burned at Constance, is said to have drawn special comfort from this passage, during the lonely imprisonment which preceded his death.

33 —[*These things...peace.*] In this concluding verse our Lord sums up the reasons why He has spoken the things contained in this whole discourse. " All these things I have spoken for this one great end,—that you may have inward peace by resting your souls on Me, and keeping up close communion with Me." It is one great secret in our religion to draw all our consolation from Christ, and live on Him. " He is our peace." (Eph. ii. 14.)

[*In the world...tribulation.*] Here our Lord tells the eleven, plainly and honestly, that they must expect trouble and persecution from the world. He does not conceal that the way to heaven is not smooth and strewed with flowers. On the contrary, "all that will live godly in Christ Jesus shall suffer persecution." (2 Tim. iii. 12.) To keep back from young beginners in religion the cross and the battle, is not teaching as Christ taught.

[*But be...good cheer...overcome...world.*] Here our Lord winds up all by bidding the disciples take courage, cheer up, be confident, and go forward without fear. The world in which they lived was a vanquished enemy. He, their Master, had "overcome the world." This means, I believe, not merely that He had given them an example of successful fighting by overcoming the fear of the world and the flattery of the world, but something far more important. He had overcome the Prince of this world, and was just about to win His final victory over him on the cross. Hence His disciples must remember that they were contending with an enemy already sorely beaten. "Ye need not fear the world, because I am just leading captive its King, and about to triumph over him on the cross."

Luther, quoted by Besser, here remarks, "Thus is the 'good-night' said, and the hand shaken. But very forcibly does He conclude with that very thing around which His whole discourse has turned. Let not your heart be troubled. Be of good cheer."

No devout commentator, I think, can leave this wonderful chapter without deeply feeling how little we understand of the depths of Scripture. There are many words and sentences in it about which we can only give conjectures, and must admit our inability to speak positively. Nowhere in Scripture, I must honestly confess, do commentators appear to me to contribute so little light to the text, as in their interpretation of this chapter.

JOHN XVII 1—8

1 These words spake Jesus, and lifted up his eyes to heaven, and said, Father, the hour is come; glorify thy Son, that thy Son also may glorify thee:

2 As thou hast given him power over all flesh, that he should give eternal life to as many as thou hast given him.

3 And this is life eternal, that they might know thee the only true God, and Jesus Christ, whom thou hast sent.

4 I have glorified thee on the earth: I have finished the work which thou gavest me to do.

5 And now, O Father, glorify thou me with thine own self with the glory which I had with thee before the world was.

6 I have manifested thy name unto the men which thou gavest me out of the world: thine they were, and thou gavest them me; and they have kept thy word.

7 Now they have known that all

things whatsoever thou hast given me are of thee.

8 For I have given unto them the words which thou gavest me ; and they have received *them*, and have known surely that I came out from thee, and they have believed that thou didst send me.

THESE verses begin one of the most wonderful chapters in the Bible. It is a chapter in which we see our Lord Jesus Christ addressing a long prayer to God the Father. It is wonderful as a specimen of the communion that was ever kept up between the Father and the Son, during the period of the Son's ministry on earth.— It is wonderful as a pattern of the intercession which the Son, as an High Priest, is ever carrying on for us in heaven.—Not least it is wonderful as an example of the sort of things that believers should mention in prayer. What Christ asks for His people, His people should ask for themselves. It has been well and truly said by an old divine, that "the best and fullest sermon ever preached was followed by the best of prayers."

It is needless to say that the chapter before us contains many deep things. It could hardly be otherwise. He that reads the words spoken by one Person of the blessed Trinity to another Person, by the Son to the Father, must surely be prepared to find much that he cannot fully understand, much that he has no line to fathom. There are sentences, words, and expressions, in the twenty-six verses of this chapter, which no one probably has ever unfolded completely. We have not minds to do it, or to understand the matters it contains, if we could. But there are great truths in the chapter which stand out clearly and plainly on its face, and to these truths we shall do well to direct our best attention.

We should notice, firstly, in these verses, *what a glorious account* they *contain of our Lord Jesus Christ's office and dignity*. We read that the Father has " given Him power over all flesh, that He should give eternal life." The keys of heaven are in Christ's hands. The salvation of every soul of mankind is at His disposal.— We read, furthermore, that "it is life eternal to know the only true God, and Jesus Christ whom He has sent." The mere knowledge of God is not sufficient, and saves none. We must know the Son as well as the Father. God known without Christ is a Being whom we can only fear, and dare not approach. It is "God in Christ, reconciling the world unto Himself," who alone can give to the soul life and peace.—We read, furthermore, that Christ "has finished the work which the Father gave Him to do." He has finished the work of redemption, and wrought out a perfect righteousness for His people. Unlike the first Adam, who failed to do God's will and brought sin into the world, the second Adam has done all, and left nothing undone that He came to do.—Finally, we read that Christ "had glory with the Father before the world was." Unlike Moses and David, He existed from all eternity, long before He came into the world ; and He shared glory with the Father, before He was made flesh and born of the Virgin Mary.

Each of these marvellous sayings contains matter which our weak minds have not power fully to comprehend. We must be content to admire and reverence what we cannot thoroughly grasp and explain. But one thing is abundantly clear: sayings like these can only be used of one who is very God. To no patriarch, or prophet, or king, or apostle, is any such language ever applied in the Bible. It belongs to none but God.

Forever let us thank God that the hope of a Christian rests on such a solid foundation as a Divine Saviour. He to whom we are commanded to flee for pardon, and in whom we are bid to rest for peace, is God as well as man. To all who really think about their souls, and are not careless and worldly, the thought is full of comfort. Such people know and feel that great sinners need a great Saviour, and that no mere human redeemer would meet their wants. Then let them rejoice in Christ, and lean back confidently on Him. Christ has all power, and is able to save to the uttermost, because Christ is divine. Office, power, and pre-existence, all combine to prove that He is God.

We should notice, secondly, in these verses, *what a gracious account they contain of our Lord Jesus Christ's disciples.* We find our Lord Himself saying of them, "'They have kept Thy Word,—they have known that all things Thou hast given Me are of Thee,—they have received Thy words,—they have known surely that I came out from Thee,—they have believed that Thou didst send Me."

These are wonderful words when we consider the character of the eleven men to whom they were applied. How weak was their faith ! How slender their knowledge ! How shallow their spiritual attainments ! How faint their hearts in the hour of danger ! Yet a very little time after Jesus spoke these words they all forsook Him and fled, and one of them denied Him three times with an oath. No one, in short, can read the four Gospels with attention, and fail to see that never had a great master such weak servants as Jesus had in the eleven apostles. Yet these very weak servants were the men of whom the gracious Head of the Church speaks here in high and honorable terms.

The lesson before us is full of comfort and instruction. It is evident that Jesus sees far more in His believing people than they see in themselves, or than others see in them. The least degree of faith is very precious in His sight. Though it be no bigger than a grain of mustard seed, it is a plant of heavenly growth, and makes a boundless difference between the possessor of

it and the man of the world. Wherever the gracious
Saviour of sinners sees true faith in Himself, however
feeble, He looks with compassion on many infirmities,
and passes by many defects. It was even so with the
eleven apostles. They were weak and unstable as water ;
but they believed and loved their Master when millions
refused to own Him. And the language of Him who
declared that a cup of cold water given in the name of
a disciple should not lose its reward, shows clearly that
their constancy was not forgotten.

The true servant of God should mark well the feature
in Christ's character which is here brought out, and rest
his soul upon it. The best among us must often see in
himself a vast amount of defects and infirmities, and
must feel ashamed of his poor attainments in religion.
But do we simply believe in Jesus ? Do we cling to
Him, and roll all our burdens on Him ? Can we say
with sincerity and truth, as Peter said afterwards, " Lord,
Thou knowest all things: Thou knowest that I love
Thee ? " Then let us take comfort in the words of Christ
before us, and not give way to despondency. The Lord
Jesus did not despise the eleven because of their feebleness, but bore with them and saved them to the end,
because they believed. And He never changes. What
He did for them, He will do for us.

NOTES JOHN XVII 1—8

1 —[*These words spake Jesus.*] The chapter we have now begun
is the most remarkable in the Bible. It stands alone, and there
is nothing like it. A few introductory remarks will not be out
of place.

Henry remarks that this was a prayer after sermon, a prayer
after sacrament, a family prayer, a parting prayer, a prayer before a sacrifice, a prayer which was a specimen of Christ's intercession.

We have here the only long prayer of the Lord Jesus, which
the Holy Ghost has thought good to record for our learning.

That He often prayed we know well ; but this is the only prayer reported. We have many of His sermons, parables, and conversations ; but only this prayer.

We have here the prayer of one who spake as never man spake, and prayed as never man prayed,—the prayer of the second Person in the Trinity to the Father : the prayer of one whose office it is, as our High Priest, to make intercession for His people.

We have a prayer offered up by the Lord Jesus on a specially interesting occasion,—just after the Lord's Supper,—just after a most striking discourse,—just before His betrayal and crucifixion,—just before the disciples forsook Him and fled,—just at the end of His earthly ministry.

We have here a prayer which is singularly full of deep and profound expressions ; so deep, indeed, that we have no line to them. The wisest Christian will always confess that there are things here which he cannot fully explain.

The Bible reader who attaches no weight to such considerations as these must be in a very strange state of mind.

Augustine remarks, " The prayer which Christ made for us, He hath also made known to us. Being so great a Master, not only what He saith in discoursing to the disciples, but also what He saith to the Father in praying for them, is their edification."

Calvin remarks, " Doctrine has no power, unless efficacy is imparted to it from above. Christ holds out an example to teachers, not to employ themselves only in sowing the Word, but by mingling prayers with it, to implore the assistance of God, that His blessing may render their labor fruitful."

Bullinger remarks that it was the duty of the Jewish priest to pray for the people, as well as to offer sacrifice for them.

About the place where this prayer was offered we know nothing certain. Some, as Alford, have conjectured that it was in the upper room where the Lord's Supper was held. This, however, seems inconsistent with "Arise, let us go hence." (Ch. xiv. 31.) It seems more likely that it was prayed in some quiet place outside the walls, before our Lord " crossed the brook Cedron." (John xviii. 1.) One thing at least is almost certain. It is a totally different prayer from that which our Lord prayed in the Garden of Gethsemane, although Rupertus asserts it was the same.

About the hearers of this prayer, there seems no reason to doubt that all the eleven apostles were present, and all heard it. All heard the discourses of the last three chapters, and I cannot see why all should not have heard the concluding prayer.

About the general plan and order and arrangement of the prayer, I decline to express any opinion, thinking it more reverent not to define too closely such a matter. We can all see at a glance that our Lord prays about Himself, prays about the disciples, and prays about those who were after to be disciples. But it is best to pause here, and not to dissent and analyze and systematize too minutely such a prayer. One thing only may be remarked, and that is, the singular frequency with which "the world" is mentioned. The phrase occurs no less than nineteen times.

I conclude these introductory observations by advising all who wish to study thoroughly this wonderful chapter of Scripture, to consult, if they can, the following works specially devoted to the elucidation of it: viz., "Manton's Sermons on Seventeenth John," 400 folio pages;" George Newton's Exposition of Seventeenth John," 560 pages folio; and "Burgess's Expository Sermons on Seventeenth John," 700 pages folio. These three books, having been written by Puritans 200 years ago, are ignored by some and despised by others. I simply venture the remark, that he who cares to examine them will find that they richly repay perusal. Manton's work especially will bear a comparison with anything written on this chapter since his days. It is curious that the other prayer, commonly called the "Lord's Prayer," has been frequently made the subject of books and expositions, while this much larger "prayer" has been comparatively little handled.

Melancthon says, " There is no voice which has ever been heard, either in heaven or earth, more exalted, more holy, more fruitful, more sublime, than this prayer.

Luther says, " In proportion as this prayer sounds plain and simple, it is in reality deep, rich, and wide, that which none can fathom."

[*And lifted up His eyes to heaven.*] This sentence shows that bodily gestures in prayer and worship of God are not altogether to be overlooked as unmeaning. There is a decent and reverent manner and gesture which suits the action of addressing God. It also seems clearly to show that the prayer was prayed before witnesses. John writes as one describing what he saw and heard. It is perhaps too much to say that the expression proves the prayer to have been in the open air. A person may look upward and heavenward even in a room. Yet it certainly rather increases the probability that our Lord was in the open air.

Calvin says, " If we desire to imitate Christ, we must take care that our outward gestures do not express more than is in our mind, but that inward feeling shall direct the eyes, the hands, the tongue, and everything about us."

Newton observes that gesture and demeanor in God's worship, though not everything, are something.

[*And said, Father, the hour is come.*] The "hour" here named is the hour appointed in God's eternal counsels for the sacrifice of the death of Christ, and the final accomplishment of His atonement. That time, which had been promised by God, and expected by saints for 4000 years, ever since Adam's fall, had at length arrived ; and the seed of the woman was actually about to bruise the serpent's head, by dying as man's Substitute and Redeemer. Up to this night " the hour was not yet come " (John vii. 30; viii. 20); and till it had come, our Lord's enemies could not hurt Him. Now, at last, the hour had come, and the Sacrifice was ready.

Augustine says here, " Time did not force Christ to die, but Christ chose a time to die. So also the time at which He was born of the Virgin He settled with the Father, of whom He was begotten without time."

Let us remember, though in a far lower sense, that believers are all immortal till their hour is come ; and till then they are safe, and cannot be harmed by death.

Let us note how our Lord addresses God as " Father." In a lower sense we may do the same, if we have the Spirit of adoption, and are His children in Christ. The Lord's prayer teaches us to do so.

It is worth notice that our Lord uses the phrase " Father " six times in this one prayer.

[*Glorify Thy Son...glorify Thee.*] I think the meaning of this sentence must be this : " Give glory to Thy Son, by carrying Him through the cross and the grave, to a triumphant completion of the work He came to do, and by placing him at Thy right hand, and highly exalting Him above every name that is named. Do this, in order that He may glorify Thee and Thy attributes. Do this, that He may bring fresh glory to Thy holiness, and justice, and mercy, and faithfulness, and prove to the world that Thou art a just God, a holy God, a merciful God, and a God that keepeth His word. My vicarious death and my resurrection will prove this, and bring glory to Thee. Finish the mighty work. Glorify Me, and in so doing glorify Thyself. Finish Thy work, not least, that Thy Son may glorify Thee by bringing many redeemed souls to heaven, to the glory of Thy grace."

Stier remarks, " These words prove the Son is equal to the Father, as touching His Godhead. What creature could stand before his Creator, and say, ' Glorify Me, that I may glorify Thee ? ' "

The glory of God and His attributes is the grand end of all creation, and of all God's arrangements and providences. No-

thing brings such glory to God as the completion of the redeeming work of Christ, by His death, resurrection, and ascension into heaven. Our Lord seems to me to ask that His death
may at once take place, that He through death may be taken
up to glory, and that there the justice, holiness, mercy, and
faithfulness of the Father may be glorified and exhibited to all
creation, and many souls be at once saved and glorify the Divine wisdom and power.

Augustine remarks, " Some take the Father's glorifying the
Son to consist in this,—that He spared Him not, but delivered
Him up for us all. But if He be said to be glorified by passion,
how much more by resurrection? For in the passion it is more
His humility than His glory that is shown forth, as the Apostle
says in Phil. ii. 7—11.''

2 —[*As Thou hast given Him power, etc.*] The Greek of part of
this verse is peculiar, as it contains a nominative absolute ; and
a literal translation seems impossible. It would be, " That with
regard to all that body or thing which Thou hast given Him,
He should give eternal life to them." There seems a distinction between the whole body and the particular individual members. The body is given to Christ, in the mass, from all eternity. The members of that body are called in time, separately
and one by one, and eternal life given to them.

There certainly seems a connection between this verse and
the concluding clause of the preceding verse. " Let Thy Son
glorify Thee by saving souls, even as Thou hast appointed He
should do, seeing that Thou hast given Him power and authority over all flesh, to give eternal life to all the members of that
mystical body which Thou hast given Him."

When we read here of " the Father giving power to the Son,"
we must carefully remember that it is not the giving of a superior to an inferior. It signifies that arrangement in the counsels of the eternal Trinity, by which the Father gives to the
Son especially the carrying out of the work of redemption.
Newton thinks the " power" includes the dignity of judgment
at the last day, as in John v. 22.

The expression "all flesh" seems to me, as it does to Augustine, Bullinger, Newton, and others, to denote all mankind.
All are not saved, but Christ has power and authority over all.
Some confine it to the " elect," but I cannot see the force of
their argument. To my eyes it is like John iii. 16, where
" world" and " believers" are in contradistinction. So it
seems here, " all flesh " and " given ones."

Chrysostom thinks that the phrase " all flesh " had special
reference to the calling of the Gentiles into the Church ; and
that our Lord meant that henceforward He was to be " Saviour
of Gentiles as well as Jews."

The phrase " eternal life " includes everything that is necessary to the complete salvation of a soul,—the life of justification, sanctification, and final glory.

The Son gives " eternal life " to none but those who are " given to Him," in the everlasting counsels of the Trinity, from all eternity. Who these are man cannot say. " Many of the *given* ones," says Traill, " do not for a long time know it." All are invited to repent and believe, without distinction. No one is warranted in saying, " I was not given to Christ, and cannot be saved." But that the last day will prove that none are saved except those given to Christ by the Father, is clear and plain.

Poole remarks, " We need not ascend up to heaven to search the rolls of the eternal counsels. All whom the Father hath given to Christ shall come to Christ ; and not only receive Him as Priest, but give themselves up to be ruled and quickened by Him. By such a *receiving* of Christ we shall know whether we are of the number of those that are *given* to Christ."

Traill remarks, " This giving of men to the Son to be redeemed and saved is the same thing with election and predestination."

" There is a twofold giving of men to the Son by the Father. One is eternal, in the purpose of His grace ; and this is mainly meant here. The other is in time ; when the Father by His Spirit draws men to Christ. (John vi. 44.) All the elect are given from eternity to the Son, to be redeemed by His blood ; and all the redeemed are in due time drawn by the Father to the Son, to be kept to eternal life."

3 —[*And this is life eternal, etc.*] This verse is mercifully given to us by our Lord as a description of saved souls. " The secret of possessing eternal life,—of being justified and sanctified now, and glorified hereafter,—consists simply in this : in having a right saving knowledge of the one true God, and of that Jesus Christ whom He has sent to save sinners." In short, our Lord declares that he who rightly knows God and Christ is the man who possesses eternal life.

Of course we must distinctly understand that mere head-knowledge, like that of the devil, is not meant by our Lord in this verse. The knowledge He means is a knowledge which dwells in the heart and influences the life. A true saint is one who " knows the Lord." To know God on the one hand—His holiness, His purity, His hatred of sin ; and to know Christ on the other hand—His redemption, His mediatorial office, His love to sinners,—are the two grand foundations of saving religion.

Right knowledge after all lies at the root of all vital Christianity, as light was the beginning of creation. We need to be " renewed in knowledge." (Col. iii. 10.) We must know what we believe, and we cannot properly worship an unknown God.

Do we know God, and do we know Christ aright ? are the two great questions to be considered. God known out of Christ is a consuming fire, and will fill us with fear only. Christ known without God will not be truly valued : we shall see no meaning in His Cross and passion. To see clearly at the same time a holy, pure, sin-hating God, and a loving, merciful, sin-atoning Christ, is the very A B C of comfortable religion. In short, it is life eternal to know rightly God and Christ. " To know God without Christ," says Newton, " is not to know Him savingly."

Traill remarks, " The secret moth and poison in many people's religion is, that it is not Christianity at all. God out of Christ is a consuming fire ; God not worshipped in Christ is an idol ; all hopes of acceptance out of Christ are vain dreams ; a heaven out of Christ is little better than the Turk's paradise."

The Greek of the phrase, " that they might know," would have been better rendered, " to know." It is the same phrase that is so rendered in John iv. 34 : " My meat is to do the will." Literally, this is, " My meat is that I may do the will."

Let us learn that knowledge is the chief thing in religion, though we must not make it an idol. Most wicked men are what they are because they are ignorant. Godly people are often described in Scripture by one single phrase : " They know God."

The argument which Arians and Socinians have always loved to found on this verse appears to me extremely weak. Their idea, that our Lord did not lay claim to divinity, because He speaks of the Father as the " only true God," is foolish and unreasonable. Chrysostom, Cyril, Toletus, and others, remark very sensibly, that the word " only " was not meant to exclude the Son and the Holy Ghost, but only those idols and false gods with which the heathen religions had filled the earth when Christ appeared. The very fact that eternal life consists in knowing not only God, but Christ, goes far to prove Christ's divinity.

Manton remarks that the expression in this verse had a two-fold object ; firstly, to exclude the idols and false gods ; and secondly, to show the order and economy of salvation."

Let us note that this is the only place in the New Testament where our Lord calls Himself " Jesus Christ."

4 —[*I have glorified Thee on the earth.*] The meaning of these words I take to be this. " I have now glorified Thee during my life on earth by keeping Thy law perfectly, so that Satan can find no defect or blemish in Me,—by witnessing faithfully to Thy truth in opposition to the sins and false teaching of the Jews,—by showing Thee and Thy mind towards man in a way that was never known before."

[*I have finished the work...to do.*] The meaning of these

words I take to be this. "I have completed the work of redemption which Thou didst send Me into the world to accomplish,—My death and resurrection being so near that to all intents and purposes it is finished."

On the use of the past tense here instead of the future, Augustine remarks, "Christ saith He *has* finished that which He most surely knows He *will* finish. Thus long before in prophecy he used verbs of past tense, when that which He said was to come to pass after many years. 'They pierced,' says He, 'my hands and my feet:' not they will pierce." (Psalm xxii. 16.)

It has been truly remarked that Christ alone, of all born of woman, could say literally "I have finished the work Thou gavest Me to do." He did what the first Adam failed to do, and all the saints in every age fail to do: He kept the law perfectly, and by so keeping it brought in everlasting righteousness for all them that believe. Yet here is the model we ought to keep before our eyes continually. We must aim to finish the work our Father appoints for us, whether great or small.

Musculus remarks, that true godly obedience is to be seen not merely in doing such work as we arbitrarily take up, but in doing such work as God appoints us to do.

It admits of doubt, whether there is not a latent reference in the end of this verse to Daniel's prophecy, that Messiah would "finish transgression, make an end of sins, make reconciliation for iniquity, and bring in everlasting righteousness." (Dan. ix. 24.)

Let it be carefully noted that Christ's redeeming work on earth was " work which the Father gave Him to do." He was the Person commissioned in the counsels of the everlasting Trinity to do this work.

"On the earth" must include the whole period of Christ's incarnation, from His birth until His ascension. During all that period He glorified the Father by perfect unvarying holiness.

5 —[*And now, O Father, glorify Thou Me, etc.*] Having briefly recited His work on earth, or, as it were, rendered an account of His ministry, our Lord now repeats the one prayer with which He began: "Glorify Me." The meaning of this verse I take to be as follows: "Father, my earthly work being now finished, I ask to be restored to that heavenly glory which in an unspeakable manner I had with Thee, as one of the co-equal and undivided Trinity, long before this world existed. The period of my humiliation and self-imposed weakness being accomplished, let Me once more share Thy glory, and sit with Thee on Thy throne as I did before my incarnation."

It is needless to say that the things asked in this prayer both here **and** elsewhere, are very deep, and reach far beyond man's **understanding**. The glory which the Son had with the Father, in the time before the creation of the world, is a matter passing our comprehension. But the pre-existence of Christ, the doctrine that Father and Son are two distinct persons, and the equal glory of the Father and the Son, are at any rate taught here very plainly. It seems perfectly impossible to reconcile the verse with the Socinian theory,—that Christ was a mere man, like David or Paul, and did not exist before He was born at Bethlehem.

Let us also learn the practical lesson, that a prayer for glory comes best from those who have done work upon earth for God. A lazy wish to go to glory without working is not according to Christ's example.

6.—[*I have manifested Thy name.*] In this part of the prayer our Lord begins to speak of His believing people: directly of the eleven apostles, but indirectly and partially of all believers in every age. And the rest of the prayer from this point is entirely taken up with the case of the disciples.

The sentence before us means, " I have made known Thyself, Thy character, and Thine attributes to my disciples." The word " name " is continually used in this sense in the Bible. Thus: Psalm xxii. 22; lii. 9; cxix. 55; Is. xxvi. 8; Acts ix. 14; Prov. xviii. 10. A right knowledge of God the Father was the first thing which Chr t revealed and taught to His disciples.

Burgon remarks, " The word *name* is here used in that large signification, so well known to readers of Scripture, whereby it is made to stand for God himself. (Psalm xx. 1.) The evangelist says, " They shall call His name Emmanuel;" meaning, that our Saviour would be what the name Emmanuel means: viz, ' God with us.' As often thus as our Lord made known to men the mind and will of the eternal Father, so often did He manifest His name."

Traill remarks, " What is the Father's name? Many think they know it, to whom Christ never revealed it. If you ask them whether they know Christ's Father's name, they have a ready answer. He is the first Person in the Trinity. He is the Almighty, the maker and ruler of heaven and earth. Yes: but this is the name of God only, and that in general! The name of Christ's Father is that name and discovery of God wherein He stands related to the Son."

[*Unto the men...gavest them Me.*] In this sentence our Lord describes His disciples. He calls them " men whom the Father gave Him out of the world,—men who were the elect children of the Father, and whom the Father committed and entrusted to His care as to a good Shepherd." Lampe thinks that " men " are emphatically mentioned here to the seclusion of angels.

Believers are "given" to Christ by the Father, according to an everlasting covenant made and sealed, long before they were born; and taken out from the world, by the calling of the Spirit, in due time. They are the Father's peculiar property, as well as the property of the Son. They were of the world, and nowise better than others. Their calling and election out of the world to be Christ's people, and not any foreseen merit of their own, is the real foundation of their character.

These are deep things, things to be read with peculiar reverence, because they are the words of the Son addressed to the Father, and handling matter about believers, which the Eternal Trinity alone can handle with positiveness and certainty. Who those are who are given to Christ by the Father, we can only certainly know by outward evidences. But that all believers are so given by the Father, predestined, elect, chosen, called by an everlasting covenant, and their names and exact number known from all eternity, is truth which we must reverently believe, and never hesitate to receive. So long as we are on earth we have to do with invitations, promises, commands, evidences, and faith ; and God's election never destroys our responsibility. But all true believers, who really repent and believe and have the Spirit, may fairly take comfort in the thought, that they were known and cared for and given to Christ by an eternal covenant, long before they knew Christ or cared for Him. It is an unspeakable comfort to remember that Christ cares for that which the Father has given Him.

[*And they have kept Thy word.*] Here our Lord continues the description of His disciples, and names things about them which may be seen by men as well as God. He says, " They have kept, or observed, or attended to, the Word of the Gospel, which thou didst send them by Me. While others would not attend to or keep that Word, these eleven men had hearing ears and attentive hearts, and diligently obeyed Thy message." Practical obedience is the first great test of genuine discipleship.

7 —[*Now they have known, etc.*] In this verse our Lord proceeds to give an account of His disciples. The meaning seems to be, " They have now attained such a degree of knowledge, that they know that the words they have heard and the works they have seen from Me, are words and works given Me to speak and do by Thee."

The idea is that they know my mission to be divine. " They know that Thou hast sent Me to be the Messiah, and hast commissioned Me to speak and act as I have done."

Here, as elsewhere, it is striking to observe how Jesus dwells on a right knowledge of the Father as the great truth which He came into the world to reveal.

8 —[*For I have given...words...gavest Me.*] In this sentence our Lord declares what He had done in teaching His disciples : He had given them the words, doctrines or truths, which the Father had given Him to proclaim to the world. The words which our Lord spoke, and the works which He did, were both alike given Him by the Father to speak and to do, in the eternal counsels of the Trinity about man's salvation.

For the peculiar use of the phrase, " words," to denote the truths or doctrines taught by our Lord, see John iii. 34; vi. 68; xii. 48; xiv. 10. Specially we should remark Peter's saying, " Thou hast the words of eternal life."

[*They have received, etc., etc.*] Our Lord here declares three remarkable things about His disciples. They had willingly received and embraced the truths He brought them from the Father. They had known and acknowledged that their Master came from God the Father. They believed and were persuaded that the Father sent Him to be the Messiah. And all this had taken place when the vast majority of their countrymen neither acknowledged nor believed anything of the kind.

We should carefully note the high character given to the disciples by our Lord. It seems wonderful, at first sight, when we remember their many defects in faith and knowledge, that our Lord should commend them for " knowing " and " believing." Yet when we think of their immensely difficult position, and the opposition they had to meet, we shall see it was no light matter to believe at all. It is after all a very comfortable reflection that our Lord does not despise weak grace ; and that He honors reality and sincerity of faith, although it may be very small. Believers make a better appearance in heaven than they do upon earth.

The word rendered " surely " is literally " truly." It is translated " surely " in Matt. xxvi. 73; Mark xiv. 70. The idea is, " They have known for a sure and undoubted truth."

Manton observes, " The faith of the Apostles was weak. They had but a confused view of Christ's Godhead and eternal generation. They knew little of His death, were filled with the thought of a terrene kingdom and a pompous Messiah, and understood not His prediction of His death and passion. Though they knew Him to be the Redeemer and Saviour of the world, yet the manner of His death and passion they knew not. ' We trusted that it had been He that should have redeemed Israel.' Yet observe how Christ commendeth their weak faith ! Certainly He loveth to encourage poor sinners, when He praiseth their mean and weak beginnings."

Traill observes, " Christ tells all the good He can of His disciples, and covers their failings. How poorly had they received Christ's Word! How weak and staggering was their faith! How oft had Christ reproved them sharply for their unbelief and other faults! Yet not a word of all this in Christ's representing them to His Father! This is the constant, gracious way of our High Priest. He makes no mention of His Israel's faults in heaven, but for their expiation."

JOHN XVII 9—16

9 I pray for them: I pray not for the world, but for them which thou hast given me; for they are thine.

10 And all mine are thine, and thine are mine: and I am glorified in them.

11 And now I am no more in the world, but these are in the world, and I come to thee. Holy Father, keep through thine own name those whom thou hast given me, that they may be one, as we *are*.

12 While I was with them in the world, I kept them in thy name: those that thou gavest me I have kept, and none of them is lost, but the son of perdition: that the Scripture might be fulfilled.

13 And now come I to thee: and these things I speak in the world, that they might have my joy fulfilled in themselves.

14 I have given them thy word; and the world hath hated them, because they are not of the world, even as I am not of the world.

15 I pray not that thou shouldest take them out of the world, but that thou shouldest keep them from the evil.

16 They are not of the world, even as I am not of the world.

THESE verses, like every part of this wonderful chapter, contain some deep things which are "hard to be understood." But there are two plain points standing out on the face of the passage which deserve the special attention of all true Christians. Passing by all other points, let us fix our attention on these two.

We learn, for one thing, that *the Lord Jesus does things for His believing people which He does not do for the wicked and unbelieving.* He helps their souls by special intercession. He says, " I pray for them: I pray not for the world, but for them which Thou hast given Me."

The doctrine before us is one which is specially hated by the world. Nothing gives such offence, and stirs up such bitter feeling among the wicked, as the idea of God making any distinction between man and man, and

loving one person more than another. Yet the world's
objections to the doctrine are, as usual, weak and unreasonable. Surely a little reflection might show us that
a God who regarded good and bad, holy and unholy,
righteous and unrighteous, with equal complacency and
favor, would be a very strange kind of God! The
special intercession of Christ for His saints is agreeable
to reason and to common sense.

Of course, like every other Gospel truth, the doctrine before us needs careful statement and Scriptural
guarding. On the one hand, we must not narrow the
love of Christ to sinners, and on the other we must not
make it too broad. It is true that Christ loves all sinners, and invites all to be saved ; but it is also true that
He specially loves the " blessed company of all faithful
people," whom He sanctifies and glorifies. It is true
that He has wrought out a redemption *sufficient* for all
mankind, and offers it freely to all ; but it is also true
that His redemption is *effectual* only to them that believe. Just so it is true that He is the Mediator between
God and man ; but it is also true that He intercedes
actively for none but those that come unto God by Him.
Hence it is written, " I pray for them: I pray not for the
world."

This special intercession of the Lord Jesus is one
grand secret of the believer's safety. He is daily
watched, and thought for, and provided for with unfailing care, by One whose eye never slumbers and
never sleeps. Jesus is " able to save them to the uttermost who come unto God by Him, because He ever
liveth to make intercession for them." (Heb. vii. 25.)
They never perish, because He never ceases to pray for
them, and His prayer must prevail. They stand and persevere to the end, not because of their own strength and
goodness, but because Jesus intercedes for them. When

Judas fell never to rise again, while Peter fell, but repented, and was restored, the reason of the difference lay under those words of Christ to Peter, "I have prayed for thee, that thy faith fail not." (Luke xxii. 32.)

The true servant of Christ ought to lean back his soul on the truth before us, and take comfort in it. It is one of the peculiar privileges and treasures of a believer, and ought to be well known. However much it may be wrested and abused by false professors and hypocrites, it is one which those who really feel in themselves the workings of the Spirit should hold firmly and never let go. Well says the judicious Hooker,— "No man's condition so safe as ours: the prayer of Christ is more than sufficient both to strengthen us, be we never so weak; and to overthrow all adversary power, be it never so strong and potent." ("Hooker's Sermons." Nisbet's edit., 1834, p. 171.)

We learn, for another thing, in these verses, that *Christ does not wish His believing people to be taken out of the world, but to be kept from the evil of it.*

We need not doubt that our Lord's all-seeing eye detected in the hearts of His disciples an impatient desire to get away from this troubled world. Few in number and weak in strength, surrounded on every side by enemies and persecutors, they might well long to be released from the scene of conflict, and to go home. Even David had said in a certain place, "Oh, that I had wings like a dove, then would I flee away and be at rest!" (Psalm lv. 6.) Seeing all this, our Lord has wisely placed on record this part of His prayer for the perpetual benefit of His Church. He has taught us the great lesson that He thinks it better for His people to remain in the world and be kept from its evil, than to be taken out of the world and removed from the presence of evil altogether.

Nor is it difficult on reflection to see the wisdom of our Lord's mind about His people, in this as in every thing else. Pleasant as it might be to flesh and blood to be snatched away from conflict and temptation, we may easily see that it would not be profitable. How could Christ's people do any good in the world, if taken away from it immediately after conversion?—How could they exhibit the power of grace, and make proof of faith, and courage, and patience, as good soldiers of a crucified Lord?—How could they be duly trained for heaven, and taught to value the blood and intercession and patience of their Redeemer, unless they purchased their experience by suffering?—Questions like these admit of only one kind of answer. To abide here in this vale of tears, tried, tempted, assaulted, and yet kept from falling into sin, is the surest plan to promote the sanctification of Christians, and to glorify Christ. To go to heaven at once, in the day of conversion, would doubtless be an easy course, and would save us much trouble. But the easiest course is not always the path of duty. He that would win the crown must carry the cross, and show himself light in the midst of darkness, and salt in the midst of corruption. "If we suffer, we shall also reign with Him." (2 Tim. ii. 11.)

If we have any hope that we are Christ's true disciples, let us be satisfied that Christ knows better than we do what is for our good. Let us leave "our times in His hand," and be content to abide here patiently as long as He pleases, however hard our position, so long as He keeps us from evil. That He will so keep us we need not doubt, if we ask Him, because He prays that we may be "kept." Nothing, we may be sure, glorifies grace so much as to live like Daniel in Babylon, and the saints in Nero's household,—in the world and yet not of the world,—tempted on every side and yet conquerors of temptation, not taken out of the reach of evil and yet kept and preserved from its power.

NOTES   JOHN XVII 9—16

9 —[*I pray for them, etc. etc.*] In this verse our Lord begins that part of His prayer which is specially intercessory, and proceeds to name things which He asks for His disciples, from this point down to the end of the chapter. It may be convenient to remember that the things He asks may be divided under four heads. He prays that His disciples may be (*a*) kept, (*b*) sanctified, (*c*) united, (*d*) and be with Him in glory. Four more important things cannot be desired for believers.

To say, as some have said, that our Lord's intercessory prayer is an exact specimen of what He does in heaven as our High Priest, is straining a point, and going too far. To suppose that the Son literally *asks* things of the Father by prayer in heaven, is in my judgment unreasonable, and a very limited, narrow view of Christ's intercession. We are reading a prayer made by our Lord during the time of His earthly ministry, before His ascension and session at God's right hand ; and we are not reading an account of what He does for us, as our Priest, within the veil. Let it suffice us to believe that the intercession of this chapter exhibits accurately Christ's mind toward believers, His desires for believers, the active interest He takes in believers, and the graces He would fain see in believers. Above all, let us believe that if we seek for ourselves the same four things that Jesus here names, we have a Friend in heaven who will take care that we do not seek in vain and will make our prayer effectual.

There are two interpretations of our Lord's meaning, when He speaks of praying for the disciples, and " not praying for the world."

Some, as Bengel and Alford, think that our Lord meant, "At this present moment I pray specially for my disciples, and not for the world." They will not admit that our Lord does not pray and intercede in any way for the wicked and unbelieving ; and they quote with some show of reason His prayer at the crucifixion for His murderers,—" Father, forgive them." (Luke xxiii. 34.)

Others, as Hutcheson and Lampe, think that our Lord meant, " I pray specially for my disciples, because now and always it is their special privilege to be prayed for and interceded for by Me." The advocates of this view maintain that it is derogatory to our Lord's honor to suppose that He can ever ask anything in vain ; and that His intercession specially belongs to " those who come unto God by Him." (Heb. vii. 25.)

The point in dispute is a nice and delicate one, and will probably never be settled. On the one hand we must take care that we do not forget that our Lord Jesus Christ does take a special interest in His believing people, and does do special things for them which He does not do for the wicked and unbelieving.—On the other hand we must not forget that our Lord pities all, cares for all, and has provided salvation *sufficient* for all mankind. There is no escaping the text which says of the wicked that they "deny the Lord that bought them." (2 Peter ii. 1.) The most fair and honest interpretation of the text, "God so loved the world" (John iii. 16), is to regard "the world" as meaning all mankind.

The whole dispute turns, as is often the case in such disputes, on the meaning we put on a word. If by "intercession" we mean vaguely and generally the whole mediatorial work of Christ on behalf of mankind, it is then true that Christ intercedes for all, both good and bad ; and this text before us must mean, " I pray at this moment specially for my people, and am only thinking of them."—If, on the other hand, we mean by "intercession" that special work which Christ does for His people, in order to carry them to heaven, after calling, pardoning, justifying, renewing, and sanctifying them, it is then plain that Christ intercedes for none but believers, and that the words before us mean, "I pray now, as always, specially for my disciples, and not for the world."

If I must give an opinion, I must own that I decidedly hold the second or last view of which I have spoken. I believe that Christ never, in the fullest sense of the word, " makes intercession ". for the wicked. I believe that such intercession is a peculiar privilege of the saints, and one grand reason of their continuance in grace. They stand, because there is One in heaven who actively and effectually intercedes.

I will give place to no one in maintaining that Jesus loves all mankind, came into the world for all, died for all, provided redemption sufficient for all, calls on all, invites all, commands all to repent and believe ; and ought to be offered to all—freely, fully, unreservedly, directly, unconditionally—without money and without price. If I did not hold this, I dare not get into a pulpit, and I should not understand how to preach the Gospel.

But while I hold all this, I maintain firmly that Jesus does special work for those who believe, which He does not do for others. He quickens them by His Spirit, calls them by His grace, washes them in His blood—justifies them, sanctifies them, keeps them, leads them, and continually intercedes for them—that they may not fall. If I did not believe all this, I should be a very miserable, unhappy Christian.

Holding this opinion, I regard the text before us as one which describes our Lord's special intercession for His people ; and I take the meaning to be simply, " I pray for them, as my peculiar people, that they may be kept, sanctified, united, and glorified ; but I do not pray for the world."

The famous text, " Father, forgive them " (Luke xxiii. 34), is at best a doubtful one. Will any one undertake to say, that those for whom our Lord prayed were never forgiven and saved ?—Have we forgotten that within fifty days after that prayer 3,000 souls were converted at Pentecost, of whom Peter said, " By wicked hands ye crucified and slew Jesus of Nazareth " ? (Acts ii. 23.) Who can prove that the very men who crucified our Lord were not among the number converted, and were thus the answer to our Lord's prayer ?—These however are conjectures at the very best. The matter is one which is not necessary to salvation, and one about which Christians must agree to differ, and must not excommunicate one another. " Let every man be fully persuaded in his own mind." (Rom. xiv. 5.)

Hengstenberg remarks, " The world may be viewed under two aspects. First, there is the susceptibility of grace, which, despite the depths of the sinful depravation of Adam's race, still remains in it. Of the world in this sense Jesus says, ' I came not into the world to condemn the world, but to save the world.' (John i. 29 ; iii. 17.) Viewed under this aspect, the world is the subject of Christ's intercession. The disciples themselves were won from the world. But the world may also be viewed as ruled by predominantly ungodly principles. Of the world in this sense we read that it cannot receive the ' Spirit of truth.' (John xiv. 27.) To pray for the world, thus viewed, would be as vain as to pray for the prince of this world."

Manton suggests that we must draw some distinction between the intercession of Christ as a Divine Mediator, and the prayers of Christ as a man, wherein He is an example to His people. Yet, however just this remark, it hardly seems to apply to this peculiarly solemn prayer.

[*For them...given Me...thine.*] Our Lord here repeats the description of His disciples which He had given before. They were men whom " the Father had given Him " to teach and feed, and save. They were His Father's sheep, intrusted to His charge. Therefore, He seems to argue, " I am specially bound to pray for them, and ask for them everything that their souls need. Like a good Shepherd, I must give an account of them one day."

10.—[*And all mine...thine...mine.*] This sentence seems to come in parenthetically, and to be a reassertion of the great truth of the perfect unity of the Father and the Son. The words in the Greek mean literally " things," and not " persons." " All my things are Thy things, and all Thy things are my things. As with everything else, these eleven disciples are not mine more than Thine, or Thine more than mine." This continual assertion of the doctrine of the perfect unity of the Godhead, and the distinction of the Persons in the Trinity, is very remarkable and instructive.

[*I am glorified in them.*] In this sentence our Lord seems to return to the disciples. " I have been and am glorified in them, by their faith, and obedience and love, when the vast majority of their countrymen have hated and rejected Me. They have honored Me and brought glory to Me, by continuing with Me in my tribulation. Therefore I now make special prayer and intercession for them."

Let us mark here that the weakest faith and love to Christ brings Him some glory, and is not overlooked by Him.

11 —[*And now I am...come to Thee.*] In the beginning of this verse our Lord describes the position of the disciples, and shows the special reason why they required prayer and intercession to be made for them. They were about, for the first time, to be left alone like orphans, and thrown on their own resources, in a certain sense. Hitherto they had always had their Master at their side, and could turn to Him in every case of need. Now they were about to enter on a totally different condition of things.—" The time of my departure from the world is at hand. I am very soon about to ascend into heaven and come to Thee. But these few sheep, these weak disciples, are not coming to heaven with Me. They are going to be left alone in a wicked, cold, persecuting world."

Poole observes, " Christ here speaks of Himself as one who had already died, and was already risen, and ascended, though none of all these things were past, because they were so soon and suddenly to come."

Let us not fail to note how our Lord remembers the position of His people here on earth,—cares tenderly for them, and will make all needful provision for their safety and comfort. " I know thy works, and where thou dwellest." (Rev. ii. 13.)

[*Holy Father.*] This is the only place in the Gospel where we find our Lord addressing the Father by this epithet. There is doubtless some good reason for it. It may be that there is a fitness in asking the " Holy " Father to keep the disciples holy and free from the dominion of evil. "As Thou art holy, so keep these my disciples holy."

[*Keep through Thine...name...given Me.*] Here is the first petition that our Lord puts up for His disciples. He asks that they may be kept and preserved from evil, from falling away, from false doctrine, from being overcome by temptation, from being crushed by persecution, from every device and assault of the devil. Danger was around them on every side. Weakness was their present characteristic. Preservation was what He asked.

The expression, " Keep through Thine own name," is remarkable. I take it to mean, " Through Thine own attributes of power, love, and wisdom." The " name " of God, as before remarked, is frequently used in Scripture to signify His character and attributes.

[*That they may be one, as we are.*] Here our Lord mentions one special object for which He desires that His people may be kept : viz., their unity : that they may be one.—"Keep them, that they may be of one heart and one mind, striving together against common foes and for common ends, and not broken up, weakened, and paralyzed by internal quarrels and divisions."

He adds the highest model and pattern of unity,—" one, as we are,"—the unity of the Father and the Son. Of course there cannot be literally such union between Christian and Christian, as there is between two Persons in the Trinity. But the unity which Jesus prays the disciples may aim at, should be a close, intimate, unbroken unity of mind, and will, and opinion, and feeling.

Burgon remarks here, " The word rendered ' as,' both here and in ver. 21, does not denote strict correspondence, but only general resemblance ; as in the Athanasian Creed, where the union of two natures in the one Person of Christ, is popularly illustrated by the union of the ' reasonable soul and flesh ' in man." (Comp. Matt. v. 48 ; Luke vi. 36.)

The importance attached by our Lord to " unity " among Christians, is very strikingly illustrated by the prominent place assigned to it in this verse. The very first object for which He desires the preservation of the disciples, is that they may be kept from division. Nor can we wonder at this, when we consider the interminable divisions of Christians in every age, the immense harm they have done in the world, and the astounding indifference with which many regard them, as if they were perfectly innocent things, and as if the formation of new sects was a laudable work !

12 —[*While...with them...kept... Thy name.*] Our Lord here recites what He had done for the disciples during His ministry : " Throughout the three years in which I have been with these eleven disciples in the world, I used to keep them from all harm, through Thy power and name."—I can see no reason why the same Greek words should not be rendered " *through* Thy name," in this verse, as well as in the preceding one. In both cases the idea seems the same,—a preservation through the grace, power, and attributes of God the Father.

[*Thou...gavest...kept...none...lost.*] The word rendered " kept " in this clause, is quite different from the word so rendered in the first part of the verse. There it means simply, " I have preserved." Here it means, " I have guarded," like a shepherd guarding a flock, or a soldier guarding a treasure. " I have so carefully guarded those disciples whom Thou hast given Me, that not one of them has perished, or is lost."

[*But the son of perdition.*] This remarkable expression of course refers to Judas Iscariot, the traitor, the only one of the Apostles who was lost and cast away in hell. The name given to Judas is a strong Hebraism, and means " a person worthy of perdition, or only fit to be lost and cast away, by reason of his wickedness." David says to Saul's servants, " Ye are worthy to die : " or, as the margin says, "sons of death." (1 Sam. xxvi. 16.) Again, he says to Nathan, " The man that hath done this thing shall surely die," or, "is a son of death." (2 Sam. xxvi. 5 ; see also Ps. lxxix. 11 ; Matt. xiii. 38 ; Luke xvi. 8.) It is a tremendously strong expression to come from the lips of our merciful and loving Saviour. It shows the desperate helplessness of any one who, living in great light and privileges like Judas, misuses his opportunities, and deliberately follows the bent of his own sinful inclinations. He becomes the "child of hell." (Matt. xxiii. 15.)

A question of very grave importance arises out of the words before us. Did our Lord mean that Judas was originally one of those that the Father " gave to him," and was primarily a true believer? Did he therefore fall away from grace ?—Many maintain, as Hammond, Alford, Burgon, and Wordsworth, that Judas was at one time a true believer, like Peter, James, and John,—that the text is an unanswerable proof that grace may be *lost*,—and that a man may be converted, and have the Holy Ghost, and yet finally fall away, and perish forever in hell.— This is not only a very uncomfortable doctrine, but one which it is hard to reconcile with many plain texts of Scripture, to say nothing of the seventeenth Article of our own Church.— But does the text before us clearly prove that Judas was one of those who were " given" to Christ by the Father? I believe firmly that it does not. I maintain that the " but " in the text is not an " exceptive " word, but an " adversative " one. I hold the right meaning to be, " Those whom Thou gavest Me I have kept, and out of them not one is lost. But there is one man who is lost, even Judas, the son of perdition ; not one who was ever given to Me, but one whom I declared long ago to be a ' devil,' a man whose hardened heart fitted him for destruction."

It is easy of course to say that this view is a far-fetched and non-natural one. I ask those who say this to observe, that the same Greek words here rendered " but," are used in other places in the New Testament, where it is impossible to put an " exceptive " sense on them, and where the "adversative" meaning is the only one they can possibly bear.—I challenge any one to deny that " but," in such texts as Matt. xii. 4, " but only for the priests,"—Mark xiii. 32, " but the Father,"—Rev. ix. 4, " but only those men,"—Rev. xxi. 27, " but they which are written,"—must be interpreted as an " adversative," and cannot possibly be an " exceptive " word. (See also Acts xxvii. 22 and 2 Kings v. 17.) And so it is here. Our Lord does not mean, " No one of those given to Me is lost EXCEPT the son of perdition."—What He does mean is, " Not one of those given to Me is lost. On the other hand, and in contrast, Judas, a man not given to Me, a graceless man, is lost."

Let me add, in confirmation of the view I maintain, that in the very next chapter the expression here used is referred to by St. John, in his account of our Lord's capture. He says, " The saying was fulfilled which He spake: Of them which Thou gavest Me have I lost none " (John xviii. 9) ; and not one hint does he give of any exception having been made by our Lord, when he heard Him use the expression before.

The view I advocate is maintained by De Dieu, Gomarus, Lampe, Hutcheson, and Manton.

It is a curious fact that even in our own English language, Milton, writing in the seventeenth century, when the last re- vision of our Bible took place, has used the word " except " in the same way. He says of Satan, in " Paradise Lost : "—

> " God and His Son *except*, created thing
> Nought valued He or shunned."

" Except " there must clearly be " adversative." God and His Son are not *created* things ! Both Brown (on xvii. John) and Doddridge quote this sentence of Milton.

Bishop Beveridge, quoted by Ford, remarks, " Judas, here called the son of perdition, though he seemed to be given to Christ, and to come to Him, yet really did not. Therefore, though he was lost, as the Scripture had foretold, yet Christ's word is still true, that He never casts out, nor loseth any, that really come to Him."

[*That Scripture...fulfilled.*] Here, as in many places, it does not mean that Judas was lost in order to fulfill Scripture, but that the Scripture was fulfilled by the loss of Judas. The place referred to is Psalm cix. 8.

Let us not fail to note the high honor put on Scripture in this place. Even in a prayer of the utmost solemnity address- ed by the Son to the Father, we find reverent allusion to the written word of the Old Testament, and to that oft-quoted book, the Psalms.

13 —[*And now I come to Thee, etc.*] This is a somewhat ellipti- cal verse. I take the meaning to be something of this kind : " I am now soon leaving the world, and coming to Thee. Be- fore leaving the world, I speak these things openly in prayer in the hearing of these my disciples, in order that they may be cheered and comforted, and feel the joy which I give to them filled up and abounding in their hearts."

I can hardly think that our Lord is referring to the discourse which preceded this prayer. It seems more natural to apply " these things I speak " to His prayer.

The expression, " my joy," occurs before, in chapter xv. 11. It must mean that peculiar, inward sense of comfort that Christ imparts to believers, and which no one knows excepting him who receives it.

14 —[*I have given them Thy Word, etc.*] In this verse our Lord appears to describe more fully the position of the disciples as an introduction to a more full repeated prayer for their preservation. It is as though He said, " I do not pray that my disciples may be kept without good reason. I have given them the Word of the Gospel, and they have received it, and have been at once persecuted and ill-treated for receiving it. In short, the world has hated them ever since they became my disciples, because, like myself, they are not of the world, neither holding the world's principles, nor walking in the world's ways."

Let us not fail to remark that true believers must expect the hatred and enmity of the wicked in every age. They must not be surprised at it. Christ and His disciples had to endure it, and all real Christians must endure it too. The reason of this enmity is the continual testimony which believers bear against the world's opinions and practices. The world feels itself condemned, and hates those whose faith and lives condemn it. If believers were more bold, decided, and consistent, they would soon find these things out more than they do now. The good opinion of the world is about the last thing a true Christian should expect or desire. If all men speak well of his opinions and ways in religion, he may well doubt whether there is not something very wrong and defective about them. We are not to court the world's enmity. A narrow, morose, uncourteous, and exclusive spirit, is downright wrong. But we are never to be the least surprised by the world's enmity if we meet with it ; and the more holy we are, the more we shall meet with it. Christ was perfect in holiness ; but the world hated Him.

15 —[*I pray not that Thou, etc., etc.*] In this verse our Lord repeats, and develops more fully, His prayer that His disciples may be kept. His meaning appears to be this :—" Wicked and persecuting as the world is, I pray not that Thou wouldst take my disciples immediately out of it. Such removal would be bad for themselves and bad for the world. What I do pray is, that remaining in the world, Thou wouldst keep them from the evil of the world. Though in it, let them not be spoiled or corrupted by it."

The deep wisdom of this prayer is very instructive. There are few Christians who would not like to go to heaven without trouble, conflict, and persecution. Yet it would not be for their own sanctification, and it would deprive the world of the benefit of their teaching and example. Believers would never value Christ and heaven as much as they will do one day, if they were not kept here on earth a good deal, taught to know their own hearts, and, like their Master, "perfected by suffering." (Heb. ii. 10.)

Hutcheson remarks, "However much we ought to have our eye upon our rest, and make ready for it, yet we are not anxiously to long for it till God's time come, nor to be weary of life because of any trouble, persecution, or inconvenience we meet with in His service."

There is a strong indirect argument here, as Bullinger and Gaulter remark, against the favorite theory of many, that entire retreat from the world, by going into monasteries and convents, is the secret of eminent holiness. Eminent holiness is most seen by publicly winning a victory over evil, and not by a cowardly desertion of our post in society.

Three of the only prayers not granted to saints, recorded in Scripture, are the prayers of Moses, Elijah, and Jonah, to be "taken out of the world."

Gerhard remarks that the Apostles were to be the first preachers of the Gospel and the light of the world. If they had been taken away immediately after their Lord, the world would have been left in darkness. Moreover, the cross is the school of faith and patience, and without remaining in the world they could not have become eminent saints.

George Newton remarks, "The world is the place where we bring glory to the Lord; in the world to come we are glorified by Him. Oh, let us be so ingenuous as to desire to be awhile where we may glorify God, rather than where we may have glory from Him. Let us not be so eager for our wages and our rest, till we have finished our work and served our generation. When we have done so God will glorify us with Himself for ever."

The meaning of the phrase, "the evil," is a point on which there is much difference of opinion.

Some think that it means simply, as our translation of the Bible has it,—evil in the abstract,—all evil of every kind,—like "deliver us from evil" in the Lord's prayer; and they think that it includes all evil that may assail us from the world, the flesh, and the devil.

Others think that the words would have been better rendered, "the evil one," and apply the expression to the devil, as the first great cause and beginner of evil. The word is so rendered in Matt. xiii. 19—38; 1 John ii. 13, 14; iii. 12; v. 18.

The question is one which will probably never be settled, and the Greek phrase may be translated either way. Nevertheless I decidedly incline to think that our translation is right. It is "evil" in the abstract, and not the devil, that our Lord means. I think so, partly because the devil is not anywhere brought forward in this prayer, and partly because it is more consistent to reason to suppose our Lord would have His disciples kept from all kind of "evil," than from the devil only. This is the more clear to my mind, from the fact that it is "the world," and its hatred and enmity, which our Lord has just been speaking of, and not the devil. However, I freely admit that it is an open question.

16 —[*They are not of the world, etc.*] These words are a literal repetition of the end of the fourteenth verse, and need no further comment. Our Lord seems to repeat them in order to add emphasis to the request He has just made ; and the repetition strengthens my opinion that it is "the evil in the world" which He specially desires His people to be kept from. "They need to be specially kept and preserved, because, I repeat, there is an entire want of harmony, a gulf of separation between them and this wicked world, in which I leave them. They are much hated, and need to be much kept."

Repetitions in real, earnest prayer, we may observe, are not wrong : Christ's example warrants them. It is "vain repetitions," such as were common among the heathen, repeating the same words over and over again, without thought or feeling, against which we are warned in the Sermon on the Mount. (Matt. vi. 7.)

JOHN XVII 17—26.

17 Sanctify them through thy truth : thy word is truth.

18 As thou hast sent me into the world, even so have I also sent them into the world.

19 And for their sakes I sanctify myself, that they also might be sanctified through the truth.

20 Neither pray I for these alone, but for them also which shall believe on me through their word ;

21 That they all may be one : as thou, Father, *art* in me, and I in thee, that they also may be one in us : that the world may believe that thou hast sent me.

22 And the glory which thou gavest me I have given them : that they may be one, even as we are one :

23 I in them, and thou in me, that they may be made perfect in one ; and that the world may know that thou hast sent me, and hast loved them, as thou hast loved me.

24 Father, I will that they also, whom thou hast given me, be with me where I am : that they may behold my glory, which thou hast given me : for thou lovedst me before the foundation of the world.

25 O righteous Father, the world hath not known thee : but I have known thee, and these have known that thou hast sent me.

26 And I have declared unto them thy name, and will declare *it :* that the love wherewith thou hast loved me may be in them, and I in them.

THESE wonderful verses form a fitting conclusion of

the most wonderful prayer that was ever prayed on earth,—the last Lord's prayer after the first Lord's Supper. They contain three most important petitions which our Lord offered up in behalf of His disciples. On these three petitions let us fix our attention. Passing by all other things in the passage, let us look steadily at these three points.

We should mark, first, *how Jesus prays that His people may be sanctified.* "Sanctify them," He says, " through thy truth : Thy word is truth."

We need not doubt that, in this place at any rate, the word " sanctify " means " make holy." It is a prayer that the Father would make His people more holy, more spiritual, more pure, more saintly in thought and word and deed, in life and character. Grace had done something for the disciples already,—called, converted, renewed, and changed them. The great Head of the Church prays that the work of grace may be carried higher and further, and that His people may be more thoroughly sanctified and made holy in body, soul, and spirit,—in fact more like Himself.

Surely we need not say much to show the matchless wisdom of this prayer. More holiness is the very thing to be desired for all servants of Christ. Holy living is the great proof of the reality of Christianity. Men may refuse to see the truth of our arguments, but they cannot evade the evidence of a godly life. Such a life adorns religion and makes it beautiful, and sometimes wins those who are not " won by the Word." Holy living trains Christians for heaven. The nearer we live to God while we live, the more ready shall we be to dwell for ever in His presence when we die. Our entrance into heaven will be entirely by grace, and not of works; but heaven itself would be no heaven to us if we entered it with an unsanctified character. Our hearts must be in tune for heaven if we are to enjoy it. There must be a moral "meetness for the inheritance of the saints in light," as well as a title. Christ's blood alone can give us a title to enter the inheritance. Sanctification must give us a capacity to enjoy it.

Who, in the face of such facts as these, need wonder that increased sanctification should be the first thing that Jesus asks for His people? Who that is really taught of God can fail to know that holiness is happiness, and that those who walk with God most closely, are always those who walk with Him most comfortably? Let no man deceive us with vain words in this matter. He who despises holiness and neglects good works, under the vain pretence of giving honor to justification by faith, shows plainly that he has not the mind of Christ.

We should mark, secondly, in these verses, *how Jesus prays for the unity and oneness of His people.* "That they all may be one,—that they may be one in Us,—that they may be one even as We are one,"—and "that so the world may believe and know that Thou hast sent Me,"—this is a leading petition in our Lord's prayer to His Father.

We can ask no stronger proof of the value of unity among Christians, and the sinfulness of division, than the great prominence which our Master assigns to the subject in this passage. How painfully true it is that in every age divisions have been the scandal of religion, and the weakness of the Church of Christ! How often Christians have wasted their strength in contending against their brethren, instead of contending against sin and the devil! How repeatedly they have given occasion to the world to say, "When you have settled your own internal differences we will believe!" All this, we need not doubt, the Lord Jesus foresaw with prophetic eye. It was the foresight of it which made Him pray so earnestly that believers might be " one."

Let the recollection of this part of Christ's prayer abide in our minds, and exercise a constant influence on our behavior as Christians. Let no man think lightly, as some men seem to do, of schism, or count it a small thing to multiply sects, parties, and denominations. These very things, we may depend, only help the devil and damage the cause of Christ. "If it be possible, as much as lieth in us, let us live peaceably with all men." (Rom. xii. 18.) Let us bear much, concede much, and put up with much, before we plunge into secessions and separations. They are movements in which there is often much false fire. Let rabid zealots who delight in sect-making and party-forming, rail at us and denounce us if they please. We need not mind them. So long as we have Christ and a good conscience, let us patiently hold on our way, follow the things that make for peace, and strive to promote unity. It was not for nothing that our Lord prayed so fervently that His people might be " one."

We should mark, finally, in these verses, *how Jesus prays that His people may at last be with Him and behold His glory.* " I will," He says, " that those whom Thou hast given Me, be with Me where I am : that they may behold my glory."

This is a singularly beautiful and touching conclusion to our Lord's remarkable prayer. We may well believe that it was meant to cheer and comfort those who heard it, and to strengthen them for the parting scene which was fast drawing near. But for all who read it even now, this part of his prayer is full of sweet and unspeakable comfort.

We do not see Christ now. We read of Him, hear of Him, believe in Him, and rest our souls in His finished work. But even the best of us, at our best, walk by faith and not by sight, and our poor halting faith often makes us walk very feebly in the way to heaven. There shall be an end of all this state of things one day. We shall at length see Christ as He is, and know as we have been known. We shall behold Him face to face, and not through a glass darkly. We shall actually be in His presence and company, and go out no more. If faith has been pleasant, much more will sight be ; and if hope has been sweet, much more will certainty be. No wonder that when St. Paul has written, " We shall ever be with the Lord," he adds, " Comfort one another with these words."   (1 Thess. iv. 17, 18.)

We know little of heaven now. Our thoughts are all confounded, when we try to form an idea of a future state in which pardoned sinners shall be perfectly happy. "It does not yet appear what we shall be." (1 John iii. 2.) But we may rest ourselves on the blessed thought, that after death we shall be " with Christ." Whether before the resurrection in paradise, or after the resurrection in final glory, the prospect is still the same. True Christians shall be " with Christ." We need no more information. Where that blessed Person is who was born for us, died for us, and rose again, there can be no lack of anything. David might well say, " In Thy presence is fulness of joy, and at Thy right hand are pleasures forevermore."   (Psalm xvi. 11.)

Let us leave this wonderful prayer with a solemn recollection of the three great petitions which it contains. Let holiness and unity by the way, and Christ's company in the end, be subjects never long out of our thoughts or distant from our minds. Happy is that Christian who cares for nothing so much as to be holy and loving like his Master, while he lives, and a companion of his Master when he dies.

Notes John xvii 17—26

17 —[*Sanctify them, etc.*] In this verse our Lord proceeds to name the second thing He asks for His disciples in prayer. Preservation was the first thing, and sanctification the second. He asks His Father to make the disciples more holy, to lead them on to higher degrees of holiness and purity. He asks Him to do it " through the truth,"—by bringing truth to bear more effectually and powerfully on their hearts and consciences and inner man. And to prevent mistake as to what He meant by truth, he adds, " Thy Word, Thy revealed Word, is the truth that I mean."

Some, as Maldonatus, maintain that the sentence only means " sanctify them truly,"—in opposition to ,that legal sanctification of priests, of which we read in Exodus and Leviticus. This, however, seems a very cold, thin, shallow sense to put on the words.

Some, again, as Mede, Pearce, and Burgon, maintain that our Lord is only praying that His Apostles may be consecrated, fitted, and set apart for the great work of the ministry, and that this is all the meaning of " sanctify." This appears to me an imperfect and defective view of the sentence.

No doubt the word "sanctify" originally and primarily means " set apart, separate for religious uses ;" and it might be used of a vessel, a house, or an animal. But inasmuch as in human beings this separation is principally evidenced by holiness and godliness of life and character, the secondary sense of "sanctify" is " to make holy," and holy and godly people are " sanctified." This I hold to be the meaning here most decidedly. It is a prayer for the increased holiness and practical godliness of Christ's people. In short, the petition comes to this : " Separate them more and more from sin and sinners, by making them more pure, more spiritual-minded, and more like Thyself." This is the view of Chrysostom and all the leading commentators.

Four great principles may be gathered from this text.

a) The importance of sanctification and practical godliness. Our Lord specially asks it for His people. Those that despise Christian life and character, and think it of no importance so long as they are sound in *doctrine*, know very little of the mind of Christ. Our Christianity is worth nothing, if it does not make us value and seek practical sanctification.

(*b*) The wide difference between justification and sanctification. Justification is a perfect and complete work obtained for us by Christ, imputed to us, and external to us, as perfect and complete the moment we believe, as it can ever be, and admitting of no degrees.—Sanctification is an inward work wrought in our hearts by the Holy Spirit, and never quite perfect so long as we live in this body of sin. The disciples needed no prayer for justification ; they were completely justified already. They did need prayer for their sanctification; for they were not completely sanctified.

(c) Sanctification is a thing that admits of growth ; else why should our Lord pray, " Sanctify them "? The doctrine of imputed sanctification is one that I can find nowhere in the Word of God. Christ's imputed righteousness I see clearly, but not an imputed holiness. Holiness is a thing imparted and inwrought, but not imputed.

(d) The word is the great instrument by which the Holy Ghost carries forward the work of inward sanctification. By bringing that Word to bear more forcibly on mind and will, and conscience, and affection, we make the character grow more holy. Sanctification from without by bodily austerities and asceticism, and a round of forms, ceremonies, and outward means, is a delusion. True sanctification begins from within. Here lies the immense importance of regularly reading the written Word, and hearing the preached Word. It surely, though insensibly, promotes our sanctification. Believers who neglect the Word will not grow in holiness and victory over sin.

Calvin remarks, " As the apostles were not destitute of grace, we ought to infer from Christ's words that sanctification is not instantly completed in us on the first day, but that we make progress in it through the whole course of our life."

Hutcheson remarks, " It is not enough that men have a begun work of sanctification in them, unless they grow up in it daily more and more. Christ prayeth for those who were already converted and sanctified."

Augustine thinks that " Thy Word " in this place means the Personal Word, Christ Himself. But in this opinion I can find no one holding with him, except Rupertus.

18 —[*As thou hast sent Me, etc.*] The connection between this verse and the preceding one seems to me to be this : " I ask for the increased sanctification of my disciples, because of the position they have to occupy on earth. Just as Thou didst send Me to be Thy Messenger to this sinful world, so have I now sent them to be my messengers to the world. It is therefore of the utmost importance that they should be holy—the holy messengers of a holy Master,—and so stop the mouths of their accusers." Believers are Christ's witnesses, and the character of a witness should be spotless and blameless. For this reason our Lord specially prays that His disciples may be " sanctified."

19 —[*And for their sakes I sanctify myself.*] This is a rather hard passage. In one sense, of course, our Lord needed no sanctification. He was always perfectly holy and without sin.

I believe, with Chrysostom, the meaning must be, " I consecrate myself, and offer myself up as a sacrifice and a priest, for one special reason, to say nothing of others : in order that these my disciples may be sanctified by the truth, and made a holy people."—Is it not as good as saying, " The sanctification no less than the justification of my people is the end of my sacrifice ? I want to have a people who are sanctified as well as justified. So much importance do I attach to this that this is one principal reason why I now offer myself to die as a sacrifice."—The same idea seems to lie in the text : " He gave Himself for us that He might redeem us from all iniquity, and purify unto himself a peculiar people." And again : " Christ loved the Church, and gave Himself for it, that He might sanctify it." (Titus ii. 14 ; Eph. v. 26 ; 1 Pet. ii. 24.)

Melancthon remarks, " The word ' I sanctify myself,' in this place, without doubt, is taken from priests and victims."

20 —[*Neither pray I for these alone, etc.*] In this and the three following verses our Lord proceeds to name another thing that He prays for His people. He asks that they may be " one." He had already named this on behalf of the eleven Apostles. But He takes occasion now to enlarge the prayer, and to include others beside the eleven,—the whole company of future believers. " I now pray also for all who shall believe on Me through the preaching of my disciples in all future time, and not for my eleven apostles only." All believers needed preservation and sanctification in every age ; but none so much as the eleven, because they were the first to attack the world and bear the brunt of the battle. In some respects it was more easy to be " one " at the first beginnings of the Church, and harder to be kept and " sanctified." As the Church grew, it would be more difficult to keep unity.

Let us mark how wide was the scope of our Lord's intercessory prayer. He prayed not only for present, but for future believers. So should it be with our prayers. We may look forward and pray for believers yet to be born, though we may not look back and pray for believers who are dead.

George Newton observes what an encouragement it should be to us in praying for others, for a child or a friend, to remember that perhaps Christ is asking him or her of God too. He here prays for those who did not yet believe, but were to believe one day.

Let us mark how the " word " preached is mentioned as the means of making men believe. Faith cometh by hearing. The Church which places Sacraments above the preaching of the Word, will have no blessing of God, because it rejects God's order.

Hengstenberg thinks that the " word " here must include the writings of the Apostles as well as their sermons.

21 —[*That they all...one in us.*] The meaning of this sentence I take to be, " I pray that both these my disciples, and those who hereafter shall become my disciples, may all be of one mind, one doctrine, one opinion, one heart, and one practice, closely united and joined together, even as Thou, Father, and I are of one mind and one will, in consequence of that ineffable union whereby Thou art in Me and I in Thee."

Here, as in verse 11, we must carefully remember that the unity between the Father and the Son is one which the unity of believers cannot literally attain to. They must however imitate it.

The true secret of the unity of believers lies in the expression, " one in us." They can only be thoroughly " one " by being joined at the same time to one Father and to one Saviour. Then they will be one with one another.

Ferus thinks that one thing in our Lord's mind in this sentence was the union of Jew and Gentile into one Church, and the removal of the " wall of partition."

[*That the world...believe...sent Me.*] Here our Lord brings in one important reason why He prays for His people to be " one." It will help to make the world believe His Divine mission. " When the world sees my people not quarrelling, not divided, but one in judgment, heart, and life, then the world will begin to believe that the Saviour, who has such a people, must really be a Saviour sent from God."

Let us carefully note how well our Lord foresaw the effect which the lives, ways, and opinions of professing Christians have on the world around them. The want of unity, and consequent strife among English Christians in the last 300 years, has been a miserable example of the enormous damage that believers may do their Master's cause by neglecting this subject. " How much," says George Newton, " Our blessed Saviour and His Gospel suffer by the hot contentions of those who call themselves saints."

22 —[*And the glory, etc., etc.*] In this verse our Lord repeats His deep desire for the unity of His people. He declares, " that in order that they may be one, He has given them the glory which the Father gave Him." This is a very difficult expression, and one which seems to puzzle all commentators. The whole question is, what did our Lord mean by " the glory " which He gave.

(*a*) Some, as Calvin, think that " glory " means the image and likeness of God, by which the disciples were renewed. (2 Cor. iii. 18.)

(*b*) Some, as Bengel, think that " glory " means that insensible power, influence, and authority, which accompanied all our Lord did and said during His earthly ministry. Thus Moses had

" glory " in his countenance when coming down from the mount.
(2 Cor. iii. 7.) This same power and influence Christ gave to
the Apostles. (See Acts iv. 33.)

(c) Some, as Zwingle, Brentius, Gualter, and Pearce, think
that " glory " means the power of working miracles, which was
the special and peculiar glory of our Lord while He was on
earth. Thus, we read, " Christ was raised from the dead by
the glory of the Father." (Rom. vi. 4.)

(d) Some, as Augustine, Ecolampadius, Bullinger, and Manton, think that " glory " means the heavenly glory and immor-
tality which our Lord promised to His disciples,—a glory which
they should have after faithfully serving Him on earth. (Rom.
viii. 18.)

(e) Toletus makes the strange suggestion, that the " glory "
means that which is communicated to us in the Lord's Supper !
Burgon seems to take the same view.

(f) Stier and Hengstenberg hold that the " glory " means
unity of mind and heart.

(g) Some, as Gregory Nyssen, Ammonius, Theophylact, and
Bucer, think that " glory " means the Holy Ghost, who is else
where called " the Spirit of glory." (1 Pet. iv. 14.)

The question will probably never be settled. If I must give
an opinion, I prefer the last view to any other. It suits the
end of the verse better than any other. Nothing was so likely
to make the disciples " one " as the gift of the Holy Ghost.

23 —[*I in them and Thou in Me, etc.*] In this verse our Lord sim-
plifies His declarations about unity, and expands them more
fully, in order to show emphatically how great importance He
attached to unity. I take the meaning to be something of this
kind : " I pray that my disciples may be so closely united—I
dwelling in them, and Thou dwelling in Me,—that they may be
compacted and perfected into one body,—having one mind, one
will, one heart, and one judgment, though having many members,—and that then the world, seeing this unity, may be
obliged to confess that Thou didst send Me to be the Messiah,
and that Thou lovest my people even as Thou lovest Me."

In leaving this deep and difficult passage about unity, it is
well to remember that the Church, whose unity the Lord desires and prays for, is not any particular or visible Church, but
the Church which is His Body, the Church of the elect, the
Church which is made up of true believers and saints alone.

Moreover, the unity which our Lord prays for is not unity of
forms, discipline, government, and the like ; but unity of heart,
and will, and doctrine, and practice. Those who make uniformity the chief subject of this part of Christ's prayer, entirely miss the mark. There may be uniformity without unity, as
in many visible Churches on earth now. There may be unity

without uniformity, as between godly Episcopalians and godly Presbyterians. Uniformity no doubt may be a great help to unity, but it is not unity itself.

The unity which our Lord prays about here is that true, substantial, spiritual, internal, heart unity, which undoubtedly exists among all members of Christ of every Church and denomination. It is the unity which results from one Holy Ghost having made the members of Christ what they are. It is unity which makes them feel more of one mind with one another than with mere professors of their own party. It is unity which is the truest freemasonry on earth. It is unity which shakes the world, and obliges it to confess the truth of Christianity.—For the continued maintenance of this unity, and an increase of it, our Lord seems to me in this prayer specially to pray. And we need not wonder. The divisions of mere worldly professors are of little moment. The divisions of real true believers are the greatest possible injury to the cause of the Gospel. If all believers at this moment were of one mind, and would work together, they might soon turn the world upside down. No wonder the Lord prayed for unity.

24 –[*Father, I will...my glory...given Me.*] In this verse our Lord names the fourth and last thing which He desires for His disciples in His prayer. After preservation, sanctification, and unity, comes participation of His glory. He asks that they may be " with Him " in the glory yet to be revealed, and " behold," share, and take part in it.

" I will " is a remarkable phrase, though it must not be pressed and strained too far. (See Mark vi. 25 ; x. 35.) The daughter of Herodias asking the head of John the Baptist, said, " I will that thou give me." It may be nothing more than the expression of a strong " wish." Yet it is the wish of Him who is one with the Father, and only wills what the Father wills. It is probably used to assure the mind of the disciples. " I will," and it will be done.

Hutcheson says, " ' I will ' doth not import any imperious commanding way, repugnant to His former way of humble supplication ; but it only imports that in this His supplication, He was making His last will and Testament, and leaving His legacies, which He was sure would be effectual, being purchased by His merits, and prosecuted by His affectionate and earnest requests and intercessions."

Traill remarks, " Christians, behold the amazing difference betwixt Christ's way of praying against His own hell (if I may so call it) and His praying for our heaven ! When praying for Himself, it is, ' Father, if it be Thy will, let this cup pass from Me.' But when Christ is praying for His people's heaven, it is, ' Father, *I will* that they may be with Me.' "

Stier maintains that " I will " " is no other than a testament-
ary word of the Son, who in the unity of the Father, is appointing what He *wills*, at the second limit of the prayer where
petition ceases."

Alford says " this is an expression of will founded on acknowledged right."

The expression, " Be with Me where I am," is one of those
deeply interesting phrases which show the nature of the future dwelling-place of believers. Wherever it may be, whether before or after the resurrection, it will be in the company
of Christ. It is like " with Me in Paradise," " depart and be
with Christ," and " forever with the Lord." (Luke xxiii. 43 ;
Phil. i. 23 ; 1 Thess. iv. 17.) The full nature of the future state
is wisely hidden from us. It is enough for believers to know
that they will be " with Christ." It is company, and not place,
which makes up happiness.

Traill remarks, " Heaven consists in the perfect immediate
presence of Christ. Perfect presence is, when all on both
sides is present ; all of Christ, and all of the Christian. But
now all of Christ is not with us, and all of us is not with Him.
On His part we have Christ's Spirit, word, and grace. On our
part there is present with Him our hearts, and the workings of
our faith and love and desire towards Him. But the presence
is imperfect, and mixed with much distance and absence."

The expression, " Behold my glory," of course must not be
confined to the idea of " looking on as spectators." It includes
participation, sharing, and common enjoyment. (Compare
John iii. 3—36 ; viii. 51 ; Rev. xviii. 7.)

The expression, " Which Thou hast given Me," seems to
point to that special glory which the Father, in everlasting
covenant, has appointed for Christ as the reward of the work
of redemption. (Philip. ii. 9.)

[*For Thou lovedst Me...foundation...world.*] This sentence
seems specially inserted in order to show that the glory of
Christ in the next world is a glory which had been prepared
from all eternity, before time began, and before the creation of
man, and that it was not only something which, like Moses or
John the Baptist, He had obtained by His faithfulness on
earth ; but something which He had, as the eternal Son of the
eternal Father, from everlasting. " Thou lovedst Me, and did
assign Me this glory long before this world was made," that is,
from all eternity. This is a very deep saying, and contains
things far above our full comprehension.

25 —[*O righteous Father, etc.*] In this verse our Lord begins the
final winding up of His wonderful prayer. He does it by declaring the position of things in which He was about to leave
the world and His disciples. I take the meaning to be this : " I

come to Thee from a world which knows Thee not, and has refused to know Thee throughout my ministry.   But in the
midst of this world I have known Thee and steadily adhered
to Thee.   And these my disciples have acknowledged and confessed that Thou didst send Me to be the Messiah."

It is not clear why our Lord uses the expression, " Righteous
Father."   It is one which stands alone.   It may possibly be
intended to bring out in strong contrast the wickedness of a
world which " knew not the Word," when the Word was in it
(see John i. 10), and the justice of God in punishing this world,
which refused to know Christ while the disciples received
Him.

The expression, " I have known Thee," seems to point to the
veil of humiliation which covered our Lord during the whole
period of His incarnation.   " Even then," He seems to say, " I
never ceased to know and honor Thee."

The high testimony borne to the disciples once more deserves
notice.   With all their infirmity, " they have KNOWN my Divine mission."

26 —[*And I have declared...declare it.*]   In this sentence our Lord
briefly sums up what He had done, and was still doing for the
disciples : " I have made known to them Thy name and character and attributes, as the sender of salvation to a lost world,
and will continue to declare it after my ascension, by the Holy
Spirit."

Here, as elsewhere, our Lord again declares that to make
known the Father was one great object of His ministry.

The expression, " I will declare it," says George Newton, is
a proof that " Jesus Christ will be continually making further
declarations of His Father's name to other nations and other
persons, to the end of the world.   He will be ever teaching
new scholars to spell it and understand it, in every generation,
while the world endureth."

[*That...in them...I in them.*]   Our Lord ends His prayer by
expressing His wish that the Father's love may dwell in the
hearts of His disciples, and that He Himself may dwell in their
hearts.   " My great desire is that they may know and feel the
love wherewith Thou dost love Me, and that I may ever dwell
in their hearts by faith."

Let us not forget that one great wish of St. Paul in his Epistle to the Ephesians, was that " Christ might dwell in their
hearts by faith." (Eph. iii. 15.)   He also tells the Romans
" The love of God is shed abroad in our hearts." (Rom. v. 5.)

The expression, " I will declare my love," is a difficult one.
It can only mean, " I will declare it personally during the interval between my resurrection and my ascension," or " I will
continue to declare it by my Spirit's continual teaching after

I leave the world." The latter seems the more probable meaning.

The expression, " Thy love may be in them," is another grave difficulty. It must either be " That Thy love, the same love wherewith Thou lovest Me, may be directed on and toward them ; " or else, " That they may feel in their own hearts a sense of that same love toward them wherewith Thou lovest Me." I prefer the latter sense.

George Newton remarks on this verse, " If Christ is in you, let me give you this caution : let Him live quiet in your hearts. Do not molest Him and disturb Him ; do not make Him vex and fret. Let it not be a penance to Him to continue in you. But labor every way to please Him, and give Him satisfaction and content, that so the house He hath chosen may not be dark and doleful, but delightful to Him."

Manton remarks, " If an earthly King lie but one night in a house, what care there is taken that nothing be offensive to him, and that all be neat and sweet and clean. How much more careful ought you to be to keep your hearts clean, to perform service acceptable to Him, to be in the exercise of faith, love, and other graces, that so you may entertain, as you ought, your heavenly King, who comes to take up His continual abode in your hearts."

We may well feel humbled, as we leave this chapter, when we think of our ignorance of the true meaning of many of its phrases. How much of our exposition is nothing better than feeble conjecture ! We seem only to scratch the surface of the field. Let us only remember that the four things prayed for by our Lord are things that every Christian should daily desire, —preservation, sanctification, unity, and final glory in Christ's company.

George Newton closes his Exposition of the whole chapter with these touching words :—" How earnest and importunate is Christ with God the Father, that we may be one here, and that we may be in one place hereafter ! Oh, let us search into the heart of Jesus Christ, laid open to us in this abridgment of His intercession for us, that we may know it and the workings of it more and more, until at length the precious prayer comes to its full effect, and we be taken up to be for ever with the Lord, and where He is there we may be also ! "

JOHN XVIII 1—11

1 When Jesus had spoken these words, he went forth with his disciples over the brook Cedron, where was a garden, into the which he entered, and his disciples.

2 And Judas also, which betrayed him, knew the place : for Jesus ofttimes resorted thither with his disciples.

3 Judas then, having received a

band *of men* and officers from the chief priests and Pharisees, cometh thither with lanterns and torches and weapons.

4 Jesus therefore, knowing all things that should come upon him, went forth, and said unto them, Whom seek ye?

5 They answered him, Jesus of Nazareth. Jesus said unto them, I am *he.* And Judas also, which betrayed him, stood with them.

6 As soon then as he had said unto them, I am *he,* they went backward, and fell to the ground.

7 Then asked he them again, Whom seek ye? And they said, Jesus of Nazareth.

8 Jesus answered, I have told you that I am *he ;* if therefore ye seek me, let these go their way:

9 That the saying might be fulfilled which he spake, Of them which thou gavest me have I lost none.

10 Then Simon Peter having a sword drew it, and smote the high priest's servant, and cut off his right ear. The servant's name was Malchus.

11 Then said Jesus unto Peter, Put up thy sword into the sheath: the cup which my Father hath given me, shall I not drink it?

THESE verses begin St. John's account of Christ's sufferings and crucifixion. We now enter on the closing scene of our Lord's ministry, and pass at once from His intercession to His sacrifice. We shall find that, like the other Gospel-writers, the beloved disciple enters fully into the story of the cross. But we shall also find, if we read carefully, that he mentions several interesting points in the story, which Matthew, Mark, and Luke, for some wise reasons, have passed over.

We should notice, first, in these verses, *the exceeding hardness of heart to which a backsliding professor may attain.* We are told that Judas, one of the twelve Apostles, became guide to them that took Jesus. We are told that he used his knowledge of the place of our Lord's retirement, in order to bring His deadly enemies upon Him; and we are told that when the band of men and officers approached his Master, in order to make Him prisoner, Judas "stood with them."—Yet this was a man who for three years had been a constant companion of Christ, had seen His miracles, had heard His sermons, had enjoyed the benefit of His private instruction, had professed himself a believer, had even worked and preached in Christ's name!—"Lord," we may well say, "what is man?" From the highest degree of privilege down to the lowest depth of sin, there is but a succession of steps. Privileges misused seem to paralyze the conscience. The same fire that melts wax, will harden clay.

Let us beware of resting our hopes of salvation on religious knowledge, however great, or religious advantages, however many. We may know all doctrinal truth and be able to teach others, and yet prove rotten at heart, and go down to the pit with Judas. We may bask in the full sunshine of spiritual privileges, and hear the best of Christian teaching, and yet bear no fruit to God's glory, and be found withered branches of the vine, only fit to be burned. "Let him that thinketh he standeth, take heed lest he fall." (1 Cor. x. 12.) Above all, let us beware of cherishing within our hearts any secret besetting sin, such as love of money or love of the world. One faulty link in a chain-cable may cause a shipwreck. One little leak may sink a ship. One allowed and unmortified sin may ruin a professing Christian. Let him that is tempted to be a careless man in his religious life, consider these things, and take care. Let him remember Judas Iscariot. His history is meant to be a lesson.

We should notice, secondly, in these verses, *the entire voluntariness of Christ's sufferings*. We are told that the first time that our Lord said to the soldiers, "I am He, they went backward, and fell to the ground." A secret invisible power, no doubt, accompanied the words. In no other way can we account for a band of hardy Roman soldiers falling prostrate before a single unarmed man. The same miraculous influence which tied the priests and Pharisees powerless at the triumphant entry into Jerusalem,—which stopped all opposition when the temple was purged of buyers and sellers,—that same mysterious influence was present now. A real miracle was wrought, though few had eyes to see it. At the moment when our Lord seemed weak, He showed that He was strong.

Let us carefully remember that our blessed Lord suffered and died of His own free will. He did not die because He could not help it; He did not suffer because He could not escape. All the soldiers of Pilate's army could not have taken Him, if He had not been willing to be taken. They could not have hurt a hair of His head, if He had not given them permission. But here, as in all His earthly ministry, Jesus was a willing sufferer. He had set His heart on accomplishing our redemption. He loved us, and gave Himself for us, cheerfully, willingly, gladly, in order to make atonement for our sins. It was "the joy set before Him" which made Him endure the cross, and despise the shame, and yield Himself up without reluctance into the hands of His enemies. Let this thought abide in our hearts, and refresh our souls. We have a Saviour who was far more willing to save us than we are willing to be saved. If we are not saved, the fault is all our own. Christ is just as willing to receive and pardon, as He was willing to be taken prisoner, to bleed, and to die.

We should notice, thirdly, in these verses, *our Lord's tender care for His disciples' safety.* Even at this critical moment, when His own unspeakable sufferings were about to begin, He did not forget the little band of believers who stood around Him. He remembered their weakness. He knew how little fit they were to go into the fiery furnace of the High Priest's Palace, and Pilate's judgment-hall. He mercifully makes for them a way of escape.—"If ye seek Me, let these go their way."—It seems most probable that here also a miraculous influence accompanied his words. At any rate, not a hair of the disciples' heads was touched. While the

Shepherd was taken, the sheep were allowed to flee away unharmed.

We need not hesitate to see in this incident an instructive type of all our Saviour's dealings with His people even at this day. He will not suffer them "to be tempted above that which they are able to bear." He will hold the winds and storms in His hands, and not allow believers, however sifted and buffeted, to be utterly destroyed. He watches tenderly over every one of His children, and, like a wise physician, measures out the right quantity of their trials with unerring skill. "They shall never perish, neither shall any one pluck them out of His hand." (John x. 28.) For ever let us lean our souls on this precious truth. In the darkest hour the eye of the Lord Jesus is upon us, and our final safety is sure.

We should notice, lastly, in these verses, *our Lord's perfect submission to his Father's will.* Once, in another place, we find Him saying, "If it be possible, let this cup pass from Me : nevertheless, not as I will, but as Thou wilt." Again, in another place, we find Him saying, "If this cup may not pass away from Me except I drink it, Thy will be done." Here, however, we find even a higher pitch of cheerful acquiescence : "The cup that my Father hath given Me, shall I not drink it? " (Matt. xxvi. 39—42.)

Let us see in this blessed frame of mind, a pattern for all who profess and call themselves Christians. Far as we may come short of the Master's standard, let this be the mark at which we continually aim. Determination to have our own way, and do only what we like, is one great source of unhappiness in the world. The habit of laying all our matters before God in prayer, and asking Him to choose our portion, is one chief secret of peace. He is the truly wise man who has learned to say at every stage of his journey, " Give me what thou wilt, place me where Thou wilt, do with me as Thou wilt ; but not my will, but Thine be done." This is the man who has the mind of Christ. By self-will Adam and Eve fell, and brought sin and misery into the world. Entire submission of will to the will of God is the best preparation for that heaven where God will be all.

NOTES   JOHN XVIII 1—11

1 —[*When Jesus...these words.*] This would have been more literally rendered, " Jesus having said these things." The " things " referred to, seem to me to include the discourse of the fifteenth and sixteenth chapters, as well as the prayer of the seventeenth.

Henry observes, " the office of the priest was to teach and pray and offer sacrifice. Christ, after teaching and praying, applies Himself to make atonement. He had said all He had to say as a prophet. He now addresses Himself to His work as priest."

[*He went forth...disciples.*] The question arises, " From what place did He go forth ? " and it receives very different answers.

Many, as Cyril, Ecolampadius, Maldonatus, Doddridge, and Ellicott, think that it only means He went forth from the room where He had held the Lord's Supper and delivered His part ing address and prayer. The advocates of this view hold that our Lord did not actually go out of the room, when He said, at the end of the fourteenth chapter, " Arise, let us go hence," and that He probably continued His discourse, and prayed standing. This, to say the least, seems a very unnatural view.

Some, as Burgon, think that our Lord spoke the latter part of His address and prayer within the precincts of the temple, and that the words before us mean that He moved away from the temple. This, however seems hardly probable. It was night, we know. There is no evidence that gatherings of people by night were held within the temple precincts.

The most probable view, in my opinion, seems to be that Jesus went forth out of the city, after concluding His discourse and prayer, and that after leaving the room where our Lord's Supper was held, at the end of the fourteenth chapter, He spoke and prayed near the gates, or within the city walls. He left the room when He said, " Arise, let us go hence." Then having reached some quiet spot near the walls, He continued His discourse and prayed. Then after that he went out of the city. This seems to me the more natural account.

[*Over the brook Cedron.*] The Cedron here mentioned, is the same as the Kidron named more than once in the Old Testament. The word " brook " means, literally, a " winter torrent," and this, according to all travellers, is precisely what the Kidron is. Excepting in winter, or after rains, it is merely the dry bed of a water-course. It lies on the east side of Jerusalem, between the city and the Mount of Olives. It is the same Kidron which David passed over weeping, when obliged to flee from Jerusalem by the rebellion of Absalom. (2 Sam. xv. 23.) It is the same Kidron by the side of which Asa burnt the idol of his mother Maachah (2 Chron. xv. 16), and into which Josiah cast the dust of the idolatrous altars which he destroyed. (2 Kings xxiii. 12.)

Lampe says that the way by which our Lord left the city, was the way by which the scape-goat, Azazel, was annually sent out into the wilderness on the great day of atonement.

Bishop Andrews says that " the first breach made by the Romans, when Titus took Jerusalem, was at the brook Cedron, where they took Christ."

[*Where was a garden...disciples.*] There can be little doubt that this garden is the same as the " place called Gethsemane." What kind of a garden it was we know not, unless a garden of olive trees. Probably it was neither a garden of flowers nor of herbs, but simply a place enclosed, where trees were sheltered and encouraged to grow, in order to provide a quiet shady retirement away from the bustle of the city. Whether it was a public garden, or private property, we know not. Hengstenberg conjectures that " the owner of the place must have stood in some special relation to Jesus," and that this accounts for His frequent and free resort to the place. He also conjectures that the " young man " named in Mark xiv. 51, 52, must have belonged to the family of the owner. This however, is pure conjecture.

Almost all commentators notice the curious fact that the fall of Adam and Eve took place in a garden, and Christ's passion also began in a garden, and the sepulchre where Christ was laid was in a garden, and the place where He was crucified was in a garden. (John xix. 41.)

Augustine remarks, " It was fitting that the blood of the Physician should there be poured out, where the disease of the sick man first commenced."

Gualter remarks that the first Adam had everything that was pleasant in the Garden of Eden, and yet fell. The second Adam had everything that was painful and trying in the Garden of Gethsemane, but was a glorious conqueror.

The agony in Gethsemane, we may observe, is entirely passed over by John in His Gospel; and for wise reasons, we need not doubt. But it is evident that it took place at this point of the narrative. The order of things is : first, the Lord's Supper,—then the long discourse recorded by John alone,—then the marvellous prayer,—then the going over Cedron into the garden,—then the agony,—and then the arrival of Judas and the capture of our Lord. It is plain therefore that there is a pause in the narrative of John's Gospel at this point, and that we must allow a little space of time for the agony, after our Lord " went out " of the city and crossed the Cedron. This would make the arrival of Judas and the soldiers far on in the night.

Lightfoot mentions a curious fact which he draws from a Jewish writer,—that the blood from the sacrifices in the temple ran down a drain into the brook Kidron, and was then sold to the gardeners for the purpose of dressing their gardens. The blood having been consecrated, could not be put to common uses without sin, and therefore the gardeners paid for it as much as would buy a trespass offering. This is curious, if true.

2 —[*And Judas also, etc.*] This verse is one of John's peculiar explanatory comments. He tells us that this garden was a place where our Lord and His disciples were in the habit of assembling together, when they went up to Jerusalem at the great Jewish feasts. At such seasons the crowd of worshippers was very great ; and many had to content themselves with such shelter as they could find under trees, or rocks, in the open air. This is what Luke means when he says, "At night He went out and abode in the mount that is called the Mount of Olives." (Luke xxi. 37.) Excepting at the celebration of the first Lord's Supper, we have no mention of our Lord ever being in any *house* in Jerusalem.

Chrysostom remarks, " It is evident from this that Jesus generally passed the night out of doors."

Bucer thinks that Judas specially knew the place where our Lord used to pray. Our Lord's habits of prayer were as well known as those of Daniel.

The fact that the traitor Judas " knew the place," while our Lord deliberately went there, shows three things. One is, that our Lord went to His death willingly and voluntarily ; He went to the " garden," knowing well that Judas was acquainted with the place.—Another thing is, that our Lord was in the habit of going to this garden so " often," that Judas felt sure He would be found there.—Another thing is, that the heart of Judas must have been desperately hard, when, after so many seasons of spiritual refreshment as he must have seen in this garden, he could use his knowledge for the purpose of betraying his Master. He "knew the place," because he had often heard his Master teaching and praying there. He knew it from spiritual associations, and yet turned his knowledge to wicked ends !

May we not learn from this verse that there is nothing to be ashamed of, nothing wrong, in loving one place more than another, and choosing one place more than another, for communion with God? Even our blessed Lord had one special place, near Jerusalem, more than other places, to which He often resorted. The common idea of some, that it matters not where or in what place we worship, and that it is unspiritual and wrong to care for one seat in church more than another, can hardly be reconciled with this verse.

The Greek words rendered " resorted thither," are literally " were gathered together there."

2 —[*Judas then having received, etc.*] This verse begins John's circumstantial account of the taking and subsequent passion of our Lord Jesus Christ. A careful reader will not fail to observe that John entirely passes over several points in this history which are mentioned by the three other Gospel writers, and not least the bargaining of Judas with the priests to betray our Lord for money. But it is evident that John assumes that his readers were acquainted with the other three Gospels, and purposely dwells on points which they had not mentioned.

The expression "a band of men," can only mean " the detachment of Roman soldiers " which had been lent by Pilate to the priests for the occasion. Some think that it means literally " a cohort," which was the tenth part of a legion, and consisted of four or five hundred men. This, however, seems doubtful. Yet Matthew speaks of Judas coming, and " a great multitude with him." (Matt. xxvi. 47.)

The " officers " mean the Jewish servants of the priests and Pharisees, who accompanied the Roman soldiers. The party, therefore, which Judas led consisted of two distinct elements, —Romish soldiers detached from the garrison of Jerusalem, and Jewish servants got together by the leaders of the Jews. Gentiles and Jews were, therefore, equally concerned in the arrest. The number of the party was probably large, from the fear of an attempt at a rescue by the Galilean Jews, who were supposed to favor our Lord. They would be at Jerusalem in large numbers at the Passover, and after our Lord's recent triumphal entry into Jerusalem, the priests might well feel doubts whether they would allow Him to be made a prisoner without a struggle.

Chrysostom remarks that " these men had often, at other times, been sent to seize Him, but had not been able. Hence it is plain that at this time He voluntarily surrendered Himself."

The " lanterns and torches " at first sight may seem to have been needless, as the moon at Passover time was full. But they were doubtless intended to assist the party in searching for our Lord if he endeavored to hide Himself among the rocks and trees. And in a deep valley there would be many dark and shady places.

The " weapons " most probably apply to the Jewish servants of the priests. It is unreasonable to suppose that Roman soldiers would ever move without their arms. For fear of resistance the Jewish portion of the party took arms also.

.Burkitt remarks on the activity and energy of wicked men, " At the very time when Peter, James, and John were sleeping in the garden, Judas and his bloody followers were gathering, marching, and planning a murder."

The confidence of Judas that our Lord would be in the garden, shows plainly how familiar he was with our Lord's habits on the occasion of his visits to Jerusalem.

4 —[*Jesus...knowing...come upon Him.*] This sentence shows our Lord's perfect foreknowledge of everything that was about to happen to Him. Never was there a more willing, deliberate, and voluntary sufferer than our Lord. The words " things that should come " would be more literally rendered " the things coming," in the present tense.

The best of martyrs, like Ridley and Latimer, did not know for certain, up to the moment of their deaths, that something might not occur to alter the mind of their persecutors and save their lives. Our Lord knew perfectly well that His death was sure, by the determinate counsel and foreknowledge of God.

Ford quotes a saying of Pinart, that " what rendered Christ's sufferings most terrible was the perfect foreknowledge He had of the torments He should endure. From the first moment of His life He had present to His mind the scourge, the thorns, the cross, and the agonizing death which awaited Him. Saw He a lamb in the meadow or a victim in the temple, the sight reminded Him that He was the lamb of God, and that He was to be offered up a sacrifice."

[*Went forth.*] This must mean that our Lord came forward from that part of the garden where He was, and did not wait for the party of Judas to find Him. On the contrary he suddenly showed Himself, and met them face to face. The effect of this action alone must have been startling to the soldiers. They would feel at once that they had to do with no common person.

Henry remarks, " When the people would have forced Him to take a crown and wished to make Him a king he withdrew and hid Himself. (John vi. 15.) But when they came to force Him to His cross He offered Himself. He came to this world to suffer, and went to the other world to reign."

Lampe remarks that the first Adam hid himself in the garden. The second Adam went forth to meet His enemies. The first felt guilty, the second innocent.

[*And said... Whom seek ye ?*] Jesus Himself was the first to speak, and did not wait to be challenged or commanded to surrender. This sudden question no doubt would take the party of Judas by surprise, and prepare the way for the mighty miracle which followed. The soldiers must needs have felt, " this is not the language or manner of a malefactor or a guilty man."

5 —[*They answered...Jesus...Nazareth.*] This would be more literally rendered " Jesus the Nazarene." It is certainly hard to suppose that those who said this could have known that Jesus Himself was speaking to them. It looks as if they did not know our Lord by sight, or could not believe that the bold speaker before them could be the prisoner they came to apprehend. That many of the party did not know our Lord by sight, is clear from the fact mentioned by Matthew and Mark, that Judas had given them a sign : " Whomsoever I kiss, that same is He : hold Him fast." This sign, therefore, had not yet been given. Probably there was no time for it. The coming forward and question of our Lord had taken place so suddenly that they took the whole party by surprise.

Chrysostom, Cyril, Theophylact, Gualter, Brentius, Gerhard, and Ferus, think that our Lord miraculously blinded the eyes of the party, so that they did not recognize him, as Elisha blinded the Syrians. (2 Kings vi. 18.) They had lights, and they must have known his voice. But they seem to have been unable to know him. Musculus thinks they did not recognize Him, and thought Him a disciple.

[*Jesus saith...I am He.*] Our Lord here makes a plain, bold, full avowal that He is the very person whom they seek. It must have been a most startling announcement.

The words in the Greek are literally " I am." Some have thought that there was an intentional reference to the famous passage in Exodus, where the Lord says, " I AM hath sent you." (Exodus iii. 14), to which also our Lord certainly did refer in John viii. 58. But it seems very doubtful whether such a reference would have been used in speaking to such a party as those who came to seize our Lord.

[*And Judas...stood with them.*] It is not quite clear why this little sentence is put in here. It may be meant to show the desperate wickedness of Judas. He stood side by side with the enemies of Jesus.—It may be meant to show that even Judas himself was staggered and confounded by our Lord's boldness, and did not give his companions the promised sign, not recognizing him any more than the others. The false apostle stood there like one struck dumb.—It may be meant to show that Judas himself was a witness and a subject of one of the last great miracles our Lord wrought. He himself was once more to feel, and experience proof, that the Master he betrayed had divine power. There seems to me much probability in this last idea.

6 —[*As soon then as He had said, etc.*] I cannot doubt that the thing here related was a great miracle. I have not the slightest sympathy with Alford and others, who try to explain it away partially, by reminding us of the awe and reverence which a great and good man sometimes inspires in inferior minds. Such an explanation will never account for the fact here recorded,—that the band of Roman soldiers and the servants of the priests, in fact the whole body of armed men who came to seize on our Lord, "went backward and fell on the earth," on hearing our Lord say, " I am He." The Roman soldiers, especially, knew nothing about our Lord, and had no cause to fear Him. The only reasonable account of the event is that it was a miracle. It was an exercise for the last time of that same Divine power by which our Lord calmed the waves, stilled the winds, cast out devils, healed the sick, and raised the dead. And it was a miracle purposely wrought at this juncture, in order to show the disciples and their enemies that our Lord was not taken because He could not help it, or crucified because He could not prevent it ; but because He was willing to suffer and die for sinners. He came to be a willing sufferer for our sins, that the Scriptures might be fulfilled. (Comp. Matt. xxvi. 53.) The effect of the miraculous influence put forth by our Lord, seems to have been that the party who came to seize Him were for a little time struck down to the ground, like men struck down, but not killed, by lightning, and rendered so helpless that our Lord and His disciples might easily have escaped. How long they lay on the ground we are not told, but there certainly seems to be some pause at the end of the verse. It seems clear to me that the miracle saved the disciples from being taken prisoners, and so far awed the party of Judas that they were satisfied to seize our Lord only, and either intentionally let the eleven go, or in their fear of some further display of miraculous power, neglected them, and gave them time to escape. That it also made the whole party of Judas without excuse, is equally clear. They could never say they had no evidence of our Lord's divine power. They had felt it in their own persons.

Burgon sees in this incident something which recalls to mind the prophetic words of the Psalmist : " When the wicked, even mine enemies and my foes, came upon me to eat up my flesh, they stumbled and fell." (Psal. xxvii. 2.)

Augustine remarks, " What shall He do when He comes to judge, who did this when about to be judged ? What shall be His might when He comes to reign, who had this might when He was at the point to die ? "

The effort of some to lessen the miraculous character of this circumstance, by quoting such a case as the classical story of the soldier being daunted by the appearance of the Roman General Caius Marius, is weak and evasive. A whole cohort of Roman soldiers would not fall down without miraculous interference. If not a miracle, the event is utterly inexplicable and contrary to experience.

7 —[*Then asked He them again, etc.*] Our Lord repeats His question, as if to test the effect of the miraculous exhibition of power which He had just given to His enemies. But they were hardened, like Pharaoh and the Egyptians under the miraculous plagues of Egypt. As soon as they rose from the ground, they proved, that though frightened, they were not turned from their purpose. They still seek to take Jesus of Nazareth.

8 —[*Jesus answered...I am He.*] The dignity and calmness of our Lord at this point are very striking. Knowing full well all the insults and barbarous usage about to begin in a few minutes, He repeats His declaration. " I am He whom you seek. Behold Me : here I am, ready to surrender myself into your hands."

[*If therefore...Me...let them...way.*] The tender thoughtfulness of our Lord for His weak disciples is strikingly shown in this sentence. Even at this trying moment He thought more of others than of Himself. " If I alone am the person you seek to make prisoner, if your commission is to seize Me only, then let these my followers go away, and do not harm them." Once more, we need not doubt that the miraculous power accompanied these words, and that insensibly a restraint was laid upon our Lord's enemies, so that they felt obliged to let the disciples escape.

The tender sympathy and consideration of our great High Priest for His people come out very beautifully in this place, and would doubtless be remembered by the eleven long afterwards. They would remember that the very last thought of their Master, before He was made a prisoner, was for them and their safety.

Christ's protecting power over all His believing people is plainly taught in this passage.

Jansenius remarks, that to this saying we may attribute the safety of Peter, though he smote with the sword and got inside the high priest's palace, and of John, though he stood by the cross.

Besser quotes a saying of Luther, that this was as great a miracle as that of casting the party to the ground. To tie the hands of the party of Judas and prevent them touching His disciples, was a mighty exercise of Divine power.

9 —[*That the saying might be fulfilled, etc.*] In this verse we have one of those parenthetical comments or explanations

which are so often found in John's Gospel. He reminds us
that our Lord's interference to secure the safety of His disciples at this crisis was a fulfilment in fact of His expression in
prayer, " none of them is lost."

Some persons see a difficulty here, and object that in the
prayer our Lord speaks of eternal salvation, while here He is
only speaking of temporal safety. Yet there seems no solid
ground for the objection. Our Lord's preservation of His disciples included the means as well as the end. One means of
preserving them from making shipwreck of the faith altogether,
was to keep them from being tempted above what they could
bear. Our Lord knew that they would be so tempted, and that
their souls were not strong enough to bear the trial. If they
had been taken prisoners and brought before Caiaphas and
Pilate, with Himself, their faith would have failed entirely.
He therefore provides for their escape, and overrules the plans
of His enemies, so that the eleven were " let go." And thus
He literally carried out what he had mentioned in prayer. He
prevented any of them being lost. They would have been lost
so far as man's eye can judge, if He had not provided a way of
escape, and prevented them being tempted beyond their strength.
The care of Jesus over His people provides the means of perseverance and continuance in the faith, as well as the great end
of eternal salvation.

Chrysostom remarks, " By loss He doth not here mean temporal death, but eternal.

Calvin remarks, " The Evangelist does not speak merely of
their bodily life, but means that Christ, sparing them for a
time, provided for their eternal salvation. Consider how great
their weakness was. What do we think they would have done
alone, if brought to the test? Christ did not choose they should
be tried beyond the strength He had given, and rescued them
from eternal destruction."

It seems to me most probable that at this point of the history
the " kiss " of Judas and His " Hail Master " come in. At any
rate it is difficult to suppose that Judas could have kissed our
Lord, when he first " went forth," and surprised the band by
meeting them. There does not seem time for the salutation,
nor does it seem probable that Judas would first kiss our Lord
and then fall to the ground. Nor does the repeated answer of
the band to the question " Whom seek ye ? " give the idea that
they had as yet recognized our Lord, or had any sign from
Judas. I give this as my own conjecture, and admit that the
matter is doubtful. But I must think that as soon as the band
of soldiers recovered their presence of mind, Judas came forward and kissed our Lord, and then the capture took place.
This is the order of events maintained by Chrysostom, Cyril,
Theophylact, Gerhard, Jansenius, Lightfoot, Stier, and Alford.

10 —[*Then Simon Peter having a sword, etc.*] The event here

mentioned is recorded by all the four Gospel-writers, but John alone gives the name of Peter as the striker, and of Malchus as the person struck. The reason commonly assigned for this is probably correct. John's Gospel was written long after the other three, when Peter and Malchus were both dead, and their names could, therefore, be safely mentioned.

Peter's impetuous temperament comes out in the action before us. Impulsive, earnest, zealous, and inconsiderate of consequences, he acted hastily, and his zeal soon cooled down and was changed into fear. It is not those who are for a time most demonstrative and fervent, whose religion is deepest. John never smote with the sword ; but John never denied his Lord, and was at the foot of the cross when Christ died.

The use of the article " the" before " servant " would seem to indicate that Malchus was some person well known as an attendant of Caiaphas.

Whether the ear was cut off entirely, or only so cut as to hang down by the skin, may be left to conjecture. In any case we know that it gave occasion for the last miracle of bodily cure which our Lord ever wrought. Luke tells us that He " touched " the ear, and it was instantaneously healed. To the very end of His ministry our Lord did good to His enemies, and gave proof of His divine power. But His hardened enemies gave no heed. Miracles alone convert no one. As in the case of Pharaoh, they only seem to make some men harder and more wicked.

We cannot doubt that Peter meant to kill Malchus with this blow, which was probably aimed at his head. His own agitation probably, and the special interposition of God, alone prevented him taking away the life of another, and endangering his own life and that of his fellow-disciples. What might have happened if Malchus had been killed, no one can tell.

Musculus remarks how entirely Peter seems to have forgotten all His Master's frequent predictions that He would be delivered to the Gentiles and be condemned to death, and acts as if he could prevent what was coming. It was clearly an impulsive act, done without reflection. Zeal not according to knowledge often drives a man into foolish actions, and makes work for repentance.

11 —[*Then said Jesus...the sheath.*] This was the language of firm and decided rebuke. It was meant to teach Peter, and all Christians in every age, that the Gospel is not to be propagated or maintained by carnal weapons, or by smiting and violence. Matthew adds the solemn words "All they that take the sword shall perish with the sword." How needful the rebuke, and how true the comment, have often been proved by the history of the Church of Christ. The appeal to the sword can rarely be justified, and has often recoiled on the head of its promoters.

The wars of the Protestants on the Continent after the Reformation, and the American war between North and South, furnished melancholy proofs of this. Some of the best Christians have died on battle-fields. Taking the sword, they perished by the sword.

St. John, for wise reasons, does not mention the miraculous healing of Malchus. Burgon takes occasion to remark that even in the hour of our Lord's apparent weakness He gave His enemies a miracle of power and a miracle of mercy,—power in striking them to the ground, mercy in healing.

[*The cup...Father...given...drink it.*] This beautiful saying is peculiar to St. John's Gospel. It was meant to show our Lord's perfect willingness and readiness to drink the bitter cup of suffering which was before Him. It should always be read in connection with the two other expressions about "the cup" which our Lord had very shortly before used in the garden of Gethsemane. First came the prayer, "If it be possible let this cup pass from Me." Then came the resigned declaration, "If this cup may not pass from Me except I drink it, Thy will be done." And last of all comes the firm and composed assertion of perfect readiness for anything: "Shall I not drink the cup given to Me by my Father?" The three expressions taken together are deeply instructive. They show that our Lord in His agony prayed for relief. They show that His prayer was first answered by His being able to submit entirely to His Father's will. They show that His prayer was finally answered by His being able to show complete willingness to suffer. What an example this is for all believers in the time of trouble! Like our Master we may pray about it, and hope that like Him we shall obtain help by prayer. What a proof this is of our Lord's power to sympathize with suffering believers. He knows their conflicts by experience.

The absolute voluntariness of Jesus Christ's suffering for us is nowhere perhaps more remarkably brought out than in this passage. He resents and rebukes the effort of a zealous disciple to repel force by force. He speaks of His sufferings as "a cup" given to Him by His Father, and appointed in the everlasting counsels of the Trinity, and as one which He cheerfully and willingly drinks. "Shall I not drink it? Would you have me refuse it? Would you prevent my dying for sinners?" It is the more marvellous when we reflect that He who thus willingly suffered was God Almighty as well as man. Nothing can account for the whole scene but the doctrine of atonement and substitution.

To the eye of some, our Lord's sufferings were forced on Him by the Jews. Yet when He speaks of them here, He looks far above second causes. He says, His sufferings were "the cup given to Him by the Father." Are not all the sufferings of God's children to be regarded in the same light?

Calvin warns us here that while we ought to be ready to drink any cup appointed by our Father, " we must not listen to those fanatics who tell us that we may not seek remedies for diseases and any other kind of distresses, lest we reject the cup presented to us by our heavenly Father."

Henry observes on the word " cup " as applied to affliction : " It is but a cup, a small matter comparatively, be it what it will.—It is not a sea, a Red sea, or a Dead sea, for it is not hell ; it is light, and but for a moment.—It is a cup that is *given* us : sufferings are gifts.—It is given us by a Father, by one who has a Father's authority, and does us no wrong,—a Father's affection, and means us no hurt."

Bengel remarks that John here evidently pre-supposes the particulars detailed by Matthew about " the cup," named by our Lord in prayer, to be things known by his readers. Paley also notices the expression as one of the undesigned coincidences of Scripture.

JOHN XVIII 12—27

12 Then the band and the captain and officers of the Jews took Jesus, and bound him,

13 And led him away to Annas first ; for he was father in law to Caiaphas, which was the high priest that same year.

14 Now Caiaphas was he, which gave counsel to the Jews, that it was expedient that one man should die for the people.

15 And Simon Peter followed Jesus, and *so did* another disciple : that disciple was known unto the high priest, and went in with Jesus into the palace of the high priest.

16 But Peter stood at the door without. Then went out that other disciple, which was known unto the high priest, and spake unto her that kept the door, and brought in Peter.

17 Then saith the damsel that kept the door unto Peter, Art not thou also *one* of this man's disciples ? He saith I am not.

18 And the servants and officers stood there, who had made a fire of coals ; for it was cold : and they warmed themselves : and Peter stood with them, and warmed himself.

19 The high priest then asked

Jesus of his disciples and his doctrine.

20 Jesus answered him, I spake openly to the world ; I ever taught in the synagogue, and in the temple, whither the Jews always resort ; and in secret have I said nothing.

21 Why askest thou me ? ask them which heard me, what I have said unto them : behold, they know what I said.

22 And when he had thus spoken, one of the officers which stood by struck Jesus with the palm of his hand, saying, Answerest thou the high priest so ?

23 Jesus answered him, if I have spoken evil, bear witness of the evil : but if well, why smitest thou me ?

24 Now Annas had sent him bound unto Caiaphas the high priest.

25 And Simon Peter stood and warmed himself. They said therefore unto him, Art thou not also *one* of his disciples ? He denied *it*, and said, I am not.

26 One of the servants of the high priest, being *his* kinsman whose ear Peter cut off, saith, Did not I see thee in the garden with him ?

27 Peter then denied again : and immediately the cock crew.

IN this part of St. John's history of Christ's sufferings, three wonderful things stand out upon the surface of the narrative. To these three let us confine our attention.

We should mark, for one thing, *the amazing hardness of unconverted men.* We see this in the conduct of the men by whom our Lord was taken prisoner. Some of them most probably were Roman soldiers, and some of them were Jewish servants of the priests and Pharisees. But in one respect they were all alike. Both parties saw our Lord's divine power exhibited, when they "went backward, and fell to the ground." Both saw a miracle, according to St. Luke's Gospel, when Jesus touched the ear of Malchus and healed him. Yet both remained unmoved, cold, indifferent and insensible, as if they had seen nothing out of the common way. They went on coolly with their odious business. "They took Jesus, bound Him, and led Him away."

The degree of hardness and insensibility of conscience to which men may attain, when they live twenty or thirty years without the slightest contact with religion, is something awful and appalling. God and the things of God seem to sink out of sight and disappear from the mind's eye. The world and the things of the world seem to absorb the whole attention. In such cases we may well believe miracles would produce little or no effect, as in the case before us. The eye would gaze on them, like the eye of a beast looking at a romantic landscape, without any impression being made on the heart. He who thinks that seeing a miracle would convert him into a thorough Christian has got much to learn.

Let us not wonder if we see cases of hardness and unbelief in our own day and generation. Such cases will continually be found among those classes of mankind, who from their profession or position are completely cut off from means of grace. Twenty or thirty years of total irreligion, without the influence of Sunday, Bible, or Christian teaching, will make a man's heart hard as the nether mill-stone. His conscience at last will seem dead, buried, and gone. He will appear past feeling. Painful as these cases are, we must not think them peculiar to our own times. They existed under Christ's own eyes, and they will exist until Christ returns. The Church which allows any portion of a population to grow up in practical heathenism, must never be surprised to see a rank crop of practical infidelity.

We should mark, for another thing, *the amazing condescension of our Lord Jesus Christ.* We see the Son of God taken prisoner and led away bound like a malefactor,—arraigned before wicked and unjust judges, —insulted and treated with contempt. And yet this unresisting prisoner had only to will His deliverance, and He would at once have been free. He had only to command the confusion of His enemies, and they would at once have been confounded. Above all He was One who knew full well that Annas and Caiaphas, and all their companions, would one day stand before His judgment seat and receive an eternal sentence. He knew all these things, and yet condescended to be treated as a malefactor without resisting.

One thing at any rate is very clear. The love of Christ to sinners is " a love that passeth knowledge." To suffer for those whom we love, and who are in some sense worthy of our affections, is suffering that we can understand. To submit to ill-treatment quietly, when we have no power to resist, is submission that is both graceful and wise. But to suffer voluntarily, when we have the power to prevent it, and to suffer for a world

of unbelieving and ungodly sinners, unasked and un-
thanked,—this is a line of conduct which passes man's
understanding. Never let us forget that this is the peculiar beauty of Christ's sufferings, when we read the
wondrous story of His cross and passion. He was led
away captive, and dragged before the High Priest's
bar, not because He could not help Himself, but because
He had set His whole heart on saving sinners,—by bearing their sins, by being treated as a sinner, and by being punished in their stead. He was a willing prisoner,
that we might be set free. He was willingly arraigned
and condemned, that we might be absolved and declared innocent.—"He suffered for sins, the just for the
unjust, that He might bring us unto God."—"Though
He was rich, yet for our sakes He became poor, that we
through His poverty might be rich."—"He was made
sin for us who knew no sin, that we might be made the
righteousness of God in Him." (1 Peter iii. 18 ; 2 Cor.
viii. 9 ; v. 21.) Surely if there is any doctrine of the
Gospel which needs to be clearly known, it is the doctrine of Christ's voluntary substitution. He suffered and
died willingly and unresistingly, because He knew that
He had come to be our substitute, and by substitution
to purchase our salvation.

We should mark, lastly, the *amazing degree of weakness that may be found in a real Christian.* We see
this exemplified in a most striking manner, in the conduct of the Apostle Peter. We see that famous disciple forsaking his Master, and acting like a coward,—
running away when he ought to have stood by His side,
—ashamed to own Him when he ought to have confessed Him,—and finally denying three times that He knew
Him. And this takes place immediately after receiving
the Lord's Supper—after hearing the most touching
address and prayer that mortal ear ever heard—after

the plainest possible warnings—under the pressure of no very serious temptation. "Lord," we may well say, "what is man that Thou art mindful of him?" "Let him that thinketh he standeth, take heed lest he fall." (1 Cor. x. 12.)

This fall of Peter is doubtless intended to be a lesson to the whole Church of Christ. It is recorded for our learning, that we be kept from like sorrowful overthrow. It is a beacon mercifully set up in Scripture, to prevent others making shipwreck. It shows us the danger of pride and self-confidence, If Peter had not been so sure that although all denied Christ, he never would, he would probably never have fallen.—It shows us the danger of laziness. If Peter had watched and prayed, when our Lord advised him to do so, he would have found grace to help him in the time of need.—It shows us, not least, the painful influence of the fear of man. Few are aware, perhaps, how much more they fear the face of man whom they can see, than the eye of God whom they cannot see. These things are written for our admonition. Let us remember Peter and be wise.

After all let us leave the passage with the comfortable reflection that we have a merciful and pitiful High Priest, who can be touched with the feeling of our infirmities, and will not break the bruised reed. Peter no doubt fell shamefully, and only rose again after heartfelt repentance and bitter tears. But he did rise again. He was not left to reap the consequence of his sin, and cast off for evermore. The same pitiful hand that saved him from drowning, when his faith failed him on the waters, was once more stretched out to raise him when he fell in the High Priest's hall. Can we doubt that he rose a wiser and better man? If Peter's fall has made Christians see more clearly their own great weakness

and Christ's great compassion, then Peter's fall has not
been recorded in vain.

NOTES. JOHN XVIII 12—27

12 —[*Then the band and the captain, etc.*] This verse begins the
story of our Lord when He was actually in the hands of His
deadly enemies. For the first time in His earthly ministry we
see Him not a free agent, but submitting to be a passive sufferer,
and allowing His foes to work their will. The last miracle
had been wrought in vain. Like a malefactor He is seized and
put in chains.

The " captain " must mean the Roman officer who commanded the " band," cohort, or detachment, which was sent to
apprehend our Lord. The " officers " must mean the civil servants of the priests who accompanied them. The " binding "
must mean the putting of chains or handcuffs on our Lord's
arms and wrists.

13 —[*And led Him away to Annas, etc.*] This is a fact which is
mentioned by no Gospel-writer except John. The explanation
of it is probably something of this kind. In the time when our
Lord Jesus was on earth, the office of the high priest among
the Jews was filled up with the utmost disorder and irregularity. Instead of the high priest being high priest for life, he
was often elected for a year or two, and then deposed, and his
office given to another. There were often living at one time
several priests who had served the office of high priest, and
then ceased to hold it, like sheriffs or mayors among ourselves.
In the case before us Annas appears, after ceasing to be high
priest himself, to have lived in the same palace with his son-in-
law Caiaphas, and to have assisted him as an assessor and ad-
viser in the discharge of his duties, which from his age and
official experience he would be well qualified to do. Remembering this, we may understand our Lord being " led away to
Annas first," and then passed on by him to Caiaphas. So intimate were the relations between the two, that in Luke iii. 2 we
are told that " Annas and Caiaphas were high priests." In Acts
iv. 6, Annas is called " the high priest." Yet it is very certain
that Caiaphas was the acting high priest the year that our Lord
was crucified. John distinctly asserts it.

The gross inconsistency of the Jews in making such ado
about the law of Moses, while they permitted and tolerated
such entire departures from its regulations about the high
priest's office, is a curious example of what blindness unconverted men may exhibit. As to there being two high priests at
the same time, we must in fairness remember that even in holy
David's time " Zadok and Abiathar were the priests." (2 Sam.
xx. 25.) The gross irregularity in our Lord's time consisted in
making the high priest's office an annual one.

The object of the Jews in bringing our Lord before the high priest and in the Sanhedrim first, is very plain. They wished to convict him of heresy and blasphemy, and then after that to denounce him to the Romans.

Augustine thinks that Caiaphas arranged that our Lord should be taken to Annas first, because he was his father-in-law. He also thinks that these two held the office of high priest, each in his turn, year by year. Calvin thinks that our Lord was only taken to Annas first, because his house happened to be convenient, till the high priest and council assembled. Cyril and Musculus think that Annas was the contriver and designer of all done against Christ.

Cyril here interposes the verse which in most Bibles comes in as twenty-fourth : " Annas at once sent Him bound to Caiaphas the high priest." Luther, Flacius, and Beza, incline to approve of this. But it is fair to say that there is great lack of authority for this change.

Many commentators think that Jesus was taken to Annas first, by way of exhibiting to that old " enemy of all righteousness " the triumphant success of the attempt to capture the prisoner, whom the Sanhedrim had agreed to slay. They think that he was just shown to Annas, and then passed on to Caiaphas. But I cannot think this probable. I hold, with Alford and Ellicott, that our Lord was examined by Annas.

Cornelius a'Lapide suggests that Annas was very likely the person with whom Judas bargained to betray our Lord for money ; and that when the capture was effected, Judas brought the prisoner to the house of Annas, and remained there to claim his price, after Annas had seen Him. He observes with some acuteness that Judas does not appear after this in the history of the examination of our Lord.

Lightfoot quotes a Jewish writer, who says that " in the second temple, which only stood four hundred and twenty years, there were in that time more than three hundred high priests ! "

Henry remarks, " It was the ruin of Caiaphas that he was high priest that year, and so became a ringleader in putting Christ to death. Many a man's advancement has lost him his reputation ; and he would not have been dishonored if he had not been preferred and promoted."

14.—[*Now Caiaphas was he, etc.*] This verse contains one of John's peculiar explanatory comments, and as such comes in parenthetically. It is as though he said, " Let us not forget that this was the very Caiaphas, who after the raising of Lazarus, had said publicly that it was expedient that one man should die for the people. Behold how he is made the unconscious instrument of bringing that saying to pass, though in a widely different sense from that which he intended ! " Calvin compares him to Balaam.

Let us note how the great wicked men of this world—the Sennacheribs and Neros, and bloody Marys, and Napoleons—are used by God as His saws and axes and hammers to do His work and carry out the Building of His Church, though they are not themselves in the least aware of it. Indeed Caiaphas helps forward the one great sacrifice for the sins of the world !

15 —[*And Simon Peter followed Jesus.*] The first flight and running away of the disciples is passed over entirely by John. He simply mentions that Peter followed his Master, though at a distance, lovingly anxious to see what was done to Him, yet not bold enough to keep near Him like a disciple. Any one can see that the unhappy disciple was under the influence of very mixed feelings. Love made him ashamed to run away and hide himself. Cowardice made him afraid to show his colors, and stick by his Lord's side. Hence he chose a middle course, the worst, as it happened, that he could have followed. After being self-confident when he should have been humble, and sleeping when he ought to have been praying, he could not have done a more foolish thing than to flutter round the fire, and place himself within reach of temptation. It teaches the foolishness of man when his grace is weak. No prayer is more useful than the familiar one : " Lead us not into temptation." Peter forgot it here.

[*And so did another disciple.*] This would be more literally rendered, " the other disciple." The opinion of many commentators is, that this disciple was John. Precisely the same expression is used in four successive verses (John xx. 2, 3, 4, and 8), where John is clearly referred to. This is the view of Chrysostom, Cyril, Alford, Wordsworth, and Burgon.

Chrysostom and Cyril observe that it was John's humility that made him conceal his name both here and elsewhere. Here he would not proclaim that he stood while Peter fell. Ferus suggests that the presence of a disciple is mentioned in order to show that John saw with his own eyes all that went on at our Lord's examination.

[*That disciple....known...priest.*] How and in what manner this acquaintance originated we are not told, nor is there any clue to a knowledge of it. On the face of things it certainly seems strange that a humble Galilean fisherman, like John, should be personally known to Caiaphas ! On the other hand we must not forget that every devout Jew went up to Jerusalem at the three great feasts ; and on these occasions might easily have become acquainted with the high priest ; and the more likely to get acquainted, if a conscientious and godly man. Moreover we must remember that John was once a disciple of John the Baptist, and that there was a time when " Jerusalem and all Judea " attended on John's ministry. Acquaintance might have been formed then. Some have thought that John's calling as a fisherman might easily bring him into

communication with the family of Caiaphas, when he visited
Jerusalem on business. All these, it must be confessed, are
only conjectures; and it is perhaps the safest to admit our ignorance. Enough for us to read that the high priest knew
John; but why and how we cannot tell.

Hengstenberg suggests an explanation, which is so singular
that I think it best to give it in his own words: "The character of John leads to the obvious supposition that his acquaintance with the high priest rested on religious grounds. Searching for goodly pearls, John had earlier sought from the high
priest what, after the intervening ministry of the Baptist, he
found in Christ. With what eyes he had formerly regarded
the position of high priest, is shown by the fact that though a
disciple of Christ, he nevertheless assigned to the word of the
high priest a prophetic significance. (John xi. 51.) John, by
his internally devout nature, had so attracted the good will of
the high priest, that he did not wholly cast him off even after
he had gone over to the true High Priest. Nor had John entirely abandoned Caiaphas. Real love cannot be so easily rooted from the heart; and it is characteristic of John to retain a
pious regard to earlier relations. In the love which hopeth all
things, he might hope yet to win the high priest to Christ."
I make no comment on this extraordinary suggestion. I cannot see the slightest warrant for it; but others, perhaps, who
like the Athenians love new things, may see more in it than I
can.

After all, it is only fair to remember that Augustine, Gerhard, Calovius, Lightfoot, Lampe, and many others, think it
quite uncertain who this disciple, "known to the high priest,"
was. Grotius and Poole think it may have been the master of
the house where Jesus had the Lord's Supper. Toletus thinks
it was one of those to whom the garden belonged. Bengel
thinks it was Nicodemus. One German commentator suggests
that it was Judas Iscariot. Calvin thinks it most improbable
that a proud high priest would have known so mean a person
as a fisherman. Yet, singularly enough, Gualter and others
lean strongly to the theory that John's business as a fisherman
may have made him acquainted with the high priest. It certainly is rather remarkable that when John was brought before Annas and Caiaphas shortly after, they do not appear to
have known much of him, except that he was unlearned and
ignorant, and had been with Jesus. (Acts iii. 13.) The question, "who it was," is one which will probably never be settled.

[*And went in with Jesus...palace...priest.*] This sentence
would seem to indicate that John went together with our Lord,
either by His side, or in the crowd around Him, from the garden where He was taken, to the house of Annas and Caiaphas.
We can hardly doubt that at first he fled, when we read, "All
forsook Him and fled;" but we must suppose that he soon

turned back, and mixed with the multitude escorting our Lord, which he might easily do by night, and amidst the confusion of the whole event.

It is noteworthy that some think the houses of Caiaphas and Annas were adjacent, and that " the hall " was common to both of them. I am strongly disposed to think that this is a correct view, and a remembrance of it may help us over several difficulties in the narrative of the four evangelists when compared.

16 —[*But Peter stood...door without.*] This seems to indicate that at first Peter stood outside the door of the palace, not daring to go in. It is a little detail in the story of his fall which the three other Gospel-writers omit to mention. Again we see in him the mixture of good and bad feelings, cowardice and love contending for the mastery. Happy would it have been for him if he had stayed outside the door !

Rollock remarks that when Peter found the door shut, he ought not to have stood there, but gone away. " It was by God's providence the door was shut. He got a warning then to leave off, but would not. These impediments, cast in our way when we purpose to do a thing, should not be idly looked at, but should make us carefully try the deed, whether it be lawful."

[*Then went out that other...brought in Peter.*] Here we see how Peter got inside the palace. It was through the mistaken, though well-meant, kindness of John. He must have seen through the door, when it occasionally opened, the well-known figure of his brother disciple, and with the best intentions got him admission. It is plain that John must have been well known to the household of the high priest, or else we should not be told that he had only to speak to the door-keeper, to get admission for Peter.

Let us mark what mistakes even the best believers make in dealing with their brethren. John thought it would be a kind and useful thing to bring Peter into the high priest's house. He was perfectly mistaken, and was unintentionally one link in the chain of causes which led to his fall. People may harm each other with the best intentions.

Quesnel remarks, " Men sometimes imagine they do a considerable piece of service to their friends who are clergymen, by introducing them to the great ; and thereby they undesignedly expose them to sin and eternal damnation."

17 —[*Then saith...damsel...door...Peter.*] Those who are best acquainted with Jewish customs say that it was a common practice to employ women as door-keepers. Thus a damsel named Rhoda went to the gate, when Peter knocked at the door of Mary's house in Jerusalem, after his miraculous escape from

prison. (Acts xii. 13.) It is the same in large houses in Paris to this very day.

[*Art not thou...I am not.*] This was the first trial of Peter's faith and courage. A woman asks him a simple question. There is nothing to show that she does it in a threatening manner, as if she desires to harm him. But at once the Apostle's courage breaks down. He answers with a direct lie: " I am not."—How little we know our own hearts! Twelve hours before Peter would have told us this lie was impossible. " Is Thy servant a dog that he should do this thing ? "—Why this door-keeper should have asked the question we know not. Perhaps Peter's dress and appearance, like a Galilean fisherman of the very same stamp and style as John, made her guess that, like John, he was a disciple.—Perhaps Peter's manner and demeanor made her guess it. There may have been agitation, anxiety, fear in the apostle's countenance.—Perhaps the woman may have seen him in Jerusalem in company with Jesus.—Perhaps the mere fact that John knew him, and asked her to admit him, made her assume that he was a friend of John, and like John a disciple of Christ.—Perhaps the Galileans were marked men, not often seen in high priests' houses, and known to be specially favorable to the cause of Jesus of Nazareth.—Any one of these solutions, or all, may be correct. In any case the woman only asked a simple question, and perhaps from no other motive than curiosity, and at once the great apostle falls into sin. How weak we are, when left to reap the consequence of self-confidence, and laziness, and neglect of prayer. Even an apostle, we see, could tell a cowardly lie.

Chrysostom observes, " What sayest thou, Peter ? Didst not thou declare but now, ' I will lay down my life for Thee ' ? What hath happened then that thou canst not endure the questioning of a door-keeper ? Is it a soldier who questions thee ? Is it one of those who seized Him ? No ; it is a mean and abject door-keeper. Nor is the questioning of a rough kind. She saith not, Art thou a disciple of that cheat and corrupter,—but *of that man ;* which was the expression rather of pitying and relenting. But Peter could not bear any of these words. The expression ' Art not thou *also,*' is used because John was already within."

Augustine remarks, " Behold that most firm pillar of the Church, touched but by one breath of danger, trembles all over. Where is now that boldness of promising,—that confident vaunting of himself ? "

Brentius remarks how the impulsive, unstable character of the apostle Peter comes out here. One hour he draws his sword against a whole multitude of armed men. Another hour he is frightened out of his Christian profession, and driven into lying by one woman.

18 —[*And...servants...officers...stood there.*] This seems to indicate that when Peter entered the hall, he found the common servants, and the higher attendants of the high priest, standing round a fire. It is the pluperfect tense, "they had stood," or "had been standing there" some little time.

[*Who had made...fire...coals...cold...themselves.*] It is remarked by all travellers in Palestine, that the nights in that country about Easter time, are often so extremely cold that a fire is very acceptable. The servants and officers were in the act of warming themselves when Peter entered.

It is worth notice that the Greek word rendered "a fire of coals" is only used here and at John xxi. 9, in the marvellous account of Jesus appearing to the disciples at the sea of Galilee. Some have thought that the "fire of coals" on that latter occasion was purposely intended by our Lord to remind Peter of his fall.

[*And Peter stood with them...himself.*]—The Greek words here would be more literally rendered "and there was among them Peter, standing and warming himself." The tense is imperfect, and conveys the idea of continuous action for a little time. The apostle stood among the crowd of his Master's enemies, and warmed himself like one of them, as if he had nothing to think of but his bodily comfort; while his beloved Master stood in a distant part of the hall, cold, and a prisoner. Who can doubt that Peter, in his miserable cowardice, wished to appear one of the party who hated his Master, and thought to conceal his real character by doing as they did? And who can doubt that while he warmed his hands he felt cold, wretched, and comfortless in his own soul? "The backslider in heart is filled with his own ways."

How many do as others do, and go with the crowd, while they know inwardly they are wrong!

Cyril suggests that Peter wished to conceal his discipleship by warming himself, and trying to look comfortable among the high priest's servants.

19 —[*The high priest...asked...disciples...doctrine.*] This verse describes the first judicial examination that our Lord underwent. He was questioned concerning "His disciples,"—that is, who they were, how many, what position they occupied, and what were their names. And concerning "His doctrine,"—that is, what were the principal points or truths of His creed, what were the peculiar things He called on man to believe. The object of this preliminary inquiry seems manifest. It was meant to elicit some admission from our Lord's mouth, on which some formal charge of heresy and blasphemy before the Sanhedrim might be founded. There are two grave difficulties growing out of this verse, both of which require consideration.

(*a*) Who was the "High Priest" in this verse? Most commentators think it was Caiaphas. He alone is called by John "the high priest," that same year in which Jesus was crucified. Some few think it was "Annas," because John says Jesus was brought to him. (Ver. 13.) This at first sight seems the plain meaning of the narrative, and is confirmed by verse 24. Yet this theory is open to the serious objection, that it makes John call Annas the high priest, and that it makes John omit altogether our Lord's examination before Caiaphas and the Sanhedrim. Yet notwithstanding all these difficulties, I own to the opinion that this is the true view of the history. Augustine, Chrysostom, Casaubon, Ferus, Besser, Stier, Alford, and Ellicott maintain this view, but most of the commentators do not. We must remember that "Annas" is distinctly called " the High Priest" in Acts iv. 6, and this probably before the year of the crucifixion had completely run out. Even in David's time Zadok and Ahimelech are called " the priests " (2 Sam. viii. 17), as if both were high priests.

(b) What was the examination recorded in this verse? It seems to be one entirely passed over by Matthew, Mark, and Luke. They only record what took place before Caiaphas, which, on the other hand, is a part of the history passed over by John. It seems a kind of preliminary inquiry, intended to prepare the case for the Sanhedrim. In spite, therefore of the common opinion, I decidedly hold the theory, that the examination here related is only described by John. It seems moreover to have been an examination conducted by Annas only, and quite of a separate character from that which took place at " day-break " before the whole Sanhedrim. This at any rate seems to my mind by far the most reasonable account of the passage, and the difficulties in the way of any other interpretation appear to me insuperable.

Ellicott remarks, " It only requires the simple and reasonable supposition that Annas and Caiaphas occupied one common official residence, to unite their testimony, and to remove many of the difficulties with which this portion of the sacred narrative is specially marked. Be this as it may, we can scarcely doubt, from the clear statement in St. John's Gospel, that a preliminary examination of an inquisitorial nature, in which our Lord was questioned, perhaps conversationally, about His followers and His teaching, and which the brutal conduct of one attendant present seems to show was private and informal, took place in the palace of Annas. There, too, it would seem, we must place the three denials of St. Peter."

20 —[*Jesus answered him, etc.*] This verse contains a calm, dignified statement from our Lord, of the general course of His ministry. He had done nothing in a clandestine or underhand way. He had always spoken openly " to the world," and not confined His teaching to any one class. He had always taught publicly in synagogues, and in the temple where the Jews re-

sorted. He had said nothing privately and secretly, as if He had any cause to be ashamed of it.

The verse is mainly remarkable for the strong light it throws on our Lord's habit of teaching throughout the three years of His ministry. It shows that He was eminently a public teacher, —kept back no part of His message from any class of the population,—and proclaimed it with equal boldness in every place. There was nothing whatever of reserve about His Gospel. This is His own account, and we therefore know that it is correct. " I have spoken in the most public manner, and taught in the most public places, and done nothing in a corner."

Calvin remarks, " When Jesus says that He spoke nothing in secret, this refers to the substance of His doctrine, which was always the same, though the form of teaching it was various."

We should observe that our Lord did not refuse to use the synagogue and the temple on account of the corruption of the Jewish Church ! Four times we read in St. John of our Lord being at Jerusalem at the feasts (John ii. 13, v. 1, vii. 14, x. 22), and each time speaking in the temple.

21 —[*Why askest thou Me, etc.*] This verse is a remonstrance against the gross injustice of Annas's line of examination. Our Lord appeals to him whether it is reasonable, and just, and fair to call upon a prisoner to criminate himself, and to supply evidence which may be used against himself. " Why dost thou, the judge, ask information of Me, the prisoner, about my disciples and my doctrine ? Ask rather of those who have heard Me teach and preach, what I have said to them. These know well, and can tell you what things I have said."

Cyril thinks there may be a reference here to those servants of the priest, who were sent on a former occasion to take Jesus, and returned, saying, " Never man spake like this Man." (John vii. 46.)

The boldness and dignity of our Lord's reply to Annas in this verse are very noteworthy. They are an example to all Christians of the courageous and unflinching tone which an innocent defendant may justly adopt before the bar of an unrighteous judge. " The righteous is bold as a lion."

The wide difference between the language of our Lord here, and that which He uses before Caiaphas and the Sanhedrim, as recorded in Matthew, Mark, and Luke, is very remarkable. It affords strong additional evidence that we are reading an account of an examination of a more private kind before Annas, quite distinct from that which took place before Caiaphas. The careful reader of the other three Gospels cannot fail to observe that not a word of all this is recorded in them.

Bengel and Stier think that the expression, " these," points to the people there in the court, hearing and standing by.

22 —[*And when He had thus spoken, etc.*] This verse mentions an event which John alone has recorded. One of the attendants standing by rudely interrupts our Lord by striking Him, and coarsely taxing Him with impertinence and disrespect in so speaking, as He had spoken to the high priest.

The Greek words literally rendered, mean " gave a blow on the face ;" but whether with the palm of the hand, or with a stick, cannot be determined. The marginal reading renders it quite uncertain. Some see in the action a fulfilment of the prophecy, " They shall smite the judge of Israel with a rod upon the cheek." (Micah v. 1.)

Stier remarks that this was the first blow which the holy body of Jesus received from the hands of sinners.

We may learn from this circumstance what a low, degraded, and disorderly condition the Jewish courts of Ecclesiastical law must have been in at this period, when such a thing as publicly striking a prisoner could take place, and when violence could be shown to a prisoner in a full court of justice for answering boldly for himself. It supplies strong evidence of the miserably fallen state of the whole Jewish nation, when such an act could be done under the very eyes of a judge. Nothing is a surer index of the real condition of a nation than the conduct of its courts of justice, and its just or unjust treatment of prisoners. The sceptre had clearly fallen from Judah, and rottenness was at the core of the nation, when the thing mentioned in this verse could happen. Our Lord's assailant evidently held that a prisoner must never reply to his judge, however unjust or corrupt the judge might be.

Theophylact suggests that the man who struck our Lord was one who had heard our Lord preach, and was now anxious to free himself from the suspicion of being one of His friends.

There is a striking resemblance between the treatment our Lord received here, and the treatment which Latimer, Ridley, Rogers, and other English martyrs, received at their examination before the Popish bishops.

Hutcheson remarks, "Corrupt masters have generally corrupt servants."

23 —[*Jesus answered him, etc.*] Our Lord's reply to him who smote is a calm and dignified reproof. " If I have spoken wickedly, bear witness in a just and orderly way becoming a court of law ; but do not strike Me. If on the contrary I have spoken well, what reasonable cause canst thou allege for striking Me either here or out of court ?"

Let us note that our Lord's conduct at this point teaches that His maxim, " If any one smite thee on thy right cheek, turn to him the other also" (Matt. v. 39), is a maxim which must be taken with reserve, and is not of unlimited application. There may be times when, in defence of truth and for the honor of justice, a Christian must firmly protest against violence, and publicly refuse to countenance it by tame submission.

Augustine observes, " Our Lord here showed that His great precepts of patience are to be put in practice, not by outward show of the body, but by preparedness of heart. Visibly to present the other cheek is no more than an angry man can do. How much better then that with mild answer he speak the truth, and with tranquil mind endure worse outrages."

24 —[*Now Annas had sent Him...Caiaphas...priest.*] This verse undoubtedly contains a difficulty. Most commentators seem to think that it states a fact which ought to come in after the thirteenth verse ; and that the questioning and smiting of the last four verses took place before Caiaphas and the Sanhedrim, and not before Annas. Some think that up to this point John only describes what took place before Annas ; and that he entirely passes over all that took place before Caiaphas, as being well known to his readers. The question is undoubtedly rather a puzzling one, and there is much to be said on both sides.

On the one hand, it seems curious that the examination of our Lord before Caiaphas and the Sanhedrim should be so completely omitted by John in his Gospel, as it must be, if we take the high priest of the nineteenth verse to be Annas.

On the other hand, we cannot see why John should so carefully mention our Lord being " led to Annas first," if after all Annas did not examine Him at all, and sent Him at once to Caiaphas.

If I must give an opinion, I must say that I agree with Stier, Ellicott, and Alford, and consider that this twenty-fourth verse describes our Lord's first appearance before Caiaphas,—that for some wise reason John entirely omits, and silently passes over, our Lord's examination before the Sanhedrim,—and that the examination of the nineteenth and four following verses was a kind of private, preliminary examination before Annas, which Matthew, Mark, and Luke entirely omit. My grounds for this conclusion are as follows :—

(*a*) The whole tone of John's narrative would make any ordinary reader suppose that Annas, and not Caiaphas, was the examiner and high priest of the nineteenth verse. The story reads straight on upon this theory ; while upon the other it is most awkward and seemingly contradictory, and the twenty-fourth verse seems to come in at the wrong place.

(*b*) The tone of the high priest's examination in John, is entirely different from that of the other three Gospels, and so also are our Lord's answers.

(*c*) There is nothing uncommon in John omitting something

which is fully recorded in the other three Gospels. The institution of the Lord's Supper is an example. His Gospel was eminently supplementary. Writing later than the others, he was
specially inspired to dwell at great length on the examination
of Jesus before Pilate the Gentile ruler, and to say comparatively little about the proceedings in the Jewish courts.

(*d*) Last, but not least, the Greek of the twenty-fourth verse
cannot fairly and honestly bear the same sense which our
translators have put upon it. They have really strained the
words to make the sense square with their evident interpretation. The word " sent " is not a pluperfect at all in the Greek!
The verse literally translated is, " Annas sent Him bound to
Caiaphas the high priest." It is rather " did then send Him,"
than " now had sent Him." The natural sense that any ordinary reader would put on it is, that " Annas having asked our
Lord about His disciples and His doctrine, and having found
by His reply that he could make nothing of Him, did then send
Him bound to Caiaphas." As to what THEN took place before
Caiaphas and the Sanhedrim John tells us NOTHING, and leaves
us to learn it from Matthew, Mark, and Luke.

Such are my reasons for the view which I adopt. If the
reader does not think them valid, he must regard the twenty-
fourth verse as one of John's parenthetical explanations or
comments, and carry the true place of the fact mentioned backwards to verse thirteenth ; and must suppose that the examination of our Lord in the nineteenth and four following verses is
the examination before Caiaphas and the Sanhedrim, and only
another part of what Matthew, Mark, and Luke describe!
—Not least, he must suppose that " did send " in the twenty-
fourth verse, means " had sent " some time before!

Chrysostom says, " Annas questioned Jesus about His doctrine ; and having heard Him, sent Him to Caiaphas ; and he
having in his turn questioned Him, and discovered nothing,
sent Him to Pilate."

25 —[*And Simon Peter...warmed himself.*] This would be more
literally rendered, " was standing and warming himself." The
expression seems to indicate, that all the time during which
Annas was questioning and examining our Lord, Peter was
standing by the fire in another part of the hall, and warming
himself comfortably among the enemies of our Lord, like one
of them. May not the light of the fire, as it burned up, have
made Peter's face and appearance more easily recognizable?

[*They said...art not thou...disciple ?*] Here comes Peter's second trial. After a time, when the fire had burned up, and men
could see better and felt more warm, they looked at Peter standing among them, and recognizing either by his dress and talk
that he was a Galilean, or suspecting by his anxious manner
that he was a friend of our Lord, they asked him plainly, " Art

thou not one of this prisoner's disciples?" We see what trials people bring on themselves by going where they ought not.

[*He denied it...I am not.*] A second time we find the unhappy Apostle telling a lie, and this time it is added emphatically, "he denied it." The further a backslider goes, the worse he becomes. The first time he seems to have said quietly, "I am not." The second time he flatly "denies." Even an apostle can fall into being a liar!

Bloomfield suggests that Peter heard our Lord's examination, and was terrified at hearing inquiry made about His *disciples.* This, he supposes, hastened his fall.

26 —[*One of the servants, etc., etc.*] Here comes Peter's last trial. Attention seems to have been roused by his strong denial, and eyes were fixed on him. And the one who had seen him in the garden, and marked him as a forward man among the disciples by his using the sword, presses home the painful question, "Did not I see thee?"

27 —[*Peter then denied again.*] This denial we know from the other Gospels, was more loud and emphatic than any, and was made with cursing and swearing! The further a man falls, the heavier his fall.

Calvin remarks on the course of a backslider, "At first the fault will not be very great; next, it becomes habitual; and at last, after the conscience has been laid asleep, he who has accustomed himself to despise God will think nothing unlawful, but will dare to commit the greatest wickedness."

Henry remarks, "The sin of lying is a fruitful sin, and therefore exceeding sinful. One sin needs another to support it, and that needs another."

[*And immediately the cock crew.*] There was nothing uncommon in this, of course. Every one knows that cocks crow at night. But the bird's familiar crow no doubt sounded in Peter's ear like a clap of thunder, because it awoke him to a sense of his sin and his fall.

It will be noted that for wise reasons John says nothing about Peter's weeping, or about our Lord turning and looking at him, or about Peter going out. He seems to have left the hall when the cock crew, without any attempt being made to detain him. This too MAY have been the overruling work of his gracious Master.

As long as the world stands, Peter's fall will be an instructive example of what even a great saint may come to if he neglects to work and pray,—of the mercy of Christ in restoring such a backslider,—and of the honesty of the Gospel writers in recording such a history.

Let it never be forgotten that Peter's fall is one of those few

facts which all four Gospel writers carefully record for our
learning.

28 Then led they Jesus from Caiaphas unto the hall of judgment:
and it was early; and they themselves went not into the judgment
hall, lest they should be defiled;
but that they might eat the passover.

29 Pilate then went out unto
them, and said, What accusation
bring ye against this man?

30 They answered and said unto
him, If he were not a malefactor,
we would not have delivered him
up unto thee.

31 Then said Pilate unto them,
Take ye him, and judge him according to your law. The Jews therefore said unto him, It is not lawful
for us to put any man to death:

32 That the saying of Jesus might
be fulfilled, which he spake, signifying what death he should die.

33 Then Pilate entered into the
judgment hall again, and called
Jesus, and said unto him, Art thou
the King of the Jews?

34 Jesus answered him, Sayest
thou this thing of thyself, or did
others tell it thee of me?

35 Pilate answered, Am I a Jew?

Thine own nation and the chief
priests have delivered thee unto
me: what hast thou done?

36 Jesus answered, My kingdom
is not of this world: if my kingdom
were of this world, then would my
servants fight, that I should not be
delivered to the Jews: but now is
my kingdom not from hence.

37 Pilate therefore saith unto him,
Art thou a king then? Jesus answered, Thou sayest that I am a
king. To this end was I born, and
for this cause came I into the world,
that I should bear witness unto the
truth. Every one that is of the
truth heareth my voice.

38 Pilate saith unto him, What is
truth? And when he had said
this, he went out again unto the
Jews, and saith unto them, I find in
him no fault *at all.*

39 But ye have a custom, that
I should release unto you one at
the passover: will ye therefore that
I release unto you the King of the
Jews?

40 Then cried they all again,
saying, Not this man, but Barabbas. Now Barabbas was a robber.

THE verses we have now read contain four striking
points, which are only found in St. John's narrative of
Christ's passion. We need not doubt that there were
good reasons why Matthew, Mark, and Luke were not
inspired to record them. But they are points of such
deep interest, that we should feel thankful that they
have been brought forward by St. John.

The first point that we should notice is *the false con-
scientiousness of our Lord's wicked enemies.* We are
told that the Jews who brought Christ before Pilate
would not go into "the judgment hall, lest they should
be defiled; but that they might eat the passover."

That was scrupulosity indeed! These hardened men were actually engaged in doing the wickedest act that mortal man ever did. They wanted to kill their own Messiah. And yet at this very time they talked of being " defiled," and were very particular about the passover!

The conscience of unconverted men is a very curious part of their moral nature. While in some cases it becomes hardened, seared, and dead, until it feels nothing; in others it becomes morbidly scrupulous about the lesser matters of religion. It is no uncommon thing to find people excessively particular about the observance of trifling forms and outward ceremonies, while they are the slaves of degrading sins and detestable immoralities. Robbers and murderers in some countries are extremely strict about confession, and absolution, and prayers to saints. Fastings and self-imposed austerities in Lent, are often followed by excess of worldliness when Lent is over. There is but a step from Lent to Carnival. The attendants at daily services in the morning are not unfrequently the patrons of balls and theatres at night. All these are symptoms of spiritual disease, and a heart secretly dissatisfied. Men who know they are wrong in one direction, often struggle to make things right by excess of zeal in another direction. That very zeal is their condemnation.

Let us pray that our consciences may always be enlightened by the Holy Ghost, and that we may be kept from a one-sided and deformed Christianity. A religion that makes a man neglect the weightier matters of daily holiness and separation from the world, and concentrate his whole attention on forms, sacraments, ceremonies, and public services, is to say the least, very suspicious. It may be accompanied by immense zeal and show of earnestness, but it is not sound in the sight of God. The Pharisees paid tithe of mint, anise, and cummin, and compassed sea and land to make proselytes, while they neglected "judgment, mercy, and faith." (Matt. xxiii. 23.) The very Jews who thirsted for Christ's blood were the Jews who feared the defilement of a Roman judgment hall, and made much ado about keeping the passover! Let their conduct be a beacon to Christians, as long as the world stands. That religion is worth little which does not make us say, " I esteem all Thy commandments concerning all things to be right, and I hate every false way." (Ps. cxix. 128.) That Christianity is worthless which makes us compound for the neglect of heart religion and practical holiness, by an extravagant zeal for man-made ceremonies or outward forms.

The second point that we should notice in these verses, is *the account that our Lord Jesus Christ gives of His kingdom.* He says, " My kingdom is not of this world." These famous words have been so often perverted and wrested out of their real sense, that their true meaning has been almost buried under a heap of false interpretations. Let us make sure that we know what they mean.

Our Lord's main object in saying " My kingdom is not of this world," was to inform Pilate's mind concerning the true nature of His kingdom, and to correct any false impression he might have received from the Jews. He tells him that He did not come to set up a kingdom which would interfere with the Roman Government. He did not aim at establishing a temporal power, to be supported by armies and maintained by taxes. The only dominion He exercised was over men's hearts, and the only weapons that His subjects employed were spiritual weapons. A kingdom which required neither money nor servants for its support, was one of which the Roman Emperors need not be afraid. In the highest sense it was a kingdom " not of this world."

But our Lord did not intend to teach that the kings of this world have nothing to do with religion, and ought to ignore God altogether in the government of their subjects. No such idea, we may be sure, was in His mind. He knew perfectly well that it was written, " By Me kings reign " (Prov. viii. 15), and that kings are as much required to use their influence for God, as the meanest of their subjects. He knew that the prosperity of kingdoms is wholly dependent on the blessing of God, and that kings are as much bound to encourage righteousness and godliness, as to punish unrighteousness and immorality. To suppose that He meant to teach Pilate that, in His judgment, an infidel might be as good a king as a Christian, and a man like Gallio as good a ruler as David or Solomon, is simply absurd.

Let us carefully hold fast the true meaning of our Lord's words in these latter days. Let us never be ashamed to maintain that no Government can expect to prosper which refuses to recognize religion, which deals with its subjects as if they had no souls, and cares not whether they serve God, or Baal, or no God at all. Such a Government will find, sooner or later, that its line of policy is suicidal, and damaging to its best interests. No doubt the kings of this world cannot make men Christians by laws and statutes. But they can encourage and support Christianity, and they will do so if they are wise. The kingdom where there is the most industry, temperance, truthfulness, and honesty, will always be the most prosperous of kingdoms. The king who wants to see these things abound among his subjects, should do all that lies in his power to help Christianity and to discourage irreligion.

The third point that we should notice in these verses

is *the account that our Lord gives of His own mission.*
He says, "To this end was I born, and for this cause
came I into the world, that I should bear witness unto
the truth."

Of course we are not to suppose our Lord meant that
this was the *only* end of His mission. No doubt He
spoke with special reference to what He knew was passing through Pilate's mind. He did not come to win a
kingdom with the sword, and to gather adherents and
followers by force. He came armed with no other
weapon but "truth." To testify to fallen man the truth
about God, about sin, about the need of a Redeemer,
about the nature of holiness,—to declare and lift up
before man's eyes this long lost and buried " truth,"—
was one great purpose of His ministry. He came to be
God's witness to a lost and corrupt world. That the
world needed such a testimony, He does not shrink from
telling the proud Roman Governor. And this is what
St. Paul had in view, when he tells Timothy, that "before Pontius Pilate Christ witnessed a good confession."
(1 Tim. vi. 13.)

The servants of Christ in every age must remember
that our Lord's conduct in this place is meant to be their
example. Like Him we are to be witnesses to God's
truth, salt in the midst of corruption, light in the midst
of darkness, men and women not afraid to stand alone,
and to testify for God against the ways of sin and the
world. To do so may entail on us much trouble, and
even persecution. But the duty is clear and plain. If
we love life, if we would keep a good conscience, and
be owned by Christ at the last day, we must be "witnesses." It is written, " Whosoever shall be ashamed of
Me and of my words in this adulterous and sinful generation, of him also shall the Son of man be ashamed,

when He cometh in the glory of His Father with the holy angels." (Mark viii. 38.)

The last point that we should notice in these verses is *the question that Pontius Pilate addressed to our Lord.* We are told that when our Lord spoke of the truth, the Roman Governor replied, " What is truth ? " We are not told with what motive this question was asked, nor does it appear on the face of the narrative that he who asked it waited for an answer. It seems far more likely that the saying was the sarcastic, sneering exclamation of one who did not believe that there was any such thing as " truth." It sounds like the language of one who had heard, from his earliest youth, so many barren speculations about " truth " among Roman and Greek philosophers, that he doubted its very existence. " Truth indeed! What is truth ? "

Melancholy as it may appear, there are multitudes in every Christian land whose state of mind is just like that of Pilate. Hundreds, it may be feared among the upper classes, are continually excusing their own irreligion by the specious plea that, like the Roman Governor, they cannot find out " what is truth." They point to the endless controversies of Romanists and Protestants, of High Churchmen and Low Churchmen, of Churchmen and Dissenters, and pretend to say that they do not understand who is right and who is wrong. Sheltered under this favorite excuse, they pass through life without any decided religion, and in this wretched, comfortless state, too often die.

But is it really true that truth cannot be discovered ? Nothing of the kind ! God never left any honest, diligent inquirer without light and guidance. Pride is one reason why many cannot discover truth. They do not humbly go down on their knees and earnestly ask God to teach them.—Laziness is another reason. They do not honestly take pains, and search the Scriptures. The followers of unhappy Pilate, as a rule, do not deal fairly and honestly with their consciences. Their favorite question,—What is truth?—is nothing better than a pretence and an excuse. The words of Solomon will be found true as long as the world stands : " If thou criest after knowledge, and liftest up thy voice for understanding ; if thou seekest her as silver, and searchest for her as for hid treasures ; then shalt thou understand the fear of the Lord, and find the knowledge of God." (Prov. ii. 4, 5.) No man ever followed that advice and missed the way to heaven.

NOTES JOHN XVIII 28—40

28 —[*Then led they Jesus from Caiaphas.*] A careful reader of the Gospels will not fail to observe here, that John entirely passes over the examination of Caiaphas and the Sanhedrim of the Jews, which is so fully described by Matthew, Mark, and Luke. Specially he omits our Lord's confession, when adjured, that He was the Christ. He takes it all for granted, as a thing well known, and passes on to dwell on his far more important examination before Pilate, the Roman Governor. In this he brings out many striking pârticulars, which, for wise reasons, Matthew, Mark, and Luke did not record. Writing, as John did, long after the other three, and writing more especially for Gentile readers, we can well understand that he would give far more prominence to the proceedings before the Gentile Governor, than to those before the Jewish Ecclesiastical Court. Yet it cannot be denied that there is a remarkable curtness and brevity in his statement of facts at this point. The Greek is literally they " lead,"—in the present tense.

[*Unto the hall of judgment.*] This is a Latin word, and admits of two views. The marginal reading, according to Schleusner and Parkhurst, is the correct translation. It is the " Governor's palace," rather than the hall of judgment. According to Josephus, the prætors, or governors of Judæa, who ordinarily lived at Cæsarea, when they were at Jerusalem, used Herod's palace, in the upper part of the city, as their residence. Some say it was the famous tower of Antonia.

[*And it was early.*] The precise time here meant we cannot exactly tell. It cannot have been so early as day-break, because we are especially told by Luke that the elders and chief priests and the Sanhedrim assembled to examine our Lord " as soon as it was day." (Luke xxii. 66.) Considering that the day begins at the equinox about six, we may assume that " early " cannot mean sooner than seven or eight o'clock.

⌊*And they went not...judgment hall...defiled.*⌋ The meaning of this sentence is, that the Jews would not go within the walls of Pilate's palace, lest by so doing they should contract ceremonial uncleanness. Pilate was a Gentile. Peter says in the Acts, " It is unlawful for a man that is a Jew to keep company or come unto one of another nation." (Acts x 28.) If the Jews had gone inside Pilate's house, they would have been made ceremonially unclean, and would have considered themselves defiled.

The sentence is an extraordinary example of the false scru-pulosity of conscience which a wicked man may keep up, about forms and ceremonies and trifling externals in religion, at the very time when he is deliberately committing some gross and enormous sin. The notorious fact that Italian bandits and mur-derers will make much of fasting, keeping Lent, confession, absolution, Virgin Mary worship, saint worship, and image worship, at the very time when they are arranging robberies and assassinations, is an accurate illustration of the same prin-ciple. The extent to which formality and wickedness can go side by side is frightful, and little known. The Jews were afraid of being defiled by going into a Gentile's house, at the very moment when they were doing the devil's work, and mur-dering the Prince of life !—Just so, many people in England will attach immense importance to fasting and keeping Lent and attending saints'-day services, while they see no harm in going to races, operas, and balls, at other times ! Persons who have very low notions about the Seventh Commandment, will actually tell you that it is wrong to be married in Lent ! The very same persons who totally disregard Sunday abroad, will make much ado about saints'-day at home ! Absurd strict-ness about Lent, and excess of riot and licentiousness in carni-val, will often go together.

Chrysostom remarks, " Though they had taken up a deed which was unlawful, and were shedding blood, they are scru-pulous about the place, and bring forth Pilate unto them."

Augustine remarks, " O impious blindness ! They would be defiled, forsooth, by a dwelling which was another's, and not be defiled by a crime which was their own. They feared to be defiled by the prætorium of an alien judge, and feared not to be defiled by the blood of an innocent brother."

Bishop Hall remarks, " Woe unto you priests, scribes, elders, hypocrites ! can there be any roof so unclean as that of your own breasts ? Not Pilate's walls, but your own hearts, are im-pure. Is murder your errand, and do you stick at a local infec-tion ? God shall smite you, ye whited walls ! Do you long to be stained with blood—with the blood of God ? And do ye fear to be defiled with the touch of Pilate's pavement? Doth so small a gnat stick in your throats, while ye swallow such a camel of flagitious wickedness? Go out of Jerusalem, ye false disbelievers, if ye would not be unclean! Pilate hath more cause to fear, lest his walls should be defiled with the presence of such prodigious monsters of iniquity."

Poole remarks, " Nothing is more common than for persons over zealous about rituals to be remiss about morals."

[*That...eat...passover.*] This sentence contains an undeniable difficulty. How could the Jews eat the passover now, when our Lord and His disciples had eaten it the evening before? That our Lord would eat the passover at the right time we may assume as a matter of course, and that time was Thursday evening. What then can be meant by the chief priests, and elders, and leaders of the Jews, eating the passover on Friday? This is a question which has received various answers.

(*a*) Some think that in our Lord's time the whole Jewish Church had fallen into such disorder, and had so fallen away from original purity, that the passover was not kept strictly according to the primary institution, and might be eaten on almost any day within the passover feast.

(*b*) Some think that it was considered allowable to eat the passover at any time between sunset one day and sunset the next day, so long as it was eaten within the twenty-four hours.

(*c*) Some think that the passover eating here mentioned was not the eating of the passover lamb, but the eating of the passover feast, called " chagigah," which took place every day during the passover week.—This is Lightfoot's view.

(*d*) Some think that as there is no law without an exception, and even the law of the passover admitted of alteration in case of necessity (see Num. ix. 11), so the chief priests persuaded themselves that as they had been occupied by duty—the duty (forsooth!) of apprehending our blessed Lord—throughout the night when they ought to have kept the passover, they were justified in deferring it till the next day.

All these, it must be confessed, are only conjectures. There is probably some explanation which, at this distance of time, we are unable to supply. For the present the third and fourth suggestions seem to me the most reasonable.

Chrysostom observes, " Either John calls the whole feast the passover, or means that they were then keeping the passover; while Jesus delivered it to His followers one day sooner, reserving His own sacrifice for His preparation day, when also of old His passion was celebrated."

One thing at any rate is very plain and noteworthy. The chief priests and their party made much ado about eating the passover lamb and keeping the feast, at the very time when they were about to slay the true Lamb of God, of whom this passover was a type! No wonder that Samuel says, "To obey is better than sacrifice." (1 Sam. xv. 22.)

Bullinger calls attention here to the wide difference between inward sanctification of the heart, and outward sanctimoniousness about forms, ordinances, and ceremonies.

Calvin remarks, that it is one mark of hypocrisy, "that while it is careful in performing ceremonies, it makes no scruple of neglecting matters of the highest importance."

29 —[*Pilate then went out...said, etc.*] This "going out" means that Pilate hearing that the chief priests had brought a prisoner to the courtyard, or open space before his palace, and knowing from experience, as a governor of Judæa, that they would not come into his palace for fear of defilement, but waited for him to come out to them, went out and spoke to them. His first question is one which became his office as a magistrate and judge. He inquires what is the charge or accusation brought against the prisoner before him. "Of what crime do you accuse this man?"

The well-known Valerian law among the Romans made it unlawful to judge or condemn any one without hearing the charge against him stated.

30 —[*They answered and said, etc.*] The reply of the chief priests to Pilate's inquiry, as given by John, is peculiar and elliptical. They began by saying that the prisoner was a convicted evil-doer according to their law, or else they would not have brought Him there. They had found Him, by examination before the Sanhedrim, to be a breaker of the law, and they only came there to have sentence pronounced on Him by Pilate. "If He were not a person guilty and worthy of death, we would not have delivered Him up to thee. We have discovered Him to be such a person, and we now ask thee to sentence Him to death. We have convicted Him, and we ask thee, as our chief ruler, to slay Him." There is a proud, haughty, supercilious tone, we may remark, about this answer, which was not likely to please a Roman Governor.

It is plain, by a comparison with St. Luke's Gospel, that at this point the Jews added a statement which St. John has omitted. "If thou wouldst know the precise nature of this prisoner's evil-doing, we tell thee that we found Him perverting the nation, and forbidding to give tribute to Cæsar, and saying that He is a King." (Luke xxiii. 2.) Why St. John omitted this we cannot tell, but he evidently takes it for granted that his readers knew this accusation was made, by telling us in verse thirty-three, that Pilate asked Him if He was " the King of the Jews."

Tholuck remarks, that " if the authorities had not regarded

the prisoner as worthy of death, they would not have brought him to the procurator, as none but criminal cases needed confirmation by him."

31 —[*Then said Pilate....take..judge...law.*] This sentence indicates a desire on Pilate's part to have nothing to do with the case. From the very first he evidently wished to put it away from him, and, if he could, to avoid condemning our Lord. How this feeling originated, we cannot tell. Matthew and Mark say that he knew Jesus was delivered to him from " envy." Matthew says that his wife warned him to do nothing to do with that " just person." (Matt. xxvii. 18; xxvii. 19; Mark xv. 10.) It is quite possible that the fame and character of Jesus had reached Pilate's ears long before He was brought before him. It is hard to suppose that such miracles as our Lord wrought, would never be talked of within the palace of the chief ruler of Judæa. The raising of Lazarus must surely have been reported among his servants. Our Lord's triumphal entry into Jerusalem, attended by myriads of people shouting, " Blessed is the King," must surely have been noted by the soldiers and officers of Pilate's guard. Can we wonder that all this made him regard our Lord with something like awe? Wicked men are often very superstitious. His language now before us is that of one who would gladly evade the whole case, and leave the responsibility entirely with the Jews. " If He is, as you say, a malefactor, take Him into your own hands, and condemn Him to death according to your own law. Do as you like with Him ; but do not trouble me with the case." The word we render "judge," is literally much stronger in sense. It is rather condemn to death. The only punishment the Jews might inflict, if any (which is more than doubtful), was death by stoning.

The pitiable and miserable character of Pilate, the Roman Governor, begins to come into clear light from this point. We see him a man utterly destitute of moral courage,—knowing what was right and just in the case before him, yet afraid to act on his knowledge,—knowing that our Lord was innocent, yet not daring to displease the Jews by acquitting Him,— knowing that he was doing wrong, and yet afraid to do right. " The fear of man bringeth a snare." (Prov. xxix. 25.) Wretched and contemptible are those rulers and statesmen whose first principle is to please the people, even at the expense of their own consciences, and who are ready to do what they know to be wrong rather than offend the mob! Wretched are those nations which for their sins are given over to be governed by such statesmen ! True godly rulers should lead the people, and not be led by them, should do what is right and leave consequences to God. A base determination to keep in with the world at any price, and a slavish fear of man's opinion, were leading principles in Pilate's character. There are many like him. Nothing is more common than to see statesmen evading the plain line of duty, and trying to shuffle responsibility on others, rather than give offence to the mob. This is precisely what Pilate did here. The spirit of his reply to the Jews is, " I had rather not be troubled with the case : cannot you settle it yourselves, without asking me to interfere ?"

Ellicott remarks, " It seems clear that from the first the sharp-sighted Roman perceived that this was no case for his tribunal, that it was wholly a matter of religious difference and religious hate, and that the meek prisoner who stood before him was at least innocent of the political crime laid to his charge with such an unwonted and suspicious zeal." He also quotes the just and pertinent remark of a German writer, " Pilate knew too much of Jewish expectations to suppose that the Sanhedrim would hate and persecute one who would free them from Roman authority."

Calvin thinks that Pilate said this ironically, as he would not have allowed them to inflict capital punishment. Gerhard also regards the saying as sarcastic and sneering. " If this prisoner has done anything against your Jewish superstitions, settle it yourselves." Yet a comparison with Luke makes this rather improbable in my opinion. The Jews there tell him plainly that Christ made Himself a King. (Luke xxiii. 1.) This, even a Roman must allow, was a serious charge.

Henry suggests that perhaps Pilate thought they did not really want to kill Jesus, but only to chastise Him.

[*The Jews...not lawful for us...death.*] This answer of the Jews completely defeated the wretched Pilate's attempt to put away the case before him, and avoid the necessity of judging our Lord. They reminded the Roman Governor that the power of taking away life was no longer in their hands, and that it was impossible for them to do as he suggested, and settle our Lord's case in their own way.

Let us mark here what a striking confession the Jews here made, whether they were aware of it or not. They actually admitted that they were no longer rulers and governors of their own nation, and that they were under the dominion of a foreign power. They were no longer independent, but subjects of Rome. He that has power of condemning to death, and taking away the life of a prisoner, he is the governor of a country. " It is not lawful for us," said the Jews, " to take away life. You, the Roman Governor, alone can do it, and therefore we come to thee about this Jesus." By their own mouth and their own act they publicly declared that Jacob's prophecy was fulfilled, " that the sceptre had departed from Judah," that they had no longer a lawgiver of their own stock, and that consequently the time of Shiloh, the promised Messiah, must have come. (Gen. xlix. 10.) How unconscious wicked men are that they fulfil prophecy !

The idea of Chrysostom and Augustine, that the sentence only means that the Jews could not put any one to death during the passover feast, looks to me utterly improbable.

32 —[*That the saying...fulfilled, etc.*] This verse is one of John's peculiar parenthetical comments, which are so frequent in his Gospel. Here, as in many other instances, the meaning is, " By this the saying of Jesus was fulfilled ; " and not " The thing took place, in order that the saying might be fulfilled." What precise saying is referred to, is a point on which commentators have not quite agreed.

(*a*) Some think, as Theophylact, Bullinger, Musculus, and Gerhard, that St. John refers to the saying recorded in this very Gospel (John xii. 33) ; and that the expression, " what death," only refers to the particular manner of His death by crucifixion.

(*b*) Others think, as Augustine, Calvin, and Beza, that St. John refers to the fuller saying in Matt. xx. 19, where our Lord foretells His own delivery to the Gentiles as well as His crucifixion.

Of the two views, the second seems to me the preferable one. The previous verse distinctly points to the inability of the Jews to put Jesus to death, and the necessity of the Gentiles doing the murderous work. And John remarks that this was just what Jesus had predicted,—that He would die by the hand of the Gentiles. I think, at the same time, that the crucifixion was probably included, being the death which the Gentiles inflicted, in contradistinction to the Jewish custom of stoning.

33 —[*Then Pilate entered into the judgment hall.*] The meaning of this must be that Pilate, disappointed in his attempt to put away the case from him, retired into his palace again, where he knew the Jews would not follow him, from fear of contracting ceremonial defilement, and resolved to have a private interview with our Lord, and examine Him alone.—It is quite clear that the conversation which follows, from this point down to the middle of the thirty-eighth verse, took place within the Roman Governor's walls, and most probably without the presence of any Jewish witnesses. If that was so, the substance of it could only be revealed to John by the inspiration of the Holy Ghost. Pilate's soldiers and a few guards of the prisoner may have been present. But it is highly improbable that John, or any friend of our Lord's, could have got inside the Governor's palace. If the beloved Apostle did manage to get in and hear the conversation, it is a striking example of his attachment to his Master. " Love is strong as death." (Cant. viii. 6.)

[*And called Jesus.*] This expression literally means, that he called Jesus with a loud voice to follow him inside the palace ; and came out of the outer court, or area, where he had first met the party which had brought the Prisoner to him. It is as though he said, "Come in hither, Prisoner, that I may speak with thee privately!"

[*And said...art Thou...King...Jews?*] The first question that Pilate asked of our Lord, was whether he really admitted that He was what the Jews had just accused Him of being. "Tell me, is it true that Thou art the King of the Jews? Dost thou really profess to be the King of this ancient people, over whom I and my soldiers are now rulers?"—It is far from improbable that Pilate, living so long in Jerusalem, may have often heard of the old Jewish kings, and of the dominion they received. It is far from unlikely, moreover, that he thought it possible he had before him one of those mock Messiahs, who, like Theudas, rose up at this period, and kept the minds of the Jews in agitation. "They accuse Thee of setting up Thyself as a King? Art Thou really a King? Dost Thou lay claim to any royal authority?" The humble attire and lowly appearance of our Lord can hardly fail to have struck Pilate. "Can it be true, that Thou, a poor man, with no signs of a kingdom about Thee, art the King of the Jews?"

In order to estimate aright this question which Pilate put, we must remember that Suetonius, the Roman historian, distinctly says that a rumor was very prevalent throughout the East at this period, that a King was about to arise among the Jews, who would obtain dominion over the world. This singular rumor, originating no doubt from Jewish prophecies, had of course reached Pilate's ears, and goes far to account for his question.

It is noteworthy that each of the four Gospel writers distinctly records that this was the first question that Pilate put to our Lord. It seems to show that the chief thing impressed on the mind of Pilate about Jesus, was that He was *a King*. As a King he examined Him, as a King he sentenced Him, and as a King he crucified Him. And one main object that he seems to have had in view in questioning our Lord, was to ascertain what kind of a kingdom He ruled over, and whether it was one that would interfere with the Roman authority. On the whole, the question seems a mixture of curiosity and contempt.

34.—[*Jesus answered him, Sayest thou, etc.*] Our Lord's motive in this answer to Pilate was probably to awaken Pilate's conscience: "Dost thou say this of thine own independent self, in consequence of any complaints thou hast heard against Me as a seditious person? Or dost thou only ask it because the Jews have just accused Me of being a King? Hast thou, during all the years thou hast been a Governor, ever heard of Me as a leader of insurrection, or a rebel against the Romans? If thou hast never heard anything of this kind against Me, and hast no personal knowledge of my being a rebel, oughtest thou not to pay very little attention to the complaint of my enemies? Their bare assertion ought not to weigh with thee."

Grotius paraphrases the verse thus : " Thou hast been long a ruler, and a careful defender of the Roman majesty. Hast thou ever heard anything that would impeach Me of a desire to usurp authority against Rome ? If thou hast never known anything of thyself, but others have suggested it, beware lest thou be deceived by an ambiguous word."

There is undoubtedly some little obscurity around the verse, and it becomes us to handle it reverently. It certainly looks like an appeal to the Roman Governor's conscience. " Before I answer thy question let Me ask thee one. For what reason and from what motive art thou making this inquiry about my being a King ? Canst thou say, from thy own personal knowledge, that thou hast ever heard Me complained of as setting up a kingdom ? Thou knowest thou canst not say that. Art thou only asking Me because thou hast heard the Jews accuse Me of being a King to-day ? If this is so, judge for thyself whether such a King as I appear to be is likely to interfere with thy authority."

Poole says, " Our Saviour desired to be satisfied from Pilate, whether he asked Him as a private person for his own satisfaction, or as a judge, having received any such accusation against Him. If he asked Him as a judge, he was bound to call others to prove what they had charged Him with."

Burgon remarks that Jesus did not need information in asking this question. He asked, as the Lord asked Adam, " Where art thou ?" (Gen. iii. 9) in order to arouse Pilate to a sense of the shameful injustice of the charge.

35 —[*Pilate answered, etc.*] The answer of Pilate exhibits the haughty, high-minded, supercilious, fierce spirit of a Roman man of the world. So far from responding to our Lord's appeal to his conscience, he fires up at the very idea of knowing anything of the current opinions about Christ.—" Am I a Jew ? Thinkest thou that a noble Roman like me knows anything about the superstitions of Thy people. I only know that Thine own countrymen, and the very leaders of Thy nation, have brought Thee unto me as a prisoner worthy of death. What they mean I do not pretend to understand. But I suppose there is some ground for their accusation. Tell me plainly what Thou hast done."

Pilate's answer seems tantamount to an acknowledgment that he knew nothing against our Lord. But as He had been brought before him as a prisoner, and he was pressed to condemn Him, he asks Him what He has done to bring this hatred of the Jews upon Him.

He that would know the depth of scorn contained in that sentence, " Am I a Jew ?" should mark the contemptuous way in which Horace, Juvenal, Tacitus, and Pliny speak of the Jews.

Stier remarks, " The Romans were only concerned with what was DONE; not with dreams, like the Jews ; nor with wisdom, like the Greeks." Pilate's question was characteristic of his nation.

36 —[*Jesus answered.. kingdom...not...world.*] In this famous sentence our Lord begins His answer to Pilate's question, " Art Thou the King of the Jews ? " " Thou askest whether I am a King. I reply that I certainly have a kingdom, but it is a kingdom entirely unlike the kingdoms of this world. It is a kingdom which is neither begun, nor propagated, nor defended by the power of this world, by the world's arms or the world's money. It is a kingdom which took its origin from heaven, and not from earth,—a spiritual kingdom,—a kingdom over hearts and wills and consciences,—a kingdom which needs no armies or revenues,—a kingdom which in no way interferes with the kingdoms of this world."

The literal rendering of the Greek would be " out of this world." But it evidently means " belonging to, dependent on, springing from, connected with." It is the same preposition that we find in John viii. 23 : " Ye are from beneath; I am from above : ye are of this world ; I am not of this world."

That the above was our Lord's plain meaning, when He spoke the words before us, is to my mind as evident as the sun at noonday. The favorite theory of certain Christians that this text forbids Governments to have anything to do with religion, and condemns the union of Church and State, and renders all Established Churches unlawful, is, in my judgment, baseless, preposterous, and utterly devoid of common sense. Whether the union of Church and State be right or wrong, it appears to me absurd to say that it is forbidden by this text. The text declares that Christ's kingdom did not spring from the powers of this world, and is not dependent on them ; but the text does not declare that the powers of this world ought to have nothing to do with Christ's kingdom. Christ's kingdom can get on very well without them ; but they cannot get on very well without Christ's kingdom.

The following leading principles are worth remembering, in looking at this vexed question :—

(*a*) Every Government is responsible to God, and no Government can expect to prosper without God's blessing. Every Government therefore is bound to do all that lies in its power to obtain God's favor and blessing. The Government that does not strive to promote true religion, has no right to expect God's blessing.

(*b*) Every good Government should endeavor to promote truth charity, temperance, honesty, diligence, industry, chastity, among its subjects. True religion is the only root from which these things can grow. The Government that does not labor to promote true religion cannot be called either wise or good.

(*c*) To tell us that a Government must leave religion alone, because it cannot promote it without favoring one church more than another, is simply absurd. It is equivalent to saying that, as we cannot do good to everybody, we are to sit still and do no good at all.

(*d*) To tell us that no Government can find out what true religion is, and that consequently a Government should regard all religions with equal indifference, is an argument only fit for an infidel. In England at any rate a belief that the Bible is true is a part of the Constitution; an insult to the Bible is a punishable offence, and the testimony of an avowed atheist goes for nothing in a court of law.

(*e*) It is undoubtedly true that Christ's kingdom is a kingdom independent of the rulers of this world, and one which they can neither begin, increase, nor overthrow. But it is utterly false that the rulers of this world have nothing to do with Christ's kingdom, may safely leave religion entirely alone, and may govern their subjects as if they were beasts and had no souls at all.

Chrysostom says that our Lord's reply meant, " I am indeed a King; but not such a King as thou suspectest, but one far more glorious."

[*If my kingdom...servants fight...Jews.*] Our Lord proceeds to give proof that His kingdom was not of this world, and therefore not likely to interfere with the Roman authority. " If the kingdom of which I am head, were like the kingdoms of this world, and supported and maintained by worldly means, then my disciples would take up arms and fight, to prevent my being delivered to the Jews. This, as thou mayest know by inquiry, is the very thing which I forbade last night. Thine own soldiers can tell thee that they saw Me reprove a disciple for fighting, and heard Me tell him to put up his sword."

Let us mark that a religion propagated by the sword, or by violence, is a most unsatisfactory kind of Christianity. The weapons of Christ's warfare are not carnal. Even true Christians who have appealed to the sword to support their opinions, have often found themselves losers by it. Taking the sword, they have perished by the sword. Zwingle dying in battle, and the Scotch Covenanters, are examples.

Stier thinks that by "my servants" in this verse our Lord meant the angels! This, however, seems very improbable.

Bullinger makes some good remarks on this sentence, in reply to the Anabaptists of his time. He says, among other things, " Just as it does not follow that the Church is worldly, because we who are flesh and blood, and are the world, are members of the Church,—so no one, unless he wants common sense, will say that the Church is worldly, because in it Kings and Princes serve God, by defending the good and punishing the bad."

Calvin observes that this sentence "does not hinder Princes from defending the kingdom of Christ; partly by appointing external discipline, and partly by lending their protection to the Church against wicked men." Beza says much the same.

Hutcheson observes, "This text is not to be understood as if Christ disallowed that they to whom He has given the sword should defend His kingdom therewith; for if magistrates were as magistrates should be, nursing parents to the Church, and ought to kiss the Son, then certainly they may and should employ their power as magistrates for removing idolatry, and setting up the true worship of God, and defending it against violence."

[*But now...my kingdom not...hence.*] The true meaning of this little sentence is not very clear. May it not mean, "Now, in this dispensation, my kingdom is not an earthly one, and is not of this world. A day will come by and by, after my second advent, when my kingdom will be a visible one over the whole earth, and my saints shall rule over the renewed world."—This may seem fanciful to some; but I have a strong impression that it is the true meaning. The adverb "now" is very decided and emphatical.

37 —[*Pilate therefore...Art Thou a King ?*] Here Pilate returns to his question, though he puts it in a different way : "Art Thou in some sense a King, if not such a King as the Kings of this world? Thou speakest of Thy kingdom and Thy servants. Am I to understand that Thou art a King?" We should observe the distinction in the language here, compared with that of verse thirty-three. There it was, "Art Thou the King of the Jews?" Here it is simply, "Art Thou a King?"

[*Jesus answered, Thou sayest...I am a King.*] This sentence is a direct acknowledgment from our Lord's lips that He is a King; a King only over hearts, consciences, and wills, but still a real true King. "Thou sayest," is equivalent to an affirmation. "Thou sayest truly: I am what thou askest about. I admit that I am a King."

There can be no doubt that this "is the good confession before Pontius Pilate," which St. Paul specially impresses on the attention of the timid disciple Timothy, in his pastoral epistle. (1 Tim. vi. 13.)

[*To this end...born...witness...truth.*] Here our Lord informs Pilate what was the great end and purpose of His incarnation. "It is true that I am a King, but not a King after the manner of the world. I am only a King over hearts and minds. The principal work for which I came into the world, is to be a witness of the truth concerning God, concerning man, and concerning the way of salvation. This truth has been long hidden and lost sight of. I came to bring it to light once more, and to be the King of all who receive it."

I think the " truth " in this sentence must be taken in the widest and fullest sense. The true doctrine about man, and God, and salvation, and sin, and holiness, was almost buried, lost, and gone, when Christ came into the world. To revive the dying light, and erect a new standard of godliness in a corrupt world, which neither Egypt, Assyria, Greece nor Rome could prevent rotting and decaying, was one grand end of Christ's mission. He did not come to gather armies, build cities, amass treasure, and found a dynasty, as Pilate perhaps fancied. He came to be God's witness, and to lift up God's truth in the midst of a dark world. He that would know how miserably small is the amount of truth which even the most civilized nations know without Christianity, should examine the religion and morality of the Chinese and Hindoos in the present day.

Some think that " I was born " points to Christ's humanity, and " came into the world," to His divinity.

[*Every one...of truth...heareth my voice.*] I think that in this sentence our Lord tells Pilate who are His subjects, disciples, and followers. " Wouldest thou know who are the members of my kingdom ? I tell thee that it consists of all who really love the truth and desire to know more of God's truth. All such hear my voice, are pleased with my principles, and subjects of my kingdom." It is like our Lord's words to Nicodemus: " He that doeth truth cometh to the light." (John iii. 21.)

Thus our Lord shows Pilate that His kingdom was not an earthly kingdom, that His business was not to wear a crown and found an earthly monarchy, but to proclaim truth ; and that His followers were not soldiers and warriors, but all earnest seekers after truth. Pilate therefore might dismiss from his mind all idea of His kingdom interfering with the authority of Rome.

Let us note that the position of Christ in the world must be the position of all Christians. Like our Master we must be witnesses for God and truth against sin and ignorance. We must not be afraid to stand alone. We must testify.

The expression " every one that is of the truth " is remarkable. It must mean every one that really and honestly desires to know the truth, receives my teaching, and follows Me as a Master. Does it not show that our Lord, when He appeared, gathered around Him all who were true-hearted lovers of God's revealed will, and were seeking, however feebly, to know more of it ? (Compare John iii. 20 ; and viii. 47.) That there were many such, like Nathanael, among the Jews, anxiously looking for a Redeemer, we cannot doubt. " These," says our Lord, " are my subjects and make up my kingdom." Just as when

He speaks of Himself as a shepherd, He says, " My sheep hear my voice;" so when He speaks of Himself as God's great witness to truth, He says, " All friends of truth hear my voice."

The wise condescension with which our Lord adapts His language to Pilate's habits of thought as a Roman, is very noteworthy. If He had used Jewish figures of speech, drawn from Old Testament language, Pilate might well have failed to understand Him. But every Roman in high position must have heard the arguments of philosophers about "the truth." Therefore our Lord says, " I am a witness to truth." In speaking to unconverted people, it is wise to use terms which they can understand.

Theophylact suggests that here is an appeal to Pilate's conscience: " If you are a real seeker after truth you will listen to Me."

38 —[*Pilate saith... What is truth?*] This famous question, in my judgment, can only admit of one interpretation. It is the cold, sneering, sceptical interjection of a mere man of the world, who has persuaded himself that there is no such thing as truth, that all religions are equally false, that this life is all we have to care for, and that creeds and modes of faith are only words and names and superstitions, which no sensible person need attend to. It is precisely the state of mind in which thousands of great and rich men in every age live and die. Expanded and paraphrased, Pilate's question comes to this:—" Truth indeed ! What is truth ? I have heard all my life of various philosophical systems, each asserting that it has found the truth, and each differing widely from the others. Who is to decide what is truth and what is not ? "—The best proof that this is the right view of the sentence is Pilate's behavior when he has asked the question. He does not, as Lord Bacon remarked two centuries ago, wait for an answer, but breaks off the conversation and goes away.—The supposition that he asked a question, as an honest inquirer, with a real desire to get an answer, is too improbable and unreasonable to require any comment. The right way to understand Pilate's meaning is to put ourselves in his place, and to consider how many sects and schools of philosophers there were in the world at the time when our Lord appeared,—some Roman, some Grecian, and some Egyptian,—all alleging that they had got the truth, and all equally unsatisfactory. In short Gallio, who thought Christianity a mere " question of words and names,"—Festus, who thought the dislike of the Jews to Paul arose from " questions of their own superstition,"—and Pontius Pilate, were all much alike. The worldly-minded Roman noble speaks like a man sick and weary of philosophical speculations ;—" What is truth indeed ? Who can tell ? "—Nevertheless truth was very near him. If he had waited he might have learned !

Lightfoot alone thinks that Pilate only meant, " What is the

true state of affairs? How can one so poor as Thou art be a
King? How canst Thou be a King and yet not of this world!"

[*And when...said this...went out...Jews.*] The meaning of this
sentence is that Pilate " went out " of the palace where he had
been conversing with our Lord apart from the Jews, and returned to the courtyard, or open space at the gate, where he
had left the Jews at the thirty-third verse. He broke off the
conversation at this point. Very likely the mention of " truth "
touched his conscience, and he found it convenient to go out
hurriedly, and cover his retreat with a sneer. A bad conscience
generally dislikes a close conversation with a good man.

Augustine says, " I suppose that when Pilate said, ' What is
truth?' the Jews' custom, that one should be released at the
passover, came into his mind at that instant, and for this reason he did not wait for Jesus to tell him what truth was, that
no time might be lost!" This, however, seems rather improbable.

[*And saith...I find...no fault at all.*] In this sentence comes
out the true impression of Pilate about our Lord.—" After examining this man I can discern in Him no guilt, and nothing
certainly to warrant me in condemning Him to death. He says,
no doubt, and does not hesitate to avow it, that He is a King.
But I find that His kingdom is not one which interferes with the
authority of Cæsar. Such Kings as this we Romans do not
care for, or regard as criminals. In short, your charge against
Him entirely breaks down, and I am disposed to dismiss Him
as not guilty."

Our Lord, we may remember, came to be a sacrifice for our
sins. It was only fitting that he who was one of the chief
agents in killing Him, should publicly declare that, like a lamb
without blemish, there was " no fault in Him."

39 —[*But ye have a custom, etc.*] In this verse we see the cowardly, weak, double-minded character of Pilate coming out. He
knows in his own conscience that our Lord is innocent, and
that if he acts justly he ought to let Him go free. But he fears
offending the Jews, and wants to contrive matters so as to
please them. He therefore prepares a plan by which he hoped
that Jesus might be found guilty and the Jews satisfied, and
yet Jesus might depart unhurt, and his own secret desire to
acquit Him be gratified.—The plan was this. The Jews had a
custom that at passover time they might obtain from the Roman
Governor the release of some notable prisoner. Pilate craftily
suggests that the prisoner released this passover should be our
Lord Jesus Christ.—" Let us suppose that Jesus is guilty," he
seems to say : " I am willing to condemn Him, and declare Him
a criminal worthy of death, and a malefactor, in order to please
you. But having pronounced Him a guilty criminal, what say
you to my letting Him go free, according to the passover custom?"--This cowardly and unjust judge hoped in this way to

please the Jews, by declaring an innocent person guilty, and yet at the same time to please himself by getting His life spared. Such are the ways of worldly and unprincipled rulers. Between the base fear of men, the desire to please the mob, and the secret dictates of their own conscience, they are continually doing wicked things, and pleasing nobody at all, and least of all themselves.

About this "custom," and when it began, we know nothing. St. Mark's account would lead us to suppose that as soon as Pilate came out of his palace, the multitude cried out for the usual passover favor to be granted to them. (See Mark xv. 8.) Pilate would seem to have caught at the idea at once, and to have suggested that Jesus should be the person released.

There seems a latent meaning in Pilate's use of the expression "the King of the Jews." Some think that it is a sneer.— "This miserable, poor, lowly King; will you not have Him let go?"—Others think that Pilate had in view our Lord's claim to be the Messiah. "Would it not be better to release this man who asserts that He is your own Messiah? Would it not be a scandal to your nation to kill Him?"—A desire to release our Lord, side by side with a cowardly fear of offending the Jews by doing what was just and right, runs through all Pilate's dealings. He evidently knows what he ought to do, but does not do it.

Henry thinks Pilate must have heard how popular Jesus was with some of the Jews, and must have known of His triumphal entry into Jerusalem a few days before. "He looked on Him as the darling of the multitude, and the envy of the rulers. Therefore he made no doubt they would demand the release of Jesus; and this would stop the prosecution, and all would be well." But he had not reckoned on the influence of the priests over the fickle multitude.

40.—[*Then cried they all, etc.*] This verse describes the complete failure of Pilate's notable plan, by which he hoped to satisfy the Jews and yet release Jesus. The fierce and bigoted party of Caiaphas would not listen to his proposal for a moment. They declared they would rather have Barabbas, a notorious prisoner in the hands of the Romans, released than Jesus. Nothing would content them but our Lord's death. Barabbas, we know from St. Luke (xxiii. 19), was a murderer as well as a robber. The Jews were asked to decide whether the holy Jesus or the vile criminal should be let go free and released from prison.—Such was their utter hardness, bitterness, cruelty, and hatred of our Lord, that they actually declare they would rather have Barabbas set free than Jesus! Nothing in short would satisfy them but Christ's blood. Thus they committed the great sin which Peter charges home on them not long after: "Ye denied Jesus in the presence of Pilate, when he was determined to let Him go.—Ye denied the Holy One

and the Just, and desired a murderer to be granted unto you."
(Acts iii. 13, 14.) They publicly declared that they liked a robber and a murderer better than Christ !

The Greek word rendered " cried," signifies a very loud cry
or shout. It is the same word that occurs at the raising of
Lazarus. " He cried, Lazarus, come forth ! " (John xi. 43.)

The expression " again " must either refer to the loud cries
the Jews had raised, when they first brought Jesus to Pilate
and demanded His condemnation ; or else it must refer to a
former cry for Barabbas to be released. According to Matthew
they TWICE demanded this, with an interval of time between.
(Compare Matt. xxvii. 15—26.)

The singularly typical character of all this transaction should
be carefully noticed. Even here at this juncture we have a
lively illustration of the great Christian doctrine of *substitution*. Barabbas, the real criminal, is acquitted and let go free.
Jesus, innocent and guiltless, is condemned and sentenced to
death. So is it in the salvation of our souls. We are all by
nature like Barabbas, and deserve God's wrath and condemnation ; yet he was accounted righteous and set free. The Lord
Jesus Christ is perfectly innocent ; and yet He is counted a
sinner, punished as a sinner, and put to death that we may live.
Christ suffers, though guiltless, that we may be pardoned. We
are pardoned, though guilty, because of what Christ does for
us. We are sinners, and yet counted righteous. Christ is
righteous, and yet counted a sinner. Happy is that man who
understands this doctrine, and has laid hold on it by faith for
the salvation of his own soul.

In leaving this chapter, it is vain to deny that there are occasional difficulties in harmonizing the four different accounts of
our Lord's examination and crucifixion. This of course arises
from one Gospel writer dwelling more fully on one set of facts,
and another on another. But we need not doubt that all is perfectly harmonious, and that if we do not see it, the reason lies
in our present want of perception. If each Evangelist had told
the story in precisely the same words, the whole result would
have been far less satisfactory. It would have savored of imposture, concert, and collusion. The varieties in the four accounts are just what might have been expected from four honest independent witnesses, and, fairly treated, admit of explanation.

Augustine remarks, " How all the Evangelists agree together
and nothing in any one Evangelist is at variance with the truth
put forth by another,—this whosoever desires to know, let him
seek it in laborious writings, and not in popular discourses, and
not by standing and hearing, but by sitting and reading, or by
lending a most attentive ear and mind to him that readeth. Yet
let him believe, before he knows it, that there is nothing writ-

ten by any one Evangelist, that can possibly be contrary either to his own or another's narration."

Melancthon suggests that the whole history of the passion, in this chapter, is a vivid typical picture of the history of Christ's Church in every age. He bids us observe what a multitude of portraits it contains! Saints both weak and strong,—enemies of many kinds—traitors, hypocrites, tyrants, priests, rulers, mobs, violence, treachery, the flight of friends, the bitter language of foes. What is it but a kind of prophetic history of Christ's Church?

The character of Pontius Pilate is so ably drawn out by Ellicott, that it may be well to quote it, in concluding this chapter. " Pilate was a thorough and complete type of the later-Roman man of the world. Stern, but not relentless,—shrewd and world-worn,—prompt and practical,—haughtily just,—and yet, as the early writers correctly observed, self-seeking and cowardly,—able to perceive what was right, but without moral strength to follow it out,—the Procurator of Judæa stands forth a sad and terrible instance of a man whom the fear of endangered self-interest drove not only to act against the deliberate convictions of his heart and conscience, but further to commit an act of cruelty and injustice, even after those convictions had been deepened by warnings and strengthened by presentiment."

JOHN XIX. 1—16

1 Then Pilate therefore took Jesus, and scourged *him*.

2 And the soldiers platted a crown of thorns, and put *it* on his head, and they put on him a purple robe.

3 And said, Hail, King of the Jews! and they smote him with their hands.

4 Pilate therefore went forth again and saith unto them, Behold I·bring him forth to you, that ye may know that I find no fault in him.

5 Then came Jesus forth, wearing the crown of thorns, and the purple robe. And *Pilate* saith unto them, Behold the man!

6 When the chief priests therefore and officers saw him, they cried out, saying, Crucify *him*, crucify *him*. Pilate saith unto them, Take ye him, and crucify *him*: for I find no fault in him.

7 The Jews answered him, We have a law, and by our law he ought to die, because he made himself the Son of God.

8 When Pilate therefore heard that saying, he was the more afraid;

9 And went again into the judgment hall, and saith unto Jesus, Whence art thou? But Jesus gave him no answer.

10 Then saith Pilate unto him, Speakest thou not unto me? knowest thou not that I have power to crucify thee, and have power to release thee?

11 Jesus answered, Thou couldest have no power *at all* against me, except it were given thee from above: therefore he that delivered me unto thee hath the greater sin.

12 And from thenceforth Pilate sought to release him: but the Jews cried out, saying, If thou let this man go, thou art not Cæsar's friend: whosoever maketh himself a king speaketh against Cæsar.

13 When Pilate therefore heard that saying, he brought Jesus forth, and sat down in the judgment seat in a place that is called the Pavement, but in the Hebrew, Gabbatha.

14 And it was the preparation of the passover, and about the sixth hour: and he saith unto the Jews, Behold your King!

15 But they cried out, Away with *him*, away with *him*, crucify him. Pilate saith unto them, Shall I crucify your King? The chief priests answered, We have no king but Cæsar.

16 Then delivered he him therefore unto them to be crucified. And they took Jesus, and led *him* away.

THESE verses exhibit to our eyes a wonderful picture, a picture which ought to be deeply interesting to all who profess and call themselves Christians. Like every great historical picture, it contains special points on which we should fix our special attention. Above all, it contains three life-like portraits, which we shall find it useful to examine in order.

The first portrait in the picture is that of our Lord Jesus Christ Himself.

We see the Saviour of mankind scourged, crowned with thorns, mocked, smitten, rejected by His own people, unjustly condemned by a judge who saw no fault in Him, and finally delivered up to a most painful death. Yet this was He who was the eternal Son of God, whom the Father's countless angels delighted to honor. This was He who came into the world to save sinners, and after living a blameless life for thirty years, spent the last three years of His time on earth in going about doing good, and preaching the Gospel. Surely the sun never shone on a more wondrous sight since the day of its creation!

Let us admire that love of Christ which St. Paul declares, " passeth knowledge," and let us see an endless depth of meaning in the expression. There is no earthly love with which it can be compared, and no standard by which to measure it. It is a love that stands alone. Never let us forget when we ponder this tale of suffering, that Jesus suffered for *our* sins, the Just for the unjust, that He was wounded for *our* transgressions and bruised for *our* iniquities, and that with His stripes we are healed.

Let us diligently follow the example of His patience in all the trials and afflictions of life, and specially in those which may be brought upon us by religion. When He was reviled, He reviled not again ; when He suffered, He threatened not, but committed Himself to Him that judgeth righteously. Let us arm ourselves with the same mind. Let us consider Him who endured such contradiction of sinners without a murmur, and strive to glorify Him by suffering well, no less than by doing well.

The second portrait in the picture before us, is that of the unbelieving Jews who favored our Lord's death.

We see them for three or four long hours obstinately rejecting Pilate's offer to release our Lord,—fiercely demanding His crucifixion, savagely claiming His condemnation to death as a right,—persistently refusing to acknowledge Him as their King,—declaring that they had no King but Cæsar,—and finally accumulating on their own heads the greater part of the guilt of His murder. Yet these were the children of Israel and the seed of Abraham, to whom pertained the promises and the Mosaic ceremonial, the temple sacrifices and the temple priesthood. These were men who professed to look for a Prophet like unto Moses, and a son of David who was to set up a kingdom as Messiah. Never, surely, was there such an exhibition of the depth of human wickedness since the day when Adam fell.

Let us mark with fear and trembling the enormous danger of long-continued rejection of light and knowledge. There is such a thing as judicial blindness ; and it is the last and sorest judgment which God can send upon men. He who, like Pharaoh and Ahab, is often reproved but refuses to receive reproof, will finally have a heart harder than the nether mill-stone, and a conscience past feeling, and seared as with a hot iron. This was the state of the Jewish nation during the time of our Lord's ministry; and the heading up of their sin was their deliberate rejection of Him, when Pilate desired to let Him go. From such judicial blindness may we all pray to be delivered ! There is no worse judgment from God than to be left to ourselves, and given over to our own wicked hearts and the devil. There is no surer way to bring that judgment upon us than to persist in refusing warnings and sinning against light. These words of Solomon are very awful : " Because I have called, and ye refused; I have stretched out my hand, and no man regarded ; but ye have set at nought all my counsel, and would none of my reproof : I also will laugh at your calamity ; I will mock when your fear cometh." (Prov. i. 24–26.) Never let it be forgotten, that, like the Jews, we may at length be given up to strong delusion, so that we believe lies, and think that we are doing God service while we are committing sin. (2 Thess. ii. 11.)

The third, and last portrait in the picture before us, is that of Pontius Pilate.

We see a Roman Governor,—a man of rank and high position,—an imperial representative of the most powerful nation on earth,—a man who ought to have been the fountain of justice and equity,—halting between two opinions in a case as clear as the sun at noonday. We see him knowing what was right, and yet afraid to act up to his knowledge,—convinced in his own conscience that he ought to acquit the prisoner before him, and yet afraid to do it lest he should displease His accusers,—sacrificing the claims of justice to the base fear of man,—sanctioning from sheer cowardice, an enormous crime,—and finally countenancing, from love of man's good opinion, the murder of an innocent person. Never perhaps did human nature make such a contemptible exhibition. Never was there a name so justly handed down to a world's scorn as the name which is embalmed in all our creeds,—the name of Pontius Pilate.

Let us learn what miserable creatures great men are, when they have no high principles within them, and no faith in the reality of a God above them. The meanest laborer who has grace and fears God, is a nobler being in the eyes of his Creator than the King, ruler, or statesman, whose first aim it is to please the people. To have one conscience in private and another in public,— one rule of duty for our own souls, and another for our public actions,—to see clearly what is right before God, and yet for the sake of popularity to do wrong,—this may seem to some both right, and politic, and statesmanlike, and wise. But it is a character which no Christian man can ever regard with respect.

Let us pray that our own country may never be without men in high places who have grace to think right, and courage to act up to their knowledge, without truckling to the opinion of men. Those who fear God more than man, and care for pleasing God more than man, are the best rulers of a nation, and in the long run of years are always most respected. Men like Pontius Pilate, who are always trimming and compromising, led by popular opinion instead of leading popular opinion, afraid of doing right if it gives offence, ready to do wrong if it makes them personally popular, such men are the worst governors that a country can have. They are often God's heavy judgment on a nation because of a nation's sins.

NOTES   JOHN XIX 1—16

1 —[*Then Pilate...took Jesus...scourged Him.*] The cruel injury inflicted on our Lord's body, in this verse, was probably far more severe than an English reader might suppose. It was a punishment which among the Romans generally preceded crucifixion, and was sometimes so painful and violent that the sufferer died under it. It was often a scourging with rods, and not always with cords, as painters and sculptors represent. Josephus, the Jewish historian, in his "Antiquities," particularly mentions that malefactors were scourged, and tormented in every way before they were put to death. Smith's Dictionary of the Bible says, that under the Roman mode of scourging, "the culprit was stripped, stretched with cords or thongs on a frame, and beaten with rods."

As to Pilate's reason for inflicting this punishment on our Lord, there seems little doubt. He secretly hoped that this tremendous scourging, in the Roman fashion, would satisfy the Jews ; and that after seeing Jesus beaten, bleeding, and torn with rods, they would be content to let Him go free. As usual, he was double-minded, cruel and deceitful. He tried to please the Jews by ill-treating our Lord as much as possible, and at the same time he hoped to please his own conscience a little by not putting Him to death. He told the Jews, indeed, according to Luke's account, what he wanted : "I will chastise Him and release Him." (Luke xxiii. 16.) How entirely this weak design failed we shall see by-and-by.

Chrysostom says, "Pilate scourged Jesus, desiring to exhaust and soothe the fury of the Jews. Being anxious to stay the evil at this point, he scourged Him, and permitted to be done what was done, and the robe and crown to be put on Him, in order to relax their anger." Augustine and Cyril say much the same.

The importance of this particular portion of our Lord's sufferings is strongly shown by the fact that Isaiah specially says, "by His stripes we are healed ;" and that St. Peter specially quotes that text in his first epistle. (Isaiah liii. 5. 1 Peter ii. 24.) Our Lord Himself particularly foretold that He would be scourged. (Luke xviii. 33.)

It may seem needless to say that Pilate did not scourge Jesus with his own hands. Any plain reader will at once conclude that the scourging was inflicted by his soldiers or attendants. Yet the venerable Bede thinks that Pilate himself scourged Jesus. And it is worth remembering that a modern sceptical writer has actually argued that the book of Leviticus must be uninspired, because in that book the priest is commanded to lift, and move, and offer up the bodies of slain sacrifices, which alone he could not do ! Surely he might have recollected that a man is said to do things, when he does them by the hands of servants and attendants! It was thus, no doubt, that Pilate scourged Jesus. The word "took" probably means, "commanded Him to be seized."

Hengstenberg thinks that the remarkable incident of Pilate's "washing his hands" (Matt. xxvii. 24), and declaring his innocence of Christ's blood, comes in between this verse and the preceding chapter. I would rather place it after the fifteenth verse of this nineteenth chapter.

The place where this horrible indignity was inflicted on our Lord's holy person (according to St. Matthew xxvii. 27) was the prætorium, or common hall, which was probably a kind of guard-room, where the Roman soldiers used to spend their time, and keep themselves in readiness to do anything the Governor wished. What kind of a place the guard-room of a body of rough Roman soldiers can have been we can hardly conceive, even if we visit the worst regimental guard-rooms of modern days.

Some think that our Lord was scourged twice; once at the beginning of Pilate's examination, and once after His final condemnation. This however seems to me very doubtful. The idea probably arises from not carefully observing that the proceedings before Pilate, after the scourging recorded here, are peculiar to St. John's Gospel, and omitted by Matthew, Mark, and Luke.

Besser remarks, " Before the message, ' Christ our righteousness' was revived, and the Lutheran ' Christ for us ' was again the refreshment of weary souls, men could not draw much refreshment from Christ's scourging. Before the Reformation whole hosts of self-bewailing penitents came forth from Italy and spread over Germany. They were called ' Flagellants ;' and naked to the waist they roamed through towns and villages, singing penitential hymns like Dies Iræ, and flogging one another."

2 —[*And...soldiers...crown...thorns...head.*] About the object of the soldiers in this act there can be no doubt. It was done in mockery and ridicule of our blessed Lord, and to pour contempt on the idea of His being a King. These rude men would show how they defied such a King. We can well believe that rough heathen soldiers, like Roman legionaries, were expert and trained by practice in the best way of torturing a prisoner.

Thorns, according to Tristram, are so common in Palestine, that the soldiers would have no difficulty in finding materials for weaving this crown. Hasselquist, quoted in Smith's Dictionary, says, " The plant called ' nebk ' (*zizyphus spina Christi*) was very suitable for the purpose, as it has many sharp thorns, and its flexible, pliant, and round branches, might easily be plaited in the form of a crown; and what, in my opinion, seems the greatest proof is, that the leaves most resemble those of ivy, as they are of a very deep green. Perhaps the enemies of Christ would choose a plant like that with which Emperors and Generals used to be crowned, that there might be calumny even in the punishment." How painful and irritating such a crown of thorns would be, sticking into the forehead or head of one whose hands were bound, we can easily imagine.

Here, as in every step of Christ's passion, we see His complete and perfect substitution for sinners. He, the innocent sin-bearer, wore the crown of thorns, that we, the guilty, might wear a crown of glory. Vast is the contrast which there will be between the crown of glory that Christ will wear at His second advent, and the crown of thorns which He wore at His first coming.

Lightfoot remarks that " it was a most unquestionable token that Christ's kingdom was not of this world, when He was crowned only with thorns and briars, which are the curse of the earth." It was, moreover, a striking symbol of the consequences of the fall being laid on the head of our divine Substitute. In Leviticus it is written that Aaron shall lay his hands " upon the *head* of the live goat, and confess over him all the iniquities of the Children of Israel, and all their transgressions in all their sins, putting them upon the head of the goat." (Lev. xvi. 21.)

History says that in the Crusades, when Godfrey of Bouillon, the Christian General, was made King of Jerusalem, he refused to be crowned with a golden crown,—saying that " it did not become him to wear a crown of gold, in the city where his Saviour had worn a crown of thorns."

Rollock observes, " Ye shall find these soldiers even worse inclined than Pilate was. This falls out: if the master command them to do one evil deed, often the servants will do two."

When John Huss, the martyr, was brought forth to be burned, they put a paper over his head, on which were pictured three devils, and the title " heresiarch." When he saw it, he said, " My Lord Jesus Christ, for my sake, did wear a crown of thorns: why should not I, therefore, for His sake, wear this ignominious crown ? "

[*And they put...purple robe.*] This again was done as a mark of contempt and derision. A mock royal robe was thrown over our Lord's shoulders, in order to show how ridiculous and contemptible was the idea of His kingdom. The color, " purple," was doubtless meant to be a derisive imitation of the well-known imperial purple, the color worn by Emperors and Kings. Some have thought that this robe was only an old soldier's cape, such as a guard-house would easily furnish. Some, with more show of probability, have thought that this " robe " must be the " gorgeous robe " which Herod put on our Lord mentioned by St. Luke, when he sent Him back to Pilate (Luke xxiii. 11), a circumstance which John has not recorded. In any case we need not doubt that the " robe " was some shabby, cast-off garment. It is worth remembering that this brilliant color, scarlet or purple, would make our blessed Lord a most conspic-uous object to every eye, when He was led through the streets from Herod, or brought forth from Pilate's house to the assem-bled multitude of Jews.—Once more we should call to mind the symbolical nature of this transaction also. Our Lord was clothed with a robe of shame and contempt, that we might be clothed with a spotless garment of righteousness, and stand in white robes before the throne of God.

3 —[*And said, Hail, King of the Jews!*] This again was evi-dently done to pour contempt upon our Lord. The words of the soldiers were spoken in contemptuous imitation of the words addressed to a Roman Emperor, on his assuming Impe-rial power : "Hail, Emperor! *ave Imperator!*" It was as much as saying, "Thou a King indeed! Thou and thy king-dom are alike base and contemptible."

Hengstenberg observes, "It was the kingdom of the Jews it-self that the soldiers laughed at. They regarded Jesus as the representative of the Messianic hope of the Jews. They would turn to ridicule these royal hopes, which were known far in the heathen world, more especially as they aspired to the do-minion of the whole earth."

Let us not fail to remark at this point that ridicule, scorn, and contempt, were one prominent portion of our blessed Mas-ter's sufferings. Any one who knows human nature, must know that few things are more difficult to bear than ridicule, especially when we know that it is undeserved, and when it is for religion's sake. Those who have to endure such ridicule may take comfort in the thought that Christ can sympathize with them ; for it is a cup which He Himself drank to the very dregs. Here again He was our Substitute. He bore contempt, that we might receive praise and glory at the last day.

Henry remarks, "If at any time we are ridiculed for well-doing, let us not be ashamed, but glorify God ; for thus we are partakers of Christ's sufferings."

[*And they smote...hands.*] The words so rendered would be equally well translated, "they gave Him blows with a rod or stick." The same Greek word in the singular is so translated in the marginal reading of John xviii. 22. When we compare Matt. xxvii. 27, 30, where it says the soldiers took a reed and smote Him with it on the head, it seems highly probable that this was the action here recorded. According to Matthew, the soldiers put the reed in our Lord's hand as a mock sceptre ; and when, as Lampe observes, "He refused to retain it in His right hand, because He came to suffer indignities, but not to perform them," they snatched it out of His hand, and brutally struck

Him with it on the head. This appears to me a reasonable and satisfactory supposition, and makes it most likely that the blow here was not "with the hand."

If the blows were inflicted on the head, whether with hand or reed, we can readily conceive what acute bodily pain they might occasion to a head crowned with thorns. The thorns would be driven into the skin, till the blood ran down the face and forehead and neck of our Lord. Truly "He was bruised for our iniquities." (Isaiah liii. 5.)

4 --[*Pilate therefore went forth, etc.*] This verse opens a new scene of the painful story of the passion. The scourging being over, and the mockery of the soldiers having gone on as long as Pilate thought it worth while, the Roman Governor went forth outside the palace where he lived, to the Jews, who were waiting to hear the result of his private interview with our Lord. We must remember that, under the influence of hypocritical scrupulosity, they would not go inside the Gentile Governor's house, lest forsooth they should be "defiled," and were therefore waiting in the court outside. Now Pilate comes out of his palace and speaks to them. The words of the verse seem to show that Pilate came out first, and that our Lord was led out behind him.—" Behold I am bringing Him outside again, that you may know that I can find no fault or cause of condemnation in Him, and no ground for your charge that He is a stirrer up of sedition and a rebel King. He is only a weak, harmless fanatic, who lays claim to no kingdom of this world, and I bring Him forth to you as a poor, contemptible person worthy of scorn, but not one that I can pronounce worthy of death. I have examined Him myself, and I inform you that I can see no harm in Him."

It seems to me quite plain that Pilate's private interview with our Lord has completely satisfied the Governor that He was a harmless, innocent person, and made him feel a strong desire to dismiss Him unhurt ; and he secretly hoped that the Jews would be satisfied when they saw the prisoner whom they had accused brought out beaten and bruised, and treated with scorn and contempt, and that they would not press the charge any further. How thoroughly this cowardly double-dealing man was disappointed, and what violence he had to do to his own conscience, we shall soon see.

It is very noteworthy that the expression, "I find no fault in Him," is used three times by Pilate, in the same Greek words, in St. John's account of the passion. (John xviii. 38 ; xix. 4–6.) It was meet and right that he who had the chief hand in slaying the Lamb of God, the Sacrifice for our sins, should three times publicly declare that he found no spot or blemish in Him. He was proclaimed a Lamb without spot or fault, after a searching examination, by him that slew Him.

5 —[*Then...Jesus forth...thorns...robe.*] The language of this sen-

tence appears to me to show that Pilate went outside the palace first, and announced that he was going to bring out the prisoner, and that then our Lord followed him. The word " forth," both in this and the preceding verse, means literally, " outside," or " without." It is the same that is used in the texts, " His brethren stood without " (Matt. xii. 46); and " Without are dogs." (Rev. xxii. 15.)

That our blessed Lord, the eternal Word, should have meekly submitted to be led out after this fashion, as a gazing-stock and an object of scorn, with an old purple robe on His shoulders and a crown of thorns on His head, His back bleeding from scourging and His head from thorns, to feast the eyes of a taunting, howling, blood-thirsty crowd, is indeed a wondrous thought! Truly, " though He was rich, yet for our sakes He became poor." (2 Cor. viii. 9.) Since the world began, the sun never shone on a more surprising spectacle both for angels and men.

[*And Pilate...Behold the Man.*] This famous sentence, so well known as " Ecce Homo," in Latin, admits of two views being taken of it. Pilate may have spoken it in *contempt :* " Behold the Man you accuse of setting Himself up as a King ! See what a weak, helpless, contemptible creature He is."—Or else Pilate may have spoken it in *pity :* " Behold the poor feeble Man whom you want me to sentence to death. Surely your demands may be satisfied by what I have done to Him. Is He not punished enough? "—Perhaps both views are correct. In any case there can be little doubt that the latent feeling of Pilate was the hope that the Jews, on seeing our Lord's miserable condition, would be content, and would allow Him to be let go. In this hope, again, we shall find he was completely deceived.

Pilate probably threw a strong emphasis on the expression " Man," indicative of contempt. This may have led to the Jews saying so strongly, in the seventh verse, that the prisoner " made Himself the *Son of God*," and claimed to be Divine, and not a mere " man," as Pilate had said. He probably also meant the Jews to mark that he said, " Behold the man," not " your King," but a mere common man.

6 —[*When the chief priests...crucify Him.*] We see in this verse the complete failure of Pilate's secret scheme for avoiding the condemnation of our Lord. The pitiful sight of the bleeding and despised prisoner had not the effect of softening down the feelings of His cruel enemies. They would not be content with any thing but His death, and the moment He appeared they raised the fierce cry, " Crucify Him, crucify Him."

Let it be noted that the chief priests were the foremost in raising the cry for crucifixion. It is a painful fact that in every age, none have been such hard, cruel, unfeeling, and bloodyminded persecutors of God's saints, as the ministers of religion.

The conduct of Bishop Bonner, in the reign of bloody Mary, towards some of our martyred Reformers, is a melancholy proof of this.

The "officers" here mentioned were the attendants, and servants, and immediate followers of the priests, who would naturally take up any cry raised by their masters.

The word rendered "cried out," means a loud shout or clamorous cry, and is peculiar to John's account of this part of the passion. It is the same word that is used of our Lord at the grave of Lazarus: "He cried, Lazarus, come forth." (John xi. 43.) It is the same that is used of the multitude at Jerusalem, when they would no longer listen to Paul speaking to them on the stairs: "They cried out, and cast off their clothes, and threw dust into the air." (Acts xxii. 23.)

The cry "Crucify" was equivalent to a demand that our Lord might be put to death after the Roman manner.

Cyril remarks, "When the multitude would perhaps have blushed with shame at the sight of what had been done, remembering Christ's miracles, the priests are the first to cry out, and so inflame and stir up the mob."

He who would know to what an extraordinary degree of blood-thirstiness a mob may be stirred up when once excited, should study the history of the Reign of Terror at Paris, during the first French revolution.

[*Pilate saith...Take ye... in Him.*] This, as Cyril justly argues, is the language of one vexed, and irritated, and made impatient by the pertinacity with which the priests stuck to their point. "Do your bloody work yourselves, if you must needs have it done. Take your prisoner away, and do not trouble me with the case. I find no fault in Him, and I dislike being made your tool in this matter." It seems impossible to put any other construction on Pilate's words. He could not have meant gravely and seriously that he would allow the Jews to put the prisoner to death, and thus admit the precedent of letting them inflict capital punishment. Temper, vexation, and irony, seem to lie at the bottom of his words; and the chief priests seem to have taken his words in this sense. We cannot doubt that they would gladly have taken away our Lord and crucified Him at once, if they had thought Pilate really meant they should do so.

For the third time we should notice Pilate's emphatic declaration: "I find no fault in Him." Three times he vainly tried to evade condemning our Lord, or to make the Jews desist from their bloody design: once by asking the Jews to choose between · Christ and Barabbas,—once by sending Him to Herod, —once by scourging Him, and exhibiting Him in a contemptible light before the people. Three times he failed utterly.

Burkitt remarks, " Hypocrites within the pale of the visible Church may be guilty of such monstrous acts of wickedness, as even the consciences of heathens without the Church may boggle at and protest against."

7 —[*The Jews answered him, etc.*] In this verse we find the priests taking up a new ground of accusation against our Lord. They saw that their political accusation had failed. Pilate would not condemn Him as a King, and refused to see any fault in Him on that score. They, therefore, charge our Lord with blasphemy, and committing an offence against their law. As to Pilate's ironical words, " Take ye Him and crucify Him," they made no remark on them, as though they knew they were not meant to be taken seriously. The whole sense must be filled up in some such way as this,—" It is no use telling us to crucify this prisoner ourselves, because you well know that it is not lawful for us to put any man to death ; but seeing that you will not condemn Him as a political offender, we now charge Him with an offence against our religion, which, as our Governor, you are bound to defend and protect. We call upon you to condemn Him to death for claiming to be the Son of God, which, according to our law, is blasphemy, and a capital crime." This is a lengthy paraphrase, undoubtedly, but one which is necessary, if we would fill up the sense of the verse, and understand what the Jews meant.

The "law" referred to by the Jews is probably Levit. xxiv. 16. But it is curious that " stoning " is the punishment there mentioned, and not a word is said of crucifixion. This they do not tell Pilate. There is, perhaps, more fullness in the expression " a law " than appears at first. It may mean, " we Jews have a law given us by man from God, which is our rule of faith in religion. It is a law, we know, not binding on Gentiles, but it is a law which we feel bound to obey. One of the articles of that law is, that " He that blasphemeth the name of the Lord shall be stoned.' We ask that this article may be enforced in the case of this man. He has blasphemed by calling Himself the Son of God, and He ought to be put to death. We, therefore, demand His life." There certainly seems an emphasis in the Greek on the word " we," as if it meant " we Jews," in contradistinction to Gentiles.

The expression " He ought " is literally, " he owes it," he is a debtor, he is under an obligation or penalty of death, according to the terms of our code of law.

The expression " made Himself," must mean appointed, constituted, or declared Himself the Son of God. Compare Mark iii. 14, John vi. 15—viii. 53, Acts ii. 36, Heb. iii. 2, Rev. i. 6.

The expression " Son of God" meant far more to a Jewish mind than it does to us. We see in John v. 18 that the Jews considered that when our Lord said that God was His Father He made Himself " equal with God." See also John x. 33.

One thing at any rate is very clear : whatever Socinians may say, our Lord distinctly laid claim to divinity, and the Jews distinctly understood Him to mean that He was God as well as man.

Cyril well remarks that if the Jews had dealt justly, they would have told the Gentile ruler that the person before him had not only claimed to be the Son of God, but had also done many miracles in proof of His divinity.

Rollock observes, " Look, what blinds them ! The Word of God that should make them see, blinds them so that they use it to their ruin. The best things in the world, yea, the Word of God itself, serve to wicked men for nothing else but their induration. The more they read, the blinder they are. And why ? Because they abuse the word, and make it not a guide to direct their affections and actions."

8 —[*When Pilate...heard...was afraid.*] In this verse we see Pilate in a different frame of mind. This new charge of blasphemy against our Lord threw a new light over his feelings. He began to be really frightened and uncomfortable. The thought that the meek and gentle Prisoner before him might after all be some superior Being, and not a mere common man, filled his weak and ignorant conscience with alarm. What if he had before him some God in human form ? What if it should turn out that he was actually inflicting bodily injuries on one of the Gods ? As a Roman he had doubtless heard and read many stories, drawn from the heathen mythology of Greece and Rome, about Gods coming down to earth, and appearing in human form. Perhaps the prisoner before him was one ! The idea raised new fears in his mind. Already he had been made very uncomfortable about Him. Our Lord's calm, dignified, and majestic demeanor had doubtless made an impression. His evident innocence of all guilt, and the extraordinary malice of His enemies, whose characters Pilate most likely knew well, had produced an effect. His own wife's dream had its influence. Even before the last charge of the Jews the Roman judge had been awe-struck, and secretly convinced of our Lord's innocence, and anxious to have Him set free, and actually " afraid " of his prisoner. But when he heard of His being the " Son of God," he was made more afraid.

Burgon remarks, " Like Gamaliel in the Acts, Pilate was seized with a salutary apprehension, lest haply he be found even to fight against God."

The " saying " referred to must mean the expression, " Son of God."

The word "more " deserves attention. It shows clearly that from the first Pilate had been " afraid," and uneasy in conscience. He had never liked the case being brought before him at all. To have such an extraordinary preacher, and a worker of such miracles as our Lord, brought to his bar, frightened him. But now when he heard that He laid claim to divinity, he was " *more* afraid." We must never forget that Pilate, as Roman Governor of Judæa, charged with the management of a most -turbulent and troublesome province, was doubtless informed by spies, as well as by the officers of his army, of everything that went on in Judæa. Can we doubt for a moment that he must have heard many accounts of our Lord's ministry, and specially of His miracles and astonishing power over the sick and the dead ? Can we doubt that he heard of the raising of Lazarus at Bethany, within a walk of Jerusalem ? Remembering all this, we may well suppose that he regarded the whole case brought before him by the Jews with much anxiety from the very first, and we can well understand that when he heard that Jesus was " the Son of God," he was more than ever alarmed. Unprincipled rulers have an uneasy position.

Bishop Hall thinks that the cause of Pilate's fear was only the increased rage and excitement of the people. He was afraid of a riot and tumult !

9 —[*And went again...judgment hall.*] This means, thït, on hearing this fresh charge of blasphemy, Pilate retired again from the outside of the palace into the inner part, where he had before conversed with our Lord, once more leaving the Jews outside. This new charge was so serious that he did not care to enter into it publicly, and preferred examining our Lord about it privately.

[*And saith... Whence art Thou ?*] This question I think can admit of only one meaning. It meant,—" Who art Thou ? What art Thou ? Art Thou from heaven ? Art Thou one of the gods come down to earth, of whom I have heard the priests talk ? What is Thy real nature and history ? If Thou art some superior being, more than a common man, tell me plainly, that I may know how to deal with Thy case. Tell me privately, while these Jews are not present, that I may know what line to take up with Thine enemies."—We may well believe that Pilate caught at the secret hope that Jesus might tell him something about Himself, which would enable Him to make a firm stand and deliver Him from the Jews. In this hope, again, the Roman Governor was destined to be disappointed.

[*But Jesus gave him no answer.*] Our Lord's silence, when this appeal was made to him by Pilate, is very striking. Hitherto He had spoken freely and replied to questions ; now He refused to speak any more. The reason of our Lord's silence must be sought in the state of Pilate's soul. He deserved no answer, and therefore got none. He had forfeited his title to any further revelation about his Prisoner. He had been told plainly the nature of our Lord's kingdom, and the purpose of our Lord's coming into the world, and been obliged to confess publicly his innocence. And yet, with all this light and knowledge, he had treated our Lord with flagrant injustice, scourged Him, allowed Him to be treated with the vilest indignities by his soldiers, and held Him up to scorn, knowing in his own mind all the time that He was a guiltless person. He had, in short, sinned, away his opportunities, forsaken his own mercies, and turned a deaf ear to the cries of his own conscience. Hence our Lord would have nothing more to do with him, and would tell him nothing more. " He gave him no answer."

Here, as in many other cases, we learn that God will not force conviction on men, and will not compel obstinate unbelievers to believe, and will not always strive with men's consciences. Most men, like Pilate, have a day of grace, and an open door put before them. If they refuse to enter in, and choose their own sinful way, the door is often shut, and never opened again. There is such a thing as a " day of visitation," when Christ speaks to men. If they will not hear His voice, and open the door of their hearts, they are often let alone, given over to a reprobate mind, and left to reap the fruit of their own sins. It was so with Pharaoh, and Saul, and Ahab; and Pilate's case was like theirs. He had his opportunity, and did not choose to use it, but preferred to please the Jews at the expense of his conscience, and to do what he knew was wrong. We see the consequence. Our Lord will tell him nothing more.

In saying all this, I think we must not forget that Pilate's wicked refusal to listen to his own conscience, and our Lord's consequent refusal to speak to him any more, were all overruled by the eternal counsels of God to the carrying out of His purpose of redemption. In handling such a point we must speak with reverence. But it is plain that if our Lord had revealed to Pilate who He was, and forced Pilate to see it, the crucifixion might perhaps never have taken place, and the great sacrifice for a world's sins might never have been offered up on the cross. Our Lord's silence was just and well merited. But it was also part of God's counsels about man's salvation.

Let us note that there is " a time to be silent," as well as " a time to speak." This is a matter in the social intercourse of daily life, about which we all need to pray for wisdom. To be always saying to everybody everything we know, is not the line of a wise follower of Christ.

Let us note that if we do not make a good use of light and opportunities,—and if we resist Christ speaking to our conscience,—a time may come when, like Pilate, we may speak to Christ, and ask things of Him, and He may give us no answer. It is written in a certain place, " They would none of my counsel, they despised all my reproof; therefore shall they eat of the fruit of their own way." " Then shall they call upon Me, but I will not answer." (Prov. i. 24—32.)

Chrysostom observes, " Christ answered nothing, because He knew that Pilate asked all the questions idly."

Besser remarks, "A petition to Christ for enlightenment, even when offered up in a man's last moments from a death bed, never fails of being answered, if offered in sincerity and from the heart ; and obtains for the suppliant as much grace as is needful for salvation. But to a Pilate Jesus is silent."

10 —[*Then saith Pilate, etc.*] In this verse we see the imperious, fierce, haughty, arrogant temper of the Roman Governor breaking out. Accustomed to see prisoners cringing before him, and willing to do anything to obtain his favor, he could not understand our Lord's silence. He addresses him in a tone of anger and surprise combined :—" Why dost Thou not answer my question ? Dost Thou know what Thou art doing in offending me ? Dost Thou not know that Thou art at my mercy, and that I have power to crucify Thee or release Thee, according as I think right ?"—I can see no other reasonable construction that can be put on Pilate's words. The idea that he was only persuading our Lord, and gently reminding Him of his own power, seems utterly unreasonable, and inconsistent with the following verse.

This high-minded claim to absolute power is one which ungodly great men are fond of making. It is written of Nebuchadnezzar, " Whom he would he slew, and whom he would he kept alive ; and whom he would he set up, and whom he would he put down." (Dan. v. 19.) Yet even when such men boast of power, they are often like Pilate, mere slaves, and afraid of resisting popular opinion. Pilate talked of " power to release ; " but he knew in his own mind that he was afraid, and so unable to exercise it.

It is only fair to remember that the Greek word rendered " power," might be rendered " authority," or " commission ; " and in this sense Pilate might only mean, " I have commission from the Roman Government to sentence prisoners to death or let them go free : would it not be for Thine interest to speak to me ? "

11 —[*Jesus answered, etc.*] Our Lord's reply to Pilate in this verse is remarkably calm and dignified, though not without some difficulties, because of its elliptical construction. It may be paraphrased thus : " Thou speakest of power. Thou dost not know that both thou and the Jews are only tools in the hand of a higher Being, and that thou couldst have no power whatever against Me, if it were not given thee by God. This, however, thou dost not understand, and art therefore less guilty than the Jews. The Jews who delivered Me into thine hand, do know that all power is from God. Thus their knowledge makes them more guilty than Thou. Both thou and they are committing a great sin ; but their sin is a sin against knowledge, and thine is comparatively a sin of ignorance. You are both unconsciously mere instruments in the hand of God, and you could do nothing against Me, if God did not permit and overrule it." The logical

connection of the former and latter parts of the verse is by no means clear. The precise object of " therefore," and the reason why God's overruling providence made the Jews more guilty than the Gentiles, are things which it is not easy to explain. But I must think that the latent idea of our Lord was to remind Pilate how ignorantly he was acting, and how little he knew what he was about compared to the Jews.

That the possession of superior knowledge increases the sinfulness of a sinner's sin, seems taught by implication in this verse. It was more sinful in the Jews, with all their knowledge of the law and the prophets, to deliver up Christ to be crucified, than it was in Pilate, an ignorant heathen, to condemn Him and put Him to death.

The word " he " is differently interpreted. Some think that it must refer to Caiaphas, as the high priest and chief actor in the whole affair of our Lord's murder. Some even think it refers to Judas Iscariot. The more probable idea is that it refers to the whole Jewish people, personified by " he," and represented by their high priest.

One thing, at any rate, is very certain. This was the last word that Jesus spoke during His trial. Henceforth He was " like a lamb before his shearers, dumb."

Hengstenberg remarks, that in apportioning the comparative guilt of Pilate and of the Jews, our Lord shows Himself even at this crisis the true Judge of mankind.

Lampe remarks, " The sin of the Jews was heavier than that of Pilate. Pilate was a Gentile, ignorant alike of the Messiah and His distinguishing marks : the Jews had read the prophecies about Him. Pilate could only have heard something about our Lord's great miracles by rumor and report : they were all done under the very eyes of the Jews. Pilate injured Jesus unwillingly, and from cowardice : they injured Him from hatred and envy. Finally, Pilate was only the instrument : the Jews were the impelling cause. Thus our Lord pronounces His opinion concerning His judges, an opinion according to which He will one day judge them."

The expression " therefore," or literally " on account of this," is rather a difficult one. Markland says it means, "*Because* he has not this power from above, which thou hast, the Jew has the greater sin." Pearce takes much the same view.

Rollock observes, speaking of the inquisition in Spain, " The Papists, when they have caught a Christian who confesseth Jesus Christ, after trying him, put him in the hands of the Emperor or King of Spain. Then they wash their hands, as clean of His blood ; and who took his life but the King of Spain ? But the wrath of God persecutes them, and the blood of the innocent lies on them, because they *delivered* them into their hands to be tormented."

Hutcheson observes, that " the greatest height of impiety is
found within the visible Church," where there is most knowledge.

When all has been said, we must admit that there is probably something in the verse more deep than we have line to
fathom. The two propositions of the verse are both quite intelligible ; but the connecting link, " therefore," is a hard knot,
which has not yet been fairly untied.

Augustine paraphrases this sentence thus : " He sins worse
who of ill-will delivers up the innocent to the power to be put
to death, than doth the power itself, if for the fear of another
greater power it puts to death the innocent. The Jews delivered Me unto the power, as having ill-will against Me ; but
thou art about to exercise thy power against Me, as being afraid
for thyself. Not that a man has a right to put to death an innocent person from fear ; but to put to death out of hatred is
much more evil than to put to death out of fear." Cyril says
much the same.

One thing, at any rate, is very clear. There are degrees in
sin. All are not equally sinful. The servant who knew his
master's will and did it not, was more guilty than he who knew
it not.

12 —[*And from thenceforth Pilate sought to release Him.*] This
is a remarkable sentence. It evidently means that from this
point of the case Pilate sought more diligently than ever to
have our Lord acquitted and set free. Before he wished it :
now he really took pains to effect it. Whether this was occasioned by our Lord's manner and demeanor in speaking the
words of the preceding verse, or by some meaning which He
attached to the words, we cannot tell. But so it was.

How and in what manner Pilate " sought to release " Jesus,
we are not told by John. But it is evident that he left our Lord
in the hall, where he had been asking Him, " Whence art
Thou ? " and went out alone to the Jews, to tell them he could
make nothing of their charge of blasphemy, and wished to let
the prisoner go. This must have taken place *outside* the doors,
because the Jews scrupulously refused to go *inside*. Moreover,
the Jews could not have known of this fresh desire to release
Jesus, if Pilate had not come forth and communicated it to them.
In this verse, therefore, be it remembered, we have Pilate and
the Jews alone, outside the palace, and our Lord left inside.
Pilate proposes to release Him, and the Jews protest against it.
Then we shall find Pilate goes in again, and brings Jesus out
for the last time.

[*But the Jews cried out...Cæsar.*] In these words we see the
Jews stopping Pilate short, in his weak efforts to get our Lord
released, by an argument which they well knew would weigh
heavily on a Roman mind. They tell him plainly that they will

accuse him to Cæsar, the Roman Emperor, as a governor un-friendly to the Imperial interests.—" You are no friend to Cæsar if you let off this prisoner. Every one who sets himself up as a king, be his kingdom what it may, is usurping part of Cæsar's authority, and is a rebel. If you pass over this man's claim to be a king, and set Him at liberty, we shall complain of you to Cæsar."—This was a settling and clinching argument. Pilate knew well that his own government of Judæa would not bear any investigation. He also knew well the cold, suspicious, cruel character of Tiberius Cæsar, the Emperor of Rome, which is specially mentioned by Tacitus and Suetonius, the Roman his-torians, and he might well dread the result of any appeal to him from the Jews. From this moment all his hopes of get-ting rid of this anxious case, and letting our Lord go away unharmed, were dashed to the ground. He would rather con-nive at a murder to please the Jews, than allow himself to be charged with neglect of Imperial interests and unfriendliness to Cæsar.

It is hard to say which was the more wretched and contempti-ble sight at this point of the history,—Pilate trampling on his own conscience to avoid the possible displeasure of an earthly monarch, or the Jews pretending to care for Cæsar's interests, and warning Pilate not to do anything unfriendly to him! It was a melancholy exhibition of cowardice on the one side, and duplicity on the other; and the whole result was a foul mur-der!

13 —[*When Pilate heard that saying, etc.*] The " saying " here refers to the Jews' saying about Cæsar in the preceding verse. When Pilate heard the dreaded name of Cæsar brought up, and found himself threatened with a possible complaint to Rome as a neglecter of Imperial interests, he saw plainly that nothing more could be done, and that he must give way to the demands of the Jews and sacrifice an innocent prisoner. He therefore returned to the palace, brought forth Jesus again, and for the first time took his seat on the throne of judgment outside the palace, in the courtyard, or paved area adjacent to it. The case was now over. Pilate's weak efforts to deliver an innocent prisoner from unjust accusation were useless. He dared no longer oppose the bloody demands of the Jews. There re-mained nothing to be done but to take his seat publicly on the throne of judgment and pronounce the sentence.

The word " forth " here, as in the fourth and fifth verses, means literally " outside." Pearce remarks, that " this is the fifth time that Pilate came forth and tried to prevail with the Jews that Jesus might not be crucified."

On the " judgment seat," Parkhurst remarks : " In the Roman provinces, justice was administered in the open air, the presid-ing judge sitting on a tribunal, on a raised ground covered with marble."

The " pavement " means the marble, or Mosaic levelled space
on which the judge's chair was placed. Parkhurst says that
Roman Governors used sometimes to carry with them the materials to form such a pavement.

The word "Gabbatha," according to Hammond, is more Syriac
than Hebrew; " According to the custom of the New Testament, which calls Syriac, at that time the vulgar language of
the Jews, Hebrew." Parkhurst says that the word means literally a raised place ; and remarks that John does not mean in
this verse that Gabbatha means pavement,—but that the same
place which in Greek was called " pavement," was called in
Hebrew " the raised place."

[*And it was...preparation of the passover.*]   This remarkable
expression cannot mean that " this was the hour for preparing
the passover meal," for it was not. It means, " this was the
day before the great sabbath of the passover week, a day well
known among the Jews as the preparation, or day of preparing
for the passover sabbath, which was peculiarly a high day."
St. Mark expressly says this in his account of the passion.
(Mark xv. 42.)   That all the Jewish feasts had their " eves," or
preparation days, is quite clear from Rabbinical writers.

We should observe how accurately and precisely John marks
the day of the crucifixion.

[*And about the sixth hour.*]   This expression raises a grave
difficulty, and one which in every age has perplexed the minds
of Bible readers.   The difficulty lies in the fact that Mark in
his Gospel expressly says, " it was the third hour, and they
crucified Him " (Mark xv. 25); while John in this place says
our Lord was only condemned at the sixth hour!   Yet both
Evangelists wrote by inspiration, and both were incapable of
making a mistake.   How then are we to reconcile and harmonize these two conflicting statements.   The solutions of the
difficulty suggested are many and various.

(*a*) Some say, as the rationalistic writers, that one of the two
Evangelists made a blunder, and that one of the accounts therefore is false.   This is a solution which will satisfy no reverent-
minded Christian.   If Bible writers could make blunders like
this, there is no such thing as inspiration, and there is an end
of all confidence in Scripture as an infallible guide.

(*b*) Some say, as Theophylact, Beza, Nonnus (in his poetical
paraphrase), Tittman, Leigh, Usher (vol. vii. 176), Kuinoel,
Bengel, Pearce, Alford, Scott, and Bloomfield, that the discrepancy has probably been caused by an error of the manuscript
writers, and that the true reading in St. John should be
" third," and not " sixth hour."   This, however, is a very short-
cut road out of the difficulty, and the immense proportion of
old manuscripts are flatly against it.

(c) Some say, as Augustine does in one place, and Bullinger, "that at the third hour the Lord was crucified by the tongues of the Jews, and at the sixth by the hands of the soldiers." This, however, to say the least, is a weak and childish explanation. Moreover, it is open to the grave objection that it would make out our Lord to have been only three hours on the cross, and all that time in the dark, and not seen consequently by any one! At this rate, the inscription over His head on the cross would certainly not have been read by many! "There was darkness over all the land from the sixth to the ninth hour."

(d) Some say that Mark reckoned time on the Jewish plan, by which the hours began to count from the morning, and their seven o'clock answered to our one; while John reckoned time on our English plan, which is the same as the Roman one, and John's sixth hour meant literally about six in the morning. According to this theory Jesus was condemned, in John's account of the passion, at six o'clock in the morning, and crucified, in Mark's account, at nine o'clock.

This explanation is very commonly adopted, and is supported by Wordsworth, Lee, and Burgon. But it is open to very serious objections. I see no proof whatever that John reckons time on the Roman and English plan, and not on the Jewish plan. The passage in the story of the Samaritan woman, which is commonly quoted as a proof, is no proof at all, and on reflection will cut directly the other way. If the "sixth hour," when Jesus sat on the well (see John iv. 6), meant really our English six o'clock in the evening, it makes it impossible to understand how the conversation with the woman, her return to her native village, the telling of the men to come and see Jesus, the coming of the men, the return of the disciples with meat, could all be brought into the short space of one evening! The thing would have been impossible.—Moreover, it is an additional objection, that if Jesus was condemned at six o'clock in the morning, there are left three long hours between the condemnation and the crucifixion unaccounted for and unexplained. I am obliged to say that in my judgment this way of explaining the difficulty completely fails.

(e) Some think, as Calvin, Bucer, Gaulter, Brentius, Musculus, Gerhard, Lampe, Hammond, Poole, Jansenius, Burkitt, Hengstenberg, and Ellicott, that John's sixth hour means any time after our nine o'clock in the morning; any time, in fact, within the space begun by the Jewish third hour. They say that the Jews divided the twelve hours of their day into four great portions: from six to nine, from nine to twelve, from twelve to three, and from three to six. They also say that any part of the time after our six in the morning would be called the third hour, and any time after our nine in the morning would be called the sixth hour. And they conclude that both the condemnation and the crucifixion took place soon after nine

o'clock,—Mark calling it the third hour, because it was near
our nine o'clock; John calling it the sixth hour, because it was
some time between our nine and twelve.

Grotius says, in Parkhurst, that the third, sixth, and ninth
hours, which were most esteemed for prayer and other services, were marked by the sounding of a trumpet, and that after
the trumpet sounding at the third hour, the sixth hour was
considered to be at hand. Glass and Lampe support this opinion; and Lampe shows from Maimonides, a famous Jewish
writer, that the Jews really divided the day into four quarters.
Hengstenberg also remarks that the fourth and fifth hours are
never mentioned in the New Testament.

This theory undoubtedly brings the two Evangelists near to
one another, if it does not quite reconcile them.

(*f*) Some think, as Augustine in a second place suggests, and
Harmer, quoted in Parkhurst, following him, that the "sixth
hour here does not refer to the time of day, but to the preparation of the passover;"—and that the meaning is, "It was the
preparation of the passover, and about the sixth hour after
that preparation began." But as that preparation often began
very early indeed in the morning, or about our three o'clock,
six hours counted from that time would bring us down to
Mark's third hour, or our nine o'clock. Lightfoot supports
this view, which is certainly very ingenious, and would clear
away all difficulty. But it may fairly be objected that plain
readers would hardly attach such a meaning as Harmer suggests to "the sixth hour."

The difficulty is one of those which will probably never be
solved. God has been pleased to leave it in Scripture for the
trial of our faith and patience, and we must wait for its solution. Questions of time and date, like this, are often the most
puzzling, from our inability to place ourselves in the position
of the writer, and from the widely different manner in which
measures and points of time are expressed in the language of
different nations and in different ages. This very difficulty before us, perhaps, presented no difficulty whatever to the Apostolic Fathers, such as Polycarp and Clement. Perhaps they
possessed some simple clue to its solution of which we know
nothing. It is our wisdom to be patient, and to believe that it
admits of explanation, though we have not eyes to see it.

If I must venture an opinion, I think there is more to be said
for the fifth of the six solutions I have given than for any
other. But I allow that it is incomplete. In any case we must
in fairness remember that St. John does not say, distinctly and
expressly, "it was the sixth hour," but "*about* the sixth hour."
This shows that some latitude may be allowed in interpretation, and that the acknowledged discrepancy between John and
Mark, must not be too far pressed, or made of too much importance. One thing, at all events, appears to me quite inadmis-

sible. We cannot allow ourselves to suppose that Jesus was not crucified till twelve o'clock in the day, when the miraculous darkness began, and that He only hung on the cross three hours.

[*And he saith...Behold your King!*] These words must have been spoken in bitter irony, anger, and contempt. "Behold the Man whom you accuse of setting Himself up as a King and being an enemy to Cæsar! Behold this bleeding, weak, humble, meek, helpless prisoner!—this wretched, harmless Person, you pretend to be afraid of, and want me to crucify! You wish your own King to be put to death? This, I am to understand, is what you desire. Look at Him, and say!"

15 —[*But they cried...away...crucify Him.*] As on former occasions, Pilate's public appeal had not the slightest effect on the Jews. Once more they raised their fierce, relentless, obstinate, cry, and demanded the Prisoner's death by crucifixion. Nothing but His blood would satisfy them. The horrible excesses of the Parisian mob, during the infamous Reign of Terror in the first French revolution, give us some faint idea of the savage spirit which can run through a crowd, by a kind of infection, when their hatred is stirred up against an individual.

The Greek word rendered "away with him," is literally, "take him away;" and often means, "take him away to execution or destruction."

Henry remarks, that this public rejection of Christ fulfilled two prophecies of Isaiah: "Him whom the nation abhorreth" (Isa. xlvii. 7); and "We hid as it were our faces from Him." (Isa. liii. 2.)

[*Pilate saith...crucify your King?*] For the last time Pilate put the question to the Jews, and gave them a last chance of relenting. In bitter irony he asked,—"Shall I then really crucify your own King? Shall I, a Roman, order a King of the Jews to be put to an ignominious death? Is this your wish and desire?"

[*The chief priests...no king but Cæsar.*] These memorable words inflicted indelible disgrace on the leaders of the Jews, and stamped the Jews forever as a fallen, blinded, God-forsaking, God-forsaken, and apostate nation. They, who at one time used to say, "The Lord God is our King," renounced the faith of their forefathers, and publicly declared that Cæsar was their king, and not God. They stultified themselves, and gave the lie to their own boasted declaration of independence of foreign powers. Had they not said themselves, "We be Abraham's seed, and were never in bondage to any man"? (John viii. 33.) Had they not tried to entrap our Lord into saying something in favor of Cæsar, that they might damage His reputation? "Is it lawful to give tribute to Cæsar?" (Matt. xx. 17.) And now, forsooth, they shout out, "We have no king

but Cæsar!" Above all they madly proclaimed to the world,
though they knew it not, that "the sceptre had departed from
Judah," and that Messiah must have come. (Gen. xlix. 10.)
Truly the sceptre had departed, when chief priests could say,
"We have no king but Cæsar."

Cyril remarks, that "while other nations, all over the world,
cling tenaciously to their own religion, and honor those whom
they call gods, and will not forsake them, Israel revolted from
God, cast off His authority, and claimed Cæsar as their king.
Justly therefore they were delivered over into Cæsar's hands,
and endured the heaviest calamities."

Henry remarks,—"They would have no king but Cæsar, and
never have they had any other to this day, 'but have been
many days without a king, and without a prince' (Hos. iii. 4),
that is, without any of their own, and the kings of the nations
have ruled over them. Since they will have no king but Cæsar,
so shall their doom be: themselves have decided it."

Lampe compares the conduct of the priests in this place to
that of the trees in Jotham's parable, who said to the bramble,
"Come and reign over us." (Judges ix. 14.) The very men
who ought to have taught the people to hope for the Messiah,
here publicly renounce the Messiah's kingdom, and declare
themselves contented with Cæsar!

I cannot but think that Pilate's public washing of his hands
before the people, and saying, "I am innocent of the blood of
this just person" (Matt. xxvii. 24), must come in at this part of
St. John's narrative.

16.—[*Then delivered, etc.*] This verse describes the conclusion of
the most unjust trial of our blessed Lord, when, "in His humiliation, His judgment was taken away." (Acts viii. 33.) All
was now over. The last appeal had been made to the Jews,
and for the last time they had rejected it. What happened is
described by Luke, but passed over by John. "Pilate gave
sentence that it should be as they required." (Luke xxiii. 24.)
He then formally delivered over our Lord into the hands of the
chief priests, and formally gave them permission to put Him to
death by crucifixion. These hardened and wicked men at
once "took Jesus and led Him away."—Of course we must
not suppose that the "chief priests" *themselves* laid hands
on our Lord, and with their own hands led Him away. No
doubt the Roman soldiers of Pilate were the executioners, and
a centurion had charge of all the bloody transaction of the execution. But inasmuch as the soldiers only carried out the
wishes of the priests, the priests were the responsible persons
and prime agents in this judicial murder. Luke says, "He delivered Jesus to their *will*." (Luke xxiii. 25.)

Let us remember, when we read that word "delivered," that
it is expressly written, He was "delivered for our offences,"

and that God " spared not His own Son, but delivered Him up for us all." (Rom. iv. 25 ; viii. 30.) Christ was delivered to death, that we might be delivered from death and set free. Here is substitution.

Let us remember, as we read the word " led," that Isaiah expressly foretold that Messiah should be brought, or led, as a Lamb to the slaughter." (Isaiah liii. 7 ; Acts viii. 32.)

Alford thinks it possible that at this point the scourging of our Lord was repeated. But I see no satisfactory proof of this. Considering what a Roman scourging was, it is not probable that any body could have endured it twice in one day.

Let us note, that according to the narrative of John, there seems no delay between the condemnation of our Lord and His crucifixion. He went at once from Gabbatha to Golgotha, and from the judgment to execution. At this rate the theory, supported by Burgon and others, that there was a delay of three hours, between six o'clock and nine, after condemnation, is completely overthrown. If we looked at Matthew and Mark alone, we might fancy that Pilate saw nothing more of our Lord after He had been scourged and mocked by the soldiers. But it appears plain to me, if we carefully compare John's account with that of Matthew and Mark, that they have not recorded our Lord's last appearance before Pilate, which John relates. Nor can I feel surprised at this, when I remember that throughout John's Gospel, he supplies what the other evangelists have omitted. In particular he supplies our Lord's examination before Annas, and His private conversation with Pilate, when the Jews would not enter Pilate's palace, and entirely omits the examination before Caiaphas. So likewise I think he supplies the last scene in our Lord's trial, which Matthew and Mark entirely omit, for some wise reason. Holding this theory, which to me seems the most natural account of the order of things, I cannot see any room for an interval of time between the final condemnation and the crucifixion.

Henry remarks with much shrewdness, " Judgment was no sooner pronounced, than with all possible expedition the prosecutors, having gained their point, resolved to lose no time, lest Pilate should change his mind and order a reprieve, and also lest there should be an uproar among the people."

How St. John became acquainted with all the details of our Lord's trial, and the private conversations between Him and Pilate, is a question which none can answer satisfactorily who do not hold the doctrine of plenary inspiration. That John was in and about the palace of the high priest, and not far from our Lord all the time, from the seizure in Gethsemane up to His death, we may well believe ; but that he could have overheard the private conversations between Jesus and Pilate, seems simply impossible. How then could he know anything about them, and write them down? There is but one answer. He wrote them by inspiration of the Holy Ghost.

Why the common people, who always " heard Jesus gladly," permitted our Lord's crucifixion so easily, and made no resistance, is at first sight rather hard to understand. The Galileans, who would have made Jesus King at one time, were of course at Jerusalem in great numbers, on account of the passover feast. The triumphal entry into Jerusalem, when an immense multitude cried, " Hosanna to the Son of David !—blessed is the King that cometh !" had happened only a few days before. The priests themselves were afraid of an uproar among the " people." Yet there is not a symptom of any opposition to the judicial murder which was arranged, and carried into execution, How was this?

In reply, we must probably take into account the following considerations. (1) There was a superstitious reverence for the priests among all Jews. The mere fact that the high priests accused Jesus would have immense weight. (2) The fear of the Roman garrison kept the people back. (3) The followers and friends of Jesus were almost entirely the poor and lower orders. (4) All multitudes are fickle and capricious

---

JOHN XIX 17—27

17 And he bearing his cross went forth into a place called *the place* of a skull, which is called in the Hebrew Golgotha:

18 Where they crucified him, and two other with him, on either side one, and Jesus in the midst.

19 And Pilate wrote a title, and put *it* on the cross. And the writing was, JESUS OF NAZARETH THE KING OF THE JEWS.

20 This title then read many of the Jews: for the place where Jesus was crucified was nigh to the city: and it was written in Hebrew, *and* Greek, *and* Latin.

21 Then said the chief priests of the Jews to Pilate, Write not, The King of the Jews; but that he said, I am King of the Jews.

22 Pilate answered, What I have written I have written.

23 Then the soldiers when they had crucified Jesus, took his garments, and made four parts, to every soldier a part; and also *his* coat: now the coat was without seam, woven from the top throughout.

24 They said therefore among themselves, Let us not rend it, but cast lots for it, whose it shall be: that the scripture might be fulfilled, which saith, They parted my raiment among them, and for my vesture they did cast lots. These things therefore the soldiers did.

25 Now there stood by the cross of Jesus his mother, and his mother's sister, Mary the *wife* of Cleophas, and Mary Magdalene.

26 When Jesus therefore saw his mother, and the disciple standing by, whom he loved, he saith unto his mother, Woman, behold thy son !

27 Then saith he to the disciple, Behold thy mother ! And from that hour that disciple took her unto his own *home.*

HE that can read a passage like this without a deep

sense of man's debt to Christ, must have a very cold, or
a very thoughtless heart. Great must be the love of the
Lord Jesus to sinners, when He could voluntarily endure
such sufferings for their salvation. Great must be the
sinfulness of sin, when such an amount of vicarious suffering was needed in order to provide redemption.

We should observe, first, in this passage, *how our
Lord had to bear His cross when He went forth from the
city to Golgotha.*

We need not doubt that there was a deep meaning
in all this circumstance. For one thing, it was part of
that depth of humiliation to which our Lord submitted
as our substitute. One portion of the punishment imposed on the vilest criminals, was that they should carry their own cross when they went to execution; and
this portion was laid upon our Lord. In the fullest sense
He was reckoned a sinner, and counted a curse for our
sakes.—For another thing, it was a fulfilment of the
great type of the sin-offering of the Mosaic law. It is
written, that "the bullock for the sin-offering, and the
goat for the sin-offering, whose blood was brought in to
make atonement in the holy place, shall one carry forth
without the camp." (Lev. xvi. 27.) Little did the
blinded Jews imagine, when they madly hounded on the
Romans to crucify Jesus *outside* the gates, that they
were unconsciously perfecting the mightiest sin-offering
that was ever seen. It is written, "Jesus, that He might
sanctify the people with His own blood, suffered without the gate." (Heb. xiii. 12.)

The practical lesson which all true Christians should
gather from the fact before us, is one that should be
kept in continual remembrance. Like our Master, we
must be content to go forth "without the camp," bearing
His reproach. We must come out from the world and
be separate, and be willing, if need be, to stand alone.

Like our Master, we must be willing to take up our cross daily, and to be persecuted both for our doctrine and our practice. Well would it be for the Church if there was more of the true cross to be seen among Christians! To wear material crosses as an ornament, to place material crosses on churches and tombs, all this is cheap and easy work, and entails no trouble. But to have Christ's cross in our hearts, to carry Christ's cross in our daily walk, to know the fellowship of His sufferings, to be made conformable to His death, to have crucified affections, and live crucified lives,—all this needs self-denial ; and Christians of this stamp are few and far between. Yet, this, we may be sure, is the only cross-bearing and cross-carrying that does good in the world. The times require less of the cross outwardly and more of the cross within.

We should observe, secondly, in this passage, *how our Lord was crucified as a King.*

The title placed over our Lord's head made this plain and unmistakable. The reader of Greek, or Latin, or Hebrew, could not fail to see that He who hung on the central cross of the three on Golgotha, had a royal title over His head. The overruling hand of God so ordered matters, that the strong will of Pilate overrode for once the wishes of the malicious Jews. In spite of the chief priests our Lord was crucified as " the King of the Jews."

It was meet and right that so it should be. Even before our Lord was born, the angel Gabriel declared to the Virgin Mary, "The Lord God shall give unto Him the throne of His father David: and He shall reign over the house of Jacob for ever; and of His kingdom there shall be no end." (Luke i. 32, 33.) Almost as soon as He was born, there came wise men from the East, saying, "Where is He that is born King of the Jews?" (Matt. ii. 2.) The very week before the crucifixion, the multitude who accompanied our Lord at His triumphal entry into Jerusalem, had cried, " Blessed is the King of Israel that cometh in the name of the Lord." (John xii. 13.) The current belief of all godly Jews was, that when Messiah, the Son of David came, He would come as a King. A kingdom of heaven and a kingdom of God was continually proclaimed by our Lord throughout His ministry. A King indeed He was, as He told Pilate, of a kingdom utterly unlike the kingdoms of this world, but for all that a true King of a true kingdom, and a Ruler of true subjects. As such He was born. As such He lived. As such He was crucified. And as such He will come again, and reign over the whole earth, King of kings and Lord of lords.

Let us take care that we ourselves know Christ as our King, and that His kingdom is set up within our hearts. They only will find Him their Saviour at the last day, who have obeyed Him as King in this world. Let us cheerfully pay Him that tribute of faith, and love, and obedience, which He prizes far above gold. Above all, let us never be afraid to own ourselves His faithful subjects, soldiers, servants and followers, however much He may be despised by the world. A day will soon come when the despised Nazarene who hung on the cross, shall take to Himself His great power and reign, and put down every enemy under His feet. The kingdoms of this world, as Daniel foretold, shall be swept aside, and become the kingdom of our God and of His Christ. And at last every knee shall bow to Him, and every tongue confess that Jesus Christ is Lord.

We should observe, lastly, in these verses, *how tenderly our Lord took thought for Mary, His mother.*

We are told that even in the awful agonies of body and mind which our Lord endured, He did not forget her of whom He was born. He mercifully remembered her desolate condition, and the crushing effect of the sorrowful sight before her. He knew that, holy as she was, she was only a woman, and that, as a woman, she must deeply feel the death of such a Son. He therefore commended her to the protection of His best-loved and best-loving disciple, in brief and touching words: "Woman," He said, "behold thy son! Then saith He to the disciple, Behold thy mother! And from that hour that disciple took her unto his own home."

We surely need no stronger proof than we have here, that Mary, the mother of Jesus, was never meant to be honored as divine, or to be prayed to, worshipped, and trusted in, as the friend and patroness of sinners. Common sense points out that she who needed the care and protection of another, was never likely to help men and women to heaven, or to be in any sense a mediator between God and man! It is not too much to say, however painful the assertion, that of all the inventions of the Church of Rome, there never was one more utterly devoid of foundation, both in Scripture and reason, than the doctrine of Mary-worship.

Let us turn from points of controversy to a subject of far more practical importance. Let us take comfort in the thought that we have in Jesus a Saviour of matchless tenderness, matchless sympathy, matchless consideration for the condition of His believing people. Let us never forget His words, "Whosoever shall do the will of God, the same is my brother, and my sister, and mother." (Mark iii. 35.) The heart that even on the cross felt for Mary, is a heart that never changes. Jesus never forgets any that love Him, and even in their worst estate remembers their need. No wonder that Peter says, "Casting all your care upon Him; for He careth for you." (1 Pet. v. 7.)

17 —[*And He bearing His cross.*] It was the Roman custom to compel criminals, sentenced to crucifixion, to carry their own cross. Our Lord was thus treated like the vilest felon. " Furcifer," was the Latin name of ignominy and contempt given to the worst criminals. It means, literally, " cross-bearer."

Besser observes that our Lord, when a workman in the carpenter's shop at Nazareth, had willingly carried pieces of timber in the service of His foster-father. Here, with no less cheerfulness, He bears to Golgotha the timber of the cross, in order to raise the altar on which He is to be sacrificed, and to do the will of his Father in heaven.

Whether the " cross" that our Lord bore, was a straight piece of timber, with another transverse piece fixed across it, for the hands of the criminal to be nailed to,—or whether it was a tree with two forked arms, admits perhaps of some little doubt. The almost universal tradition of the Churches is that it was the former: viz., a cross made of two pieces. Yet it is worth remembering that it was very common to crucify on a tree such as I have described,—that the Latin word for " crossbearer," means, literally, " forked-tree-bearer,"—and that our Bible translators have four times spoken of the " wood " on which our Lord was crucified as " the tree." (Acts v. 30 ; x. 39 ; xiii. 29 ; 1 Peter ii. 24.) The matter therefore is not quite so clear as some may think, though of course it is one of no consequence. The cross of two pieces at right angles, is certainly more picturesque than a common tree shaped like the letter Y, and the habitual use of the cross in Christian art, and the general tradition of ecclesiastical history, have combined to make most people regard the question as a settled one. Yet the undeniable use of forked trees in crucifying criminals, and the equally undeniable difficulty of carrying a cross of two transverse pieces, compared with a forked tree, are points that really ought not to be overlooked. The matter, after all, is one of pure conjecture. But, to say the least, it is quite a disputable point whether the cross with which Christendom is so familiar, on the gable ends of churches, on tombs, in painted windows, in crucifixes, or in the simple ornamental form which ladies are so fond of wearing,—the cross, I say, of two transverse pieces at right angles, is really and truly the kind of cross on which Christ was crucified ! There is no proof positive that the whole of Christendom is not mistaken. Of course, if the cross itself had been preserved and found, it would settle the dispute. But there is not the slightest reason to suppose that it was preserved, or treated with any respect, either by Jews, Romans, or disciples. The famous story of the " discovery or invention of the cross " by the Empress Helena in 326 A. D., is a mere apocryphal legend invented by man, and deserves no more attention than the many pretended pieces of the true cross, which are exhibited in Romish churches as sacred relics.

Ambrose says, quaintly enough, that the form of the cross is that of a sword with the point downward; above is the hilt toward heaven, as if in the hand of God; below is the point toward earth, as if thrust through the head of the old serpent the devil.

One thing only is very certain. Whatever was the shape of the cross on which Jesus was crucified, it could not have been the huge, tall, heavy thing which painters and sculptors have continually represented it to be. To suppose that any man could carry such an enormous weight of timber, as the cross is made to be in Rubens' famous picture of the "Descent from the Cross," is preposterous and absurd. A cross was manifestly not a larger thing than could be lifted and borne on the shoulders of one person. Some get over the difficulty by maintaining the theory that the transverse piece was the only part of the cross which the criminal carried. But there is no sufficient evidence that this was the case.

It is noteworthy that John is the only Evangelist who says that our Lord bore His own cross. Matthew, Mark and Luke, all say that Simon the Cyrenian was compelled to bear it. The explanation is probably this. Our Lord bore the cross for a short part of the way from the judgment-seat to Golgotha. Weakness and physical exhaustion, after all the mental and bodily suffering of the last night, rendered it impossible for Him to carry it all the way. Just at the moment when His strength failed, perhaps at the city gate, the soldiers saw Simon coming into the city, and pressed him into the service. As on other occasions, John records a fact which the other Evangelists for wise reasons passed over. It is interesting to remember that the circumstance is one which John must have seen in all probability with his own eyes.

That our blessed Lord, who had a body like our own, and not a body of superhuman vigor, should have been unable to carry the cross more than a little way, need not surprise us at all, if we consider all that He had gone through to try His physical strength, and tax His nervous system to the uttermost, in the eighteen hours preceding His crucifixion.

It is hardly necessary to remark that the type of Isaac bearing the wood for the sacrifice on Moriah, in which he himself was to be the victim, was here fulfilled by our Lord. It is moreover a curious circumstance, mentioned by Bishop Pearson, that a Jewish commentator on Gen. xxii. 6, speaks of Isaac carrying the wood for the burnt offering, "as a man carries his cross upon his shoulders."

[*Went forth.*] That expression shows clearly that our Lord

went out of the city to be crucified. He was condemned in the
open air, and " went forth " cannot mean out of Pilate's house,
but went outside of Jerusalem, without the gates. Trifling as
this incident may seem to a careless reader, it as a striking
fulfilment of one of the great types of the Mosaic law. The
sin offering on the great day of atonement was to be carried
forth " without the camp." (Lev. xvi. 27.) Our Lord came to
be the true sin offering, to give His soul an offering for our
sins. Therefore it was divinely overruled of God, that, in order to fulfil the type perfectly, He should suffer outside the
city. (See also Lev. vi. 12—21.) St. Paul specially refers to
this when he tells the Hebrew Christians, who were familiar
with the law of Moses, that " Jesus suffered without the gate."
(Heb. xiii. 12.)   The minutest details of our Lord's passion
have a deep meaning.

[*Into a place...skull...Golgotha.*]   The precise position of this
place is not known certainly, and can only be conjectured. We
only know (from verse twenty) that it was " nigh to the city "
that it was " outside " the walls of Jerusalem at the time of
our Lord's crucifixion, and that it was near some public road,
as there is mention in one Gospel of them " that passed by."
(Matt. xxvii. 39.)   So many changes have taken place, during
the long period of 1800 years, in the boundary walls and the
soil of Jerusalem, that no wise man will speak positively as to
the exact whereabouts of Golgotha at this day. Though outside the walls 1800 years ago, it is far from unlikely that it is
within the walls at this time.

(*a*) Some maintain, as most probable, that Golgotha was a
place between the then existing wall of Jerusalem, and the descent into the valley of the Kidron, on the east side of the city,
near the road leading to Bethany. In this case the cross must
have been in full view of any one standing on the tower of
Antonia, in the temple courts, on the Mount of Olives, or upon
the eastern wall of the city. If this is correct, the crucifixion
might have been seen by hundreds of thousands of people at
once with perfect ease ; and from the sufferer being lifted up,
as it were, in the air, must have been an event of extraordinary publicity. According to the advocates of this theory, the
traditional site now assigned to the Holy Sepulchre is the true
one.

(*b*) Others, however, who have carefully examined the topography of Jerusalem, and are extremely likely to be wise and
impartial judges, are decidedly of opinion that Golgotha was
on the north side of Jerusalem, near the Damascus gate; and
they repudiate altogether the site commonly assigned to the
holy sepulchre at the present time.   An old and valued friend,
who has walked repeatedly over this " debateable land," says,
" I think the crucifixion took place on the north side of the
city, near the present Damascus gate, on a platform of rock,
just above a valley which runs on in endless tombs nearly two

miles.   Beneath this platform is a garden of olives still, full of excavations. In one of these, I think, was the sepulchre."

(c) Others, and among them another friend, who has travelled much in Palestine, and published the results of his travels, inclined to think that Golgotha was on the west side of Jerusalem, near the Jaffa gate.   The friend I refer to says, in a letter to me on this subject, " When I was first in Jerusalem in 1857, I visited some extraordinary fissures and cracks in the rocks west of the city, reminding me of the expression, *the rocks rent.* (Matt. xxvii. 51.)   These fissures are now all filled up."   Much, he adds, depends on the question whether Pilate resided in the tower of Antonia, and had his judgment hall there, or in the tower of Hippicus. This, however, we have no means of ascertaining.

In the face of such conflicting opinions I dare not speak positively, and I must leave my readers to judge for themselves. The question is one about which no one, it is clear, has any right to be heard, unless he has actually seen Jerusalem.

Why the place was called "the place of a skull" we are not told, and are left entirely to conjecture.

(a) Some think, as Gualter, Bullinger, Musculus, Gerhard, Burgon, Alford, Besser, and others, that the verse points to the bones, skeletons, and skulls, of executed criminals, which were lying about on Golgotha, as the common place of execution. This theory, however, is open to the grave objection, that it is most unlikely that dead men's bones would be left lying above ground, so near the city, when, according to the Mosaic law, they made any Jew unclean who touched them.   The Pharisees, with their excessive scrupulosity about externals, were not likely to tolerate such a source of defilement close to the holy city!—Moreover, John expressly says, that in the place where Jesus was crucified "there was a garden." (John xix. 41.)   This does not look like a place where dead men's bones and the skulls of criminals would be left lying about!   The very mention of this "garden" would suggest the idea that the place was not ordinarily used for execution, and that the Pharisees chose it only for its singular publicity. If it was on the east side, we can well believe that they felt a diabolical pleasure in tormenting our Lord to the last, by making Him die with the temple, the Mount of Olives, and His favorite Gethsemane before His eyes.

(b) Some think, as Lampe, Ellicott, and others, that the name, " place of a skull," arose from the shape of the small rising ground, like a skull, on which the cross was fixed. That such small elevations of limestone rock are to be found in that vicinity, is asserted by some travellers. To me there seems more probability in this theory than in the other. The name " Calvary," we should remember, is never used in the Greek ; and the marginal reading in Luke xxiii. 33 ought certainly to be in the text.

One thing alone is very certain. There is not the slightest authority for the common idea, that the place where our Lord was crucified was a hill, or mountain. The common expression in hymns and religious poetry, " Mount Calvary," is utterly incorrect and unwarrantable, and the favorite antithesis, or comparison between Mount Sinai and Mount Calvary, is so completely destitute of any Scriptural basis, that it is almost profane. Anything more unlike, as a matter of fact, than Sinai and Golgotha, cannot be conceived.

Origen, Cyprian, Epiphanius, Augustine, Jerome, and Theophylact, all mention an old tradition, that Golgotha was the place where the first Adam, our forefather was buried, and that the second Adam was buried near the first! This of course is a ridiculous, lying fable, as Noah's flood must have swept away all certainty about Adam's grave.

18 —[*Where they crucified Him.*] This famous mode of execution is so well known to every one that little need be said of it. The common mode of inflicting it, in all probability, was to strip the criminal,—to lay him on the cross on his back,—to nail his hands to the two extremities of the cross-piece, or fork of the cross,—to nail his feet to the upright piece, or principal stem of the cross,—then to raise the cross on end, and drop it into a hole prepared for it,—and then to leave the sufferer to a lingering and painful death. It was a death which combined the maximum of pain with the least immediate destruction of life. The agony of having nails driven through parts so full of nerves and sinews as the hands and feet, must have been intense. Yet wounds of the hands and feet are not mortal, and do not injure any great leading blood-vessel. Hence a crucified person, even in an eastern climate, exposed to the sun, might live two or three days, enduring extreme pain, without being relieved by death, if he was naturally a very strong man and in vigorous health. This is what we must remember our blessed Lord went through, when we read " they crucified Him." To a sensitive, delicate-minded person, it is hard to imagine any capital punishment more distressing. This is what Jesus endured willingly for us sinners. Hanging, as it were, between earth and heaven, He exactly filled the type of the brazen serpent, which Moses lifted up in the wilderness. (John iii. 14.)

Whether the person crucified was bound to the cross with ropes, to prevent the possibility of his breaking off from the nails in convulsive struggling,—whether He was stripped completely naked, or had a cloth round His loins,—whether each foot had a separate nail, or one nail was driven through both feet, —are disputed points which we have no means of settling. Some think, following Irenæus, Tertullian, and Justin Martyr, that there was a kind of seat or projection in the middle of the stem of the cross, to bear up the weight of the body, and also a place for the feet to rest on. Jeremy Taylor thinks, in support of this view, that the body of a crucified person could not rest only on the four wounds of hands and feet. Bishop Pearson also quotes a passage from Seneca, which seems to favor the idea.—As to the nails, Nonnus and Gregory Nazianzen say there were only three, and that one was driven through both feet at once. Cyprian says there were four.—But these are matters about which we really know nothing, and it is useless to guess and speculate about them. Of one thing however we may be very sure. The feet of a crucified person were much nearer the ground than is commonly supposed, and very likely not more than a foot or two from the earth. In this, as in other points, most pictures of the crucifixion are grossly incorrect, and the cross is made out to be a piece of timber so long and so thick that no one mortal man could ever have carried it.

Concerning the precise amount of physical suffering, and the precise effect on the human body in a crucifixion, the following medical account by a German physician, named Richter, quoted in Smith's Dictionary of the Bible, can hardly fail to interest a Bible reader. He says, "(1) The unnatural position and violent tension of the body caused a painful sensation from the least motion. (2) The nails being driven through parts of the hands and feet which are full of nerves and tendons, and yet at a distance from the heart, created the most exquisite anguish. (3) The exposure of so many wounds and lacerations brought on inflammation, which tended to become gangrene, and every moment increased the poignancy of suffering. (4) In the distended parts of the body more blood flowed through the arteries than could be carried back into the veins : and hence too much blood found its way from the aorta into the head and stomach, and the blood vessels of the head became pressed and swollen. The general obstruction of circulation caused an internal excitement, exertion, and anxiety, more intolerable than death itself. (5) There was the inexpressible misery of gradually increasing and lingering anguish. (6) To all this we may add burning and raging thirst." (Smith's Dictionary of the Bible : article, Crucifixion.) On the whole subject of the cross, and the sufferings connected with crucifixion, " Lipsius de Cruce " (published in 1595) is a most exhaustive book.

When we remember, beside all this, that our Lord's head was crowned with thorns, His back torn with savage scourging, and His whole system weighed down by the mental and bodily agony of the sleepless night following the Lord's Supper, we may have some faint idea of the intensity of His sufferings.

When we read " they " crucified, we are left to conjecture who it can refer to. It cannot be the Jews, because they could only stand by, and superintend at the most, as the Roman soldiers would certainly not let the punishment be inflicted by any other hands than their own. It must either be the four soldiers who were the executioners, or else it must be interpreted generally after the manner of other places, for " He was crucified." Thus in John xvi. 2, "*They* shall put you out of the synagogues." In that sentence " they " cannot refer to any person in particular. The simplest plan is to refer it generally to the whole party,—Jews and Gentiles together.

[*And two others with Him, etc.*] We know from the other Gospels that these other two were malefactors and thieves. The object of crucifying our Lord between them is plain. It was intended as a last indignity and injury. It was a public declaration that He was counted no better than the vilest criminals.

Little as our Lord's enemies meant it, this very crucifixion between two thieves did two great things. One was, that it precisely fulfilled Isaiah's prophecy about Messiah : " He was numbered with the transgressors." (Isai liii. 12.) The other was, that it gave our Lord the opportunity of working one more mighty miracle, even in His last hours,—the miracle of converting the penitent thief, forgiving his sins, and opening to him paradise. If His enemies had been content to crucify Him alone, this last trophy could not have been won, and our Lord's power over sin and the devil would not have been exhibited. So easy is it for God to bring good out of evil, and to make the malice of His enemies work round to His praise.

Augustine remarks, that three very different persons hung together on the three crosses on Golgotha. One was the Saviour of sinners. One was a sinner about to be saved. One was a sinner about to be damned. (On Psa. xxxiv.)

Cyril sees in the two malefactors a type of the Jewish and Gentile Churches : the one rejected, impenitent, and lost ; the other believing at the eleventh hour, and saved.

Many pious commentators remark, that even on the cross our Lord gave an emblem of His kingly power. On His right hand was a saved soul whom He admits into His kingdom ; on His left hand, a lost soul whom He leaves to reap the fruit of his own ways. There was right and left on the cross, even as there will be right and left, saved and unsaved, when He sits on the judgment-seat, wearing the crown at the last day.

It only remains to add that the cruel punishment of crucifixion was formally abolished by the Emperor Constantine, towards the end of his reign. It is an awful historical fact that when Jerusalem was taken by Titus, he crucified so many Jews around the city, that Josephus says that space and room failed for crosses, and crosses could not be found in sufficient number for bodies ! Reland well remarks, " They who had nothing but ' crucify ' in their mouths, were therewith paid home in their bodies."

19 —[*And Pilate wrote a title...cross.*] To fix a board with an inscription over the head of the person crucified, appears to have been a well-known custom, and is mentioned as such by classical writers. Some say it was a board covered with white gypsum, with letters of black, and others say that the letters were red. Pilate therefore did nothing unusual. In our Lord's case it served two ends, whether Pilate meant them or not. For one thing, it proclaimed to all passers-by, all who saw the crucifixion, that Jesus did really suffer, that He was not at the last moment released, and another punished in His stead, and that He was not taken away by miraculous interference from His enemies' hands. For another thing, it drew the attention of all witnesses and passers-by to our Lord, and made it quite certain on which of the three crosses He hung. Without this, a person looking at three naked figures hanging on their crosses, from a little distance off, might well have doubted which of the three was Jesus. The title made it plain. That our Lord was regarded as no common every-day criminal, and that it was thought right to call special attention to Him, is evident from this title being put on His cross.

[*Jesus...Nazareth...King...Jews.*] Pilate's reasons for choosing to place this description of our Lord over His cross, we are left to conjecture. My own decided opinion is that he worded the title as he did, in anger and vexation, and with an intention to annoy and insult the Jews. He publicly held up to scorn their King, as a poor criminal from a mean village in Galilee, a fitting *king* for such a people !—Whatever his motive may have been, it was curiously overruled by God that even on the cross our Lord should be styled a " King." He came to be a King, and as a King He lived and suffered and died, though not acknowledged and honored by His subjects. " Nazarene " identified our Lord as the well-known Teacher from Galilee, who for three years had stirred the Jewish mind. " King " identified Him as the Person accused by the chief priests for claiming a kingdom, and formally rejected by them, on the plea that they had no king but Cæsar. It was a very full and significant title.

A careful reader of the Gospels will not fail to observe, that each Gospel writer gives this title in a slightly different form, and that there are in fact four versions of it. The question naturally arises, Which is correct ? The versions do not at all contradict one another ; but that of Mark, " the King of the Jews," is much shorter than that of John. No two, in a word, are exactly alike.—In reply, it is fair to remind the reader, that the inscription was written in three languages ; and that it is far from unlikely that it was in one form in one language, and in another form in another. The one common point in all the four versions is, " the King of the Jews," and this was probably the only point that Mark, in his brief and condensed history, was taught to record. John gives the whole inscription, because he alone narrates the dispute between the priests and

Pilate about it. If I may venture a conjecture, I should guess that Mark gives the Latin inscription, Luke the Greek, and Matthew and John the Hebrew one. But why it seemed good to the Holy Ghost that Matthew should omit the expression "of Nazareth," which John mentions, I do not pretend to say. It is precisely one of those things in which it is wisest to confess our ignorance, and to be willing to wait for more light.

St. John alone records that Pilate " wrote " and " put " on the cross this title. We are not obliged to suppose that he did both with his own hands. The writing was almost certainly his own act. The putting the title on the cross he probably left to the soldiers.

The common pictures of the crucifixion, showing a kind of scroll, or parchment over our Lord's head on the cross, are most probably in this, as in other details, most incorrect representations of the real facts. Moreover most painters seem to forget that it was written three times over, being in three languages !

20 —[*This title then read many, etc.*] This seems to be one of John's parenthetical comments. It also reads like the report of an eye-witness ; and this we know John was. He stood by and saw all that happened. It is as though he said, " I can testify that many of the Jews saw and read this title,—some as they passed along the road which ran by,—some from the walls of the city, for the place was near the walls. It was an inscription moreover so contrived, that hardly any one in Jerusalem could fail to understand it ; for it was written in the three languages most likely to be known,—in Hebrew, Greek, and Latin."

It is almost needless to say that the title was in Hebrew, because every Jew would know it, the oldest language in the world, and the language of the Old Testament,—in Greek, because this was the language most known in all eastern countries, and the language of all literary and educated people,—in Latin, because this was the language of the Romans, the ruling nation in the world. The Roman soldiers would all understand the Latin ; the Greek proselytes and Hellenistic Jews would all understand the Greek ; and the pure Jews from Galilee and Judæa, and every part of the earth, assembled for the passover, would all understand the Hebrew. All would go away to spread the tidings that one Jesus, the King of the Jews, had been put to death by crucifixion at the passover feast.

Henry remarks, " In the Hebrew, the oracles of God were recorded ; in Greek, the learning of the philosophers ; and in Latin, the laws of the empire. In each of these languages Christ is proclaimed King, in whom are hid all the treasures of revelation, wisdom and power."

To this very day it is certain that no three languages can be more useful for a Christian minister to know, if he would be familiar with his Bible, than Hebrew, Greek, and Latin.

The last day alone, perhaps, will disclose the effect this title had on those who read it. When the priests and their companions saw it, they mocked and scoffed : " King indeed ! Let Christ the King of Israel descend from the cross, and we will believe." (Mark xv. 32.) But there was one man who saw the title probably with very different eyes. The penitent thief perhaps grasped at the word " King," and believed. Who can tell that this was not the root of his cry, " Lord remember me, when Thou comest into *Thy kingdom*." (Luke xxiii. 42.) Perhaps Pilate's title helped to save a soul !

Brentius remarks, that when we think of the cross of Christ, and the title on it, which so many read, we should remember there was another handwriting nailed to that cross spiritually, which no mortal could read. Jesus Christ, by His vicarious death for us, " Blotted out the handwriting of ordinances that was against us, which was contrary to us, and took it out of the way, nailing it to His cross." (Col. ii. 14.)

21 —[*Then said the chief priests, etc.*] This verse brings out the feeling which the sight of Pilate's title excited in the minds of the chief priests. They were annoyed and angry. They did not like the idea of this crucified criminal being publicly declared " the King of the Jews." They detected the latent scorn and irony which guided Pilate's hands, and lay at the bottom of his mind. They did not like so public an announcement that they had crucified their own King, and wanted " no King but Cæsar." They were vexed at the implied reflection on themselves. Besides this, they were probably uncomfortable in conscience. Hardened and wicked as they were, they had, many of them, we may be sure, a secret conviction which they vainly tried to keep down, that they were doing a wrong thing, and a thing which by and by they would find it hard to defend either to themselves or others. Hence they tried to get Pilate to alter the title, and to make it appear that our Lord was only a pretended King,—an impostor who " said that He was King." This, they doubtless thought, would shift some of the guilt off their shoulders, and make it appear that our Lord was crucified for usurping a title to which He was legally proved to have no claim.

When and where the chief priests said this to Pilate does not appear. It must either have been when the whole party was leaving the judgment-seat for Golgotha, or after our Lord was nailed to the tree, or while the soldiers were nailing Him. Looking at St. John's account, one might fancy that the centurion sent word to Pilate that the prisoner was being nailed to the cross, and asked for a title to put over His head, before the cross was reared. If we do not suppose this, we must believe that Pilate actually accompanied the party outside the walls, and was only at a little distance off during the last horrible preparations. In that case he might easily write a title, and the

priests might easily be standing by. The difficulty is to understand where the parties could be, when the priests said " write
not ; " and it is one which must be left unsettled. It seems,
however, certain that once put over our Lord's head, the title
was not expected to be taken down ; and the request was not
to alter it, after being put up, but to write a different title before it was put up.

Bengel observes, that this is the only place in St. John's Gospel where the chief priests are called " the chief priests *of the
Jews.*" He thinks it is intended to mark emphatically the bitter hatred with which the *priests* of the Jews regarded the
King of the Jews.

We may well believe that even the wickedest men at their
worst, are often more sore and uncomfortable inwardly than
they appear outwardly. This it was that probably lay at the
bottom of the chief priests' remonstrance about the title.
Herod's cry, " It is John the Baptist," after John was dead, is
another case in point.

22 —[*Pilate answered...1 have written.*] The hard, haughty, imperious character of the wicked Roman Governor comes out
forcibly in these words. They show his contempt for the
Jews :—" Trouble me not about the title : I have written it, and
I shall not alter it to please you."—They suggest the idea that
he was willing enough to be revenged on them for their obstinate refusal to meet his wishes, and consent to our Lord's release. He was glad to hold them up to scorn and contempt, as
a people who crucified their own king. It is likely enough that
between his wife and his own conscience and the chief priests,
the Roman Governor was vexed, worried, and irritated, and
savagely resolved not to gratify the Jews any further in any
matter. He had gone as far as he chose, in allowing them to
murder an innocent and just person. He would not go an inch
further. He now made a stand, and showed that he could be
firm and unyielding and unbending when he liked. It is no
uncommon thing to see a wicked man, when he has given way
to the devil and trampled on his conscience in one direction,
trying to make up for it by being firm in another.

Calvin observes that Pilate, by publishing in three languages
Christ's title, was " by a secret guidance made a herald of the
Gospel." He contrasts his conduct with that of the Papists
who prohibit the reading of the Gospel and the Scriptures by
the common people. Gualter says much the same.

Bullinger remarks that Pilate acted like Caiaphas when he
said, " It is expedient that one die for the people, not knowing
what he said." Just so Pilate little knew what testimony he
was bearing to Christ's kingly office.

Leigh quotes a saying of Augustine : "If a man like Pilate
can say, what I have written I have written, and will not alter,

can we think that God doth write any in His book and blot it out again?"

23 —[*Then the soldiers, etc.*] The soldiers having now finished their bloody work, having nailed our Lord to the cross, put the title over His head and reared the cross on end, proceeded to do what they probably always did,—to divide the clothes of the crucified criminal among themselves. In most countries the clothes of a person put to death by the law are the perquisite of the executioner. So it was with our Lord's clothes. They had most likely first stripped our Lord naked, before nailing his hands and feet to the cross, and had laid his clothes on one side till they had finished their work. They now turned to the clothes, and, as they had done many a time on such occasions, proceeded to divide them. All four Evangelists particularly mention this, and evidently call our special attention to it.

The division into four portions shows clearly that there were four soldiers employed, beside the centurion, in the work of crucifixion. Many commentators see in them emblems of the four quarters of the Gentile world. This, however, seems to me fanciful. A quaternion, a small party of four, was a common division of soldiers in those days, just as "a file" of men is among ourselves. (See Acts xii. 4.)

What the four portions of garments were we are left to conjecture. Hengstenberg thinks that they consisted of the covering of the head, the girdle, the shoes, and the under garment fitting to the body. Matthew's report of the Sermon on the Mount contains a clear distinction between a coat and a cloak. (Matt. v. 40.) For these four portions the soldiers probably cast lots, in order that each one might have his part decided, and to prevent wrangling about the unequal value of the portions.

Others think that the language of St. John about the coat which was "not rent," is strong evidence that all the rest of our Lord's clothes were rent into four pieces, and that Hengstenberg's division of them will not stand. It must be admitted that there is much probability in this. It seems very unlikely that so much should be said about this seamless garment being not rent, if the other garments had not been torn in dividing them.

Concerning the "coat" here mentioned, it is not easy to say positively what part of our Lord's dress it was.

(*a*) Most commentators say that it was the long inner tunic, girt about the waist, and reaching almost to the feet, which was the principal garment of an inhabitant of the East,—a kind of loose smock-frock with sleeves, such as any one may see a pattern of, in Leonardo da Vinci's famous picture of the Lord's Supper. The objection to this view, to my mind, is the grave difficulty of explaining how such a garment could be seamless and woven throughout,—though I doubt not our Lord wore it, and it was the hem of such a garment the woman touched.

(b) Some few commentators think it was the outer garment, a loose mantle or cape, thrown over the shoulders, which many wore above the tunic. Such a garment, having no sleeves, might easily be made in one piece without any seam, and perhaps was only drawn together or clasped about the shoulders. It is fair, nevertheless, to say that the Greek word here rendered " coat," ordinarily means the inward garment or tunic. (See Suicer and Parkhurst.) Becker's Charicles, however, on this Greek word, shows some reason for thinking it sometimes means the outward coat.

The reader must judge for himself. The question is one which cannot be settled positively either way, and happily is not of any moment. To my own mind, the objection to the first and common view is very serious indeed, if not insuperable ; but it may not appear so to others. The only thing we know for certain is that one portion of our Lord's dress was not rent, but made the subject of casting lots as to who should have it. As to the ancient fable that our Lord's coat was woven by his mother Mary when He was a child, grew with His growth, and never waxed old or wore out, it is a foolish apocryphal legend.

Bengel observes that we never read of our Lord " rending " His own garments in desperate sorrow, like Job, Jacob, Joshua, Caleb, Jephthah, Hezekiah, Mordecai, Ezra, Paul, and Barnabas. (See Gen. xxxvii. 9 ; Numb. xiv. 6 ; Judges xi. 35 ; 2 Kings xix. 3 ; Esther iv. 1 ; Ezra ix. 3 ; Job i. 20 ; Acts xiv. 14.)

On the incident recorded in this verse, Luther remarks, " This distribution of garments served for a sign that everything was done with Christ, just as with one who was abandoned, lost, and to be forgotten forever." Even among ourselves, the division, sale, or giving away of a man's clothes, is a plain indication of his being dead, or given up for lost ; just as among soldiers and sailors, when dead or missing, the effects are sold or distributed.

Henry thinks that " the soldiers hoped to make something more than ordinary out of our Lord's clothes, having heard of cures wrought by the touch of the hem of His garment, or expecting that His admirers would give any money for them." But this seems unlikely and fanciful.

Our Lord was treated, we should observe, just like all common criminals,—stripped naked, and His clothes sold under His eyes, as one dead already and cast off by man.

It is noteworthy that in this, as in many other things, our Lord was, in a striking manner, our substitute. He was stripped naked, and reckoned, and dealt with as a guilty sinner, in order that we might be clothed with the garment of His perfect righteousness and reckoned innocent.

24 —[*They said therefore among themselves, etc.*] In this verse we are told that the conduct of the soldiers was a precise fulfilment of a prophecy delivered a thousand years before. (Ps. xxii. 18.) That prophecy foretold not only that Messiah's garments should be parted and distributed, but that men should " cast lots for His vesture." Little did the four rough Roman soldiers think that they were actually supplying evidence of the truth of the Scriptures ! They only saw that our Lord's " coat " was a good and serviceable garment, which it was a pity to rend or tear and therefore they agreed to cast lots who should have it. And yet, in so doing, they added to the great cloud of witnesses who prove the divine authority of the Bible. Men little consider that they are all instruments in God's hand for accomplishing His purposes.

The importance of interpreting prophecy literally, and not figuratively, is strongly shown in this verse. The system of interpretation which unhappily prevails among many Christians—I mean the system of spiritualizing away all the plain statements of the prophets, and accommodating them to the Church of Christ—can never be reconciled with such a verse as this. The plain, literal meaning of words should evidently be the meaning placed on all the statements of Old Testament prophecy. This remark of course does not apply to symbolical prophecies, such as those of the seals, trumpets, and vials in Revelation.

The typical meaning of this seamless and unrent coat of our Lord is a point on which fanciful theological writers have loved to dwell in every age of the Church of Christ. It represented, we are told by Augustine and many others, the unity of the Church, and it was an allusion to the priesthood of the Divine wearer! I frankly confess that I am unable to believe such notions, and I doubt extremely whether they were intended by the Holy Ghost. But it is a fact mentioned by Henry, that "those who opposed Luther's separation from the Church of Rome, urged much this seamless coat as an argument, and laid so much stress on it, that they were called Inconsutilistæ,—the seamless ones ! "

As to the lying legend that this seamless coat was preserved and handed down to the Church as a precious relic, it is scarcely worth while to mention it, except as a melancholy illustration of the corruption of man, and the apostacy of the Church of Rome. The holy coat of Trèves, and its exhibition, are a scandal and disgrace to Christianity. Suffice it to say, that any one who can seriously believe that our Lord's seamless coat, after falling into the hands of a heathen Romish soldier, was finally treasured up as a relic, or that the cross itself was kept safe and escaped destruction, must be so credulous a person that argument is thrown away on him.

It is worth remembering, that when the first Adam fell by sin and was cast out of Eden, God mercifully clothed him and covered his nakedness. When the second Adam died as our substitute, and was counted " a curse " for us on the cross, He was stripped naked and His clothes sold.

The object for which John concludes the verse with the words, " These things therefore the soldiers did," is not very apparent. Burgon suggests it may mean, " Such was the part which the soldiers played in this terrible tragedy. Uninfluenced by the Jews, without any direction from Pilate, these things the soldiers did." This however seems hardly satisfactory, because this was not all that the soldiers did.—I prefer thinking that St. John means to say, that he was actually an eye-witness of the soldiers unconsciously fulfilling an ancient prophecy : " I myself saw, with mine own eyes, the four soldiers casting lots on my Lord's coat ; and I can testify that I saw the words of the Psalmist literally fulfilled."

Lampe thinks that St. John makes this remark, in order to show how literally Scripture was fulfilled by men who were totally ignorant of Scripture. The Roman soldiers of course knew nothing of the Psalms, yet did the very things predicted in the Psalms.

25 —[*Now there stood by the cross, etc.*] A wonderfully striking incident is recorded in this and the two following verses, which is not found in the other three Gospels. St. John tells us that at this awful moment, Mary, the mother of Jesus, and other women, two if not three, stood by the cross on which our Lord hung. " Love is strong as death ; " and even amidst the crowd of taunting Jews and rough Roman soldiers, these holy women were determined to stand by our Lord to the last, and to show their unceasing affection to Him. When we remember that our Lord was a condemned criminal, peculiarly hated by the chief priests, and executed by Roman soldiers, the faithfulness and courage of these holy women can never be sufficiently admired. As long as the world stands they supply a glorious proof of what grace can do for the weak, and of the strength that love to Christ can supply. When all men but one forsook our Lord, more than one woman boldly confessed Him. Women, in short, were the last at the cross and the first at the tomb.

It is interesting to consider who and what they were, that stood by our Lord's cross as He hung upon it. John, the beloved disciple, was there, we know ; though with characteristic modesty he does not directly name it. But the twenty-sixth verse shows clearly that he was one of the party. He might well be the one that " Jesus loved." No Apostle seems to have had such deep feeling towards our Lord as John.—Mary, the mother of our Lord (*never called the Virgin Mary in Scripture*) was there. We must suppose that she had come up from Galilee to the feast of the passover, in company with the other women who ministered to our Lord. She must now have been comparatively old, at least forty-eight years old. To represent her in pictures as a beautiful young woman at the time of the crucifixion is absurd. Who can doubt that when she saw her Son hanging on the cross, she must have realized the truth of old Simeon's prophecy, " A sword shall pierce through thine own soul also." (Luke ii. 35.) Very striking and instructive is it to observe how very rarely she is named in the Gospel history.—Mary, the wife of Cleophas, or Alpheus, was there. The Greek leaves it uncertain whether it means daughter or wife; but nearly all think it must be wife. She seems to have been the mother of James and Jude the Apostles, and to have been related in some way to the Virgin Mary, either as sister or sister-in-law. Hence James is called the " Lord's brother." She too must have been nearly as old as the Virgin Mary, if we may judge by her having two sons who were Apostles.—Mary of Magdala, in Galilee, commonly called Mary Magdalene, was also there. Of her we only know that Jesus had cast out of her seven devils, and that none of all the women who ministered to our Lord, seem to have felt such deep gratitude to our Saviour, and to have demonstrated such deep affection. The common doctrine that she had once been a notorious breaker of the seventh commandment has no foundation in Scripture. She probably was the youngest of all the party, and as such had to risk more, and sacrifice her own feelings more than any, in pressing through a crowd of enemies to the foot of the cross.

But were there only three women at the cross ? This is a disputed question, and one which will probably never be settled, since the Greek wording of the verse before us leaves the point open either way.

(a) Most commentators think that the words, " His mother's sister," belongs to " Mary the wife of Cleophas," and are meant to define the relationship between that Mary and Mary the mother of our Lord.

(b) Others, as Pearce, Bengel, and Alford, think that " His mother's sister " means a fourth woman, and that this woman was Salome, the mother of James and John. The strongest argument in favor of this view is the distinct statement in Matthew's account of the crucifixion, that many women beheld the sight, " among which was Mary Magdalene, and Mary the mother of James and Joses, and the mother of Zebedee's children,"—that is, Salome. (Matt. xxvii. 56.) If she stood with Mary Magdalene looking on, why should we doubt that she stood with her at the cross ? The suppression of her name is quite characteristic of John. She was his own mother, and he modestly keeps back her name, as he keeps back his own. In what way she was the " sister " to the mother of our Lord we do not know. But there is no reason against it, that I know of. According to this view, the women at the foot of the cross were four: viz, (1) Mary, the mother of Jesus. (2) The sister of our Lord's mother: *i.e.*, Salome, the mother of John, who wrote this Gospel. (3) Mary, the wife of Alpheus and mother of two Apostles. (4) Mary Magdalene.

The reader must decide for himself. The question happily is not one affecting our salvation. For myself I must frankly declare my belief that the second view is the right one, and that there were four women, and not three only, at the foot of the cross. The objection that the word " and " is omitted before " Mary the wife of Cleophas " is worthless. In almost every catalogue of the Apostles the same omission may be noticed. (See Acts i. 13; Matt. x. 2; Luke vi. 14.)

Whether all Christian women should always come forward and put themselves in such public and prominent positions as these holy women took up, is a grave question, about which each Christian woman must judge for herself. Considerations of *physical* strength and nervous self-command must not be overlooked. The four women who stood by the cross neither fainted nor went into hysterics, but were self-controlled, and calm. Let every one be persuaded in their own minds. Some women can do what others cannot.

Why the fierce enemies of our Lord among the Jews, and the rough Roman soldiers, permitted these holy women to stand undisturbed by the cross, is a question we have no means of deciding. Possibly the Romans may have thought it only fair and reasonable to let a criminal's relatives and friends stand by him, when he could do the State no more harm, and they could not rescue him from death. Possibly the centurion who superintended the execution, may have felt some pity for the little weeping company of weak women. Who can tell but his kindness was a cup of cold water which was repaid him a hundredfold? He said before the day ended, " Truly this was the Son of God." (Matt. xxvii. 54.) Possibly John's acquaintance with the high priest, already mentioned, may have procured him and his companions some favor. All these, however, are only conjectures, and we cannot settle the point.

The Greek word rendered " stood " is literally " had stood " Does not this mean from the beginning of the crucifixion?

26, 27.—[*When Jesus therefore saw His Mother, etc.*] The incident recorded in these two verses is wonderfully touching and affecting. Even in this trying season of bodily and mental agony, our blessed Lord did not forget others.—He had not forgotten His brutal murderers; but had prayed for them: " Father forgive them, for they know not what they do."—He had not forgotten His fellow-sufferers by His side. When one of the crucified malefactors cried to him, " Lord, remember me," He had at once answered him, and promised him a speedy entrance into Paradise.—And now He did not forget His mother. He saw her standing by the cross, and knew well her distress, and felt tenderly for her desolate condition, left alone in a wicked world, after having lost such a Son. He therefore commended her to the care of John, His most loving and tender-hearted and faithful disciple. He told John to look on her as his mother, and told His mother to look on John as her son. No better and wiser arrangement could have been made in every way. None would care so much for the mother of Jesus as the disciple whom Jesus loved, and who lay in His bosom at the last supper. No home could be so suitable to Mary, as the home of one who was, according to the view maintained above, son to her own sister Salome.

The lessons of the whole transaction are deeply instructive.

(a) We should mark the depth and width of our Lord's sympathies and affections. The Saviour on whom we are bid to repose the weight of our sinful souls is one whose love passeth knowledge. Shallow, skin-deep feelings in others, we all know continually chill and disappoint us on every side in this world. But there is one whose mighty heart affection knows no bottom. That one is Christ.

(b) We should mark the high honor our Lord puts on the fifth commandment. Even in His last hour He magnifies it, and makes it honorable, by providing for His mother according to the flesh. The Christian who does not lay himself out to honor father and mother—both one and the other parent, is a very ignorant religionist.

(c) We should mark that when Jesus died Joseph was probably dead, and that Mary had no other children beside our Lord. It is absurd to suppose that our Lord would have commended Mary to John, if she had had a husband or son to support her. The theory of some few writers, that Mary had other children by Joseph after Jesus was born, is very untenable, and grossly improbable.

(d) We should mark what a strong condemnation the passage supplies to the whole system of Mary-worship, as held by the Roman Catholic Church. There is not here a trace of the doctrine that Mary is patroness of the saints, protectress of the Church, and one who can help others. On the contrary, we see her requiring protection herself, and commended to the care and protection of a disciple! Hengstenberg remarks, " Our Lord's design was not to provide for John, but to provide for His mother." Alford observes, " The Romanist idea that the Lord commended all His disciples, as represented by the beloved one, to the patronage of His mother, is simply absurd."

(e) Finally, we should mark how Jesus honors those who honor and boldly confess Him. To John, who alone of all the eleven stood by the cross, He gives the high privilege of taking charge of His mother. As Henry pleasantly remarks, it is a sign of great confidence, and a mark of great honor, to be made a trustee and a guardian by a great person, for those he leaves behind at his death. To the women Jesus gives the honor of being specially named and recorded for their faithfulness and love, in a Gospel which is read all over the world in 200 languages.

The Greek words rendered " his own home," mean literally, "his own things." It is a thoroughly indefinite expression. We can only suppose it means, that in future, from that day, wherever John abode the mother of our Lord abode also. His home, in a word, became her home. There is no evidence whatever that John had any home in Jerusalem. If he had any home at all, it must have been in Galilee, near the lake of Gennesaret.

Bengel, Besser, Ellicott, and Alford, from the phrase " hour," suggest that John took Mary home *immediately*, so that she did not see our Lord die, and then returned to the cross. This, however, seems to me very improbable. The mother of our Lord would surely stay by the cross to the last, if any woman did. John would not leave the cross, in my opinion, for a minute. His narrative of the crucifixion reads like that of an eyewitness from first to last.

Hengstenberg takes the same view that I do.

The word " woman " in the twenty sixth verse, is noteworthy. It must not be pressed too far as implying the slightest disrespect or want of affection. The whole transaction here narrated overthrows such an idea. But I think it is remarkable that our Lord does not say " Mother." And I cannot help thinking that, even at this awful moment, He would remind her that she must never suffer herself or others to presume on the relationship between her and Him, or claim any supernatural honor on the ground of being His mother. Henceforth she must daily remember, that her first aim must be to live the life of faith as a believing woman, like all other Christian women. Her blessedness did not consist in being related to Christ according to the flesh, but in believing and keeping Christ's Word. I firmly believe that, even on the cross, Jesus foresaw the future heresy of " Mary-worship." Therefore he said " Woman," and did not say " Mother."

Besser remarks, " Some old writers, as Bonaventura, say that Christ perhaps avoided the sweet name of *mother*, that He might not lacerate Mary's heart with such a tender word of farewell. Others see in Christ's manner of speaking a reference to the seed of the *woman* who was to bruise the serpent's head. The most obvious view is, that the Lord, through this name *woman*, would direct His mother into that love which knows Christ no more after the flesh (2 Cor. v. 16), and would also declare to us that in the midst of His work of atonement He felt Himself equally bound close to all sinners, and that He was not nearer to His mother than He was to thee and me."

JOHN XIX 28—37

28 After this, Jesus knowing that all things were now accomplished, that the scripture might be fulfilled, saith, I thirst.

29 Now there was set a vessel full of vinegar : and they filled a sponge with vinegar, and put *it* upon hyssop, and put *it* to his mouth.

30 When Jesus therefore had received the vinegar, he said, it is finished: and he bowed his head and gave up the ghost.

31 The Jews therefore, because it was the preparation, that the bodies should not remain upon the cross on the sabbath day, (for that sabbath day was an high day,) besought Pilate that their legs might be broken; and *that* they might be taken away.

32 Then came the soldiers and brake the legs of the first, and of the other which was crucified with him.

33 But when they came to Jesus, and saw that he was dead already, they brake not his legs :

34 But one of the soldiers with a spear pierced his side, and forthwith came there out blood and water.

35 And he that saw *it* bare record, and his record is true : and he knoweth that he saith true, that ye might believe.

36 For these things were done, that the scripture should be fulfilled, A bone of him shall not be broken.

37 And again another scripture saith, they shall look on him whom they pierced.

THIS part of St. John's narrative of Christ's passion, contains points of deep interest, which are silently passed over by Matthew, Mark, and Luke. The reason of this silence we are not told. Suffice it for us to remember that, both in what they recorded and in what they did not record, all four Evangelists wrote by inspiration of God.

Let us mark, for one thing, in these verses, *the frequent fulfilments of prophetic Scripture throughout every part of Christ's crucifixion.* Three several predictions are specially mentioned, in Exodus, Psalms, and Zechariah, which received their accomplishment at the cross. Others, as every well-informed Bible-reader knows, might easily be added. All combine to prove one and the same thing. They prove that the death of our Lord Jesus Christ at Golgotha was a thing foreseen and predetermined by God. Hundreds of years before the crucifixion, every part of the solemn transaction. was arranged in the Divine counsels, and the minutest particulars were revealed to the Prophets. From first to last it was a thing foreknown, and every portion of it was in accordance with a settled plan and design. In the highest, fullest sense, when Christ died, He " died according to the Scriptures." (1 Cor. xv. 3.)

We need not hesitate to regard such fulfilments of prophecy as strong evidence of the Divine authority of God's Word. The Prophets foretell not only Christ's death, but the particulars of His death. It is impossible to explain so many accomplishments of predicted circumstances upon any other theory. To talk of luck, chance, and accidental coincidence, as sufficient explanation, is preposterous and absurd. The only rational account is the inspiration of God. The Prophets who foretold the particulars of the crucifixion, were inspired by Him who foresees the end from the beginning ; and the books they wrote under His inspiration ought not to be read as human compositions, but Divine. Great indeed are the difficulties of all who pretend to deny the inspiration of the Bible. It really requires more unreasoning faith to be an infidel than to be a Christian. The man who regards the repeated fulfilments of minute prophecies about Christ's death, such as the prophecies about His dress, His thirst, His pierced side, and His bones, as the result of chance, and not of design, must indeed be a credulous man.

We should mark, secondly, in these verses, *the peculiarly solemn saying which came from our Lord's lips just before He died.* St. John relates that " when He had received the vinegar, He said, it is finished ; and He bowed His head and gave up the ghost." It is surely not too much to say, that of all the seven famous sayings of Christ on the cross, none is more remarkable than this, which John alone has recorded.

The precise meaning of this wondrous expression, " It is finished," is a point which the Holy Ghost has not thought good to reveal to us. There is a depth about it, we must all instinctively feel, which man has probably no line to fathom. Yet there is perhaps no irreverence in conjecturing the thoughts that were in our Lord's mind, when the word was spoken. The finishing of all the known and unknown sufferings which He came to endure, as our Substitute,—the finishing of the ceremonial law, which He came to wind up and fulfil, as the true Sacrifice for sin,—the finishing of the many prophecies, which He came to accomplish,—the finishing of the great work of man's redemption, which was now close at hand,—all this, we need not doubt, our Lord had in view when He said, "It is finished." There may have been more behind, for aught we know. But in handling the language of such a Being as our Saviour, on such an occasion, and at so mysterious a crisis of His history, it is well to be cautious. "The place whereon we stand is holy ground."

One comfortable thought, at all events, stands out most clearly on the face of this famous expression. We rest our souls on a "finished work," if we rest them on the work of Jesus Christ the Lord. We need not fear that either sin, or Satan, or law shall condemn us at the last day. We may lean back on the thought, that we have a Saviour who has done all, paid all, accomplished all, performed all that is necessary for our salvation. We may take up the challenge of the Apostle, "Who is he that condemneth? It is Christ that died: yea, rather that is risen again; who is even at the right hand of God; who also maketh intercession for us." (Rom. viii. 34.) When we look at our own works, we may well be ashamed of their imperfections. But when we look at the finished work of Christ, we may feel peace. We "are complete in Him," if we believe. (Colos. ii. 10.)

We should mark, lastly, in these verses, *the reality and truth of Christ's death.* We are told that " one of the soldiers with a spear pierced His side, and forthwith came there out blood and water." This incident, small as it may seem at first sight, supplies probable proof that the heart of our blessed Lord was pierced, and that life was consequently extinct. He did not merely faint, or swoon away, or become insensible, as some have dared to insinuate. His heart actually ceased to beat, and He actually died. Great, indeed, was the importance of this fact. We must all see, on a moment's reflection, that without a real death there could be no real sacrifice; that without a real death there could be no real resurrection ; and that without a real death and real resurrection, the whole of Christianity is a house built on sand, and has no foundation at all. Little indeed did that reckless Roman soldier dream that he was a mighty helper of our holy religion, when he thrust his spear into our Lord's side.

That the " blood and water " mentioned in this place had a deep spiritual meaning, we can hardly doubt. St. John himself seems to refer to them in his first Epistle, as highly significant. " This is He that came by water and blood." (1 John v. 6.) The Church in every age has been of one mind in holding that they are emblems of spiritual things. Yet the precise meaning of the blood and water is a subject about which Christians have never agreed, and perhaps will never agree until the Lord returns.

The favorite theory that the blood and water mean the two Sacraments, however plausible and popular, may be reasonably regarded as somewhat destitute of solid foundation. Baptism and the Lord's Supper were ordinances already in existence when our Lord died, and they needed no reappointing. It is surely not necessary to drag in these two blessed, Sacraments on every occasion, and to insist on thrusting them forward, as the hidden sense of every disputed text where the number "two" is mentioned. Such pertinacious application of hard places in Scripture to Baptism and the Lord's Supper does no real good, and brings no real honor to the Sacraments. It is questionable whether it does not tend to vulgarize them, and bring them into contempt.

The true meaning of the blood and water is probably to be sought in the famous prophecy of Zechariah, where he says, "In that day there shall be a fountain opened to the house of David, and to the inhabitants of Jerusalem, for sin and uncleanness." (Zech, xiii. 1.) When was that fountain so truly and really opened as in the hour when Christ died? What emblem of atonement and purification was so well known to the Jews as blood and water? Why then should we hesitate to believe that the flow of "blood and water" from our Lord's side was a significant declaration to the Jewish nation, that the true fountain for sin was at length thrown open, and that henceforth sinners might come boldly to Christ for pardon, and wash and be clean? This interpretation, at any rate, deserves serious thought and consideration.

Whatever view we take of the blood and water, let us make sure that we ourselves are "washed and made white in the blood of the Lamb." (Rev. vii. 14.) It will matter nothing at the last day, that we held during life the most exalted view of the sacraments, if we never came to Christ by faith, and never had personal dealings with Him. Faith in Christ is the one thing needful. "He that hath the Son hath life, and he that hath not the Son of God hath not life." (1 John v. 12.)

Notes John xix 28—37

28 —[*After this.*] When our Lord had commended His mother, Mary, to John, I believe that the miraculous darkness for three hours came on. During those three hours I believe our Lord said nothing, except " My God, my God, why hast Thou forsaken Me ? " As the darkness was passing away, He said, " I thirst." This, and the two last sayings, " It is finished," and " Father, into Thy hands I commend my spirit," were all that He said during the last three hours. Thus three of His seven sayings on the cross were before the darkness, and four after it, or during it.

The order of the famous seven sayings was as follows:—

1. " Father, forgive them ; for they know not what they do."
2. " To-day shalt thou be with Me in paradise."
3. " Woman behold thy son. Behold thy mother."
4. " My God, my God, why hast thou forsaken me."
5. " I thirst."
6. " It is finished."
7. " Father, into thy hands I commend my spirit."

[*Jesus knowing...accomplished, etc.*] In order to understand this verse aright, there is one point concerning our Lord's death which must be carefully remembered. His death was entirely a voluntary act on His part. In this one respect His death was unlike that of a common man ; and we need not wonder at it when we consider that He was God and man in one Person. The final separation between body and soul, in His case, could not take place until He willed it ; and all the power of Jews and Romans together could not have effected it against His will. We die because we cannot help it ; Christ died because He willed to die, and not until the moment arrived when He saw it best. He said Himself, " No man taketh life from Me, but I lay it down of myself. I have power to lay it down, and I have power to take it again." (John x. 18.) As a matter of fact, we know that our Lord was crucified about nine o'clock in the morning, and that He died about three o'clock in the afternoon of the same day. Mere physical suffering would not account for this. A person crucified in full health was known sometimes to linger on alive for three days ! It is evident therefore that our Lord willed to give up the ghost in the same day that He was crucified, for some wise reason. This reason, we can easily suppose, was to secure the fullest publicity for His atoning death. He died in broad daylight, in the sight of myriads of spectators ; and thus the reality of His death could never be denied. This voluntariness and free choice of His death, and of the hour of His death, in my judgment, lie at the bottom of the verse before us.

Remembering all this, I believe that the sense of the verse before us must be paraphrased in the following way: " After this, Jesus knowing in His own mind that all things were now practically accomplished, which he came into the world to do, and knowing that it was expedient that His death should be a most public event, in the face of the crowds assembled to view His crucifixion, proceeded to say the last words which He intended to say, before giving up the ghost at three o'clock, and by saying them fulfilled a prophecy of Scripture."—Nothing in the details of our Lord's death, we must always remember, was accidental or by chance. Every part of the great sacrifice for sin was foreordained and arranged in the eternal counsels of the Trinity, even to the words which He was to speak on the cross.

The expression " I thirst," was chiefly used, I believe, in order to afford a public testimony of the reality and intensity of His bodily sufferings, and to prevent any one supposing, because of His marvellous calmness and patience, that He was miraculously free from suffering. On the contrary, He would have all around Him know that He felt what all severely wounded persons, and especially what all crucified persons, felt, —a burning and consuming thirst. So that when we read that " He suffered for sins," we are to understand that He really and truly suffered.

Henry observes, " The torments of hell are represented by a violent thirst, in the complaint of the rich man who begged for a drop of water to cool his tongue. To that everlasting thirst we had all been condemned, if Christ had not suffered on the cross, and said, ' I thirst.' "

Scott observes that Christ suffered thirst, in order that we might drink the water of life for ever, and thirst no more.

Quesnel remarks, " The tongue of Jesus Christ underwent its own particular torment, in order to atone for the ill-use which men make of their tongues by blasphemy, evil-speaking, vanity, lying, gluttony, and drunkenness."

The theory that Christ only said " I thirst," in order to fulfil Scripture, is to my mind unsatisfactory and unreasonable. His saying " I thirst," was a fulfilment of Scripture, but He did not merely say it in order to fulfil Scripture. St. John, according to his style of writing, only meant that by His saying " I thirst," and having His thirst relieved by vinegar, the words of Psalm lxix. 21, were fulfilled.

The Greek word which is rendered " accomplished," is the same that is rendered " finished " in the thirtieth verse. This difference, within two verses, in translating the same word, is one of those blemishes in our authorized version which must be regretted.

The connection of the sentence, " that the Scripture might be fulfilled," is not very clear to my mind. Is it to be taken with the words that follow in the verse, or with those that immediately precede it ?—The common view taken, undoubtedly, is to connect the sentence with " I thirst." The sense will then be " Jesus saith, I thirst, so that by this the Scripture was fulfilled." But is it necessary to make this connection ? Might not the sentence be connected with the one which precedes ? The sense will then be, " Jesus knowing that all things were now accomplished, so that the Scripture was fulfilled concerning Himself, said, I thirst." In three other places in St. John where the sentence occurs, " that the Scripture might be fulfilled," the connection is with what goes before, and not with what follows., (John xvii. 12 ; xix. 24—36.) Semler and Tholuck incline to take this view. But I admit that the matter is doubtful, and it certainly is not one of vital importance. One thing only we must remember. Our Lord did not say, " I thirst," for no other purpose than to fulfil the Scriptures. He spoke with far deeper and stronger reasons, and yet by His speaking and afterwards drinking vinegar, a passage in the prophetical Psalms was fulfilled.

29 —[*Now there was set...vessel...vinegar.*] This would be more literally rendered " there was lying " a vessel. In all probability this was a vessel full of the sour wine in common use among the Roman soldiers.

[*And they filled a sponge, etc.*] The persons here spoken of seem to be the Roman soldiers who carried out the details of the crucifixion. The vinegar was theirs, and it is not likely that any one would have dared to interfere with the criminal hanging on the cross, except the soldiers. The act recorded here must be carefully distinguished from that recorded in Matt. xxvii. 34, and is the same as that recorded in Matt. xxvii. 48. The first drink of vinegar and gall, commonly given to criminals to deaden their pains, our Lord refused. The second, here mentioned, was given, I believe, notwithstanding what some writers say, in kindness and compassion, and our Lord did not refuse to accept it. A sponge filled with vinegar and put on the end of a stick, was far the easiest and most convenient way of giving drink to one whose head was at least seven or eight feet from the ground, and whose hands, being nailed to the cross, were of course unable to take any cup, and put it to his mouth. From a sponge full of liquid, pressed against the lips, a crucified person might suck some moisture, and receive some benefit.

What this " hyssop " here mentioned was, is a point by no means clearly ascertained. Casaubon speaks of the question as a proverbial difficulty. Some think that it was a branch of the plant hyssop fastened to the end of a reed. This seems very improbable, because of the "sponge." Dr. Forbes Royle maintains that it was the caper plant, which bears a stick about three or four feet long. Hengstenberg gives evidence from Talmudic writers that the hyssop was among the branches used at the feast of tabernacles, and that its stalk was an ell long. Like many other questions of Bible natural history, the point must probably be left obscure. Some see deep meaning in the mention of hyssop, as the plant used in the ceremonial sprinklings of the law of Moses. (See Heb. ix. 19.) Hyssop, moreover, was used at the passover in sprinkling the door posts with blood. (Exod. xii. 22.) Yet the allusion, to say the least, seems doubtful, nor is it quite clear how any typical meaning can be got out of the mention of the plant in this place.

It is very noteworthy that even in the roughest, hardest kind of men, like these heathen soldiers, there is sometimes a tender and compassionate spot in the breast. According to Matthew's account the cry, "I thirst," must have followed soon after the cry, "My God, my God, why hast Thou forsaken Me." This exhibition of great mental and bodily agony combined, in my opinion, touched the feelings of the soldiers, and one of them at least ran to give our Lord vinegar. We should remember this in dealing with men. Even the worst have often a soft place, if we can find it out, in their inward nature.

Cyril maintains strongly, I must admit, that the act of the soldiers in giving our Lord the sponge full of vinegar, was not an act of kindness, but of mockery and insult. I cannot however, agree with him. He does not appear to distinguish between the first drink which our Lord refused at the beginning of His crucifixion, and the last which He accepted ; but speaks of them as one and the same. Theophylact agrees with Cyril.

30 —[*When Jesus therefore...finished.*] Our Lord having now given plain proof that He had endured intense bodily suffering, and that like any other human sufferer He could appreciate a slight relief of thirst, such as the vinegar afforded, proceeded to utter one of His last and most solemn sayings : "It is finished."

This remarkable expression, in the Greek, is one single word in a perfect tense, "It has been completed." It stands here in majestic simplicity, without note or comment from St. John, and we are left entirely to conjecture what the full meaning of it is. For eighteen hundred years Christians have explained it as they best can, and some portion of its meaning in all likelihood has been discovered. Yet it is far from unlikely that such a word spoken on such an occasion, by such a person, at such a moment, just before death, contains depths which no one has ever completely fathomed. Some meanings there are, which no one perhaps will dispute, belonging to this grand expression, which I will briefly mention. No one single meaning, we may be sure, exhausts the whole phrase. It is rich, full, and replete with deep truths.

(*a*) Our Lord meant that His great work of redemption was

finished. He had, as Daniel foretold, " finished transgression, made an end of sin, made reconciliation for iniquity, and brought in everlasting righteousness." (Dan. ix. 24.) After thirty-three years, since the day when He was born in Bethlehem, He had done all, paid all, performed all, suffered all that was needful to save sinners, and satisfy the justice of God. He had fought the battle and won it, and in two days would give proof of it by rising again.

(b) Our Lord meant that God's determinate counsel and fore-will concerning His death was now accomplished and finished. All that had been appointed from all eternity that He should suffer, He had now suffered.

(c) Our Lord meant that He had finished the work of keeping God's holy law. He had kept it to the uttermost, as our head and representative, and Satan had found nothing in Him. 'He had magnified the law and made it honorable, by doing perfectly all its requirements. " Woe unto us," says Burkitt, " if Christ had left but one farthing of our debt unpaid. We must have lain in hell insolvent to all eternity."

(d) Our Lord meant that He had finished the types and figures of the ceremonial law. He had at length offered up the perfect sacrifice, of which every Mosaic sacrifice was a type and symbol and there remained no more need of offerings for sin. The old covenant was finished.

(e) Our Lord meant that He had finished and fulfilled the prophecies of the Old Testament. At length, as the Seed of the woman, he had bruised the serpent's head, and accomplished the work which Messiah was engaged by covenant to come and perform.

(f) Finally, our Lord meant that His sufferings were finished. Like His Apostle, He had " finished His course." His long life of pain and contradiction from sinners, and above all His intense sufferings, as bearer of our sins on Gethsemane and Calvary, were at last at an end. The storm was over, and the worst was passed. The cup of suffering was at last drained to the very dregs.

Thoughts such as these come to my own mind, when I read the solemn phrase, " It is finished." But I am far from saying that the phrase does not contain a great deal more. In interpreting such a saying, I am deeply conscious that there is an inexhaustible fulness in our Lord's words. I am sure we are more likely to make too little of them than to make too much.

Luther remarks, " In this word, ' It is finished,' will I comfort myself. I am forced to confess that all *my* finishing of the will of God is imperfect, piecemeal work, while yet the law urges on me that not so much as one tittle of it must remain unaccomplished. Christ is the end of the law. What it requires, Christ has performed."

To the objection of some persons, that all things were not completely finished and accomplished, until Jesus rose again and ascended into heaven, Calvin replies that Jesus knew that all things were now *practically* accomplished, and that nothing now remained to hinder His finishing the work He came to do.

[*And He bowed His head.*] This is the action of one dying. When the will ceases to exercise power over muscles and nerves, at once those parts of the body which are not rigid like the bones, collapse and fall in any direction to which their centre of gravity inclines them. The head of a crucified person would naturally in death droop forward on the breast, the neck being no longer kept stiff by the will. This is what seems to have happened in the case of our Lord.

May we not gather from this expression, that our Lord up to this moment held up His head erect, firm, steady, and unmoved, even under extreme pain ?

Alford remarks how this little incident was evidently recorded by an eye-witness. The miraculous darkness must have now passed away, in order to let this movement of the head be seen.

[*And gave up the ghost.*] These words mean, literally, " delivered up the spirit." It is an expression never used of any dying person in the Bible except our Lord. It is an expression denoting voluntary action. He delivered up His spirit of His own free will, because the hour was come when He chose to do it. He had just said, after using the phrase, " It is finished," — " Father into Thy hands I commend my spirit,"—and then He proceeded to deliver up His spirit into the hands of God the Father. It is the Father, and none else, to whom the words, " He delivered up," must apply.

Augustine observes, " Not against His will did the Saviour's spirit leave His flesh, but because He would, and when He would, and how He would. Who is there that can even go to sleep when He will, as Jesus died when He would ? Who thus puts off his clothes when he will, as Jesus unclothed Himself of His flesh when He would ? Who goes thus out of his door when he will, as Jesus, when He would, went out of this world ? "

In death, as well as in life, our Lord has left us an example. Of course we cannot, like Him, choose the moment of our death, and in this, as in everything else, we must be content to follow Him at an enormous distance. The best of saints is a miserable copy of his Master. Nevertheless, we too, as Cyril observes, must endeavor to put our souls into God's hands, if God is really our Father, when the last hour of our lives comes ; and like Jesus, to place them by faith in our Father's keeping, and trust our Father to take care of them.

Above all, let us never forget, as we read of Christ's death, that He died for our sins, as our Substitute. His death is our life. He died that we might live. We who believe on Christ shall live forevermore, sinners as we are, because Christ died for us, the innocent for the guilty. Satan cannot drag us away to everlasting death in hell. The second death cannot harm us. We may safely say,—" Who can condemn me, or slay my soul ? I know well that I deserve death, and that I ought to die, because of my sins. But then my blessed Head and Substitute died for me, and when He died, I, His poor weak member, was reckoned to die also. Get thee behind me, Satan, for Christ was crucified and died. My debt is paid, and thou canst not demand it twice over."—Forever let us bless God that Christ " gave up the ghost," and really died upon the cross, before myriads of witnesses. That " giving up the ghost " was the hinge on which all our salvation turned. In vain Christ's life and miracles and preaching, if Christ had not at last died for us ! We needed not merely a teacher, but an atonement, and the death of a Substitute. The mightiest transaction that ever took place on earth since the fall of man, was accomplished when Jesus " gave up the ghost." The careless crowd around the cross saw nothing but the common death of a common criminal. But in the eyes of God the Father the promised payment for a world's sin was at last effected, and the kingdom of heaven was thrown wide open to all believers. The finest pictures of the crucifixion that artists have ever painted, give a miserably insufficient idea of what took place when Jesus " gave up the ghost." They can show a suffering man on a cross, but they cannot convey the least notion of what was really going on,—the satisfaction of God's broken law, the payment of sinners' debt to God, and the complete atonement for a world's sin.

The precise physical cause of the death of Christ is a very interesting subject, which must be reverently approached, but deserves attention. Dr. Stroud, in his book on the subject, takes a view which is supported by the opinions of three eminent Edinburgh physicians, the late Sir James Simpson, Dr. Begbie, and Dr. Struthers. This view is that the immediate cause of our Lord's decease was rupture of the heart. Dr. Simpson argues that all the circumstances of our Lord's death, —His crying with a loud voice just before death, not like an exhausted person, and His sudden giving up the ghost,—confirm this view very strongly. He also says that " strong mental emotions produce sometimes laceration or rupture of the walls of the heart ; " and he adds, " If ever a human heart was riven and ruptured by the mere amount of mental agony endured, it would surely be that of our Redeemer." Above all, he argues that the rupture of the heart would go far to account for the flow of blood and water from our Lord's side, when pierced with a spear. Dr. Simpson's very interesting letter on the subject, will be found in the appendix to "Hanna's Last Days of our Lord's Passion."

Concerning the deep question as to what became of our Lord's soul when He gave up the ghost, it must suffice to believe that His soul went to paradise, the place of the departed spirits of believers. He said to the penitent thief, "To-day shalt thou be *with Me* in Paradise." (Luke xxiii. 43.) This is the true meaning of the article, "descended into hell," in the Belief. "Hell" in that clause certainly does not mean the place of punishment, but the separate state or place of departed spirits.

Some theologians hold that, between His death and resurrection "He went and preached to the spirits in prison" (1 Peter iii. 19); and proclaimed the accomplishment of His work of atonement. This, to say the least, is doubtful. But Athanasius, Ambrose, Zwingle, Calvin, Erasmus, Calovius, and Alford hold this view.

Concerning the miraculous signs which accompanied our Lord's death,—the darkness from twelve o'clock to three, the earthquake, the rending of the temple veil,—St. John is silent, and doubtless for some wise reason. But we may well believe that they struck myriads with awe and astonishment, and perhaps smoothed the way for our Lord's burial in Joseph's tomb, without opposition or objection.

31 —[*The Jews therefore, because it was, etc.*] The "Jews" in this verse, as in many other places in St. John's Gospel, can only mean the chief priests and leaders of the nation at Jerusalem ; the same men who had pressed on Pilate our Lord's crucifixion,—Annas, Caiaphas, and their companions.

The "preparation" means the day preceding the passover sabbath. That sabbath being pre-eminently a "high day," or, to render the Greek literally, a "great" day in the year, the Friday, or day preceding it, was devoted to special preparations. Hence the day went by the name of "the preparation of the sabbath." The expression makes it certain that Jesus was crucified on a Friday. The Jews saw clearly that, unless they took active measures to prevent it, the body of our Lord would remain all night hanging on the tree of the cross, the law would be broken (Deut. xxi. 23), and a dead body would hang throughout the sabbath in full view of the temple, and close by the city walls. Therefore they made haste to have Him taken down from the cross and buried.

The "breaking of the legs" of crucified criminals, in order to despatch them, seems to have been a common accompaniment of this barbarous mode of execution, when it was necessary to make an end of them, and get them out of the way. In asking Pilate to allow this breaking of the legs, they did nothing but what was usual. But for anything we can see, the thing would not have been done if the Jews had not asked.—The verse supplies a wonderful example of the way in which God can make the wickedest men unconsciously carry out His purposes, and promote His glory. If the Jews had not interfered this Friday afternoon, for anything we can see, Pilate would have allowed our Lord's body to hang upon the cross till Sunday or Monday, and perhaps to see corruption. The Jews procured our Lord's burial the very day that He died, and thus secured the fulfilment of His famous prophecy: " Destroy this temple of my body, and in three days I will raise it up." (John ii. 19.) If He had not been buried till Sunday or Monday, He could not have risen again the third day after His death. As it was, the Jews managed things so that our Lord was laid in the grave before the evening of Friday, and was thus enabled to fulfil the famous type of Jonah, and give the sign He had promised to give of His Messiahship, by lying three days in the earth, and then rising again the third day after He died. All this could not have happened if the Jews had not interfered, and got Him taken from the cross and buried on Friday afternoon!—How true it is that the wickedest enemies of God are only axes and saws and hammers in His hands, and are ignorantly His instruments for doing His work in the world. The restless, busy, meddling of Caiaphas and his companions, was actually one of the causes that Christ rose the third day after death, and His Messiahship was proved. Pilate was their tool: but they were God's tools! The Romans, in all probability, would have left our Lord's body hanging on the cross till sun and rain had putrefied and consumed it, had such a thing been possible. Bishop Pearson says it was a common rule of Roman law not to permit sepulture to the body of a crucified person. The burial, therefore, was entirely owing to the request of the Jews. The providence of God ordered things so that they who interceded for His crucifixion interceded for His burial. And by so doing they actually paved the way for the crowning miracle of His resurrection !

Let us mark the miserable scrupulosity that is sometimes compatible with the utmost deadness of conscience. Thus we see men making ado about a dead body remaining on the cross on the Sabbath, at the very time when they had just murdered an innocent living person with the most flagrant injustice and monstrous cruelty. It is a specimen of " straining out a gnat, and swallowing a camel."

32 —[*Then came the soldiers, etc.*] Pilate having given his consent to the request of the Jews, the Roman soldiers proceeded to break the legs of the criminals, and began with the two thieves. Why they began with them is by no means clear. If the three crosses were all in a row, it is hard to see why the two outer criminals of the three should have their legs broken first, and the one in the centre be left to the last. We must suppose one of three things in order to explain this.

(*a*) Possibly two of the soldiers broke the legs of one male-factor, and the other two the legs of the other. Reason and common sense point out that it does not require four men to do this horrid work on a helpless, unresisting, crucified person. Thus, having finished their work at the two outward crosses, they would come last to the centre one.

(*b*) Possibly the two outward crosses may have been rather forwarder in position than the central one, so that the sufferers might see each others' faces. In that case the soldiers would naturally begin with the crosses they came to first. This, per-haps, would account for the penitent thief having read the word "King" over our Lord's head on the cross.

(*c*) Possibly the soldiers saw that our Lord was dead, even before they came up to Him. At any rate they probably saw that He was still and motionless, and thus suspecting that He was dead, they did not trouble themselves with His body, but began with the two who evidently were yet alive.

It is noteworthy that the penitent thief, even after his con-version, had more suffering to go through before he entered paradise. The grace of God and the pardon of sin did not de-liver him from the agony of having his legs broken. When Christ undertakes to save our souls, He does not undertake to deliver us from bodily pains and a conflict with the last enemy. Penitents, as well as impenitents, must taste death and all its accompaniments. Conversion is not heaven, though it leads to it.

Scott remarks that those who broke the legs of the penitent thief, and hastened his end, were unconscious instruments of fulfilling our Lord's promise, "*To-day*-shalt thou be with me in Paradise."

How the legs of crucified criminals were broken we do not know; but it was probably done in the roughest manner. With such tools at hand as the hammers used for driving in the nails, and the mattocks and spades used for putting the cross in the ground, the soldiers could hardly want instru-ments. It must be remembered that a simple fracture would not cause death. The Greek word which we render "break," means, literally, "shiver to pieces." May it not be feared that this is the true meaning here?

33 —[*But when they came to Jesus, etc.*] This verse contains the first proof of the mighty fact that our Lord really died. We are told that the soldiers did not break His legs, because they "saw that He was dead already." Accustomed as Roman sol-diers necessarily were to see death in every form, wounds of every kind, and dead bodies of every description, and trained to take away human life by their profession, they were of all men least likely to make a mistake about such a matter. Thus we have it most expressly recorded, that the soldiers "saw

that He was dead already," and therefore did not break His legs. Our salvation hinges so entirely on Jesus Christ's vicarious death, that a moment's reflection will show us the divine wisdom of the fact being thoroughly proved. His unbelieving enemies could never say that He did not really die, and that He was only in a swoon, or fainting-fit, or state of insensibility. The Roman soldiers are witnesses that on the centre cross of the tree they saw a dead man.

34 —[*But one...spear...pierced His side.*] Here we have the second proof that our Lord did really die. One of the soldiers, determined to make sure work and leave nothing uncertain, thrust his spear into our Lord's side, in all *probability* directing his thrust at the heart, as the seat of vitality. That thrust made it certain, if there had been any doubt before, that the body on the central cross was actually dead. They believed it from appearance, and perhaps from touch, when they first came up to the cross. They made it quite certain by the thrust of the spear. The body of a person in a swoon would have given some sign of life, when pierced with a spear.

The gross inaccuracy of those pictures which represent this soldier as a horseman, is worth noticing. Our Lord's body was easily within reach of the thrust of a spear in the hand of a foot soldier. There is no evidence whatever that any Roman cavalry were near the cross !

The theory of Bishop Pearson, that this soldier pierced our Lord's side in anger and impatience, as if provoked to find Him dead, does not appear to me well-founded. It is not likely that the soldiers would be angry at finding a state of things which saved them trouble. To me it seems far more likely that the thrust was the hasty, careless act of a rough soldier, accustomed to prove in this way whether a body was alive or dead. I have heard it said by an eye-witness, that some of the Cossacks who followed our retreating cavalry, after the famous Balaclava charge, in the Crimean war, were seen to prick the bodies of fallen soldiers with their spears, in order to see whether they were dead or alive.

Theophylact suggests that this soldier thrust the spear into our Lord's side in order to gratify the wicked Jews who stood by.

Besser remarks most sensibly, " Even the soldier's spear was guided by the Father's hand."

[*And forthwith...blood and water.*] The remarkable fact here recorded has given rise to considerable difference of opinion.

(*a*) Some, as Grotius, Calvin, Beza, and others, hold that this issue of blood and water was a proof that the heart or pericardium was pierced, and death in consequence quite certain. They say that the same result would follow from a thrust into the side of any person lately dead, and that blood and water, or

something closely resembling it, would immediately flow out.
They maintain, therefore, that there was nothing supernatural
in the circumstance recorded.

(b) Others, as most of the Fathers, Brentius, Musculus, Calovius, Lampe, Lightfoot, Rollock, Jansenius, Bengel, Horsley,
and Hengstenberg, hold that this issue of blood and water was
supernatural, extraordinary, unusual, and contrary to all experience ; and they maintain that it was a special miracle.

The question is one of those which will probably never be
settled. We are not in possession of sufficiently precise information to justify a very positive opinion. We do not know for
a certainty that the left side of our Lord was pierced and not
the right. We do not know exactly how much blood and water flowed out, whether a large quantity or a very little. That
a miracle might take place at such a death, on such an occasion, and in the body of such a Person, we have no right to deny. The mere facts that, when our Lord hung on the cross,
the sun was darkened, and, when He gave up the ghost, the
veil of the temple was rent in twain, and the rocks rent, and
the earth quaked, might well prepare our minds to see nothing
extraordinary in a miracle taking place, and almost to expect
it. Perhaps the safest line to adopt is to combine both views.
The thrust of the spear into the side caused blood to flow, and
proved that the seat of vitality in the body was pierced. The
extraordinary and unusual flow of blood and water was a supernatural event, and meant to teach spiritual lessons.

I may be allowed to say that three eminent medical men in
large practice, whom I have ventured to consult on this verse,
are all of one mind,—that any large flow of blood and water
from a dead body is contrary to all ordinary experience. Each
of them, singularly enough, has expressed this opinion independently, and without any communication with the other
two.

Concerning the symbolical meaning of this flow of " blood
and water " from our Lord's side much has been written in
every age of the Church. That it had a deep spiritual sense
appears almost certain from St. John's words in his first Epistle. (1 John v. 6—8.) But what the real symbolical meaning
was, is a very disputable question.

(a) The common opinion is, that the blood and water symbolized the two sacraments of baptism and the Lord's Supper, both
given by Christ and emanating from Him, and both symbols of
atonement, cleansing, and forgiveness. This is the view of
Chrysostom, Augustine, Andrews, and a large body of divines,
both ancient and modern. I cannot myself receive this opinion.
In matters like this I dare not call any man master, or endorse
an interpretation of Scripture, when I do not feel convinced that
it is true. I cannot see the necessity of dragging in the sacra-

ments at every point in the exposition of God's Word, as some
do.

(b) My own opinion is most decided, that the flow of blood
and water, whether supernatural or not, was meant to be a symbolical fulfilment of the famous prophecy in Zechariah : " In
that day there shall be a fountain opened to the house of David
and to the inhabitants of Jerusalem for sin and for uncleanness." (Zech. xiii. 1.) It was a practical declaration, by fact
and deed, to all Jews, that by Christ's death that famous prophecy was fulfilled, and that now at last there was a fountain
opened by Christ's death.   The moment He was dead this fountain was opened and began to flow.   Over the bleeding side of
our Lord there might have been written, " Behold the fountain
for all sin."   It is no small evidence to my mind, in favor of
this view, that this famous prophecy occurs only five verses
after the text immediately quoted by St. John in this very chapter, " they shall look on Him whom they pierced." (Zech.
xii. 10.)

Augustine sees a type of this wound in our Lord's side, from
which flowed blood and water, in the door in the side of Noah's
ark, by which the living creatures entered in and were preserved from drowning!   He also sees another type of the
transaction in the first Adam sleeping and Eve being formed
out of his side.

The opinion held by some, that this " blood and water " warrant the mixture of water and wine in the Lord's Supper,
seems to me utterly untenable.   As Musculus sensibly observes,
it was not " wine and water," but " blood and water " that
flowed from our Lord's side.   There is not the slightest evidence that our Lord used water at the institution of the Lord's
Supper.

That " blood " was the symbol of atonement, and " water " of
cleansing, every careful reader of the Old Testament must
know.   The two things are brought together by St. Paul in
Heb. ix. 19.   The smiting of the rock by Moses, and water
flowing forth, was also typical of the event before us.   Lightfoot mentions a Jewish tradition that blood and water flowed
from the rock at first.

Henry says, " The blood and water signified the two great
benefits which all believers partake of through Christ,—justification and sanctification.   Blood stands for remission, water
for regeneration ; blood for atonement, water for purification.
The two must always go together.   Christ hath joined them
together, and we must not think to put them asunder.   They
both flowed from the pierced side of our Redeemer."

35 —[*And he that saw it bare record, etc.*]   This singular verse,
by common consent, can only refer to St. John.   It is as though
he said, " The fact that I now testify to I saw with my own

eyes ; and my testimony is true, and accurate, and trustworthy, and I know that I say true things in recording the fact, so that you to whom I write need not hesitate to believe me. I stood by. I saw it. I was an eye-witness, and I do not write by hear-say."

The Greek word rendered "true" in the second place in this verse, means literally, "true things."

The question arises naturally, To what does John refer in this peculiar verse ? (a) Does he refer only to the issue of blood and water from our Lord's side, as a singularly miraculous event ? (b) Or does he refer to the thrust of the spear into our Lord's side, as a convincing proof that our Lord really died ? (c) Or does he refer to the fact that our Lord's legs were not broken, and that he thus saw the great type of the passover-lamb fulfilled ?

I decidedly lean to the opinion that the verse refers to all the three things I have mentioned together, and not to any one of them only. All three things were so remarkable, and so calculated to strike the mind of a pious and intelligent Jew, and all happened in such close and rapid succession, that John emphatically records that he saw all the three with his own eyes. He seems to say, " I saw myself that not a bone of the Lamb of God was broken, so that He fulfilled the type of the passover. I saw myself a spear thrust into His heart, so that He was a true Sacrifice, and really died. And I saw myself that blood and water came out of His side, and I beheld a fulfilment of the old prophecy of a fountain for sin being opened." When we consider the immense importance and significance of all these three things, we do not wonder that John should have been inspired to write this verse, in which he emphatically tells his readers that he is writing down nothing but the plain naked truth, and that he actually saw these three things,—the unbroken legs, the pierced side, the flow of blood and water,— with his own eyes.

Pearce and Alford think that the expression "that ye might believe," signifies that ye might believe that Jesus did really die on the cross. Others decidedly prefer thinking that it means, "that ye may believe that blood and water did really flow from the side of Jesus after His death." Others take the phrase in a general sense, "that ye may believe more firmly than ever on Christ, as the true sacrifice for sin."

36, 37 —[*For these things were done, etc.*] In these two verses John explains distinctly to his readers why two of the facts he has just mentioned, however trifling they might seem to an ignorant person, were in reality of great importance. By one of these facts,—the not breaking a bone of our Lord's body,— the text was fulfilled which said that not a bone of the passover-lamb should be broken. (Ex. xii. 46.) By the other fact, —the piercing of our Lord's side,—the prophecy of Zechariah was fulfilled, that the inhabitants of Jerusalem " should look on him whom they pierced." (Zech. xii. 10.)

Alford observes that the expression, " they shall look," does not refer to the Roman soldiers, but to the repentant in the world, who at the time this Gospel was written had begun to fulfil this prophecy ; and that it also contains a prophetic reference to the future conversion of Israel, who were here the real piercers, though the act was done by the hands of others."

It is almost needless to say that the passage, like many others, does not mean that these things were done in order that Scripture might be fulfilled, but that by these things being done the Scripture was fulfilled, and God's perfect foreknowledge about the least details of Christ's death was proved. Nothing in the great sacrifice happened by chance, luck, or accident. All was arranged as appointed, from first to last, many centuries before, by the determinate counsel of God. Caiaphas, Pilate, the Roman soldiers, were all unconscious instruments in carrying into effect what God had long predicted and foretold to the least jot and tittle.

Let us carefully note here what strong evidence these verses supply in favor of a literal, and not a merely spiritual, fulfilment of Old Testament prophecies.

Rollock observes, " If God have ordained and said anything, it lies not in the hands of any man to disannul it. If God shall say, " There shall not be one bone of my anointed broken," great Cæsar and all the kings of the earth, the King of Spain, and the Pope, and all their adherents, shall not be able to do the contrary. So, in the midst of all fear and danger, let us depend on the providence of God.

JOHN XIX 38—42

38 And after this Joseph of Arimathæa, being a disciple of Jesus, but secretly for fear of the Jews, besought Pilate that he might take away the body of Jesus : and Pilate gave *him* leave. He came therefore, and took the body of Jesus.

39 And there came also Nicodemus, which at the first came to Jesus by night, and brought a mixture of myrrh and aloes, about an hundred pound *weight*.

40 Then took they the body of Jesus, and wound it in linen clothes with the spices, as the manner of the Jews is to bury.

41 Now in the place where he was crucified there was a garden : and in the garden a new sepulchre, wherein was never man yet laid.

42 There laid they Jesus therefore because of the Jews' preparation *day;* for the sepulchre was nigh at hand.

THERE is a peculiar interest attached to these five verses of Scripture. They introduce us to a stranger, of whom we never heard before. They bring in an old friend, whose name is known wherever the Bible is read. They describe the most important funeral that ever took place in this world. From each of these three points of interest we may learn a very profitable lesson.

We learn, for one thing, from these verses, that *there are some true Christians in the world of whom very little is known.* The case of Joseph of Arimathæa teaches this very plainly. Here is a man named among the friends of Christ, whose very name we never find elsewhere in the New Testament, and whose history, both before and after this crisis, is completely withheld from the Church. He comes forward to do honor to Christ, when the Apostles had forsaken Him and fled. He cares for Him and delights to do Him service, even when dead, —not because of any miracle which he saw Him do, but out of free and gratuitous love. He does not hesitate to confess himself one of Christ's friends, at a time when Jews and Romans alike had condemned Him as a malefactor, and put Him to death. Surely the man who could do such things must have had strong faith ! Can we wonder that, wherever the Gospel is preached, throughout the whole world, this pious action of Joseph is told of as a memorial of him ?

Let us hope and believe that there are many Christians in every age, who, like Joseph, are the Lord's hidden servants, unknown to the Church and the world, but well known to God. Even in Elijah's time there were seven thousand in Israel who had never bowed the knee to Baal, although the desponding prophet knew nothing of it. Perhaps, at this very day, there are saints in the back streets of some of our great towns, or in the lanes of some of our country parishes, who make no noise in the world, and yet love Christ and are loved by Him. Ill-health, or poverty, or the daily cares of some laborious calling, render it impossible for them to come forward in public; and so they live and die comparatively unknown. Yet the last day may show an astonished world that some of these very people, like Joseph, honored Christ as much as any on earth, and that their names were written in heaven. After all, it is special circumstances that bring to the surface special Christians. It is not those who make the greatest show in the Church, who are always found the fastest friends of Christ.

We learn, for another thing, from these verses, that *there are some servants of Christ whose latter end is better than their beginning.* The case of Nicodemus teaches that lesson very plainly. The only man who dared to help Joseph in his holy work of burying our Lord, was one who at first " came to Jesus by night," and was nothing better than an ignorant inquirer after truth. At a later period in our Lord's ministry we find this same Nicodemus coming forward with somewhat more boldness, and raising in the Council of the Pharisees the question, " Doth our law judge any man, before it hear him, and know what he doeth ? " (John vii. 51.) Finally, we see him in the passage before us, ministering to our Lord's dead body, and not ashamed to take an active part in giving to the despised Nazarene an honorable burial. How great the contrast between the man who timidly crept into the Lord's lodging to ask a question, and the man who brought a hundred pounds weight of myrrh and aloes to anoint His dead body ! Yet it was the same Nicodemus. How great may be a man's growth in grace, and faith, and knowledge, and courage, in the short space of three years.

We shall do well to store up these things in our minds, and to remember the case of Nicodemus, in forming our estimate of other people's religion. We must not condemn others as graceless and godless, because they do not see the whole truth at once, and only reach decided Christianity by slow degrees. The Holy Ghost always leads believers to the same foundation truths, and into the same highway to heaven. In these there is invariable uniformity. But the Holy Ghost does not always lead believers through the same experience, or at the same rate of speed. In this there is much diversity in His operations. He that says conversion is a needless thing, and that an unconverted man may be saved, is undoubtedly under a strange delusion. But he that says that no one is converted except he becomes a full-blown and established Christian in a single day, is no less under a delusion. Let us not judge others rashly and hastily. Let us believe that a man's beginnings in religion may be very small, and yet his latter end may greatly increase. Has a man real grace? Has he within him the genuine work of the Spirit? This is the grand question. If he has, we may safely hope that his grace will grow, and we should deal with him gently, and bear with him charitably, though at present he may be a mere babe in spiritual attainments. The life in a helpless infant is as real and true a thing as the life in a full-grown man: the difference is only one of degree. "Who hath despised the day of small things?" (Zech. iv. 10.) The very Christian who begins his religion with a timid night-visit, and an ignorant inquiry, may stand forward alone one day, and confess Christ boldly in the full light of the sun.

We learn, lastly, from these verses, that *the burial of the dead is an act which God sanctions and approves.* We need not doubt that this is part of the lesson which the passage before us was meant to convey to our minds. Of course, it supplies unanswerable evidence that our Lord really died, and afterwards really rose again; but it also teaches that, when the body of a Christian is dead, there is a fitness and meetness in burying it with decent honor. It is not for nothing that the burials of Abraham, and Isaac, and Jacob, and Joseph, and Moses are carefully recorded in holy writ. It is not for nothing that we are told that John the Baptist was laid in a tomb ; and that "devout men carried Stephen to his burial, and made great lamentation over him." (Acts viii. 2.) It is not for nothing that we are told so particularly about the burial of Christ.

The true Christian need never be ashamed of regarding a funeral with peculiar reverence and solemnity. It is the body, which may be the instrument of committing the greatest sins, or of bringing the greatest glory to God. It is the body, which the eternal Son of God honored by dwelling in it for thirty and three years, and finally dying in our stead. It is the body, with which He rose again and ascended up into heaven. It is the body, in which He sits at the right hand of God, and represents us before the Father, as our Advocate and Priest. It is the body, which is now the temple of the Holy Ghost, while the believer lives. It is the body, which will rise again, when the last trumpet sounds, and, re-united to the soul, will live in heaven to all eternity. Surely, in the face of such facts as these, we never need suppose that reverence bestowed on the burial of the body is reverence thrown away.

Let us leave the subject with one word of caution. Let us take care that we do not regard a sumptuous funeral as an atonement for a life wasted in carelessness and sin. We may bury a man in the most expensive style, and spend hundreds of pounds in mourning. We may place over his grave a costly marble stone, and inscribe on it a flattering epitaph. But all this will not save our souls or his. The turning point at the last day will not be how we are buried, but whether we were "buried with Christ," and repented and believed. (Rom. vi. 4.) Better a thousand times to die the death of the righteous, have a lowly grave and a pauper's funeral, than to die graceless, and lie under a marble tomb!

NOTES JOHN XIX 38—42

38 —[*And after this Joseph of Arimathæa.*] This verse begins St. John's account of our Lord's burial. The manner of that burial was one of the things predicted by Isaiah (ch. liii. 9), in a verse which is not correctly translated. It should be, "His grave was appointed with the wicked : but with the rich man was His tomb." The details of His burial are carefully recorded by all the four Evangelists. Each of them names Joseph as the prime agent in the transaction, and, singularly enough, each mentions something that the other three Gospel-writers do not mention. St. Matthew alone says that he was "a rich man." (Matt. xxvii. 51.) St. Mark alone says that he was "an honorable counsellor, which also waited for the kingdom of God." (Mark xv. 43.) St. Luke alone says that he was "a good man and a just," who had "not consented to the counsel and deed of them, . . . who himself waited for the kingdom of God." (Luke xxiii. 50, 51.) St. John alone says here, that he was "a disciple of Jesus, but secretly, for fear of the Jews." It is another singular fact about Joseph, that we never hear a word about him in Scripture, except on this occasion of our Lord's burial. Both before and after this interesting event, the Bible, for some wise reason, is entirely silent about him. Nor can we explain how an inhabitant of Arimathæa happened to have a new tomb at Jerusalem. We must either suppose that, as a rich man, he had two residences, or else that, though born at Arimathæa, he had lately removed to Jerusalem. The utmost we know is that the article in the Greek before "Joseph," and before "of Arimathæa," seems to indicate that he was a person well known by history to the readers of St. John's Gospel.

About the place whence Joseph came, "Arimathæa," nothing certain is known. Some think that it is Ramah, where Samuel dwelt. (1 Sam. vii. 17.) The Septuagint Greek translator certainly calls Ramah "Armathaim," which looks like it. St. Luke calls it a "city of Judæa." Nothing certain seems to be known about it.

[*Being a disciple...secretly...Jews.*] The Greek word rendered "secretly," is literally "a concealed" disciple,—a past participle. The expression teaches the interesting fact that there were Jews who secretly believed that Jesus was the Messiah, and yet had not courage to confess Him before His crucifixion. We are distinctly told in John xii. 42, that "many of the chief rulers believed, but did not confess Christ, because of the Pharisees." But the character given of them, that "they loved the praise of men more than the praise of God," is so condemnatory, that we may well doubt whether Joseph was one of these. Want of physical or moral courage was probably the flaw in his character. It is only fair to remember that, as "a rich man and a counsellor," he had far more to sacrifice, and far more opposition to encounter, than poor fishermen or publicans would have. His backwardness to confess Christ cannot of course be defended. But his case teaches us that there is sometimes more spiritual work going on in men's minds than appears. We must not set down every one as utterly graceless and godless, who is not bold and outspoken at present. We must charitably hope that there are some secret disciples, who at present hold their tongues and say nothing, and yet, like Joseph, will one day come forward, and be courageous witnesses for Christ. All is not gold that glitters, and all is not dross that now looks dirty and makes no show. We must be charitable and hope on.—His case should also teach us the great power of that mischievous principle, the fear of man. Open sin kills its thousands, but the fear of man its tens of thousands. Let us watch and pray against it. Faith is the grand secret of victory over it. Like Moses, we must ever live as those who "see Him that is invisible." (Heb. xi. 27.) And to faith must be added the expulsive power of a new principle,—the fear of God. "I fear God," said holy Col. Gardiner, "and there is none else that I need fear."

[*Besought Pilate...take...body...Jesus.*] The conduct of Joseph deserves our praise and admiration, and his name will be held in honor by the Church of Christ, in consequence of it, as long as the world stands. Whatever Joseph was at first, he shone brightly at last. "The last are first" sometimes. Let us see what he did.

(*a*) Joseph honored Christ, when our Lord's own apostles had forsaken Him. He showed more faith and courage than His nearest and dearest friends.

(*b*) Joseph honored Christ, when it was a dangerous thing to do Him honor. To come forward and avow respect for one condemned as a malefactor, for one cast out by the High Priests and leaders of the Jews,—to say practically, "I am Christ's friend," was bold indeed. St. Mark particularly says, "He went in boldly unto Pilate" (Mark xv. 43), showing plainly that it was an act of uncommon courage.

(*c*) Joseph honored Christ, when He was a lifeless corpse, and to all appearance could do nothing for Him. It was not when Jesus was doing miracles and preaching wonderful sermons, but when there remained nothing of Him but a dead body, that he came forward and asked leave to bury Him.

Why Joseph's " fear " departed, and he acted with such marvellous boldness now, is a question which we have no means of settling. But reason points out that in all probability he had been an eye-witness of much that had happened this eventful day. He had possibly stood within a short distance of the cross, and seen all that took place, and heard every one of our Lord's seven sayings. The miraculous darkness for three hours, and the earthquake, must have arrested his attention. Surely it is not presumptuous to conjecture, that all this must have had a mighty effect on Joseph's soul, and made him resolve at once to cast fear away, and avow himself openly one of Christ's friends. It is almost certain that he must have been near the cross at three o'clock, when our Lord gave up the ghost, or else how could he have known of His death, and had time to think of burying Him ?

After all it is a deep truth, that circumstances bring out character in an extraordinary way. Just as the developing liquid brings out of the dull grey glass in the photographer's hands, a latent image which you never suspected before, so do circumstances bring out in some men a decision and power of character, which before you would have thought impossible.

Rollock remarks, " When Christ was working wonders, and speaking as never man spake, all this moved not Joseph to come forth and show himself. But now, Christ being dead and in shame, he comes out. Whereunto do I ascribe this ? I ascribe it to the force that comes from the death of Christ. There was never a living man in the world that had such power as that dead body had. More mighty was His death than His life."

[*And Pilate gave him leave.*] The entire absence of difficulties in Joseph's way is, at first sight, rather remarkable. We may easily believe that Pilate was willing enough to grant Joseph's request. He did not grant it till the centurion certified that Jesus was actually dead, and the ends of justice (so called) attained. Then at once he gave permission. It is fair to remember that he had regarded our Lord as guiltless all along, that if left to his own free will he would have released Him. It is probable, moreover, that he was vexed and annoyed at the obstinate pertinacity with which the Jews pressed for our Lord's death against his wish, and that he would be glad enough to pay them off, and spite them, by gratifying any friend of our Lord. But we must also remember that to the burial of our Lord's body the Jews themselves had no objection, and had even asked that the death of the criminals might be hastened and the dead bodies got out of the way. What they would have done with the body of our Lord, if Joseph had not come forward, we cannot certainly tell. Lightfoot says there was a common grave for the bodies of malefactors. In any case Joseph's request was not likely to meet with objection either from Gentile or Jew. But, for all that we must not forget that it made him a marked man, as a friend of Christ, and utterly ruined his character with Caiaphas and the high priests.

[*He came therefore...took...body...Jesus.*] The word rendered " took " here, is the same that is rendered " took away " just above.—Some think, as Tholuck and Ellicott, that the Roman soldiers took the body down from the cross. But I see no certain proof of this, and I think it unlikely they would take the trouble to do it, if others were willing to undertake the task. The meaning, in my opinion, is that Joseph came up to the cross, raised and lifted from it the lifeless corpse of our Lord and took it away for burial. Whether this was done by rearing a ladder against the cross, as Rubens' famous picture represents, and so letting down the body after drawing out the nails; or, whether by taking up the cross out of the hole in which it was fixed, laying it on the ground, and then taking out the nails, is a question which we have no means of deciding. To me it seems far more probable that the latter plan would be adopted than the former, and that as the cross was most likely reared up with the body on it, so it was taken down again with the body on it. But every reader must judge for himself.

In whatever way the body was taken down, or taken off the cross, everything seems to me to indicate that Joseph was the person who did it with his own hands. This is the more remarkable, when we consider that to touch a dead body made a Jew ceremonially unclean, and that this was the afternoon preceding the passover Sabbath. There seems, however, no reason why we should suppose that no one helped Joseph. He could hardly lift the cross, or reverently lift off the body of a full-grown person in the prime of life, without some aid. Why should we hesitate to believe that John and Nicodemus helped him ?

It is a curious coincidence, though perhaps only a coincidence, that it was a " Joseph," who probably first touched and received our Lord's body when He was born into the world at Bethlehem, and again a " Joseph," who was the last to hold, and lift, and handle the dead body of the same Lord, when He was buried.

39 —[*And there came also Nicodemus...night.*] The fact here recorded is quite peculiar to St. John's Gospel. For wise reasons, neither Matthew, Mark, nor Luke, ever mention the name of Nicodemus. John mentions him three times,—first as a secret inquirer (John iii. 1) ; secondly, as a timid advocate of justice towards our Lord in the Jewish Council (John vii. 10); and lastly, in this place. Both here and on the second occasion, he emphatically inserts the explanatory comment, that it was the same Nicodemus which " at first came to Jesus by night."

The verse before us seems to show that Nicodemus came forward as a volunteer, and helped to bury our Lord, and did not shrink to take part with Joseph in his good work. I can hardly think that he went with Joseph to Pilate. There is not a word to show this in any of the four Gospels.

Some think that by agreement Nicodemus went to fetch the hundred pounds' weight of spice (no slight burden to carry), while Joseph went to Pilate.

I should rather conjecture, that when Nicodemus saw Joseph coming boldly forward and showing anxiety to honor our Lord's body,—Joseph, whom doubtless as a Pharisee and counsellor, he knew well,—his own heart was stirred within him, his own timidity fell to the ground, and he came forward and offered to aid. In so doing he deserves praise and honor, though in a lower degree, like Joseph. He showed more reverence and love to our Lord when dead than he had ever done when alive. Once more we see that circumstances bring out character in very unexpected ways. The man that began seeking Jesus by night, at last confesses Jesus openly before the world, in the full light of day.

The case of Nicodemus is deeply instructive. It shows us how small and weak the beginning of true religion may be in the soul of man. It shows us that we must not despair of any one because he begins with a little timid, secret inquiry after Christ. It shows us that there are wide differences and varieties in the characters of believers. Some are brought into full light at once, and take up the cross without delay. Others attain light very slowly, and halt long between two opinions. It shows us that those who make the least display at first, sometimes shine brightest and come out best at last. Nicodemus confessed his love to Christ when Peter, James, and Andrew, had all run away. What need we have for patience and charity in forming an estimate of other people's religion! There are more successors of Nicodemus in the Church of Christ than we are aware of. We may see some marvellous changes in some persons, if we live with them a few years. The strongest, hardiest trees, are often the slowest in growth. He that sets down men and women as graceless and godless, if they do not profess full assurance of hope the first day they take up religion and hear the Gospel, forgets the case of Nicodemus, and exhibits his own ignorance of the ways of the Spirit. All God's elect are led to Christ, undoubtedly, but not all at the same speed, or through the same experience.

Calvin remarks on the conduct of Joseph and Nicodemus, "Here we have a striking proof that Christ's death was more quickening than His life. So great was the efficacy of that sweet savor which the death of Christ conveyed to the minds of these two men, that it quickly extinguished all the passions of the flesh."

Quesnel observes, "Wonderful is the power of Christ's death, which gives courage to confess Him in His deepest humiliation, to those who, when He was doing miracles, came to Him only in secret."

Henry observes that Joseph and Nicodemus showed weak faith, but strong love. " A firm faith in Christ's resurrection would have saved them this cost and expense." But they showed their deep love to our Lord's person and teaching.

[*And brought...myrrh...aloes...weight.*] The mixture here mentioned was probably in the shape of powder. The two ingredients were strongly aromatic and antiseptic. The large quantity brought shows the wealth and the liberal mind of Nicodemus. It also shows his wise forethought. A dead body so torn and lacerated as that of our blessed Lord, would need an unusually large quantity of antiseptics or preservatives, to check the tendency to corruption which such a climate would cause, even at Easter. Considering also that everything must have been done with some haste, the large quantity of spices used was probably meant to compensate for the want of time to do the work slowly and carefully.

40 —[*Then took...body...wound...clothes...spices.*] Here we are told the precise manner of the preparation of our Lord's body for burial. As always in that time and country, He was not put into a coffin. He was simply wrapped up in linen cloths, on which the preparation of myrrh and aloes had been laid. Thus the powder would be next to our Lord's body, and interpose between the linen and His skin. How the linen clothes were provided, we are told by St. Mark. Joseph " bought fine linen." (Mark xv. 46.) Joseph, being a rich man, had no difficulty in supplying funds for this purpose.

The word " wound " means literally " bound."

The sentence before us supplies one more strong evidence of the reality of Christ's death. Joseph and Nicodemus could not possibly be deceived. When they touched and handled the body, and wrapped it in linen clothes, they must have felt convinced that the heart had ceased to beat, and that life was extinct. There is no mistaking the feel of a dead body.

[*As the manner...Jews...bury.*] This is one of those occasional comments or explanatory remarks, which St. John sometimes makes in his Gospel, supplying strong internal evidence that he wrote for all the Church of Christ in every land, Gentiles as well as Jews, and that he thought it wise to explain Jewish customs. The reference appears to be to the wrapping of the body in linen, rather than to the use of the spices. Lazarus at Bethany came out of the grave wrapped around with cloths.

The wise foresight of the Spirit of God appears strongly in the details here given of our Lord's burial. The quantity of spices used was so great, that it anticipates the objection that our Lord's body might possibly "see corruption" in some degree before His resurrection. At the same time the special mention of Joseph being "a rich man," and Nicodemus "a ruler" helping him, completely stops the mouths of those who would have said that the followers of our Lord could never have found means to prevent the wounds of His body corrupting. By God's superintending providence, inclining rich men to come forward, the difficulty was obviated, and the means provided.

Besser says, "Twice was Jesus Christ rich in the days of His poverty. Once, immediately after His birth, when the wise men from the East offered Him gold and frankincense, and myrrh; and now, after His ignominious death, when a rich man buries him, and a distinguished man provides spices to anoint Him. Yea, a rich Joseph has taken the place of that poor Joseph who stood by the manger."

41 —[*Now in the place...crucified...garden.*] This verse tells us the place where our Lord was buried. It was in "a garden" close to the spot called Golgotha, where He was crucified. This fact alone seems to dispose of the theory, that the "place of a skull" meant a place where the skeletons and bones of executed criminals were lying about! Reason and common-sense point out, that, even if there were no argument against the theory from the Jewish customs about bones, it is very unlikely that "a garden" would have been near such a loathsome place. Golgotha could hardly be a place of execution, or a place where criminals were frequently crucified, if there was a garden near! The pictures that commonly represent the scene of the crucifixion as a bleak desolate-looking rocky hill, are manifestly quite incorrect. It was a place near to which, or where "there was a garden."

The curious coincidence that the fall of the first Adam, the agony, the cross, and the sepulchre of the second Adam, were all alike connected with a garden, can hardly fail to strike a reflecting mind.

[*And in the garden...new sepulchre...laid.*] Here we have the very receptacle described in which our Lord's sacred body was laid. Matthew, Mark, and Luke, all tell us it was "hewn out of a rock,"—the limestone rock, which is the rock of the place. John tells us that it was "new;" and, like St. Luke, adds that "never man was laid in" it before.

It is curious that Matthew alone tells us that this tomb was Joseph's own, "which he had hewn out of a rock." (Matt. xxvii. 60.) Theophylact remarks, that it is a striking proof of our Lord's poverty, that while He lived He had no house of His own, and when He died He was buried in another's tomb.

It is almost needless to say that both the conditions of the sepulchre above mentioned are of great importance, and deserve careful notice. (*a*) Our Lord's tomb was hewn out of a hard limestone rock. This made it clearly impossible for any one to say, that the disciples made a subterraneous entrance into the tomb by night and stole the body away. By the entrance that it was carried into the sepulchre, by the same it must be carried out.—(b) Our Lord's tomb was a new one, in which no one had ever been laid. This made it impossible for any one to say, after the resurrection, that there was no proof that Jesus rose from the dead, and that it might possibly be some one else. This could not be, when His body was the first and only body that was ever laid in this grave. Wonderful is it to see how at every turn the overruling wisdom of God has stopped, obviated, and frustrated, by wise provisions, the objections of infidels.

42 —[*Then laid they Jesus, etc.*] In order to see the full meaning of this verse, we should slightly invert the order of the words, and paraphrase them in some such way as this :—" In this new rock-hewn tomb, therefore, Joseph and Nicodemus laid the body of Jesus, because it was conveniently nigh at hand, and because the Jews' preparation day, or day preceding the passover sabbath, left them little time, and made it necessary to hasten their proceedings."—We may well believe that these two holy men had but little time, when we consider that our Lord did not give up the ghost till three o'clock, that the day ended at six, and that only three hours were left for Joseph to go to Pilate and get leave to remove the body from the cross, for Joseph and Nicodemus to take the nails out and lift the body from the tree, for wrapping the body in linen with a hundred pounds of myrrh and aloes, and for finally carrying it to the tomb and rolling a huge stone to the mouth of the tomb. When we remember, besides this, that the body of a full-grown man wrapped in linen with a hundred pounds of additional weight in myrrh and aloes, would be a most awkward and difficult burden for two men to carry, we may well believe that nothing but severe exertion could have enabled Joseph and Nicodemus to finish their labor of love before six o'clock. The wonder is that they managed to do it at all. It certainly could not have been done if they had not got a sepulchre nigh at hand. Again the Holy Ghost appears to me to foresee the objection that there was not time to bury our Lord, and mercifully supplies the words which answer it: "the sepulchre was nigh at hand." Even then we can hardly doubt that John and the women from Galilee must have lent some help. At all events it is distinctly recorded that the women were present, and that they were sitting by and beheld where the body was laid.

Thus ended the most wonderful funeral the sun ever shone upon. Such a death and such a burial,—so little understood by man and so important in the sight of God,—there never was, and never can be again. Who need doubt the love of Christ, when we consider the deep humiliation that Christ went through for our sakes ! To tabernacle in our flesh at all, to die after the manner of a man, to allow his holy body to hang naked on a cross, to suffer it to be lifted, handled, carried like a lump of cold clay, and shut up in a dark, silent, solitary tomb,—this was indeed love that passeth knowledge. What true believer need fear the grave now? Solemn as is the thought of our last narrow bed, we must never forget that " it is the place where the Lord lay." (Matt. xxviii. 6.) " The sting of death is sin, and the strength of sin is the law. But thanks be to God who giveth us the victory through our Lord Jesus Christ." (1 Cor. xv. 56.)

Henry observes, " Christ's death should comfort us against the fear of death. The grave could not long keep Christ, and it shall not long keep us. It was a loathsome prison before, it is a perfumed bed now. He whose Head is in heaven, need not fear to put his feet into the grave."

Every Bible reader knows that Isaiah's famous prophecy contains the words, " He made His grave with the wicked, and with the rich in His death." (Isa. liii. 9.) But not every one knows the interesting fact that the more correct translation of the Hebrew words would be, " His grave was appointed to be with the wicked ; but with the rich man was His tomb." This is the opinion of such eminent scholars as Capellus, Vitringa, Bishop Lowth, and Bishop Horsley.

JOHN XX 1—10

1 The first *day* of the week cometh Mary Magdalene early, when it was yet dark, unto the sepulchre, and seeth the stone taken away from the sepulchre.

2 Then she runneth, and cometh to Simon Peter, and to the other disciple, whom Jesus loved, and saith unto them, They have taken away the Lord out of the sepulchre, and we know not where they have laid him.

3 Peter therefore went forth, and that other disciple, and came to the sepulchre.

4 So they ran both together: and the other disciple did outrun Peter, and came first to the sepulchre.

5 And he stooping down, *and look-ing in*, saw the linen clothes lying ; yet went he not in.

6 Then cometh Simon Peter following him, and went into the sepulchre, and seeth the linen clothes lie,

7 And the napkin, that was about his head, not lying with the linen clothes, but wrapped together in a place by itself.

8 Then went in also that other disciple, which came first to the sepulchre, and he saw, and believed.

9 For as yet they knew not the scripture, that he must rise again from the dead.

10 Then the disciples went away again unto their own home.

THE chapter we have now begun takes us from Christ's death to Christ's resurrection. Like Matthew, Mark, and Luke, John dwells on these two great events with peculiar fulness and particularity. And we need not wonder. The whole of saving Christianity hinges on the two facts, that Christ died for our sins, and rose again for our justification. The chapter before our eyes deserves special attention. Of all the four evangelists, none supplies such deeply interesting evidence of the resurrection, as the disciple whom Jesus loved.

We are taught in the passage before us, *that those who love Christ most are those who have received most benefit from Him.*

The first whom St. John names among those who came to Christ's sepulchre, is Mary Magdalene. The history of this faithful woman, no doubt, is hidden in much obscurity. A vast amount of needless obloquy has been heaped upon her memory, as if she was once an habitual sinner against the seventh commandment. Yet there is literally no evidence whatever that she was anything of the kind! But we are distinctly told that she was one out of whom the Lord had cast " seven devils " (Mark xvi. 9 ; Luke viii. 2),—one who had been subjected in a peculiar way to Satan's possession,—and one whose gratitude to our Lord for deliverance was a gratitude that knew no bounds. In short, of all our Lord's followers on earth, none seem to have loved Him so much as Mary Magdalene. None felt that they owed so much to Christ. None felt so strongly that there was nothing too great to do for Christ. Hence, as Bishop Andrews beautifully puts it,—" She was last at His cross, and first at His grave. She staid longest *there*, and was soonest *here*. She could not rest till she was up to seek Him. She sought Him while it was yet dark, even before she had light to seek Him by." In a word, having received much, she loved much ; and loving much, she did much, in order to prove the reality of her love.

The case before us throws broad and clear light on a question, which ought to be deeply interesting to every true-hearted servant of Christ. How is it that many who profess and call themselves Christians, do so little for the Saviour whose name they bear? How is it that many, whose faith and grace it would be uncharitable to deny, work so little, give so little, say so little, take so little pains, to promote Christ's cause, and bring glory to Christ in the world? These questions admit of only one answer. It is a low sense of debt and obligation to Christ, which is the account of the whole matter. Where sin is not felt at all, nothing is done ; and where sin is little felt, little is done. The man who is deeply conscious of his own guilt and corruption, and deeply convinced that without the blood and intercession of Christ he would sink deservedly into the lowest hell, this is the man who will spend and be spent for Jesus, and think that he can never do enough to show forth His praise. Let us daily pray that we may see the sinfulness of sin, and the amazing grace of Christ, more clearly and distinctly. Then, and then only, shall we cease to be cool, and lukewarm, and slovenly in our work for Jesus. Then, and then only, shall we understand such burning zeal as that of Mary ; and comprehend what Paul meant when he said, "The love of Christ constraineth us; because we thus judge that if One died for all, then were all dead : and that He died for all, that they which live should not henceforth live unto themselves, but unto Him which died for them, and rose again." (2 Cor. v. 14, 15.)

We are taught, secondly, in these verses, *that there are widely different temperaments in different believers.*

This is a point which is curiously brought out in the conduct of Peter and John, when Mary Magdalene told them that the Lord's body was gone. We are told that they both ran to the sepulchre ; but John, the disciple whom Jesus loved, outran Peter, and reached the empty grave first. Then comes out the difference between the two men. John, of the two more gentle, quiet, tender, reserved, retiring, deep-feeling, stooped down and looked in, but went no further. Peter, more hot, and zealous, and impulsive, and fervent, and forward, cannot be content without going down into the sepulchre, and actually seeing with his own eyes. Both, we may be sure, were deeply attached to our Lord. The hearts of both, at this critical juncture, were full of hopes, and fears, and anxieties, and expectations, all tangled together. Yet each behaves in his own characteristic fashion. We need not doubt that these things were intentionally written for our learning.

Let us learn, from the case before us, to make allowances for wide varieties in the inward character of believers. To do so will save us much trouble in the journey of life, and prevent many an uncharitable thought. Let us not judge brethren harshly, and set them down in a low place, because they do not see or feel things exactly as we see and feel, and because things do not affect or strike them just as they affect and strike us. The flowers in the Lord's garden are not all of one color and one scent, though they are all planted by one Spirit. The subjects of His kingdom are not all exactly of one tone and temperament, though they all love the same Saviour, and are written in the same book of life. The Church of Christ has some in its ranks who are like Peter, and some who are like John ; and a place for all, and a work for all to do. Let us love all who love Christ in sincerity, and thank God that they love Him at all. The great thing is to love Jesus.

We are taught, finally, in these verses, *that there may be much ignorance even in true believers.*

This is a point which is brought out here with singular force and distinctness. John himself, the writer of this Gospel, records of himself and his companion Peter, " As yet they knew not the Scripture, that He must rise again from the dead." How truly wonderful this seems! For three long years these two leading Apostles had heard our Lord speak of His own resurrection as a fact, and yet they had not understood Him. Again and again He had staked the truth of His Messiahship on His rising from the dead, and yet they had never taken in His meaning. We little realize the power over the mind which is exercised by wrong teaching in childhood, and by early prejudices imbibed in our youth. Surely the Christian minister has little right to complain of ignorance among his hearers, when he marks the ignorance of Peter and John, under the teaching of Christ Himself.

After all we must remember that true grace, and not head knowledge, is the one thing needful. We are in the hands of a merciful and compassionate Saviour, who passes by and pardons much ignorance, when He sees "a heart right in the sight of God." Some things indeed we must know, and without knowing them we cannot be saved. Our own sinfulness and guilt, the office of Christ as a Saviour, the necessity of repentance and faith,—such things as these are essential to salvation. But he that knows these things may, in other respects, be a very ignorant man. In fact, the extent to which one man may have grace together with much ignorance, and another may have much knowledge and yet no grace, is one of the greatest mysteries in religion, and one which the last day alone will unfold. Let us then seek knowledge, and be ashamed of ignorance. But above all let us make sure that, like Peter and John, we have grace and right hearts.

Notes John xx 1—10

The two last chapters of St. John's Gospel are taken up with accounts of our Lord's appearances after His resurrection. Like Matthew, Mark, and Luke, St. John dwells very fully on the history of the crucifixion and resurrection. But, as in other parts of his Gospel, so here also, he supplies many deeply interesting details, which the other Evangelists, for some wise reasons, have not recorded. A few preliminary remarks on the whole subject will not perhaps be found uninteresting. The matter is one about which every Christian ought to have very clear and correct views.

(a) Concerning the importance of Jesus Christ's resurrection from the dead, it would be hard to speak too strongly. It is a cardinal article of the Christian faith, second to none in value.—It is the grand proof that He was the promised Messiah whom the Prophets had foretold. It is the one great sign which He named to the Jews when asked to give convincing evidence of His Divine mission,—the sign of the Prophet Jonas, the rebuilding of the temple after destruction. (Matt. xii. 39 ; John ii. 19—21.) If He did not rise again after three days, they were not to believe Him.—It is the completion of the work of redemption which He came into the world to accomplish. It proved that the ransom was accepted, and the victory over sin and death obtained. Christ " was delivered for our offences, and raised again for our justification."—" We are begotten again unto a lively hope, by the resurrection of Jesus Christ from the dead."—(Rom. iv. 25 ; Pet. i. 3.) If He had not risen again, our hope would have been a huge uncertainty.—It is a fact which has the closest connection with the spiritual life, and position before God, of all believers. They are counted by God as " risen with Christ," and they should regard themselves as partakers of Christ's resurrection life, and sitting in heavenly places.—Not least, it is the pledge and assurance of our own resurrection at the last day. We need not fear death, and look at the grave with despair, when we remember that Jesus Christ rose again in the body. As surely as the Head rose, so shall the members be raised.—Let these points never be forgotten. When we think of them we may understand why the Apostles, in their preaching and Epistles, dwell so much upon the resurrection. Well would it be if modern Christians thought more about it. Myriads seem unable to look at anything in the Gospel except the sacrifice and death of Christ, and altogether pass over His resurrection.

(b) Concerning the evidences of Christ's resurrection,—the proofs that He actually did rise again from the grave with His body,—it is most remarkable to observe how full and various they are. He was seen at least eleven times after He rose again, at different times of day, in different ways, and by different witnesses. He was seen first by one woman alone, then by several women together, then by one man, then by two men, and each time in the open air. Then He was seen by ten disciples in the evening in a room, then by eleven disciples again in a room, and afterwards on five different occasions, at one of which no less than five hundred people were present. Those to whom He appeared, touched Him, talked with Him, and saw Him eat and drink. (Matt. xxviii. 9 ; John xx. 27 ; Luke xxiv. 42.) Nor must it be forgotten that all who saw Him were most unwilling at first to believe, and most slow to credit the report of His resurrection. Yet they were all finally convinced ! If there is any fact in Christianity that is well supported by evidence, it is the fact of Christ rising again from the dead. It is the one fact that no infidel has ever fairly grappled with. One thing at any rate is most undeniably certain, and no infidel can escape it. The Apostles a few weeks after our Lord's crucifixion, were utterly and entirely different men in every way from what they were before the crucifixion, —bolder, more decided, more unhesitating followers of Jesus of Nazareth, than they used to be, to a most enormous extent. Even such men as the German Rationalists, Paulus and Strauss, according to Tholuck, are obliged to make the curious admission,—" Something extraordinary must have occurred."

(c) Concerning the best mode of harmonizing the accounts which the four Evangelists give of our Lord's appearances, after He rose again from the dead, there is undeniably some difficulty. But it is probably far more apparent than real. Matthew, Mark, Luke, and John, each tell their own story. There is a most decided absence of any appearance of concert or collusion about them. How to reconcile the seeming discrepancies in their narratives, has exercised the skill of commentators in every age. Dean Alford says flatly, that he " attempts no harmony of the accounts, and that he believes all such attempts to be fruitless." I do not agree with him at all, and I think the statement to be unworthy of the able writer who makes it. I think the accounts can be harmonized and reconciled, and that too without any unfair violence to the narratives of the four Gospels.

The order of Christ's eleven appearances between His resurrection and ascension, I believe to be as follows: (1) to Mary Magdalene alone (Mark xvi. 9 ; John xx. 14) ; (2) to certain women returning from the sepulchre (Matt. xxviii. 9, 10) ; (3) to Simon Peter alone (Luke xxiv. 34) ; (4) to two disciples going to Emmaus (Luke xxiv. 13) ; (5) to ten Apostles at Jerusalem, and some other disciples, Thomas being absent (John xx. 19) ; (6) to eleven Apostles at Jerusalem, Thomas being present (John xx. 26—29) ; (7) to seven disciples fishing at the sea of Tiberias (John xxi. 1) ; (8) to eleven Apostles on a mountain in Galilee, and perhaps some others with them (Matt. xxviii. 16) ; (9) to above five hundred brethren at once (1 Cor. xv. 7) ;

(10) to James only (1 Cor. xv. 7); (11) to all the Apostles, and probably some others, on Mount Olivet, at His ascension.

Most of these eleven appearances require little or no explanation. The ninth and tenth in the list are only recorded by St. Paul; and some think that the appearance to five hundred at once, is the same as that to the eleven in Galilee, though I doubt it. The appearance to Peter is one of which we know nothing except the fact; and, in my judgment, it certainly is not the same as the appearance to the two who were walking to Emmaus. The only appearances, after all, about which there is any difficulty, are the two first in the list, and to my own mind the difficulty is by no means insuperable. The knot to be untied is this. St. Mark expressly says that our Lord appeared first to Mary Magdalene. (Mark xvi. 9.) St. John also describes this appearance; and it is quite plain from his account that Mary Magdalene was alone. (John xx. 11—13.) Yet St. Matthew says that Mary Magdalene and the other Mary came to the sepulchre together,—saw an angel, and heard that our Lord had risen,—ran to bring the tidings to the disciples, and were met on the way by Jesus, and both saw Him at the same time. Now how is this to be explained? How can the account of these three witnesses be made to harmonize and agree? I will try to show.

(1) I believe that Mary Magdalene and the other Mary did not go alone to the sepulchre, on the morning of the resurrection. By comparing Mark xvi. 1, and Luke xxiii. 55, and xxiv. 1, with Matt. xxviii. 1, it is quite evident that several " other women " accompanied them.

(2) I believe that, on drawing nigh the sepulchre, the company of women saw the stone rolled away from its mouth. At once, on seeing this, it flashed on the mind of Mary Magdalene that the body of Jesus had been removed from the tomb, and, without waiting a moment, she ran off to Peter and John, and told them, as recorded in John xx. 1, 2. This is the view of Chrysostom and Cyril.

(3) I believe that, while Mary Magdalene ran off to tell Peter and John, the other women went up to the sepulchre, found the body gone, saw a vision of angels, were told that Jesus had risen, and were commanded to go and tell the disciples. They departed to tell the news. Some went in one direction and some in another; Mary and Salome with one party; Joanna with another.

(4) I believe that while this was going on, Mary Magdalene, who had run off alone to tell Peter and John, had found them, and that they all three came to the sepulchre shortly after the other women went away. Whether Mary got there so soon as Peter and John, perhaps admits of doubt.

(5) I believe that Peter and John saw the empty sepulchre, and went away, leaving Mary Magdalene weeping there.

(6) I believe that, as soon as Peter and John went away, Mary Magdalene saw the two angels, and immediately after saw our Lord Himself, and was told to carry a message to His brethren. (John xx 17.)

(7) I believe that in the meantime the other women had gone in two or three directions, to tell the other disciples who lived in a different part of Jerusalem from that where Peter and John lived. Mary the wife of Cleophas, and Salome, were yet on their way when Jesus met them, very shortly after He had appeared to Mary Magdalene.

(8) I believe that one party of the women, with Joanna at their head, saw nothing of our Lord, but went to the disciples and told them the message of the angels.

(9) I believe that, shortly after this, our Lord appeared to Simon Peter, who very likely had gone again to the grave on hearing Mary Magdalene's report.

(10) I believe that in the course of the same day our Lord appeared to the two disciples on the way to Emmaus, who had left Jerusalem after Joanna and the women reported the vision of angels, but before our Lord had appeared to Peter.

(11) Finally, I believe that in the evening of the same day our Lord appeared to the Apostles, and others with them, Thomas being absent. Luke says, " The *eleven* Apostles were gathered together." But he evidently means the Apostles generally, as *a body*. (See my note on Luke xxiv. 34.) This was our Lord's fifth appearance on the day that He rose.

I know not whether this scheme of reconciliation will satisfy all my readers. On a point so much controverted, it becomes a commentator to speak humbly and diffidently. I content myself with saying that I see far fewer difficulties in it than in any other scheme that I have met with. I see, moreover, nothing unfair or unreasonable about it, and nothing which is not consistent with the variety that may justly be expected from the testimony of four independent witnesses.

To those who wish to study the subject more fully, I strongly recommend a careful study of " West on the-Resurrection," and " Birks's Horæ Evangelicæ."

1 —[*The first day of the week.*] This, I need hardly say, means our Sunday, the Lord's day, the first day following the Jewish sabbath. Between the end of the nineteenth chapter and these words, we must suppose an interval of thirty-six hours to have passed away. During these hours our blessed Lord's body lay still in the tomb, and His soul was in paradise, while the disciples were quiet in their respective abodes, and honored the fourth commandment. The chief and principal breakers of this Sabbath were the priests and Pharisees, who came to Pilate and obtained leave to set a watch around the tomb, and put a

seal on the stone which lay at its mouth. The very men who made a boast of the law, through breaking of the law dishonored God, and disgraced themselves. The very followers of Him whom they had slain, kept the law more strictly than they did.

[*Cometh Mary Magdalene...early...dark...sepulchre.*] St. John names none but Mary. Yet it is clear, by examining the account of the other three Gospel writers, that she did not come alone. She was only one among several women from Galilee,—including Mary the wife of Cleophas, or Alpheus, Salome the mother of John and James, and Joanna the wife of Chuza, Herod's steward. These all appear to have been near our Lord when He was crucified, and to have looked on, if they did not actively help, when He was buried. They then probably agreed to come to the tomb early on the morning after the sabbath in order to do more for our Lord's body than there was time to do on Friday afternoon. On the sabbath they rested according to the commandment. They now came as early as they could, even before the sun was up, in order to begin their pious work as soon as they had light to do it. Foremost among the whole party was Mary Magdalene.

Rupertus and Ferus maintain that Mary Magdalene lived at Bethany, and therefore came alone to the sepulchre, from a different road to that by which the other women came. But this seems pure conjecture, and probably arises from confounding Mary Magdalene with Mary the sister of Lazarus.

[*And seeth...stone...sepulchre.*] It seems to me, from these words, that Mary Magdalene was the first who detected in the dim twilight that the stone was rolled away from the mouth of the tomb. It may be that she was in advance of the other women, and thus saw it first. It may be that strong feeling and anxiety made her more quick-sighted and keen of observation than her companions. Indeed we do not know for a certainty that all the women came together in a body. For anything I can see they may have come separately, or by twos and threes, and Mary may have been the first of the party. It is quite consistent with her character to suppose this. In any case her conduct this memorable morning was so remarkable and prominent, that St. John speaks of her alone. All the women showed faith and courage and love, he seems to intimate ; but none so pre-eminently as Mary Magdalene. She was first to come near the tomb, first to discover that the stone was rolled away, first to conjecture that something remarkable had happened, and first to act at once on what she saw.

Let us note Mary's courage, and zeal to honor her buried Lord. Not every woman would have dared to go outside the city while it was yet dark, to a grave, and specially during the passover feast, when thousands of strangers were probably sleeping under any slight shelter near the walls of Jerusalem.

Let us note how St. John takes it for granted that his readers were acquainted with the other three Gospels, and knew that "a stone" had been rolled to the door of the sepulchre. He here speaks of "the stone." Yet he has said nothing about it before.

There seems strong internal evidence that Mary, and the other women who agreed to come with her to the sepulchre, could not have known of the Roman guard having been placed around it. It seems, at all events, highly improbable that they would have gone there before the sun was up, if they had expected to find Roman soldiers at the place.

Andrews observes that four special favors were granted to Mary in one day : (1) To see the angels; (2) To see Christ at all; (3) To see Him first of all; (4) To be employed by Christ to carry a heavenly errand. And why? Because she loved much. He adds, " We cannot say that she believed much. By her thrice repeated saying her Lord was ' taken away ' (2, 13, 15 verses), it seems she believed no more than the high priest would have had the world believe, that He was taken away by night."

2 — [*Then she runneth.*] I believe this expression means that Mary Magdalene, the moment she saw the stone rolled away from its place, ran off alone to tell the news to Peter and John. She did not go a step nearer the tomb, but left the other women to go up to the grave and look in, and thus missed seeing the angel whom they saw. She waited for nothing. The stone was moved. The body, she at once concluded, had been taken away. She turned on her heel at once and ran off to tell the two chief Apostles. The rest of the party probably drew near to the grave slowly and hesitatingly, not knowing what to think or expect ; and Mary was probably a long way on the road to the dwelling of Peter and John, before they finally turned away from the tomb. This should be carefully noticed, if we would reconcile the narratives of Matthew and John. It is clear to my own mind that there was something peculiar and striking in the conduct of Mary Magdalene this wonderful morning, and St. John desires on that account to direct our special attention to it. " Mary," he seems to say, " was the first to come to the tomb, the first to see that the stone was removed, and the one that ran off alone to tell me and Peter. Many of the Galilean women showed faith, and love, and zeal that morning, but none more than Mary."

[*And cometh...Peter...other disciple...loved.*] The other disciple here mentioned was unquestionably John. Mary's reasons for running to tell these two first were probably these. (*a*) They were chief men among the Apostles. (*b*) They had been the two who had stuck most closely to Jesus up to the last, and shown most faith and love, and were naturally most anxious to know about His body. (*c*) Wherever John was, Mary the mother of our Lord was. Can we doubt that Mary Magdalene would think of her as one among the first to be told about the stone being rolled away? It is moreover highly probable, though a matter of conjecture only, that Peter and John were staying at some house very near the sepulchre. It is most likely that the other Apostles were "scattered," according to our Lord's prophecy, in different parts of Jerusalem, and none were so near the tomb as Peter and John.

It is interesting to notice how, all through the Gospels and Acts, Peter and John seem to have been peculiarly drawn together, and to have been close friends and companions. As fishermen, we are told that James and John were partners with Simon. (Luke v. 10.) Three times the name of James is joined with theirs,—on the Mount of Transfiguration, at the house of Jairus, and in the garden of Gethsemane. But the special intimacy between Peter and John comes out at the last supper, in the high priest's house, on the occasion now before us, at the Sea of Tiberias, at the end of this Gospel, and in the third of Acts, where the lame man was healed. All point to that mysterious drawing together between two men of widely different temperaments, which every observing eye must occasionally see in the world. John alone, of all the Apostles, had witnessed Peter's sad fall in the high priest's house, and observed his bitter weeping afterwards. Can we not understand that from Friday night to Sunday morning John would be lovingly employed in binding up the broken heart of his brother, and telling him of our Lord's last words? Can we doubt that they were absorbed and occupied in converse about their Master on this very morning, when Mary Magdalene suddenly ran in with her wonderful news?

The love and tender charity of John's character come out beautifully in his affection for Peter, even after his denial of Christ. How many modern Churches would have excommunicated Peter, and put him in a low place for months. John clings to him, and has him under his own roof, wherever that was. When Judas fell, he had no friend to raise and cheer him. When Peter fell, there was a "brother born for adversity," who did not despise him.

Bengel thinks, from the repetition of the preposition " to," in the Greek,—" to Peter, to John,"—that the disciples were not together. But I cannot think this at all likely.

[*And saith...taken away...know not...laid Him.*] Mary's announcement was a very short one. Whether she had actually looked inside the tomb and seen that it was empty, seems more than doubtful. It would rather appear, by comparison of the four Gospels, that she had only seen the stone rolled away from the door. But that was enough for her. She had at once jumped to the conclusion that the body of "the Lord" was taken away, and so she announces it. And after all she had reason on her side. Who would have taken the trouble of rolling away the stone, but one who wanted to take away the body ? If the stone was rolled away, she justly concluded the body was gone.

One thing, at any rate, will be observed by every one who carefully compares St. John's narrative with that of the other three Evangelists. Mary Magdalene had evidently not seen " the vision of angels " which the other women saw, or else she would certainly have mentioned it to Peter and John. She does not say a word about it ! She had not heard the comfortable tidings that the Lord had " risen," or else she would surely have told it. She clearly knew nothing of all this; and the conclusion is plain to my mind, that she ran off as soon as she saw the stone rolled away, and waited for no companion.

Another thing should be observed. St. John's narrative here lets out the fact that Mary Magdalene did not go to the sepulchre alone. For what does she say ? She speaks in the plural number: " *We* know not where they have laid Him." That " we " can only apply to herself and the other women who had gone with her to the grave.

We should notice that Mary's mournful announcement is almost the same that she made to the angels, when they asked her why she wept. (Verse 13.) Her repeated dwelling on the body being gone, and her wanting to know where it was " laid," should be noticed. May we not suspect that this holy woman, with all her faith and love, had not yet realized the great truth that Jesus was to rise again. She talks of His *body*, and longs to know where it is laid, and seems to think it must be a cold dead corpse still, and wishes to do it more honor. But she has forgotten altogether His repeated prediction that He would rise again ! Alas, how little of Christ's teaching the best of us take in ! How much we let fall !

By the word " they " we must suppose Mary meant our Lord's enemies,—the chief priests, or the Roman soldiers. Perhaps we should not press the word too closely. It may be that the good woman, in her excitement and trouble, hardly knew whom she meant, and spoke indefinitely ;—" somebody " has taken away. She can hardly have meant that the chief priests had taken away the body, in order to exhibit it as the dead corpse of a conquered, wicked impostor.

It is fair to say that Ecolampadius actually thinks that Mary saw the angels, talked with them, and received the message for the disciples that Christ had risen, but quite forgot it ! This, however, seems to me an extremely improbable view.

3. -[*Peter therefore went forth, and that other disciple, etc.*] The announcement of Mary Magdalene was so startling, that the two disciples arose at once, and went to the sepulchre, in order to find out what this rolling away of the stone meant, and to

make sure that the Lord's body was gone. We need not doubt that they would at once ask Mary, " How do you know the body is gone ? " and would receive the answer, " Because the stone is rolled away." But finding then, that Mary had not actually been inside the sepulchre, and seen it empty, they judged it best to go and see for themselves. When we remember that Mary the mother of our Lord was, in all human probability, in the house where Peter and John were, we may well imagine that she would be deeply anxious to have the whole matter cleared up at once.

St. Luke, we may recollect, only mentions Peter going to the sepulchre. The verse before us fills up the narrative, and tells us that John went with him. Two witnesses would be better than one.

4.--[*So they ran both together, etc.*] The simple fact here mentioned shows the anxiety and excitement of the two loving Apostles. We can well suppose that Mary Magdalene's sudden announcement completely overwhelmed them, so that they knew not what to think. Who can tell that thoughts did not come into their mind, as they ran, about our Lord's oft-repeated prediction of His resurrection ? Could it really be true ? Could it possibly prove that all their deep sorrow was going to turn to joy ? These are all conjectures, no doubt. Yet a vast quantity of thoughts may run through a mind, at a great crisis, in a very few minutes. Those who have had a narrow escape from drowning know that very well.

Why John outran Peter we know not. The common opinion is that John was the younger man of the two, and so he has been always represented by painters in every age of the Church. The only evidence, however, we have of this difference of age, is the fact that John's father is mentioned as being alive, following his calling as a fisherman with his sons, while Peter's father, Jonas, is not mentioned in the same way. Moreover, John outlived all the rest of the Apostles by many years. So he may have been a comparatively young man, when our Lord called him to be an Apostle.

After all, the matter is of little importance. Bodily strength and agility are no evidence that a man possesses superior grace. The holiest saints have often had very weak and infirm bodies. Holy and zealous as John was, we have no right to contend that he felt more zeal than penitent, broken-hearted Peter, when he outran him on this eventful morning.

Lampe thinks it just possible that Peter was troubled in conscience by reason of his recent fall, and therefore went to the grave with a slow and hesitating step. But I doubt this.

5 --[*And he stooping down, etc.*] The opinion of well-informed persons who have seen the tombs near Jerusalem, is, that our Lord's sepulchre was a kind of cave hewn out of the side of a

rocky hill, and that there was either a hollow place, hewn out at a little distance within the entrance of the cave, to receive the body, or that the grave sloped gradually backwards, and the body was laid at the back part of the cave. In either case we may understand that a person coming to the door of the cave (which must have been small, if a single stone could close it), could only see what was inside, by "stooping down," as we are here told John did.

When John looked in, he saw nothing whatever but the empty grave, and the linen clothes in which our Lord's body had been wrapped lying together. Not going in, it is evident that he could not see very clearly the precise state of a dark cave, with only one small entrance. He only saw enough to satisfy him at a glance that the body of Christ was not there, and that the linen clothes were there.

Why the beloved apostle "went not in," we do not know, and are left to conjecture. It may be that he was at once satisfied that the body of his Master was gone, and that was all he cared to know. It may be that he felt a holy reverence for the place where our Lord had lain, and shrunk from going in. It may possibly be that he felt some fear, and hardly knew what to expect next, remembering the earthquake and the rending of graves on the previous Friday. It may be that, being the younger man of the two, he waited for his elder brother to take the lead, and would touch nothing, do nothing, and take no step, without another witness besides himself. We cannot tell. The incident is precisely one of those little circumstantial details which bring out men's natural temperament.

It is noteworthy that John himself is the writer who records that he "went not in." Be the motive what it may, he generously gives his brother Peter the whole honor and credit of being the first of the two to go inside the grave, and thoroughly investigate the condition of it in every particular.

We should not forget that the simple fact of the "linen clothes lying," was enough to satisfy any thinking mind, that something extraordinary must have occurred. No enemy or thief, in removing our Lord's body, would have taken the trouble to remove the linen clothes in which he was wrapped. Reason points out that it would save time and trouble to take the body as it was, with the linen wrapped around it.

Lampe thinks it possible that John did not go in from fear of being made unclean by a dead body. But I can hardly think this.

6 —[*Then cometh Simon Peter, etc.*] In this verse we see how differently different men act under the same circumstances. Grace does not alter natural temperaments, when it changes hearts. What John for some reason would not do, Peter did. On arriving, he went down at once through the mouth of the

cave into the inside of the sepulchre. Then he saw, as John had seen, that the body of our Lord was not there, and that the linen clothes in which the body had been wrapped were lying there, and had been removed in some way from the body. How much linen was used by Joseph and Nicodemus we cannot tell. But when we consider that one hundred pounds of aromatic powder had been used in wrapping up the body, it is not unreasonable to suppose that many yards of linen had been employed. The quantity of linen wrapped round the corpse of an Egyptian, we know from the mummies, was prodigious. It is probable that the linen wrapped round our Lord's body, which Peter saw " lying," was no small heap.

It is noteworthy that two different Greek words are used, in this and the preceding verse, to express *seeing*. St. John " saw" at a glance. St. Peter saw as a spectator, looking round and examining. The Greek word rendered " lying " in one verse and " lie " in the other, is precisely the same, and without reason our translation varies. In both it should be " lying."

7 —[*And the napkin, etc., etc.*] The object of this verse seems to be to show that Peter found in the empty tomb the clearest evidence of a deliberate, orderly, and calmly-done transaction. The linen clothes, in which our Lord's body had been wrapped, were lying by themselves. The napkin which had been tied round his head was rolled up by itself in another place, separate from the linen clothes. There were no symptoms of hurry, haste, or fear. All had been done decently and in order. Everything that Peter saw contradicted the idea that the body had been stolen. No thief would have taken so much trouble about the clothes and napkin. In fact the person who had removed the body, whoever it was, must have entailed on himself needless labor, if he removed it as a dead corpse, by unwrapping the linen clothes in which the corpse was buried. The easiest plan would have been to carry away the body just as he found it, wrapped up in linen. Why were the linen clothes taken off and left behind? Why were the removers of the body so careful to take away nothing but the body? Questions like these must have sorely perplexed Peter's mind. The body, he saw plainly, was gone. But there was something in the whole appearance of things which he could not understand.

Chrysostom observes, " The linen cloths lying was a sign of the resurrection. For neither if any person had removed the body, would they, before doing so, have stripped it; nor if any had stolen it, would they have taken the trouble to remove the napkin, and roll it up, and lay it in a place by itself. They would have taken the body as it was. On this account, John tells us, by anticipation, that it was buried with much myrrh, which glues linen to the body not less firmly than lead, in order that when thou hearest that the napkin lay apart, thou mayest not endure those who say He was stolen. A thief would not have been so foolish as to spend so much time on a superfluous matter. Why should he undo the cloths? How could he have escaped detection if he had done so? He would probably have spent much time in doing it, and been found out by delaying. But why did the clothes lie apart while the napkin was wrapped together by itself? That thou mayest learn that it was not the action of men in confusion or haste, the placing some in one place and some in another, and the wrapping them together."

Theophylact, as usual, follows Chrysostom; and adds, that linen cloths wrapped round the body with myrrh, would stick to it like pitch.

The word translated "napkin," is only used four times in the New Testament. On one occasion, and one only, it is rendered "handkerchief." (Acts xix. 12.)

8.—[*Then went in also that other disciple, etc.*] We are here told how John at last followed Peter, and went inside the tomb. He does not seem to have gone in at first with Peter, but to have waited without, while his brother Apostle investigated and examined everything. Then, on hearing his report, he resolved to go inside himself, and see with his own eyes. Why he hesitated at first, we are left to conjecture. Perhaps, like Mary Magdalene, he was so absorbed and overwhelmed by the fact that his Master's body was gone, that he could pay no attention to the minor details of the transaction. But when he did go inside the tomb, and saw with his own eyes the clear evidence of a deliberate, orderly removal of the body only, and the cloths left behind, it seems to have flashed across his mind that the Lord must have risen. For we are told that he "believed."

Concerning the true meaning of this word "believed" in this place, there has been some dispute, but without good cause. It cannot of course mean that John became a true believer now for the first time. Such an idea is absurd. Nor yet can it only mean, I think, that John at last believed that the body of our Lord was not there. Such an interpretation seems to me cold, tame, and shallow. I hold that it can only bear one meaning, and that is, that John, when he saw the state of the tomb, believed that Christ had really risen from the dead. In short, he was the first of all our Lord's followers that believed His resurrection.

9 —[*For as yet they knew not, etc.*] This parenthetical comment of the Evangelist is hardly rendered with accuracy in our English version. It would be more literally translated, "As yet they had not known," in the pluperfect tense. The meaning obviously is,—" Up to this time these two disciples, like all the rest of our Lord's followers, had not fully understood the meaning of the Scriptures, which taught that Christ must rise again from the dead, after dying for our sins."

Augustine suggests that one reason why the disciples did not understand our Lord's prediction of His own resurrection, was His custom of using parables in His teaching. "Being accustomed to be spoken to in parables by Him, they supposed Him to be signifying some other thing." But the worthy Father rather seems to forget that although our Lord spoke parables to the multitude, "when He was alone He expounded all things to His disciples." Yet the suggestion is worth remembering. Dwellers in the cold prosaic north, can have little idea of the enormous quantity of figurative and flowery language used in oriental countries. An Englishman going for the first time among Orientals, finds it hard to know whether those around him are using flowery expressions which mean nothing, or speaking of facts.

Whether St. John referred to any particular text, in using this expression about "Scripture," is matter of doubt. To me it is far more likely that he had in view the general teaching of the whole Old Testament, both in types and typical events, as well as in direct texts. I suspect that he refers to such things as the receiving back of Isaac by Abraham on Moriah after he had offered him, the whale casting up Jonah on the dry land, the living bird being let go free in cleansing the leper, the scape-goat being let go alive on the day of atonement, and other like things written for our learning.

The subject, I must honestly say, is a very deep one. It is vain to deny that the manner in which texts are quoted from the Old Testament in the New Testament, is sometimes very puzzling. The safest and most reverent line of thought is to believe that there is a fulness in Scripture which many of us have never realized ; and that scores of texts refer to Christ's life, death, and resurrection, though we know it not.

When it says here, "He must rise again," the meaning is literally, "It is necessary, or it is becoming that He should rise." It was necessary for the accomplishment of man's redemption, and for the completion of the work which Jesus came to do as our Substitute and Representative. The second Adam must die and rise again, in order to win back what the first Adam lost.

The case of the Apostles is a striking example of the extent of spiritual ignorance there may be in a man, while his heart is right with God. Who would think of denying that Peter and John were true believers, and loved Christ, and were on the way to heaven ? Yet here we are plainly told that up to this time they had not understood that Jesus must rise again on the third day, after dying for our sins on the cross. Surely we must take care that we do not hastily condemn men as heretics, and set them down as graceless and godless, because they are deficient in head-knowledge. After all, how many Christians there are in the present day, who talk about Christ's blood and Christ's death, but seem to know nothing of Christ's resurrection, and hardly give it a place in their religion, except as a fact.

It is very noteworthy, that while Peter and John and their companions seem to have overlooked and forgotten our Lord's predictions that He would rise again the third day, there were certain Jews who did not forget them at all. And who were they ? The very last men that we might have expected,—the chief priests and Pharisees ! It is written in Matthew (ch. xxvii. 62—64), that they went to Pilate, and said, " We *remember* that deceiver said, while He was yet alive, after three days I will rise again." What a curious fact is that ! Peter and John forgot their Lord's predictions, while Caiaphas and his wicked companions remembered them !

Burgon quotes from Ainsworth, a saying of a Jew, commenting on Gen. xxii. 4: " There are many a three things in the Holy Scripture, of which one is the resurrection of the Messiah."—I add to this, that any one who examines Ainsworth's commentary on this verse will find, that he gathers together as many as fifteen places in the Old Testament where " three " is spoken of as a mystical number.

10 —[*Then the disciples went...their own house.*] This verse describes the end of the visit which Peter and John made to the grave. They had seen with their own eyes proofs positive that Mary Magdalene's report was true. The grave was empty, and their Master's body was gone. They both felt that there was no need for tarrying at an empty sepulchre, and resolved to return to their lodging. They could do no good by staying longer. They might do good by going away. They therefore went home : Peter confounded and perplexed, and unable to account for what he had seen ; John convinced and persuaded by what he had seen, that his Master had risen from the dead. Doubtless he could not prove it yet, had not seen Him alive, and could not convince Peter of it. But for all that he believed it.

The Greek words which we render, " To their own home," mean literally, " To themselves." It can only signify, in my judgment, the lodging which they occupied in Jerusalem. Though John was acquainted with the high priest, and may have occasionally visited Jerusalem on the business of his fisherman's calling, there is not the least likelihood that he had a house there. Wherever John was in Jerusalem it is interesting to remember, in looking at the events of this wonderful morning, that Mary, the mother of our Lord, was probably under his roof, in accordance with our Lord's last command. May we not fairly suppose that one reason why the disciples did not linger at the tomb, like Mary Magdalene, was their earnest desire to return home, and tell the mother of our Lord what they had seen ? I see nothing fanciful or unreasonable in the thought.

Cyril suggests, with some probability, that one reason why Peter and John went away from the tomb so soon, was fear of the Jews. They might well expect that the anger of Caiaphas and his companions on finding the sepulchre was empty, and the body of Jesus gone, would be very great, and they would naturally turn their wrath on the helpless disciples. The day was breaking, and the sooner they got home the better. Mary Magdalene might stay near the tomb with more safety.

Beza thinks that this verse leaves John, Peter, and Mary in three different states of mind. John was convinced, and believed that Jesus was risen from the dead. Peter was uncertain, wondering, and amazed. Mary could not yet believe it at all.

JOHN XX 11—18

11 But Mary stood without at the sepulchre weeping: and as she wept, she stooped down *and looked* into the sepulchre,

12 And seeth two angels in white sitting, the one at the head, and the other at the feet, where the body of Jesus had lain.

13 And they say unto her, Woman, why weepest thou? She saith unto them, Because they have taken away my Lord, and I know not where they have laid him.

14 And when she had thus said, she turned herself back, and saw Jesus standing, and knew not that it was Jesus.

15 Jesus saith unto her, Woman, why weepest thou? whom seekest thou? She, supposing him to be the gardener, saith unto him, Sir, if thou have borne him hence, tell me where thou hast laid him, and I will take him away.

16 Jesus saith unto her, Mary. She turned herself, and saith unto him, Rabboni; which is to say, Master.

17 Jesus saith unto her, touch me not; for I am not yet ascended to my Father: but go to my brethren, and say unto them, I ascend unto my Father, and your Father; and *to* my God, and your God.

18 Mary Magdalene came and told the disciples that she had seen the Lord, and *that* he had spoken these things unto her.

THE interview between the Lord Jesus and Mary Magdalene immediately after His resurrection, described in these verses, is a narrative peculiar to St. John. No other Evangelist has been inspired to record it. Of all the accounts of the appearances of our Lord, after He rose from the dead, none perhaps is so pathetic and touching as this. He that can read this simple story without a deep interest, must have a very cold and unfeeling heart.

We see, first, in these verses, *that those who love*

Christ most diligently and perseveringly, are those who receive most privileges from Christ's hand. It is a touching fact, and one to be carefully noted, that Mary Magdalene would not leave the sepulchre, when Peter and John went away to their own home. Love to her gracious Master would not let her leave the place where He had been lain. Where He was now she could not tell. What had become of Him she did not know. But love made her linger about the empty tomb, where Joseph and Nicodemus had lately laid Him. Love made her honor the last place where His precious body had been seen by mortal eyes. And her love reaped a rich reward. She saw the angels whom Peter and John had never observed. She actually heard them speak, and had soothing words addressed to her. She was the first to see our Lord after He rose from the dead, the first to hear His voice, the first to hold conversation with Him. Can any one doubt that this was written for our learning? Wherever the Gospel is preached throughout the world, this little incident testifies that those who honor Christ will be honored by Christ.

As it was in the morning of the first Easter day, so will it be as long as the Church stands. The great principle contained in the passage before us, will hold good until the Lord comes again. All believers have not the same degree of faith, or hope, or knowledge, or courage, or wisdom; and it is vain to expect it. But it is a certain fact that those who love Christ most fervently, and cleave to Him most closely, will always enjoy most communion with Him, and feel most of the witness of the Spirit in their hearts. It is precisely those who wait on the Lord, in the temper of Mary Magdalene, to whom the Lord will reveal Himself most fully, and make them know and feel more than others. To know Christ is good; but to "know that we know Him" is far better.

We see, secondly, in these verses, *that the fears and sorrows of believers are often quite needless.* We are told that Mary stood at the sepulchre weeping, and wept as if nothing could comfort her. She wept when the angels spoke to her ; " Woman," they said, " why weepest thou ? "—She was weeping still when our Lord spoke to her: " Woman," He also said, " why weepest thou ? "—And the burden of her complaint was always the same: " They have taken away my Lord, and I know not where they have laid Him."—Yet all this time her risen Master was close to her, with "body, flesh, and bones, and all things pertaining to the perfection of man's nature." (Article IV.) Her tears were needless. Her anxiety was unnecessary. Like Hagar in the wilderness, she had a well of water by her side, but she had not eyes to see it.

What thoughtful Christian can fail to see, that we have here a faithful picture of many a believer's experience? How often we are anxious when there is no just cause for anxiety ! How often we mourn over the absence of things which in reality are within our grasp, and even at our right hand ! Two-thirds of the things we fear in life never happen at all, and two-thirds of the tears we shed are thrown away, and shed in vain. Let us pray for more faith and patience, and allow more time for the full development of God's purposes. Let us believe that things are often working together for our peace and joy, which seem at one time to contain nothing but bitterness and sorrow. Old Jacob said at one time of his life, "all these things are against me" (Gen. xlii. 36); yet he lived to see Joseph again, rich and prosperous, and to thank God for all that had happened. If Mary had found the seal of the tomb unbroken, and her Master's body lying cold within, she might well have wept ! The very absence of the body which made her weep, was a token for good, and a cause of joy for herself and all mankind.

We see, thirdly, in these verses, *what low and earthly thoughts of Christ may creep into the mind of a true believer.* It seems impossible to gather any other lesson from the solemn words which our Lord addressed to Mary Magdalene, when He said, " Touch Me not ; for I am not yet ascended to my Father."—No doubt the language is somewhat mysterious, and ought to be delicately and reverently handled. Yet it is only reasonable to suppose that the first surprise, and the reaction from great sorrow to great joy, was more than the mind of Mary could bear. She was only a woman, though a holy and faithful woman. It is highly probable that, in the first excess of her joy, she threw herself at our Lord's feet, and made greater demonstrations of feeling than were seemly or becoming. Very likely she behaved too much like one who thought all must be right if she had her Lord's bodily presence, and all must be wrong in His bodily absence. This was not the highest style of faith. She acted, in short, like one who forgot that her Master was God as well as man. She made too little of His divinity, and too much of His humanity. And hence she called forth our Lord's gentle rebuke, "Touch Me not! There is no need of this excessive demonstration of feeling. I am not yet ascending to my Father for forty days : your present duty is not to linger at my feet, but to go and tell my brethren that I have risen. Think of the feelings of others as well as of your own."

After all, we must confess that the fault of this holy woman was one into which Christians have always been too ready to fall. In every age there has been a tendency in the minds of many, to make too much of Christ's bodily presence, and to forget that He is not a mere earthly friend, but one who is "God over all, blessed forever," as well as man. The pertinacity with which Romanists and their allies cling to the doctrine of Christ's real corporal presence in the Lord's Supper, is only another exhibition of Mary's feeling when she wanted Christ's body, or no Christ at all. Let us pray for a right judgment in this matter, as in all other things concerning our Lord's person. Let us be content to have Christ dwelling in our hearts by faith, and present when two or three are met in His name, and to wait for the *real presence* of Christ's body till He comes again. What we really need is not His literal flesh, but His Spirit. It is not for nothing that it is written, "It is the Spirit that quickeneth: the flesh profiteth nothing." "If we have known Christ after the flesh, yet henceforth know we Him no more." (John vi. 63 ; 2 Cor. v. 16.)

We see, lastly, in these verses, *how kindly and graciously our Lord speaks of His disciples.* He bids Mary Magdalene carry a message to them as "His brethren." He bids her tell them that His Father was their Father, and His God their God. It was but three days before that they had all forsaken Him shamefully, and fled. Yet this merciful Master speaks as if all was forgiven and forgotten. His first thought is to bring back the wanderers, to bind up the wounds of their consciences, to reanimate their courage, to restore them to their former place. This was indeed a love that passeth knowledge. To trust deserters, and to show confidence in backsliders, was a compassion which man can hardly understand. So true is that word of David : "Like as a Father pitieth his children, so the Lord pitieth them that fear Him. For He knoweth our frame; He remembereth that we are dust." (Psalm ciii. 13, 14.)

Let us leave the passage with the comfortable reflection that Jesus Christ never changes. He is the same yesterday, to-day, and forever. As He dealt with His erring disciples in the morning of His resurrection, so will He deal with all who believe and love Him, until He comes again. When we wander out of the way He will bring us back. When we fall He will raise us again. But he will never break His royal word: "Him that cometh to Me I will in no wise cast out." (John vi. 37.) The saints in glory will have one anthem in which every voice and heart will join: "He hath not dealt with us after our sins, nor rewarded us according to our iniquities." (Psalm ciii. 10.)

NOTES JOHN XX 11—18

11 —[*But Mary stood without...weeping.*] The question naturally arises, "Why did not Mary go away from the tomb with Peter and John?"—The answer to that question must probably be found in the curiously different temperaments of men and women. Mary acted like a woman, and Peter and John acted like men. The head of a woman is generally weaker than that of a man, but the affections are generally stronger.—In the case before us the heart of Mary was not satisfied. Her mind was not convinced, like that of John, that our Lord had risen from the dead. It was not enough for her to know that the body was gone, and the tomb empty, and something wonderful had occurred, as it was for Peter. Her strong love and gratitude towards our Lord made her linger near the tomb, in the faint hope that something might yet turn up to explain where the body was gone. At any rate she could not tear herself away from the place where her Master's body had last been seen, and when Peter and John departed she stayed behind, like a real warm-hearted woman, and gave a natural vent to her feelings in tears. She felt as if she must see something, before she could be satisfied, and so lingered near the grave, perhaps hardly knowing what she expected to see. The Lord had compassion on her. Her deep love was richly rewarded.

On Mary staying at the sepulchre, Andrews remarks, "The going away of Peter and John commends Mary's staying behind. To the grave she came before them, from the grave she went to tell them, to the grave she returned with them, at the grave she remains behind them." "To stay, while others do so, while company stays, that is the world's love. But Peter is gone, and John too; all are gone and she left alone. Thus to stay is love, and constant love."

Epiphanius an ancient writer (A. D. 390), according to Heinsius, maintains the monstrous theory that the Mary here spoken of is the mother of our Lord, and not Mary Magdalene !
It is well to know that the ancient Fathers were not always
wise, and are certainly not infallible in expounding Scripture.

Tholuck thinks that Mary did not go to the sepulchre with
Peter and John, but followed them alone, more slowly. This
is possible ; but I rather doubt it.

[*And as she wept...stooped...sepulchre.*] How long Mary wept,
after she was left alone, we are left to conjecture. Probably
not very long. At last it came into her mind to stoop down
and look into the grave, through the small door or opening
against which the stone had been rolled. It is worth noticing
that we are not told that she had either entered, or looked into
the sepulchre, before. Up to this time apparently she had
only heard the report of Peter and John. Now, left alone, she
probably felt a natural curiosity and anxiety to see with
her own eyes what they had reported, and so, in the middle of
her weeping, she stooped down and looked in, and at once saw
a wondrous sight.

I think Mary's case teaches us that heart is of more value in
God's sight than intellect. Those who feel most and love most
get most privileges. The more we love, the more we are like
to Christ.

12 —[*And seeth two angels...white...sitting. etc.*] The incident here
recorded is very remarkable and interesting. Mary saw figures
in white sitting inside the grave. They evidently looked like
men, but they were in reality angels,—two of those mysterious
ministering spirits whom the Bible teaches us God is pleased
to employ on great occasions. An angel announced the coming
birth of John Baptist and of Christ himself. Angels told the
shepherds that Christ was born. Angels ministered to our Lord
after the temptation, and an angel strengthened him in Gethsemane. And now also angels appeared in the day of our Lord's
resurrection. They first announced that He was born, and
they again, after thirty-three years, announced that He was
risen.

The whole subject of angels is very deep and mysterious,
and one about which we must beware of holding anything that
is not revealed. But the case before us teaches one or two
wonderful things, which we should do well to remember.
These angels evidently came and went away, appeared and
disappeared, after a manner supernatural, invisible, and inexplicable to our minds. It is clear that angels were at the tomb,
when the party of women arrived there, after Mary Magdalene
had run to tell Peter and John. It is equally clear that they
were not to be seen, when Peter and John ran to the grave on
hearing Mary's report. Not one word do we read of their seeing angels. Yet it is equally clear that when Mary Magdalene

looked in, after Peter and John went away, she saw two angels and talked with them. These are very deep things. They prove plainly that the angels of God appear and disappear, are visible or invisible, instantaneously and supernaturally, according as God commissions them. In short they are beings of a totally different nature to our own, and are in all the conditions of their constitution totally unlike us. For anything we know, they were in the tomb when Peter and John inspected it, but at that moment were invisible. For anything we know, they are now very near us every minute of our existence, and doing God's will concerning us, though we are utterly unaware of their presence. All this no doubt is very mysterious, and past the power of man to explain and comprehend. One thing, however, is very certain. Neither here nor elsewhere do we ever find the slightest warrant in Scripture for praying to angels, any more than to dead saints, or for giving them the smallest portion of worship, as if they were divine. Like ourselves, after all, they are only God's creatures.

The expression " in white," means literally " in white robes or garments." It is an adjective and we are left to supply the substantive. The Holy Ghost here abstains from telling us the precise fashion of apparel which these angels wore. The garment worn by the angel mentioned in Mark, at the resurrection, was a long stole or flowing robe. (Mark xvi. 5.) It is worth noticing that " white " was the color of the Lord's raiment in the transfiguration, and which is the color in which the angels always seem to have appeared. It need hardly be said that the color is symbolical of that perfect purity and freedom from defilement, which is the character of the inhabitants of heaven. It will be the garment of the saved souls in glory. (Rev. iii. 4 ; vii. 9.)

The attitude in which the angels were seen by Mary deserves attention. " Sitting one at the head and the other at the feet," where our Lord's body had lain, they would seem to have been placed there by God as watchmen and guards over the sacred body of our Lord, during the time He was in the grave. It is written, " He shall give His angels charge over Thee." (Psalm xci. 11.)

Some have thought that the position of the angels points to that of the Cherubim, who sat on the two ends of the mercy-seat, over the ark, with their faces toward each other. (Exod. xxv. 20 ; 2 Chron. iii. 13.)

Bengel thinks that this " sitting " was meant to intimate that their work was done. This seems to me doubtful, because angels need no rest.

Cyril thinks that the attitude of the two angels was meant to show Mary, that our Lord's body had been safely guarded by them, and that no one could have stolen it away against their consent. If one angel could slay 180,000 of Sennacherib's army, what could two do ?

Andrews observes, " We learn that between the angels there was no striving for places. He that sat at the feet was as well content with his place, as he that sat at the head. We should learn from their example. With us both angels would have been at the head, and never a one at the feet. With us none would be at the feet by his good will: we must be head-angels all ! "

13 —[*And they say unto her, Woman, why, etc.*] The address of the angels to Mary is that of gentle and kind inquiry. We cannot doubt that they knew well why she wept. They ask the question in order to stir up in her mind self-inquiry, as to whether she had cause to weep or not. " What is the reason of this excessive lamentation ? Search your own heart. Are you quite sure that this empty tomb does not show that you ought to be rejoicing ? "

Mary's reply to the angels is almost word for word what she had told Peter and John, only in the singular number. It shows plainly that the one thing that weighed on her mind was the disappearance of our Lord's body, and her ignorance what had become of it. Of His resurrection she evidently had no idea at present. Her only thought was that his body was dead, that it had been taken away, and that she wanted to know where it was. To this one notion she sticks, and not even the appearance of angels can make her give it up. And yet the good woman must have often heard our Lord foretell His death and resurrection. How slow we are to give up long-standing prejudices ! How backward to receive truths which contradict our little private systems of religion !

It should be observed that Mary told Peter and John that " the Lord " was taken away. When she speaks to the angels here, she says, " My Lord." In both cases she speaks indefinitely of " they," without indicating whom she means.

The calmness of manner with which Mary speaks to these two angels can hardly fail to strike us. She cannot have supposed that they were two men only, whether enemies or friends. The mere fact that Peter and John had not seen them in the grave, must surely have shown her that they were angels. Yet she answers their question without hesitation, like one who feared nothing in her anxiety about her Lord. May we not however consider that a belief in the reality and ministry of angels was far more common among Jews than it is among Christians ? They perhaps believed too much about them. It may be feared that we go into the opposite extreme, and believe too little.

Andrews remarks on Mary's needless weeping, " All was in error : tears of grief,—but false grief, imagining that to be

which was not, and Him to be dead which was alive. She
weeps, because she finds the grave empty, which, God forbid she
should have found full, for then Christ must have been dead
still, and there would be no resurrection. And this case of
Mary Magdalene is our case oftentimes. It is the error of our
conceit to weep when we have no cause, and to joy when we
have as little. False joys and false sorrows, false hopes and
false fears, this life of ours is full of. God help us!"

14 —[*And when...turned...back...saw Jesus standing.*] Why Mary
turned back at this moment we are not told. I feel no doubt
there was some reason. The Greek words are very emphatical : "She turned to the things or places behind her." (*a*) It
may be that she turned away from the questioners, as not caring to continue conversation with them. (*b*) It may be that she
heard a footstep behind her, and turned to see who it was. (*c*) It
may be that the shadow of some one behind her fell on the entrance to the tomb. The sun would be in the east, and if the
tomb faced that way, its horizontal rays would throw the
shadow of any person behind her on the tomb. (*d*) It may be
that she observed some gesture or motion on the part of the
angels with whom she was talking, which told her that some
one was behind her. Who can tell but these holy spirits, who
doubtless recognized the Lord, rose respectfully from their sitting position, as soon as they saw Jesus appear. I like this
last solution best, for my own part. I cannot for a moment
suppose that the angels would remain sitting motionless, when
Jesus appeared. And I believe that Mary, as she talked with
them, detected at once by their altered manner, that there was
some one behind her. This it was that made her " turn herself
back." Such little touches give a wonderful life and reality to
the whole narrative, in my judgment.

Chrysostom observes, " While Mary was speaking, Christ
suddenly appearing behind her, struck the angels with awe ;
and they, beholding their Ruler, showed immediately by their
bearing, their look, their movements, that they saw the Lord.
This drew the woman's attention, and caused her to turn."

The same view is taken by Athanasius, Theophylact, Brentius,
Gerhard, and Andrews.

[*And knew not that it was Jesus.*] There are but three ways
in which we can explain Mary not recognizing Christ at once.
(*a*) She was weeping bitterly, and her eyes were dim with tears.
This, however, seems very improbable. (*b*) It was not broad
day-light yet, and it was too dusky to distinguish any one.
This is Cyril's view; but it can hardly be correct, considering
all that had already occurred this Sunday morning. (*c*) Her
eyes were holden supernaturally, like those of the disciples
walking to Emmaus, so that she did not distinguish the figure
before her to be that of our Lord. This appears to me by far
the most likely solution, miraculous as the circumstance cer-

tainly was. But the condition of our Lord's risen body was altogether different from that of His body before crucifixion. We cannot pretend to explain in the least where He was, and what He was doing in the intervals between His various appearances, during the forty days before His ascension. We need not therefore hesitate to believe that He could assume such an appearance, that even a disciple like Mary did not recognize Him at first, or that He could cause her eyes to be unable to distinguish Him, even when close to her.

After all, what a striking emblem this little incident supplies of the spiritual experience of hundreds of Christ's believing people even at this very day. How many are ever mourning and sorrowing, and have no comfort in their religion, while Christ is close to them. But they do not know it, and, like Mary, go on weeping.

15 —[*Jesus saith... Why weepest thou...seekest thou.*] The first question that Jesus asked of Mary was precisely the same that the angels had asked. " Woman, why art thou weeping ? Art thou quite sure that thou art right to weep over this empty grave, and oughtest not rather to rejoice ? "—The second question was even more searching than the first. " Whom seekest thou ? Who is this person that thou art seeking among the dead ? Hast thou not forgotten that He whom thou seekest is one who has power to take life again, and who predicted that He would rise ? "—I must think that in both these questions there was a gentle latent reproof intended for this holy woman. Faithful and loving as she was, she had too much forgotten her Master's teaching about His death and resurrection. These questions were meant to rouse her to a recollection of things often said in her hearing. Of course our Lord knew perfectly well why she was weeping, and whom she was seeking. He needed not to ask her. He asked for her benefit rather than His own information. But excessive grief has an absorbing and stupefying effect on the mind and memory. Mary could think of nothing but that her Lord's body was gone, and this swallowed up all her thoughts.

[*She supposing Him, etc.*] Here we see what Mary's first thought was, when she heard a strange voice, and saw a strange figure. She catches at the idea that this person may be the keeper of the garden in which Joseph's sepulchre was, and that, having probably been keeping watch over the garden all night, he may know what had become of her Master's body, or may even have removed it himself. " Sir," she says, " If thou art the person who has taken away my Lord out of the tomb, only tell me where thou hast carried His body, and I will take Him away."—Once more we see that this holy woman could only think of her Master as one dead, and that her one absorbing idea was how she could recover His corpse and do it honor. As for His resurrection and victory over death, she seems utterly unable to get hold of it at present. Wonderful is it to see how much of Christ's teaching was apparently thrown away on His disciples, and clean forgotten! Ministers who complain of the ignorance of their hearers, should learn patience, when they mark the imperfect knowledge of Christ's own followers.

The Greek word rendered "Sir," in this verse, might have been equally correctly rendered "Lord." But it is rendered "Sir," in like manner, in the conversation between our Lord and the Samaritan woman, in the fourth chapter of this Gospel. In both cases it is a term of respect, such as a Jewish woman would address to a man.

It is noteworthy that Mary does not name her Master to the supposed gardener. She simply says "Him,"—"if thou hast borne *Him* hence, I will take *Him* away." It is the language of one so absorbed in the thought of our Lord, that she thinks it needless to name Him ; and assumes, as a matter of course, that the gardener will understand whom she means.

It is noteworthy that Mary talks of "taking Him away." How one weak woman like her could suppose that she was able to lift and carry away the dead body of a man, we cannot of course understand. It is clear that she either meant (*a*) that she would soon find friends who would remove the body, or else (*b*) that she spoke hurriedly, fervently, impulsively, and passionately, without reflecting on what she was saying. I incline to think the latter view is the correct one.

Luther, quoted by Besser, remarks on this verse, "Mary's heart was so filled up with Christ and thoughts about Christ, that besides Him she neither hears nor sees anything. She is not frightened at the sight of angels. She addresses Christ abruptly, supposing Him to be the gardener ; and if he has taken Him away, she is ready to carry Him back to the sepulchre."

Andrews observes, "*Him* is enough with love. Who knows not who it is, though we never tell His name, nor say a word more?"

16.—[*Jesus saith unto her, Mary, etc.*] We are here told how our Lord at last revealed Himself to this faithful disciple, after her patience, love, and boldness had been fully proved. Little as she had shown herself able to understand the great truth of her Saviour's resurrection, she had at any rate shown that none loved Him more, or clung to Him more tenaciously, than she did. And she had her reward. One single word was enough to open her eyes, to let the whole truth shine in upon her mind, and to reveal the great fact that her Saviour was not dead but alive, and that He had won a victory over the grave.—Speaking in His usual well-known voice, our Lord addressed her by her name,—the name by which, no doubt, He had often addressed her before. That single word touched a spring, as it were, and opened her eyes in a moment. Need we doubt that at once the whole world seemed turned upside down to the astonished woman ; and that under the influence of such an amazing revulsion of feeling as that much-loved voice must have caused, her mind could only find expression in one passionate word—" Rabboni," or Master.

The expression, " turned herself," in this verse, is rather curious. We know, from the fourteenth verse, that Mary had already turned once from the grave, when Jesus appeared behind her. Here again we are told that she " turned herself." The simplest explanation seems to be, that when she did not recognize the person who spoke to her, and thought He had been the gardener, she partially turned away, as a woman naturally would from a strange man, and hardly looked at Him, while she spoke of taking the body away. But the moment the voice of Jesus sounded in her ears, she turned again directly to Him, aad made some movement towards Him, as she uttered the cry, " Rabboni."—Thus there were three movements : first, a turning round to see who was behind her ; second, a partial turning away, when she heard a voice she did not recognize ; and finally, a quick, passionate turning round entirely, when the well-known voice of her. Master said, " Mary." So at least it appears to me.

Chrysostom says, " It seems to me that after having said, ' Where hast thou laid Him ? ' she turned to the angels to ask why they were astonished ; and that then Christ, by calling her by name, turned her back to Himself from them, and revealed Himself by His voice."

The boundless compassion of our Lord Jesus Christ to His believing people comes out wonderfully in this verse. He can be touched with the feeling of our infirmities. He knows how weak our bodily frame is, and how much excessive sorrow can unnerve and stupefy our minds. He can pass over much darkness of understanding, much slowness of comprehension, when He sees real, genuine, hearty, bold, persevering, thorough love to Himself and His Person. We see this prominently brought out in His dealing with Mary Magdalene, when He revealed Himself to her. He graciously pardons her forgetfulness of His oft-repeated declaration that He would rise again after His death, pities her deep sorrow, and abundantly rewards her love. These things are written for our learning. Jesus never changes. What He was, when He revealed Himself to Mary Magdalene, He is at this day.

Rabboni, according to Parkhurst, " is nearly of the same import as Rabbi. St. John explains both by the same word,— teacher. But Lightfoot and others say it was a term of higher respect." Parkhurst thinks it is formed from the Chaldee, and includes the idea, " MY Master."

17 —[*Jesus saith...Touch Me not...my Father.*] This saying of our Lord is undeniably a very " deep thing," and the real meaning

of it is a point which has greatly perplexed commentators. I
suspect it is one of those things which will never be fully settled
until the Lord comes. In the meantime we must be content to
make humble conjectures. It will clear our way to remember
that our Lord could not possibly mean by saying, " Touch Me
not," that there was anything sinful or wrong in Mary touching
His risen body. The mere fact that a few minutes after this
interview with Mary, he allowed the other women who had
been to the grave to " hold Him by the feet" (Matt. xxviii. 9),
completely settles that point. Moreover, within a week after this
very day, He says to Thomas, " Reach hither thy hand and thrust
it into my side." (John xx. 27.) This alone entirely contradicts
the notion that our Lord's body might not be touched before
His ascension. But having cleared the way negatively, the
question yet remains, " What did our Lord mean positively ? "

In order to understand the meaning of " Touch Me not," we
must try to realize the state of mind in which Mary Magdalene
was, when our Lord revealed Himself to her. A very slight
knowledge of human nature, and especially of woman's nature,
will tell us that the sudden discovery that Jesus was alive and
standing before her, would throw her into a violent state of
excitement, and produce an immense revulsion of feeling, from
deep despondency to extravagant joy. May we not well believe that under the influence of this excitement, this holy woman might be more demonstrative than was seemly, and might
exhibit her feelings by actions and gestures that our Lord saw
it absolutely needful to repress ? Can we not understand that
a warm-hearted, impulsive Jewish woman, holy and pure-
minded as she certainly was, would be likely to cast herself at
our Lord's feet, to say the least, in a passionate ecstasy of delight, and to hold them fast, kissing and embracing them, like
the woman in Simon's house, as if she would never let them go ?
—And can we not well understand that our wise Master, who
knew all hearts, thought it good to check and repress her, and
therefore, for her soul's benefit, and not unkindly, said, " Touch
Me not."—Nothing would be more likely to calm the good woman's mind, and to recall her to a reverent sense of what was
due to herself and to her Lord, than this prohibition to " touch."
Such is my view of this wonderful expression. It is to my
mind a very suggestive one, and deserves the especial attention
of ministers, in carrying on their private pastoral work. But
I forbear. Let it however never be forgotten (and I desire to
speak with the utmost reverence and delicacy), that when our
Lord allowed the women, mentioned by St. Matthew (Matt.
xxviii. 9), to " hold Him by the feet," there were several women
present together, and some of them mothers and not young.
When, on the contrary, He said to Mary Magdalene, " Touch
Me not," He spoke to one who in all probability was a young
woman, and He and she were alone !

The Greek word we render " touch," according to Liddell

and Scott's Lexicon, frequently means "fasten oneself to, cling to, hang on by, lay hold of, or grasp." Homer constantly uses the word in this sense. This deserves special notice. Schleusner and Parkhurst agree with Liddell and Scott.

The words, "for I am not yet ascended to my Father," are even more difficult than " Touch Me not;" and the connection between the two sayings is the hardest knot of all the sentence.

(a) Some think that the sense is, "I have not yet ascended to my Father. Till I håve ascended and taken my seat at His right hand, my work as your Saviour is not perfect and complete. Do not therefore touch Me and fasten upon Me, as if you would fain keep Me upon earth forever, now that I have risen again. Remember that my ascension is as much a part of my great work of redemption as my crucifixion and resurrection. I have not yet ascended. Do not, therefore, behave as though you wished to detain Me here below, and never to part with Me again."

(b) Some think that the sense is, "I am not yet ascending to my Father. I shall not ascend for forty days. There will, therefore, be abundant time for seeing, touching, hearing, and conferring with Me. Do not therefore now waste precious time on this eventful morning by embracing my feet, and demonstrating your affection to my person. Rather rise, and lose no time in going to my brethren, and telling them that I am risen. Think of others; and do not occupy yourself, as you are disposed to do, in touching my feet and gratifying your own feelings. Natural as it is, there is other work to do now. Go and do it, and do not linger here. Touch Me not." This is the view of Beza, Brentius, and Bishop Hall.

(c) Some think, as Melancthon, that our Lord had in view His second advent and kingdom, when all who have known and loved Him on earth, shall at length dwell with Him in holy familiarity, and go out from His presence no more. Melancthon says, "It is as if Christ would say, Then shall you touch Me, when I have ascended to my Father : that is, when I shall bring thee and all my Church to the Father at the last day. Another kingdom and another life remains yet to be given, in which you shall enjoy fellowship with Me and my Father."

I honestly confess that I find it almost impossible to say which of the three opinions I have here described deserves most attention. If I must decide, I incline to prefer the second one, and I think it is more in keeping with the latter part of the verse. The weakest point of this view is the future sense which it puts on the words, "I am not ascended." The Greek word is in the perfect tense, and the perfect is undoubtedly used sometimes in the sense of a future. (Compare Rom. xiv. 23, John xvii. 10; and see Telf's Greek Grammar, vol. ii., p.

65 ; and Winer's Grammar, p. 288. Clark's edition.) But it is rather awkward that "I ascend" comes immediately after in the present tense. The reader must decide for himself which view he prefers.

Chrysostom says, "Methinks Mary wished still to converse with Jesus as before, and in her joy perceived nothing great in Him, although He had become far more excellent in the flesh. To lead her therefore from this idea, and that she might speak to Him with awe (for neither with the disciples doth He henceforth appear so familiar as before), He raiseth her thoughts, that she should give more reverent heed to Him. To have said, ' Approach Me not as you did before, for matters are not in the same state ; nor shall I henceforth be with you in the same way,' would have been harsh and high-sounding. But the saying, ' I am not yet ascended to my Father,' though not painful to hear, was the same thing. For by saying, ' I am not yet ascended,' He showeth that He hasteth and passeth thither, and that it was not meet that one about to depart thither, and no longer to converse with men, should be looked on with the same feelings as before."

Augustine says, " There is a spiritual meaning latent here.— Either this is so spoken, 'Touch Me not, for I am not yet ascended,' that the woman is a figure of the Church of the Gentiles, which did not believe on Christ until He was ascended unto the Father ;—or else Jesus would have men so believe in Him, or touch Him spiritually, as knowing that Himself and the Father are one.—Mary might believe in such a way as if she thought Him unequal to the Father, which thought is forbidden to her. ' Touch Me not ' : *i. e.*, ' Do not believe in Me in such wise as thou art yet minded in thy thoughts of Me : let not thy perception reach only to the thing I was made for thee, without passing beyond to that by which thou wast made. I am not yet ascended to my Father. Then shalt thou touch Me, when thou believest Me to be God not unequal to the Father."

Calvin says, " The meaning of these words is, that Christ's state of resurrection would not be full and complete, until He should sit down in heaven at the right hand of the Father. Therefore Mary did wrong in satisfying herself with having nothing more than the half of His resurrection, and desiring only to enjoy His presence in the world."

Lightfoot says, " These words relate to what Christ had spoken formerly about sending the Comforter, and that He would not leave them comfortless, but would come to them. Christ says to Mary, ' I must first ascend to my Father, before I can bestow those things upon you which I have promised. Do not therefore touch Me, and *detain* Me upon any expectation of that kind. Rather wait for my ascension, and go and tell the same thing to my brethren for their encouragement."

Poole says, " The best opinion seems to be the opinion of those who think our Saviour saw Mary too fond, as if she thought He had been raised up to such a converse with them as He had before His death. This error is all He tasks her of, not forbidding any kind of touching, so as to satisfy herself He was truly risen, but restraining any gross conception.—He reminded Mary that He was about to ascend to His Father, though He had not yet ascended, and was therefore not to be enjoyed by them with so much freedom and familiarity as before."

Bishop Hall says, " There may be a kind of carnality in spiritual notions. " If I have known Christ after the flesh, from henceforth I know Him no more.' That Thou livedst here, my Saviour, in this shape, that color, this stature, that habit, I should be glad to know : nothing that concerns Thee can be unuseful. Could I say, here Thou satest, here Thou layest, here Thou wast crucified, here Thou wast buried, I should with much content see and recount those ceremonials of Thy presence. But if I shall so fasten my thoughts on them, as not to look higher, to the spiritual part of these achievements, to the power and issue of Thy resurrection, I am none the better.' "

Rollock says, " The meaning in effect is this. It is not time for thee to touch Me now, till that time I be in glory, and then touch Me by the arm of faith as much as thou canst or mayest. Ye must consider that she was too much addicted to His bodily presence. She thought He should have remained and dwelt on earth as He did before. Therefore He would not let her come near Him, until He instructed her of a spiritual touching, and that He was not to stay here, but to dwell with His Father in heaven.

" Mark this lesson. Some men love the Lord entirely, and yet when they come to His service they fail : for such is the grossness of our nature that we cannot incline to that spiritual service which He chiefly requires. Popery is full of this grossness. They can do nothing if they have not His carnal presence, either in Himself, or in a stock or stone, or in a piece of bread, and therefore they draw a bodily presence of Him in the sacrament. All their religion is earthly,—no grace, no spirit in it. But did the Lord accept that gross service that Mary offered ? I am certain He loved Mary better than the Pope and all his priests ; yet well as He liked Mary, He liked not her service. He says to her, Touch Me not ! The Lord keep us from gross service, and make us touch Him by faith."

Andrews says, " The most we can make is that here Mary failed in somewhat. Not that she did it in any immodest or indecent manner. God forbid ! Never think of that. But she was only a little too forward, it may be : not with the due respect that was meet."—" I tell you plainly I do not like her Rabboni. It was no Easter-day salutation ; it should have been some better term, expressing more reverence."—" The touch was not the right touch, and all for want of expressing more regard ; not for want of reverence at all, but of reverence enough."—" It is no excuse to say it was all out of love. Never lay it upon that. Love, Christ loves well. But love, if it be right, doth nothing uncomely, keeps decorum, forgets not what belongs to duty and decency, carries itself accordingly." —" A strange kind of love, when for very love to Christ we care not how we use Him, or carry ourselves toward Him. Which, being Mary's case, she heard and heard quickly. Touch Me not,—you are not now in case till you shall have learned to touch after a more regardful manner.

Sibbes says, " Mary was too much addicted to Christ's bodily presence. It is this that men have labored for from the beginning of the world,—to be too much addicted to present things and to sense. They will worship Christ ; but they must have a picture before them. They will adore Christ ; but they must bring His body down to a piece of bread : they must have a presence. And so instead of raising their hearts to God and Christ in a heavenly manner, they pull down God and Christ to them. And, therefore, saith Christ, ' Touch Me not in that manner : it is not with Me as it was before.' We must take heed of mean and base conceits of Christ."

Sherlock, in his " Trial of the Witnesses," says, " The natural sense of this place is this : Mary Magdalene, upon seeing Jesus, fell at His feet and laid hold on them, and held them as if she never meant to let them go. Then Christ said to her, " Touch Me not, or hang not about Me now. You will have other opportunities of seeing Me, for I go not yet to my Father. Lose no time then, but go quickly with my message to my brethren."

West, on the Resurrection, says, " I take Christ's forbidding Mary to touch Him, to have been meant as a signification of His intention to see her and the disciples again ; just as in ordinary life, when one friend says to another, ' Do not take leave for I am not going yet,' he means to let him know that he purposes to see him again before he sets out on his journey."

Lampe mentions a strange view of " Touch Me not " maintained by Bauldry, a German professor. He would put a full stop at " not," and place it first in the sentence, rendering it thus, " No ! I am not the gardener. Touch Me, and see that I am Thy Saviour risen." He also mentions a view held by many, that it means, " Do not try whether I am risen by touching Me. It is I myself." Both views, however, seem very improbable.

Paulus, the German theologian, maintains the monstrous notion that our Lord meant, " Do not lay a finger on Me, because my wounds still smart." This is simply ridiculous, to say the least.

Hengstenberg says, " The reason of the prohibition must be sought in the personal character of Mary, and in the passionate nature of the touch which sprang from that character. She thought that the limits which had formerly existed between herself and the Lord (*the old style of confidence is a very incorrect idea*) were, now that the Saviour had passed into another form of existence, removed, and that she might now give free course to her feelings without fearing the admixture of anything human in her sentiment toward her Lord. But her Lord repelled her : Touch Me not."

Wordsworth says, " The term (in the Greek) indicates not only a prohibition of a particular act, but forbids a habit : *i. e.*, of clinging to Him with a bodily touch. And the words, ' I have not ascended,' contain a precept concerning the time when the habit of touching Christ may be exercised. He is to be touched after He has ascended,— that is, He is then to be truly touched, when He is beyond the reach of the bodily touch. And one of the purposes of His absence and His ascension into heaven was to elicit and exercise that touch,—the touch of faith."

Burgon remarks what a strange thing it is, that " both the old world and the new should have begun with the same prohibition, *Touch not*."

[*But go...my brethren...say unto them.*] This sentence is strikingly full of wisdom, tender thoughtfulness, and kindness. Wisely our Lord summons Mary Magdalene to an act of duty to others. He bids her not spend time in demonstrations of affection, but arise and be useful.—Thoughtfully our Lord's first consideration is for His poor scattered disciples. Weak and erring as they had been, He still loved them, and at once sends them a message. He did not mean to cast them off, or forget them.—Kindly He calls them " my brethren." All was pardoned and forgiven. He still regarded them as His dear brethren,—risen, conqueror over the grave as He was,—and would have them look on Him as an elder brother. This is the first time our Lord ever called the disciples " brethren."

Bucer thinks that " my brethren " in this place really means " my brethren according to the flesh : " *i. e.*, James and others, whose faith was weaker perhaps than that of the other Apostles. But the vast majority of commentators see in the expression nothing of the kind, and regard it only as a term of affection applied to all the Apostles. Calvin properly refers us to Psalm xxii. 22 : " I will declare thy name unto my brethren." See also Heb. ii. 11.

Andrews remarks that the words " my brethren " was " a word to be touched and taken hold of. It was so once when Benhadad's servant laid hold on the word of the King of Israel, ' He is my brother.' " (1 Kings xx. 32, 33.) He adds that it implied identity of nature, and identity of love and affection after the resurrection, and no change.

Let us mark what a strong proof we have here of the duty of telling others the good news of the Gospel. The very first work that a risen Christ proposes to the first disciple to whom He revealed Himself is the work of telling others. It was a deep saying of the four leprous men : " This day is a day of good tidings, and we hold our peace : if we tarry till the morning light, some mischief will come upon us." (2 Kings vii. 9.)

Cyril remarks what an honor was put on woman, when a woman was commissioned to be the first person to proclaim the tidings of the resurrection.

[*I ascend...my Father...your God.*] The message which our Lord desires Mary to carry to His disciples is remarkable. He does not bid her say " I have risen," but "I ascend." He would evidently have them understand that His resurrection was only a step towards His ascension, and that He did not rise again in order to tarry with them upon earth, but in order to go up to heaven as a conqueror, and sit down at God's right hand as their forerunner, representative, priest, advocate, and friend. The message is clearly elliptical. It is as though our Lord said, " Say unto them that I have risen from the dead, and that I am soon about to ascend into heaven, to Him who is my Father and my God, and their Father and their God also."

When our Lord dwells on His ascension more than His resurrection, it seems to me that He names it as the great conclusion and accomplishment of the work He came to do, and the necessary consequence of His rising again. It is as though He said, " My work is finished, my battle is won, and I shall not be much longer with you in the world. Get ready to receive my last instructions."

Calvin says, " Christ forbids the Apostles to fix their whole attention on His resurrection viewed simply in itself, but exhorts them to proceed further, until they come to the spiritual kingdom, the heavenly glory, and God Himself."

Andrews remarks, " We ourselves had better lie still in our graves, better never rise, than rise and rising not ascend."

Flavel remarks, " If Christ had not ascended, He could not have interceded, as He now does in heaven for us. And do but take away Christ's intercession, and you starve the hope of the saints."

When our Lord speaks of God as " My Father and my God," He seems as usual, to point to the close and intimate union which He always declared to exist between Himself and the First Person in the Trinity. " The God and Father of our Lord Jesus Christ" (1 Peter i. 3), is a kindred expression.—He does not, we should observe, say, I ascend unto " our Father," etc., but "my Father and your Father." He thus shows that there is a certain distinction between His relation to the Father and ours. Believers are not naturally sons of God: they only become so by grace, by adoption, and by virtue of union with Christ. Christ, on the contrary, is in His nature the Son of God by an eternal generation.

When our Lord speaks of "Your Father and your God," He seems to me to speak with a special view to the consolation of His disciples. It is as though He said, "Do not be troubled because I go away. He to whom I go is *your* Father and *your* God as well as mine. All that He is to me, the Head, He is also to you, the members."

It may well be doubted, when we read this verse, whether Christians, as a rule, assign sufficient importance to the great truth of Christ's ascension into heaven. Let us never forget that if our Lord had not ascended into heaven, and sat down on the right hand of God, His resurrection would have been but of little value. It is His going into heaven itself, to appear in the presence of God for us, that is the great secret of Christian comfort. It is not for nothing that St. Paul answers the question, "Who is he that condemneth?" by saying, "Christ hath died,—yea, rather hath risen again, who is even at the right hand of God, who also maketh intercession for us." (Rom. viii. 34.) The death, the resurrection, the ascension, the intercession of Christ, are four great facts that should never be separated.

It ought not to be forgotten that there seems to be a close connection between the ascension of Christ and the outpouring of the Holy Ghost. This, at least, seems to be the meaning of the text in the Psalms, quoted by St. Paul: "When He had ascended up on high, He led captivity captive, and received gifts for men." (Psalm lxviii. 18. Ephes. iv. 8.)

18 —[*Mary Magdalene came and told, etc.*] In this verse we see the effect that our Lord's words had on the loving disciple to whom He first appeared. She meekly accepts the reproof of her over-forward zeal to touch Him, without gainsaying or answering again. Like a good servant, she proceeds at once to do what she is told. The use of the present tense shows the promptness of her obedience. The Greek words would be more literally rendered, "Mary Magdalene cometh, telling or declaring to the disciples that she has seen the Lord, and that He has said these things to her,"—that He has given her this message to carry to them, and that He calls them His brethren. The use of the participle makes the words sound as if she went open-mouthed, telling every disciple as she went, and hardly stopping to sit down, till she had told every one whom she could find in Jerusalem. We need not doubt that the first house she went to was that where Peter and John lodged, and one of the first persons to whom she told the joyful news was

the mother of our Lord. A few minutes after she departed on her joyful errand—running, we need not doubt, as she had run before,—our Lord appeared to the other women, as is recorded by St. Matthew. (Matt. xxviii. 9.)

Brentius remarks what honor this passage puts on women. Sin came into the world by Eve, a woman. Yet God, in mercy, ordered things so that of a woman Christ was born, to a woman Christ first appeared after He rose from the dead, and a woman was the first to carry the news of His resurrection. He quaintly says, " Jesus made Mary Magdalene an Apostle to the Apostles."

Cecil remarks, " Singular honor is reserved for solitary faith. Mary has the first personal manifestation of Christ after His resurrection. She is the first witness of this most important and illustrious fact, and the first messenger of it to His disciples."

JOHN XX 19—23

19 Then the same day at evening, being the first *day* of the week, when the doors were shut where the disciples were assembled for fear of the Jews, came Jesus and stood in the midst, and saith unto them, Peace *be* unto you.

20 And when he had so said, he shewed unto them *his* hands and his side. Then were the disciples glad, when they saw the Lord.

21 Then said Jesus to them again, Peace be unto you : as *my* Father hath sent me, even so send I you.

22 And when he had said this, he breathed on *them*, and saith unto them, Receive ye the Holy Ghost:

23 Whose soever sins ye remit, they are remitted unto them; *and* whose soever *sins* ye retain, they are retained.

THE verses we have now read contain things hard to be understood. Like all the events which followed our Lord's resurrection, there is much in the facts before us which is mysterious, and requires reverent handling. Our Lord's actions, in suddenly appearing among the disciples when the doors were closed, and in breathing upon them, might soon draw us into unprofitable speculation. It is easy, in such cases, to darken counsel by words without knowledge. We shall find it safer and wiser to confine our attention to points which are plain and instructive.

We should observe, for one thing, the *remarkable language with which our Lord greeted the apostles, when*

He first met them after His resurrection. Twice over he addressed them with the kindly words, "Peace be unto you." We may dismiss as untenable, in all probability, the cold and cautious suggestion, that this was nothing better than an unmeaning phrase of courtesy. He who "spake as never man spake," said nothing without meaning. He spoke, we may be sure, with special reference to the state of mind of the eleven apostles, with special reference to the events of the last few days, and with special reference to their future ministry. "Peace" and not blame,—"peace" and not fault-finding,—"peace" and not rebuke,—was the first word which this little company heard from their Master's lips, after He left the tomb.

It was meet, and right, and fitting, that it should be so, and in full harmony with things that had gone before. "Peace on earth" was the song of the heavenly host, when Christ was born. Peace and rest of soul, was the general subject that Christ continually preached for three years. Peace, and not riches, had been the great legacy which He had left with the eleven the night before His crucifixion. Surely it was in full keeping with all the tenor of our Lord's dealings, that, when He revisited His little company of disciples after His resurrection, His first word should be "Peace." It was a word that would soothe and calm their minds.

Peace, we may safely conclude, was intended by our Lord to be the key-note to the Christian ministry. That same peace which was so continually on the lips of the Master, was to be the grand subject of the teaching of His disciples. Peace between God and man through the precious blood of atonement,—peace between man and man through the infusion of grace and charity,—to spread such peace as this was to be the work of the Church. Any religion, like that of Mahomet, who made converts with the sword, is not from above but from beneath. Any form of Christianity which burns men at the stake, in order to promote its own success, carries about with it the stamp of an apostasy. That is the truest and best religion which does most to spread real, true peace.

We should observe, for another thing, in these verses, *the remarkable evidence which our Lord supplied of His own resurrection.* He graciously appealed to the senses of His trembling disciples. He showed them "His hands and His side." He bade them see with their own eyes, that He had a real material body, and that He was not a ghost or a spirit. "Handle Me and see," were His words, according to St. Luke : "a spirit hath not flesh and bone, as ye see Me have." Great indeed was the condescension of our blessed Master, in thus coming down to the feeble faith of the eleven Apostles ! But great also was the principle which He established for the use of His Church in every age, until He returns. That principle is, that our Master requires us to believe nothing is contrary to our senses. Things *above* our reason we must expect to find in a religion that comes from God, but not things contrary to reason.

Let us lay firm hold on this great principle, and never forget to use it. Specially let us take care that we use it, in estimating the effect of the sacraments and the work of the Holy Ghost. To require people to believe that men have the quickening power of the Holy Spirit, when our eyes tell us they are living in habitual carelessness and sin, or that the bread and wine in the Lord's Supper are Christ's real body and blood, when our senses tell us they are still bread and wine,—this is to require more belief than Christ ever required of His disciples. It is to require that which is flatly contradictory to reason and common sense. Such requisitions

Christ never made. Let us not try to be wiser than our Lord.

We should observe, lastly, in these verses, *the remarkable commission which our Lord conferred upon His eleven Apostles.* We are told that He said, "As my Father hath sent Me, even so send I you. And when He had said this, He breathed on them, and saith unto them, Receive ye the Holy Ghost: whose soever sins ye remit, they are remitted unto them; and whose soever sins ye retain, they are retained." It is vain to deny that the true sense of these solemn words has been for centuries a subject of controversy and dispute. It is useless perhaps to expect that the controversy will ever be closed. The utmost that we can hope to do with the passage is to supply a probable exposition.

It seems then highly probable that our Lord in this place solemnly commissioned His Apostles to go into all the world, and preach the Gospel as He had preached it. He also conferred on them the power of *declaring* with peculiar authority whose sins were forgiven, and whose sins were not forgiven. That this is precisely what the Apostles did is a simple matter of fact, which any one may verify for himself by reading the book of the Acts. When Peter proclaimed to the Jews, "Repent ye, and be converted,"—and when Paul declared at Antioch of Iconium,—"to you is the word of this salvation sent,"— "Through this man is preached the forgiveness of sins, and by Him all that believe are justified,"—they were doing what this passage commissioned the Apostles to do. They were opening with authority the door of salvation, and inviting with authority all sinners to enter in by it and be saved. (Acts iii. 19; xiii. 26—38.)

It seems, on the other hand, most improbable that our Lord intended in this verse to sanction the practice of private absolution, after private confession of sins.

Whatever some may please to say, there is not a single instance to be found in the Acts of any Apostle using such absolution after confession. Above all, there is not a trace in the two pastoral Epistles to Timothy and Titus, of such confession and absolution being recommended, or thought desirable. In short, whatever men may say about private ministerial absolution, there is not a single precedent for it in God's Word.

Let us leave the whole passage with a deep sense of the importance of the minister's office, when that office is duly exercised according to the mind of Christ. No higher honor can be imagined than that of being Christ's ambassadors, and proclaiming in Christ's name the forgiveness of sins to a lost world. But let us ever beware of investing the ministerial office with one jot more of power and authority than Christ conferred upon it. To treat ministers as being in any sense mediators between God and man, is to rob Christ of His prerogative, to hide saving truth from sinners, and to exalt ordained men to a position which they are totally unqualified to fill.

NOTES JOHN XX. 19—23

19 —[*Then the same day at evening, etc.*] This verse describes our Lord Jesus Christ's first appearance to the Apostles, in a body, after He rose from the dead. It took place in the evening of the same Sunday when He had appeared to Mary Magdalene in the morning. Between that morning and that evening He had already appeared three times,—once to the company of women returning from the sepulchre, as described by St. Matthew,—once to Simon Peter, as we are told by St. Luke and St. Paul,—and once to the two disciples walking to Emmaus. (Matt. xxviii. 9; Luke xxiv. 34; 1 Cor. xv. 5; Luke xxiv. 13, etc.) This, therefore, was the fifth appearance which our Lord graciously vouchsafed. Each of the five appearances, we should observe, was peculiar in its circumstances, and unlike the others. We need not wonder that this Sunday, from the earliest ages, was always marked by the Church as a day which ought to be had in remembrance, and kept with peculiar honor.

The beginning of the verse would be more literally rendered,

"When it was evening on that day, the first day of the week." The precise *hour* is not specified ; but, considering all things, it seems probable that it was after sunset, and when it was dark, in order to avoid observation.—The *cause* of the disciples assembling, we may reasonably suppose, was the tidings received from no less than four distinct sets of witnesses, that Jesus had risen from the dead, and was alive. It would have been strange indeed if they did not assemble on hearing such news.—The *place* where the disciples assembled is not mentioned. But at a time like the passover feast it would not be difficult to find some " upper room," where ten men might meet together. I can see no improbability in the supposition that the very room where the Lord's Supper was instituted on the previous Thursday evening, might be the same room where the disciples gathered together on Sunday night. The words of St. Mark incline me to think that the person to whom the " upper room " belonged was one of those Jews who were friendly to Christ, though they had not courage to confess Him openly. (Mark xiv. 13—15.)

That the " doors" should be " shut, where the disciples were assembled, for fear of the Jews," is a circumstance that need not surprise us. The Apostles might well regard their lives as being in imminent danger, when they remembered how their Master had just been treated. Moreover, the story of the guard placed round the sepulchre, that " the disciples had stolen the body of Jesus," might reasonably incline them to expect further ill-treatment themselves. They did their best therefore to avoid observation, and closed the doors of the room where they assembled after sunset.

Concerning the precise manner in which our Lord appeared to the disciples, there is no little difference of opinion. (*a*) Some think. as Calvin, and many of the divines of the seventeenth century, that He suddenly caused the doors to open, passed through them when open, and suddenly stood in the midst of the company assembled. (*b*) Some think, as Chrysostom, Cyril, Augustine, the Romanists, and nearly all Lutherans, that the doors continued fastened, and that our Lord miraculously appeared standing in the room where the disciples were, instantaneously, in a moment, and without notice. I do not know that it signifies much which view we take. *In either case a miracle was wrought.* Our Lord's risen body must evidently have had a power of moving from one place to another, and of being visible or invisible, as He thought fit, according to His good pleasure, after a manner that we cannot understand. In any case, we must carefully remember that it was a real, material body,—a body that could be touched, and felt, and seen, and handled, and yet a supernatural and peculiar body. With such a body it was as easy for our Lord to appear suddenly standing in the middle of the room, while the doors remained fastened, as it was to open the doors (as He did the

doors of Peter's prison), and to walk into the room, like another
man. To my own mind there is no proof positive either way,
and I must leave it to my readers to choose for themselves.
One thing alone we must not forget. Even if our Lord did appear in the room, without unfastening the doors, it is no proof
that He can be literally, and locally, and corporally present in
the Lord's Supper, under the forms of bread and wine. Moreover, it does not follow, because He could move from place to
place invisibly, that His body could ever be in more than one
place at one and the same time. When He rose from the dead,
He rose with a body of a far more spiritual kind than He had
before, but a body for all that which was a real human body,
and not a mere seeming and shadowy body, like that of a ghost
or a spirit.

The first words that our Lord spake to the disciples afford a
beautiful proof of His loving, merciful, tender, thoughtful,
pitiful, and compassionate spirit. He said, " Peace be unto
you." That expression, in my opinion, must on no account be
taken as a mere formal salutation, without meaning. It was
intended to reassure and cheer the minds of the disciples, by
exhibiting at once His mind towards them. Not a word of reproof, or rebuke, or fault-finding, or blame falls from our Lord's
lips, notwithstanding all their sad faint-heartedness and desertion on the preceding Thursday night. All is forgiven and forgotten. The very first word is " Peace." This was almost the
last word that our Lord had spoken on Thursday night before
He prayed : " These things I have spoken, that in Me ye might
have peace." (John xvi. 33.) This was the last legacy He had
left His disciples : " Peace I leave with you : my peace I give
unto you. Let not your hearts be troubled." (John xiv. 27.)
Can we doubt that this comfortable word would cheer and calm
the minds of the little company, when our Lord suddenly appeared ?—" Once more I stand among you : and once more I
proclaim peace ;—not excommunication, not rejection from my
friendship, not rebuke, but peace." We cannot realize the fulness of comfort which the word would supply, unless we bear
in mind the events of the last few days, and especially the conduct of the Apostles on the night before the crucifixion, when,
after loudly professing their faithfulness, they all " forsook Him
and fled."

The parallel account in St. Luke would lead us to conclude
that there were others present on this occasion beside the Apostles. He speaks of " Them that were with them." (Luke
xxiv. 33.)

20.—[*And when He had so said, etc.*] After speaking, our Lord
proceeded most graciously to supply tangible evidence that He
had really risen from the dead, and stood before His disciples
with a material living body. When it says He " showed them
His hands and side," we cannot doubt that He bade them touch
Him. In fact St. Luke, when describing this very same inter-

view, expressly records that our Lord said, " Behold my hands and my feet, that it is I myself : handle me, and see ; for a spirit hath not flesh and bones, as ye see Me have." (Luke xxiv. 39.)

The mention of the "hands and side" points clearly to the wounds made by the nails on the one, and by the spear in the other. Those wounds appeared visibly and unmistakably in His risen body, and our blessed Master was not ashamed of them. Even in the glory of heaven, according to Revelation, John saw Him appear as a " Lamb that had been slain." (Rev. v. 6.) I think we need not doubt that when He ascended up into heaven, those wounds went with Him, and are a perpetual witness to angels that He has actually suffered for man's sins. When we see His real presence in the day of His appearing, we shall see " the man Christ Jesus," and see the marks of His crucifixion. I give this however as my private opinion, and I think it is fair to say that many divines think differently. For instance, Calvin strongly holds that our Lord's " use of the wounds was only temporary, until the Apostles were fully convinced, and that His glorified body is without them." I cannot, however, agree with him. After a great victory, the scars of a conqueror are marks of honor.

Concerning the actual condition of our Lord's wounds it becomes us to speak reverently. A very slight acquaintance with surgery will tell us, of course, that a lacerated wound in the hand or foot, or a deep wound in the side inflicted on Friday, would naturally, to say the least, be very painful and inflamed on Sunday night. But we must carefully remember that our Lord's risen body, though a real and material body, was evidently not subject to all the conditions of an ordinary human body, or of His own body before His death. It was in fact such a body, as we may hope to have when we rise again. We may, therefore, conclude that the wounds made by the nails and spear were not wounds that were sore and inflamed, though it is equally certain that they were not closed up, and only scars left behind.

How it was that the two disciples going to Emmaus did not recognize our Lord by the wounds in His hands and feet, is a question that admits of two answers. Either we must suppose that " their eyes were holden," and that they were miraculously unable to discern who it was that walked with them, and did not even know Him by His voice ; or else we must suppose that our Lord's hands and feet were covered during the walk, and that they only saw the wounds in His hands when He broke the bread. St. Mark's account would lead us to believe that our Lord was pleased to assume another body on the way to Emmaus. He says, " He appeared in another form." (Mark xvi. 12.)

The expression " were glad when they saw," would be more

literally rendered "rejoiced seeing," and "having seen." I cannot myself think that these words fulfilled our Lord's saying, "1 will see you again, and your heart shall rejoice." (John xvi. 22.) That joy, I believe, is the joy of the whole Church at the Lord's second advent, and is yet to come. It is a joy of which our Lord said, "No man taketh it from you." I believe the phrase before us simply means that the disciples were greatly delighted and rejoiced, when they saw before them their risen Master. It relieved their anxious minds, revived their hopes, and set at rest all their fears. "Our Master is actually alive again and has overcome death. Now all will be right."

We should not fail to observe how our Lord condescended to satisfy the senses of His disciples,—the sense of sight, and the sense of touch,—when He showed Himself to them after His resurrection. If their senses had contradicted the news that His body had risen again to life, He would not have required them to believe it. Things above reason and sense the Gospel calls on us to believe often, things contrary to reason and sense never. This is precisely what we should remember when a Romanist bids us believe that the consecrated wafer in the Lord's Supper is the real Body of Christ. Sense, sight, taste, and chemical analysis, combine to tell us that the wafer is still bread. The Romanist, therefore, has no right to demand our belief.

Rollock remarks, "When I mark this place, I see in it what then shall be the estate of the godly, when they shall meet with their Lord. The first sight shall so ravish them, that they shall wonder there ever could be such glory.'

21 —[*Then said Jesus...again, etc.*] In this verse our Lord proceeds to tell the disciples the work which He now wished them to do, but in general terms. He meant to send them forth into the world to be His ministers, messengers, and witnesses, even as the Father had sent Him into the world to be His messenger and witness. (Heb. iii. 1; John xviii. 37.) As He had gone up and down preaching the Gospel, testifying against the evil of the world, and proclaiming rest and peace to the heavy laden, so He intended them to go up and down, as soon as He had ascended up into heaven. In short, He at once prepared their minds for the work which was before them. They were to dismiss from their minds the idea that the day of ease and reward had come, now that their Master had risen and was with them once more. So far from that being the case, their real work was now to begin. He Himself was about to leave the world, and He meant them to take His place. And one purpose for which He appeared among them was to give them their commission.

The repetition of the salutation, "Peace be unto you," is very noteworthy. I cannot doubt that it was specially intended to cheer, and comfort, and animate the disciples. Glad as they doubtless were to see the Lord, we may easily believe that they were frightened, and overcome by a mixture of feelings ; and the more so when they remembered how they had behaved when they had last seen their Lord. Jesus read the condition of· their hearts, and mercifully makes assurance doubly sure by repeating the gracious words, " Peace be unto you." As Joseph said to Pharaoh, " the thing was doubled," in order to make it sure and prevent the possibility of mistake.

Augustine says, "The iteration is confirmation. It is the ' peace upon peace ' promised by the prophet." (Isa. lvii. 19.)

It is curious that two entirely different Greek words are used to express the English " sent " and " send " in this verse. Parkhurst says that the word used where our Lord says " My Father hath sent Me," is a more *solemn* word than the one used when our Lord says, " I send you." Yet I do not think this is proved ; and certainly Liddell and Scott flatly contradict the idea. At any rate the second or less solemn word is repeatedly used in St. Luke in the most solemn sense. (John v. 23, 24, 30.) It is just one of those things which we ought to notice, but cannot explain. There is doubtless some reason why two words are used, but what it is has not yet been discovered.

22 —[*And when He had said...breathed, etc.*] In this verse our Lord proceeds to confer a special gift on the disciples, and, as it were, to ordain them for the great work which He intended them to do. And we have in it a remarkable emblematical action, and a no less remarkable saying.

The action of our Lord, " He breathed on them," is one that stands completely alone in the New Testament, and the Greek word is nowhere else used. On no occasion but this do we find the Lord " breathing " on any one. Of course it was a symbolical action, and the only question is, What did it symbolize? and Why was it used ? My own belief is that the true explanation is to be found in the account of man's creation in Genesis. There we read, " The Lord God formed man of the dust of the ground, and *breathed* into his nostrils the breath of life, and man became a living soul." (Gen. ii. 7.) Just as there was no life in man until God breathed into him the breath of life, so I believe our Lord taught the disciples, by this action of breathing on them, that the beginning of all ministerial qualification is to have the Holy Spirit breathed into us ; and that, until the Holy Ghost is planted in our hearts, we are not rightly commissioned for the work of the ministry.

I do not however feel sure that this view completely exhausts the meaning of our Lord when He breathed on the disciples. I cannot forget that they had all forsaken their Master the night that He was taken prisoner, fallen away from their profession, and forfeited their title to confidence as Apostles. May we not therefore reasonably believe that this breathing pointed to a *revival of life* in the hearts of the Apostles, and to a restoration of their privileges as trusted and commissioned messengers, notwithstanding their grievous fall ?—I cannot help suspecting that this lesson was contained in the action of breathing. It not only symbolized the infusion for the first time of special ministerial gifts and graces. It also symbolized the restoration to complete power and confidence in their Master's eyes, even after their faith had so nearly breathed its last, and given up the ghost. The first symptom of returning life, when a man is recovered from drowning, is his beginning to breathe again. To set the lungs breathing, in such cases, is the first aim of a skilful doctor.

When we remember that the wind is pre-eminently an emblem of the Holy Ghost (John iii. 8 ; Ezek. xxxvii. 9 ; Acts. ii. 2), we cannot fail to see that there is a beautiful fitness in the symbolical action which our Lord has employed.

Lampe thinks that our Lord breathed on all the disciples at once, and not on each one separately. It is probable that it was so, in my judgment.

Hooker remarks (Eccles. Pol. 6, v. c. 77), " The cause why we breathe not, as Christ did on the disciples unto whom He imparted power, is that neither Spirit nor spiritual authority may be thought to proceed from us, who are but delegates and assigns to give men possession of His grace."

The words, " Receive ye the Holy Ghost," are almost as deep and mysterious as the action of breathing. They can only signify, " I bestow on you the Holy Ghost." But in what sense the Holy Ghost was bestowed, is a point that demands attention, and we must beware that we do not run into error.

(a) Our Lord cannot have meant that the disciples were now to " receive the Holy Ghost " for the first time. They had doubtless received Him in the day when they were first converted and believed. Whether they realized it or not, the Holy Ghost was in their hearts already. " No man can say that Jesus is the Lord, but by the Holy Ghost." (1 Cor. xii. 3.)

(b) Our Lord cannot have meant that the disciples were now to " receive the Holy Ghost," for the purpose of working miracles and speaking with tongues. They had worked many miracles already, and the gift of speaking with tongues was specially conferred afterwards, on the day of Pentecost, when they were endued with power from on high.

(c) Our Lord, in my opinion. must have meant, " Receive the Holy Ghost as the Spirit of knowledge and understanding." He must have meant that He now conferred on them a degree of light and knowledge of divine truth, which hitherto they had not possessed. They had been greatly deficient in light and knowledge up to this time. With all their faith and love towards our Lord's Person, they had been sadly ignorant of many things, and particularly of the true purpose of His coming, and

the necessity of His death and resurrection.—" Now," says our
Lord, " I bestow on you the Spirit of knowledge. Let the time
past suffice to have seen through a glass darkly. Receive the
Holy Ghost, open your eyes and see all things clearly."—In fact
I believe the words point to the very thing which, St. Luke
says, our Lord did on this occasion : " then opened He their
understanding that they might understand the Scriptures."
(Luke xxiv. 45.) Light was the first thing made in the day of
creation. Light in the heart is the first beginning of true conversion. And light in the understanding is the first thing required in order to make a man an able minister of the New
Testament. Our Lord was commissioning His first ministers,
and sending them out to carry on His work. He begins by
giving them light and knowledge :—" Receive ye the Holy
Ghost. I commission you this day, and confer on you the office
of ministers. And the first gift I confer on you is spiritual
knowledge." That this is the true view of the words, is proved
to my own mind by the extraordinary difference in doctrinal
knowledge which from this day the Apostles exhibited.

Theophylact thinks that our Lord only meant, " Become fit
for receiving the Holy Ghost." This seems weak and poor.

The expression before us is one of those which seem to me
to supply strong indirect proof of the doctrine of the procession
of the Holy Ghost from the Son, as well as from the Father. It
seems to me that when the Lord Jesus Christ could say with
authority, " Receive the Holy Ghost," it is very strange to say
that the Holy Ghost does not proceed from Him! Yet the
Greek Church does not admit this.

The expression before us is one which, strictly speaking, no
one but our Lord Jesus Christ could use. It is evident that no
mortal man has the power of conferring the Holy Ghost upon
another. This is a prerogative of God alone and of His Christ.
When, therefore, the ordination service for Presbyters, in the
Church of England Prayer-book, puts into the Bishop's mouth
these solemn words, " Receive the Holy Ghost." I have never
felt a doubt that the compilers of our Liturgy only meant the
words to be used as in an optative, and not a positive sense, as *a
prayer* : " I pray that thou mayest receive the Holy Ghost."—
Archbishop Whitgift, in his Reply to the objections of the famous Cartwright, says, " To use these words in ordaining of
ministers, which Christ Himself used in appointing His Apostles, is no more ridiculous and blasphemous than it is to use
the words that he used in the Lord's Supper."—" The Bishop,
by speaking these words, doth not take upon him to give the
Holy Ghost, no more than he doth to remit sins, when he pro-
nounceth the remission of sins; but by speaking these words
of Christ, he doth show the principal duty of a minister, and
assureth him of the assistance of God's Holy Spirit, if he labor
in the same accordingly." (See Blakeney on the Common
Prayer, p. 513.) While, however, I say this, I shall never

shrink from expressing my regret that the words, " receive the Holy Ghost," were adopted by the compilers of our Prayer-book. They do not trouble my conscience, but I consider them likely to offend the consciences of many, and I think it would have been wiser to throw them distinctly and unmistakably into the form of a prayer. It is a simple historical fact which ought not to be forgotten, that these words were never used, in the ordination of ministers, for more than a thousand years after Christ ! (See Nicholls and Blakeney on the Common-Prayer.)

One practical lesson, at any rate, is very plain in this expression. The first thing that is necessary, in order to make a man a true minister of the Gospel, is the indwelling of the Holy Ghost. Bishops and presbyters can lay hands on men, and make them clergymen. The Holy Ghost alone can make a " man of God," and a minister of God's Word.

23 —[*Whose soever sins ye remit, etc.*] In this verse our Lord continues and concludes the commission for the office of ministers, which He now gives to His Apostles after rising from the dead. His work as a public Teacher was now finished. The Apostles henceforth were to carry it on.—The words which form this commission are very peculiar, and demand close attention. The meaning of the words, I believe, may be paraphrased thus : " I confer on you the power of declaring and pronouncing authoritatively whose sins are forgiven, and whose sins are not forgiven. I bestow on you the office of pronouncing who are pardoned, and who are not, just as the Jewish high priest pronounced who were clean, and who were unclean, in cases of leprosy."—I believe that nothing more than this *authority to declare* can be got out of the words, and I entirely repudiate and reject the strange notion maintained by some, that our Lord meant to depute to the Apostles, or any others, the power of absolutely pardoning or not pardoning, absolving or not absolving, any one's soul. My reasons for maintaining this view of the text are as follows :

(*a*) The power of forgiving sins, in Scripture, is always spoken of as the special prerogative of God. The Jews themselves admitted this, when they said, " Who can forgive sins but God only ?" (Mark ii. 7, Luke v. 21.) It is monstrous to suppose that our Lord meant to overthrow and alter this great principle when He commissioned His disciples.

(*b*) The language of the Old Testament Scripture shows conclusively, that the Prophets were said to " DO " things, when they " DECLARED " them about to be done." Thus Jeremiah's commission runs in these words, " I have this day set thee over the nations, and over the kingdoms, to root out, and to pull down, and to destroy, and to throw down, to build, and to plant," (Jer. i. 10.) This can only mean to *declare* the rooting out and pulling down, etc.—So also Ezekiel says, " I came to destroy the city " (Ezek. xliii. 3 ;) where the marginal reading is, " I came to prophesy the city should be destroyed." The Apostles were doubtless well acquainted with prophetical language, and I believe they interpreted our Lord's words in this place accordingly.

(c) There is not a single instance in the Acts or Epistles, of an Apostle taking on himself to absolve, pardon, or forgive any one. The Apostles and preachers of the New Testament declare in the plainest language whose sin is pardoned and absolved, but they never take on themselves to pardon and absolve. When Peter said to Cornelius and his friends, " Whosoever believeth in Him shall receive remission of sins" (Acts xvi. 43); when Paul said at Antioch, in Pisidia, " We declare unto you glad tidings ; " " Through this Man is preached unto you the forgiveness of sins " (Acts xiii. 32, 38); and when Paul said to the Philippian jailor, " Believe on the Lord Jesus Christ, and thou shalt be saved " (Acts xvi. 31),—in each case they fulfilled the commission of the text before us. They " declared whose sins were remitted, and whose were retained."

(d) There is not a single word in the three pastoral Epistles, written by St. Paul to Timothy and Titus, to show that the Apostle regarded absolution as part of the ministerial office. If it was he would surely have mentioned it, and urged the practice of it on young ministers, for the relief of burdened souls.

(e) The weakness of human nature is so great, that it is grossly improbable that such a tremendous power as that of absolutely pardoning and absolving souls, would ever be committed to any mortal man. It would be highly injurious to any man to trust him with such a power, and would be a continued temptation to him to usurp the office of a Mediator between God and man.

(f) The experience of the Romish Church, in which the priests are practically regarded as having the power to absolve sinners, and shut heaven against persons not absolved, affords the strongest indirect evidence that our Lord's words can only have meant to bear a " declarative " sense. Anything worse or more mischievous, both to minister and people, than the results of the Romish system of penance and absolution, it is impossible to conceive. It is a system which has practically degraded the laity, puffed up and damaged the clergy, turned people away from Christ, and kept them in spiritual darkness and bondage.

A question of no small interest arises out of the text before us, which it may be well to consider. Was the ministerial office and commission conferred on the Apostles by our Lord in this place an office which they transmitted to others, with all its privileges and powers?

I answer, without hesitation, that in the strictest sense the commission of the Apostles was not transmitted, but was confined to them and St. Paul. I challenge any one to deny that the Apostles possessed certain ministerial qualifications which were quite peculiar to them, and which they could not transmit, and did not transmit to others. (1) They had the gift of declaring the Gospel without error, and with infallible accuracy, to an extent that no one after them did. (2) They confirmed their teaching by miracles. (3) They were, some of them, plenarily inspired by the Holy Ghost to write portions of the New Testament. (4) They had the power of discerning spirits, and knowing the hearts of others to an extent that no one after them possessed, as we see in the case of Peter's dealing with Ananias, Sapphira, and Simon Magus. In all these respects they stood alone, and had no successors. *In the strictest sense there is no such thing as Apostolical succession.* Modern ministers are not successors of the Apostles, but of Timothy and Titus. The Apostles were peculiarly qualified, and gifted, and furnished for the very peculiar work they had to do, as the first founders of Churches. But, in the strictest and most accurate sense, their office was one which was not transmitted. With them it began, and with them it ended.

But while I say all this, I maintain as strongly as any one, that there is a sense in which the verse now before us applies to all Christian ministers, and in this sense their commission resembles that of the Apostles. It is the office of every minister of Christ to declare boldly, authoritatively, and with decision, out of God's Word, who they are whose sins are forgiven, and who they are whose sins are retained. This is his commission, and this the work for which he is set apart and ordained. Whenever a minister in his pulpit proclaims the full Gospel of Christ faithfully, he does the work which our Lord in this verse commissioned the Apostles to do, and may take comfort in the thought that he may expect our Lord's blessing. He cannot do it with such infallible power as the Apostles, but in a sense he is really their follower and successor.

The whole subject opened up in this verse is so important in modern days, that I make no apology for quoting the following passage from Bishop Jewell's Apology, which throws light on it:—

Jewell says, " We say, that Christ has given to His ministers the power of binding and loosing, of opening and shutting. And we say, that the power of loosing consists in this, that the minister, by the preaching of the Gospel, offers to dejected minds and true penitents, through the merits of Christ, absolution, and doth assure them a certain remission of their sins, and the hopes of eternal salvation; or, secondly, reconciles, restores, and receives into the congregation and unity of the faithful, those penitents, who by any grievous scandal or known and public offence have offended the minds of their brethren, and in a sort alienated and separated themselves from the common society of the Church and the body of Christ. And we say the minister doth exercise the power of binding or shutting, when he shutteth the gate of the kingdom of heaven against unbelievers and obstinate persons, and denounceth to them the vengeance of God and eternal punishment; or excludeth out of the bosom of the Church, those that are publicly excommunicated; and that God Himself doth so far approve whatever sentence His ministers shall so give, that whatsoever is either loosed or bound by their ministry here on earth, He will in like manner bind or loose and confirm in heaven. The key with which these ministers do shut or open the kingdom of heaven, we say, with St. Chrysostom, is *the knowledge of the Scripture ;* with Tertullian, is *the interpretation of the law ;* and with Eusebius, is *the Word of God.* We say the disciples of Christ received this power (from Him) not that they might hear the private confessions of the people, and catch their whispering murmurs, as the Popish priests everywhere now do, and that in such a manner as if all the force and use of the keys consisted only in this; but that they might go and preach and publish the Gospel, that so they might be a savor of life unto life, to them that did believe; and that they might be also a savor of death unto death, to those that did not believe; that the minds of those who were affrighted with the sense of their former ill lives and errors, after they beheld the light of the Gospel, and believed in Christ, might be opened by the Word of God, as doors are with a key: and that the wicked and stubborn, who would not believe and return into the way, might be left, shut up, and locked, and, as St. Paul expresseth it (2 Tim. iii. 13), might " wax *worse and worse.*" *This* we take to be the meaning of the *keys,* and that in this manner the consciences of men are either bound or loosed."

Calvin observes, " When Christ enjoins the Apostles to forgive sins, He does not convey to them what is peculiar to Himself. It belongs to Him to forgive sins. This honor, so far as it belongs peculiarly to Himself, He does not surrender to the Apostles. He only enjoins them, in His name, to proclaim the forgiveness of sins, that through their agency He may reconcile men to God."

Brentius says, " This is the true and heavenly mode of remitting sins: to wit, the preaching of the Gospel of Jesus Christ. Those who do not preach the Gospel of Christ have no power of either remitting or retaining sins."

Bullinger says, " The Apostles remitted men's sins, when by the preaching of the Gospel they taught that the sins of believers were remitted, and eternal life granted through the death and resurrection of Jesus Christ. They retained men's sins when they announced that the wrath of God remained on those who believed not."

Gualter says, " At this day ministers are said to remit sins when they promise remission of them in Christ to those who believe, and to retain sins when they denounce damnation on the unbelieving and obstinately impenitent."

Musculus says that this promise does not belong " to every and any minister, but to the real minister of the Gospel, who teaches nothing, promises nothing else but this,—that those who repent and believe on Christ have remission of sin and eternal life, and that those who are impenitent and unbelieving remain in their sins and death. Doctrine like this is ratified and confirmed before God, because it is agreeable to the Gospel of the Son of God."

·Lightfoot thinks that, in interpreting these words, we must carefully remember that they were probably spoken in close connection with our Lord's words in St. Luke, when He says that " repentance and remission of sins should be preached in His name, beginning at Jerusalem." (Luke xxiv. 46.) He thinks that on hearing these words, scruples might arise in the Apostles' minds: " Is this so indeed ? Must remission of sin be really preached in Jerusalem to men stained with Messiah's blood ? " And then he thinks these words are spoken to encourage them. " Yes: you are to begin at Jerusalem. For whose soever sins ye remit, they are remitted unto them." Finally, Lightfoot asks, with much sense, " On what foundation and with what confidence could the Apostles have preached remission of sins to such wretched men as the murderers of their Lord, unless authorized by a peculiar commission granted by the Lord Himself ? "

Poole says, " The question among divines is whether Christ in this text has given authority to His ministers actually to discharge men of the guilt of their sins; or only to declare to them that if their repentance and faith be true, their sins are really forgiven. The former view is contended for by many. But it does not seem reasonable (1) that God should betrust man with such a piece of His prerogative ; and (2) that God who knoweth the falsehood of men's hearts, and the inability of the best minister to judge of the truth of any man's repentance and faith, as also the passions to which they are subject, should give to any of the sons of men an absolute power under Him to discharge any from the guilt of sin. Certain it is that without true repentance and faith in Christ no man hath his sins forgiven ; so that no minister, who knoweth not the hearts of men, can possibly say to any man with certainty, *Thy sins are forgiven*. What certainty the Apostles might have had by the Spirit of discernment, we cannot say. But certain it is, that none hath now such certainty of any man's faith and repentance. Hence it is to me apparent, that no man hath any further power from Christ than to declare to men, that if they truly repent and believe, their sins are really forgiven. Only the minister, being Christ's interpreter and ambassador, and better able to judge of true faith and repentance than others (though not certainly and infallibly), such declarations from a faithful, able minister are of more weight and authority than from others. This is the most, I conceive, should be in this matter."

I leave the whole passage with one general word of caution. Whatever sense we place on the words, let us beware that we do not give to ministers, of any name or denomination, a place, power, authority, position, or privilege, which Christ never gave them. Putting ministers out of their proper place has been the root of endless superstition and corruption in Christ's Church. To regard ministers as mediators between Christ and the soul, to confess to them privately and receive private absolution from them, is a system for which there is no authority in the New Testament, and the high road to every kind of evil. It is a system equally mischievous to ministers and to people, utterly subversive of the Gospel, and thoroughly dishonoring to the priestly office of Christ.

The three absolutions found in the Liturgy of the Church of England, (1) that in the Morning and Evening Prayer, (2) that in the Communion Service, and (3) that in the Visitation for the Sick, were all, in my judgment, intended to bear only a *declarative* sense. But I can never refrain from saying that the absolution in the Visitation Service is liable to be misunderstood, and its wording is to be regretted.

Shepherd, on the Common Prayer, remarks, " The Church of England neither maintains nor countenances the opinion, that a priest, by virtue of his ordination, has an absolute, unconditional power to forgive sin. The power that the clergy have received and exercised, is purely ministerial, being defined and limited by the Word of God, which expressly declares upon what condition sin shall be remitted, and upon what retained. To suppose that any minister of Christ, since the Apostles, possesses the power of remitting or retaining sin at his discretion, is repugnant to the whole tenor of Scripture, as well as to every dictate of reason and common sense."

JOHN XX 24—31

24 But Thomas, one of the twelve, called Didymus, was not with them when Jesus came.

25 The other disciples therefore said unto him, We have seen the Lord. But he said unto them, Except I shall see in his hands the print of the nails, and put my finger into the print of the nails, and thrust my hand into his side, I will not believe.

26 And after eight days again his disciples were within, and Thomas with them : *then* came Jesus, the doors being shut, and stood in the midst, and said, Peace *be* unto you.

27 Then saith he to Thomas, Reach hither thy finger, and behold my hands ; and reach hither thy hand, and thrust *it* into my side : and be not faithless, but believing.

28 And Thomas answered and said unto him, My Lord and my God.

29 Jesus saith unto him, Thomas, because thou hast seen me, thou hast believed : blessed *are* they that have not seen, and *yet* have believed.

30 And many other signs truly did Jesus in the presence of his disciples, which are not written in this book :

31 But these are written, that ye might believe that Jesus is the Christ, the Son of God ; and that believing ye might have life through his name.

THE story of the unbelief of Thomas, related in these verses, is a narrative peculiar to the Gospel of St. John. For wise and good reasons it is passed over in silence by Matthew, Mark, and Luke, and was probably not given to the world till Thomas was dead. It is precisely one of those passages of Scripture which supply strong internal evidence of the honesty of the inspired writers. If impostors and deceivers had compiled the Bible for their own private advantage, they would never have told mankind that one of the first founders of a new religion behaved as Thomas here did.

We should mark, for one thing, in these verses, *how much Christians may lose by not regularly attending the assemblies of God's people.* Thomas was absent the first time that Jesus appeared to the disciples after His resurrection, and consequently Thomas missed a blessing. Of course we have no certain proof that the absence of the Apostle could not admit of explanation. Yet, at such a crisis in the lives of the eleven, it seems highly improbable that he had any good reason for not being with his brethren, and it is far more likely that in some way he was to blame. One thing, at any rate, is clear and plain. By being absent he was kept in suspense and unbelief a whole week, while all around him were rejoicing in the thought of a risen Lord. It is difficult to suppose that this would have been the case, if there had not been a fault somewhere. It is hard to avoid the suspicion that Thomas was absent when he might have been present.

We shall all do well to remember the charge of the Apostle St. Paul : "Forsake not the assembling of yourselves together, as the manner of some is." (Heb. x. 25.) Never to be absent from God's house on Sundays, without good reason,—never to miss the Lord's Supper when administered in our own congregation,—never to let our place be empty when means of grace are going on, this is one way to be a growing and prosperous Christian. The very sermon that we needlessly miss, may contain a precious word in season for our souls. The very assembly for prayer and praise from which we stay away, may be the very gathering that would have cheered, and stablished, and quickened our hearts. We little know how dependent our spiritual health is on little, regular, habitual helps, and how much we suffer if we miss our medicine. The wretched argument that many attend means of grace and are no better for them, should be no argument to a Christian. It may satisfy those who are blind to their own state, and destitute of grace, but it should never satisfy a real servant of Christ. Such an one should remember the words of Solomon: "Blessed is the man that heareth me, watching daily at my gates, waiting at the posts of my doors." (Prov. viii. 34.) Above all he should bind around his heart the Master's promise: "Wheresoever two or three are gathered together in my name, there am I in the midst of them." (Matt. xviii. 20.) Such a man will rarely be left like Thomas, shut out in the cold chill of unbelief, while others are warmed and filled.

We should mark for another thing in this verse, *how kind and merciful Christ is to dull and slow believers.* Nowhere, perhaps, in all the four Gospels, do we find this part of our Lord's character so beautifully illustrated as in the story before our eyes. It is hard to imagine anything more tiresome and provoking than the conduct of Thomas, when even the testimony of ten faithful brethren had no effect on him, and he doggedly declared, "Except I see with my own eyes and touch with my own hands, I will not believe." But it is impossible to imagine anything more patient and compassionate, than our Lord's treatment of this weak disciple.

He does not reject him, or dismiss him, or excommunicate him. He comes again at the end of a week, and apparently for the special benefit of Thomas. He deals with him according to his weakness, like a gentle nurse dealing with a froward child:—" Reach hither thy finger, and behold my hands ; reach hither thy hand, and thrust it into my side." If nothing but the grossest, coarsest, most material evidence could satisfy him, even that evidence was supplied. Surely this was a love that passeth knowledge, and a patience that passeth understanding.

A passage of Scripture like this, we need not doubt, was written for the special comfort of all true believers. The Holy Ghost knew well that the dull, and the slow, and the stupid, and the doubting, are by far the commonest type of disciples in this evil world. The Holy Ghost has taken care to supply abundant evidence that Jesus is rich in patience as well as compassion, and that He bears with the infirmities of all His people. Let us take care that we drink into our Lord's spirit, and copy His example. Let us never set down men in a low place, as gracious and godless, because their faith is feeble and their love is cold. Let us remember the case of Thomas, and be very pitiful and of tender mercy. Our Lord has many weak children in His family, many dull pupils in His school, many raw soldiers in His army, many lame sheep in His flock. Yet He bears with them all, and casts none away. Happy is that Christian who has learned to deal likewise with his brethren. There are many in the Church, who, like Thomas, are dull and slow, but for all that, like Thomas, are real and true believers.

We should mark, lastly, in these verses, *how Christ was addressed by a disciple as " God," without prohibition or rebuke on His part.* The noble exclamation which burst from the lips of Thomas, when convinced that his Lord had risen indeed,—the noble exclamation, "My Lord and my God,"—admits of only one meaning. It was a distinct testimony to our blessed Lord's divinity. It was a clear, unmistakable declaration that Thomas believed Him, whom he saw and touched that day, to be not only man, but God. Above all, it was a testimony which our Lord received and did not prohibit, and a declaration which He did not say one word to rebuke. When Cornelius fell down at the feet of Peter and would have worshipped him, the Apostle refused such honor at once: "Stand up; I myself also am a man." (Acts x. 26.) When the people of Lystra would have done sacrifice to Paul and Barnabas, "they rent their clothes, and ran in among the people, saying, Sirs, why do ye these things? We also are men of like passions with you." (Acts xiv. 14.) But when Thomas says to Jesus, "My Lord and my God," the words do not elicit a syllable of reproof from our holy and truthloving Master. Can we doubt that these things were written for our learning?

Let us settle it firmly in our minds that the divinity of Christ is one of the grand foundation truths of Christianity, and let us be willing to go to the stake rather than let it go. Unless our Lord Jesus is very God of very God, there is an end of His mediation, His atonement, His advocacy, His priesthood, His whole work of redemption. These glorious doctrines are useless blasphemies, unless Christ is divine. Forever let us bless God that the divinity of our Lord is taught everywhere in the Scriptures, and stands on evidence that can never be overthrown. Above all, let us daily repose our sinful souls on Christ with undoubting confidence, as one who is perfect God as well as perfect man. He is man, and therefore can be touched with the feeling of our in-

firmities. He is God, and therefore is "able to save to
the uttermost all who come unto God by Him." That
Christian has no cause to fear, who can look to Jesus by
faith, and say with Thomas, "My Lord and my God."
With such a Saviour we need not be afraid to begin the
life of real religion, and with such a Saviour we may
boldly go on.

NOTES   JOHN XX. 24—31

24 —[*But Thomas one...twelve...Didymus.*] The story of the second appearance of Christ to the whole company of the Apostles,
for the special benefit of Thomas, is one of those narratives
which are only found in St. John's Gospel. We ought to feel
thankful that it has been recorded. It is precisely one of those
stories which supply strong indirect evidence of the divine inspiration of the Scriptures and the genuine honesty of the Gospel writers. An uninspired man, much less a dishonest
impostor, would not have told us of the unbelief of a chosen
Apostle. Moreover it is one of those stories which throw most
useful light on a very interesting subject. That subject is the
great variety of temperament which may be found among true
Christians.

Chrysostom remarks, " Observe the truthfulness of the disciples. They hide no faults, either their own or others; but record them with great veracity."

Cardinal Bellarmine, according to Gerhard, goes so far as to
say that the history of Thomas, like that of Noah's drunkenness, David's adultery, and Peter's denial, is a reason why the
laity ought not to read the Bible, lest forsooth they should get
harm! The worthy Cardinal forgets that we need beacons to
warn us against danger, and examples of Christ's mercy to sinful and dull people in order to encourage us to repent.

Concerning the Apostle Thomas we know little. Twice in
the Gospel of St. John we find him saying something, and on
each occasion he appears in the same character. When our
Lord declared His intention of going to Bethany, and says
plainly that Lazarus is dead, Thomas says to his fellow-disciples, " Let us also go, that we may die with Him." (John xi.
16.) When our Lord in His parting address to His disciples
said, " Whither I go ye know, and the way ye know. Thomas
saith unto Him, Lord, we know not whither Thou goest; and
how can we know the way?" (John xiv. 4, 5.) He always
seems to be one of those desponding, fearful, gloomy-minded
Christians, who look at the dark side of every subject and condition, and can never see a bit of blue sky,—who go on their

way to heaven with real faith and true grace, but are so full of doubts and fears that they are unable to enjoy religion, and are a trouble to themselves and all around them. This I believe to be the true account of his character. The modern theory that he was a man of *free thought and wide range of intellect,* who wisely required reasonable evidence of everything in religion, and properly dreaded taking anything on trust, is a theory which I believe to be utterly without foundation, and I cannot receive it for a moment. He was simply a good man with a very doubting and gloomy turn of mind ;—a man that really loved Jesus and was willing to die with Him, but a man who saw little but the dangers attending everything that a disciple had to do, and the difficulties belonging to everything which a disciple had to believe. There are many like him. It is a very useful picture. John Bunyan's " Fearing," " Despondency," and " Much afraid," in Pilgrim's Progress, are types of a large class of Christians, who are successors of the Apostle Thomas.

[*Was not with them...Jesus came.*] The reasons why Thomas was not with the other ten Apostles on Sunday night when Jesus appeared to them, are not given, and we have no clue whatever to them. Most commentators consider that he was to blame ; and that by his absence he missed a blessing, and was kept in suspense a week. I admit that this may be true, and I think his example teaches indirectly that it is unwise to be ever absent from the assembly of God's people without good cause. But I believe we must not press this point too far, and must not lay too much blame on the Apostle, in the absence of direct evidence that he was in fault. For anything we know, he may have lodged at a greater distance from the place of meeting than any of the eleven, and thus been unable to reach the place at an earlier hour ; or he may have been detained by necessary business. One thing is very certain : the disciples found no fault with Thomas for his absence when they said, " We have seen the Lord." Moreover, our Lord Himself, when He appears, does not blame Thomas for having been absent on a former occasion, but only chides his unbelief. The simplest view of the subject appears to me to be, that Thomas's absence was a part of his character. He was slow and dull in action as well as in perception,—the sort of man would always have been last in Church, and last in a meeting. In the present instance I venture to conjecture that he meant no harm, and intended to have been present when the ten Apostles met ; but that he probably started late, walked slow, and was so absorbed in doubts, and fears, and anxious meditations about the prospects of Christ's disciples, that he never reached the place of meeting till Christ had withdrawn Himself.

The question has been needlessly raised by some, whether Thomas was not deprived of the gifts and privileges conferred on the other Apostles by his absence ? Lightfoot sensibly re-

plies, " Surely not : it was a privilege common to the whole
Apostolate, and peculiar to them as Apostles. St. Paul was
distant, while these things happened, both from apostleship
and religion. Yet, when made an Apostle, he was at once
adorned with this privilege." Some think that his case is like
Eldad and Medad, who had their share of the Spirit, though
absent, like the rest of the seventy elders. (Num. xi. 27.)

25 —[*The other disciples...said...seen the Lord.*] We are not told
when and where the disciples said this. I incline to believe
that they said it the very evening that our Lord first appeared
to them, and that Thomas came into the assembly very shortly
after the Lord disappeared. To my eyes it reads as if the ten
Apostles all exclaimed together, full of joy and delight at what
they had seen and heard, " Thomas, we have just seen our Lord
and Master ! If you had been here a little sooner, you also
would have seen Him." I think this for two reasons. (*a*) The
words of the twenty-sixth verse, " after eight days," seem to
indicate that there were eight days between our Lord's first appearance and his second, and also eight days between Thomas's
expression of unbelief and his being convinced. (*b*) It seems
highly improbable that Thomas would allow a whole day and
night to pass away, after the rumor of our Lord's body having
been removed from the sepulchre had spread through Jerusalem, without seeking out the other Apostles and inquiring what
it meant. Slow and dull in faith as he was, he would hardly
sleep without finding out something about it. These considerations incline me to believe, that before the ten Apostles had
time to separate, after our Lord's appearance to them, Thomas
came in. Then they told him immediately, that they had just
seen the Lord. And then came the remarkable declaration
which the doubting Apostle made.

[*But he said unto them, Except, etc.*] The unbelief of Thomas,
expressed in this famous sentence, was a sad fault in a good
man, which cannot be explained away. He refused to believe
the testimony of ten competent witnesses, who had seen Christ
in the body with their own eyes. He refused to believe the
testimony of ten true friends and brethren, who could have no
object in deceiving him. He passionately declares that he will
not believe, unless he himself sees and touches our Lord's
body. He presumes to prescribe certain conditions, which must
be fulfilled before he can credit the report of his brethren. He
uses singularly emphatic language to express his scepticism :
—" Others may believe if they like ; but I shall not and will
not believe until I see and touch for myself."—All this was
very sad and very sinful. Thomas might have remembered
that at this rate nothing could ever be proved by witnesses ;
and that he himself, as a teacher, could never expect men to
believe him. His case shows us how foolishly and weakly a
believer may speak sometimes, and how, under the influence of
depression and doubt, he may saw things of which afterwards
he is heartily ashamed.

After all, the case of Thomas is not an uncommon one. Some people are so strangely constituted that they distrust everybody, regard all men as liars, and will believe nothing except they can see it all, and work it all out for themselves. They have a rooted dislike to receive anything on trust, or from the testimony of others, and must always go over the ground for themselves. In people of this kind, though they know it not, there is often a vast amount of latent pride and self-conceit; and it is almost ludicrous to observe how entirely they forget that the business of daily life could never go on, if we were always doubting everything which we could not see for ourselves. Nevertheless they exist in the Church, and always will exist; and the case of Thomas shows what trouble they bring on themselves.

Two things must, in fairness, be remembered, which form some slight extenuation of Thomas's unbelief. For one thing it does not appear that any one of our Lord's Apostles ever understood, up to the time of our Lord's crucifixion, that he was really going to be crucified, buried, and rise again. Simple as these great facts appear to us now, it is perfectly certain that they formed no part of the creed of the Apostles, so long as our Lord was with them. This may seem astonishing, but it is true. They believed that Christ was the Messiah, but they did not realize a crucified Messiah. Of these Apostles, I would remind the reader, Thomas was one. Does not all this throw a little light on his extraordinary scepticism about the reality of the resurrection? For another thing we must remember, that Thomas, like all Jews, had a firm belief in the reality of spirits and ghosts, and the possibility of their appearing. Even after this, when Peter was delivered from prison, and came to the house of John, surnamed Mark, the disciples said, "It is his angel." (Acts xii. 15.) May we not therefore conceive it possible that Thomas, overwhelmed and confounded at the astounding news that Christ had been seen, would cling, with his characteristic incredulity, to the notion that the Apostles had only seen Christ's spirit or ghost? That they had seen something he did not dispute, but that what they had seen was the real material body of his Lord, he could not bring himself to believe. These things are worth considering. I do not for a moment excuse or defend Thomas. I only remind those who condemn him wholesale, and can find no words strong enough to use about his unbelief, that it was not quite so easy for a pious Jew, brought up and trained as Thomas had been, to receive at once the resurrection of our Lord as a proved thing, as it may appear at first sight to an English mind.

Musculus remarks, how extraordinary the unbelief of Thomas seems, when we consider that he not only had heard our Lord frequently foretell His resurrection, but had actually within a few weeks seen Lazarus raised from the dead at Bethany!

Bengel remarks, "No doubt Thomas seemed to himself to be

entertaining and expressing sentiments altogether judicious. But unbelief, while it attributes defects in judgment to others, often itself discovers and betrays hardness of heart, and in that hardness slowness of belief."

26 —[*And after eight days again, etc.*] This verse describes how Jesus was graciously pleased to appear again to the company of the Apostles, for the express purpose of convincing and satisfying the mind of Thomas.

He came " after eight days." That means a week according to the Jewish manner of expressing a space of time, by which the first and last days were always reckoned in, if any part of them was employed. Thus our Lord was buried on Friday afternoon and rose again on Sunday morning, and was actually only thirty-six hours in the grave. But a Jew would say that He was " three days " buried. It thus appears that, both on the first and second times when our Lord appeared to the Apostles, it was a Sunday. Poole remarks that we have here the beginning of keeping holy the first day of the week.

He came when the disciples were " within." That means that they were assembled in a room, and probably in the same house where they had assembled before. The conviction and reproof of a weak disciple was a thing which was mercifully transacted in private, and among friends. We cannot doubt, moreover, that at this period the disciples would hardly dare to assemble in the open air anywhere about Jerusalem. The rumor that they stole the body of our Lord would still be rife in the city, and they might well feel the necessity of caution.

He came when " Thomas was with them." That means that He timed His visit, so that not one of the Apostles were missing. He knew exactly who were assembled, and where they were assembled, and He ordered His appearance accordingly. It should be a great comfort to believers to remember that their Lord's eye is always upon them, and that He knows exactly in what place and in what company they are.

He came " when the doors were shut." That means that He appeared exactly under the same circumstances under which He appeared a week before, in an evening, when the doors were carefully closed for fear of the Jews. Thus, as on the previous Sunday, He suddenly, without a moment's notice, stood in the midst of the assembled disciples.

He came with the same gracious salutation with which He had appeared before. Once more, the first word that fell from His lips is " Peace be unto you." Thomas was there. The disciple who made his emphatic declaration of unbelief, might well expect to hear some word of rebuke. But our Lord makes no exception. He saw Thomas, and well knew all that Thomas had said ; and yet to him, as well as to the other ten, He once more says " Peace."

We should note carefully the amazing kindness of our Lord Jesus Christ to a weak disciple, and the trouble He was pleased to take, if I may use such a phrase with due reverence, about one single soul. The unbelief of Thomas was most provoking and inexcusable, and if he had been cast out of the company of disciples we could not have said His excommunication was undeserved. But our Lord cares tenderly for this weak member of His mystical body, and specially appears in order to heal and restore him. What a wonderful example He gives to all His people! How kind we ought to be to weak brethren, and how ready to take any pains and trouble if we can only do them good! The Christian of modern times, who is ready to excommunicate every one who cannot speak his shibboleth, and see every point of doctrine and ceremonial with his eyes,—the Christian who is ready to turn away from every brother who is overtaken in a fault, as graceless, godless, and unconverted,— such a Christian may flatter himself that he is very zealous and faithful. But he is a Christian who has not got the mind of Christ. What Christ did for Thomas, we ought to be ready to do for others.

Let us not forget that Thomas continued a whole week in unbelief and doubt, while his brethren around him were rejoicing. We may well believe that it was not a very happy week with him. He that sows a short period of scepticism often reaps a long period of trouble.

Rupertus, almost alone, maintains that the second appearance of our Lord, for the special benefit of Thomas, was in Galilee, in Nazareth, at the house of Mary. But the vast majority of commentators think that it was at Jerusalem.

Musculus observes how kind and brotherly was the dealing of the ten Apostles with Thomas. They did not excommunicate him, and cast him out of their society for his unbelief, but allowed him to assemble with them as before.

Rollock observes, "The loving dealing of the Lord with Thomas teaches us this comfortable lesson. The Lord marks not narrowly the infirmities and wants that are in His own. He looks not narrowly to the weakness of their faith, to the imperfections and wants of their prayers and requests, for their prayers are full of imperfections, He oversees their infirmities, He misknows the corruption wherein their faith and prayers and desires are involved, and hath a regard to their faith, albeit they have it in small measure."

27 —[*Then saith He to Thomas, etc.*] The verse before us is a wonderful instance of Christ's pitifulness and condescension. To come into the world at all, and take a body on Him,—to allow that body to be scourged, crowned with thorns, nailed to the cross, and laid in the grave,—all this, beyond doubt, was astonishing condescension. But when the victory over sin and death was won, and He had taken on Him His resurrection

body, to come to a doubting, sceptical disciple, and bid him touch Him, put his finger into the nail-prints on His hands, and put his hand into the great wound in His side,—all this was a condescension which we can never sufficiently admire and adore.

The last sentence of the verse is a rebuke and an exhortation at the same time. It would have been more literally rendered, " Be not an unbeliever, but a believer." It is not merely a reproof to Thomas for his scepticism on this particular occasion, but an urgent counsel to be of a more believing turn of mind for time to come.—" Shake off this habit of doubting, questioning, and discrediting every one. Give up thine unbelieving disposition. Become more willing to believe and trust, and give credit to testimony for time to come."—No doubt the primary object of the sentence was to correct and chastise Thomas for his sceptical declaration on the preceding Sunday. But I believe our Lord had in view the further object of correcting Thomas's whole character, and directing his attention to his besetting sin. How many there are among us who ought to take to themselves our Lord's words! How faithless we often are, and how slow to believe !

Let us note here, as already remarked, that the wounds on our Lord's body must have been still open, from the language He addresses to Thomas, and that the wound in His side must have been a very large wound, from His telling Thomas to thrust in *his hand*.

Let us not fail to observe our Lord's perfect knowledge of all that passed on the previous Sunday, of all that the Apostles had said, and of the sceptical declaration which Thomas had made. Such knowledge showed clearly that He was God and not man. He hears every idle word that we say, and notes all our conversation.

Let us observe our Lord's thorough acquaintance with the special faults and besetting sins of every one of His people. He saw that Thomas's defect was his unbelief, and so He says, " Be not faithless, but believing."

28 —[*And Thomas...my Lord...my God.*] The famous answer of Thomas, contained in this verse, is precisely the short interjectional exclamation of a man taken by surprise, convinced at once of his own grievous mistake, and so overwhelmed by a variety of feelings that he is unable for the moment to use many words. It is the language of amazement, delight, repentance, faith and adoration, all combined in one sentence.

Whether it is to be taken in the third person, as an exclamation, " It is my Lord and my God!" or in the second person, as an adoring, loving, believing address, " Thou art my Lord and my God," is an open question which the original Greek does not settle. If I must give an opinion, I prefer the second person. But in either case the sense is good.

The text before us is one of those which are justly quoted, as an unanswerable proof of the divinity of our Lord Jesus Christ. He is called " God " in the presence of ten witnesses, and He accepts the language, and does not say one word to reprove the person who uses it. Unless a person is prepared to deny the inspiration of St. John's Gospel generally, or the genuineness and correctness of this text in particular, it is hard to see how the force of the sentence in favor of Christ's divinity can be evaded. The suggestion of Theodorus of Mopsuestia, and some modern Socinians, that Thomas only used a kind of oath or exclamation, which he did not mean to apply to Christ Himself, is utterly untenable, and almost profane. It is unreasonable to suppose that a pious Jew, like Thomas, would take God's name in vain and break the third commandment, however much he might be surprised. Moreover, there is no proof whatever, although a careless Greek, Roman, or Englishman, might say " *My God*," when suddenly taken by surprise, that any such expression was in use among the Jews. In short there is, in my judgment, but one way of regarding the text, if we treat it honestly. It is an incontrovertible proof that Thomas looked on Christ as God, and addressed Him to His face as God, and that our Lord made no objection, and did not reprove him.

Bullinger remarks how emphatically Thomas says, " MY Lord and MY God," showing the reality of his faith.

Rollock says, " If we compare Thomas with the other Apostles, we shall see that as he surpassed them all in unbelief, so he surpassed them far in ' believing and confessing the Lord." But he adds, " Jesus praises not Thomas for his faith, because he tied his faith to his senses. He calls him not blessed for it, but pronounces them blessed who believe without seeing."

Whether, after all, Thomas did actually touch our Lord's wounds, as he was told to do, is an open question, which we have no means of deciding. There is certainly, as Augustine observes, no proof that he did, and his exclamation reads as if it was sudden and immediate, and not the result of examination and deliberation. May we not well believe that the discovery of our Lord's perfect acquaintance with every word that he had said on the previous Sunday, combined with the evidence of his own eyes that he saw before him a material body, and not a spirit, would be enough to convince him ? The question is an open one, and every reader must form his own opinion about it. We are neither told that Thomas did touch our Lord, nor yet that he did not. Certainly our Lord says in the next verse, " Because thou hast *seen Me*, thou hast believed."

29 —[*Jesus saith unto him, Thomas. etc.*] This verse contains a grave and solemn rebuke to Thomas, and a warning to all who are disposed to demand an excessive amount of evidence before they believe. The first part of our Lord's words would be

translated more literally, " Because thou hast seen Me, Thomas, thou hast believed." The whole sentence may be thus paraphrased and expounded. " Thomas, thou hast at last believed my resurrection, because thou hast seen Me with thine own eyes, and touched Me with thine own hands. It is well. But it would have been far better if thou hadst believed a week ago, on the testimony of thy ten brethren, and not waited to see Me. Remember from henceforth, that in my kingdom they are more blessed and honorable who believe on good testimony, without seeing, than those who insist first on seeing, before they believe."

The sentence " Blessed are they that have not seen and yet have believed," would be rendered literally, " Blessed are those persons not having seen and having believed,"—consisting, as it does, of two participles connected with " blessed." The idea that our Lord had in view any particular person, such as Abraham, Moses, David, the prophets, and, generally, the Old Testament saints, appears to me utterly untenable. I believe our Lord had in view no individual case, but only laid down a great general principle which Thomas had forgotten, as a lesson to him and the whole Church in every age. The construction of the Greek language allows us to regard the past tense as a present, in such a sentence as this. (See Jelf's Greek Grammar, 401, 403 ; and Farrar's Greek Syntax, 130.)

Gregory well says, " The incredulity of Thomas has done us more good than the faith of Mary." He means that if Thomas had never doubted, we should not have had such full proof that Christ rose from the dead.

The principle contained in the sentence before us, is one of vast importance in every age, and specially in our own. In a day of scepticism, free inquiry and rationalism, so-called, when hundreds are continually railing against creeds, and dogmatism, and priestcraft, the sentence deserves close attention and consideration. Nothing is more common now-a-days than to hear people say, that they " decline to believe things above their reason, that they cannot believe what they cannot entirely understand in religion, that they must see everything clearly before they can believe." Such talk as this sounds very fine, and is very taking with young persons and superficially educated people, because it supplies a convenient reason for neglecting vital religion altogether. But it is a style of talking which shows a mind either proud, or foolish, or inconsistent.

In matters of science, what sensible man does not know that we must begin by believing much which we do not understand, taking many positions on trust, and accepting many things on the testimony of others? Even in the most exact science the scholar must begin with axioms and postulates. Faith and trust in our teachers is the very first condition of acquiring knowledge. He that begins his studies by saying " I

shall not believe anything which I do not see clearly demonstrated from the very first," will make very little progress.

In the daily business of life, what sensible man does not
know that we take many important steps on no other ground
than the testimony of others? Parents send sons to Australia,
New Zealand, China, and India, without ever having seen
these countries, in faith that the report about them is dependable and true. Probability, in fact, is the only guide of most
parts of our life.

In the face of such facts as these, where is the common sense
of saying, as many rationalists and sceptics now do, that in
such a mysterious matter as the concern of our souls, we ought
to believe nothing that we do not see, and ought to receive
nothing as true which will not admit of mathematical demonstration?—Christianity does not at all refuse to appeal to our
intellects, and does not require of us a blind, unreasoning faith.
But Christianity does ask us to begin by believing many things
that are above our reason, and promises that, so beginning, we
shall have more light and see all things clearly.—The would-
be wise man of modern times says, " I dislike any religion
which contains any mystery. I must first see, and then I will
believe." Christianity replies, "You cannot avoid mystery,
unless you go out of the world. You are only asked to do with
religion what you are always doing with science. You must
first believe and then you will see."—The cry of the modern
sceptic is, " If I'could see I would believe." The answer of
the Christian ought to be, " If you would only believe, and
humbly ask for Divine teaching, you would soon see."

The plain truth is that modern freethinkers are like the
Jews, who were always demanding some visible sign that our
Lord was the Messiah, and pretended that they would believe
if they only saw it. Just in the same way there are hundreds
of people in this latter age of the world, who tell us they can
believe nothing which is above their reason, and that they
want stronger evidences of the truth of the doctrine and fact
of Christianity than probability. Like Thomas they must first
see before they believe.—But what an extraordinary fact it is
that the very men who say all this, are continually acting all
their lives on no better evidence than probability! They are
continually doing things on no other ground than the report of
others, and their own belief that this report is probably true.
The very principle on which they are incessantly acting, in the
affairs of their bodies, their families, and their money, is the
principle on which they refuse to act in the affairs of their
souls! In the things of this world they believe all sorts of
things which they have not seen, and only know to be probable, and act on their belief. In the things of the eternal world
they say they can believe nothing which they do not see, and
refuse the argument of probability altogether. Never, in fact,
was there anything so unreasonable and inconsistent as ration-

alism, so called! No wonder that our Lord laid down, for the benefit of Thomas and the whole Church, that mighty principle, "Blessed are they that have not seen and yet have believed."

The remarks of Richard Cecil, on the subject before us, are so apposite, that I make no apology for quoting them. They will be found in his "Original Thoughts." (Vol. i., p. 440—442.)

"When a man doubts, after proper evidence, God calls it folly. When we complain and want more evidence, the fault is in us and not in God's dispensations. A humble spirit will accept a glimmering light, and not refuse to walk because it has not the noonday sun. Incredulity, as to divine truth, has its root in pride and self-sufficiency, and is accompanied by much rashness and ignorance. It presumes to understand and comprehend everything that is proposed to it. The incredulous man calls for demonstration. The feeble creature, who cannot explain the nature of his own formation, would have things made out as plain as that 'two and two make four.' The true believer receives the truths of the Bible as he receives the kingdom of heaven,—with the simplicity of a little child."—

—"Let us beware of the danger of following our own imaginations. A man may make one demand after another, till, at last, nothing will satisfy him; and the next step is, that, when he will not be content with what God shows him, he shall be left in darkness and perplexity.—Consider the nature of believing; it is not like believing that two and two make four. Do not men believe on probability in other things? God has given all the evidence that man requires or needs; and if in a right mind, we shall thank God for the dispensation of light we have, willing to walk by faith and not by sight. If we do not get on in this way, we shall not get on at all. Divine justice punishes incredulity by credulity; by giving up the unbelieving to the dominion and bondage of strong delusions. When men get into a high mind and an unbelieving spirit, and reject the truth, God punishes them by letting them 'believe a lie.' Let us take heed how we say, like Thomas, we will not walk at all without such light as we think proper."

The opinion expressed by Dean Stanley, following Dr. Arnold (in Smith's "Bible Dictionary," Article "Thomas"), that Thomas is a remarkable example of "free inquiry combined with fervent belief," is one which I only mention in order to express my dissent from it.—I see nothing like "free inquiry" in this Apostle. I read of no question he asked of his brethren. I see no trace of any willingness to investigate, sift, weigh, and consider the testimony which they bore. I discover no readiness to go to the grave, to examine the linen clothes, to talk with Mary Magdalene, to question the two disciples who journeyed to Emmaus. All this would have been "free inquiry." But I see nothing of the kind. I only see a dull, obstinate, desponding declaration that, whatever his ten friends may say, he will not believe till he sees. This cannot surely deserve the name of "free inquiry!"—As to the "fervent belief" of Thomas, no doubt, at last, when his most compassionate Saviour almost forced conviction on him, in pity for his dulness, and made unbelief quite impossible, he made a most beautiful confession of faith. But it was a confession, we must remember, that came out only at the last moment, and was extracted, as it were, by a miracle of kindness. Above all, beautiful as it was, it did not prevent his gracious Master speaking words of grave and solemn rebuke. Beyond doubt, Thomas lay down that night a pardoned and forgiven man,—a man raised from faithlessness to strong faith. But we must not forget that he was not praised and commended, though raised, convinced, and pardoned. If words mean anything, he had received a reproof, and one that I doubt not he felt deeply. To me therefore it appears that, to represent him as an example of "free inquiry combined with fervent belief," is an entire mistake, and a misapprehension both of his character and of the whole drift of the remarkable narrative of this passage.

If, as I believe, St. Mark's remarkable words apply to this appearance of our Lord for the special benefit of Thomas, it is impossible to regard our Lord's language to Thomas in any other sense than that of rebuke. St. Mark says, "He appeared unto the eleven as they sat at meat, and upbraided them with their unbelief and hardness of heart, because they believed not them which had seen Him after He was risen." (Mark xvi. 14.) Most commentators certainly take this view. Chrysostom says that Thomas received a "sharp rebuke."

30, 31 —[*And many other signs, etc.*]   The two last verses in this chapter contain one of those parenthetical comments, or glosses, which are so peculiar to the Gospel of St. John. It must be admitted that they seem to break the thread of the narrative, and come in with a rather startling effect. We need not, therefore, wonder that the right meaning of the two verses has long been a subject of dispute.

(a) Some think, as Calvin, Ecolampadius, Brentius, Poole, Rollock, Lampe, Hengstenberg, Pearce, and Alford, that St. John refers to the whole history of Christ's ministry, and is comparing his own Gospel with the Gospels of Matthew, Mark, and Luke. They would paraphrase the two verses in the following way : —"Jesus did many other miracles during His ministry, under the eyes of His disciples, which are not recorded in this Gospel of mine, though they are recorded in the other three. But those few which are recorded in this, my Gospel, are recorded in order that you who read it may be convinced that Jesus is the Messiah, the Christ of God, and that believing on Him you may have eternal life through His name."—It is a heavy objection to this interpretation, that the two verses, on this view, appear to come in rather abruptly, and without much connection with what goes either before or after. In short, it is not very easy to explain why they come in here at all.—Moreover, it is not very easy to see the drift of the expression, "signs in presence of His disciples," considering that many of our Lord's greatest miracles were worked before people who were not disciples at all.—Furthermore, it is not very clear what St. John can mean by saying " other " signs. That word " other " seems to point to miracles just performed, yet there was no special miracle performed at this particular, beyond, of course, our Lord's miraculous appearances.

(b) Others, as Chrysostom, Theophylact, Rupertus, Beza, Bullinger, Calovius, Musculus, Gerhard, Ferus, Toletus, Maldonatus, Henry, Tholuck, Scott, Bloomfield, and Olshausen, think that St. John writes these two verses with a special reference to the wondrous signs and evidences which the Lord had just given to the disciples of His own resurrection from the dead. They would paraphrase the two verses in this way :—" Many other wondrous proofs did the Lord give to the Apostles of His own resurrection, which are not written down in this Gospel, though they are written in Matthew, Mark, and Luke. But the three appearances which I have narrated, are written down in order to convince you that Jesus is the true Messiah, the Christ of God, and that, believing this firmly, you may have eternal life through faith in His name."—According to this view the two verses refer to nothing but this twentieth chapter, and are a parenthetical comment on it. It is as though John would say, " Do not suppose that these three appearances of Christ are the only wondrous signs and proofs of His resurrection. There are others which you will find recorded in the other three Gospels. But I have related these three in order to confirm your faith, and to show you that in believing on a risen Saviour you are resting on solid ground."

Of the two views I prefer the second one, as involving the fewest difficulties. It is more probable, considering John's peculiar style of writing, to suppose that he makes a short parenthetical remark about a single chapter, than to suppose that he makes it about the whole of his Gospel. Above all this second view gets over the heavy objection that, after bringing his whole Gospel to a conclusion by a general remark on the whole of it as compared to the other three Gospels, St. John seems to begin again in the twenty-first chapter, and to write a postscript or appendix.—In short the common theory, that these two verses apply to the whole Gospel, makes St. John finish his history, lay down his pen, complete his work, and then suddenly take up his pen again, and add the twenty-first chapter as a kind of after-thought. To say the least, this is an undignified, not to say rather irreverent, view of the composition of an inspired writer !—The other theory, or the theory which strictly confines the application of the two concluding verses of the twentieth chapter to the matter contained in that chapter, viz., the signs which our Lord gave of His resurrection, is entirely in keeping with St. John's style of writing his Gospel. He simply remarks parenthetically that there are other proofs of Christ's resurrection, which are to be found in the other Gospels, and that he has only written down such accounts as he was guided by the Spirit to consider most calculated to stablish the faith of his readers.

I frankly confess that the passage appears to come in abruptly under any view, and I cannot expect that all will adopt the explanation which I have advocated. If the Gospel of St. John had ended with this twentieth chapter, I might perhaps have acquiesced in the theory that the two verses were meant to form a brief concluding remark about the whole of the Evangelist's work ; and a brief admission of the fact that he passed over many miracles recorded by Matthew, Mark, and Luke. But I cannot acquiesce in the theory, when I see that St. John goes on to write the twenty-first chapter. The existence of that chapter alone satisfies me that, in the two verses before us, St. John is only speaking of the signs of Christ's resurrection, which he has supplied, and is admitting that there are others in the other Gospels. As a rule, moreover, when I find a parenthetical comment or gloss in St. John's Gospel, I prefer to apply it to the immediate subject of which he is speaking. It is the habit of this Evangelist to turn aside for a moment, and make a short explanatory remark ; and then to take up the thread again, and go on with his history. Of this habit, I think the two verses before us are an example. When the Holy Ghost plenarily inspired the writer of any Book of Scripture, both as to his faith and his words, He did not prevent him writing in his own peculiar style.

Whatever view we may take of the matter in dispute about these two verses, there are things in them which are abundantly clear and ought never to be forgotten. For one thing, St. John generously recognizes the existence of other books beside his own, and disclaims the idea of his own Gospel being the only one which Christians ought to read. Happy is that author who can humbly say, " My book does not contain everything about the subject it handles. There are other books about it. Read them."—For another thing, we should note the grand end and object for which this and all the books of the New Testament were written. They were written to glorify Christ, to make us believe on Him as the only Saviour of sinners, and to lead us to eternal life through faith in His name.

It is interesting to remember that ecclesiastical historians assign to Thomas the honor of being the Apostle who first preached the Gospel in India ; and they also say that he there suffered martyrdom. A society of Christians in Malabar is

said to be still known by his name. Unhappily, the truth of
all this is very doubtful, and rests on a very sandy foundation.

JOHN XXI 1—14

1 After these things Jesus shewed himself again to the disciples at the sea of Tiberias; and on this wise shewed he *himself*.

2 There were together Simon Peter, and Thomas called Didymus, and Nathanael of Cana in Galilee, and the *sons* of Zebedee, and two other of his disciples.

3 Simon Peter saith unto them, I go a fishing. They say unto him, We also go with thee. They went forth, and entered into a ship immediately; and that night they caught nothing.

4 But when the morning was now come, Jesus stood on the shore: but the disciples knew not that it was Jesus.

5 Then Jesus saith unto them, Children, have ye any meat? they answered him, No.

6 And he said unto them, Cast the net on the right side of the ship, and ye shall find. They cast therefore, and now they were not able to draw it for the multitude of fishes.

7 Therefore that disciple whom Jesus loved saith unto Peter, It is the Lord. Now when Simon Peter heard that it was the Lord, he girt *his* fisher's coat *unto him* (for he was naked), and did cast himself into the sea.

8 And the other disciples came in a little ship (for they were not far from land, but as it were two hundred cubits); dragging the net with fishes.

9 As soon then as they were come to land, they saw a fire of coals there, and fish laid thereon, and bread.

10 Jesus saith unto them, Bring of the fish which ye have now caught.

11 Simon Peter went up, and drew the net to land full of great fishes, an hundred and fifty and three: and for all there were so many, yet was not the net broken.

12 Jesus saith unto them, Come *and* dine. And none of the disciples durst ask him, Who art thou ? knowing that it was the Lord.

13 Jesus then cometh, and taketh bread, and giveth them, and fish likewise.

14 This is now the third time that Jesus shewed himself to his disciples, after that he was risen from the dead.

THE appearance of our Lord Jesus Christ after His
resurrection, described in these verses, is a deeply interesting portion of the Gospel history.   The circumstances attending it have always been regarded as highly
allegorical and figurative, in every age of the Church.
It may, however, be justly doubted whether commentators and interpreters have not gone too far in this direction.   It is quite possible to spiritualize and filter away
the narratives of the Gospels, until we completely lose
sight of the plain meaning of words.   In the present
case we shall find it wise to confine ourselves to the

great, simple lessons, which the passage undoubtedly contains.

We should observe, for one thing, in these verses, *the poverty of the first disciples of Christ.* We find them working with their own hands, in order to supply their temporal wants, and working at one of the humblest of callings,—the calling of a fisherman. Silver and gold they had none, lands and revenues they had none, and therefore they were not ashamed to return to the business to which they had, most of them, been trained. Striking is the fact, that some of the seven here named were fishing, when our Lord first called them to be Apostles, and again fishing, when He ap peared to them almost the last time. We need not doubt that to the minds of Peter, James, and John, the coincidence would come home with peculiar power.

The poverty of the Apostles goes far to prove the divine origin of Christianity. These very men who toiled all night in a boat, dragging about a cold wet net, and taking nothing,—these very men who found it necessary to work hard in order that they might eat,— these very men were some of the first founders of the mighty Church of Christ, which has now overspread one-third of the globe. These were they who went forth from an obscure corner of the earth, and turned the world upside down. These were the unlearned and ignorant men, who boldly confronted the subtle systems of ancient philosophy, and silenced its advocates by the preaching of the cross. These were the men who at Ephesus, and Athens, and Rome, emptied the heathen temples of their worshippers, and turned away multitudes to a new and better faith. He that can explain these facts, except by admitting that Christianity came down from God, must be a strangely incredulous man. Reason and common sense lead us to only one conclu·

sion in the matter. Nothing can account for the rise and progress of Christianity but the direct interposition of God.

We should observe, for another thing, in these verses, *the different characters of different disciples of Christ.* Once more, on this deeply interesting occasion, we see Peter and John side by side in the same boat, and once more, as at the sepulchre, we see these two good men behaving in different ways. When Jesus stood on the shore, in the dim twilight of the morning, John was the first to perceive who it was, and to say, "It is the Lord;" but Peter was the first to spring into the water, and to struggle to get close to his Master. In a word, John was the first to see; but Peter was the first to act. John's gentle loving spirit was quickest to discern; but Peter's fiery, impulsive nature was quickest to stir and move. And yet both were believers, both were true-hearted disciples, both loved the Lord in life, and were faithful to Him unto death. But their natural temperaments were not the same.

Let us never forget the practical lesson before us. As long as we live, let us diligently use it in forming our estimate of believers. Let us not condemn others as graceless and unconverted, because they do not see the path of duty from our stand-point, or feel things exactly as we feel them. "There are diversities of gifts, but the same Spirit." (1 Cor. xii. 4.) The gifts of God's children are not bestowed precisely in the same measure and degree. Some have more of one gift, and some have more of another. Some have gifts which shine more in public, and some which shine more in private. Some are more bright in a passive life, and some are more bright in an active one. Yet each and all the members of God's family, in their own way and in their own season, bring glory to God. Martha was "careful

and troubled about much serving," when Mary " sat at
the feet of Jesus and heard His word." Yet there came
a day at Bethany, when Mary was crushed and pros-
trated by overmuch sorrow, and Martha's faith shone
more brightly than her sister's. (Luke x. 39, 40; John
xi. 20—28.) Nevertheless both were loved by our
Lord. The one thing needful is to have the grace of
the Spirit, and to love Christ. Let us love all of whom
this can be said, though they may not see with our eyes
in everything. The Church of Christ needs servants of
all kinds, and instruments of every sort ; penknives as
well as swords, axes as well as hammers, chisels as well
as saws, Marthas as well as Marys, Peters as well as
Johns. Let our ruling maxim be this, " Grace be with
all them that love our Lord Jesus Christ in sincerity."
(Ephes. vi. 24.)

We should observe, lastly, in these verses, *the abundant evidence which Scripture supplies of our Lord Jesus Christ's resurrection*. Here, as in other places, we
find an unanswerable proof that our Lord rose again
with a real material body, and a proof seen by seven
grown-up men with their own eyes, at one and the
same time. We see Him sitting, talking, eating, drinking, on the shore of the lake of Galilee, and to all appearance for a considerable time. The morning sun of
spring shines down on the little party. They are alone
by the well-known Galilean lake, far away from the
crowd and noise of Jerusalem. In the midst sits the
Master, with the nail-prints in His hands,—the very
Master whom they had all followed for three years, and
one of them, at least, had seen hanging on the cross.
They could not be deceived. Will any one pretend to
say that stronger proof could be given that Jesus rose
from the dead? Can any one imagine better evidence
of a fact ? That Peter was convinced and satisfied we

know. He says himself to Cornelius, We did " eat and
drink with Him after He rose from the dead." (Acts x.
41.) Those who in modern times say they are not convinced, may as well say that they are determined not
to believe any evidence at all.

Let us all thank God that we have such a cloud of
witnesses to prove that our Lord rose again. The resurrection of Christ is the grand proof of Christ's divine
mission. He told the Jews they need not believe He
was the Messiah, if He did not rise again the third day.
—The resurrection of Christ is the top-stone of the work
of redemption. It proved that He finished the work He
came to do, and, as our Substitute, had overcome the
grave.—The resurrection of Christ is a miracle that no
infidel can explain away. Men may carp and cavil at
Balaam's ass, and Jonah in the whale's belly, if they
please, but till they can prove that Christ did not rise
again we need not be moved.—Above all, the resurrection of Christ is the pledge of our own. As the grave
could not detain the Head, so it shall not detain the
members. Well may we say with Peter, " Blessed be
the God and Father of our Lord Jesus Christ, who hath
begotten us again unto a lively hope by the resurrection of Jesus Christ from the dead." (1 Peter i. 3.)

NOTES JOHN XXI 1—14

The last chapter of St. John's Gospel requires a few preliminary observations. Certain very objectionable theories have
been propounded about it. (a) Some, as Grotius, maintain
that the chapter was not written by John at all, that his Gospel ended with the last verse of the twentieth chapter, and
that the twenty-first chapter is the work of another writer, perhaps one John, an Ephesian presbyter ! (b) Others do not go so
far as this, and yet maintain that the chapter must be regarded
as a postscript or appendix to the Gospel, and was probably
added, as an afterthought, by St. John himself, some years after the rest of the Gospel. The chief ground on which these
theories are built is the passage with which the twentieth
chapter ends. Men tell us that the two concluding verses of

that chapter were evidently intended to finish and wind up John's narrative, and that the twenty-first chapter comes in awkwardly and abruptly.

From all these theories I entirely dissent, and repudiate them altogether. I see no proof whatever that the two last verses of the twentieth chapter were intended to be a winding up of the whole Gospel. To me they appear to be a characteristic comment of the Evangelist, such as he often makes, on the account he has given in the chapter of our Lord's appearances to the disciples after His resurrection, and nothing more. To me it appears perfectly natural that he should go on writing, and give a further account of our Lord's most instructive appearance at the sea of Galilee; and I see in the narrative no abruptness or awkward fitting whatever. On the contrary, I see a peculiar beauty in the selection of the matter which the twenty-first chapter contains. It seems to me a most fitting conclusion to the whole narrative of the Gospel, to tell us our Lord's last sayings about two such Apostles as Peter and John. —Concerning Peter, it should be remembered that none of the Apostles had professed so much, and yet fallen so sadly as he had. John takes care to tell us how graciously and emphatically Jesus restores him to his commission, and specially bids him feed His Church, and foretells his end.—Concerning John, it should be remembered that he had been peculiarly mentioned, as the disciple whom Jesus loved. He meekly tells us that the only prediction about himself, if it can be called one, was that his future end was left in obscurity by his Lord. And thus he concludes his Gospel. If any one thinks that such a chapter comes in awkwardly, and is not a fitting conclusion to John's narrative after the twentieth chapter, I cannot agree with him.

Of evidence, whether external or internal, that the theories I have referred to deserve consideration, there is a conspicuous absence. There is not the slightest proof that any trustworthy ancient writer ever regarded the last chapter of St. John's Gospel, as less genuine and less inspired than the rest of the book. There is nothing in the language or style of the chapter, to create any suspicion that any other person than John composed it. Those who wish to see this subject fully investigated, are advised to study Wordsworth's Appendix to St. John's Gospel, in his Commentary.

When I add to this statement the fact that, in every age, the wisest and holiest commentators have seen in this chapter several singularly deep and interesting types of the history and position of Christ's Church in the world, I think I shall have said enough to satisfy many readers, that they may approach the last chapter of St. John's Gospel with as much reverence, and as much reasonable expectation of getting benefit from it, as any other chapter in the book.

1 — [*After these things.*] This expression is indefinite. It only means that the appearance of our Lord, about to be described in this chapter, took place "after" His appearance on the eighth day following His resurrection. The time therefore, in the verse before us, is some day between the eighth and the fortieth day, when He ascended up into heaven. But what precise day we cannot tell. One thing at any rate we may be sure of. It was not the Sabbath day, or else the disciples would not have gone fishing. Even on the day following the crucifixion, Christ's disciples "rested according to the commandment." (Luke xxiii. 56.)

[*Jesus showed Himself again...disciples.*] A deep question naturally rises out of the expression before us. Where was our Lord on the days when He did not "manifest or show Himself" to His disciples? It is evident that He was not with them always, and that He only visited them at intervals. Where was He then in the mean time ?—Not in heaven, we may be sure, because He had not yet ascended. But where was He on earth ? I speak of course of His human nature. As God, He is everywhere. But where was He, as a man ? This is a mysterious matter, and one about which it is useless to speculate. Enough for us to know that our Lord was visible, or invisible, and appeared suddenly in one place or another place, and assumed one form or another form, at His own will, after a manner that we cannot understand. But it is quite plain that, when we read the words in Acts, "being seen of them forty days" (Acts i. 3), we must not suppose them to mean that our Lord was seen every day. It only means that during forty days He was seen at intervals. Each appearance, we doubt not, had its own special purpose and intention.

Chrysostom remarks, "It is clear from the words 'showed Himself,' that Christ was not seen (after His resurrection) unless He condescended, because His body was henceforth incorruptible, and of unmixed purity."

[*At the Sea of Tiberias.*] Concerning this remarkable piece of water, sometimes called the Lake of Gennesaret, and sometimes the Sea of Galilee, I have already said something in my note on John vi. 1. (Vol. 1, "Expository Thoughts on John," p. 329.) It is a fresh-water lake, through which the river Jordan runs, twelve and a half miles long and six and three-quarters broad, and remarkable in a geological point of view, as being six hundred and fifty-five feet below the level of the Mediterranean Sea.* In a theological point of view it must always be most interesting to a Christian, because some of our Lord's mightiest miracles were wrought on it, or close to it.

---

* I give the above measurements from Tristram's "Topography of the Holy Land," as I believe they are more trustworthy than those which I gave in the first volume of this work.

Here our Lord walked on the waters, and came to the disciples toiling in rowing. Here He stilled the wind and waves with a word. Here He granted to four of His Apostles a miraculous draught of fishes. Here He provided payment of the tribute-money, out of the mouth of a fish which He commanded Peter to catch. On the banks of this lake He fed a multitude with a few loaves and fishes. On a high ground overhanging this lake He cast out the legion of devils, and allowed them to drive 2,000 swine into the sea. In the towns upon this lake, Chorazin, Bethsaida, and Capernaum, He did some of His mightiest works. Sitting in a boat on this lake, He delivered the parable of the Sower. In short, of all the districts in which our Lord preached and wrought miracles, there was none which saw and heard so much as the district round "the Sea of Tiberias."

Can we doubt, when we remember all this, that our Lord had a deep purpose and meaning, in appearing to His disciples at the Sea of Tiberias? Can we doubt that He meant to remind them of all they had seen in former days of his wisdom, love, and power, by the side of these well-known waters? He knew well the influence which scenery and places exercise over the mind of man. He would recall to the memory of His disciples all that they had witnessed in the early days of His ministry. Above all He would stir the hearts of Peter and James and John, by saying some of His last things to them, at the very place where He had first called them to leave their boats and nets, to follow Him, and to become fishers of men. Where He had begun with them, there He would have one of His last interviews with them, before leaving the world.

The exact spot where our Lord appeared at the Sea of Tiberias, is of course unknown. But when we remember that Bethsaida, at the north end of the lake, was "the city of Andrew and Peter," (John i. 44), we may safely conjecture that the scene of this chapter was somewhere near Bethsaida. The boat in which Peter went fishing would most probably either be his own boat, or the property of some relative or friend in his native city.

[*And on this wise shewed He Himself.*] This is a somewhat curious sentence. It does not, I think, only mean "The manner of His appearance was as follows." I suspect that it was inserted emphatically, in order to direct our special attention to all the little details of the occurrence, and to remind us that even the minutest parts of it have a deep spiritual meaning.

2.—[*There were together Simon Peter, etc.*] This verse contains the names of the seven witnesses, before whom the remarkable appearance of Christ, about to be described, took place. Seven, we may remember, is the number of perfection, and the evidence of seven witnesses was regarded as the most complete evidence that could be given. Two of the seven, we shall ob-

serve, are not named, and we are left entirely to conjecture
who these two were. Most commentators think they must
have been Andrew and Philip,—Andrew because he was Peter's brother, and Philip because he was an inhabitant of Bethsaida, on the lake. But we really do not know, and it is useless to guess.

Why these seven *alone*, out of the eleven, were here, we are
not told. But we need not doubt there was good reason. All
the company of the Apostles, we may believe, went into Galilee when the passover feast was over, according to our Lord's
command, and probably very soon after His appearance for the
benefit of Thomas. But where Matthew, Simon, James the
less, and Jude, were, on the present occasion, we do not know.

It is worth noting that this is the only place in St. John's
Gospel, where he mentions the name of his own father, Zebedee.

Why these seven disciples *in particular* were together, is
worth inquiry. The presence of Simon Peter, as he lived in
Galilee, and had a special message from our Lord that He was
going into Galilee, we can understand. Thomas, once convinced
that Jesus had risen, would very likely take care to stick close
to Peter and John. Nathanael lived at Cana in Galilee, and was
probably Bartholomew. Augustine, however, doubts this. The
two sons of Zebedee were Simon's partners, and are always
found together with him on great occasions.

The message of our Lord about Galilee, we must remember,
was, " Tell my brethren that they go into Galilee : there shall
they see Me." (Matt. xxviii. 10.) These were our Lord's own
words.—The angel also said to the women, " He goeth before
you into Galilee : there shall ye see Him." (Matt. xxviii. 7.)
We might reasonably expect to find the Apostles in Galilee after
this.

On Thomas being one of the party, Henry remarks, " Thomas
is named next to Peter, as if he now kept closer to the meetings
of the Apostles than ever. It is well if losses by our neglect
make us more careful afterwards not to let opportunities slip."

3 —[*Simon Peter saith unto them, etc.*] Some worthy commentators have presumed to find fault with Peter for going a fishing.
They say that he showed a disposition to return to the world,
and to follow his worldly calling once more. From this view
I entirely dissent. I see no harm whatever in Peter's conduct
on this occasion. He and his companions were poor men, and
must needs work in order to provide for their subsistence.
There was nothing wrong in the act of fishing, and it was only
natural to take up the business with which they were most familiar. The great business of going out as our Lord's messengers,
to preach the Gospel, was not to begin until His ascension, and
in the interval it was better to follow an honest calling than to

be idle. Neither in Peter's proposal, nor in the simple frank consent of his companions, can I detect a jot of proof that any·thing wrong was done. Idleness does Christians far more in·jury than work. Among the Jews every man, whatever his rank or position might be, was required to learn a worldly call ing.

Chrysostom remarks, "Since neither Christ was with them continually, nor was the Spirit yet given, nor they at that time entrusted with anything, having nothing to do, they went after their trade."

Augustine observes, "The Apostles were not forbidden to seek their necessary subsistence by the exercise of their craft, a lawful and permitted one, if at any time they had no other means of subsistence." He also remarks that they were no more to blame than St. Paul was, when he wrought with his own hands as a tent-maker. (Acts xviii. 3.)

Calvin remarks, "Peter had not yet been enjoined to appear in public, for the discharge of his office of teaching, but had only been reminded of his future calling (John xx. 21—23), that he and others might understand that they had not in vain been chosen from the beginning. Meanwhile, they were to do what they were accustomed to do, and what belonged to men in pri·vate life."

Ferus remarks that a lawful business is not sinful. If Mat·thew had gone back to a publican's life it would have been a very different thing from Peter going to fish.

Stier remarks that this going to fish was only carrying out our Lord's words. "But *now*, he that hath a purse, let him take it, and likewise his scrip: and he that hath no sword, let him sell his garment and buy one." (Luke xxii. 36.)

The expression "a boat" should have been translated "the boat." Does not the use of the article show that this was that well-known boat, which our Lord and His disciples had always used, when they went on the lake?

In the fact that "they caught nothing that night," there is nothing that would surprise a fisherman. Of all callings by which men earn their living none is more uncertain than that of a fisherman. (Luke v. 4.) "Night" is the time when most fish are caught, as all who are familiar with fishing know. That there was probably a deep typical meaning in all this, I shall hope to show when I reach the end of the passage. I think it better to reserve all remarks upon that point, until I can present them to the reader in one continuous form.—For the present, both here and throughout the passage, I shall simply comment on the facts as facts.

Burgon remarks, "One thing is certain, and the circumstance is full of interest. It must have been their *necessities* which

sent forth the Apostles on this lowly errand of fishing. And
yet these were they on whom the Church was to be built !
These seven were among the names written on the twelve
foundations of the heavenly Jerusalem."

Burgon also thinks that the words " went forth," point to the
Apostles sitting together indoors, in the evening, and very like
ly on a Sabbath evening.

4 —[*But when the morning...come.*] This probably means " When
the day began to break, so that an object at a little distance
could be seen." As soon as there was enough light, through
the grey dawn, the party in the boat saw the figure of a person
on the shore. There is little or no twilight in countries so far
south as Palestine. Night goes, and day follows, much more
suddenly than with us.

[*Jesus stood on the shore.*] This reads like a sudden and in-
stantaneous appearance, like that which took place when our
Lord appeared the first time in the midst of the disciples. Just
in the same manner, it seems to me, in a moment, in the twink-
ling of an eye, Jesus appeared standing on the shore of the
lake. The risen body of our Lord, we must remember, ap
peared or disappeared,—was present or absent, according to His
will, in a moment of time.

Grotius remarks that our Lord never went on the sea after
His resurrection. (Comp. Rev. xxi. 1.) "There was no more
sea."

[*But the disciples knew not...was Jesus.*] The disciples did
not recognize our Lord, in my opinion, because He appeared in
another form, just as He appeared to the two who were journeying to Emmaus. I reject entirely the idea that the dim light
of the early morning was the reason why they did not know
Him. It is evident to me that our Lord's risen body did not, on
any occasion, after He rose again, for some mysterious reason,
look exactly like the body He had before His crucifixion. It
was the same, and yet not the same, if I may so speak. Will
it not be so with our own bodies when we rise again at the last
day ? We shall be the same, and yet not the same.

It is noteworthy that the Greek words here used, were exactly those that were used about Mary Magdalene, when she
thought the gardener spoke to her, and " knew not that it was
Jesus." (John xx. 14.)

5 —[*Then Jesus saith unto them, etc.*] We cannot suppose for a
moment, that our Lord did not know whether the disciples had
any meat, when He asked the question of this verse. It is
clear to me that He asked it in order to raise attention in the
minds of the disciples, and to put them at ease in conversing
with them. He appeared as a stranger, who was graciously
pleased to say something familiar and friendly. Does it not remind us of the way in which He began conversation with the

woman of Samaria, and broke the ice, as it were, between Him and her ? "Give Me to drink," He said. (John iv. 7.) Nothing sets people so much at ease, when they meet as strangers, as courteous inquiries about the simple matters of daily life.

The word " meat" is a striking example of the change which comes over the meaning of English words in the course of time. It means literally " anything eatable."—Two centuries ago the word " meat " was a translation which no Englishman would misunderstand. Now, unfortunately, it is a word confined entirely to " flesh." No translation can ever be perfect. All require occasional reverent revision.

The context seems to me to show that our Lord's inquiry was specially meant to apply to the success of the disciples in fishing. " Have ye caught anything that can be eaten ? " The disciples evidently took it in this sense.

It is worth noticing that our Lord must have spoken in a very loud voice, when He addressed His disciples in this verse. We are distinctly told that the boat was two hundred cubits, at least one hundred yards, from land, in the eighth verse, and there is nothing to show that the disciples put out further into the lake, when our Lord told them to cast in their net again. I mention this, because some, as Gerhard, Henry, and Besser, think that there was something curt, rough, and rather abrupt in the answer of the disciples. But they seem to forget that a conversation carried on over a hundred yards of water, could only be carried on in very brief and abrupt phrases.

The word " children " in this verse, rendered " sirs " in the margin, is to my mind rightly rendered in the text. It is a familiar, friendly mode of address, like our English " boys " or " lads," not necessarily implying great youth in the persons addressed.

6 —[*And He said...cast...right side...find.*] Our Lord now goes a step further in order to discover Himself to His disciples. He gives a command or counsel to cast their net, which they had apparently hauled into the boat, once more into the water, and upon the right side of the ship. Such advice, and such a promise of success from a stranger, could hardly fail to strike the disciples. Would it not raise in the quick mind of John a suspicion, that this was no common stranger who spoke ? Would not he and Peter both remember a former occasion, when they " toiled all the night and took nothing," and yet, at the command of their Master, had let down their nets again with marvellous success ? I think they would.

To me it seems highly probable that the disciples had finished their night's work, had hauled up their net into the boat, and were rowing toward home, tired of their profitless toil, when our Lord appeared and spoke to them.

[*They cast, therefore, and now...fishes.*] In the fact that the
disciples found a multitude óf fishes in their net the moment
they acted on our Lord's advice, there is, in one point of view,
nothing extraordinary. Many fish swim in shoals, and it is
quite a matter of common experience among fishermen, that
one boat may take nothing, while a few yards off another boat
has an immense haul. The miracle consisted in the perfect
knowledge that our Lord ˙possessed, as to where the fish were,
and on which side of the boat to cast the net. This alone
proved that He was omniscient.

Whether it is likely that seven tired fishermen, after working all night, and hauling up their net and stowing it away,
would stop on their way home at the advice of a stranger, and
cast in their net once more in broad daylight, is a point which
admits of question. My own impression is that a secret power
and influence went with our Lord's words, and, without knowing why, the seven disciples felt irresistibly constrained to do
what the mysterious stranger advised.

7 —[*Therefore that disciple...the Lord.*] The first to recognize,
Jesus was the disciple who first believed the resurrection,—the
beloved disciple John, who as usual does not give his own name.
With characteristic quickness and sensitiveness, he at once felt
convinced that the mysterious stranger must be his beloved
Master. Love is always keen-sighted. It suddenly flashed
across his mind that the advice given by the stranger, and the
result of following the advice, had been precisely the same
three years before. The stranger must surely know what happened then, and must have been present! The stranger must
be the Lord Himself! Thoughts such as these most probably
passed through his mind far quicker than we can describe them ;
and at once he said to his friend Peter, who was most likely the
leading man in the boat, " It is the Lord."

Rollock thinks it was the wonderful draught of fishes that
made John know it was the Lord. "He saw in it not only
miraculous power, but wonderful bountifulness and liberality,"
just like His Divine Master.

[*Now when Simon Peter heard, etc.*] The conduct of the
Apostle Peter, here described, is eminently characteristic of the
man. It is just what might have been expected from the disciple who went out of the ship to walk on the water on a former occasion, and drew his sword, and began to smite, when our
Lord was surrounded by His enemies. Fervent, warm-hearted,
impulsive, impetuous, affectionate, thinking nothing of consequences, acting on the spur of present feeling, he at once
plunges into the sea, when he hears that his Lord is on the
shore, and struggles to get close to Him. Whatever we may
think of his hasty behavior, we must all admire his love. Zeal
for Christ deserves respect, even when it leads a man into
hasty action. Enthusiasm, even when it runs to seed, is better
than indifference.

We should note how Peter rushed into action, the very moment that he " heard " the words, " It is the Lord." He did not wait to see, like Thomas on another occasion, but was satisfied with a word from his brother John. A single spark is enough to kindle tinder, and a single word is enough to stir a heart, when its affections are deeply concerned.

The Greek word which is rendered " fisher's coat," is only found here in the New Testament. Theophylact says it was the upper garment of a Syrian fisherman. The context seems to show that it was a sort of garment which a fisherman laid aside when in the very act of handling his nets.

When we read that Peter was " naked," I see no reason why we should suppose that he was entirely without clothes. I think the meaning is, that he was *comparatively* naked, having laid aside all his looser garments, as a fisherman in that hot climate naturally would, in order to be able to handle wet nets and fish with greater convenience. And when we read that he girt around him his fisher's coat, I think it simply means that he took up the loose outward garment that he wore when he went on the lake to fish, and girded it tightly round his waist before jumping into the sea.

When we read that Peter " cast himself into the sea," I see no reason for supposing that he swam to land. In order to swim, it is not likely that he would put on more clothes !—I rather think that the water where he and his companions were was shallow, and that he waded to land. He knew that his large fishing-boat drew too much water to get near shore, and he was too impatient to wait for the slow process of launching the little boat, and coming ashore in it. I cannot doubt, as he jumped into the water, that he remembered going out of the same ship on a former occasion, and walking on the water " to go to Jesus."

It is only fair to say that Chrysostom thinks that Peter swam. On the other hand Brentius, Gerhard, and Archbishop Whately (see Bengel's " Gnomon," English translation), think that he walked on the water, in a miraculous manner, as on the former occasion !

8 —[*And the other disciples came, etc.*] Here we see, placed in strong contrast with Peter's action, the way in which the six remaining Apostles came to land. They came in the boat (" a little ship " is a defective translation), which means the skiff or punt which most large fishing vessels have with them. The water was evidently too shallow for the large fishing vessel to get near shore. And they came slowly, we may be sure, because, for two hundred cubits, or one hundred yards, they had to drag behind their little boat a net full of fish. How heavy a drag such a net makes on a little boat's progress through the water, those only know who have had experience.

It is noteworthy that we are not told that Peter got to shore at all sooner than his brethren. This point is, singularly enough, passed over in silence. But wading through deep water is slow work, and the fact that Peter put his coat on before plunging into the sea, is, to my own mind, strong indirect proof that he did not swim, but wade.

It is noteworthy that Peter forgot fish, and net, and boat, and everything else, in his anxiety to reach Christ. It was like the Samaritan woman who " left her waterpot." (John iv. 28.)

9 —[*As soon then...fire...coals...fish...bread.*] I cannot doubt that this verse records a miracle. Our blessed Lord made preparation for the bodily wants of His wearied disciples, and mercifully " furnished a table for them in the wilderness." (Ps. lxxviii. 19.) The burning fire, the fish lying on it, the bread, were all the creation of Him who had but to will a thing and it was done. Ever thoughtful, ever compassionate, our Lord thought good at this appearing, to show His poor toiling disciples that He cared for their bodies as well as their souls, and remembered that they were men. Who can tell but this miracle took place near the very spot where He had formerly fed five thousand men with a little bread and fish ? I cannot doubt that the bread and fish thus miraculously created would remind the Apostles of " loaves and fishes " multiplied. Once more they saw the same miraculous food, *bread and fish*, provided by the same Almighty power of their Lord.

The Greek word rendered " fire of coals," is only found in two places in the New Testament, here and in the account of the scene in the High Priest's hall at our blessed Lord's examination before Annas. (John xviii. 18.) It was a " fire of coals " at which the servants of the High Priest warmed themselves, and before which the Apostle Peter denied his Lord. Some think that our Lord had a special object in view by having a " fire of coals " in this place, and that was to remind Peter of his fall. But perhaps the idea is far-fetched.

Stier argues strongly, but needlessly in my judgment, that this provision of bread and fish was made by the angels. In any case it was a miracle, and an act of creation.

Quesnel observes, " Here are miracles upon miracles. The same power which filled the net with fishes in the midst of the sea, created others upon land, to show His disciples that it was not from want of power to give them fish that Christ asked for some, and ordered them to fish for them."

10 —[*Jesus saith unto them, Bring, etc.*] In this verse our Lord calls on the disciples to bring proof that, in casting the net at His command, they had not labored in vain. It was the second saying that He spoke, we must remember, on this occasion. The first saying was, " Cast the net on the right side, and ye shall find." The second saying was, " Bring up the fish which

ye have now caught," with a strong emphasis on the word
"now." I believe our Lord's object was to show the disciples
that the secret of success was to work at His command, and to
act with implicit obedience to His word. It is as though He
said, " Draw up the net ; and see for yourselves how profitable
it is to do what I tell you." Fish for food they did not want
now, for that was provided for them. Proof of the power of
Christ's blessing, and the importance of working under Him
was the lesson to be taught, and as they drew up the net they
would learn it.

11.—[*Simon Peter went up, etc.*] I see no reason for supposing,
in this verse, that Peter alone drew up the net. I think it reasonable to suppose that he is named as leader of the party, and
captain of the boat. But I believe that all the others helped
him. The " going up " must mean that Peter went on board
the little boat.

Once more we see two miracles recorded in this verse. One
miracle was the singularly large catch of fish which the net
contained, a quantity evidently exceeding what was generally
taken at one haul. The other miracle was the singular fact,
that, in spite of this large quantity of fish, the net was " not
broken." Miracle on miracle passed under the eyes of the astonished disciples.—Can we doubt that their minds recalled the
miraculous draught of fishes on a former occasion, when " their
net brake," and our Lord's words, " Fear not ; from henceforth
thou shalt catch men ; " and also his original saying, "Follow
Me, and I will make you fishers of men ?" And can we doubt
that some of them remembered the parable of the kingdom of
Heaven being like to " a net cast into the sea," and finally
drawn to shore ? (Luke v. 10. Matt. iv. 19 ; xiii. 47.)

Concerning the number one hundred and fifty-three, we
know nothing, and it is useless to speculate. Some have
thought that it refers to the languages, and some to the tribes
or nations of the world,—each, it is alleged, about one hundred
and fifty in number. But this is only guess-work. Yet it is
worth remembering, that the strangers whom Solomon employed in building the first temple were precisely-*one hundred
and fifty-three thousand and six hundred.* Let the remark be
taken for what it is worth. (2 Chron. ii. 17.)

Pearce calls attention to a remark of Jerome, that Oppian, a
Greek poet of Cilicia, in the second century, who wrote on fishing, " has given an account of the number of fishes known to
him in his time, being exactly one hundred and fifty-three."
This, at any rate, is curious.

Scott makes the remark, that " this draught of fishes might
be sold for a considerable sum of money, which the Apostles
would have need of, on their return to Jerusalem before the
day of Pentecost." There may be something in the idea.

12 —[*Jesus saith...Come and dine.*] The object of this gracious invitation seems to me to have been two-fold. It was meant partly to show our Lord's tender compassion for the weary bodies of His disciples. Though risen, He knew and felt for their wants, and would supply food for them when hungry and fatigued. It was meant partly to show that, though risen from the dead, with a glorified body, He would be on the same loving terms of familiarity and kindness as before with His disciples. They need not be frightened at Him. He had not forgotten them. He did not mean to keep them at a distance. He was still one who would eat and drink with them, as a man eateth and drinketh with his friends. It is written, "I will come in to him, and sup with him, and he with Me." (Rev. iii. 20.) An old divine says, "Christ loveth to deal familiarly with men."

The Greek word rendered "dine," does not necessarily mean a mid-day meal. Parkhurst shows, on the contrary, from Xenophon, that it may mean a morning repast. As things are in England now, the translation is a peculiarly unfortunate one. Two or three centuries ago, when people dined at eleven o'clock, the unfitness of it would not have been so remarkable. The meaning evidently is, "Come and partake of a morning meal."

[*And none...durst ask...the Lord.*] These words describe the state of mind in which the disciples were at this moment. They all felt convinced and satisfied that the Person before them was the Lord. They felt no doubt; and no one was the least disposed to say, "Who art thou?" Nevertheless they all felt awed and solemnized by His presence. A deep sense of the mysterious nature of their Lord, in consequence of His resurrection, filled their minds with an indefinable sensation of mingled embarrassment, reverence, and fear. Surely we can all understand this! Even when Joseph spoke lovingly to his brethren, and revealed himself to them, they were "troubled at his presence." (Gen. xlv. 3.) To sit, and eat, and drink, in the company with one who had risen from the dead, and appeared and disappeared after a supernatural manner, was no light thing. Who can wonder that they felt awed?

Chrysostom says, "Seeing that His form was altered, and full of awfulness, they were amazed, and desired to ask something concerning it. But fear, and their knowledge that He was not some other but the same, checked the inquiry; and they only ate what He, with greater exertion of power than before, created for them. For here Jesus no more looked up to heaven, nor performed those human acts, showing that those also which He did formerly were done by way of condescension."

13 —[*Jesus then cometh and taketh bread, etc.*] This verse describes what took place at this meal, or as our Bible calls it, this dinner. Our Lord came forward, as the host and entertainer of the seven astonished disciples, and gave them bread and fish, as He had doubtless often done on former occasions, and perhaps at the same place. He doubtless meant to give the disciples one more plain proof that He had risen from the dead. Alone by the Sea of Galilee, in the open air, far from the fear of interruption, in broad daylight, He eats and drinks at a social meal. Could these seven men ever doubt from that day, if they had doubted before, that Jesus rose from the dead? He meant, furthermore, to encourage them to continue looking to Him, as they had done before, as a loving, familiar, sympathizing friend. Though risen, He would have them see practical proof that He could be touched with the feeling of their infirmities, and cared for their bodies as well as their souls. He meant, not least, to remind them of His great miracle of feeding the multitude with a few loaves and fishes. He would freshen their memory of that wondrous miracle, and show them that He would continue doing for them what He had formerly done for those who followed Him in the wilderness.

Chrysostom here remarks, that we are not directly told that Jesus ate with the disciples, but that it is probable from Luke's words in Acts i. 4, that He did. "How," he remarks, " it is not ours to say. These things came to pass in too strange a manner. His nature did not even need food. It was an act of condescension in proof of the resurrection." (See Gen. xviii. 8.)

14 —[*This is now the third time, etc.*] In this verse St. John winds up the wonderful story he has just told, by one of his peculiar parenthetical comments. Concerning the meaning of the expression " third time," there has been, in my judgment, much needless dispute. No doubt it is perfectly true that this was not literally the third time that our Lord was seen by any one after His resurrection. On the contrary, we know of at least six different appearances before this one: viz. (1) to Mary Magdalene, (2) to Joanna and other women, (3) to Simon Peter, (4) to two disciples going to Emmaus, (5) to ten Apostles together, (6) to the eleven, for the special benefit of Thomas.— But it is no less true that this is strictly and literally the *third time* that Jesus appeared to any number of the disciples gathered together.—And it is also the *third day*, as Augustine remarks, that our Lord was pleased to appear at all. The first five appearances were all on the very same day when He rose from the dead. The sixth was a week afterwards, when He appeared to rebuke the unbelief of Thomas. And the appearance recorded in this chapter, though the seventh in number, took place on the third day only, that any one on earth saw Him after He rose.

The question now remains to be considered. Has the narrative contained in these fourteen verses any deep spiritual and allegorical meaning? Were we intended to read the passage simply as a description of one of our Lord's appearances after

His resurrection, and an account of one of His miracles? Or is the narrative a typical one? Is the passage intended to convey, under figures and symbols, great prophetical truths concerning the work of the ministry, and the history of the Church in every age, until the Lord comes? The question is a serious one, and demands serious consideration.

(a) On the one hand, there is undeniable danger in the habit of seeking spiritual and allegorical meanings in the plain historical facts of God's Word. We may go so far in this direction, that, like Origen, and too often Augustine, we may lose sight of the primary simple meaning of Scripture, and turn the Bible into a mere book of riddles, which is useless to any common man, and useful only to those who have very fertile and fanciful imaginations. In fact, if we are always extracting figurative meanings out of Scripture, we may destroy the usefulness of the Book altogether. There must be some limit to the system of figurative interpretation. As a rule, I shrink intuitively from putting any sense on God's Word, which is not the obvious and plain sense of its language. Hooker's words are weighty and wise: " When a literal construction of a text will stand, that which is furthest from the letter is commonly the worst."

(b) On the other hand, it is impossible to deny that all Christ's miracles were meant, more or less, to teach great spiritual truths, under allegories and figures ; and the passage before us is a miracle. In addition to this, we must remember that the occasion of the miracle before us was a peculiarly solemn one,—that the Apostles needed certain great truths to be impressed on their attention with peculiar force, by facts as well as by words,—and that, on the eve of His ascension into heaven, our Lord would be exceedingly likely to remind them of their duty, and their position as ministers, by things under their eyes as well as by instruction in their ears. Finally let us try to put ourselves in the position of the seven Apostles on the occasion before us, and try to imagine what they thought and felt about the incidents of this remarkable morning. It is very hard to imagine that they saw nothing but a simple miracle in all that happened. I cannot think so.—I think their hearts must have burned within them, and old spiritual truths, which they had heard before, must have revived in their minds with fresh power, and been written on their souls as with the point of a diamond, never to be effaced.

On the whole, then, I cannot avoid the conclusion, that the familiar verses before us probably contain, under symbolical facts, great spiritual truths. I think we are fairly justified in regarding the passage as a great parable, or vision, or allegory, intended to convey to the Church of Christ lessons for all time. And I am strengthened in this conclusion by the remarkable fact, that almost all commentators, of every school and in every age, have taken this view of the passage. Even Grotius, cold and rationalistic as his tone of exposition too frequently is, puts a figurative sense on several circumstances of the passage. Other expositors, of a more figurative and imaginative turn of mind, go into heights and depths, where I cannot pretend to follow them. I shall content myself with pointing out the more obvious spiritual lessons which I think the passage was probably meant to convey.

(a) I think that Christ's remarkable appearance to the disciples, when they were in the act of fishing, was meant to remind them and the whole Church of the primary duty of ministers. They were doing work which was strikingly emblematic of their calling. They were to be " fishers of men."

(b) I think the want of success in catching fish which the disciples had, until the Lord appeared, was meant to teach that without Christ's presence and blessing ministers can do nothing.

(c) I think the marvellous success which attended the cast of the net, when Christ gave the command, was meant to teach that, when Christ is pleased to give success to ministers, nothing can prevent souls being brought into the Gospel net, converted and saved.

(d) I think the drawing of the net to shore at last, was meant to remind the disciples and all ministers, of what will happen when the Lord comes again. The work of the Church will be completed, and the reckoning of results will take place.

(e) I think the dinner prepared and provided for the disciples, when the net was drawn to the shore, was meant to remind ministers that there will be the great "marriage supper of the Lamb" at last, when Christ Himself shall welcome His faithful servants and ministers, and " come forth and serve them." (Luke xii. 37.)

(f) I think, besides this, that the respective positions of the disciples and Christ, when they first saw Him, may *possibly* be intended to represent the respective positions of Christ and His people during this dispensation. They were on the water of the sea. He was looking at them from the land. Just so Christ is in heaven looking at us, and we are voyaging over the troublous waters of this world.

(g) Finally, I think that our Lord's sudden appearing on shore, when the morning broke, may *possibly* represent our Lord's second advent. "The night is far spent, and the day is at hand." When the morning dawns, Christ will appear.

With these conjectures I leave the passage. They may not commend themselves to some readers. I only say that they appear to me to deserve consideration and reflection.

JOHN XXI 15—17

15 So when they had dined, Jesus saith to Simon Peter, Simon, *son* of Jonas, lovest thou me more than these? He saith unto him, Yea, Lord; thou knowest that I love thee. He saith unto him, Feed my lambs.

16 He saith to him again the second time, Simon, *son* of Jonas, lovest thou me? He saith unto him, Yea, Lord; thou knowest that I love thee. He saith unto him, Feed my sheep.

17 He saith unto him the third time, Simon, *son* of Jonas, lovest thou me? Peter was grieved because he said unto him the third time, Lovest thou me? And he said unto him, Lord, thou knowest all things; thou knowest that I love thee. Jesus saith unto him, Feed my sheep.

These verses describe a remarkable conversation between our Lord Jesus Christ and the Apostle Peter. To the careful Bible reader, who remembers the Apostle's thrice-repeated denial of Christ, the passage cannot fail to be a deeply interesting portion of Scripture. Well would it be for the Church, if all "after-dinner" conversations among Christians were as useful and edifying as this.

We should notice first, in these verses, *Christ's question to Peter :* "Simon, son of Jonas, lovest thou Me?" —Three times we find the same inquiry made. It seems most probable that this three-fold repetition was meant to remind the Apostle of his own thrice-repeated denial. Once we find a remarkable addition to the inquiry : "Lovest thou Me more than these?" It is a reasonable supposition that those three words "more than these," were meant to remind Peter of his over-confident assertion : "Though all men deny Thee, yet will not I."—It is just as if our Lord would say, "Wilt thou now exalt thyself above others? Hast thou yet learned thine own weakness ?"

"Lovest thou Me" may seem at first sight a simple question. In one sense it is so. Even a child can understand love, and can say whether he loves another or not. Yet "Lovest thou Me" is, in reality, a very searching question. We may know much, and do much, and profess much, and talk much, and work much, and give much, and go through much, and make much show in our religion, and yet be dead before God, from want of love, and at last go down to the pit. Do we love Christ? That is the great question. Without this there is no vitality about our Christianity. We are no better than painted wax figures, lifeless stuffed beasts in a museum, sounding brass and tinkling cymbals. There is no life where there is no love.

Let us take heed that there is some feeling in our religion. Knowledge, orthodoxy, correct views, regular use of forms, a respectable moral life,—all these do not make up a true Christian. There must be some personal feeling towards Christ. Feeling alone, no doubt, is a poor useless thing, and may be here to-day and gone to-morrow. But the entire absence of feeling is a very bad symptom, and speaks ill for the state of a man's soul. The men and women to whom St. Paul wrote his Epistles had feelings, and were not ashamed of them. There was One in heaven whom they loved, and that One was Jesus the Son of God. Let us strive to be like them, and to have some real feeling in our Christianity, if we hope to share their reward.

We should notice, secondly, in these verses, *Peter's answer to Christ's question.* Three times we find the Apostle saying, "Thou knowest that I love Thee." Once we are told that he said, "Thou knowest all things." Once we have the touching remark made, that he was "grieved to be asked the third time." We need not doubt that our Lord, like a skilful physician, stirred up this grief intentionally. He intended to prick the Apostle's conscience, and to teach him a solemn lesson. If it was grievous to the disciple to be questioned, how much more grievous must it have been to the Master to be denied!

The answer that the humbled Apostle gave, is the one account that the true servant of Christ in every age can give of his religion. Such an one may be weak, and fearful, and ignorant, and unstable, and failing in many things, but at any rate he is real and sincere. Ask him whether he is converted, whether he is a believer, whether he has grace, whether he is justified, whether he is sanctified, whether he is elect, whether he is a child of God,—ask him any one of these questions and he may perhaps reply that he really does not know! —But ask him whether he loves Christ, and he will reply, "I do." He may add that he does not love Him as much as he ought to do; but he will not say that he does not love Him at all. The rule will be found true with very few exceptions. Wherever there is true grace, there will be a consciousness of love towards Christ.

What, after all, is the great secret of loving Christ? It is an inward sense of having received from Him pardon and forgiveness of sins. Those love much who feel much forgiven. He that has come to Christ with his sins, and tasted the blessedness of free and full absolution, he is the man whose heart will be full of love towards his Saviour. The more we realize that Christ has suffered for us, and paid our debt to God, and that we are washed and justified through His blood, the more we shall love Him for having loved us, and given Himself for us. Our knowledge of doctrines may be defective. Our ability to defend our views in argument may be small. But we cannot be prevented feeling. And our feeling will be like that of the Apostle Peter: "Thou, Lord, who knowest all things, Thou knowest my heart; and Thou knowest that I love Thee."

We should notice, lastly, in these verses, *Christ's command to Peter.* Three times we find Him saying,

" Feed " my flock : once, " Feed my lambs ; " and twice
my " sheep." Can we doubt for a moment that this
thrice-repeated charge was full of deep meaning ? It
was meant to commission Peter once more to do the
work of an Apostle, notwithstanding his recent fall.
But this was only a small part of the meaning. It was
meant to teach Peter and the whole Church the mighty
lesson, that usefulness to others is the grand test of love,
and working for Christ the great proof of really loving
Christ. It is not loud talk and high profession ; it is
not even impetuous, spasmodic zeal, and readiness to
draw the sword and fight,—it is steady, patient, laborious effort to do good to Christ's sheep scattered throughout this sinful world, which is the best evidence of being
a true-hearted disciple. This is the real secret of Christian greatness. It is written in another place, " Whosoever will be great among you, let him be your minister ;
and whosoever will be chief among you, let him be your
servant : even as the Son of man came not to be ministered unto, but to minister." (Matt. xx. 26—28.)

Forever let the parting charge of our blessed Master
abide in our consciences, and come up in the practice of
our daily lives. It is not for nothing we may be sure,
that we find these things recorded for our learning, just
before He left the world. Let us aim at a loving, doing,
useful, hard-working, unselfish, kind, unpretentious religion. Let it be our daily desire to think of others,
care for others, do good to others, and to lessen the sorrow, and increase the joy of this sinful world. This is
to realize the great principle which our Lord's command
to Peter was intended to teach. So living, and so laboring to order our ways, we shall find it abundantly true,
that " it is more blessed to give than to receive." (Acts
xx. 35.)

15 —[*So when they had dined.*] In the verses we now begin, we pass away from the region of allegory, parable, symbol, miracle, and vision, to a plain, unmistakable conversation between our Lord Jesus Christ and the Apostle Peter. It is a conversation of a deeply interesting character, of which every letter deserves to be written in gold. He that supposes that any " John," except John the Apostle, could have written these three verses, gives little evidence of possessing a sound judgment.

It is noteworthy that our Lord does not begin His conversation till the social meal was over. Trifling as this circumstance may seem, it deserves attention, and conveys a lesson. Nothing was so likely to set the Apostles at ease with their Master, and to prepare them to receive any word that fell from His lips with love and affection, as to deal familiarly and intimately with them, and let them " eat and drink " in His company.

[*Jesus saith to Simon Peter.*] The object of our Lord in addressing Simon Peter in these verses should be carefully remembered, and not misunderstood. That there was a distinct object in singling him out from the seven disciples sitting round our Lord, and specially speaking to him, I cannot doubt. But what was that object? This question can only be answered by considering the peculiar character of St. Peter, and the peculiar circumstances of his history during the last day of our Lord's ministry, before the crucifixion. None had made so high a profession. None had spoken so confidently of his own strength. None had shown such instability in the hour of trial. None had fallen so sadly, by denying his Master three times. Remembering all this, I believe that our Lord had a special object in addressing Peter on this occasion ; and I see a special wisdom in the address and conversation being recorded, as taking place before six witnesses.

(*a*) I believe our Lord's first object was to remind Peter of his sad fall, through over-confidence, and want of watchfulness and prayer. He would have him know that, though raised, pardoned and forgiven, he must never forget what had happened. Three times he had denied his Master. Three times he must be publicly asked whether he loved his Master. Hengstenberg maintains that Peter's fall was not at all in our Lord's mind in this remarkable conversation. But I cannot agree with him.

(*b*) I believe our Lord's second object was, as Cyril remarks, to restore Peter to his former position as a trusted Apostle and minister in the presence of six witnesses. The thought might possibly come across the minds of some Christians, in future days, that Peter forfeited his claim to be an Apostle and leader of the Church, by his thrice repeated denial of his Master. Our Lord in mercy guards against this possibility, by publicly commissioning Peter once more to do the work of a pastor in the Church.

(c) I believe our Lord's third object was to teach Peter what should be the primary aim of an Apostle and minister. The true qualification for the ministerial office, he must learn, was not high profession of more courage and zeal than others, not loud talk, or even readiness to fight ; but loving, patient usefulness to the souls of others, and diligent care for the sheep of Christ's flock.

Calvin remarks, " The Evangelist now relates in what manner Peter was restored to that rank of honor from which he had fallen. The treacherous denial, which has been formerly described, had undoubtedly rendered him unworthy of the apostleship ; for how could he be capable of instructing others in the faith, who had basely revolted from it ? He had been made an Apostle, but it was along with Judas ; and from the time that he acted the part of a coward and traitor, he had been deprived of the honor of apostleship. Now therefore the liberty, as well as the authority of teaching is restored to him, both of which he had lost through his own fault. And that the disgrace of his apostacy might not stand in the way, Christ blots out and destroys the remembrance of it. Such a restoration was necessary, both for Peter and his hearers ; for Peter, that he might the more boldly execute his office, being assured of the calling with which Christ had again invested him ; for his hearers, that the stain which attached to his person might not be the occasion of despising the Gospel. To us also, in the present day, it is of very great importance that Peter comes forth to us as a new man, from whom the disgrace that might have lessened his authority, is removed."

The Roman Catholic theory, that our Lord specially addressed Peter, on this occasion, in order to mark him out as head of the Church, is one which I repudiate as preposterous, unreasonable, improbable, and utterly destitute of solid foundation. Neither here, nor elsewhere, is there a tittle of evidence to show that any primacy was ever intended to be given to Peter. On the contrary, the fact that our Lord specially appeared on one occasion to James alone, and that afterwards James was the presiding Apostle in the first Council at Jerusalem, would seem to indicate that, if He conferred primacy on any Apostle, He conferred it on James. But there is no proof that primacy was conferred on any one at all.

Burgon says, " The profane and ridiculous pretentions of the Church of Rome are based in great part on the words of our Saviour addressed to St. Peter in this passage. The Papists assume (1) that He hereby appointed St. Peter to be His vicar upon earth; (2) that St. Peter was the first Bishop of Rome ;

(3) that St. Peter transmitted to the Bishops of the same See, in endless succession, his own supposed authority over the rest of Christendom. Each one of these assumptions is simply unfounded and untrue ; opposed alike to Scripture and to reason ; to the records of the Early Church and the opinions of the primitive Fathers. With such fictions, nevertheless, do Romish writers distort the true image of Christianity ; disfiguring their commentaries therewith, and betraying with a reckless eagerness to obtrude their ambitious and unscriptural theory on all occasions, their secret misgivings as to its real value."

[*Simon, son of Jonas.*] This mode of address, thrice repeated in this remarkable conversation, is only used by our Lord on this occasion, and when Peter first came to Him. (John i. 42.) I do not find that any Commentator gives a satisfactory explanation of it, and we are left to conjecture the reason. (*a*) Some think that our Lord purposely avoided the name Peter, in order to remind the Apostle how on a recent occasion he had shown himself not firm as a " rock," agreeably to his name, but weak as a reed. (*b*) Some think that our Lord meant to remind the Apostle of the memorable day when he first began to be a disciple, when Jesus said to him, " Thou art Simon, the son of Jona." (*c*) Some think that our Lord would remind the Apostle of the day when he said, " Blessed art thou, Simon Barjona," after the good confession which Peter had made. (Matt. xvi. 17.) (*d*) Some think that our Lord intended to remind Peter of the lowly origin from which he sprung, as son of one who, like Zebedee, in all probability, was only an humble fisherman. (*e*) Some think that the expression was only used to distinguish Simon Peter from the other Simon, who may *possibly* have been in company, as one of the two unnamed disciples. (Ch. xxi. 2.) My own impression is, if I must give an opinion, that our Lord intended to carry Peter's mind back to the day when he first began to be a disciple of Christ, and to all the three years that had elapsed. It is as though He said, " Simon, son of Jonas, thou rememberest the day when thou didst first come to Me, and believe on Me as the Lamb of God. (John i. 35—42.) Thou knowest all that thou hast been, and all that thou hast gone through since that day. Once more I address thee by the same name with which I began. Before sending thee forth, and commissioning thee once more, in the presence of these six brethren, as a restored and trusted disciple, I ask thee, Dost thou love Me ? " I throw out the thought as a conjecture. I see more in it than in any other view.

[*Lovest thou Me ?*] The question which Jesus asked of Peter was very simple, but very searching. It was simple, because it appealed to his feelings. Even a child knows what he feels, and whom he loves. If our Lord had asked,—" Dost thou believe ? Art thou elect ? Art thou converted ? Hast thou faith ? Hast thou grace ? Art thou born again ? Hast thou the Spirit ? Art thou sanctified ? Art thou justified ? "—any one of these questions would have been perhaps very difficult to answer.

But Peter could surely tell what he felt towards Christ.—At the same time the question was very searching. It is as though our Lord said, " Simon, I know all thy history. I know what thou hast done, and what thou hast been, about the time of my betrayal and crucifixion, and I am ready to look over all, and pardon all. But one thing I must have in my disciples, and that is, a sincere and loving heart. I can look over want of knowledge and want of faith ; but I must have love. Now, before these six brethren, before commissioning thee once more as an accredited and trustworthy Apostle, I ask thee solemnly, Dost thou love Me ? "

Cyril thinks that Peter had received such special mercy, pardon, and forgiveness, that he might be reasonably required to feel special love.

[*More than these.*] This remarkable expression, which is only used in this verse, admits of three interpretations. (*a*) It may mean, Dost thou love Me more than thou lovest these thy brethren and friends around thee, and art thou willing to give them up for my sake, and follow Me alone, if need be ? (*b*) It may mean, as Whitby says, Dost thou love Me more than these boats and fishing nets, among which thou hast spent so much of thy life, from which I did first call thee, and in the midst of which I find thee to-day ? Art thou willing for my sake to give them all up, and devote thyself to preaching the Gospel ? (*c*) It may mean, as the great majority of commentators think, Dost thou love Me more than thy brethren love Me ? Thou rememberest a certain day when thou didst confidently say, " Though all men forsake Thee, yet will not I." Thou wast confident then, that thou wast more faithful than others. Will thou say that now ? After all that has happened, art thou sure that thy heart is better than that of others ? "—I decidedly prefer this last view to either of the others. I think it was meant to teach Peter, that the two grand qualifications for a faithful pastor were love and humility.

Musculus observes, that Jesus did not ask Peter this thrice-repeated question, as if He was ignorant and desired to learn, but in order to remind him before others of his future duty.

Bullinger suggests, that one reason among others why Jesus said, " more than these ? " was Peter's forwardness to spring into the water, and come to shore, before the other six Apostles, who were in the boat with him.

Rollock observes, on our Lord's merciful and loving dealing with Peter, " Rebukers should be lovers. If thou rebuke a man, love him ; otherwise speak not to him, but close thy mouth. If thou season not thy rebukes with ' love,' then that which should have been as medicine will be turned into poison. They that would be instructors and admonishers should be lovers. Wherefore, whatever thou doest, do it in lenity and meekness. A bitter teacher is not worth a penny. This is what St.

Paul requires when he says, ' The servant of the Lord must not strive; but be gentle to all men.' (2 Tim. ii. 24.) All should be in gentleness: teaching in gentleness. Wherefore? Because, if gentleness be lacking, there will be no edification,' no comforting, no instruction."

[*He saith... Yea, Lord...knowest...I love Thee.*] The answer of Simon Peter in this verse is a beautiful example of sincerity and humility. He appeals to our Lord's knowledge of his heart : " I may be very defective in knowledge, faith, courage, wisdom. I am a debtor to mercy and grace above many. Yet, Lord, thou knowest that, with all my faults and infirmities, I do love Thee." He does not venture to say a word about others. He does not pretend to compare his love with that of his brethren. If he has done so in time past he will do so no more. —" I know not whether others love Thee more or less than I do. I only know my own heart ; and I feel sure that I love Thee."

Let us carefully note that love to Christ is one of the simplest tests of a true Christian. He may not feel sure that he is converted, or that he repents or believes aright. But if he is real, he will be able to say that he loves Christ.

[*He saith...Feed my lambs.*] Having received from Peter a public profession of his sincere love, our Lord proceeds to tell him how that love is to be shown, and to give him his commission for the future. He bids him prove the reality of his love by " feeding His lambs."—When our Lord said " feed," I believe He meant that Peter was to feed souls with the precious food of God's Word, to supply them with that bread of life which a man must eat or die, and to watch carefully and diligently over their spiritual interests, like a good shepherd watching his flock. When our Lord spoke of "lambs," I believe He meant the least, the weakest, and feeblest members of that flock which is His Church. It is as though Jesus said,— " Simon, if indeed thou dost love Me, know that the best proof of love is to devote thyself to the great work of shepherding souls. Live for others. Care for others. Minister to others. Do good to others. Seek out and search for my sheep in this wicked world, and think it not beneath thee to attend to the wants of the feeblest among them. Herein, remember, is true love. It does not consist in talking, professing, fighting, or seeking pre-eminence over others. It is best seen in walking in my steps. I came to seek and save that which was lost. I came not to be ministered unto, but to minister. Go and do likewise. He loves most who is most like Me."

I cannot think that "lambs" in this place was intended to apply to young children, as it is often interpreted. All such interpretations I regard as nothing better than pious accommodations. I believe that "lambs," in contradistinction to "sheep," mean those who are young and weak in spiritual experience. Peter was not to neglect and despise them because weak. Peter remembered these ringing words, we may be sure, when he wrote in his Epistle, " Feed the flock of God that is among you." (1 Peter v. 2.)

Augustine observes that Christ, both here and in the two following verses, says, " MY " and not " THY." The Church is His property, and not the property of ministers.

Bullinger observes that Christ passes from the calling of the fisherman to that of the shepherd, as representing, more than any other callings, the ministerial office.

16 —[*He saith to him again, etc.*] This verse is simply a repetition of the preceding one, with three exceptions.—For one thing, the expression, " more than these," is omitted.—For another thing, the word which we render " feed," in the Greek is a wider, fuller word than the one employed in the preceding verse.—For another thing, our Lord speaks of His " sheep " instead of His " lambs." By " sheep " I believe our Lord meant those members of His flock who were of more advanced experience and strength in grace, than the class He had spoken of in the preceding verse. Both classes demanded the attention of a faithful pastor.

The repetition of the inquiry was doubtless intended to rouse Peter's attention, and to impress the whole subject on his mind.

Lightfoot thinks that the "threefold repetition,—feed, feed, feed, may most fitly apply to the threefold object of St. Peter's ministry: viz., the Gentiles, the Jews, and the dispersed ten tribes." But this seems to me fanciful. Bengel thinks it refers to the three periods of Peter's ministry.

Whitby observes, " Those who argue for Peter's supremacy above other Apostles, from this passage, are vain in their imagination. If by these words Christ required Peter to feed all His sheep and lambs, it is certain he was wanting in his duty. He never exercised an act of supremacy over the rest of the Apostles; but being sent by them, obeyed (Acts viii. 14), and being reproved by St. Paul, held his peace (Gal. ii. 11—16), and was so far from feeding all Christ's sheep, that he never fed any of the province of St. Paul."

17 —[*He saith unto him the third time, etc.*] This verse again is a repetition of the two preceding verses, but contains two points of difference. For one thing we are told that " Peter was grieved," on being asked the same question three times. For another thing, Peter uses stronger language when he appeals to our Lord's knowledge of his heart. " Lord," he says, " Thou knowest all things."

I cannot for a moment doubt that our Lord asked Peter this remarkable question three times, in order to remind him that he had denied Him thrice. Our sins ought never to be forgot-

ten by us, though they are wiped out of the book of God's remembrance. The very "grief" which Peter felt at being
thrice asked about his love, was intended to do him good. It
was meant to remind him that if he was grieved to be asked
thrice, "Lovest thou Me?" how much more must his Master
have been grieved when he thrice denied Him!

Whitby observes, "Here is an argument that Christ, in Peter's judgment, was truly God. He says, 'Thou knowest all
things.' It is to God alone that the secrets of all hearts lie
open."

There are little nice distinctions in the original Greek of these
three verses, in the words that are used, which the English
language cannot convey. But they deserve notice, and are not
without meaning. Two different words are used to express
our one word "love." One of these two words means a higher, calmer, nobler kind of love than the other. This is the
word which our Lord uses in the fifteenth and sixteenth verses,
where He asks the question, "Lovest thou Me?"—The other
of the two words means a more passionate and lower kind of
love. This is the word which Peter always uses when he says,
"I love thee!" and our Lord once uses it in the seventeenth
verse.—Again: two different words are employed to express
our one English word "feed." One means simply "provide
food and pasture," and is used in the fifteenth and seventeenth
verses. The other means not only "provide food," but "govern, lead, direct, and generally do the work of a shepherd."

Some of the Roman Catholic writers try to make out that
"lambs" in this remarkable passage mean the laity, and
"sheep" the clergy; and that supremacy over clergy and laity
alike is intended, by these words, to be conferred on Peter and
his successors at Rome! Archbishop Trench (on Miracles)
justly condemns this interpretation, as "groundless and trifling." He observes, "The commission should at least have
run, 'Feed my sheep and feed my shepherds,' if any such conclusion could be drawn from Christ's words, though an infinite
deal would still remain to be proved."

The lessons which the whole passage is meant to teach the
Church of Christ, are many and deep, and have been far too
much neglected in every age. I can only indicate them, and
then leave the reader to work them out in his own mind.

(a) Love to Christ's person is one of the most important
graces that can adorn a Christian, and specially a minister.
Without it, correct doctrinal views, zeal for proselytizing,
knowledge, eloquence, liberality, diligence in visiting the sick
and relieving the poor, are worth very little, and will do very
little good. With it, God is pleased to look over many infirmities. A minister may be somewhat defective in some of his
views, and even in some of his proceedings, but if he loves

Christ and has a warm heart, God will seldom allow him to lack a blessing.

Hengstenberg shrewdly remarks, that Christ's emphatical question about love to Himself, and omission of any question about *love to God*, is strong indirect proof of Christ's divinity.

(*b*) True love to Christ is chiefly to be seen in usefulness to others, in doing as Christ did, in walking in His steps, in laboring to do good in this bad world. He that talks of loving Christ, and idles on through life, never trying to do good to others, is deceiving himself, and will find at length that he had better never have been born.

(*c*) A vast amount of so-called Christianity is perfectly useless in the sight of God, and will only add to people's condemnation. Church-goers and chapel-goers, who are content to attend services and hear sermons, but know nothing of fervent love to Christ's person, and never lay themselves out to imitate Him, are in the broad way that leads to destruction.

Rollock observes, " A profane man or woman will say, ' I love God ; ' but if it manifest not itself in an action, thou art but a liar, and lovest Him not. Faith and love must ever utter themselves in good actions. Hast thou gotten a heart, hands, and feet ? Do some good. Otherwise, if thou doest never a good deed, thy profession of faith and love is vain."

He also says,—" The pastor is not worth a penny who strives not to get a sense of the love of Christ into his heart. There are so many difficulties and impediments cast before a pastor, when he is about to discharge his duty, that he never can be able to overcome them, except he both love the Lord, and be sensible of the Lord's love to him. If the Apostles and martyrs had not loved Jesus exceedingly, they would soon have fainted."

Leighton observes, " Love is the great endowment of a true pastor of Christ's flock. He says not to Peter, ' Art thou wise ? or learned ? or eloquent ? ' but ' Lovest thou Me ? ' Then, ' feed.' Love to Christ begets love to His people's souls, which are so precious to Him, and a care of feeding them."

Scott observes, " Those who have been greatly tempted, and have had much humbling experience of their own sinfulness, and have had much forgiven them, generally prove the most tender, compassionate, and attentive pastors, of weak, bruised, and trembling believers."

(*d*) The true test of reality in our religion is to be able to appeal confidently to God's knowledge of our hearts. It matters nothing what friends, and relatives, and fellow-worshippers, may think and say of us. They may praise us, when we do not deserve it, or condemn us, when we are innocent. It matters nothing. If we have the witness of our own hearts, that we can appeal to Jesus, the Searcher of hearts, and say, "Thou, who knowest all things, knowest that I love Thee," we need not be afraid.

(e) If we really and truly feel love to Christ, we may thank God and take courage. Of our own faith, and grace, and conversion, and sanctification, we are poor judges. But do we really and sincerely feel that we love Christ? That is the great question. The very existence of such love is a good sign. We should not love Christ, if we had not got something from Him.

Brentius remarks that Peter's charge to the elders, in his epistle, clearly shows that our Lord's thrice-repeated charge, "Feed," was not meant for him only, as the Romanists say, but for all ministers of the Church of Christ, without exception. "The elders which are among you, I exhort:—Feed the flock of God." (1 Peter v. 1.)

JOHN XXI 18—25

18 Verily, verily, I say unto thee, When thou wast young, thou girdedst thyself, and walkedst whither thou wouldst: but when thou shalt be old, thou shalt stretch forth thy hands, and another shall gird thee, and carry *thee* whither thou wouldest not.

19 This spake he, signifying by what death he should glorify God. And when he had spoken this, he saith unto him, Follow me.

20 Then Peter, turning about, seeth the disciple whom Jesus loved following; which also leaned on his breast at supper, and said, Lord, which is he that betrayeth thee?

21 Peter seeing him saith to Jesus, Lord, and what *shall* this man *do*?

22 Jesus saith unto him, If I will that he tarry till I come, what *is that* to thee? follow thou me.

23 Then went this saying abroad among the brethren, that that disciple should not die; yet Jesus said not unto him, He shall not die; but, If I will that he tarry till I come, what *is that* to thee?

24 This is the disciple which testifieth of these things and wrote these things: and we know that his testimony is true.

25 And there are also many other things which Jesus did, the which, if they should be written every one, I suppose that even the world itself could not contain the books that should be written. Amen.

THESE verses form the conclusion of St. John's Gospel, and bring to an end the most precious book in the Bible. The man is much to be pitied who can read the passage without serious and solemn feelings. It is like listening to the parting words of a friend, whom we may possibly not see again. Let us reverently consider the lessons which this Scripture contains.

We learn, for one thing, from these verses, *that the*

future history of Christians, both in life and death, is foreknown by Christ. The Lord tells Simon Peter, " When thou art old, thou shalt stretch forth thy hands, and another shall gird thee, and carry thee whither thou wouldest not." These words, without controversy, were a prediction of the manner of the Apostle's death. They were fulfilled in after days, it is commonly supposed, when Peter was crucified as a martyr for Christ's sake. The time, the place, the manner, the painfulness to flesh and blood of the disciple's death, were all matters foreseen by the Master.

The truth before us is eminently full of comfort to a true believer. To obtain foreknowledge of things to come would, in most cases, be a sorrowful possession. To know what was going to befall us, and yet not to be able to prevent it, would make us simply miserable. But it is an unspeakable consolation to remember, that our whole future is known and forearranged by Christ. There is no such thing as luck, chance, or accident, in the journey of our life. Everything from beginning to end is foreseen,—arranged by One who is too wise to err, and too loving to do us harm.

Let us store up this truth in our minds, and use it diligently in all the days of darkness through which we may yet have to pass. In such days we should lean back on the thought, " Christ knows this, and knew it when He called me to be His disciple." It is foolish to repine and murmur over the troubles of those whom we love. We should rather fall back on the thought that all is well done. It is useless to fret and be rebellious, when we ourselves have bitter cups to drink. We should rather say, "This also is from the Lord : He foresaw it, and would have prevented it, if it had not been for my good." Happy are those who can enter into the spirit of that old saint, who said, " I have made a covenant with my Lord, that I will never take amiss anything that He does to me." We may have to walk sometimes through rough places, on our way to heaven. But surely it is a resting, soothing reflection, "Every step of my journey was foreknown by Christ."

We learn, secondly, in these verses, *that a believer's death is intended to glorify God.* The Holy Ghost tells us this truth in plain language. He graciously interprets the dark saying, which fell from our Lord's lips about Peter's end. He tells us that Jesus spake this, "signifying by what death he should glorify God."

The thing before us is probably not considered as much as it ought to be. We are so apt to regard life as the only season for honoring Christ, and action as the only mode of showing our religion, that we overlook death, except as a painful termination of usefulness. Yet surely this ought not so to be. We may die to the Lord as well as live to the Lord ; we may be patient sufferers as well as active workers. Like Samson, we may do more for God in our death, than we ever did in our lives. It is probable that the patient deaths of our martyred Reformers had more effect on the minds of Englishmen, than all the sermons they preached, and all the books they wrote. One thing, at all events, is certain,—the blood of the English martyrs was the seed of the English Church.

We may glorify God in death, by being ready for it whenever it comes. The Christian who is found like a sentinel at his post, like a servant with his loins girded and his lamp burning, with a heart packed up and ready to go, the man to whom sudden death, by the common consent of all who knew him, is sudden glory, —this, this is a man whose end brings glory to God.— We may glorify God in death, by patiently enduring its pains. The Christian whose spirit has complete victory over the flesh, who quietly feels the pins of his earthly tabernacle plucked up with great bodily agonies, and yet never murmurs or complains, but silently enjoys inward peace,—this, this again, is a man whose end brings glory to God.—We may glorify God in death, by testifying to others the comfort and support that we find in the grace of Christ. It is a great thing, when a mortal man can say with David, "Though I walk through the valley of the shadow of death, I will fear no evil." (Psalm xxiii. 4.) The Christian who, like Standfast in "Pilgrim's Progress," can stand for a while in the river, and talk calmly to his companions, saying, "My foot is fixed sure : my toilsome days are ended,"—this, this is a man whose end brings glory to God. Deaths like these leave a mark on the living, and are not soon forgotten.

Let us pray, while we live in health, that we may glorify God in our end. Let us leave it to God to choose the where, and when, and how, and all the manner of our departing. Let us only ask that it may "glorify God." He is a wise man who takes John Bunyan's advice, and keeps his last hour continually in mind, and makes it his company-keeper. It was a weighty saying of John Wesley, when one found fault with the doctrines and practices of the Methodists,— "At any rate our people die well."

We learn, thirdly, in these verses, *that whatever we may think about the condition of other people, we should think first about our own.* When Peter inquired curiously and anxiously about the future of the Apostle John, he received from our Lord an answer of deep meaning: "If I will that he tarry till I come, what is that to thee ? Follow thou Me." Hard to understand as some part of that sentence may be, it contains a practical lesson which cannot be mistaken. It commands every Christian to remember his own heart first, and to look at home.

Of course our blessed Lord does not wish us to neglect the souls of others, or to take no interest in their condition. Such a state of mind would be nothing less than uncharitable selfishness, and would prove plainly that we had not the grace of God. The servant of Christ will have a wide, broad heart, like his Master, and will desire the present and eternal happiness of all around him. He will long and labor to lessen the sorrows, and to increase the joys, of every one within his reach, and, as he has opportunity, to do good to all men. But, in all his doing, the servant of Christ must never forget his own soul. Charity, and true religion, must both begin at home.

It is vain to deny that our Lord's solemn caution to His impetuous disciple is greatly needed in the present day. Such is the weakness of human nature, that even true Christians are continually liable to run into extremes. Some are so entirely absorbed in their own inward experience, and their own heart's conflict, that they forget the world outside. Others are so busy about doing good to the world, that they neglect to cultivate their own souls. Both are wrong, and both need to see a more excellent way; but none perhaps do so much harm to religion as those who are busy-bodies about others' salvation, and at the same time neglecters of their own. From such a snare as this may the ringing words of our Lord deliver us! Whatever we do for others (and we never can do enough), let us not forget our own inner man. Unhappily, the Bride, in Canticles, is not the only person who has cause to complain: "They made me keeper of the vineyards; but my own vineyard I have not kept." (Cant. i. 6.)

We learn, lastly, from these verses, *the number and*

greatness of Christ's works during His earthly ministry.
St. John concludes his Gospel with these remarkable
words, " There are many other things which Jesus did,
the which, if they should be written every one, I suppose the world itself could not contain the books that
should be written."—Of course we must not torture
these words, by pressing them to an excessively *literal*
interpretation. To suppose that the Evangelist meant
the world could not hold the material volumes which
would be written, is evidently unreasonable and absurd.
The only sensible interpretation must be a spiritual and
figurative one.

As much of Christ's sayings and doings is recorded
as the mind of man can take in. It would not be
good for the world to have more. The human mind,
like the body, can only digest a certain quantity. The
world could not contain more, because it would not.
As many miracles, as many parables, as many sermons,
as many conversions, as many words of kindness, as
many deeds of mercy, as many journeys, as many prayers,
as many warnings, as many promises, are recorded, as the
world can possibly require. If more had been recorded
they would have been only thrown away. There is
enough to make every unbeliever without excuse, enough
to show every inquirer the way to heaven, enough to satisfy the heart of every honest believer, enough to condemn man if he does not repent and believe, enough to
glorify God. The largest vessel can only contain a certain quantity of liquid. The mind of all mankind would
not appreciate more about Christ, if more had been
written. There is enough and to spare. This witness
is true. Let us deny it if we can.

And now let us close the Gospel of St. John with
mingled feelings of deep humility and deep thankfulness. We may well be humble when we think how

ignorant we are, and how little we comprehend of the treasures which this Gospel contains. But we may well be thankful, when we reflect how clear and plain is the instruction which it gives us about the way of salvation. The man who reads this Gospel profitably, is he who "believes that Jesus is the Christ, and, believing, has life through His Name." Do we so believe? Let us never rest till we can give a satisfactory answer to that question!

NOTES   JOHN XXI 18—25

18 —[*Verily, verily, I say unto thee, etc.*] In this verse our Lord forewarns the Apostle Peter, what death he must expect to be the conclusion of his ministry. After restoring him to his office, and commissioning him to be a pastor, He tells him plainly what his end will be. He holds out no prospect of temporal ease and an earthly kingdom. On the contrary, He bids him look forward to a violent death. If he shows his love by feeding his Master's sheep, he must not be surprised if he is made partaker of his Master's sufferings. And so it was. Peter lived to be persecuted, beaten, imprisoned, and at length slain for Christ's sake. It happened exactly as his Master had predicted. Most ecclesiastical historians say that he suffered martyrdom at Rome, in one of the first persecutions, and was crucified with his head downwards.

Melancthon remarks that Peter, like most Jews, was probably expecting that, after our Lord's resurrection, He would take to Himself His kingdom, and reign in glory with His disciples. Jesus warns him that he must expect nothing of the kind. Tribulation and not glory, was the prospect before him in this world.

It is fair to say that some learned writers deny entirely that Peter ever was at Rome, and consequently deny the truth of the ecclesiastical tradition, that he was crucified there with his head downward. Calovius gives a long passage from Casaubon, maintaining this view. Whether it was so, or not, does not affect the passage before us. In any case, wherever he died, there is no reason to doubt that Peter died a violent death.

The expression, "Verily, verily, I say unto thee," is thoroughly characteristic of St. John's Gospel. We cannot doubt that Peter would remember how solemn were the former occasions when our Lord used this phrase, and would see a peculiar solemnity in the words of this verse. Specially would Peter remember the night when our Lord was betrayed, when His

Master said to him, " Verily, verily, I say unto thee, The cock shall not crow, till thou hast denied Me thrice." (John xiii. 38.)

The expression, " When thou wast young," is commonly thought to indicate that Peter was now an old man, when these words were spoken. Perhaps too much stress is laid on the words, especially considering the context. I think the safe plan is to interpret it as meaning, " When thou wast a younger man than thou art now."

The expression, " Thou girdedst thyself, and walkedst whither thou wouldest," appears to me a general phrase, denoting the freedom from restraint and independence of movement, which Peter enjoyed, when he followed his calling as a young fisherman, before he was called to be a disciple and Apostle. I cannot, like some commentators, see any allusion to Peter's recent action, when he put his "fisher's coat about him," cast himself into the sea, and waded to the shore. I rather regard it as a proverbial phrase. A young Jewish fisherman, when inclined to go here or there, would, according to oriental custom, gird up his loins and walk off upon his journey, at the pleasure of his own will. " This," says our Lord to Peter, " thou didst use to do when a young man."

The expression, " When thou shalt be old," seems to denote at any rate that Peter would be an older man than he then was, before he died, and would suffer martyrdom in his old age. It certainly condemns the idea entertained by many, that the Apostle Peter was an aged man, when our Lord left the world. Old age, in his case, is clearly represented as a thing future.

The expression, " Thou shalt stretch forth thine hands, and another shall gird thee," is regarded by almost all commentators, as an intimation of the manner of Peter's death. He was to stretch forth his hands at the command of another, that is, of an executioner, and, in all probability, to be bound by that executioner to the cross on which he was to suffer. If this be a correct interpretation of the words, it certainly favors the idea that crucified persons were " bound," as well as " nailed," to the cross. The phrase "gird" may possibly refer to a custom of girding a person's loins, and putting cords round his middle before crucifying him. The contrast would then be more natural between a man girding up his own loins to walk, and another girding him round the loins for execution.

The expression " carry thee whither thou wouldest not," must mean that the executioner having bound Peter to the cross, would carry him so bound to the place where the cross would be reared up, after a manner which would be repugnant and painful to flesh and blood. It cannot, of course, mean that Peter would object to his punishment and resist it. It can only mean that his punishment would be one which must needs be a heavy trial to his natural will.

Brentius thinks that "another," in this sentence, refers to "Nero," or the "executioner."

We should note, in this wonderful prophecy, the unhesitating positiveness and decision with which our Lord speaks of things to come. He knew perfectly all the circumstances of His Apostle's death, long before it took place.

We should note how faithfully and unreservedly our Lord tells Peter what the consequences of his apostleship would be. He does not tempt him onward by promises of earthly success and temporal rewards. Suffering, death, and the cross, are plainly exhibited before the eyes of his mind, as the end to which he must look forward.

We should note how even our Lord intimates that suffering is painful to flesh and blood. He speaks of it as a thing that Peter will most naturally shrink from:—"Thou wouldest not." Our Lord does not expect us to "enjoy" bodily pain and suffering, though He asks us to be willing to endure it for His sake.

Chrysostom observes, "Christ here speaks of natural feeling, and the necessity of the flesh, and shows that the soul is unwillingly torn away from the body. Though the will was firm, even then nature would be found in fault. For no one lays aside the body without feeling; God having suitably ordained this in order that violent deaths might not be many. For if, even as things are now, the devil has been able to effect this, and has led thousands (by suicide) to precipices and pits, had not the soul felt such an affection for the body, many would have rushed to this under any common discouragement."

Augustine observes, "No man likes to die : a state of feeling so natural, that not even old age had power to remove it from blessed Peter, to whom Jesus said, 'Thou shalt be led whither thou wouldest not.' For our consolation, we may remember, that even our Saviour took this state of feeling on Himself, saying, 'Father, if it be possible, let this cup pass from Me!'" —He also says, "Were there nothing, or little of irksomeness in death, the glory of the martyr would not be so great as it is."

Calvin observes, "This must be understood as referring to the conflict between the flesh and the Spirit, which believers feel within themselves. We cannot obey God in a manner so free and unrestrained, as not to be drawn, as it were, by ropes, in an opposite direction, by the world and the flesh. Besides, it ought to be remembered that the dread of death is naturally implanted in us; for, to wish to be separated from the body is revolting to nature."—Again he says, "Even the martyrs experienced a fear of death similar to our own, so that they could not gain a triumph over the enemies of truth but by contending with themselves."

Beza remarks that on one occasion, when Peter and John had been beaten and threatened by the Jewish Council, "they departed, rejoicing that they were counted worthy to suffer shame for His Name." (Acts v. 41.) The expression, " whither thou wouldest not," can therefore only refer to the natural will of flesh and blood. Flesh will feel. Holy Baxter in his last illness used to say, " I groan ; but I do not grumble."

When Bishop Ridley was being chained to the stake, before he was burned as a martyr, at Oxford, he said to the smith who was knocking in the staple, " Good fellow, knock it in hard ; for the flesh will have its way."

Ambrose, quoted by Jansenius, mentions a legend that when Peter was in prison at Rome before his martyrdom, he escaped, and was going out of the city. Then Jesus Christ Himself appeared to him in a vision, and on Peter asking, " Whither goest thou ?" replied, " To Rome, to be crucified again." On hearing this, Peter returned to prison. The whole story is apocryphal, and destitute of historical foundation. But it shows the current of feeling among early Christians.

19 —[*This spake He...what death...glorify God.*] We have here one of John's peculiar parenthetical comments, and one for which we may be specially thankful. Who can tell what Commentators might have made of our Lord's prediction to Peter, if John had not been mercifully inspired to tell us that Jesus spoke of his death?

The expression " what death " means " what kind of death," and is generally considered to indicate that the preceding verse describes death by crucifixion.

The expression " glorify God " is peculiarly interesting, because it teaches that a Christian may bring glory to God by his death, as well as by his life. He does so when he bears it patiently, does not murmur, exhibits sensible peace, enjoys evident hope of a better world, testifies to others of the truth and consolation of the Gospel, and leaves broad evidences of the reality of his religion behind him. He that so ends glorifies God. The deaths of Latimer, Ridley, Hooper, Bradford, Rogers, Rowland Taylor, and many other English martyrs, in the days of Queen Mary, were said to have done more good even than their lives, and to have had immense influence in helping forward the Protestant Reformation.

[*And when...this...saith...Follow Me.*] The precise meaning of this short and emphatic phrase is not very plain.

(a) Some think that it must be interpreted literally, and that our Lord simply meant, " Follow Me in the direction where I am now going. We have tarried here long enough. Let us be going." At first sight this seems a thin and weak interpretation. But before we reject it entirely, we should carefully observe the language of the next verse.

(*b*) Some think that "Follow Me" must be interpreted spiritually, and that our Lord used the expression as a kind of watchword for Peter's course in life from that day forward. "Walk in my steps. Do as I have done. Follow Me whithersoever I lead thee, even though it be to prison and death."

I see no reason why we should not adopt both views. There is such a depth and fulness in our Lord's sayings, that I think we may safely do so. I therefore think it most probable that our Lord not only meant, "Arise, and follow Me now;" but also meant, "Always follow Me through life, whatever be the consequences." After all, Christ's three great words to Christians are, "Come to Me,—Learn of Me,—and Follow Me." (Matt. xi. 28, 29.)

Is there not in the words, "Follow Me," a latent reference to the remarkable saying of our Lord to Peter, on the night that Peter denied Him thrice: "Whither I go, thou canst not follow Me now; but thou shalt follow Me afterwards." (John xiii. 36.)

20 —[*Then Peter, turning, seeth, etc.*] This verse brings in the Apostle John Himself, described with more than usual feeling and particularity, as "the disciple whom Jesus loved, and who leaned on his breast at supper," as if to prevent the possibility of mistake.

The expressions, "turning," and "following," seem to me to place it beyond doubt, that our Lord began to move away from the scene of the social meal, when He said, "Follow Me." No other view can explain them. There was a movement in a certain direction. As our Lord moved away, Peter followed Him. As he followed, Peter turned round, and saw John following also. After John, I believe, the other five disciples followed also, or else they could hardly have heard the remarkable saying about "tarrying till I come," which they evidently did hear.

Tittman suggests that "When Peter saw John following he was displeased, as Jesus had ordered Peter alone to follow, with the intention of saying something to him apart. He therefore asked why Jesus permitted John to follow unbidden."—He then thinks, if we adopt this interpretation, that the remarkable words of the following verse may only mean,—"If I wish him to remain with the other disciples until I return to them, that is no business of thine. Just follow Me."—This however seems to me rather a tame interpretation.

Stier observes, "There was something wrong at first in Peter's act of turning himself. He was commanded to follow, and not to look around. Thus there was certainly an uncalled-for, and not artless, looking aside, a side-glance once more of comparison with others! After his deep humiliation here is still some light trace of the ancient Simon."

21 —[*Peter seeing...Lord...what...this man do.*] The Greek words of Peter's question would be literally rendered, " Lord : and this man what ? " The precise meaning and object of the question are a point which has been much disputed.

(*a*) Some think that the question was entirely one of brotherly love, interest, and affection. They regard the inquiry as one which arose from Peter's tender feeling toward John, as the disciple whom he loved most among the Apostles. He would fain know what was to be the future lot of his beloved friend and brother.

(*b*) Some think that the question was one of unseemly curiosity. They regard it as one which Peter ought not to have asked. If our Lord did not volunteer any prediction about John, Peter ought not to have made any inquiry.

(*c*) Some think, as Flacius, that there was a latent jealousy in Peter's question, and that he seemed to suspect that John, not having denied Christ, would die an easier death than himself ! I cannot think this for a moment.

My own belief is that there is truth in both the two first views. Our Lord's reply to Peter, recorded in the next verse, certainly indicates to my mind that Peter ought not to have been so forward to ask. On the other hand, I should be sorry to say that Peter's inquiry arose entirely out of curiosity, when I mark Peter's unvarying connection with John on all occasions, and evident brotherly love towards him. In feeling concern about John's future, after hearing about his own, Peter was not to blame. Grace does not require us to be cold and unfeeling about our friends. But in the manner of Peter's inquiry there certainly seems to have been something to blame. Is there not about it a little touch of the old over-readiness to talk of others ? It was once, " Though all men,—all others,— forsake Thee yet will not I." It is now, " If I am to die a violent death, what are others to do ? "

It is certainly my own impression that Peter's question had special reference to John's end : " If I am to die a violent death, what is to be the end of my brother John ? "

Leighton, quoted by Burgon, remarks, " This was a transient stumbling in one who, but lately recovered of a great disease, did not walk firmly. But it is the common track of most, to wear out their days with impertinent inquiries. There is a natural desire in men to know the things of others, and neglect their own ; and to be more concerned about things to come than things present."

Henry remarks, " Peter seems more concerned for another than for himself. So apt are we to be busy in other men's matters, but negligent in the concerns of our own souls,—quick-sighted abroad, but dim-sighted at home,—judging others, and prognosticating what they will do, when we have enough to do to prove our own works, and understand our own ways. Peter seems more concerned about events than about duty. John was younger than himself, and in the course of nature likely to survive him. ' Lord,' he says, ' what times shall he be reserved for ?' Whereas, if God, by His grace, enable us to persevere to the end, and finish well, and get safely to heaven, we need not ask, ' What shall be the lot of those that shall come after us ?' Is it not well if peace and truth shall be in my days ? Scripture predictions must be eyed for the direction of our conscience, not for the satisfying of our curiosity."

It is a curious fact worth remembering, that John was one of the only two Apostles, whose future lot had already been spoken of by Christ. " He shall drink of the cup that I drink of, and be baptized with the baptism I am baptized with." (Mark x. 39.)

22 —[*Jesus saith unto him, If I will, etc.*] Our Lord's answer to Peter can only be taken, in my judgment, as a rebuke. It was meant to teach the Apostle that he must first attend to his own duty, mind his own soul, fulfil his own course, and leave the future of other brethren in the hands of a wise and merciful Saviour. He must not pry too curiously into God's counsels concerning John. What good would it do him to know whether John was to live a long life or a short one ; to die a violent death or a natural one ? Our Lord seems to say, " Leave off inquiring about thy brother's future lot. Thou knowest that he is one of my sheep, and as such shall never perish, and is in safe keeping. What is the rest to thee ? Have faith to believe that all will be well done about him. Look to thine own soul and be content to follow Me."—I cannot help seeing a latent resemblance between this place and the well-known passage at the end of Daniel's prophecy. " Then said I, O my Lord, what shall be the end of these things? And He said, Go thy way, Daniel : for the words are closed up and sealed till the time of the end."—" Go thou thy way till the end be : for thou shalt rest, and stand in thy lot at the end of the days." (Dan. xii. 8, 9, 13.)

Theophylact suggests that our Lord saw that Peter was vehemently attached to John, and unwilling to be separated from him, and therefore meant to teach him that he must do his own work and follow Christ, wherever He might lead him, even though separation from John might be the consequence.

After all we must take care that we do not omit the special point of our Lord's words. What our Lord rebukes is not general concern about the souls of others, but over-anxiety and restless curiosity about the future of our friends. Such over-anxiety indicates want of faith : we ought to be willing to leave their future in God's hands. To know their future would, in all probability, not make us one jot more happy. I can imagine nothing more miserable than to see in the distance tribulation and sorrow coming on our friends, and not to be able to avert it. Of what use would it have been to Peter, to know that his beloved brother John would one day be cast into a caldron of boiling oil, at Ephesus, during a persecution? What good would it have done Peter, to know that John would spend years of weary captivity on the Isle of Patmos, and finally outlive all the company of the Apostles, and be left last and latest on the stormy sea of this troublous world? To know all this would not have done Peter the slightest good, and would more likely have added to his own sorrow. Wisely and well did our Lord say, "What is that to thee?" Wisely and well does He teach us not to be over-anxious about the future of our children, our relatives, and our friends. Far better for us, and far happier, to have faith in God, and to let the great unknown future alone.

Burkitt observes, "There are two great varieties in men with reference to knowledge. The one is a neglect to know what it is our duty to know. The other is a curiosity to know what it doth not belong to us to know."

In any case, the words "Follow Me" should always teach us that our first duty in religion is to look to our own souls, and to take heed that we ourselves follow Christ, and walk with God. Whatever others may do or not do, suffer or not suffer, our own duty is clear and plain. People who are always looking at others, and considering others, and shaping their own course accordingly, commit a great mistake. Of all weak and foolish reasons assigned by some for not coming to the Lord's Supper, the weakest perhaps is that very common one,—the *conduct of others* who are communicants! To such persons the words of our Lord apply with emphatical force, " What is that to thee? Follow thou Me."

The words of our Lord, " If I will that he tarry till I come," are a deep and mysterious saying, and in every age of the Church have received different interpretations.

(*a*) Some, as Gerhard, Maldonatus, and Wordsworth, hold that Jesus meant, " If I will that he tarry a long time on earth, lingering here long after thou art gone, until I come for him at death, what is that to thee?"—I cannot, however, admit this interpretation for a moment. Death and the coming of Christ are two totally different things, and it is an entire mistake to confound them, as people often do (with very good intentions), in selecting texts for tombstones, as part of epitaphs. There is not a single passage in the New Testament, where the coming of the Lord means death. Moreover, the very next verse in this chapter seems to place the two things in strong contrast, as not the same.

(*b*) Some actually hold that Jesus meant that the Apostle John was never to die at all, but to remain alive until the second advent! This, however, is a wild and preposterous interpretation, which will satisfy no sober mind. Moreover, it is contradicted by the whole tenor of ecclesiastical history. All early writers, of any weight and authority, declare that John died a natural death in extreme old age.

Theophylact mentions a strange tradition that John is kept alive somewhere, and is to be slain, together with Elias, by Antichrist, when he appears !

(*c*) Some, as Grotius, Hammond, Lightfoot, Whitby, Scott, Alford, and Ellicott, hold that Jesus meant by His coming, not His second advent at the end of the world, but His coming spiritually in judgment, for the punishment of the Jews, the destruction of the temple, and the overthrow of the whole Jewish dispensation by the Romans.   I cannot see this at all. I find no clear proof in the New Testament, that the over-throw of the Jewish dispensation is ever called the " coming of the Lord."   Moreover, it is an awkward fact, that it is com-monly agreed that the Apostle John lived for many years after Jerusalem was taken, and the temple burned by Titus.   Ge-rhard declares positively, that there is not one instance in Scrip-ture of the destruction of Jerusalem being called the " coming of the Lord."

(*d*) Bengel and Stier think it means that John was to tarry till the Lord came to reveal to him the visions recorded in the Book of Revelation.

(*e*) Some, as Hutcheson and Trench, think that Jesus did not mean to predict anything particular about John's future, but only used a general hypothetical expression.   " Supposing I do will that he stay till I come, what is that to thee ?   I do not say that I do will him to stay.   But supposing it is my will, this is no affair of thine, and it becometh thee not to inquire."

The question is one that will never be settled, and the sen-tence seems purposely left under a veil of mystery.   If I must give an opinion, I decidedly lean to the last of the five views which I have stated.

23 —[*Then went this saying, etc.*]   In this verse John carefully de-scribes the rise of the earliest ecclesiastical tradition.   He says that it became a common saying among the brethren, that he was not to die.   Some very likely took it into their heads that, like Enoch and Elijah, he was to be translated and never see death, but pass into glory without dying.   The Apostle takes pains to point out that Jesus never said that he was not to die, and had only supposed the possibility of his " tarrying till He came."   To my own mind his manner of stating the point is strongly confirmatory of the view I have already supported : viz., that our Lord only used a hypothetical expression, and did not at all intend to make a positive prediction.

We should carefully notice in this passage how easy it is for traditions to begin ; and how soon, even with the best inten-tions, unfounded reports originate among religious men.   Noth-ing is more unsatisfactory, nothing more uncertain, nothing more destitute of solid foundation, than that huge mass of matter which the Roman Catholic Church has heaped together, and professes to respect, called " Catholic tradition." The moment a Christian departs from God's Word written, and allows " Catholic tradition" any authority, he plunges into a jungle of uncertainty, and will be happy if he does not make shipwreck of his faith altogether.

Flacius observes, that not observing our Lord's " if " gave rise to a tradition I A single word omitted in a text may do harm.

Henry remarks, " Let us learn here the uncertainty of human tradition, and the folly of building faith upon it. Here was a tradition, an apostolical tradition, a saying that went abroad among the brethren. It was early ; it was common ; it was public ; and yet it was false. How little then are those unwritten traditions to be relied upon, which the Council of Trent has decreed to be worthy to be received with a veneration and pious affection equal to that which is owing to Holy Scripture."

Henry also remarks, " Let us learn the aptness of men to misinterpret the sayings of Christ. The grossest errors have sometimes shrouded themselves under the umbrage of incontestable truth, and the Scriptures themselves have been wrested by the unlearned and unstable.   We must not think it strange if we hear the sayings of Christ misinterpreted, and quoted to patronize the errors of antichrist."

The Greek phrase which we render " should not die," is literally, " does not die."

It seems impossible to avoid the conclusion, that the words which Jesus addressed to Peter were heard by the other five Apostles. Otherwise, the saying, or report referred to in this verse, could not have gone forth.

24 -[*This is the disciple, etc.*] In this verse the Apostle John makes a solemn declaration of his own authorship of the Gospel which bears his name, and of the truth of the matters which the Gospel itself contains. As usual, with characteristic humility, he does not give his name, but modestly speaks of himself in the third person. It is as though he said,—" Finally, I, John the Apostle, who leaned on Jesus's breast, declare that I am the person who here testifies of these sayings and doings of Christ, and who has here written them down in this book, and I know that I have told nothing but what is true, and that my testimony may be implicitly trusted."

The first person plural is here used by John, we should observe, just as it is in the beginning of his first Epistle.

The verse seems written in order to assure all readers of John's Gospel that they need feel no doubt whatever that they have in this Gospel a faithful and true record of things that Jesus said and did, and that this, the last of the four narratives of Christ's history, is just as trustworthy, credible, and dependable as the books written by Matthew, Mark, and Luke.

25 —[*And there are also many other things, etc.*] In this verse John seems to wind up his book, by breaking forth into a fervent declaration about the wonderful things which his Lord and Master had done. It is as though he said, " Though I finish my Gospel here, I have not told all the marvellous things that Jesus did while He was upon earth. There are many other things which he did, and many other words which He spoke, which are not recorded in my Gospel, nor yet in the Gospels of Matthew, Mark, and Luke. Indeed, if they were written down every one, I suppose the world would not receive them, and could not comprehend their value."

The words which we render, " The books that should be written," would be more literally translated, " The books written."

Brentius calls attention to the very large number of miracles which, according to St. Matthew, were wrought by our Lord, of which we have no special record in any of the Gospels. (See Matt. iv. 23, 24 ; xi. 5.) He justly argues that if these were all put down and described, it would greatly swell the Gospel narrative. What we have recorded is only a sample of what Jesus did.

Henry observes, that books might easily have been multiplied about Christ. " Everything that Christ said or did was worth our notice, and capable of being improved. He never spoke an idle word, and never did an idle thing ; nay, He never spoke or did anything mean, little, or trifling, which is more than can be said of the wisest of men."—But he wisely adds, " If we do not believe and improve what is written already, neither should we if there had been much more."

The expression which St. John uses in this verse about " the world not receiving the books," is not without difficulty. It cannot of course mean that the material bulk of the books would be so large that the universe could not receive them. This would be absurd, as the " things " spoken of are only the things which Jesus did and said during the three years of His ministry. But what does the expression mean ?

(*a*) Some, as Heinsius and Whitby, think that it means " the world, or unconverted portion of mankind, could not receive, take in, or comprehend more, if more was written. There is enough recorded for the conviction of sinners, and for the guidance of all who honestly want to be saved."—It is a grave objection to this view, that the text does not say " the world " simply, but " the world itself." Yet in fairness it must be allowed that in this sense the expression is rather like that in

Amos: "The land is not able to bear all His words." (Amos vii. 10.)

(b) Some think that the phrase must be taken as a strong hyperbolical description of the quantity and value of Christ's works and words, during the period of His ministry, and that we must not press an excessively literal interpretation of the phrase. They argue that the figure called "hyperbole" is not at all uncommon in the Scripture, and that language is often used, when the idea to be conveyed is that of very great size, value, quantity, or number, which evidently cannot be interpreted *literally*. On the whole, I incline to think that this is the right view of the expression, and that it harmonizes well with the fervent, warm-hearted, loving character of the Apostle who lay on Jesus' breast, and was commissioned to write the fourth Gospel. He ends with a heart full of Christ, and running over with love to Him, and zeal for His glory, and so he winds up just like himself.

The objection, sometimes made, that hyperbolical language is not consistent with inspiration, does not appear to me at all valid. No intelligent and careful reader of the Bible can fail to see that the inspired writers often use hyperbolical phrases,— phrases, I mean, that cannot possibly bear a *literal* interpretation, and must be regarded as a condescending accommodation to the weakness of man. For example ; "Cities walled up to heaven." (Deut. i. 28.) "A land that flowed with milk and honey." (Josh. v. 6.) "Camels as the sand of the sea for multitude." (Judges vii. 12.) All these are phrases which cannot be interpreted *literally*, and which any sensible person knows to be figurative and hyperbolical. Our Lord Himself speaks of "Capernaum being exalted unto heaven ; " and says, "If any man come after Me, and hate not his father and mother he cannot be my disciple." (Matt. xi. 23 ; Luke xiv. 26.) In both cases His language evidently cannot be construed literally.

Calvin observes, "If the Evangelist, casting his eyes on the mightiness of the majesty of Christ, exclaims in astonishment, that even the whole world could not contain a full narrative of it, ought we to wonder? Nor is he at all to be blamed, if he employs a frequent and ordinary figure of speech for commending the excellence of Christ's works. For he knew how God accommodates Himself to the ordinary way of speaking, on account of our ignorance."

This view is adopted by Augustine, Cyril, Bucer, Musculus, Gualter, Gerhard, Flacius, Ferus, Toletus, Maldonatus, Cornelius a Lapide, Jansenius, Pearson, Henry, Pearce, Scott, Tittman, Bloomfield, Barnes, Alford, Wordsworth, and Burgon.

Lampe protests strongly against the idea of any hyperbole being used, as barely reverent. But I cannot see any force in his argument.

The Greek word which we render "contain," is the same that is rendered in Matt. xix. 11 "receive," and in the same sense that it appears used here : "All men cannot receive this saying."

The change from the plural "we know," in verse 24, to the singular "I suppose," in this verse, is undoubtedly peculiar. But there are parallel cases quoted by Doddridge. (Rom vii. 14, and 1 Thess, ii. 18.) Euthymius notes it, and thinks the insertion of "I suppose" was meant to soften down the hyperbole.

It is noteworthy that the word "Amen" is the concluding word of each of the four Gospels. It is equivalent to saying, "In truth, verily, it is so." It is equally noteworthy that our Lord is the only person who ever uses the word at the beginning of a sentence.

I have now completed my Notes on St. John's Gospel. I have given my last explanation. I have gathered my last collection of the opinions of Commentators. I have offered for the last time my judgment upon doubtful and disputed points. I lay down my pen with humbled, thankful, and solemnized feelings. The closing words of holy Bullinger's Commentary on the Gospels, condensed and abridged, will perhaps not be considered an inappropriate conclusion to my "Expository Thoughts on St. John."

"Reader, I have now set before thee thy Saviour the Lord Jesus Christ, that very Son of God, who was begotten by the Father by an eternal and ineffable generation, consubstantial and coëqual with the Father in all things ;—but in these last times, according to prophetical oracles, was incarnate for us, suffered, died, rose again from the dead, and was made King and Lord of all things.—This is He who is appointed and given to us by God the Father, as the fulness of all grace and truth, as the Lamb of God who taketh away the sins of the world, as the ladder and door of heaven, as the serpent lifted up to render the poison of sin harmless, as the water which refreshes the thirsty, as the bread of life, as the light of the world, as the redeemer of God's children, as the shepherd and door of the sheep, as the resurrection and the life, as the corn of wheat which springs up into much fruit, as the conqueror of the prince of this world, as the way, the truth, and the life, as the true vine, and finally, as the redemption, salvation, satisfaction, and righteousness of all the faithful in all the world, throughout all ages. Let us therefore pray God the Father, that, being taught by His Gospel, we may know Him that is true, and believe in Him in whom alone is salvation; and that, believing, we may feel God living in us in this world, and in the world to come may enjoy His eternal and most blessed fellowship." Amen and Amen.